FUNDAMENTAL PRINCIPLES OF
INTERNATIONAL
RELATIONS

J. MARTIN ROCHESTER

WESTVIEW
PRESS

A Member of the Perseus Books Group

Copyright © 2010 by Westview Press

Published by Westview Press,
A Member of the Perseus Books Group

All rights reserved. Printed in the United States of America. No part of this book may
be reproduced in any manner whatsoever without written permission except in the case
of brief quotations embodied in critical articles and reviews. For information, address
Westview Press, 2465 Central Avenue, Boulder, CO 80301.

Find us on the World Wide Web at www.westviewpress.com.

Every effort has been made to secure required permissions to use all images, maps, and
other art included in this volume.

Westview Press books are available at special discounts for bulk purchases in the United
States by corporations, institutions, and other organizations. For more information,
please contact the Special Markets Department at the Perseus Books Group, 2300
Chestnut Street, Suite 200, Philadelphia, PA 19103, or call (800) 810-4145, ext. 5000, or
e-mail special.markets@perseusbooks.com.

A CIP catalog record for this book is available from the Library of Congress

ISBN: 978-0-8133-4418-8

10 9 8 7 6 5 4 3 2 1

To Fred Pearson and Bob Baumann,
friends and colleagues for over thirty-five years,

To my students,
an inspiration to me over that same time,
and

To Lottie and Sholom (Bear), our future

CONTENTS

PART THREE
GLOBAL PROBLEM-SOLVING: Issue-Areas

PART FOUR
CONCLUSION: Thinking About the New Millennium

PREFACE

The philosopher Blaise Pascal once said, "I would have written a shorter letter, but I did not have time." Pascal meant that a short statement can be harder to write than a longer one, since it requires greater precision and discipline. Likewise, a short textbook can be harder to write than a long one. This is especially so in the field of international relations (IR), since the subject is so large and sprawling—literally the entire world and beyond, with treaties today covering even the rescue of astronauts in outer space as well as the placement of weapons of mass destruction on the moon.

In writing an undergraduate textbook that is briefer than most international relations texts, I attempted to distill the fundamental principles of world politics and present them in concise, readable prose. Where students tend to find most academic textbooks ponderous, I hope they will find this one lively. That said, the study of international relations is serious business involving weighty matters, ranging from the control of nuclear weapons to the control of pandemics. Even a basic primer on world affairs today necessarily involves the student in the study of difficult, perplexing problems that are as challenging as they are interesting. It is not my task to simplify the world but to make the reader appreciate and understand its great complexity.

International relations are characterized by both continuity and change. In some respects, the more things change in world politics, the more they stay the same. Many core features and patterns endure for centuries, such as the existence of nation-states seeking to preserve their sovereignty and promote their national interests. Other aspects of world politics at times undergo major changes. Today, the international system appears to be in ferment, as globalization and the growth of multinational corporations, cyberspace, and other developments threaten to play havoc with national sovereignty and interests and render those traditional, core concepts problematical if not altogether irrelevant. Given the volatility of international affairs, it is easy for an IR textbook to be overtaken by events, for example by the latest crisis in the Middle East or the latest stock market crash and global financial crisis. As I write, the current economic downturn in the United

States and elsewhere may prove to be either a short-lived interruption of a general wave of economic expansion since World War II or a long-term structural problem with the potential to transform the world order. The challenge is to separate the truly earthshaking happenings with systemic implications from the daily headlines that represent mere blips on the screen, and to try to fit all this into a coherent, accurate portrait that delineates how the world works.

I do not consider the student a passive bystander in this effort. I try to engage the student in what pedagogical experts these days call "active learning." First, a major theme of the book is that no one school of thought—as we say in IR, paradigm—captures the complexity of our times, with international reality best viewed through multiple lenses; the reader must be prepared to struggle and cope with ambiguity alongside the author in making meaning of military, economic, and other phenomena. Second, each chapter contains an *IR* Critical Thinking Box that prompts the reader to reflect more deeply about an important puzzle discussed in the chapter. Third, each chapter contains a set of questions for further discussion and study as well as suggestions for further reading.

Think of the book as a four-course meal. *Part One* is the appetizer, providing a conceptual and historical foundation for the study of contemporary international relations—defining key terms, introducing various theoretical schools, and surveying the evolution of world politics over the centuries. *Part Two* and *Part Three* are the "meat and potatoes," examining the essential "stuff" of IR. *Part Two* covers the standard fare—topics such as states and foreign policy, diplomacy and bargaining, war and the use of armed force, and international organization and law. *Part Three* focuses on three main issue-areas and efforts by the international community to develop regimes addressing problems currently confronting humanity—international security (including limiting the proliferation of weapons of mass destruction), human security (including promoting human rights and economic development), and international economics (including managing trade, investment, and other dimensions of the world economy). *Part Four* wraps up the book, covering loose ends (global governance of the environment, the Internet, and other issue-areas) and engaging the reader in some final reflections, particularly about the future; think of it as dessert or, better yet, an after-dinner drink. Some may feel they need a good stiff drink to face the future, given the daunting problems and the menu of difficult choices facing leaders and publics, although whether the glass is half full or empty is yet another matter for debate. Recalling Aristotle's observation that "the diner, not the cook, is the better judge" of a meal, I will leave it to the readers to determine if I have succeeded in whetting their appetite for further study of IR.

There are many to thank for this book. First, I wish to acknowledge the two individuals to whom the book is dedicated. Fred Pearson was my first colleague when I arrived at the University of Missouri–St. Louis over three decades ago. He coauthored the first international relations textbook I wrote, and has remained a dear friend and valued source of wisdom and wit. Bob Baumann, assistant director of the Center for International Studies at UMSL, has been a friend and an indispensable aide not only to me but to countless other faculty who have benefited from his generous donation of time and energy in support of our research and teaching; crediting him is long overdue. Second, I wish to acknowledge the many students I have taught during my career. They have helped me understand the limits of the professor's hegemonic power in the classroom, the utility of soft power alongside hard power, and the value of intellectual diversity. Third, my twin sibling, Stuart, the Pentagon's chief historian in the U.S. Department of Defense until his death this past year, is owed my eternal gratitude for always being a fount of knowledge, advice, and brotherly love. Fourth, I need to thank those at Westview—including Steve Catalano (the editor who first urged me to write another international relations textbook), Toby Wahl (his successor who provided ongoing encouragement and guidance during the project), and Brooke Kush, Kelsey Mitchell, and the excellent support staff at the press who contributed greatly to the final product—as well as the many reviewers who provided valuable recommendations on how to improve the book. Finally, for tolerating my frequent moodiness during writer's blocks, special thanks go to my wife, Ruth, and my entire family, represented in the book dedication by Lottie and Sholom—our newest grandchildren and, with Leah, Mendy, and Sara, our future.

PART ONE

INTRODUCTION
Conceptual and
Historical
Background

An introduction to the study of international relations in our time is an introduction to the art and science of the survival of mankind.
—Karl W. Deutsch, *The Analysis of International Relations*, 1988

Don't be like the student who was asked, "Which is worse, ignorance or apathy?" and who responded, "I don't know and I don't care!"
—Charles Yost, former U.S. ambassador to the United Nations, 1980

1

Understanding International Relations, or Getting a Handle on the World

The twenty-first century will encompass the longest period of peace, democracy, and economic development in history.
—Allan E. Goodman, *A Brief History of the Future,* 1993

The threat of self-destruction and planetary destruction is not something that we will pose one day in the future, if we fail to take certain precautions; it is here now, hanging over the heads of all of us at every moment.
—Jonathan Schell, *The Fate of the Earth,* 1982

It is always hard to predict anything, especially the future.
—Romanian proverb

THE CHALLENGE

This is a book about international relations in the twenty-first century. It is meant to introduce the subject and distill its key features, although even a basic primer on world affairs today necessarily involves the student in the study of perplexing problems that are as challenging as they are interesting. Indeed, the author's task here is not to simplify the world but rather to make the reader appreciate, and ultimately understand, its great complexity. We are still in the early stages of the new millennium. No generation will experience such a profound moment of reflection about the human condition for another thousand years. Hence we would

seem to have a special obligation to think not only with caring but, more importantly, with carefulness and clarity about the nature of the current world order or,
as some might say, disorder. This requires us to think about the past as well, since
"those who cannot remember the past are condemned to repeat it."[1] On the importance of this subject, it has been said that "an introduction to the study of international relations in our time is an introduction to the art and science of the
survival of mankind."[2]

Professors, policymakers, and publics in the United States and throughout the
globe are faced with many puzzles that are not easily answerable, whether through
artful speculation or, even less so, through controlled experiments conducted in
white lab coats. For example, note the question posed by political scientist John
Ikenberry that is on the minds of many contemporary observers:

> The rise of China will undoubtedly be one of the great dramas of the twenty-
> first century. China's extraordinary economic growth and active diplomacy are
> already transforming East Asia, and future decades will see even greater in-
> creases in Chinese power and influence. But exactly how this drama will play
> out is an open question. Will China overthrow the existing order or become
> a part of it? And what, if anything, can the United States do to maintain its
> position as China rises?[3]

Ikenberry argues that this situation is comparable to great power transitions in
the past, and that it can be managed peaceably as long as the United States adopts
enlightened policies. An alternative viewpoint is presented by Parag Khanna, who
sees an emergent "Big Three," with the United States having to compete for dominance with both China and Europe (the European Union) in what is "for the
first time in history" a "global, multicivilizational, multipolar battle," whose outcome may not be as sanguine as Ikenberry suggests.[4]

How does one answer the question raised by Professor Ikenberry? What are we
to make of the world in the early twenty-first century? There is great uncertainty
about the United States-China relationship and other dramas being played out on
the world stage; how will these evolve, with what denouement? Henry Luce, the
founder of *Time* magazine, writing between World War I and World War II, famously declared the twentieth century "the American century." Will the twenty-
first century also be the American century? Or will it be the Chinese century,
the European century, or a "post-international politics" century altogether?[5] In the
1970s U.S. Secretary of State Henry Kissinger asked Chinese leader Chou En-Lai
what he thought of the 1789 French Revolution. He replied, "Too soon to tell." It
is especially premature to judge the long-term implications of events occurring
in the 2000s, although in the nuclear age we may not have the luxury of sitting
back and waiting a couple hundred years for a final verdict on their meaning. We
may have to think, and act, now.

Few observers, including scholars, have done a good job of correctly assessing and anticipating events of late. I vividly recall sitting in a paneled room at the International Studies Association (ISA) annual meeting in Washington, D.C., in the spring of 1987, attending a session featuring two American diplomats engaging two Russian diplomats in a speculative discussion about "the future of U.S.-Soviet relations." This was at a time when the Cold War between the United States and the Soviet Union was still raging, when Soviet leader Mikhail Gorbachev had just come to power in Moscow, when U.S. president Ronald Reagan was continuing to characterize the USSR as an "evil empire" bent on spreading global communism, and when his secretary of defense said that "we are no longer in the postwar era but the prewar era." One of the Russian diplomats began his comments by uttering what he took to be an old Romanian proverb, that "it is always hard to predict anything, especially the future." Indeed, who in that room, or for that matter any room anywhere that day, can claim to have predicted that within a half decade the world would witness the end of the Cold War and the end of the Soviet Union itself, with hardly a shot being fired? Most people—scholars, practitioners, and laypersons alike—shared former Carter administration national security adviser Zbigniew Brzezinski's 1986 assessment that "the American-Soviet conflict is not some temporary aberration but a historical rivalry that will long endure."[6] Yet by December 1989, the Berlin Wall that had symbolized the Iron Curtain separating the free and nonfree worlds had collapsed, and the Soviet Red Army Chorus could be heard in Washington, D.C., leading Reagan's successor and a throng of dignitaries at a Kennedy Center gala in a stirring rendition of "God Bless America." By December 1991, the USSR had dissolved into Kazakhstan, Tajikistan, Uzbekistan, and assorted other independent republics. As Gorbachev proclaimed that "the world is leaving one epoch, the Cold War, and entering a new one," President George H.W. Bush proclaimed a "new world order" of peace and harmony. [7]

At that very moment, amid much fanfare and jubilation, Francis Fukuyama of the U.S. State Department wrote that we were witnessing "the end of history," as the forces of Western liberal democracy and free market capitalism had seemingly achieved their final triumph over all other competing ideologies.[8] Although not everyone agreed, there was a general sense that those ideas were on the march worldwide.[9] But the "holiday from history" was short-lived, as was the jubilant mood.[10] If 11/9 (the fall of the Berlin Wall on November 9, 1989) had been earthshaking, 9/11 was no less so: on September 11, 2001, some 3,000 people lost their lives when al Qaeda terrorists attacked the World Trade Center in New York City, leading many to wonder whether the post–Cold War era had abruptly ended and had given way to a new, as yet unnamed era. Euphoria suddenly turned to despair and a doom and gloom view of the future.

Humanity, then, in the recent past has lurched wildly between the extreme mind-sets of heaven one minute and hell the next. Despite our failure to predict

AP Photo/Thomas Kienzie

AP Photo/Carmen Taylor

A tale of two cities: The fall of the Berlin Wall on 11/9 and the attack on the World Trade Center in New York on 9/11— Is it the best and worst of times?

even five-year trends, long-term forecasting remains a growth industry. Prognosticators have offered both optimistic and pessimistic prophecies. In addition to Fukuyama, the optimists in the post–Cold War era have included Alan Goodman, whose *A Brief History of the Future* heralded the twenty-first century as an era that "will encompass the longest period of peace, democracy, and economic development in history." Another observer echoes Goodman in noting that "the series of positive trends over the last 20 years" have created "an international climate of unprecedented peace and prosperity" in much of the Northern and Southern Hemispheres, while another contends that we are witnessing the "obsolescence of major war" and that terrorist threats are "overblown."[11] The ranks of the pessimists include John Mearsheimer, who, a year after Fukuyama's pronouncement, was already lamenting "why we will soon miss the Cold War" (since he expected the historical inevitability and "tragedy" of great-power politics would take an even more virulent turn in the future), and Samuel Huntington, who hypothesized that "the clash of civilizations" pitting "the West versus the rest" (Islamic fundamentalism and other cultures) would be the successor to the East-West ideological axis of conflict that ended in 1989. Another commentator wrote of "the coming anarchy" and the "shattering of the dreams of the post–Cold War era," stemming from ecological and other catastrophes, citing the recent genocidal conflicts in Africa as a metaphor for how both the South and North will evolve.[12] Many other writers have contemplated what the future holds in terms of great-power relationships and other developments, including Ikenberry and Khanna, mentioned above.

It is hard to get a handle on the world today, and especially difficult to know whether to feel good or bad about its current state, partly because, to borrow Charles Dickens's much-quoted 1859 saying, it arguably is the best of times and the worst of times. Suffice it to say, life expectancy in most countries extends beyond anything imaginable in Dickens's day, even as the entire human species can now be extinguished in a matter of hours and maybe minutes. We have the potential for unprecedented international cooperation (the United Nations, despite its many flaws, represents the most ambitious attempt at global institution-building in the million years that *Homo sapiens* has inhabited the earth) as well as unprecedented international conflict (in the words of one commentator, "it has historically been one thing to die for your country" but, in the event of a major war in the nuclear age, "it is a different thing to die *with* your country").[13]

On the one hand, one might be forgiven for thinking that Alan Goodman's prediction above is far too optimistic. After all, the twentieth century saw the worst carnage in human history, with over 100 million people killed in wars, a record that might be dwarfed in the future as ABC (atomic, biological, and chemical) weapons—WMDs (weapons of mass destruction)—all are on the brink of proliferating dangerously; biological and chemical weaponry (the "poor person's nuclear bomb") is relatively easy to develop and especially liable to end up in the hands of terrorists. As for poverty, there remain a huge number of poor people in the world, partly as a function of an ongoing population explosion in many less developed countries and partly because of a growing rich-poor gap that finds almost 3 billion persons living on less than $2 a day. The onset of a global financial crisis in 2008–2009, which saw wild swings in the U.S., European, and Asian stock markets, only served to exacerbate economic anxieties, even among the rich. In many countries, human rights violations remain prevalent, including cases of genocide. If humanity is not exterminated by the arms buildup of WMDs, it may happen instead through the buildup of CO_2 and other greenhouse gases in the earth's atmosphere that are contributing to global warming, making the last two decades since 1990 the warmest on record.[14]

On the other hand, the glass would seem at least as half full as half empty. Almost no one currently alive has had to cope with sustained crises of the magnitude experienced by my parents' generation, which in successive decades spent the flower of their youth suffering through World War I (1914–1918), the Great Depression (1929–1939), and World War II (1939–1945). Even amid grinding poverty, average income per capita in developing countries has been rising over the past twenty years while infant mortality and illiteracy have been declining. Globalization of the international economy promises a better life for more consumers if economic growth with equity and with environmentally sustainable development can be promoted and world financial crises stabilized.[15] Recent decades have seen impressive gains in the area of democratization, repressive regimes notwithstanding; the latest Freedom House report counts ninety countries as "free" (representing roughly half of the global population), sixty "partly free," and forty-three "not free," with the number of free countries being the highest in the history of the thirty-five-year survey.[16] The president of Harvard University summed up "the remarkable opportunities inherent in the current global moment" in a recent commencement address:

> For the first time in all of human history, a majority of people now live in countries where leaders are democratically elected, where women are treated as full citizens, and where the press is free. . . . Despite all the tragedies of war that rightly preoccupy us, the fraction of the world's population killed each year in wars has, in recent times, been more than 95 percent lower than the comparable fraction for an average year of the 20th century.[17]

Amid the nightmarish possibilities relating to WMDs, it is worth remembering that the Cold War following World War II was just that, a nonhot, nonshooting war. In some important respects, the period since 1945 has been relatively peaceful and has even been characterized as "the long peace," the longest continuous stretch of time since the beginning of the modern state system (in the seventeenth century) in which there has not been a single recorded instance of direct great-power exchange of hostilities.[18] The probability of a war occurring between great powers today is perhaps closer to zero than at any point in history. That isn't to say it couldn't happen, only that it is a remote possibility. This is no small accomplishment. If only we could say the same for interstate wars involving not-so-great powers, as well as intrastate (civil) wars and extrastate violence perpetrated by terrorists, all of which remain major concerns, especially as the specter of WMD proliferation threatens to blur the distinction between who is or is not a "great power" capable of causing great harm to its neighbors and the world as a whole. For the United States, the "long peace" is precariously juxtaposed against the "long war" (the U.S. Defense Department's name for the global fight against al Qaeda and international terrorism), as it awaits the possibility of another 9/11 attack.

We cannot know for sure where humanity is headed—how various dramas will play out—precisely because it depends in large measure on what *choices* policymakers and citizens make across the globe. One hopes those choices are *informed* choices, grounded in knowledge more than ignorance. As noted above, we are obliged to make every effort to think critically about international relations in order to improve our understanding and our capacity to shape things in a positive direction. This book tries to convey what is known and theorized about in the field of international relations, including core concepts and findings developed by political scientists, and to prod students to more deeply explore the subject. Chapter 1 discusses what exactly "international relations" (IR) is, offering a definition, and what approaches have been used to make sense of it, offering competing perspectives that can help us better describe and explain such phenomena. However, before we examine those issues, we need first to dispose of one other matter: Why bother studying IR? The answer may seem obvious from our discussion thus far, but a bit further elaboration may be in order.

WHY STUDY INTERNATIONAL RELATIONS?

Knowledge About Foreign Countries and Foreign Affairs Is Weak

Citizens around the globe understandably tend to be more concerned about happenings within their own societies than outside those societies. The United States, in particular, at least among developed societies, seems to stand out in this regard. Judging from the average American's level of information about the world, one might conclude that the world holds little interest for citizens of the United States, especially its youth. For example, a 2006 *National Geographic* survey of eighteen-to twenty-four-year-olds found that "geography was Greek to young Americans."[19] Eighty-eight percent could not locate Afghanistan on a map even though it is the country that housed the 9/11 skyjackers, while 66 percent could not find Iraq, even though the United States was involved in a war there that had cost some 3,000 American military casualties; and 70 percent could not find North Korea, even though that country at the time was thought to be developing nuclear weapons capable of reaching California and other parts of the West Coast.[20] These findings reinforce an earlier nine-country survey in which young Americans rated next to last on overall geographical knowledge, trailing Sweden, Germany, Italy, France, Japan, Great Britain, and Canada, surpassing only Mexico, a developing country that spends far less on education.[21] Not just geography but world affairs generally seem "Greek" to many Americans, young and old alike, since over half the Americans interviewed in polls taken throughout the Cold War were not certain whether it was the United States or the Soviet Union that belonged to the North Atlantic Treaty Organization (NATO), a bulwark of the Western alliance (which, by the way, includes Greece).[22]

Technology Is Making International Relations Increasingly Relevant to Our Everyday Lives

One would hope that Americans would be more cognizant of the importance of international affairs to their lives. If there is one almost absolute certainty that we can count on in the future among all the unknowns, it is that the world is likely to get smaller, not bigger, that the shrinking and linking of the globe will increase, not decrease. Driven mainly by technology, human beings, for better or worse, generally are experiencing a steady, almost inexorably increasing interconnectedness across geographical, cultural, and other divides even as they seek to maintain the distinctiveness and separateness of their individual communities. Technology is a double-edged sword. It has assisted democratization by creating dramatic opportunities to enhance communication, travel, and information processing worldwide, opening up closed societies to new ideas. A three-minute telephone call between New York and London (in current dollars) cost $300 in 1930; today it costs about a dollar and is practically free over the Internet, which is now being used by over a billion people globally, a 265 percent increase since 2000.[23] The fastest mode of transportation prior to the twentieth century was the steam locomotive, which could reach a speed of 100 miles per hour; jet planes can now fly over 2,000 mph and humans in capsules can exceed 18,000 mph in outer space. (The new Airbus 380 jumbo jet, eight stories high with a wingspan the length of an American football field, can carry as many as 800 passengers between New York and London in six hours.) Of course, the same technology that disseminates democratic ideas and connects families and friends across national boundaries also can facilitate the growth of terrorist networks and speed up global violence. The mere six hours it now takes to go from New York to London is matched in travel efficiency only by the mere minutes it would take if you caught a ride on an intercontinental ballistic missile hurtling through space between New York and Moscow or Beijing.

The fact that the term **interdependence** has become a cliché does not make it any less real. It is not "globaloney." We are all potentially impacted by what happens in distant corners of the earth, whether the apocalyptic possibilities associated with nuclear proliferation and global warming or more mundane matters of the sort described by Tom Friedman in *The World Is Flat*. Friedman notes that in 2005, roughly 400,000 U.S. tax returns were done in India, compared to only 25,000 two years earlier, and that such outsourcing is likely to be the norm in the future. He adds:

> There are currently about 245,000 Indians answering phones from all over the world or dialing out to solicit people for credit cards or cell phone bargains or overdue bills. . . . Sophie Sunder worked for Delta Airline's lost-baggage department: "Some would ask which country am I from? We are supposed to tell the truth, [so] we tell them India. Some thought it was Indiana, not India. Some did not know where India is. I said it is the country next to Pakistan.[24]

In the 2006 *National Geographic* survey, less than half of the Americans polled could find either India or Pakistan on the map (the former, together with China, housing one-third of the human race, and the latter being the second-largest Muslim country in the world and possessing nuclear weapons). They would be even less likely to locate Ghana, the African country whose link to New York City dog owners and other Gotham residents is described below:

> If you are found dumping trash in Central Park or letting your dog foul a soft ball field in Queens . . . the hastily scrawled ticket thrust into your hands [by city authorities] is likely to be processed in Ghana. On a three-shift cycle, 24 hours a day in a nondescript office in Accra that is home to the busiest Internet center in West Africa, about 40 employees under contract to a data management firm based in Delaware work busily at their computer station. They get three times the Ghanaian minimum wage to decipher the handwriting on the tickets, search a data base to locate the offender's name, address, the location of the infraction, and the fine, then type in the data and send it back to the United States within 48 hours of the offense.[25]

"It's the Economy and Foreign Policy, Stupid!"

The Ghana anecdote is a window into globalization that reveals how everyday lives in America and elsewhere are becoming intertwined. For weightier examples than pooper-scooper law enforcement, pick up a copy of any newspaper, the *New York Times*, say, and you will likely find dozens of headlines reporting important stories that have some combination of international and local angles. The *New York Times* of January 29, 2008, covered President George W. Bush's final State of the Union address delivered the day before to the U.S. Congress and the American people. Nearing the end of his second term after almost eight years in office, the president attempted to focus on a few key policy concerns. Whereas his predecessor, Bill Clinton, had won election by emphasizing domestic issues and using the campaign slogan "It's the economy, stupid," George Bush's presidency, along with his last State of the Union speech, seemed preoccupied more with "It's foreign policy, stupid." Although the stupidity or wisdom of Bush's foreign policy decisions is debatable, the growing interrelatedness of domestic and foreign policy is not.

President Bush devoted a great deal of time in his speech to the Iraq War. The United States had invaded Iraq in 2003, claiming that the regime of Saddam Hussein had WMDs and terrorist connections that threatened the United States in the post-9/11 era. Aside from the thousands of military and civilian casualties incurred in Iraq, Washington was spending roughly $100 billion a year to maintain troops there. This was in addition to an almost $500 billion annual Department of Defense budget that had contributed to an enormous overall federal government budget deficit that was making it difficult to fund health care and other social welfare programs. Referring to growing fears of a recession and the need to strengthen the American economy, President Bush mentioned the importance of removing tariffs and other barriers to foreign imports into the United States in the hope that other countries would reciprocate such "free trade" policies. However, many Americans worried not only about a huge trade deficit and the outsourcing of jobs overseas but also the lax regulations on imported goods from China and elsewhere that had resulted in consumers exposing their children to toys with lead-based paints and their dogs and cats to tainted pet food. Bush alluded, also, to the need for the United States to move toward energy security, as reliance on oil not only was costly (hovering around $100 dollars a barrel at the time, translating to over $3.00 a gallon at the pump) but also made the country increasingly dependent on supplies from unreliable regimes and unstable regions. He mentioned the immigration problem and the estimated 20 million illegal aliens in the United States, who were part of a growing worldwide problem of mass migration of political and economic refugees. President Bush discussed plans to help support the Millennium Development Goals project that the United Nations had initiated in 2000, which envisioned reducing the number of poor and hungry in the world by half by 2015, along with combating AIDS and other diseases that potentially could spread across borders.

Aside from the coverage of the State of the Union speech, there was much more to read in the *Times* on January 29, 2008, including the daily ritual for many of checking the weather forecast and the stock market report. Regarding the climate, 2007 had just been cited as the second hottest year in recorded history, which many scientists traced to global warming. As for the financial markets, the entire world was somewhat jittery about U.S. economic problems, reflected in the *Times* front-page headline just a week earlier announcing "World Markets Plunge on Fears of U.S. Slowdown." Just as the Chinese and other economies depended on a strong U.S. market to purchase their exports, Washington was counting on China and other "big emerging markets" to help bail out the American economy by purchasing American-made goods. The American economy was also looking to benefit from an enormous infusion of foreign investment capital, as foreigners were spending hundreds of billions of dollars buying up American companies, factories, and real estate properties, which on the one hand, according to a U.S. Treasury official, "represented a vote of confidence in the American economy" and helped "keep Americans employed" (with 5 million Americans working for foreign firms in the U.S.). At the same time it "reinvigorated jingoistic worries about foreigners securing control of America's fortunes." The possible undermining of American national identity and national security did not concern state governors from Rust Belt states, such as the governor of Michigan, who, lamenting that "we've lost 400,000 manufacturing jobs and I've got to get jobs for our people," had just made several trips to Europe and Japan in search of investment.[26] By the end of Bush's presidency, global economic interdependence was brought home more than ever by the financial crisis in the fall of 2008, which started on Wall Street and affected Main Streets worldwide, prompting the headline "Nations Weighing Global Approach As Chaos Spreads" (*New York Times*, October 10, 2008).

How can we comprehend the myriad discrete events that are reported daily in the print and electronic media, along with the larger phenomena that Ikenberry and others are concerned about, and try to fit these into a coherent framework? In other words, how can we become more worldly? Let us begin by defining some key terms.

THE DEFINITION OF INTERNATIONAL RELATIONS

Let's start with "international relations," a seemingly straightforward term that nonetheless has been contested, at times heatedly, among scholars. In the process of defining international relations, we will also define some other core concepts.

Definitional Problems

International relations as a field of study can be traced at least as far back as ancient Greece and Thucydides' accounts of the Peloponnesian War, although it is generally considered to have arrived as a distinct academic field in the early twentieth century, following World War I. *Webster's* online dictionary defines **international relations (IR)** as "a branch of political science concerned with relations between nations and primarily with foreign policies." This sounds like a perfectly reasonable definition, except that it raises as many questions as it answers. First, although international relations is often equated with international politics, clearly we can see from the previous discussion that the field is multidisciplinary, encompassing economic and other relations as well. While it is true that the field has traditionally focused on matters of war and peace and the issue-area of **international security**, other issue-areas, such as **international political economy**, have attracted increasing attention in recent years. Not only economists but historians, sociologists, psychologists, and even climatologists, agronomists, and many other specialists find themselves involved in the study of international relations.

Second, in an interdependent world, how easy is it, as the dictionary definition suggests, to separate "foreign" policy decisions from "domestic" policy decisions? A growing number of issues seem to be **intermestic** in nature, involving both international and domestic dimensions, such as energy, agriculture, the environment, and economic development. At a time when the United States has to import over half of the oil it consumes, energy is at least as much a foreign policy matter as a domestic policy matter. Likewise, although the United States could be largely self-sufficient in feeding its population, 40 percent of the fruit and 20 percent of the vegetables consumed by Americans are now imported from abroad, while half of the U.S. farm sector depends for its prosperity on exports. Even issues that would seem to fall purely in the foreign policy category, such as arms control, can have major domestic fallout, as when U.S. diplomats negotiating the 1993 Chemical Weapons Convention (which aimed to eliminate chemical weapon arsenals) had to take into account the concerns of DuPont and other American chemical firms worried about the possibility of UN inspectors engaging in overly intrusive inspections of their plants and stealing industrial secrets.

Third, where do actors such as DuPont and the UN, along with al Qaeda and other such entities, fit in? None of these are "nations." They are seemingly excluded from the dictionary definition, yet they are not exactly irrelevant to relations between nations. DuPont is one of approximately 50,000 **multinational corporations (MNCs)** in the world—companies with headquarters in one country and subsidiary branches in other countries. Other examples include Shell, British Petroleum, and the giant multinational oil companies. The United Nations is one of 300 or so **intergovernmental organizations (IGOs)**—international organizations whose members are national governments and that are ordinarily created by a treaty between governments. In addition to the UN, among the more well-known IGOs are the World Bank, the International Monetary Fund, and the World Health Organization. Al Qaeda is one of many **nongovernmental organizations (NGOs)**—international organizations whose members are private individuals and groups. Estimates of the total number of NGOs in the world vary from 5,000 to 50,000, depending on the measures used, and include the International Red Cross, Amnesty International, and Greenpeace. All of these are considered **nonstate** actors, in contrast to the roughly 200 **nation-states** (the United States, China, Russia, India, Ghana, and others) that are demarcated by the thick, dark boundaries on a world map and that are normally treated as the chief movers and shakers in international relations. (See world map on inside cover of this book.)

When most people think of international affairs, they think in dictionary terms of interactions between national governments that act on behalf of nation-states. This is understandable, since only national governments can make foreign policy and only they have the legal authority to control interactions across national boundaries, whether involving MNCs, IGOs, or NGOs. Walmart's total revenues may exceed the gross national product of Norway, not to mention Ghana, but it cannot join the United Nations and its CEO does not enjoy diplomatic immunity while traveling abroad. In this book, we, too, will be mainly concerned with relations between national governments. However, we will also look at the role of nonstate actors, as they compete with national governments in shaping world politics. If, as Ikenberry says, international relations is a drama, nation-states may be the lead actors, but nonstate actors are hardly bit players on the world stage.

Some Further Problems: Nations, States, and Nation-States

A **nation-state** is a political unit with relatively well-defined territorial boundaries and a population over which a central government exercises sovereign rule through executive, legislative, and judicial institutions based in its national capital. **Sovereignty** refers to the existence of a single supreme authority that can claim the exclusive right to rule over that patch of real estate and people and recognizes no higher authority outside those borders (whether it be the United Nations, the pope, or any other body). As noted above, there are some 200 such units in the world, ranging from large states such as China and the United States to smaller, lesser-known ones such as Palau and Nauru. In other words, states are *political-legal* entities that enter into treaties, exchange ambassadors, and engage in other official interactions. No matter how big or small a state is (whether representing over a billion people, as in the case of China, or having fewer than 25,000 inhabitants, as in the case of Palau), its sovereignty gives it formal equality with all other states.

Some further clarification is needed here. In everyday conversation, people tend to use the words "state" and "nation" interchangeably (as does *Webster's* dictionary). However, technically speaking, they are not exactly synonyms. A **nation** refers to a group of people having a sense of shared historical experience (generally rooted in a common language, ethnicity, or other cultural characteristics) as well as shared destiny. In other words, nations are *social-cultural* entities. A nation may constitute part of a state (e.g., the Tamil constituting a distinct cultural group within the state of Sri Lanka), may be coterminous with the state (e.g., the American people and the United States), or may spill over a number of different states (e.g., the Palestinians living in Israel, Lebanon, and Jordan or the Kurds living in Iraq, Turkey, and Iran). There may be as many as 1,500 nations (nationality groups) in the world.

Some states, such as Japan, are ethnically homogeneous, with over 90 percent of their population being of the same Japanese ethnicity. Other states, such as the United States, have had to work harder at assimilating diverse immigrants (Germans, Italians, Vietnamese, and others) from around the world but have largely succeeded in getting them to identify with state symbols in the form of the country's flag and anthem. Both Japan and the United States are examples where state and nation are one in the hearts and minds of their citizens—these are nation-states in the truest sense of the term. Although various groups in Japan quarrel vociferously over state political institutions, they nevertheless consider themselves "Japanese" and do not threaten secession to form a new state; the same is true of the United States.

Many other nation-states are less cohesive. In contrast, the so-called Tamil Tigers in Sri Lanka tend not to think of themselves as Sri Lankans; the Palestinians in Israel, Lebanon, and Jordan tend not to consider themselves Israelis, Lebanese, or Jordanian; and the Kurds in Iraq, Turkey, and Iran tend not to identify themselves as Iraqis, Turks, or Iranians. In all the latter cases, the states suffer from separatist movements seeking to establish their very own state to house their nation. During the 1990s, the breakup of the Soviet Union (into the Russian Federation, Kazakhstan, Tajikistan, Ukraine, and a dozen other newly independent states), along with the disintegration of Yugoslavia (into Serbia, Croatia, Slovenia, Bosnia, and Macedonia), was due to ethnic fault-lines that fractured existing states; some "successor" states themselves experienced continued internal unrest among minority populations, as with Chechnya in Russia and Kosovo in Serbia. Many states in Africa that came into existence during the decolonialization movement after World War II were artificial creations of colonial mapmakers, whose borders did not correspond to any natural, historical, or cultural groupings; hence, these societies often have been torn by **ethnopolitical conflict**, such as the civil war between the Hutu and Tutsi tribes in Rwanda in the 1990s and the strife between the Kikuyo, Luo, and other tribes in Kenya in 2008. Even rich, long-established states can experience tensions over national identity. In Belgium, ongoing discord between the Dutch-speaking north (Flanders) and the French-speaking south (Wallonia) has led one commentator to call that nation-state "two different nations, an artificial state [created as a buffer between France and other great powers in 1830]" whose people "have nothing in common except a king, chocolate, and beer."[27] An important feature of world politics, then, has been the search by culturally distinct nations for statehood and by polyglot states for nationhood. [28]

The Essence of International Relations

What are we finally left with as a definition of international relations? The definition that I have chosen to adopt is taken from political science, reflecting my primary concern with IR as the study of the relationships between the world's governments, including not only their interactions with each other but also with transnational and subnational actors. Thus, for our purposes, international relations and international politics is a distinction without a difference. A classic definition of politics is "the study of who gets what, when, and how." [29] It follows that *international politics is the study of who gets what, when, and how in the international arena.*

As the above definition suggests, international politics is a game, a competition. Indeed, many writers have used the game metaphor to capture the essence of what international politics is all about.[30] Games typically have rules. What rules generally govern the game of international politics, as opposed to intranational politics? Is politics the same in both venues? No. There is at least one basic, critical difference. International politics plays out in a setting in which there are no central institutions with authority to regulate the players, unlike national politics, where, at least on paper, there are legislatures, courts, and other authoritative bodies that are expected to oversee the contestants. If you think of the world—over 6 billion people—as a single polity, there is, of course, no world government. Perhaps the most striking, fundamental feature of the international political system is precisely its *decentralized* character, with its members organized in some 200 territorially based units—nation-states—that are sovereign. Despite the existence of nonstate actors, the nation-state remains the primary form of political organization and the locus of authority in the world.

The term **anarchy** is often used to describe the international system, referring to the lack of any hierarchy of authority beyond the individual nation-states. World politics conjures up the image of a lawless realm, without any rules whatsoever. The anarchical nature of the international system makes it inherently prone to conflict, frequently involving violence. As we have noted, it is true that many nation-states experience their own problems of internal instability and violence stemming from ethnic and other causes; some, like Somalia, which has seen almost the complete collapse of its central governmental institutions, have been labeled **"failed states."** Still, such problems seem endemic to the international polity because of the anarchical structure that is the hallmark of the international system.

Even so, it is important to understand that the members of the international community often have found ways to "cooperate under anarchy"[31] and to achieve a degree of peace and harmony in their affairs. In international relations there is an "ever-present tension between the struggle for power and the struggle for order," the competition for ever greater national resources moderated by mutual interests in at least a modicum of stability.[32] International relations is like a two-sided coin. We usually notice only one side, the struggle for power that involves efforts to maximize **national interests**, at times resulting in war. Less noticed is the other side, the search for order, involving efforts to develop **international law** and **international regimes**—rules—in various problem areas ranging from regulating the flow of air traffic and mail across national boundaries to regulating the proliferation of nuclear weapons. The latest act of aggression makes front-page headlines in the world's newspapers, but the 500 millionth airline passenger or 6 billionth piece of mail safely and routinely crossing national frontiers (thanks to the International Civil Aviation Organization and the Universal Postal Union) is not covered. There are more treaties and more international organizations than ever, both at the regional and global level, many of which represent ambitious attempts at interstate collaboration and "pooling" of sovereignty. The development of these institutions, primitive as they may be, is a manifestation of humanity's continual quest for order in a fragmented world of politically independent but economically, socially, and otherwise interdependent units that are being drawn ever closer by technological and other forces.

We have seen here that there is a schizoid, "split personality" quality to the human condition today. First, there is the aforementioned "best of times, worst of times" aspect. Second, related to that, there is the "two-sided coin" of world politics, which in the twenty-first century could produce unparalleled conflict or unparalleled cooperation. Finally, as the backdrop to all this, the traditional "state-centric" concepts that international relationists have used over the years to make sense of IR—nation-states, national interests and national security, sovereignty, citizenship, and the like—remain fundamental to understanding how the world works, yet are becoming increasingly problematical in a world of globalization and multinational corporations, cyberspace, and other phenomena that are blurring national borders and identities. The American novelist F. Scott Fitzgerald once wrote that "the measure of a first-rate intelligence is to be able to hold two contradictory ideas in your head at once and still function." That is a real challenge for the contemporary student of international relations! If the main goal of education is to learn to cope with ambiguity, how does that work in the field of IR? To find out, we will examine several alternative theoretical perspectives that political scientists have used to try to make meaning out of the jumble of world politics.

THE PARADIGM DEBATE

Social scientists assume that although each event (e.g., World War I or World War II) is unique, we nevertheless (1) can uncover and describe patterns that include not just that specific case but also other cases that fall into a more general category of similar phenomena (e.g., war) and (2) can explain those patterns. We often refer to this as engaging in *theory*, as developing answers to *why* not only specific events but larger happenings occur. For example, earlier I noted speculation by John Ikenberry and others whether the rise of China today can be understood as having similar characteristics as previous great power transitions and whether there are lessons we can learn from those previous cases that can help the United States and other members of the international community manage such change peaceably. IR specialists debate how best to understand such puzzles in world politics. At the center of these debates is the paradigm debate.

A **paradigm** is essentially a big theory. In most fields of study, the scholarly community tends to share at any given moment a widely accepted, broad theoretical orientation that dominates the field in terms of determining the kind of research questions asked and puzzles investigated. If over time the commonly held worldview becomes increasingly at odds with empirical evidence, then a competing paradigm may emerge that replaces the former as the dominant paradigm in the discipline. For example, for centuries the dominant paradigm in the study of astronomy was the Ptolemaic paradigm, named after the second-century philosopher Ptolemy, who assumed that the earth is the center of the universe. Such thinking heavily influenced the study of astronomy until the sixteenth century, when Copernicus advanced the notion that the sun is at the center of the solar system and all the planets, including the earth, revolve around it. Although paradigms are of

particular importance to scientists, they have relevance to policymakers and laypersons as well. The Copernican revolution in thought not only paved the way for
the modern science of astronomy but also fundamentally changed many people's
outlook about the universe. Another example would be Christopher Columbus's
voyage to the Americas in 1492, which altered the conventional wisdom that the
earth was flat rather than round. Put simply, paradigms are lenses through which
we can see the world—broad frameworks that organize our overall understanding of some set of phenomena we are trying to fathom. They give general direction to our observations, steering our attention toward some things and away
from others.[33]

As applied to the study of world politics, paradigms help us "tease meaningful patterns" out of "the welter of events, situations, trends, and circumstances that
make up international affairs."[34] Three paradigms have vied for the title of dominant paradigm in IR, although they have gone through several permutations and
have been challenged by other contenders: (1) the *idealist* paradigm (more commonly called today the *liberal* paradigm), (2) the *realist* paradigm, and (3) the
Marxist paradigm. I discuss each of these below, along with more recent challengers, such as *constructivism* and *feminism*.

The Idealist (Liberal) Paradigm

The **idealist (liberal) paradigm** stresses the *cooperative* side of the IR coin. It takes
a positive, optimistic view of human nature and human progress. Its roots extend
as far back as Dante, the fourteenth-century Italian poet who wrote of the uni-
versality of man and advocated for the unification of Europe. The idealist tradition also includes Hugo Grotius, the Dutch jurist widely considered the father of
international law, whose *On the Laws of War and Peace*, written in 1625 (shortly
before the Peace of Westphalia in 1648 gave birth to the modern nation-state
system), suggested a body of rules that sovereign states might be persuaded to
abide by; Emeric Cruce, the French monk and worldly thinker who died in 1648,
having dreamed of the creation of a world court, a common meeting place for states
to work out their disputes, and the abolition of armies; Adam Smith, the Scottish
author of *The Wealth of Nations* in 1776, who argued that the increased commercial ties produced by free trade between states would inhibit war making between them; and Immanuel Kant, whose *Perpetual Peace* (1795) envisioned a
federation of democratic, pacific states sharing a harmony of interests.[35]

In the twentieth century the idealist paradigm was most closely associated with
Woodrow Wilson and other thinkers who were prominent in the interwar period
between the end of World War I in 1918 and the beginning of World War II in
1939, when idealism dominated the study of IR. Idealists argued for a focus on
legal-formal aspects of international relations, such as international law and international organizations, and on moral concerns such as democracy and human
rights. It was out of the ashes of World War I that idealists claimed to have learned
certain lessons about the dynamics of international relations and what was needed

to prevent another major war. They believed a new world order had to be constructed based on a respect for law, the acceptance of shared universal values, and
the development of international institutions such as the League of Nations.

Idealism's reign as the dominant paradigm ended with its failure to anticipate
and prevent World War II, as idealists were discredited for decades as too utopian
in their worldview. However, the idealist school remained active throughout the
postwar era, with the term "liberal" becoming a substitute label for the paradigm.
By the 1970s and 1980s, the paradigm had regained some credibility, with the
growing economic interdependence among states, the growth of the European
Union as an almost supranational organization, and the end of the Cold War
without a shot being fired. Liberals argued that, rather than viewing international
relations simply as a contest between nation-states forever locked in the struggle
for power aimed at maximizing their security—which according to critics of the
idealist paradigm was a "zero-sum" (win-lose) game not conducive to cooperation—
international relations had become more complicated in ways that offered the
potential for "positive-sum" (win-win) outcomes. In particular, "complex interdependence" was increasingly entangling states in a web of relationships involving a host of subnational actors (including rival bureaucracies within a national
government and rival domestic interest groups within a national society) and
transnational actors (MNCs, NGOs, and the like), with security and nonsecurity
issues competing equally for attention. In other words, liberals relaxed the assumption that nation-states were the only actors of importance, that they were
unitary, cohesive, "rational" actors whose rationality dictated a single-minded
pursuit of power in support of national security, and that conflict and war was
the inevitable fate of humanity.[36]

One variant of liberalism, **neoliberalism,** is especially important today. Neoliberals do not dismiss the continued potential for conflict and violence in international affairs. However, they point out that, even if one accepts a state-centric
view of the world, states' self-interests will lead them often to realize they have a
mutual stake in developing international regimes in order to optimize the security and well-being of their citizenry. Because of their emphasis on the need for
international institution-building to help manage interdependence, and the opportunities that presents for interstate collaboration, neoliberals such as Robert
Keohane and Robert Axelrod (sometimes labeled "neoliberal institutionalists")
are considered in some ways the heirs of the idealist tradition, although they see
themselves as improving on the latter by trying to ground their ideas in more rigorous formulation and testing of hypotheses.[37]

The Realist Paradigm

Whether known as idealists, liberals, or neoliberals, such thinkers adopt Jean-
Jacques Rousseau's axiom that "the powerful are never so powerful as to be master of all," that even the powerful may at times need to rely on something other
than raw power to achieve their goals. They may need to use carrots rather than

sticks to get their way and may find it rational to forgo their short-term interests in order to advance their long-term interests in a stable order. In contrast, those who subscribe to the **realist paradigm** adopt Thucydides' assumption that "the strong do what they will, and the weak suffer what they must." Realists stress the *conflictual* side of the IR coin and take a relatively negative, pessimistic view of human nature and human progress. The realist tradition can be traced back to Thucydides, whose analysis of the Peloponnesian War in the fifth century B.C. centered on the changing power dynamics between the city-states Athens and Sparta, and also includes the sixteenth-century political theorist Niccolo Machiavelli, whose *The Prince* became synonymous with a realpolitik ("might makes right") emphasis on the exercise of power rather than principle, and the seventeenth-century philosopher Thomas Hobbes, whose *Leviathan* viewed the human condition as "nasty, brutish, and short" (even though Hobbes himself lived ninety-one years).

It was the idealists' failure to comprehend the forces leading to World War II that gave rise to realism as the dominant paradigm in the immediate postwar period after 1945. Whereas the idealists argued that their ideas had not been fully implemented in the interwar period and therefore had not been fairly tested, realists such as E. H. Carr contended that they had been tested but could not stand up against Adolf Hitler's armies marching across Europe and other armies marching elsewhere.[38] What came to be known as the "classical realist" view of international relations was embodied in the leading textbook of the 1950s, Hans Morgenthau's *Politics Among Nations*, which heavily influenced the next couple generations of IR scholars and practitioners.[39] Assuming that human nature tends to be more selfish than altruistic and that this applies to groups of people (states) no less than to individuals, Morgenthau questioned how much international cooperation is possible through international law and organization.

To the realist, the ultimate goal of all countries is security in a hostile environment. Their policies usually are determined by power calculations in pursuit of national security. Alliances will be made and broken, old friends abandoned and old enemies embraced, all depending on the requirements of the moment. Realists, then, tend to focus on such topics as military strategy, the elements of national power, diplomacy and other instruments of statecraft, and the nature of national interests rather than such subjects as international regimes. The realists claim to have learned their own lessons from World War II, namely, that the way to prevent future wars is to rely not on formal-legal institutions or moral precepts but on a "balance of power" capable of deterring would-be aggressors or a "concert of powers" willing to police the world. Morgenthau's disciples warn that leaders ignore realist tenets at their own peril.

The realist paradigm has continued to exercise a strong hold on many observers of international relations. However, the paradigm has been criticized for its somewhat vague, loose conception of power and national interests, as well as its failure to account adequately for interstate cooperation, in particular, such real-world developments as the creation and expansion of the European Union and the peaceful end of the Cold War. Just as neoliberalism by the 1980s added a new wrinkle to the idealist paradigm, **neorealism** around the same time offered a new take on classical realism, partly to address these criticisms. Inspired by Kenneth Waltz's *Theory of International Politics*, neorealists have maintained the assumption that nation-states are the primary units whose interactions constitute international relations, focusing on how the individual "capabilities" of states and the resultant power distribution among them in the international system determine much of what happens in the system, at least anything of major importance. In analyzing the foreign policy behavior of states, neorealists play down the impact of domestic politics (e.g., whether a country is a democracy or a dictatorship) as well as the characteristics of individual leaders (e.g., the sex or personality of a head of state). Like classical realists, they see international politics as inherently conflictual, although they base this not on the intrinsic wickedness of human nature but rather on the anarchic structure of the international system.[40]

Neorealists concede that interstate cooperation is possible, but they insist it is much more likely in **low politics** issue-areas that do not threaten core national interests (e.g., the creation of a postal regime to regulate international mail flows) than in **high politics** issue-areas (e.g., arms control). Because security remains the paramount concern, even when all states may benefit from an agreement (i.e., even when negotiations promise *absolute* gains for all—a win-win outcome), cooperation will prove difficult if some states are perceived as winning more *relative* to others, since improved capabilities could subsequently confer military advantage.[41] Moreover, whatever international regimes develop, including international organizations, will still reflect underlying power realities, as with the United States enjoying special privileges on the UN Security Council and in such institutions as the World Bank and International Monetary Fund.[42] Although the realist paradigm has gone through further iterations (recently neoclassical realists[43] have attempted to build additional foreign policy determinants into their analysis, such as the role of domestic politics and leadership characteristics, that had been ignored by neorealists), what unites all thinkers in this tradition is a basic skepticism toward the inclusion of ethical or moral concerns in the affairs of states.

The Marxist Paradigm

Marxism shares liberalism's concern with moral, normative issues but offers a very different analysis of the dynamics of world politics. This paradigm has occupied a prominent place in comparative and international politics for well over a century. It owes its origins to Karl Marx, the nineteenth-century German philosopher whose *Capital* and *Communist Manifesto* (written with Friedrich Engels) sought to explain what he viewed as an unfair, exploitive set of relationships between capitalist economic elites and members of the working class within and across national societies. According to Marx, through their control of private property rights, the former (the bourgeoisie) were able to maintain themselves as the ruling class over the latter (the proletariat). Marx envisioned that once class distinctions and private property were eliminated in a worldwide workers' revolution, national governments and nation-states would disappear as well.

Latter-day Marxists have refined Marxist thought to account for the fact that no such revolution has occurred, while capitalist economic systems have proven quite durable. One line of Marxist thought holds that capitalist states have been able to alleviate their inner class tensions by exploiting other countries, taking advantage of cheap labor and captive markets in less developed countries to stave off economic collapse. Wealthy elites in developed capitalist states that form the "core" of the world economy co-opt elites in less developed states on the "periphery" and are together responsible for the growing gap between rich and poor worldwide. The proliferation of multinational corporations is seen as merely the latest stage in the centuries-long historical development of the "world capitalist system."[44] Marxists, then, tend to view international relations more as a class struggle than a struggle between states. Wars stem from the underlying expansionist impulses of global capitalism and the rivalries among capitalist elites. To the extent that national governments move away from free market capitalism and embrace centrally planned economies that redistribute wealth in a more equal fashion, poverty will be reduced and social harmony will be increased, domestically and internationally.

Given the opposite trend of late—the collapse of communism in the former Soviet Union, the transition of erstwhile communist states in Eastern Europe toward market economies, and the experimentation with stock markets and other capitalist features in the few remaining communist states (notably China and Vietnam)—Marxist thinkers have been put on the defensive. However, the radical tradition represented by Marxism continues to have a strong attraction for many people around the world, and especially resonates in parts of Latin America, Africa, and Asia, where those who have experienced colonialism, discrimination, and massive poverty find it a more useful prism through which to interpret international relations than either the realist or liberal lenses.

Constructivism, Feminism, and Other Challengers

There are other, newer schools of thought that have gained adherents in the international relations field. One such school is **constructivism**, which has sought to address what are thought to be failings of realism and liberalism. Both the realist and liberal paradigms, for all their differences, share essentially an interest-based explanation of international relations, which treats actors as calculating, utility-maximizing agents (whether driven by national self-interest or mutual interests) coping with various *material forces* or *structures* that limit choice. In contrast, constructivism stresses the power of *ideas*, putting the emphasis on the *agents* more than the structures.[45] Constructivists study the emergence of new normative beliefs and new knowledge that become widely accepted and that can cause a redefinition of interests and changed behavior. One way to think of this is that constructivism explores the role of paradigms in revolutionizing human affairs.

Constructivists go so far as to argue that there is no objective social reality whatsoever. For example, they consider sovereignty a social construct rather than a given; it was a concept that began to be internalized in Europe by the seventeenth century and subsequently spread across the globe, and can be unlearned just as readily as it was learned. The so-called English School, represented by scholars such as Hedley Bull and Martin Wight, "holds that the system of states is embedded in a society of states, which includes sets of values, rules, and institutions that are commonly accepted by states and which make it possible for the system of states to function."[46] The recently articulated norm of "humanitarian intervention," promoted by former UN secretary-general Kofi Annan and others who argue that the international community has a right to intervene in the internal affairs of countries where genocide and gross human rights abuses are occurring, threatens to play havoc with the norm of state sovereignty. Constructivist theorists argue that "realist and liberal theories do not provide good explanations for this behavior," referring to interventions in Somalia and elsewhere since 1990.[47] When the United States led a NATO intervention in Serbia in 1999, in order to end ethnic cleansing of Albanians in the Serbian province of Kosovo by Serb leader Slobodan Milosevic, realists and liberals chalked it up to the calculation of national interests on the part of NATO countries. One realist analysis attributed it to "the allies needing target practice"[48] while liberals attributed it to the mutual interests of America's European partners in minimizing refugee and other problems in the Balkans. Constructivists, on the other hand, insisted that interests alone could not explain such interventionist behavior, and instead saw it as further evidence of a new, selfless human rights norm taking hold in the minds of statesmen.

Likewise, other long-held ideas can give way to new ideas, based not merely on changed historical forces but on new thinking that renders the old ideas "bad." Slavery and colonialism, considered for centuries to be human institutions that would prevail forever, were eventually ended by the mid-twentieth century.[49] Although their passing might be due partly to the fact that they were no longer as profitable as in earlier days, constructivists would attribute it more to normative progress. "Free trade" is now widely accepted as the basis for international economic relations not merely because of changed congeries of interests but because it is considered a "good" idea, grounded in the collective memories of how protectionism contributed to the Great Depression and World War II. Inis Claude has noted the power of the "idea" of international organization, something that did not fully become "taken for granted" until the twentieth century; and Martha Finnemore notes that "states are socialized to accept new norms, values, and perceptions of interest by international organizations."[50] Constructivists also point to the role of **epistemic communities**—climatologists and other scientific networks—in disseminating new knowledge that leads to a rethinking of environmental and other concerns. Although constructivists are criticized for overly abstract theorizing and for suggesting that reality is whatever one wishes to make of it, they have provided some useful insights into subtle factors that shape world politics.

Feminist theory, which draws on constructivist concepts and is found across several disciplines, likewise has added important insights in the study of IR. Feminist scholars see gender-based identities and beliefs as an overlooked set of variables that have affected world politics. According to feminist thinkers, women have been excluded from both the practice and study of international relations, which has had the effect of privileging a male view of IR. Feminists argue that many core assumptions in the IR field, especially those articulated by realists, such as anarchy and sovereignty, tend to reflect masculine ways of seeing the world. They call for more careful examination of how gender can affect foreign policy decision-making, including not only how male identity relates to war making and other decisions but also how women have played a role in world politics. One strand of feminist scholarship holds that if there were more women heads of state, there would be less war, owing to the fact that men are either physiologically (due to testosterone and other hormones) or socially (due to childhood upbringing) inclined to be more aggressive and competitive. Not only war but also poverty and social injustice are thought to be correlated with male-dominated, patriarchal societies. The feminist literature finds that inadequate attention has been given to studying and addressing human trafficking, sexual discrimination, and other issues that disproportionately affect women.[51] For example, only recently has rape been included in the development of international law pertaining to war crimes and genocide.

Some Final Thoughts About Paradigms

There are still other bodies of theory one could cite, such as postmodernism and various offshoots of constructivism and Marxism, but I will spare the reader any longer excursion into IR theory, except to note that some political scientists have suggested that interdependence and the blurring of domestic and foreign affairs have accelerated to the point where an entirely novel "post-international politics" paradigm is called for.[52] The point here is that no one school has a monopoly on wisdom or knowledge in the field of international relations. All the above paradigms have some merit in helping to illuminate how world politics operates. Since experienced scholars disagree as to which paradigm best captures IR, it is probably futile for beginning students to attempt to identify the "best" paradigm. However, struggling with the pros and cons of each paradigm will sharpen your ability to cope with ambiguity and help you become a shrewd observer of world politics. (See the *IR* Critical Thinking Box "Are You a Realist or an Idealist: Are You from Mars or from Venus, or from Some Other Planet?")

Since the 1960s, when **behavioralists** initiated a movement to go beyond the reliance on such traditional research methods as participant observation and diplomatic history and make greater use of aggregate data, quantitative analysis, and mathematical models, scholars have aspired to make the international relations field more *scientific*. The goal has been to build a cumulative body of knowledge based on more sophisticated, rigorous methods, entailing the systematic

IR Critical Thinking:
Are You a Realist or an Idealist: Are You from Mars or from Venus,
or from Some Other Planet?

Read the following passage from Robert Kagan, *Of Paradise and Power* (Knopf, 2003, p. 3), written at a time when the United States was experiencing disagreements with France, Germany, and other European allies over the Iraq War and other issues. It relates to our discussion of paradigms, particularly whether a realist or an idealist (liberal) paradigm best represents the contemporary world of international relations.

It is time to stop pretending that Europeans and Americans share a common view of the world, or even that they occupy the same world. On the all-important question of power—the efficacy of power, the morality of power, the desirability of power—American and European perspectives are diverging. Europe is turning away from power, or to put it a little differently, it is moving beyond power into a self-contained world of laws and rules and transnational negotiation and cooperation. It is entering a post-colonial paradise of peace and relative prosperity, the realization of Immanuel Kant's "perpetual peace." Meanwhile, the United States remains mired in history, exercising power in an anarchic Hobbesian world where international laws and rules are unreliable, and where true security . . . [and] promotion of . . . order still depend on the possession and use of military might. That is why on major strategic and international questions today, Americans are from Mars and Europeans are from Venus. They agree on little and understand one another less and less.

Ask yourself the following questions and try to answer them:

1. Where do *you* stand in this debate? Do you subscribe to the American view—seeing the world in Hobbesian terms—and label yourself a "realist"? Or do you subscribe to the European view—seeing the world in Kantian terms—and label yourself an "idealist" ("liberal")? Is the U.S. position too cynical, self-centered, and hawkish? Is the European position too naive, unrealistic, and dovish? Alternatively, do you reject both paradigms and see things differently (perhaps taking a middle-of-the-road position) or refuse to label yourself at all?

2. Do you think Europeans lean more toward relying on international law and organization and peaceful approaches to world order because of their historical experiences—having experienced firsthand the horrible costs of two world wars and having seen the benefits of cooperation in the form of the European Union—or because, unlike the United States, they prefer not having to spend a lot on armies and hence do not have that instrument of power readily available to them?

3. Many realist thinkers argue that few, if any, recent American administrations have followed purely realist policies. Which U.S. presidents since World War II might be labeled "realist" and which "idealist"? How would you label George W. Bush? Barack Obama? What kind of president is better? What are the pros and cons of each paradigm?

4. Let's get concrete. What do you think about what happened at the prison on the U.S. naval base at Guantanamo, Cuba, following 9/11, when captured al Qaeda terrorists were apparently subjected to treatment by American interrogators that bordered on "torture"? Should the United States be concerned that it may have

violated the Geneva Convention ban against mistreatment of POWs as well as the UN Convention on Torture, undermining norms that help protect captured American soldiers and civilians from torture? Or was this offset by the pressure felt by the U.S. military and CIA to extract vital intelligence information that was needed to protect the American homeland from another possible terrorist attack? Where do *you* stand on this?

---

development of theories that could *explain* the dynamics of international relations and then testing these against hard evidence. I noted, for example, the efforts of neorealists and neoliberals to formulate more carefully stated propositions. Judging from the ongoing paradigm debate, it is clear that the science of international relations remains in its infancy. Although some quantitative political scientists believe their methods will ultimately enable them to answer the question "Why do countries go to war?" and other puzzles with a high degree of precision and confidence, even to the point of being able to *predict* various international occurrences, many other scholars argue that the complexities of the international environment and the limits of quantification are such that reasonably educated guesses (along the lines of the local weather forecaster) are the best we can hope for. Most international relationists would be willing to settle for the predictive powers of meteorologists, who deal in probabilities and tendencies and are frequently wrong, especially when looking more than a week ahead. As one IR scholar said, "The goal is not to foretell exactly what events will take place in China [in, say, 2020]" but rather "to develop skill in showing 'which way the wind is blowing' and, therefore, what might well happen under stated circumstances."[53] Here is where paradigms can be helpful. A liberal thinker such as John Ikenberry will likely project different possible scenarios accompanying China's rise to great-power status than a realist thinker such as John Mearsheimer, and both taken together can force a critical analysis of how best to deal with China.

SCHOLARS, POLICYMAKERS, AND CITIZENS

Mark Twain once remarked that "everybody talks about the weather but nobody does anything about it." We may not be able to control the weather, but we do have at least some capacity to control what happens in international relations. For this reason, paradigm debates are not mere academic, ivory tower debates of concern only to *scholars*. They have import for *policymakers*, who are empowered to make decisions that affect millions of people, as well as *citizens*, who, at least in democracies, are empowered to change policymakers if they do not like the job they are doing. Although policymakers and citizens are inclined to dismiss theoretical concerns, they cannot escape them entirely. Even if they are not fully conscious of it, their judgments are based to some extent on theories—a variety of personal assumptions about how the world works—however undeveloped and unfounded those theories may be. The more solid the theories that policymakers bring to their analysis of the problems that cross their desks, the more successful they are likely to be in responding to those problems. Similarly, the better the theories that inform citizen worldviews, the better position citizens will be in to evaluate the soundness of the decisions made by their government. In other words, paradigms (or theories) aid us not only in *explanation and prediction* but also in *prescription* (weighing policy options) and making *normative* judgments (arriving at value judgments about the morality and general rightness of some decision).

For example, much hand wringing has occurred over the decision of the Bush administration in 2003 to invade Iraq and remove the dictatorial regime of Saddam Hussein. The invasion resulted in American military forces becoming bogged down in a brutal, protracted insurgency through 2009, with little end in sight. The Bush administration claimed that Iraq under Saddam posed a threat in a post-9/11 world due to what were thought to be his WMDs development plans and ties to terrorist groups. The decision has been blamed on different mind-sets—different schools of thought. Liberals were critical of Bush's unilateralist approach and failure to fully utilize multilateral institutions like the United Nations. However, realists blamed liberals, many of whom initially had supported the war as a human rights imperative and who harbored Wilsonian notions of how exporting democracy abroad would promote global peace. Most realists opposed the war from the start, worrying that it was an unwise misuse of American military power; they criticized both the liberals for "soft Wilsonianism" and the so-called neoconservatives in the Bush administration for "hard Wilsonianism" (being critical of the neocons for sharing Woodrow Wilson's penchant for seeing world politics as a morality play and undertaking global crusades, even if neocons chose to rely on the use of American military muscle rather than international organizations as their favored instrument).[54] Supporters of the war invoked the "democratic peace" hypothesis (i.e., the proposition that democracies virtually never go to war against each other) and its corollary (i.e., the more dictatorships that are replaced by democracies, the safer place the world will be) as a justification for the decision. Because it is impossible to recall the last time two democracies fought each other, the democratic peace hypothesis has been called perhaps the closest thing to a scientific law that one can find in the field of international relations. Still, obvious questions could be raised about the relevance of such scientific knowledge to the Iraq case, given the ethnic-religious divisions and the lack of any democratic tradition in the country, and whether it made sense to risk the substantial loss of life and the alienation of the international community against the United States—especially since most empirical evidence also demonstrated that it was exceedingly rare to find any cases of successful imposition of "democracy at gunpoint."[55]

Questions could also be raised about the realist prescription for U.S. handling of the terrorist threat and other problems in the Middle East, which called for the United States simply to reduce its presence and have a "smaller footprint" in the region so as to provoke less hostility; realists seemed especially ill equipped to deal with threats posed by nonstate actors such as al Qaeda, given their paradigm's almost total preoccupation with great-power politics among states.[56] Many feminist critiques of the decision to go to war in Iraq were preoccupied with the almost all-male makeup of President Bush's inner circle, and how the presence of more women in his "war council" might have changed it into a "peace council," even though Condoleezza Rice, his female national security adviser, was a leading hawkish voice in support of the war.

Meanwhile, citizens were left in the 2008 election and beyond to make their own judgments about the soundness of the decisions of their elected officials with regard to the Iraq War and other matters. Before rushing to judgment, you should take the time to gain as thorough an understanding as possible of how world politics work. This book aims to provide at least a start.

THE PLAN OF THE BOOK

I hope I have whetted your appetite for studying international relations, since there is much to digest. To help process the large volume of information and knowledge presented in this book, the text has a simple organizational logic. *Part One* provides a conceptual and historical foundation for the study of contemporary IR. Having offered some conceptual "basics" in Chapter 1, through the examination of a number of definitional and espistemological questions, I turn in Chapter 2 to a brief overview of the evolution of the *international system*, tracing the roots of the contemporary, post–Cold War system and delineating its main features (the current distribution of power, distribution of wealth, and other properties). Throughout the book, I will refer back to some of the themes introduced in Chapter 1, particularly (1) the notion that international relations is characterized by both continuity and change, with many core features enduring over centuries but other features undergoing major metamorphosis (and the current system being particularly in ferment), and (2) the notion that no one paradigm captures the complexity of our times, with different theoretical perspectives offering alternative cuts of reality and with different aspects of IR (international security, international political economy, and other topics) best viewed through multiple lenses.

Part Two and *Part Three* are the "meat and potatoes" of the book. Here the reader will find the essential "stuff" of international relations. *Part Two* covers the subjects of foreign policy (Chapter 3), diplomacy and bargaining (Chapter 4), war and the use of armed force (Chapter 5), and international organization and law (Chapter 6), adding some fresh food for thought on some very old, traditional elements of IR. You should be able to discern the ongoing "struggle for power" occurring alongside the "struggle for order." Building on *Part Two*, *Part Three* focuses on three main issue-areas—international security (Chapter 7), human security (Chapter 8), and international economics (Chapter 9). I discuss the politics of global problem-solving in these three broad areas, that is, how the international community is attempting to reduce the proliferation of weapons of mass destruction and other instruments of violence, how it is attempting to expand human rights and human development, and how it is attempting to manage the world economy through trade, investment, and foreign aid so as to promote prosperity. Along the way, we will touch upon globalization, environmental issues, and a variety of other concerns. We will see the extent to which nation-states, in combination with subnational and transnational actors, are succeeding or failing in producing international regimes capable of overcoming or at least mitigating the effects of the anarchic structure of the global polity; in other words, we will analyze efforts to promote what many observers call "global governance" in the absence of global government.

Part Four concludes our study of IR, offering a few final tidbits that hopefully will stimulate further reflection. Chapter 10 engages the reader in critical thinking about the *future*. But before we address the future, we need first to peer into the past, which is the subject of the next chapter.

QUESTIONS FOR STUDY AND DISCUSSION

1. How would you define "international relations"?
2. What is "sovereignty"?
3. How does international politics differ from domestic (national) politics?
4. How might the glass today seem both half empty and half full, in terms of negative and positive trends in the world?
5. Give at least five examples of how global interdependence has affected your life.
6. Describe the realist, idealist (liberal), Marxist, constructivist, and feminist paradigms. Which one strikes you as the best framework for trying to understand international relations?

SUGGESTIONS FOR FURTHER READING

David Baldwin, ed., *Neorealism and Neoliberalism: The Contemporary Debate* (New York: Columbia University Press, 1993).

John Baylis et al., *The Globalization of World Politics*, 4th ed. (Oxford: Oxford University Press, 2008), pt. 2.

Nils Gleditsch, "The Liberal Moment Fifteen Years On," *International Studies Quarterly* 52 (December 2008): 691–712.

Charles W. Kegley, *Controversies in International Relations Theory: Realism and the Neoliberal Challenge* (New York: St. Martin's, 1995), pt. 1.

Robert O. Keohane and Joseph S. Nye, *Power and Interdependence*, 3rd ed. (New York: Longman, 2001).

Andrew Moravscik, "Taking Preferences Seriously: A Liberal Theory of International Politics," *International Organization* 51 (Autumn 1997): 513–553.

Hans Morgenthau, *Politics Among Nations* (New York: Knopf, 1989), chap. 1.

V. Spike Peterson and Anne Sisson Runyan, *Global Gender Issues*, 2nd ed. (Boulder, CO: Westview, 1999).

Jennifer Sterling-Folker, ed., *Making Sense of International Relations Theory* (Boulder, CO: Lynne Rienner, 2006).

John A. Vasquez, ed., *Classics of International Relations*, 3rd ed. (Upper Saddle River, NJ: Prentice-Hall, 1996), pts. 1–2.

Paul R. Viotti and Mark Kauppi, *International Relations Theory* (Boston: Allyn & Bacon, 1999).

Kenneth N. Waltz, *Theory of International Relations* (Reading, MA: Addison-Wesley, 1979).

Alexander Wendt, "Anarchy Is What States Make of It: The Social Construction of Power Politics," *International Organization* 46 (Spring 1992): 391–427.

2

The Historical Development of the International System

FROM THE BIRTH OF THE NATION-STATE TO GLOBALIZATION

You cannot step in the same river twice, for fresh waters are ever flowing in upon you.

—Heraclitus, c. 500 B.C.

It is déjà vu all over again.

—Yogi Berra, c. A.D. 1980

History, by definition, involves change. And yet there are recurring patterns that can be found. It is these recurring patterns that allow us to benefit from experience, to learn from both successes and mistakes so as to produce better decisions in the future. On the lessons of history, particularly learning from mistakes, recall George Santayana's famous admonition that "those who cannot remember the past are condemned to repeat it." However, drawing lessons from history is not easy. It has been said that "the most important thing we learn from history is that we never learn from history." Especially when it comes to international relations, leaders and publics often fail to absorb the lessons of the past. Even when we do learn lessons from history, we may misapply them to current situations. This only underscores the need to develop a better understanding of our past. The purpose of this chapter is to show how we have arrived at this current moment in the political life of the planet.

In surveying the evolution of international relations, I will not provide a detailed chronology of events but rather a short sketch of major developments and trends. I want to give the reader a sense of how certain essential aspects of international relations have changed significantly over time while others have remained relatively constant. To furnish a thumbnail account of several hundred years of history in a single chapter, it is helpful to utilize the concept of **international system**, which can be defined as the broad pattern of political, economic, and other interrelationships that impact world affairs or, if you will, the general backdrop against which the drama of international relations is performed. (If one wishes to use the game metaphor, it is the game board upon which the game of IR is played.) An examination of the international system forces us to look at world politics as a whole—IR writ large—rather than focusing on any particular region or dimension. At times, the key ingredients of world politics change so much that we say the international system has been *transformed*, and one distinct era of international politics has given way to a completely new era. For example, most observers believe that the fall of the Berlin Wall in 1989 and the disappearance of the U.S.-Soviet Cold War rivalry ended a "bipolar" international system that had lasted for almost a half century after World War II, ushering in a new system that is still a work in progress.

For purposes of discussion, I have divided international relations history into three periods: (1) the international system in the seventeenth, eighteenth, and nineteenth centuries; (2) the international system in the twentieth century; and (3) the contemporary international system. In order to compare different eras of international politics, we need to identify those properties of the international system most worthy of comparison, which include (1) the nature of the actors (nation-states and other actors), (2) the distribution of power and wealth (dominance by one or two actors or relative equality among several major actors), (3) the degree of polarization (the rigidity or flexibility of alignments and alliances), and (4) the goals of the actors (preoccupation with territorial acquisition or economic welfare goals or some other objective) and the means they use to achieve them (e.g., the nature of weapons technology). We will examine how these features of international relations have changed over the years, some substantially and some less so. But first, before examining the evolution of the nation-state system from the seventeenth century onward, we need to understand why the seventeenth century serves as our starting point for the history of the international system.

THE BIRTH OF THE NATION-STATE

In Chapter 1, I mentioned that scholars generally trace the modern nation-state and nation-state system to 1648, when the Peace of Westphalia ended the Thirty Years War in Europe and gave rise to the territorially based, *sovereign* political units we now take for granted as the main reference points on the world map and in the hearts and minds of people all across the globe. What is now the predominant form of political organization on the planet is a relatively young institution, roughly only 350 years old, not long considering that *Homo sapiens* has been on earth for more than a million years, dating to the earliest cases of stone tool creation. Even though the average person today probably cannot imagine life on earth without nation-states, it is sobering to remember that there is nothing God-given about such actors. They had to be created. Any account of the birth of the nation-state needs to go back in time and examine the birth pangs well before 1648.

The Earliest Forms of Political Organization

The first humans did not live in states of any form. For millennia, the species lived a nomadic existence, gathering and hunting for food from one locale to an-other, without any permanent settlements and, therefore, without any formal gov-ernmental structures associated with "states." The earliest form of political organization was the extended family or kinship group, which evolved into bands and tribes led by chieftains. Only around 5000 B.C., with the agricultural revolution and the domestication of plants and animals that enabled permanent settlements to be established and civilizations to flourish, did states emerge in Mesopotamia (e.g., Babylon, in the vicinity of what is now Iraq). However, these were not nation-states so much as city-states and other types of political units. It is esti-mated that some 600,000 distinct political units existed in the world in 1000 B.C., although these lacked the clearly defined boundaries, complex bureaucracies, and aspirations of nationhood of modern states.[1] The Greek city-states in Thucydides' time, around 400 B.C., were independent political communities, with Athens, Sparta, and other polities forming a state system that in some respects was a pre-cursor of the nation-state system. The ancient Greeks established diplomatic and commercial contacts on the Hellenic peninsula and beyond, made war with each other, and made peace, creating the Delian League, what amounted to an inter-national organization. Athenians introduced concepts of citizenship, democracy, and sovereignty. Around the same time, other early state systems were function-ing, such as the ancient Indian state system under the Mauryan empire described in the writings of the Brahmin minister Kautilya, as well as the Chinese state sys-tem during the Chou dynasty, "noted politically for conflict and competition among the larger states, decline of stable alliances and the polar power structure, and eventual destruction of the system itself."[2]

The Greek city-states, along with much of the Mediterranean and Central Asian areas, came under the rule of Alexander the Great in the fourth century B.C. Be-fore dying at age 33 in 323 B.C., Alexander supposedly had "wept by the riverbank of the Nile because there were no more worlds to conquer." After Alexander's death, all the roads that had led to Macedonia subsequently led to Rome, whose empire under Julius Caesar and a series of rulers ultimately stretched from West-ern Europe to the Near East. Interestingly, one writer has noted that "the tapes-tries hung in the *Palais des Nations* in Geneva, Switzerland [once the headquarters of the League of Nations] . . . picture . . . the process of humanity combining into ever larger and more stable units for the purpose of governance—first the fam-ily, then the tribe, then the city-state, and then the nation—a process which pre-sumably would eventually culminate in the entire world being combined in one political unit."[3] However, this depiction of the human story as comprising a steady, unilinear progression from small political units to bigger ones, with the timeline ultimately projecting out toward world government, seems to misrepresent the flow of history. The history of humanity can more accurately be read as the search for the optimal political unit, with the pendulum swinging between two extremes: sprawling, transregional political orders (e.g., the huge empires of Alexander the Great and Rome) and a set of much smaller, highly fragmented polities (e.g., the 600,000 units that existed in 1000 B.C. and the city-states that appeared shortly thereafter on the Greek peninsula).

The Feudal Order in Medieval Europe and the Peace of Westphalia

The tension between centripetal (centralizing) and centrifugal (decentralizing) forces was an important part of the story between the fall of Rome in A.D. 476 and the Peace of Westphalia in 1648. The following passage describes just how earth-shaking the fall of the Roman Empire was when it ushered in the Dark Ages in Europe: "In the year A.D. 120, an Acquitanian grape grower may have known very little about the life of a shepherdess in the hills of Cyprus; yet both owed their allegiance to the same government, that of Rome, and, more important, each no doubt perceived herself and imagined the other as living within a single world society, the Roman one.... The political disintegration of Europe after the fall of Rome in A.D. 476 must rank as one of the most traumatic social upheavals of all time."[4]

Efforts to resurrect the empire centered on two "universalistic" institutions that sought to govern Europe during the Middle Ages. One was the pope, who as head of Christendom claimed supremacy in religious matters. The other was the Holy Roman Emperor, who as head of the Holy Roman Empire claimed supremacy in secular affairs. Charlemagne created the latter in A.D. 800, with the pope's blessing, in an attempt to unite Western Europe and all Christianity against the Byzantine Empire in the East. In reality, the secular and theological realms were blurred, as were the geographical borders. (It has been said about the Holy Roman Empire that it "was neither holy, nor Roman, nor an empire.") Both the pope and the emperor had to contend with a splintered landscape of some 500 entities on the Continent that became known as the **feudal system**. On the eve of Westphalia, this political space was one where

> nation-states did not exist, there was no concept of ethnic nationhood that had any practical significance to the form of political organization, and even though kings [and queens, as in England] reigned on thrones, few ruled directly over a specified group of people inhabiting definable territories. Instead, there were many hierarchies in the known areas of Europe.... There also existed hundreds of semisovereign walled cities and feudal lords.... Europe was a patchwork of small quasi sovereignties, states within states, and overlapping hierarchies.[5]

However, as 1648 approached, the political landscape was changing and the feudal order was dying. The nation-state was not born overnight, precisely at the moment the Treaty of Westphalia was signed, but was the product of a gradual historical process. It had been already gestating for awhile due to various technological and other developments.

One scholar traces the roots of the "Westphalian state system" as far back as A.D. 900, noting that the growing merchant class of artisans was already finding that the feudal system, with its crazy-quilt set of juridical relationships, was an obstacle to expanded commerce and was beginning to cast its lot with kings against the prerogatives of the landed nobility. Traders were attracted to the idea of a single ruler presiding over a specified territory in which contracts could be reliably enforced and a common set of laws would apply, including a standardized currency and system of weights and measures conducive to reducing the transaction costs of doing business. But it was not just capitalism that was driving the demise of feudalism. The Concordat of Worms in 1122 dealt a critical blow to the idea of papal supremacy, since the pope grudgingly agreed to surrender to princes the right to appoint bishops in their territories, presaging the religious wars that followed Martin Luther's Protestant Reformation in 1517.[6] By the fifteenth century, the invention of gunpowder had already rendered the walled city and its parapet fortifications obsolete as a mode of political organization capable of performing the defense function. As Stephen Krasner has commented, "The driving force behind the elimination of feudal institutions . . . was changes in the nature of military technology and the growth of trade, which systematically favored states that could take advantage of siege guns and elaborate defenses, and organize and protect long-distance commerce."[7] Fifteenth-century Europe saw the emergence of Florence, Venice, and other prosperous city-states on the Italian peninsula that had the trappings of independence, but they would prove no match militarily and economically for the large-scale, national units that were forming in England, France, Spain, and Holland.[8]

These historical forces converged around Westphalia in the mid-seventeenth century. It was, in a sense, the perfect storm. What exactly happened at Westphalia, at the gathering of European diplomats in the German countryside? In a nutshell, the rulers of France, Austria, Spain, Sweden, the Netherlands, Prussia, and other adversaries in the Thirty Years War agreed to end the conflict that had devastated Europe and attempted to remove a main cause of the conflict by giving each ruler the right to designate Protestantism or Catholicism as the religion of the realm. The implications, however, went well beyond granting religious autonomy to monarchs. Whether they realized it or not, the parties to the Treaty of Westphalia were not merely ending a war but were creating a revolutionary new system of sovereign states whose rulers could claim authority over all domestic matters within their borders and authority to conduct foreign affairs abroad on behalf of their subjects. The distinction between "domestic policy" and "foreign policy" suddenly had much greater meaning than previously.

Culver Pictures

The Signing of the Treaty of Westphalia in 1648.

As K. J. Holsti puts it, Westphalia "represented a new diplomatic arrangement—an order created by states, for states."[9] The nation-state was a halfway house between the universalistic pretensions of the papacy and the Holy Roman Empire on the one hand and the fragmented realities of the feudal order on the other, as national monarchs consolidated their power against local princes and repudiated any allegiance to higher religious or other authorities outside their territory. Leo Gross memorably observed that "the Peace of Westphalia, for better or worse, marks the end of an epoch and the opening of another. It represents the majestic portal which leads from the old world into the new world."[10] Some argue that there are technological and other forces at work today (e.g., globalization), which, also for better or worse and also whether we are fully cognizant of it or not, may be producing a "Westphalian moment." Whether the early twenty-first century is a portal between two epochs, putting us on the threshold of a revolution in human affairs as profound as that which occurred in 1648, remains to be seen. But we are getting ahead of the story.

THE INTERNATIONAL SYSTEM IN THE SEVENTEENTH, EIGHTEENTH, AND NINETEENTH CENTURIES

Over time, the "idea" of the nation-state was to become firmly rooted in the psyche of people everywhere. Still, it took awhile for it to catch on. The term "international relations" was not coined until the English writer Jeremy Bentham invented it in 1789, to describe what the statesmen at Westphalia had wrought; he was the first to refer to "the law of nations."[11] Not every polity instantly qualified for membership in the Westphalian state system. Many areas in central Europe in what was to become Germany, for example, retained vestiges of feudalism for quite some time after the seventeenth century, while others, such as China, occupied a different political space altogether. Christopher Columbus's voyages to the Americas and subsequent travels by other European explorers, along with the commercial contacts of traders in the British East India Company and Dutch East India Company (Vereenigde Oost-Indische Compagnie, or VOC in Dutch) had by the time of Westphalia begun to produce a planetary perspective on a scale that Alexander the Great never knew. However, the "closing of the world frontier" would not occur until the Americas and the farthermost reaches of Africa and Asia entered the interstate system.[12] Over the next three centuries, through colonialism and imperialism, the state system was a European-dominated one. Only gradually were non-European polities recognized as members of the community of nations, as the Westphalian mode of political organization spread into every corner of the earth. The United States and the Latin American countries were the first to achieve independence from European colonial rule, China and Japan and a handful of other long autonomous societies were admitted into the club as sovereign equals (at least in a formal sense) by the latter nineteenth century, and the remaining parts of the globe in the latter twentieth century.[13]

International Politics in the Seventeenth and Eighteenth Centuries

The Westphalian state system was initially dominated by England, France, Austria, Prussia, and Russia, although a few others, such as Spain and the Netherlands, also competed for influence. These "great powers" were the chief *actors* in international relations. Within these states only the royal families and aristocratic elites were involved in decision making. Sovereignty resided not in the people but in the monarch, derived from "divine right of kings." Absolute monarchy was best exemplified by King Louis XIV, who sat on the French throne for seventy-two years until his death in 1715, and whose famous motto was *l'etat c'est moi* ("I am the state"). Only later, toward the end of the eighteenth century with the American and French revolutions, did the idea of representative government and the consent of the governed begin to gain acceptance.

Although the early European states were absolutist, the size of government was limited by the resources the ruler could command, which required either collecting taxes from subjects or acquiring gold and commodities in overseas trade and conquest or through loans. These resources were devoted primarily to the *goal* of defending the realm and expanding the ruler's power. Defensive and offensive motivations tended to blend together, as each state, operating in an anarchic environment, experienced the same **security dilemma** that successive generations were to experience as well—the felt need for more national power to enhance national security, even if the quest for power only tended to increase feelings of insecurity.

Whether rational or not, the main business of government was war. For example, it is estimated that the eighteenth-century Russian czar Peter the Great spent 90 percent of his government's revenue on war preparation and fighting, while England around the same time was spending almost 75 percent of its public budget on the military.[14] "Big government" in the form of the "welfare state" did not yet exist. Certainly poverty, pollution, and other serious societal problems were cause for concern. For example, sounding like a modern-day trade protectionist, one Englishman petitioned Queen Anne in the seventeenth century to ban Indian textile imports since "English workmen could not compete with Eastern labour . . . [because] the people in India are such slaves as to work for less than a penny a day whereas ours will not work for under a shilling."[15] Similarly, in 1659 one observer wrote that London was enveloped in "such a cloud of sea-coal, as if there be a resemblance of hell on earth."[16] But the government did not see itself as having responsibility for full employment, much less clean air.

Absolutist rulers never seemed to have enough money to fund their armed forces. Louis XIV was so starved for cash that he created superfluous judgeships and other offices for sale, contributing to the growth of the French bureaucracy. In short, in France and elsewhere during the early state-building era that followed the Peace of Westphalia, "war made the state and the state made war," a pattern that was to continue into the twentieth century.[17]

To the extent the state dealt with economic issues, it was as they related to the overriding preoccupation with military issues. Each country sought to increase its economic wealth, mainly as a basis to support a large enough military establishment to expand its power, which in turn could generate additional national wealth. States followed a policy of **mercantilism**, whereby they regulated trade through tariffs and other measures so as to limit imports and increase exports, thereby creating trade surpluses that could provide the state with gold bullion and other revenue. Only with the publication of Adam Smith's *Wealth of Nations* in 1776 would mercantilist economic doctrine be challenged by advocates of **free trade**, who urged the removal of governmental restrictions on the flow of goods and services across national boundaries.

The *distribution of power and wealth* in the international system was divided roughly equally among the half dozen or so great powers. There was no single hegemon that dominated the system, nor a duo of superpowers. There was always a concern that a particular state might not be satisfied with its power or wealth position, might threaten the sovereignty of another state, and might even harbor hegemonic aspirations. The so-called **balance of power** provided a crude mechanism for maintaining order and preventing or defeating aggression. The hope was that any states bent on committing aggression would be deterred from doing so by the prospect of facing a coalition of states at least as powerful; for example, if France was seen as posing a threat to the system by becoming too powerful, England would play a "balancer" role in restoring equilibrium by throwing its weight to those seeking to counter French ambitions.

In order for the balance of power to operate effectively, it required a low level of *polarization*—a high degree of alignment flexibility—so that countries could shift their power quickly from one side to another to thwart any would-be aggressor. The international system in the seventeenth and eighteenth centuries was **multipolar** in regard to the existence of not only multiple power centers ("poles") but also very fluid alignments. The European powers did not fall into rigid blocs but instead were capable of shifting alliances rapidly. Two factors contributed to the ease of making and breaking alliances. First, decisions could be taken quickly by a few rulers who did not have to worry about consulting legislative bodies or taking public opinion polls. Second, related to the latter factor, there were no major ideological cleavages among the great powers that, had they existed, might have inhibited certain countries from becoming alliance partners with others. The leaders of European states were all conservative monarchs, many of whom were connected by family ties.

It proved impossible to prevent wars from occurring, as neither the balance of power nor family ties provided an adequate brake to violence. However, wars were relatively small affairs normally pitting one monarchical regime against another, in contrast to the total wars among whole societies waged in subsequent eras. Monarchs relied on expensive professional armies, often consisting of foreign mercenaries who displayed little loyalty and had high desertion rates. Because of the limited *means* available to states in terms of firepower—in addition to the small size of armies, the military technology of the day had only begun to progress from the longbow and pike to the musket and cannon[18]—the stakes over which wars were fought were also fairly limited. Wars could be long and bloody. However, the masses were generally innocent bystanders during wartime. They might be subjected to rape and plunder, but they usually had no vested interest in the outcome of the conflict, given the fact that rulers generally were indifferent to the well-being of their people. The average peasant in France or elsewhere on the Continent had no reason to identify fully with the state and was not yet responsive to flag-waving and other national symbols. Nation building lagged behind state building, as nationalism and patriotism had not yet become major impulses:

> Monarchs fought for bits of territory, but the residents of disputed terrain were more concerned with protecting their crops and their daughters from marauding troops than with whom they owed allegiance to. . . . It is an exaggeration to refer to European war during this period as a sport of kings, but not a gross exaggeration.[19]

By the end of the eighteenth century, two revolutions occurred that significantly altered the nature of war, along with the nature of nation-states and the state system, precisely by forging a bond between national leaders and followers. One was the American revolt against British rule that established the independence of the United States (1776), and the other was the French revolt against absolutist rule that overthrew the monarchy in France (1789). Both had the effect of establishing the principle of popular sovereignty and ushering in the age of **nationalism**, based on a firmer relationship between the central government of the state and the people over which it presided. The emotional tie between a state and its people was to prove strongest in countries that experienced the greatest growth of mass democracy, but nationalism became a powerful force almost everywhere.

International Politics in the Nineteenth Century

Because France was in the cockpit of Europe, at the center of world politics, while the fledging United States was geographically on the periphery, the French Revolution had the greater impact on the international system. The United States adopted a somewhat isolationist posture toward world affairs through much of its early history, following the advice of George Washington in his farewell address as president in 1796, when he warned America against joining "permanent alliances with any portion of the foreign world," a sentiment echoed by Thomas Jefferson in his presidential inaugural address in 1801, as he cautioned against "entangling alliances." Preoccupied with pursuing its "manifest destiny" by expanding across the North American continent from the Atlantic to the Pacific over the course of the nineteenth century and distracted by a midcentury civil war, the United States was a marginal player in world politics until coming of age as a great power by 1898, with its victory in the Spanish-American War.[20]

France, on the other hand, was a major player in international politics, especially when Napoleon Bonaparte arrived on the scene following the French Revolution. Napoleon claimed to derive his authority as ruler not from the divine right of kings but from the will of the people, whom he referred to as French "citizens." He appealed to them to accept his rule, to pay taxes, and to fight and die on behalf of—and for the greater glory of—the *nation*. France was the first state to implement a military draft, recruiting a mass citizen army through nationwide conscription of young Frenchmen, which enabled it to mobilize an almost million-man army (although Napoleon still had to rely on foreign mercenaries for half his troops). Napoleon tried to export the French Revolution and in the process expand French power, which ended up with France fighting Britain, Austria, Prussia, and Russia during the Napoleonic Wars in the early nineteenth century. French nationalism had the unintended effect of breeding nationalism in Britain and other states in Europe that felt threatened by Napoleon. The new nationalism meant that whole societies and economies were now *actors* in world politics, including as combatants in war, in ways they had not been previously.

A watershed event in the history of the international system was the **Congress of Vienna** in 1815, the peace conference convened following the defeat of Napoleon. Britain, Austria, Prussia, and Russia permitted France a seat at the table among the other great powers and allowed it to join the **Concert of Europe**, which was not so much a formal international organization as an informal multilateral conference system intended to facilitate regular consultations among the major powers whenever their disputes threatened to escalate to war; it was, in a sense, a precursor to the United Nations Security Council, premised on a "concert of great powers" approach to world order. The aim was to avoid another conflagration such as the Napoleonic Wars, which had resulted in horrendous economic and human costs. The Concert was to meet more than thirty times over the next century and was relatively successful in averting major war, so much so that the period from 1815 to 1914 (the outbreak of World War I) has been called "the century of peace." Some wars did occur, such as the Crimean War in 1854 (known for the "Charge of the Light Brigade"), the Austro-Prussian War in 1866, and the Franco-Prussian War in 1870; but these were of short duration and were not terribly costly. The latter two wars led to the unification and creation of the modern nation-states of Italy and Germany, built around appeals to the common cultural and linguistic heritage of the peoples inhabiting Sicily, Naples, and other parts of the Italian peninsula and those inhabiting Prussia and thirty-eight other Germanic territories.

Although the nationalistic fervor of the time threatened to fan the fires of war, the great powers managed to minimize military hostilities among themselves by sublimating chauvinistic energies through overseas territorial annexations in Africa and Asia, which became one of the main *goals* of the European states. At the Congress of Berlin in 1885, Africa was carved up into spheres of influence so that the ambitions of Germany and other rising powers could be accommodated without upsetting the balance of power in Europe. **Imperialism** was a response to both a need to pacify a restless public at home and a need to gain access to raw materials and markets associated with rapid industrialization in the late nineteenth century. An added impetus was the desire by some to take up the "white man's burden," to spread Christianity and Western culture to what were thought to be less civilized peoples on the "dark continent" and in other faraway places. Whereas in 1875 only about 10 percent of Africa and half of Polynesia (Indonesia and the Pacific islands) had been colonized, by 1900 virtually all of those areas had fallen under imperial rule.

Regarding the motivation to pacify restless publics, the mid-nineteenth century witnessed great internal tensions within most European states between liberal movements attempting to expand voting rights and democratic values and reactionary forces attempting to maintain their grip on power. For example, "Germany was ruled by a domestic coalition of landed aristocrats and some very large industrialist capitalists, called the Coalition of Rye and Iron. This ruling coalition used expansionist policies to provide foreign adventures instead of domestic reform, circuses in place of bread. Expansionism was an alternative to social democracy."[21] Flag-waving and the pursuit of national prestige and honor substituted for democratic reform in many states, although as the century progressed, some states, such as Britain and France, were expanding democracy while others, such as Austria and Russia, remained autocratic. The political and ideological ferment within nation-states became even more volatile with the publication of Karl Marx's *Communist Manifesto* in 1848 and *Capital* in 1867.

The Industrial Revolution, which had begun in England in the 1700s and accelerated throughout Europe and the United States in the second half of the nineteenth century, had important effects both within countries and between them. Within the most industrialized countries, it gave rise to growing class conflict between the working class and economic elites and stimulated demands for governments to become welfare states that would provide better jobs, health care, and other social benefits. Internationally, rapid industrialization required raw materials to fuel iron and steel production and other industrial processes, along with new outlets for manufactured goods, thus contributing to imperialist designs on overseas areas that could be exploited for their resources and markets. A growing disparity of wealth occurred between societies in the Northern and Southern Hemispheres. Although a gap between rich and poor had always existed within societies, the gap that formed in the nineteenth century was unprecedented. The Industrial Revolution bypassed the southern half of the globe, leaving some societies with substantial income growth and improved living standards for their rich and poor citizens alike, while other societies saw little or no economic growth and mass improvement. The widening rich-poor gap, which had produced a 2 to 1 ratio between incomes in industrial and nonindustrial societies by 1850, was to become even more pronounced in the twentieth century, by the end of which the gap in some instances had reached 400 to 1.

Industrialization not only skewed the *distribution of wealth* in favor of certain states but also further tilted the *distribution of power* in their favor, since the new economic technology was readily converted into military superiority. The identity of the great powers remained fairly constant throughout much of the nineteenth century: England (Great Britain), France, Prussia (Germany), Austria (Austria-Hungary), and Russia dominated the international system. Although the system was still multipolar in terms of the power configuration, Britain, with its great navy, was considered "the first among equals." Indeed, the "century of peace" has often been referred to as the Pax Britannica, owing to the leadership role played by Britain in conference diplomacy as well as in the international economy, as it became the champion of free trade and the chief source of investment capital.

Toward the end of the century, two non-European countries joined the ranks of the great powers. The United States announced its arrival as a major player on the world stage with its victory in the Spanish-American War in 1898, which was accompanied by imperialist acquisition of the Philippines, Puerto Rico, and Guam. Japan, which had borrowed Western technology to build its armed forces, confirmed its arrival by defeating Russia in the Russo-Japanese War of 1905. Two other non-European states were on the margins of great power status, disadvantaged by their failure to industrialize. China had accounted for almost one-third of world economic output in 1820 but was eclipsed over the next several decades by more economically developed societies. Turkey (the Ottoman Empire) held territorial possessions in the Balkans that gave it a European presence, but its economic weakness rendered it "the sick man of Europe." Almost all of Latin America consisted of independent states, but none had the industrial capacity and wealth that translated into military power.

Through much of the nineteenth century, the international system was also multipolar in terms of the *degree of polarization*: despite widening ideological disagreements between democratic and nondemocratic states, the Concert of Europe prevented formation of rigid blocs. Although ideological conflict occurred within countries between liberal and conservative forces, it was not played out on the international plane. The battle lines in the few wars that were waged were not drawn along ideological lines (e.g., the 1866 Austro-Prussian War involved two conservative regimes). Even when the Concert collapsed by the end of the century, leading to the formation of two opposing alliances, these were not clearly based on ideological divisions. The Triple Entente included democratic Britain and France alongside arch-conservative czarist Russia, while the Triple Alliance included arch-conservative Austria-Hungary with somewhat more liberal Germany and Italy. Still, the opposing alliances created some hardening of rivalries, while the advent of mass democracy and modern military technology and planning reduced decision-making flexibility.

As the twentieth century neared, the great powers found themselves increasingly headed toward confrontation due to the fact that most of the territory in Africa and Asia had already been appropriated and their competition could no longer be contained through collective carving up of the periphery. Not only had available colonies evaporated by the turn of the century, but so also had the memories of the wreckage of the Napoleonic Wars. New generations were struck by the quick, painless victory that Prussia scored in its seven-week war with Austria, achieved through not only universal conscription but also the innovative use of the railroad for speedy deployment and the breech-loading rifle for speedy firepower. Less attention was paid to the horrendous casualties caused by the new trench warfare employed during the American Civil War. Few seemed to recognize that by 1900, the *means* used to fight wars had become increasingly deadly, owing to new technologies that had been developed and others that were on the drawing board, and that cheap victories were unlikely in the future.

Some, such as Sir Norman Angell (in his book *The Great Illusion*, written in 1910, four years before World War I started), went so far as to assume that major war was unthinkable, not because of its potential destructiveness but because economic integration among European states had become so great that nobody would want to see hostilities disrupt trade and other ties. The late nineteenth century has been called the "first era of globalization," given the enormous volume of trade and capital flows across borders along with the flow of immigrants, all driven by the steamship, the railroad, the telegraph, and other inventions of the industrial age.[22] On some measures (e.g., if one uses as an indicator of interdependence a state's imports and exports along with foreign investment as a percentage of its gross national product and if one stresses the economic linkages among the great powers), economic interdependence was greater at the turn of the century than it is today.[23] At least one commentator has called the late nineteenth century "the *belle époque* (beautiful epoch) of interdependence,"[24] although others at the time saw interdependence as a mixed blessing, noting that "the world is, more than ever before, one great unit in which everything interacts and affects everything else, but in which also everything collides and clashes."[25] Rather than being a wholly new phenomenon, interdependence was a process already under way before 1900 and had the potential for both order and disorder.

One other development in the nineteenth century is worth noting that was closely related to interdependence. This was the emergence of **international organizations** as new *actors* in world politics. *Intergovernmental organizations* (IGOs) appeared on the scene, including the Central Commission for the Navigation of the Rhine River, created in 1815 to facilitate cooperation in addressing navigation and other issues among the European states sharing the common waterway, and the International Telegraphic Union and the Universal Postal Union, created in 1865 and 1874 to help maximize the potential benefits offered by new communications innovations. A number of such organizations were to be established on both a regional and global level by member governments in response to problems that transcended national boundaries and encouraged international institutional building. In addition, there was the growth of another type of nonstate actor, *nongovernmental organizations* (NGOs), formed among private individuals and groups sharing various interests. Although NGOs could be traced at least as far back as the Catholic Church, they were to proliferate during the nineteenth century, as exemplified by the founding of the International Red Cross and the Salvation Army in the 1860s. The nineteenth century also saw the emergence of a special category of nongovernmental organization—the *multinational corporation* (MNC), a for-profit NGO represented by British Petroleum and Standard Oil. Although prototypes of the MNC had existed two centuries earlier in the form of the British East India and Dutch East India trading companies, those were modest compared to the giant economic enterprises that started to appear in the late 1800s.[26]

The IGO and NGO phenomena were interrelated. In the economic sphere especially, just as the nation-state was partly a response to the inability of the feudal system to accommodate the expansion of economic activity across medieval towns by the new merchant class, IGOs developed partly in response to the inability of national governments to accommodate the growth of interstate commerce spawned by ever-expanding commercial enterprises that had outgrown national borders; national governments and corporate elites viewed IGOs as vehicles for facilitating the creation of uniform rules and orderly economic routines and thereby optimizing economic prosperity in an emergent world capitalist economy. States also saw IGOs as necessary to regulate the growing number of labor movements, scientific unions, and others who were organizing across national boundaries, energized—like transnational firms—by improvements in communications and transportation technology.

A century that had begun with the birth of nationalism was ending with the rise of transnationalism, although the former remained the more potent force. Whatever "globalization" process had started to take shape by the late nineteenth century was to be interrupted by two systemwide cataclysms experienced in the first half of the twentieth century.

THE INTERNATIONAL SYSTEM IN
THE TWENTIETH CENTURY

The year 1900 marked the high point of European dominance of the international system, as European powers claimed sovereign control over almost 85 percent of all the land on the planet. But this dominion was to wane over the next several decades. "[While] by 1900 European civilization overshadowed the Earth," the period between 1900 and 1945 was one "of utmost confusion in which a new system was struggling to be born and the old system fighting hard for its life."[27] As was the case with previous system transformations, major war would be the engine of change.

World War I (1914–1918), the Interwar Period, and World War II (1939–1945)

The causes of World War I will be examined later in the book, when we focus on the subject of war. It is enough to note here that on the eve of World War I tensions were mounting as the great powers competed for global influence, manifested by the naval arms race between Germany and Britain and the growing frictions and polarization between the two alliance systems. The assassination of Archduke Franz Ferdinand of Austria-Hungary by a Serb nationalist in June 1914 triggered the mobilization of the Triple Alliance (the Central Powers consisting of Austria, Germany, and Italy) against the Triple Entente (the Allied Powers consisting of Russia, Britain, and France). Italy immediately joined the Allied Powers, while Turkey joined the Central Powers. The United States eventually entered the war in midconflict on the side of the former, around the same time that the Bolshevik Revolution toppled the czar and Russia left the war effort. All told, more than a dozen countries became involved in the hostilities.

As suggested earlier, all participants assumed the war would be a relatively quick, costless affair, a heroic enterprise testing the valor of European youth; the German leader, Kaiser Wilhelm, spoke for many when he predicted that "the boys would be home before the leaves fell." It took four more autumns, until 1918, before the war ended, leaving some 20 million soldiers and civilians dead. World War I (called at the time the Great War) was no mere "sport of kings" but was *total war*, engaging the entire populations and economies of the participating nations and combined primitive hand-to-hand combat, fought with rifles and bayonets, and the latest in high-tech warfare, including poison gas, machine guns, tanks, submarines, and biplanes. Waves of men were sent to their death in suicidal offensive attacks on enemy entrenchments where defenders, protected by barbed wire, could now fire up to 20 bullets per minute with modern rifles and as many as 200 to 400 rounds per minute with rapid-fire machine guns.[28] The naïveté that attended the onset of war is captured in the following description: "In 1914, graduates of the French military academy marched into battle wearing white gloves and pompons. German university graduates marched singing, with arms linked, toward British trenches. Several British contingents kicked soccer balls as they advanced through no man's land."[29] The reality was evidenced at Verdun, where "the longest battle in the history of the world was fought in 1916, with the greatest density of dead per square yard that [had] ever been known. . . . There . . . 650,000 men were killed, wounded, or gassed in a period of ten months, with no significant gain of ground for either side."[30]

The Central Powers were defeated. In addition to millions of individual casualties, World War I resulted in the death of four empires (along with their dynasties) and started the decline of the European multipolar system. With the collapse of the czarist order in Russia, Vladimir Lenin became the leader of the successor state, the Soviet Union, and the promoter of a new ideology, **communism**. The Austro-Hungarian Empire disintegrated, and Austria, Hungary, Czechoslovakia, and Yugoslavia (an enlarged Serbia) suddenly appeared on the map of Europe as sovereign states. Germany lost its colonies and witnessed the creation of a newly independent Poland. The Ottoman Empire was partitioned, with Turkey losing whatever control it had over the Arabian Peninsula and North Africa, whose territory was divided into "mandates" administered by the British and the French. Although efforts were made to create new states along ethnic lines, the borders never corresponded totally with national identities. For example, only one-third of those living in Poland spoke Polish. Yugoslavia was a volatile stew of various cultures, and what were to become the sovereign states of Saudi Arabia and Iraq in 1932 represented a mixture of religious and tribal groupings whose only logic was that of colonial mapmakers. Hence, the "peace" that followed World War I created the potential for ethno-political conflicts that were to materialize much later, including the Palestinian-Israeli conflict, which was brought on by the 1917 Balfour Declaration, whereby the British government promised the Jewish people their own homeland in the Middle East.

The "peace" also created the climate that was to produce World War II just twenty years later. The Treaty of Versailles that ended World War I in 1919 was a punitive peace that not only stripped Germany of its colonies but also forced Germany to pay over $30 billion in war reparations. It bred resentment in the German public, thus contributing to the rise of Adolf Hitler and his Nazi regime that took power in Berlin in the 1930s under the banner of **fascism**, stressing German nationalism and racial superiority and promising to create a new empire under the Third Reich. The "war to end all wars" proved to be a prelude to an even worse

48

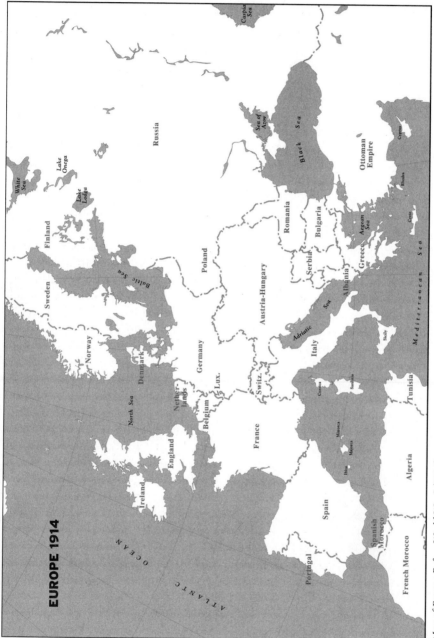

EUROPE 1914

Map of Europe Before World War I (1914)

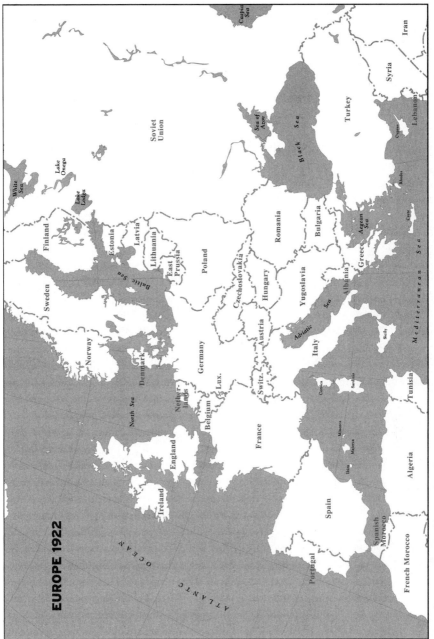

Map of Europe After World War I (1922)

systemic war within a generation, as the memory of the horrors of the Great War faded quickly. Woodrow Wilson and the leaders of the other victorious nations at Versailles had envisioned a very different scenario in the interwar period between 1919 and 1939. They had created a new *actor*, the **League of Nations**, which was designed as the first truly comprehensive, global intergovernmental organization charged with keeping the peace in place of the balance of power machinations on which previous leaders had relied. Wilson's "Fourteen Points" called for a new liberal international order, based not only on a League of Nations but the end of secret alliance pacts, the end of arms races, the further removal of economic barriers between nations and the promotion of free trade, and the promotion of democracy and self-determination for all peoples. All these aspirations failed to be realized, with Wilson himself displaying a gap between rhetoric and practice, leading later to realist critiques of idealist theories.

The *distribution of power* during the interwar period was *multipolar*, with Britain and France, the two leading powers in Europe, concerned about how other states, such as Italy, a weakened but potentially resilient Germany, and the Soviet Union might affect the power equation. Added to the mix was the United States, which emerged from World War I as the world's strongest economy, and Japan, which was expanding its domain in Asia. American power was idle in the interwar period, though, as the United States chose to "return to normalcy"—to its isolationist roots—and not join the League of Nations. As Charles Kindleberger has noted, "The United Kingdom could not [lead]," due to the decline in British power, and "the United States would not," due to its reluctance to assume a global leadership role.[31] Even when economic interdependence had the effect of enmeshing the world's economies in the Great Depression during the 1930s, the United States engaged in parochial economic nationalism, passing the Smoot-Hawley tariff and other protectionist legislation rather than championing free trade.

Despite the existence of rival ideologies that were an important feature of the interwar period—liberal democracy in Britain, France, and the United States, communism in the Soviet Union, and fascism in Germany, Italy (under Mussolini), and Japan—the international system was *not highly polarized* around competing political beliefs. One reason was continuing European efforts to maintain a balance of power. For example, League of Nations members Britain and France ignored Italy's aggression in Ethiopia in 1935, hoping to sway Mussolini to join them in a possible alliance against Hitler, whom they saw as a threat to them but also a potential bulwark against Soviet communism. The Soviet leader who followed Lenin, Joseph Stalin, feared both the democracies and the fascist states, but ultimately signed a nonaggression pact with Hitler, his fellow totalitarian dictator. The United States remained blissfully aloof and unaligned, although Japan's incursions into Manchuria in 1931 and other parts of China in 1937 started to draw Washington's attention and animosity.

The *goals* of states had not changed much despite Wilson's call for a new world order. The twentieth century saw the growth of the welfare state alongside the national security state. Either way, states were still preoccupied with advancing their national interests, which included territorial aggrandizement. The British and French continued to maintain their colonial empires. Meanwhile, Nazi Germany insisted it needed *Lebensraum*, room to expand to accommodate Germany's re-vanchist ambitions. At a meeting in Munich in 1938, British prime minister Neville Chamberlain agreed to Hitler's annexation of the Sudetenland in Czechoslovakia, hoping to satisfy his appetite and thus forestall major war. But Chamberlain's ap-peasement only signaled British weakness and emboldened Hitler to march into Poland in 1939, triggering World War II.

Given the ever more lethal *means* of conducting warfare, including aircraft carriers and strategic bombing of cities, World War II produced far more casual-ties than World War I. More than 60 million people died in the conflict, this time more civilians than soldiers. On one side were the Axis powers, including Ger-many, Italy, and Japan. On the other side were the Allies, which included Britain, France, the Soviet Union (which joined after Germany violated its nonaggression pact and invaded Russia in June 1941), and the United States (which entered the war after Japan attacked Pearl Harbor in December 1941 and Germany declared war on the United States), along with many other countries. Britain, led by Winston Churchill, held off the German military machine until the United States and the Soviet Union could tilt the balance in favor of the coalition that called itself the United Nations. The Allies eventually prevailed, with the war ending in Au-gust 1945, following the dropping of the atomic bomb on the Japanese cities of Hiroshima and Nagasaki. The A-bomb ushered in the nuclear age and an altogether new international system.

The Cold War International System (1945–1989)

There is general agreement that 1945 marked the beginning of a new era in world politics, one that some observers called "revolutionary."[32] The Westphalian state system still existed, but it was characterized by some highly unusual features, not the least of which was the fact that mankind now had the *means* to instantly erad-icate the human species. The introduction of weapons of mass destruction had profound consequences for world politics. Right away, it fostered two related de-velopments that were virtually unprecedented and that clearly distinguished the post–World War II system from earlier international systems.

One development was the emergence of only two states as the dominant *ac-tors* in the international system—the United States and the Soviet Union (USSR). The two were called *superpowers*, to distinguish them from the next tier of pow-ers (including Britain and France, which had experienced economic devastation during World War II, Germany and Japan, which had experienced military defeat, and China, which remained economically disadvantaged), and the bottom tier of states. What especially separated the superpowers from the rest of the pack were the huge nuclear arsenals the two states built after World War II, although the Soviet Union was not to achieve nuclear parity with the United States until the 1970s.

Of the two behemoths, the United States was "first among equals," accounting in 1945 for well over half of the world's industrial production and assets.

The second related development was the emergence of a highly *polarized* system in terms of alignment patterns, that is, the **East-West** axis of conflict waged between two cohesive blocs organized around rival ideologies and led by the two superpowers. One bloc ("the West") consisted of the United States and the developed, industrialized, capitalist democracies of Western Europe, Japan, Canada, Australia, and New Zealand. The other bloc ("the East") consisted of the Soviet Union and the relatively developed Marxist states of Eastern Europe along with communist China. In the immediate postwar period, the USSR established puppet "satellite" governments in Hungary, Czechoslovakia, and elsewhere in Eastern Europe behind the "Iron Curtain," while mainland China came under communist rule in 1949 after Mao Zedong forced the pro-Western government of Chiang Kai-shek to flee to the island of Taiwan. The United States created the **North Atlantic Treaty Organization** (NATO) and additional alliance arrangements with Japan and other states, while the Soviets created the **Warsaw Pact** alliance to counter NATO, as well as signing a Sino-Soviet pact with China. The **Cold War** had begun.

The U.S.-Soviet rivalry was not inevitable, since the two nations had worked closely together during World War II and thought they had reached some common understandings about the shape of the postwar order at the Yalta and Potsdam conferences toward the end of the war. The Soviet Union agreed to join the United States and the other major winners of World War II on the Security Council of the **United Nations**, the successor IGO to the League of Nations established in October 1945. The UN had even loftier aspirations than the League in hoping to promote world order through a concert of great powers approach not unlike the Concert of Europe. In addition, the United States sought to develop a liberal international economic order, becoming the champion of free trade and helping to create the International Monetary Fund and the World Bank as UN-affiliated IGOs meant to facilitate expansion of the world economy. When Washington announced the **Marshall Plan** foreign aid program in 1947, to help Europe's war-torn economies recover, it initially offered assistance to Moscow.

However, frictions between the superpowers developed immediately. Stalin, the Soviet leader, claimed that he had only defensive motives in wanting to influence the makeup of the regimes in neighboring Eastern European countries, since that region had been the invasion route into Russia twice previously, used by both Napoleon and Hitler. However, when Stalin failed to make good on allowing democratic elections in those countries, and then proceeded to threaten Greece and other states in 1947, the administration of Harry Truman (who had succeeded wartime president Franklin Roosevelt after his death) became alarmed and enunciated the Truman Doctrine. The latter called for the **containment** of Soviet aggression and stopping the spread of communism.[33] Inspired at least partly by "the lessons of Munich" and the failure of the West to confront German aggression in

1938, the United States rejected an isolationist "return to normalcy" and adopted the mantle of "leader of the free world." When communist North Korea, at the prodding of Moscow, attempted to reunify the Korean peninsula by force in 1950, the United States came to the defense of South Korea and ended up also fighting communist China. The Korean War ended in 1953 in a stalemate, with Korea remaining divided. The larger legacy was 50,000 American combat deaths and the remobilization and almost doubling of the U.S. armed forces, leaving in place "an enormously expanded military establishment, beyond anything [the United States] had ever contemplated in time of peace."[34]

Accusing each other of seeking global hegemony, Washington and Moscow solidified their two blocs into opposing alliance networks, with most members of the respective coalitions adhering rigidly to the policies of the bloc leader, at least initially. The other states in the system tended also to gravitate toward the two "poles." Hence the international system was labeled **bipolar**, to denote both the power and the alignment structure.

What started as a "tight bipolar" international system was to experience growing "fissures, larger cracks, and [ultimately] collapse" over the next several decades.[35] As the postwar era progressed, bipolarity began to morph into "tripolarity" once pressures for ending colonialism led to the proliferation of newly independent nation-states in Africa and Asia, many of which professed a nonaligned stance in the East-West conflict. These countries did not constitute a third pole or rival bloc in the system. They formed no alliance, and they were too weak to alter the world power distribution, but they did add a third ingredient to the equation of world politics. What became known as the **Third World**, composed of less developed countries located primarily in the Southern Hemisphere, owed its beginnings to a meeting in Bandung, Indonesia, in 1955, where twenty-nine African and Asian nations demanded an end to all colonialism. The decolonialization process was an important development in the history of the international system, contributing to the revolutionary character of the post–World War II era. Between 1945 and 1975, the number of nation-state actors more than doubled from roughly 60 to more than 130, completely altering the world map. In the span of one generation, a billion people and eighty nations achieved independence. Although the new nations represented enormous cultural diversity, they all agreed on their right to sovereignty based on the centuries-old rules of the European-based Westphalian system.

Both the United States and the Soviet Union attempted to add the new nations to their blocs. However, they had only mixed success, not only because the two giants tended to neutralize each other in many cases but also because the new Third World nationalism imposed limits on what even superpowers could do to force weak states to follow their lead. Because of the nearly universal aversion to foreign rule, the superpowers—more than great powers in the past—were inhibited from expanding their sphere of control through direct territorial annexation. Indeed, one of the most profound changes that had occurred in world politics was the creation of a new norm against the seizure of territory through the use of armed force. Neither the United States nor the USSR attempted to plant its flag on an inch of foreign soil after 1945, and even lesser states that sought to expand their borders through force found it difficult to make their claims stick. This norm grew more powerful as the postwar era wore on. (Mark Zacher notes that the last successful use of armed force for territorial gain was Morocco's seizure of the Spanish Sahara in 1976.)[36] Instead of acquiring territory, the *goal* of superpower competition was to gain influence over the foreign policies of Third World states, entailing at times intervention in their internal affairs to determine the nature of their governments; the regimes that one side tried to topple, the other side often tried to prop up. If the world map in earlier times had resembled a Monopoly board on which the players competed for property, the map during the Cold War looked more like a chessboard on which two players tried to move a set of pawns for maximum advantage. Third World leaders frequently learned to play off the two superpowers against each other in this game.

Fearful of the "mutual assured destruction" that a nuclear exchange between them could cause, the United States and the Soviet Union kept the Cold War cold, developing rules of the road for avoiding direct hostilities. Along the way, there were many crises, such as in Berlin and Cuba. The 1948 Berlin crisis stemmed from the fact that Germany after World War II had been temporarily divided into Western-controlled and Soviet-controlled zones of occupation, with the latter (East Germany) including the city of Berlin, itself divided into two zones. When Moscow tried to blockade land access to West Berlin, the United States and Britain airlifted supplies to the city over the next year. The crisis ended when West Germany and East Germany became separate states in 1949. Later, in 1961, in an effort to restrict the travel of East Germans to the West, the East German government aggravated tensions by erecting the Berlin Wall, a symbol of the Cold War that eventually came crashing down in 1989. The Cuban missile crisis of 1962 started when the Kennedy administration discovered that the Soviet Union had installed offensive nuclear missiles in Cuba, ninety miles from the American homeland, at least partly to deter possible U.S. efforts to unseat the Marxist government of Fidel Castro that had recently come to power on the island. The United States employed a naval blockade around Cuba to prevent Soviet ships from delivering additional missile equipment. Not knowing whether Moscow would back down, Kennedy put American forces on the highest level of alert ("cocked pistol") in preparation for a possible nuclear attack. The tremendous tensions subsided after thirteen days, when Soviet leader Nikita Khrushchev agreed to withdraw the missiles and ordered his vessels back to Russia; in the words of U.S. secretary of state Dean Rusk, "We were eyeball to eyeball, and I think the other fellow just blinked." There were also periodic thaws in the Cold War, such as Khrushchev's speech to the United Nations in 1956, in which he called for "peaceful coexistence" between the superpowers, and the American policy of "détente" during the Nixon administration in the early 1970s, calling for a relaxation of tensions.

One constant throughout the Cold War was the geopolitical struggle for the hearts and minds of people in Third World and other would-be client states, which Washington and Moscow pursued with an assortment of tactics that ranged from supplying foreign aid to engaging in either covert or direct military intervention. Covert intervention took the form of the CIA (or its Soviet counterpart, the KGB) engaging in "dirty tricks" of some sort, including plotting rebellions and even assassinations. For example, Washington had a hand in the overthrow of leftist governments in Iran in 1953, Guatemala in 1954, the Congo in 1961, and Chile in 1973, while Moscow was actively engaged in similar maneuvers against rightist, pro-Western regimes. More visible armed interventions by uniformed troops were undertaken by the United States in Lebanon in 1958, the Dominican Republic in 1965, Southeast Asia in the 1960s and 1970s, and Grenada in 1983, and by the Soviet Union in Hungary in 1956, Czechoslovakia in 1968, Ethiopia in 1977, and Afghanistan in 1979.

Nothing reflected U.S. frustrations in the Third World more than the Vietnam War. In his inaugural address as president in 1961, John Kennedy said that "we shall pay any price, bear any burden . . . oppose any foe" in defense of liberty. By 1962 the United States found itself involved in essentially a civil war between communist North Vietnam (headed by Ho Chi Minh in Hanoi) and pro-Western South Vietnam (headed by Ngo Dinh Diem in Saigon), having sent thousands of military advisers to help the Saigon regime in reaction to assistance that the Soviets and Chinese were reported to be providing Hanoi. As in Korea, there were echoes of Munich and **domino theory** assumptions that if Washington did not act to stop what was perceived as communist aggression in Vietnam, then Laos, Cambodia, and other neighboring countries might also fall prey to a global communist juggernaut. Kennedy's assassination brought Lyndon Johnson to the White House, and the war was escalated. It lasted until 1975, costing 50,000 American lives and resulting in the worst military defeat in American history. The Soviets would suffer their own Vietnam-style disaster when the Red Army invaded Afghanistan in 1979, hoping to buttress a pro-Soviet government against various tribal groups and Islamic (mujahideen) rebels seeking to overthrow the regime. Soviet troops were crushed, partly with American Stinger missiles and other weaponry supplied to the rebels, and were forced to withdraw in humiliation within a decade.

The Vietnam and Afghanistan conflicts signaled that, by the 1970s, the bipolar power structure of the international system was fracturing. One could see superpower slippage and the increasingly problematical nature of the exercise of power. Indeed, the "superpower" label seemed a misnomer. President Johnson was stunned that "the greatest power in the world" could not defeat "a band of night-riders in black pajamas," while the Soviet leadership was equally embarrassed to lose to a people considered almost medieval in their ways.[37] Not only had the "nuclear club" expanded to five members by the 1970s (adding Britain, France, and China), but, more importantly, nuclear arsenals that were once thought to confer superpower status were proving unusable and of questionable relevance to the day-to-day exercise of power in international relations. Insofar as the United States and the Soviet Union remained powerful actors, it was their economic clout—ability to provide foreign aid and trade benefits to client states—as much as military prowess that gave them leverage in world politics, although economic power, too, was becoming more diffuse. Other states, including economically revived West Germany and Japan and even some less developed countries, were learning how to make use of economic resources to assert themselves.

As the bipolar power structure fragmented, so too did the bipolar alignment structure. Tripolarity threatened to become multipolarity. Even as early as the 1960s, some observers were predicting "the end of alliance," given increasing friction within the Western and Eastern blocs.[38] French leader Charles de Gaulle proclaimed that "France has no permanent friends, only permanent interests," while Nicolae Ceausescu of Rumania and communist leaders in Europe and elsewhere were advocating "polycentrism" in place of a single party line originating from Moscow. Tensions were mounting between the Soviet leadership and the leadership of China under Mao Zedong, with minor border clashes occurring between the two communist titans in 1969. The Vietnam and Afghan conflicts further reduced the cohesion of the two alliances. The Vietnam War strained America's relations with its allies, with many European leaders and publics opposed to the war. When the United States tried to organize a worldwide boycott of the 1980 Olympic Games in Moscow as punishment for the Soviet invasion of Afghanistan, which President Jimmy Carter called "the greatest threat to world peace since World War II," Washington failed to get most of its NATO allies (and even Puerto Rico) to stay home, while China cooperated and was a no-show. Spectators needed a scorecard to keep track of the game of world politics, not only because there were now so many new players (i.e., new states, including many ministates, joining the community of nations) but also because the "teams" (i.e., coalitions) were beginning to change and become more fluid across issues. Some scholars suggested the international system had become **bimultipolar**, a term meant to convey the evolving complexity of international relations.[39]

Perhaps nothing better illustrated the growing complexity and changing nature of the Cold War system than the oil crisis of 1973, sandwiched between the Vietnam and Afghan wars. The United States and other industrialized countries had become increasingly dependent on foreign oil to meet their energy needs. Almost all the major oil exporters were less developed countries that had formed an IGO, the **Organization of Petroleum Exporting Countries (OPEC)**, to give themselves greater bargaining power over the multinational oil companies (the "Seven Sisters," such as Mobil and British Petroleum) and the governments of the oil-consuming nations. During the Israeli-Arab war in 1973, the Arab members of OPEC (Saudi Arabia, Kuwait, and others) initiated an oil embargo designed to force the United States and its oil-dependent allies to shift their support away from Israel to the Arab cause. The withholding of oil supplies caused momentary panic

"And as a last resort in hand-to-hand combat, you can always strike the enemy with your wallet."

Dunagin's People by Ralph Dunagin. Courtesy of Ralph Dunagin.

Power transitions: Was the Great Oil Sheikdown of 1973 a vision of the future?

in Western capitals, leading some states to reconsider their Middle East policy despite American efforts to maintain a united Western front in support of Israel. Oil shortages also encouraged OPEC to quadruple the price of oil from $3 a barrel to the then unheard of price of $12, causing a "shock" to the entire world economy. In the end, a group of less developed countries, some of which were tiny "statelets" and all of which were devoid of the military and other assets traditionally associated with international influence, demonstrated their ability to bring the industrialized world to a standstill and impact the entire international system. As U.S. secretary of state Henry Kissinger later remarked, "Never before in history has a group of such relatively weak nations been able to impose with so little protest such a dramatic change in the way of life of the overwhelming majority of the rest of mankind."[40]

The oil crisis episode was symptomatic of the fragmenting bipolar power and alignment structure of the Cold War system as well as other changes in the system, including the growing interdependence of nations and the rising importance of new issues and actors. One side effect of the OPEC price hike was the further widening of the rich-poor gap among countries, although here too the *distribution of wealth* had become more complicated. While some developing countries, such as OPEC states, saw their per capita incomes improve relative to developed countries, many that were least able to absorb the oil shock became even poorer and were labeled **Fourth World**, connoting the depths of their poverty. The oil crisis also reflected the emergence of a new array of issues, with traditional war and peace issues having to compete increasingly for attention with energy and other concerns. Humanity was witnessing "the move from a world dominated by a single chessboard—the strategic-diplomatic one (which either eclipsed or controlled all others)—to a world dispersed into a variety of chessboards," driven mainly by an obsession with "the quest for economic growth."[41] The 1970s saw the **North-South** axis of conflict at times claiming more attention than the East-West conflict, as the developing countries of the South, emboldened by the success of OPEC, attempted to use their large majority in the United Nations General Assembly to demand from the North a "**New International Economic Order**" that would benefit them in matters of trade, investment, and aid, although little redistribution of wealth occurred in response to southern militancy. The UN also became involved in convening a wave of global conferences on the environment, food, population, women's rights, and various other issues. Just as the oil crisis had revealed the growing importance of such *nonstate* actors as OPEC and the multinational corporations, UN conferences by the 1980s were involving not only official governmental representatives of nation-states (whose numbers had increased to over 150) but also the representatives of many NGOs (whose numbers had reached several thousand).

As already noted, the Cold War continued during much of the 1980s, with President Ronald Reagan railing against the "evil empire" based in Moscow. However, the battle lines between the Western and Eastern blocs had become more tangled than ever, as some NATO allies collaborated with the Soviet Union to build a pipeline connecting the natural gas fields of Siberia to the heart of Western Europe, while communist China, under Mao's successor, Deng Xiaoping, moved still closer to Washington. A new, more Western-oriented leader in the Kremlin, Mikhail Gorbachev, arrived on the scene in 1986, calling for *glasnost* (democratization) and *perestroika* (economic restructuring along capitalist lines), leading to arms control and other agreements with the United States. By 1989, the disintegration of the two rival alliance systems had proceeded to the point where the Warsaw Pact was moribund and NATO was searching for a new raison d'etre.

This set the stage for 11/9—the fall of the Berlin Wall in November 1989 and the end of the Cold War, which was followed by the demise of the Soviet Union in 1991, leading President George H. W. Bush to declare a "new world order." Realists attributed the end of the Cold War to the network of alliances that the United States constructed to counter Soviet power and a defense buildup that left the Soviets unable to compete; liberals attributed it to a "Pax Americana" built around the construction of global institutions; and constructivists attributed it to the greater attractiveness of Western ideas associated with free societies. In truth, almost everybody was surprised at how suddenly system transformation had occurred, without any major war as the catalyst for change, unlike previous Westphalian system transformations.

Some, like Francis Fukuyama, went so far as to declare "the end of history" due to the final triumph of capitalist democracy worldwide. He argued that the globalization trend of the late nineteenth century, which had been interrupted in the twentieth century by three wars (WWI, WWII, and the Cold War) and the Great Depression, was now poised to resume its long-term trajectory. Globalization became a ubiquitous buzzword during the 1990s, with an explosion in trade and capital flows spurred by the expansion of MNCs and the creation of a new IGO, the World Trade Organization. However, there was much history left to be written, not all triumphant, as was evidenced on 9/11, when the post–Cold War euphoria was shattered by the attack on the World Trade Center in New York City. It remained to be seen whether the new millennium would mark a more peaceful and prosperous new world order or would be so disorderly as to cause people to "miss the Cold War."[42]

THE CONTEMPORARY INTERNATIONAL SYSTEM

What are the most essential features of the contemporary international system? What characterizes international relations in the early twenty-first century? There is total agreement that the relatively neat, tidy bipolar era following World War II, which for almost a half century featured two superpowers immersed in a global struggle leading two fairly cohesive blocs—the First World (the West) and Second World (the East), separated by a Third World—is now history. There is less agreement on what has replaced the Cold War system, although trends in the direction of a more complicated system that were already discernible toward the latter stages of the Cold War have become more pronounced. We can look back and see that the trends under way in the 1970s and thereafter were the tip of the iceberg, foreshadowing the current era.

This complexity is marked by at least four key properties: (1) *a growing diffusion and ambiguity of power*, with the term "superpower" in question and the term "power" itself increasingly problematical; (2) *a growing fluidity of alignments*, with the old East-West as well as North-South axes of conflicts replaced by West-West, South-South, and other fault lines; (3) *a growing agenda of issues* facing national governments, with economic, environmental, energy, and other concerns competing for attention with traditional military security concerns, and with the nature of "security" itself changing, all this enmeshing states in ever more intricate patterns of interdependence; and (4) *a growing importance of nonstate actors*, including multinational corporations, intergovernmental organizations, and nongovernmental organizations, competing with states in shaping outcomes in world politics.

Perhaps the central question of our time is whether—based on the first two trends (the breakup of the postwar power and bloc structure)—we are witnessing merely the transformation of the international system from bipolarity back to the more normal pre-1945 historical pattern of multipolarity, *or* whether—based on the other two trends (the new agenda of issues and the new set of actors)—we are on the brink of a much more fundamental, epic transformation, namely a change not only *in* the Westphalian system but *of* the Westphalian system. In other words, is this a "Westphalian moment," a turning point in human affairs akin to 1648? Even if it is premature to reach that judgment, the fabric of the Westphalian state system does appear to be unraveling in certain respects, as discussed below.

Let us examine each of the four trends that define the contemporary international system.

The Growing Diffusion and Ambiguity of Power

Many considered the post–Cold War era, at least at first, to be a "unipolar moment."[43] Indeed, in the first decade of the twenty-first century, many scholars observed that the United States, as the lone superpower left standing, resembled the Roman Empire at its zenith, and was perhaps even superior to Rome. For example, Paul Kennedy: "Nothing has ever existed like this disparity of power. . . . No other nation comes close. . . . Charlemagne's empire was merely western European in its reach. The Roman Empire stretched further afield, but there was another great empire in Persia, and a larger one in China. There is therefore no comparison." Similarly, Stephen Walt: "The end of the Cold War left the United States in a position of power unseen since the Roman empire."[44]

Even after 9/11 and the U.S. failure in the Iraq War, many commentators view the international system as unipolar. Such a view is based on the fact that "the United States is the only Great Power in modern history to establish a clear lead in virtually every important dimension of power."[45] The United States today accounts for 40 percent of world military expenditures, outspending the next dozen countries combined. The U.S. economy accounts for more than a quarter of the planetary product and is approximately 50 percent larger than its closest competitor. In cultural terms, American cinema still dominates European and other markets, "American consumer products and brand names are ubiquitous, along with U.S. sports and media figures," and "not only is English increasingly the *lingua franca* of diplomacy, science, and international business, but the American university system is a potent mechanism for socializing foreign elites."[46]

However, some scholars see unipolarity giving way to multipolarity. As noted earlier, John Ikenberry and Parga Khanna are among those who have suggested that American hegemony is already eroding. There are several power centers thought to be potentially capable of challenging or surpassing the United States in the twenty-first century, especially if (1) American structural economic problems, such as trade and budget deficits and foreign debt obligations, aggravated by the financial crisis of 2008–2009, force a retrenchment in its overseas commitments and if (2) American "soft power"—admiration for American values—continues to slide as others see America as arrogant and bullying in its post-9/11 foreign policy behavior. Regarding the latter, while Barack Obama's election as U.S. president in 2008 was greeted warmly around the world, it is not yet clear if he will improve on the administration of George W. Bush, who was perceived in Europe and elsewhere as excessively self-centered and unilateralist in his foreign relations.[47]

One possible rival, noted by Ikenberry, is China. The People's Republic represents one-fifth of humanity and over the past two decades has been experiencing the highest annual economic growth rate of any nation in the world, which in turn has been fueling substantial increases in military spending and foreign aid and a growing presence in Africa, the Middle East, and Latin America. Still, China has weaknesses, such as environmental problems related to uncontrolled economic growth, population problems, and problems with its financial and political institutions as the communist, one-party state makes the transition to a full player in an open world economy. A second possible rival is the Russian Federation—the successor to the Soviet Union—still the largest swath of real estate on the planet (covering eleven time zones), endowed with vast oil reserves and other natural resources, and remaining in possession of thousands of nuclear weapons. Under President Vladimir Putin, Russia started flexing its muscles again, clamoring for the respect befitting a world power. However, Russia is plagued by a declining population in poor health (due partly to the AIDS epidemic and rampant alcoholism), internal ethnic strife, lack of strong political institutions, and a gross national product (GNP) roughly the size of Brazil's. A third rival is Japan, with the second-largest GNP in the world and the fourth-largest defense budget. Japan's economy, though, has been stagnant, its population has been shrinking, and its military is limited by a constitution that allows only for a "defense force" and "renounces war as a sovereign right." A final potential competitor and "pole" is the European Union (a group of over two dozen countries led by Britain, France, and Germany), which has a collective GNP larger than the U.S. GNP and may possibly evolve into a United States of Europe. Despite a single currency and growing cooperation, the main drawbacks are weak EU-wide, supranational institutions and loyalties, economic problems related to bloated welfare states, an aging and dwindling population, a reluctance to spend large sums on a military establishment, and an inability to coordinate foreign policy in European capitals. India and some other states have also been mentioned as possible counterweights to the United States.[48]

One scholar has tried to capture the complexity of the post–Cold War power structure by calling it "uni-multipolar."[49] However, talk of chief rivals may be missing the point, since world politics may no longer be revolving around great powers as much as in the past. In fact, as suggested previously, the exercise of power arguably has become so problematic and complex that labeling the contemporary international system "multipolar" might not adequately describe the current dispersion of power. It was already apparent in the Vietnam and Afghan wars and the oil crisis episode decades ago that the construction of a meaningful pecking order in international relations has become difficult. More than ever, power today seems fragmented and issue- and situation-specific.

To the extent the United States is considered the first among equals or unequals, the chief threat to American security may no longer be from great powers but from not-so-great powers, such as North Korea and Iran, which in recent years have "defied the American superpower with impunity."[50] If small or underdeveloped "rogue states" like North Korea close in on acquiring ABC (WMDs) arsenals, the international system may become a "unit veto" system of the type that was only fantasized about at the start of the atomic age in the 1950s, where each state has the ultimate instrument of warfare.[51] Moreover, it is not strong states but weak, "failed" states (such as Somalia and others whose governmental institutions have collapsed) that tend to breed terrorists. Terrorism itself has been called the weapon of the weak. Terrorists specialize in **asymmetrical warfare**, a form of combat aimed at negating a superior foe's military advantages and leveling the playing field by changing the traditional rules of engagement and norms of war fighting. Even more unsettling than rogue states getting nuclear weapons is the threat posed by "superempowered" individuals and groups obtaining them, such as Osama bin Laden and al Qaeda.[52] WMD strikes from Tehran or Pyongyang can be deterred by threats of retaliation, but terrorists do not have return addresses that allow deterrence to work.

Niall Ferguson suggests that, instead of either unipolarity or multipolarity, we may be seeing **apolarity**—a power vacuum in which there is no great power or set of great powers to ride herd over the inherent anarchy of the international system.[53] Joseph Nye says that "the bad news for Americans in this more complex distribution of power in the twenty-first century is that there are more and more things outside the control of even the most powerful state."[54] Yet he and others argue that if the United States is willing to settle for the role of "sheriff of the posse"—not going it alone but seeking to recruit help—it might be possible to achieve a better world order.[55] Whether Washington is willing to lead and whether others are willing to follow begs the question of whether the stars—in this case, nation-states—are properly aligned.

The Growing Fluidity of Alignments

Commenting on the end of the Cold War, former Israeli foreign minister Abba Eban said, "The Cold War, with all its perils, expressed a certain bleak stability; alignments, fidelities, and rivalries were sharply defined."[56] Although it is true that tight bipolarity became looser and looser as time went on, IR texts throughout the Cold War tended to conceptualize much of world politics in terms of Western, Marxist, and Third World perspectives. These categories have been replaced in the post–Cold War era by a more complex set of alignments and cleavages.

It is possible that the East-West conflict could be revived in some form if communism as a belief system is resuscitated by the failure of capitalism to make good on its promises in societies undergoing capitalist transitions. There are stirrings of a socialist revival in Venezuela under Hugo Chavez and in some other Latin American capitals. However, in much of the world Marxism-Leninism has been replaced by "market Leninism." China's brand of Marxism, for example, jokingly has been called closer to "Groucho than Karl."[57] Any East-West axis of conflict that might reappear is more likely to be the result of a Russo-Sino reaction to NATO expansion and perceived American ambitions than by competing ideologies. John Mearsheimer, a realist, has written about "the tragedy of great power politics," fearing the international system is destined to see a return to the balance-of-power politics historically associated with multipolarity. According to this logic, China may join not only with Russia but with European and other states in "resisting American hegemonism."[58] A European Union official has said that "we are building new relationships, and it's clear it's a commitment for us and for China. Both of us want a multipolar world." Russia's Putin similarly has said, "We believe here in Russia [just as the French believe]" that the future "must be based on a multipolar world. That is the main thing that unites us."[59]

Although "the West" remains a powerful idea, grounded in shared political and economic values, cracks have appeared in the NATO alliance that threaten to widen beyond those that appeared during the Cold War. This perhaps is to be expected, given the demise of the common enemy in the Soviet Union that provided the glue for the alliance. However, the cracks are also due to disagreements over policy ranging from the Iraq War to global warming and trade issues. There seems even a widening gulf between America and its European allies over basic cultural values, including the death penalty, the size of the welfare state, and the role of religion, with the United States more conservative. The chasm between Europe and America was evident in a 2006 *Financial Times* (London) poll showing that "across the continent the United States was considered a greater threat to world peace than Iran or North Korea," echoed in a comment by the mayor of London that an American president (George W. Bush) was "the greatest threat to life on this planet that we've most probably ever seen."[60] As one European commentator has remarked, "We have gone from a Cold War configuration of one West and two Europes to a current world of one Europe and two Wests."[61] This may exaggerate European unity, however, given the differences between so-called Old Europe (France, Germany, and other states opposed to American policy in Iraq and elsewhere) and New Europe (Poland, the Baltic States, and former Soviet satellites in Eastern Europe that, with Britain and a few other Western European countries, were part of the "coalition of the willing" in the Iraq War).

Just as the East-West conflict has disappeared, the North-South conflict has also largely lost its defining character, despite the persistence of the rich-poor gap. When more than 100 members of the nonaligned movement met for their annual summit in Havana, Cuba, in 2006, they had to work hard to justify their continued existence. At the conference, President Chavez of Venezuela asserted, "American imperialism is in decline. A new bipolar world is emerging. The nonaligned group has been relaunched to unite the South under one umbrella."[62] The problem Chavez faced, however, is that whatever southern solidarity had existed during the Cold War had dissipated due to growing economic diversity within the Third World. Today, instead of a North-South divide, there is the first world and "the two-thirds world," the latter constituting what some now call "**the global South**"— the grab bag of former communist states and Third World, Fourth World, or middle-income less developed countries (LDCs) as well as more prosperous "newly industrializing countries" (NICs) and next NICs, plus the BRICs set of big emerging markets (Brazil, Russia, India, and China) carving their own special niche in the world economy—all trying to join the global elite. Some observers worry that the Fourth World, composed of some fifty states that the World Bank has labeled "least developed," combined with the tier of impoverished states just above them, may represent a major fault line threatening the industrialized world:

> On the one side of the fault line will be "a relatively small number of rich, sa-tiated, demographically stagnant societies." On the other side will be "a large number of poverty-stricken, resource-depleted nations whose populations are doubling every twenty-five years or less.... How those [two] relate to each other ... dwarfs every other issue in global affairs."[63]

Although economic cleavages have the potential to play havoc in international politics, providing fertile areas for recruitment of disaffected masses into terrorist networks, there are other cleavages that may be more volatile.

If the East-West and North-South conflicts were the "dominant struggles" in the last half of the twentieth century, what is replacing them as the central global dramas?[64] Samuel Huntington, in his 1993 article "The Clash of Civilizations," posited that the East versus West axis of conflict would be replaced by the "West vs. the rest" axis, pitting Western culture against Islamic fundamentalism and other cultural traditions.[65] Huntington's article was a rejoinder to Fukuyama's more optimistic prediction about the final triumph of Western-style globalization. In the wake of 9/11, Huntington seemed to have been more prescient than Fukuyama, although, aside from "the West" itself being somewhat fractious and divided, "the rest" are even more so, particularly within Islam, given the internecine violence between Sunnis and Shiite in Iraq and elsewhere. Huntington's analysis of Hindu, Confucian, and other civilizations also has been criticized by some as simplistic.

One other point about alignments is worth making here. It is curious that, despite supposed concerns about American "hegemony," there has been no actual counteralliance formed as yet against the United States, in contrast to the "countervailing coalitions" that formed historically against such "dangerous" states as revolutionary France under Napoleon in the early nineteenth century, Nazi Germany under Hitler in the interwar period, and the Soviet Union under Stalin during the Cold War.[66] As Stephen Walt notes, despite growing contentiousness between the United States, Russia, China, and its European allies, "to date, at least, no one is making serious effort to forge a meaningful anti-American alliance." Although Mearsheimer may possibly prove correct that some sort of balancing coalition will form, Richard Haass suggests otherwise, arguing that the reason no balancing act has occurred is that "the twenty-first century is fundamentally different. For the first time in modern history, the major powers of the day ... are not engaged in a classic struggle for domination at each other's expense. There are few contests over territory. For the foreseeable future, war between or among them borders on the highly unlikely and, in some cases, unthinkable."[67]

The Growing Agenda of Issues

I noted earlier that the Cold War saw great powers no longer competing for territory, as in a game of Monopoly, but instead competing in a game of chess, and that by the 1970s there were "a variety of chessboards" in play. The post–Cold War era has seen a further widening of the range of foreign policy issue-areas that concern national governments. The line between high politics and low politics has blurred. Although national security may remain the preeminent goal of nation-states, it has been broadened beyond its classic military definition to include economic, environmental, and other dimensions that have gained increased visibility on the agendas of governments. There is now a global politics of poverty and plenty, of population, petroleum, pandemics, pollution, and other problems that face both the developed and the developing worlds.

There has been a debate since the end of the Cold War whether welfare (non-military) issues have achieved primacy over military issues. If so, that would be a truly revolutionary development in international relations. For a while it looked that way, with globalization taking off during the 1990s and finance ministers getting more newspaper coverage than defense ministers. Playing on the famous nineteenth-century Prussian military strategist von Clausewitz, economics in the 1990s was being called "the continuation of war by other means," particularly among highly developed societies, which seemed unlikely to engage in shooting wars against each other given the terrible destructiveness of armed combat in the nuclear age.[68] Wars might occur between developed and less developed societies, but the former could feel secure that they would be spared the risk of having to fight militarily menacing foes. I referred in Chapter 1 to the "long peace" that has existed among great powers since 1945 and continues to exist. However, the 9/11 attack in 2001 had the effect of restoring military concerns to the top of the agenda in the United States and elsewhere, even if the nature of military threats had changed considerably. In later chapters we will explore both the changing nature of war and the nature of economic and other issues now competing for attention on the menu of foreign policy choices entertained by national governments.

The Growing Importance of Nonstate Actors

The United Nations Charter assumed a world of states as the basis for human political organization. The post–World War II period did, in fact, witness a tremendous proliferation of new nation-states resulting from the decolonialization process. The original UN membership had more than tripled by the time the Cold War ended in 1989, with another two dozen states having been added since. (The UN membership as of 2009 totaled 192 countries.) The founders did not envision that many of these states would be of the cookie-cutter variety—microstates smaller in size than not only a typical American state but a typical American city and, in some cases, a typical American town.

What was envisioned even less was the proliferation of *nonstate* actors and their growing importance in world politics, including subnational actors (e.g., the overseas trade missions maintained by virtually every state in the United States) as well as transnational actors (e.g., the now more than 300 IGOs, 20,000 NGOs, and 50,000 MNCs). There was almost no mention of these actors in the UN Charter, and the realist paradigm that came to dominate scholarship following

World War II tended to ignore them as well. Yet our history of the international system has revealed how nonstate actors have grown in number and significance over the centuries. Today, few would deny that a nonstate actor such as al Qaeda has far greater potential to impact world politics than do many nation-states.

I noted previously that nonstate actors have been directly involved in a host of issues discussed recently at United Nations conferences. In some instances, they have been the catalyst for convening the conference and have been invited to the bargaining table in a "consultative" role, even if not given a vote at the table. As just one example, the Millennium Summit, held at the behest of UN secretary-general Kofi Annan in New York City in September 2000, brought together not only 187 member states (including 150 heads of state and government) but also officials from the UN Secretariat, the World Bank, the International Monetary Fund, and other UN-affiliated IGOs, representatives from 1,350 NGOs (including various human rights, environmental, and other advocacy groups), and assorted other players to discuss a new agenda for action "at the dawn of a new millennium." A special Millennium NGO Forum preceded the summit, giving voice to what some observers have referred to as "global civil society." Microsoft and other multinational corporations had already been involved in a joint endeavor with Kofi Annan, several UN agencies, and several NGOs called the Global Compact, which aimed to close the "digital divide" between rich and poor countries in computer usage and to address other rich-poor gaps as well. State-centric analysts would retort that IGOs are little more than assemblages of states that tend to be dominated from a few national capitals, that NGOs are no match for the power and authority of governments, and that MNCs lack autonomy and tend to be tied to their headquarters country. However, the point is not that nonstate actors played the dominant role at the Millennium Summit, only that they played a meaningful part of the equation that produced the set of "millennium development goals" that included reducing by half the number of people living on less than a dollar a day and suffering from hunger and lack of safe drinking water by 2015. Nonstate actors have played an even more important role at some other conferences, such as the Earth Summit in Rio de Janeiro in 1992 and the Montreal Conference on the Ozone Layer in 1987, where transnational "epistemic communities" of scientists successfully called attention to climatic problems leading to environmental treaties.[69]

The rise of nonstate actors has potentially far-reaching implications, captured in the following quote: "If the state remains at the centre of governance in the world, what has changed? In a word, everything. Never have so many different nonstate actors competed for the authority and influence that once belonged to states alone."[70] As far back as the 1970s, around the time of the oil crisis and the heightened importance of MNCs and interdependence, some seasoned observers were hinting about "sovereignty at bay"[71] and writing that "the state is about through as an economic unit"[72] and that "the nation-state is a very old-fashioned idea and badly adapted to serve the needs of our complex modern world."[73] Ruminations about "the end of the nation-state" and "the end of sovereignty"[74] have only gotten louder of late. Scholars can be found emphatically stating that "like a mothball, which goes from solid to gas directly, I expect the nation-state to evaporate" and "the era of the nation-state is over."[75]

Those who envision the demise of the nation-state disagree as to whether the primary threat to its viability comes from *integrative* trends (transnational links associated with globalization, cyberspace, and other phenomena that are causing "loss of control" and erosion of sovereignty) or *disintegrative* trends (the proliferation of so many small, barely sustainable polities, spurred especially by the surge in ethnic conflicts and separatist movements), or *both*. We could be witnessing the emergence of either a global village or the exact opposite—global villages. (See the *IR* Critical Thinking Box "Back to the Future: Are We on the Brink of a 'New Feudalism'?")

IR Critical Thinking:
Back to the Future: Are We on the Brink of a "New Feudalism"?

Many people have remarked that we are living in an age of contradictions, of the sort that I described in Chapter 1. Among the more intriguing contradictions are the competing integrative and disintegrative forces operating in the world today, that is, "how the planet is both falling apart and coming together"—what Benjamin Barber has called "Jihad vs. McWorld."[1] James Rosenau has referred to this as "fragmegration."[2] Former UN secretary-general Boutros Boutros-Ghali has described this condition as follows:

> We have entered a time of global transition marked by uniquely contradictory trends. Regional and continental associations of states are evolving ways to deepen cooperation and ease some of the contentious characteristics of sovereign and nationalistic rivalries. . . . At the same time, however, fierce new assertions of nationalism and sovereignty spring up, and the cohesion of states is threatened by ethnic, religious, social, cultural, or linguistic strife.[3]

These contradictions may not be wholly unique to our times—we have seen how centralizing and decentralizing forces have competed with each other throughout history—but they do seem to occupy a special place in the contemporary international system. On the one hand, we have efforts to promote unprecedented regional integration through such efforts as the European Union (EU) project involving over two dozen European states, as well as the North American Free Trade Agreement (NAFTA) involving the United States, Canada, and Mexico. In addition, there is a movement toward unprecedented "global governance" through such IGOs as the World Trade Organization, designed to go beyond regional trade blocs and facilitate global free trade. On the other hand, we have localizing pressures as well, for example, the recent breakup of Yugoslavia and the Soviet Union, demands by Wales and Scotland for greater home rule from London, Basque separatists seeking independence from Spain, the governor of California (frustrated with Washington's foot dragging on global warming and seeking to formulate his own policies apart from the U.S. government) declaring "we are a nation-state,"[4] and the emergence of sub-states within states (as with Hezbollah control of southern Lebanon)[5] or states collapsing due to tribal or religious feuds (as in Somalia and some other African states). A quintessential example of this phenomenon is the case of Kosovo fighting to gain

(continues)

(continued)

independence for its Albanian majority from Serbia in 2008, at the same time it was signaling its eventual desire to become a member of the European Union, which might entail some loss of sovereignty to EU supranational governance processes.

Given the rich blend of overlapping governance arrangements and multiple loyalties described above, some observers have suggested that we may be returning to yesteryear as humanity organizes itself into "a new feudalism" or "new medievalism."[6]

How would you answer the following:

1. What is the dominant trend in the world today—integration or disintegration? What anecdotal and empirical evidence supports your answer?

2. Normatively speaking, which trend is preferable—greater centralization or decentralization? Why?

3. It has been said that the nation-state "has become too big for the small things [such as overseeing education policy] and too small for the big things [such as regulating weapons of mass destruction or global warming]." Discuss.

4. A common catchphrase is "think globally, act locally." What does this mean in the context of the trends discussed here?

5. How do you see the future of the "nation-state"?

Notes
1. Benjamin Barber, *Jihad vs. McWorld* (New York: Times Books, 1995).
2. James N. Rosenau, *Turbulence in World Politics* (Princeton, NJ: Princeton University Press, 1990).
3. Boutros Boutros-Ghali, *An Agenda for Peace*, UN Doc. A/47/277 and S/24111, June 17, 1992, 3.
4. Arnold Schwarzenegger, quoted in *Newsweek*, April 16, 2007, 60; "California, Britain to Address Global Warming," *New York Sun*, August 1, 2006.
5. Henry A. Kissinger, "After Lebanon," *Washington Post*, September 3, 2006.
6. James A. Nathan, "The New Feudalism," *Foreign Policy,* Spring 1981, 156–166; Susan Strange, "The Defective State," *Daedalus*, Spring 1995, 55–74; John Rapley, "The New Middle Ages," *Foreign Affairs*, May–June 2006, 95–103.

Mark Twain once said that the report of his death was greatly exaggerated. Likewise, we must be careful not to exaggerate the report of the death of the Westphalian nation-state. It is not ready to be mothballed. You need only glance at any world map or globe to see that the Westphalian mode of organization continues to define political life on the planet. It bears repeating that nation-states "remain the key actors in the drama of contemporary world politics, although they are being buffeted by both centrifugal and centripetal forces, which in the short run may undermine the ability of national governments to control events fully in international relations and in the long run may pose challenges to their very existence."[76]

CONCLUSION

It was not possible to do justice to tracing the history of the world in the space of one chapter. That was not the purpose here. The purpose was to paint only a broad-brush portrait of the evolution of the state system, so that the reader might have some historical perspective for better understanding our current situation and some substantive background for examining various aspects of contemporary international relations in the chapters that follow. We now turn to *Part Two*, where we focus on foreign policy, diplomacy, war, and other "fundamentals" of international relations.

QUESTIONS FOR STUDY AND DISCUSSION

1. What is meant by the term "international system"?
2. What is the significance of the Peace of Westphalia in 1648?
3. What were the key features of the international system in the seventeenth, eighteenth, and nineteenth centuries (in terms of power distribution and other important characteristics)? What about the twentieth century, from 1900 until 1945, and from 1945 until the end of the Cold War in 1990?
4. How would you characterize the contemporary, post–Cold War international system? What are the major trends?
5. How can we reconcile the traditional way of thinking about international relations—that is, as a "game" played mainly by nation-states, revolving around such concepts as national interests, national security, sovereignty, and citizenship—with the growing contemporary reality of cyberspace, a globalized world economy of multinational corporations, and other phenomena that seem to be blurring national boundaries and identities and rendering the traditional concepts problematical and perhaps anachronistic?

SUGGESTIONS FOR FURTHER READING

Hedley Bull and Adam Watson, eds., *The Expansion of International Society* (Oxford: Oxford University Press, 1985).

Peter Calvocoressi, *World Politics Since 1945*, 6th ed. (New York: Longman, 1991).

Rupert Emerson, *From Empire to Nation* (Cambridge, MA: Harvard University Press, 1960).

Francis Fukuyama, "The End of History?" *National Interest* 16 (Summer 1989): 3–16.

John Lewis Gaddis, *We Now Know: Rethinking Cold War History* (New York: Oxford University Press, 1997).

Edward Gulick, *Europe's Classical Balance of Power* (Ithaca, NY: Cornell University Press, 1955).

Richard Haass, "The Age of Nonpolarity," *Foreign Affairs* (May–June 2008): 44–56.

Samuel P. Huntington, "The Clash of Civilizations," *Foreign Affairs* 72 (Summer 1993): 22–49.

Stephen Krasner, "Westphalia and All That," in Judith Goldstein and Robert Keohane, eds., *Ideas and Foreign Policy* (Ithaca, NY: Cornell University Press, 1993).

Margaret Macmillan, *Paris 1919: Six Months That Changed the World* (New York: Random House, 2002).

John J. Mearsheimer, "Why We Will Soon Miss the Cold War," *Atlantic,* August 1990.

F. S. Northedge and M. J. Grieve, *A Hundred Years of International Relations* (New York: Praeger, 1971).

J. Martin Rochester, *Between Two Epochs* (Upper Saddle River, NJ: Prentice-Hall, 2002), chap. 1.

Henrik Spruyt, *The Sovereign State and Its Competitors* (Princeton, NJ: Princeton University Press, 1994).

Charles Tilly, ed., *The Formation of National States in Western Europe* (Princeton, NJ: Princeton University Press, 1975).

Mark Zacher, "The Decaying Pillars of the Westphalian Temple," in James N. Rosenau and Ernst-Otto Czempiel, eds., *Governance Without Government* (Cambridge: Cambridge University Press, 1992).

PART TWO

FOREIGN POLICY AND

INTERNATIONAL POLITICS

The Dynamics of Conflict

and Cooperation

*The nation-state remains the primary locus of identity of most people;
regardless of who their employer is and what they do for a living, individuals
pay taxes to the state, are subject to its laws, serve (if need be) in its armed
forces, and can travel only by having its passport. . . . If there is to be coordinated action by the peoples of the world . . . to halt the destruction of
the tropical rainforests or reduce methane emissions (or address other problems), then international agreements, negotiated by the participating governments, are clearly required.*

—Paul Kennedy, *Preparing for the Twenty-First Century,* 1993

*Our country: in her intercourse with foreign nations may she always be in
the right; but our country right or wrong.*

—Stephen Decatur, a toast made in 1816

*In relations between nations, the progress of civilization may be seen in the
movement from force to diplomacy, from diplomacy to law.*

—Louis Henkin, *How Nations Behave,* 1979

3

States and
Foreign Policy

The 14 people involved [in the U.S. decision to blockade Cuba during the missile crisis in October 1962] were very significant. If 6 of them had been President, I think that the world might have blown up.

—Robert F. Kennedy

I cannot forecast to you the action of Russia. It is a riddle wrapped in a mystery inside an enigma, but perhaps there is a key. That key is Russian national interest.

—Winston Churchill, radio broadcast, 1939

A natural assumption is that governments—including that of the United States—tailor their national security decisions to what is happening abroad or what they hope to achieve abroad. The truth is apparently more complicated. The decisions and actions of governments result from the interplay among executive and legislative organizations, public and private interests, and, of course, personalities. This interplay becomes a determinant of foreign policy no less than events abroad.

—Morton Halperin, *Bureaucratic Politics and Foreign Policy,* 1974

The essence of ultimate decision remains impenetrable to the observer—often, indeed, to the decider himself. . . . There will always be the dark and tangled stretches in the decision-making process—mysterious even to those who may be most intimately involved.

—John F. Kennedy

In Chapter 1, international politics was defined as the study of who gets what, when, and how in the international arena. IR, in other words, can be conceptualized as a game or competition, one that at times can involve bloodshed. In *Part Two*, we will examine various aspects of this game, bloody as well as non-bloody. It is well to remember that international politics tends to be characterized by a mix of conflict and cooperation, and that even when conflict does occur, more often than not such disputes are resolved without resort to violence. In this chapter, we examine what lies behind the moves that players make in the game of IR, focusing on what is commonly called "foreign policy." As we will see, these moves are not always as carefully calculated and planned as many people think; more grand strategy can go into the preparation and execution of a football game plan by gridiron coaches than often attends the making and conduct of foreign policy. The epigraphs that appear above (the quotes from Robert Kennedy, Winston Churchill, Morton Halperin, and John Kennedy) suggest how important, and how difficult, it is to understand the determinants of foreign policy and why states and statesmen act as they do. If it is hard even for scholars and policymakers themselves to understand fully what drives foreign policy decisions and behaviors, it is all the more daunting for ordinary citizens to try to do so. However, in recent years a large body of literature on comparative foreign policy and related subjects has developed that has improved our understanding considerably.

When Robert Kennedy commented, in his reflections on the 1962 Cuban missile crisis, that if six of the fourteen U.S. officials involved in the high-level group that made the blockade decision had been president, "I think that the world might have blown up,"[1] he may have been exaggerating somewhat and overstating his brother's role. But he was nonetheless calling attention to the huge effects that potentially flow from foreign policy decisions made by governments. Graham Allison, also reflecting on the Cuban missile crisis, pointedly notes how the study of such concerns should be of profound interest to us all:

> The Cuban missile crisis is a seminal event. For thirteen days of October 1962, there was a higher probability that more human lives would end suddenly than ever before in history. Had the worst occurred, the death of 100 million Americans, over 100 million Russians, and millions of Europeans as well would make previous natural calamities and inhumanities appear insignificant. Given the probability of disaster—which President Kennedy estimated as "between one out of three and even"—our escape seems awesome. The event symbolizes a central, if only partially thinkable, fact about our existence. That such consequences could follow from the choices and actions of national governments obliges students of government as well as participants in governance to think hard about these problems.[2]

Let us proceed, then, with the study of foreign policy, first adding a few observations about the national governments Allison mentions.

STATES AS PLAYERS

Although a variety of players (actors) engage in the game of IR, at the center of the game are nation-states and the national governments that act on their behalf. It is hard to quarrel with the assertion that "the starting point of international relations is the existence of states, of independent political communities."[3] Even when it comes to promoting "global governance," IGO heads and others understand that "the foundation-stone of this work is and must remain the State."[4] After all, only nation-states make and conduct foreign policy; no matter how important they may be to the game of IR, neither the UN nor al Qaeda nor British Petroleum nor any other nonstate actor makes and conducts foreign policy, at least not in the normal sense of the term. Much of the game of IR revolves around the *foreign policy* decisions and behaviors of nation-states, whose resultant interactions, in conjunction with the actions of nonstate actors, we call *international politics*.

The nation-states of the world include familiar names such as the United States and others commonly mentioned as jockeying for position as great powers, along with less familiar ones such as Burkina Faso (formerly Upper Volta) and Vanuatu. It is symptomatic of the decentralized nature of the international system that there is no universally accepted "list" of nation-states in the world. For example, ask officials and citizens of the People's Republic of China how many countries there are in the world, and they will certainly not count the Republic of China (Taiwan) as a sovereign state, since they consider the latter to be part of the PRC; yet, visit Taiwan, and most inhabitants will insist otherwise, as will a few states that have recognized Taiwan as a member of the "community of nations." The closest thing there is to an official roster of nation-states is the United Nations membership, although even that is not definitive—note that Switzerland, a nation-state by any measure, waited until 2002 before finally joining the UN, while Vatican City (the Holy See) remains outside the UN despite the fact it essentially has all the attributes of statehood, including membership in some other IGOs as well as the right to exchange ambassadors and enter into treaties with other states. Given the large number of ministates in the world, size obviously is not a criterion for statehood. As just one example, five European states—Andorra, Monaco, San Marino, Liechtenstein, and the Vatican—have a combined population smaller than Little Rock, Arkansas (170,000 people), while Monaco itself is only slightly larger in land area than the Mall between the Capitol and the Lincoln Memorial in Washington, D.C. (2 square kilometers). The governments of many states lack economic and other resources—what political scientists call state *capacity*—to participate fully in "global governance," evidenced by Tajikistan, which, upon entering the UN as a sovereign state in 1993, was so poor that its UN ambassador had to serve as a one-man diplomatic corps and had to cook his own state dinners.[5]

Allowing for some disagreement, there are roughly 200 actors in the world today that are widely considered nation-states. The disparities in size and wealth

TABLE 3.1. Characteristics of Selected Countries (by Size and Wealth)

Country	Population (thousands)	Land Area (square km.)	Total Armed Forces	Gross National Income (millions of U.S. dollars)	Per Capita GNI (U.S. dollars)
Antigua and Barbuda	84	443	170	937	11,210
Bangladesh	144,345	144,000	126,500	69,921	480
Brazil	188,694	8,511,965	287,870	892,806	4,730
Canada	32,556	9,984,670	62,500	1,177,445	36,170
Chad	9,987	1,284,000	25,350	4,746	480
China (PRC)	1,311,798	9,596,960	2,255,000	2,641,587	2,010
Egypt	75,397	1,001,450	468,500	101,658	1,350
Germany	82,411	357,021	245,702	3,018,036	36,620
India	1,109,811	3,287,590	1,316,000	906,537	820
Indonesia	223,042	1,919,440	302,000	315,759	1,420
Iran	67,153	1,648,000	545,000	207,643	3,000
Israel	7,039	20,770	168,000	128,667	18,580
Japan	127,565	377,835	240,400	4,899,966	38,410
Mali	13,911	1,240,000	7,350	6,128	440
Micronesia	111	702	——	264	2,380
Monaco	33	2	——	1,000	11,116
Nigeria	144,749	923,768	85,000	92,358	640
Norway	4,644	323,802	23,400	308,948	66,530
Pakistan	159,002	803,940	619,000	122,295	770
Russia	142,368	17,075,200	1,027,000	822,364	5,780
Saudi Arabia	23,681	2,149,690	224,500	289,194	12,510
Tajikistan	6,652	143,100	7,600	2,572	390
Turkey	72,935	780,580	514,850	393,903	5,400
United Kingdom	60,361	244,820	191,030	2,425,210	40,180
United States	298,988	9,826,630	1,506,757	13,446,031	44,970
United Arab Emirates	4,636	83,600	50,500	103,460	23,950

SOURCES: Population data are from World Bank, *World Development Indicators 2007*. Land area data are from U.S. Central Intelligence Agency, *CIA World Factbook 2008*. Data on armed forces are from International Institute for Strategic Studies, *The Military Balance 2007*. Per capita GNI (gross national income) data and GNI data are from World Bank, *World Development Indicators 2007*, using the World Bank atlas method.

can be seen in Table 3.1, which lists the characteristics of some two dozen states. Not surprisingly, these differences in national characteristics help account for differences in foreign policy patterns exhibited by states, although we will see that there are other variables, also, that affect foreign policy.

WHAT IS FOREIGN POLICY?

Foreign Policy as a Guide to Action in World Affairs

Trying to define **foreign policy** is reminiscent of the judge in the obscenity case who said, "I can't define it, but I know it when I see it." If the word "foreign" denotes the external, international arena as the target of action, the word "policy" implies conscious, purposeful decision as a basis for action. A reasonable definition is the following: a set of strategies used by governments to guide their actions in the international arena that includes both their general *objectives* as well as the *means* whereby the objectives are to be achieved.

However, this definition begs the question I raised at the start: How thoughtful and well planned is any country's foreign policy? Indeed, does any country, whether the United States or China or Vanuatu, actually have "a foreign policy," if by that is meant a carefully crafted and faithfully implemented "guide" to action—a road map—in world affairs? Six months after Ronald Reagan assumed the U.S. presidency, a newspaper headline read: "Reagan Pressed to Spell Out Foreign Policy." After a year in the White House, Reagan's successor, George H.W. Bush, also was being criticized for not having a game plan and for passively reacting to events rather than trying to shape them, until one headline trumpeted: "A Bolder Bush Foreign Policy Emerges." Similarly, Bill Clinton was criticized for a lack of foreign policy direction, with one magazine complaining about "The Clinton Foreign Policy: Is There a Doctrine in the House?" After 2000, George W. Bush was roundly criticized for "no grand strategy, no design to guide the ship of state." In the 2008 presidential campaign, the candidates were likewise quizzed as to their overall foreign policy approach or lack thereof, with one weekly news publication examining "The Evolution of the McCain Doctrine" (an uneasy blend of "consummate pragmatism and zealous crusading") and another inviting the reader to "Meet the Obama Doctrine" (mostly reflecting an idealist view of foreign policy).[6]

The above headlines evoke an image of foreign policy as a master blueprint containing an explicit list of ends and means designed to inform all future, smaller decisions and actions. We often hear references to the "architects" of American (or Russian or Iranian) policy, and leaders themselves either assure their populace they have such a plan or accuse leaders of other states of such machinations. To what extent does this reflect reality?

George Harvey, the American ambassador to Great Britain in 1923, was quoted as saying, "The national American foreign policy is to have no foreign policy."[7] Among others who have doubted whether states have such blueprints in any meaningful sense is Henry Kissinger. In his scholarly writings in the 1960s, Kissinger stated: "Foreigners looking at American policy have a tendency to assume that anything that happened was intended and that there is a deep, complicated purpose behind our actions. I wish this were true, but I don't believe that it is. . . . In fact, this is probably the case with the Soviet Union also."[8]

Kissinger was overstating the point. As the chief national security adviser and later U.S. secretary of state in the Nixon administration in the 1970s, Kissinger was credited with fashioning a grand policy toward the Soviet Union that became known as *détente*, aimed at relaxing superpower tensions in order to build a "structure for peace." Détente was part of the larger "containment" doctrine that started with President Truman and became the overarching rationale of American foreign policy throughout the Cold War era. After the Cold War ended, American leaders tried to give new definition and orientation to U.S. foreign policy, with George H. W. Bush envisioning "a new world order" and Bill Clinton urging "enlargement" of the number of free markets and democracies. These themes represented an attempt, however sketchy, to give some general direction to U.S. foreign affairs. Indeed, since 1986, under the Goldwater-Nichols Act, each new American administration has been required by law to release its national security strategy publicly within its first five months in office and to report annually to Congress on any changes in the strategy. Whether mandated by law or not, national leaders frequently make major pronouncements articulating their broad foreign policy vision.

It is not that leaders make no effort to think of the big picture and develop a comprehensive framework for action. The gist of the Kissinger quotation is that no matter how much a leadership tries to conceive and adhere to a single, coherent foreign policy, it is unlikely to have the luxury of indulging in abstract formulations. Instead, it inevitably finds itself having to make decisions about more discrete things—in the case of the United States, whether to recognize Kosovo as a newly independent state, whether to sell more cluster bombs to Israel, whether to boycott the opening ceremony of the Beijing Olympic Games to protest the Chinese crackdown on Tibetan dissidents, and a host of other concerns. As John Ruggie says, "Policymakers generally do not get to choose on the future of the state system; they confront choices on exchange rates, trade deficits, arms-control treaties . . . terrorist attacks on airports and embassy compounds, and garbage that floats down a river."[9] The implication is that "often policy is the sum of a congeries of separate or only vaguely related actions."[10]

Types of Decisions

Foreign policy is best thought of not as a single driving worldview or game plan but, more realistically, as a series of hundreds of decisions that have to be made, which may or may not hold together in a logically consistent, seamless fashion. These myriad decisions confronting a national government can be categorized in a number of ways. One way to classify foreign policy decisions is according to **issue-area**. As Ruggie's observation above suggests, some decisions fall under national security policy, others under economic policy, and still others under environmental policy or some other category. Although national security issues traditionally have attracted the greatest attention from foreign policy analysts, increasingly economic, environmental, and other nondefense issues are competing for attention. I noted earlier how a growing number of issues are "intermestic" in nature—straddling both foreign and domestic policy. Another typology, also suggested by Ruggie, is based more on the **situational setting** in which decisions are made, for example, crisis as opposed to noncrisis decisions. Both the issue-area and the situation will heavily influence "who makes foreign policy decisions and how."[11]

Regarding the situational typology, at least three types of decisions can be identified. **Higher-order decisions** conform most closely to what is ordinarily implied by the term "policy." Some of the big decisions that a government has to consider relate to such matters as level of defense spending, level and type of foreign aid to be given or sought, and trade policy. A country such as the United States must also make decisions on Middle East policy, Asian policy, Latin American policy, and African policy, as well as more focused matters such as reevaluating U.S. policy toward China and Taiwan, or India and Pakistan. These are higher-order decisions in the sense that they involve relatively large, general concerns and are meant to establish rough guidelines to be applied to specific circumstances as they arise. These decisions normally occur in a setting in which (1) the need to make a decision has been *anticipated* and is not in response to some sudden, surprise occurrence in the environment, (2) there is a relatively *lengthy time frame* in which to reach a decision, (3) the decision involves a *major*, if not grave, concern, and (4) a *large variety of domestic political actors* inside and outside the government can become involved in the decision process, although the decision may ultimately be made by top-level officials.

Many other foreign policy decisions, in contrast, can be labeled **administrative decisions**, which are more concrete and detailed in nature. The vast majority of foreign policy decisions made by a government are of this type. "The American State Department on any one day receives about 2,300 cables from American diplomatic and consular officials abroad . . . requesting directions or seeking permission to make certain decisions in the field. But . . . the Secretary of State will read only . . . 2 percent of the total. The State Department also sends out approximately 3,000 cables daily . . . of these, the Secretary of State may see only six, and the President will have only one or two of the most important communications referred to his office."[12] These may or may not involve the element of surprise and may or may not allow for lengthy deliberation. Such decisions normally involve concerns that are (1) relatively *narrow* in scope, (2) *low-threat* in seriousness, and (3) handled at the *lower levels of the government bureaucracy*. An example might be the determination of seating arrangements at a diplomatic reception for a visiting dignitary. Although such decisions by themselves are unlikely to have significant consequences (even if a minor diplomatic incident may be created, for example, by an errant choice of dining utensils, as happened when some "made in Taiwan" chopsticks turned up at a Carter White House dinner honoring officials from mainland China), taken together they can add up to important foreign policy developments.

One special category of decisions that has attracted the attention of many scholars involves crisis situations. **Crisis decisions** are made in situations normally characterized by (1) a *high degree of threat* and potential gravity, (2) some element of *surprise*, at least in regard to timing, (3) a *finite time interval in* which to reach a decision, or at least a felt sense of *urgency*, and (4) involvement of the *very highest level* of the foreign policy establishment in the decision process (often in a small group setting).[13] Some analysts add the existence of hostilities to the definition.[14] Although a crisis tends to be associated with a short response time, some crises can drag on for a long time, such as the Iranian hostage crisis faced by the Carter administration in 1979–1980, which lasted 444 days. Most are shorter in duration, such as the Cuban missile crisis—arguably the most studied single case in history, recounted in Robert Kennedy's *Thirteen Days* and numerous other writings.

It is sometimes said that much of what we take to be foreign policy is really crisis management, that is, responding to the latest press of events as they unfold. As two authors put it, "talk of crisis is everywhere in contemporary international relations."[15] At times multiple crises can occur simultaneously and compete for attention, as in the case of the bombing of the barracks of a U.S. Marine peacekeeping force in Lebanon and the American invasion of Grenada within the same week in 1983. One study counts 980 states having been involved in 451 international crises between 1918 and 2008.[16] However, it is simplistic to characterize the foreign policy process as consisting of one round after another of putting out fires. Foreign policymakers do not spend all their time lunging from one crisis to another anymore than they do sitting at their desks pondering their philosophy of world politics.

In the foreign policy process, the various types of decisions blend together, often imperceptibly. Some decisions, as when the Kennedy administration committed 10,000 American troops to Vietnam as "advisory" counterinsurgency personnel in 1961, can set in motion a plethora of smaller administrative decisions, breed more than one crisis, and even come to dominate a country's foreign policy agenda for more than a decade, beyond anyone's expectations or intentions.[17]

Types of Behaviors

We have seen that one approach to defining foreign policy is to treat it as a set of grand designs and stratagems that guide a country's entire external relations and that another approach, which is closer to the truth, is to treat it as a collection of decisions, large and small, which do not necessarily fit neatly together. Yet another way to think about foreign policy, given the frequent gap between intentions and actual results, is to examine a country's *behavior* vis-à-vis other countries: What does it actually *do* in the world?

For example, it has often been noted that, whether intended or not, American foreign policy behavior over the years has exhibited a pattern of idealist tendencies competing with realist tendencies. Although the foreign policy of almost all countries contain such contradictions, the United States has evidenced them from its very beginning, reflected in Thomas Jefferson's oxymoronic reference to the United States as "an empire of liberty."[18] As Robert Osgood has written, from the start "the American nation demonstrated that, while it was indeed inspired by an unusual degree of idealism, it was also strongly motivated by egoism and was, in fact, no more capable of completely transcending its self-interest than other nations."[19] As I noted in Chapter 1, realists have been critical recently of both liberal internationalists ("soft Wilsonians") and neoconservatives ("hard Wilsonians") for what they believe is an overly moralistic, crusading view of world politics that results in imprudent American interventions in other countries' affairs.[20]

Intervention is one type of behavior in which countries engage. Interventionism can be diplomatic, economic, or something more intrusive. Some interventions may take the form of clandestine subversion ("covert action") through intelligence agencies such as the American CIA or Russian KGB, while others may be actual armed intervention by uniformed troops. Perhaps the most common behavior that political scientists have attempted to study is war. Not all states are equally prone to war. States differ in numerous other behaviors as well. Not all belong to the same number of international organizations, not all belong to the same number of military alliances or have overseas military bases, not all are equally supportive of free trade, not all have embassies worldwide and exhibit a foreign policy that is global in scope as opposed to mainly regional or isolationist, and so forth. The analysis of foreign policy includes an examination of not only *how* states differ in their behavior (sometimes called *dependent variables*) but also *why* they differ (sometimes called *independent variables*). When state behavior does not mesh with a grand foreign policy scheme, it is due not only to the press of events that can overtake the best-laid plans of policymakers but also to the complex forces that operate on decision making. The discussion that follows provides a framework for understanding the range of variables that affect foreign policy.

THE ANALYSIS OF FOREIGN POLICY

Recalling Graham Allison's plea that all of us have an obligation to "think hard" about "the choices and actions" governments take in the realm of foreign policy, what exactly does this entail? Whether one is interested in examining a country's foreign policy behavior patterns (e.g., interventionist versus noninterventionist tendencies) or examining a specific foreign policy decision (e.g., the Kennedy administration's decision to institute a naval blockade around Cuba during the 1962 missile crisis), several types of analysis are possible. One may merely wish to *describe* a country's foreign policy actions, establishing the facts surrounding some behavior or decision. Alternatively, one may examine the external and domestic factors impacting foreign policy, in an effort to *explain* why those actions occurred. Finally, one may *evaluate* the soundness of those actions, using various normative and other criteria, and offer prescriptions for future policy.[21]

In other words, there are several different purposes that can be served by the study of foreign policy, related to my earlier remarks about the varied modes of analysis engaged in by scholars, policymakers, and citizens (explanation and prediction along with prescriptive and normative analysis). Although this chapter will touch on prescriptive and normative concerns, here we are most interested in explanation (and ultimately prediction), in exploring the "why" question—establishing causal links between various determinants and behaviors. To quote Arnold Wolfers, "As in all fields of human activity, decisions and actions in the international arena can be understood, predicted, and manipulated only insofar as the factors influencing the decision can be identified and isolated."[22] On the importance of establishing causation, an ancient philosopher once said, "I would rather understand a single cause than be king of Persia."[23] The problem is that in international relations, especially, there are usually multiple causes. Fortunately the international relations field has developed a framework for helping students navigate through the welter of factors that affect foreign policy decisions and behaviors.

EXPLAINING FOREIGN POLICY: THE "LEVELS OF ANALYSIS" FRAMEWORK

In *Essence of Decision: Explaining the Cuban Missile Crisis*, Graham Allison "thinks hard" about a specific U.S. foreign policy decision that he endeavors to explain—the decision to impose a naval blockade around Cuba in October 1962, in response to a Soviet nuclear missile threat.[24] As mentioned in the history of the Cold War system in Chapter 2, the Kennedy administration discovered that the Soviet Union was installing offensive nuclear weapons on the island of Cuba, ninety miles from the U.S. mainland, and decided to enforce a naval blockade against Soviet ships sailing toward Cuba carrying equipment that would complete the installation. The United States ultimately succeeded in forcing the Russian ships to turn back to the Soviet Union and to remove the missiles from Cuba, but only after thirteen days of intense debate among Kennedy and his advisers and feverish diplomacy between Washington and Moscow. There is a temptation to look back and treat the blockade decision as the only viable decision that could have been made, in that it seemed the path of least resistance—a moderate option situated somewhere between doing nothing or launching air strikes against the Soviet missiles. But the blockade decision was not foreordained. Why was that option chosen as opposed to some other? Allison offers three different explanatory models—three different "cuts of reality"—that may account for U.S. foreign policy behavior during the crisis.

The first model that he uses, a **rational actor model**, is based on the same **national interest** concept that Winston Churchill alluded to in explaining Russian behavior (see the epigraph at the beginning of this chapter). Churchill was assuming that Russia as a nation-state had a set of interests that the Russian leadership pursued above all else, notably the physical survival and independence, if

The Billiard Ball Model

Josh Korenblat

not primacy, of the Soviet Union. "National interest" is commonly invoked to explain most countries' foreign policy behavior. Along the lines of the realist paradigm, there is a tendency on the part of practitioners, scholars, and laypersons alike to view foreign policy as the product of a *unitary* actor (a national government acting on behalf of a nation-state). When we speak of "the United States" or "Washington" (or "Russia" or "Moscow") having "decided" or "done" something, we are not merely employing convenient shorthand wording but are evidencing a natural inclination to adopt a states-as-actors perspective. According to one author, states can be thought of as "billiard balls," colliding with one another and reacting to each other's moves like the objects on a pool table.[25] States are conceptualized here as monolithic entities producing foreign policy decisions based on rational calculations geared toward maximizing the national interest, with the observer not having to look beneath the surface at the internal dynamics of the policymaking process, whether it be the individual decision makers themselves or their domestic environment. It is presumed here that all states, no matter who their leaders are (a Joseph Stalin or a Winston Churchill) and no matter whether they are democratic or nondemocratic polities, tend to operate in accordance with the dictates of realpolitik, each driven by similar impulses regarding the promotion of national security, power, and wealth.

Applying the rational actor model to the "missiles of October" crisis, Allison notes, for example, "on confronting the problem posed by the installation of strategic missiles in Cuba . . . [the] analyst frames the puzzle: Why did the Soviet Union decide to install missiles in Cuba? . . . The analyst has 'explained' this event when he can show how placing missiles in Cuba was a reasonable action, given Soviet strategic objectives."[26] According to this model, the Kennedy administration, having (1) defined the situation as a high-threat problem posing major security risks to the United States, (2) specified the goal as the removal of Soviet missiles, (3) considered an exhaustive menu of possible means of response, ranging from diplomatic efforts through the United Nations to all-out use of military force, and (4) weighed the costs and benefits of each option, finally settled on the blockade decision as the one likely to maximize its own strategic objectives. The rest, we are told, is history.

A good deal of foreign policy can be understood in these simple, parsimonious rational actor terms. However, there are many nonrational factors that also can affect foreign policy, since the decisions and actions of governments not only are responses to challenges and opportunities in the international environment but also "result from the interplay among executive and legislative organizations, public and private interests, and, of course, personalities. This interplay becomes a determinant of foreign policy no less than events abroad."[27] We have already noted that the entire foreign policy establishment does not become activated every time there is a foreign policy decision to be made; depending on the issue-area and situation, certain units and certain persons rather than others will become involved.

Accordingly, Allison offers a second model, the **governmental politics model,** that treats foreign policy not as the deliberate response of a single-minded government to a strategic threat or opportunity outside its national borders, but, instead, as the result of bargaining and compromise among different officials within the government who see the situation from competing bureaucratic and other perspectives. Allison points out that the members of ExCom, the small group of high-level advisers (Secretary of Defense Robert McNamara, Air Force General Curtis LeMay, Attorney General Robert Kennedy, and others) that President Kennedy convened to cope with the Cuban missile crisis, disagreed among themselves as to the gravity of the threat, as where one "stood" depended to an extent on where one "sat" in the bureaucracy and which "face" of the situation one saw. (One of the president's closest advisers warned of "the very real possibility that if we allow Cuba to complete installation . . . of missile bases, the next House of Representatives [after the upcoming November congressional elections] is likely to have a Republican majority.")[28] Allison adds a third explanatory model, the **organizational process model,** which interprets the Cuban missile crisis decision as the outcome of various organizational procedures and routines that affected the collection and analysis of intelligence data and other aspects of the decision process.

In presenting alternative explanations beyond the rational actor account of the Cuban missile crisis, Allison introduces frequently overlooked factors, focusing our

FIGURE 3.1 An Alternative to the Billiard Ball Model: A Multi-Causal Framework

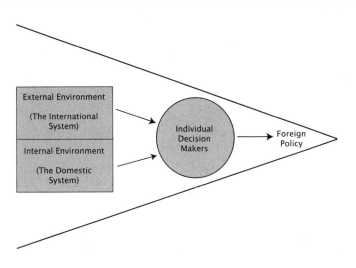

THE MAKING OF U.S. (OR RUSSIAN) FOREIGN POLICY

attention on **individual decision makers** (possessing personality quirks, self-interested motivations, divergent perceptions, and other **idiosyncrasies**) responding to stimuli not only from their **external environment** (threats and opportunities in the **international system**) but also from their **internal environment** (public opinion, electoral, interest group, and other **domestic political influences**). These clusters of variables, found at different **levels of analysis**, are depicted in Figure 3.1, which can be thought of as a "funnel of causality," with inputs streaming into a country's foreign policy establishment from its domestic and international environment, filtered through and processed by flesh-and-blood decision makers, who ultimately produce outputs in the form of foreign policy.

Among the first scholars to suggest that causation in international relations can be understood in terms of levels of analysis was Kenneth Waltz, who in *Man, the State, and War* posited that unlocking the mystery of warfare and explaining why wars occur was possible by examining world politics through three different "images": the individual (the personality and other characteristics of individual leaders), the state (political, economic, and other characteristics of the nation-state), and the state system (the distribution of power and other characteristics of the international system).[29] As a realist, Waltz ultimately concluded that the *system level* provides the most compelling explanations of foreign policy behavior, including war decisions, since, in his judgment, it contains "constraints and imperatives to which all individuals and states, regardless of their uniqueness, must abide."[30] Certainly system characteristics are important variables, as reflected in the discussion of the historical development of the international system in the previous chapter. However, so are other sets of variables. Domestic-level and individual-level variables have tended to get overlooked, relative to international system-level variables, because the very definition of foreign policy steers us to the system level. Also, the former are hardly ever cited by a government as the official explanation of a foreign policy decision. When was the last time you heard a leader say he or she made a particular decision because "I wanted to get re-elected" or because "I have an authoritarian personality"?

In the sections that follow, we will look at determinants of foreign policy that operate at each of the three levels Waltz mentions, starting with the international system level, then the nation-state level, and finally the individual level. Other analysts have added more elaborate explanatory schemes, identifying as many as six different levels of analysis, but three will suffice for our purposes here.[31]

THE INTERNATIONAL SYSTEM LEVEL

Rational actor, national interest explanations of foreign policy are rooted in the international system level. The system level includes (1) relationships between pairs of nation-states (e.g., geographical distance between them) and (2) broader characteristics of the international system as a whole (e.g., the global power structure, such as balance or imbalance of power).

Dyadic Relationships

Realist theory has been criticized for reducing international relations to a series of billiard ball-type action-reaction sequences, where states do nothing more than take cues from their external environment and formulate policies to cope with "what is happening abroad." However, realists are not alone in pointing to external, systemic factors as shapers of foreign policy. Neoliberals often see international relations in a similar light, with states reciprocating in tit-for-tat fashion either the friendship or hostility that other states display toward them.[32] The foreign policies of the United States and the Soviet Union during the Cold War have been at least partly explained simply as responses by each superpower to the hostility of the other, creating a conflict spiral that both had trouble ending.[33] Dyadic relations can change as a function of triangular relations, as in the case of the American-Soviet-Chinese triangle during the Cold War. Despite continued ideological differences, Washington and Beijing gradually realized they shared mutual interests in limiting any expansionist objectives Moscow might have. Based on the maxim "my enemy's enemy is my friend," they began to open up a dialogue, breaking the ice with an exchange of table tennis teams (the so-called ping-pong diplomacy) in 1971, followed a year later by President Nixon's visit to China to meet with Mao Zedong.

Among the frictions China experienced in its relations with the Soviet Union was a long-standing boundary dispute along the Ussuri River. The number of borders a country shares with other states is a system-level variable that can impact foreign policy significantly. One study notes that "contiguity enjoys wide empirical support as one of the key factors influencing the likelihood of war in dyads"; the author cites research demonstrating that in an "analysis of 'dangerous dyads' between 1815 and 1965, contiguous states [were] 35 more times likely to experience war than noncontiguous states."[34] Relying not on empirical research but intuition, the fourth-century realist thinker Kautilya advised Indian leaders that neighbors are always enemies and neighbors' neighbors are therefore friends, based on his conception of

> a circle of states forming a kind of political solar system and tending to gravitate toward one another as friends or come into collision as enemies according to their respective positions in the circle. Thus, states adjacent to each other, and therefore in the nature of things bound to have a greater number of points of friction, are to be regarded as natural enemies.[35]

Although historically some of the greatest rivalries in international relations have occurred between neighbors (e.g., France and Germany, Russia and Japan, Iran and Iraq), common borders can also produce considerable interstate cooperation in trade, tourism, and other areas. Note the century-old 5,500 mile demilitarized frontier between the United States and Canada—the longest common border in the world—as well as the growing political and economic integration of European countries today in the European Union.

The so-called **geopolitics** school, represented by Alfred Mahan and Sir Halford Mackinder in the late nineteenth and early twentieth centuries, attributed special importance to an array of geographical factors thought to affect foreign policy, including a state's location, topography, and natural resources. The isolationist foreign policy behavior in early U.S. history was largely attributed to its continental location. As George Washington remarked, "Our detached and distant situation invites and enables us to pursue a different course." The French ambassador to the United States put it more bluntly, following the country's expansion to the Pacific: "America is blessed among the nations. On the north she had a weak neighbor; on the south another weak neighbor; on the east, fish, and the west, fish." As late as 1939, former president Herbert Hoover was reassuring Americans that they were protected by "a moat of three thousand miles of ocean on the east, and six thousand miles on the west."[36] Given its island position, Britain, too, historically had maintained relative autonomy from continental European politics. However, as both Britain and the United States were to discover as the twentieth century wore on and gave way to the twenty-first century, airplanes, intercontinental ballistic missiles, and other technologies have rendered geography arguably a less critical shaper of policy (and the geopolitics school a less important school), even if it certainly still remains a factor in interstate relations.

Economic interdependence is another system-level variable that has been tied to foreign policy behavior. I have already noted Sir Norman Angell's prediction on the eve of World War I that European states had so many trade connections that war between them would be impossible. Although economic interdependence obviously has not always prevented war, there is evidence that it can help reduce conflict.[37] Similarly, it has been found that "democracy is a strong force for international peace."[38] What is called the **democratic peace** hypothesis stresses the *dyadic* nature of the peace—it is not so much that democracies are peaceful but that they rarely, if ever, fight each other. We will examine the democratic peace hypothesis more closely when we look at the nation-state level of analysis and how national characteristics affect foreign policy.

The Structure of the Global System: Polarity and Polarization

Realists stress how the inherent structure of the international system, particularly its anarchic character, constrains state behavior, since the lack of any central order-giver creates a "security dilemma" for all states, which inclines them more toward conflict than cooperation. However, as noted in Chapter 2, some elements of the international system, such as power and alignment configurations, change over time and impact foreign policy.

Regarding power relationships, Bruce Russett and John Oneal write:

> The balance of military capabilities undoubtedly influences decision makers contemplating the use of force against a rival. States seek to constrain their adversaries by increasing their military strength. . . . The line of thought runs like this: "I will make myself strong enough to deter others from attacking me. I will create military capabilities that will deny them the ability to invade me successfully. Or if that is not possible, I will at least be able to impose such a high cost on an attacker that the potential gains will not be worth the price."[39]

States form **alliances** mainly to add to their ability to deter aggression or defeat the aggressor. The overall power and alignment structure of the international system at any given moment often informs these sorts of calculations.

Political scientists use the term **polarity** to refer to the number of major powers, or *poles*, in the international system. If there are several great powers, as was the case throughout most eras discussed in our international relations history, the system is said to be **multipolar**. If there are only two major powers, as was the case during the Cold War, the system is labeled **bipolar**.[40] There has never been a **unipolar** international system, unless one counts either the brief immediate aftermath of World War II, when the European powers, including the Soviet Union, were totally exhausted and the United States momentarily enjoyed a monopoly possession of nuclear weapons, or the aftermath of the Cold War, when some commentators compared the United States to the Roman Empire. Scholars have a long-running debate over whether bipolar or multipolar systems are more prone toward war, something we will examine in Chapter 5.

Closely related to polarity is **polarization**, the flexibility or rigidity of alignments. Because polarization has to do with "the tendency for actors to cluster around the system's most powerful states," at times polarity and polarization can appear to be indistinguishable.[41] However, power structure and bloc structure are not exactly the same. For example, on the eve of World War I, the multipower international system had become considerably more polarized than it was during the Concert of Europe period due to the formation of two competing alliances, the Triple Entente and the Triple Alliance. During the Cold War era featuring the two superpowers, tight bipolarity, manifested by the opposing NATO and Warsaw Pact alliances, gradually gave way to loose bipolarity. There is disagreement over what to call the contemporary system, both in terms of power and alignment patterns; as noted in Chapter 2, some observers have suggested that the post–Cold War system is so complex as to be labeled "uni-multipolar," in that American dominance (at least on paper) seems offset by the growing ambiguity of power and fluidity of alignments.

Realists argue that the international system creates certain "rules of the game" that states tend to follow. According to **balance of power** theory, states seek to avoid domination by any one actor in the system; as long as a balance is maintained, not only will hegemony be prevented but the system will remain in stable equilibrium and major war can be averted. The corollary is that power imbalances often trigger war. In the early life of the international system, Britain saw itself as playing the balancer role against would-be hegemons such as France or the Hapsburg Empire, throwing its weight behind the weaker state or coalition when the balance was threatened. Realists contend that **balancing** is the logical, rational strategy for states to follow in such situations, since if states ally with a rising hegemon and help the latter gain domination, they may be setting themselves up next for conquest. However, history is replete with small and medium powers engaging instead in **bandwagoning**—joining the aspiring hegemon in hopes of sharing in the fruits of victory, as in the case of Italy allying with Nazi Germany in the 1940s.[42] (One of the problems with realist theory is that it is not always clear if it is aimed at offering predictions on how countries can be expected to behave, or rather prescriptions on how they *should* behave.) [43]

Within the realist school itself, there are differences between "balance of power realists" and "hegemonic realists" over, empirically, which theories best describe actual state behavior and, normatively, which ones are preferable in promoting peace, with hegemonic realists arguing that hegemony frequently occurs and is actually stabilizing insofar as the lead state often forges a degree of world order around a new set of norms (e.g., the role of the Pax Britannica in the nineteenth century and the Pax Americana after World War II in promoting a liberal international economic order that served the interests of both the hegemon and a majority of states).[44] Balance of power realists have an especially difficult time explaining the phenomenon noted in the previous chapter's discussion of the contemporary international system (under fluidity of alignments), namely, how no new alliance has formed against the United States despite what many see as its hegemonic status today; explanations range from the United States not being viewed as a "predatory state," to other states being content to be "free riders" letting America supply "collective goods," to the changed norms of international relations relating to the end of territorial aggrandizement by great powers and the development of the long peace among them.[45]

Changed systemwide norms (stressed by constructivists), the distribution of wealth (stressed by liberal and Marxist thinkers), and many other features of the global system impact foreign policymaking. Then, too, *regional* subsystems exhibit certain dynamics that influence war and other behaviors, as in the case of the rivalries between various Arab states, Iran, and Israel in the Middle East, although such regional systems also are touched by global great-power competition. For example, one study has found that the greater the "state to nation imbalance" in a region, the greater the likelihood of regional war, that is, regions in which there are many multiethnic states (where state and nation boundaries do not coincide much) are especially ripe for violence, which may explain why there is relatively little warfare in Latin America compared to, say, the Middle East.[46]

THE NATION-STATE LEVEL

The degree of ethnic homogeneity within a nation-state is a variable found at the nation-state level of analysis, where we are interested in how the characteristics of the state itself impact foreign policy. The nation-state level includes many sets of variables: (1) domestic political and governmental factors (e.g., whether a country is a democracy or a dictatorship), (2) economic factors (e.g., type of economic system or level of economic development), and (3) societal factors (e.g., the aforementioned degree of ethnic homogeneity). Before examining these clusters of variables, let us briefly consider a topic that follows from the previous focus on the power structure of the international system. What national characteristics tend to make one country more powerful than another?

The Bases of National Power

A favorite pastime of observers of international relations over the years has been to rank-order states according to their power, with some states labeled great powers and others medium powers, and so forth. I have done so in this book as well. It is not hard to find vast differences between nation-states in terms of size, wealth, and other measures of the sort shown in Table 3.1, on page 76. Most attempts to construct pecking orders assume that certain national attributes confer power and that the statistics presented in the table (on population, land area, total armed forces, gross national income, and per capita income) are among the leading indicators—determinants—of who exercises power in international relations. Other sources of national power not listed in the table commonly include self-sufficiency in natural resources, degree of industrial production, and more qualitative elements such as the quality of one's educational system and workforce.[47]

Although international relations textbooks have long included mention of "the bases of national power," constructing meaningful pecking orders is not as simple as it sounds. Historically, a relatively large population has been a necessary condition for achieving great-power status. However, population alone is not a sufficient condition; few analysts today would consider Indonesia, Pakistan, and Bangladesh (the fourth, sixth, and tenth most populous countries on earth) major powers. Small, rich states with highly educated, skilled human resources, including many trained scientists and engineers, can often compensate for inferior demographic size by exercising influence as foreign aid donors or in some other capacity (e.g., Norway and Canada). Similarly, smaller armies equipped with the latest high-tech weaponry can measure up to larger armies in many instances, as Israel has done in its many wars with Arab states. China has the largest army in the world but is no match for the U.S. army technologically, while some other top-ten armies in size (North Korea, South Korea, Vietnam, and Iran) do not necessarily represent the greatest firepower. Iceland has no army to speak of, yet it leads the world in energy research in the form of hydrogen power. One reason it is difficult to construct meaningful pecking orders based on hard indicators of power, then, is that qualitative assets may be at least as important to the exercise of influence in world politics. Still more intangible assets might include societal unity and morale, quality of leadership, reputation, and the will to use power.

However, even if we confine our analysis of power to hard, aggregate data on national characteristics, the utility of pecking order exercises is questionable, especially today. The United States is powerful on almost every measure. It is by far the largest country in gross domestic product (over $13 trillion), the third largest in population (after China and India), the third largest in land area (after Russia and Canada), and among the richest (its roughly $45,000 per capita income is exceeded only by Norway and a few other states with considerably smaller populations). Yet it has suffered numerous setbacks in recent times from Vietnam to Iraq. Clearly power is best conceptualized not as an aggregate national capability that can be hypothetically mobilized but rather as an influence *relationship* in which the ability of one state to influence another depends less on the sum of their respective potential resources than on contextual factors, such as whether one has the right resources to apply to a given problem. In other words, power more than ever is *issue-* or *situation-specific*. For example, Saudi Arabia may be more powerful today in shaping the global politics of oil than the United States or any other actor, but there are few other issue-areas where Riyadh exercises that kind of clout. We should not conclude that there is no stratification in world politics. A pecking order of sorts exists—it is safe to say that the United States is generally more powerful than Micronesia—but it is given to frequent collapse.

Domestic Political and Governmental Characteristics

As suggested by the democratic peace hypothesis, type of political system has long been considered an important variable affecting foreign policy behavior. From Immanuel Kant to Woodrow Wilson and more recent thinkers, a common assumption, especially among liberals, is that democracies are more peaceful than dictatorships, presumably because mass publics serve as a brake on war, given their incentive to avoid having their sons and daughters killed and tax dollars wasted, and because democracies are used to resolving disputes through a political culture based on give-and-take and the rule of law rather than violence. However, most empirical studies have not found a clear correlation between type of government and war propensity. Following up earlier studies such as Quincy Wright's *A Study of War*, Melvin Small and J. David Singer, using data from the Correlates of War Project covering the period from 1815 to 1965, found that democracies initiated as many wars as nondemocracies, and hence their frequent war participation was not simply a function of responding to aggression.[48] Other scholars have reinforced these findings, concluding, based on more extensive data analysis of "militarized disputes," that democracies are no less inclined than other kinds of states to threaten or use force in crises short of war.[49] On the other hand, it is almost "a law of nature" that, as Bill Clinton said in his 1994 State of the Union speech, "democracies don't attack each other."[50] Whether due to shared values or the political fallout that leaders in a democracy might suffer from fighting an unpopular war against a sister democracy, there seem to be enormous inhibitions against democracies fighting each other, even if there are fewer inhibitions against fighting other opponents. These ambiguous findings about the role of regime type in explaining foreign policy behavior do not mean that domestic variables are irrelevant, only that they must be examined carefully before conclusions are reached about the nature and magnitude of their impact.

The treatment of states as billiard balls neglects to take into account the fact that leaders make decisions based not only on national interest calculations but on a more complex set of criteria that includes an assessment of how their foreign policy decisions might affect their *own* personal interests, particularly in regard to reelection chances (in a democracy) or staying in power (in an authoritarian regime).[51] Although it is often said that domestic politics does not heavily affect foreign policymaking, since "politics stops at the water's edge" as a country tends to unite behind its leadership in pursuit of national goals, there are many examples of the politicization of foreign policy.[52] While "petty politics" and partisanship may play less of a role in crisis situations than noncrisis situations, and in the national security issue-area (for example, arms control) than other areas, politics can be found operating across all situations and issue-areas.

U.S. secretary of state Condoleezza Rice, in a 2007 *New York Times* op-ed, went so far as to say, "Forget grand strategy. Foreign policy is shaped by domestic concerns."[53] One of the reasons Henry Kissinger said that foreign policy cannot be as neatly conceived and executed as one might wish is precisely because of the constraints imposed on decision makers by their domestic surroundings. Kissinger explains that "what is presented by foreign critics as America's quest for dominance is very frequently a response to domestic pressure groups," such as the Cuban lobby, Jewish lobby, textile industry lobby, or some other interest group.[54] The United States is not alone in having its foreign policy influenced by domestic politics, whether interest groups, public opinion, or other domestic influences. Although nondemocratic regimes might seem more impervious to domestic political pressures than democratic governments, internal factors always operate to some extent in foreign policymaking, even in dictatorships.

One such domestic source is *bureaucratic politics*, which, according to Graham Allison, operated during the Cuban missile crisis. At one point during the Cuban missile crisis, Soviet leader Nikita Khrushchev, anxiously awaiting President Kennedy's reaction to his latest proposal for defusing the crisis and wondering why there was a delay, is reported to have sighed, "I guess he [Kennedy] has his bureaucracy to contend with also."[55] One of the most striking examples of bureaucratic politics in the Soviet Union was the competition between different subunits within the Kremlin's defense ministry in developing weapons systems, not unlike the legendary battles fought within the U.S. Defense Department between the Army, Navy, and Air Force over the slicing of the pie in the DOD budget. As one article noted, "New Soviet missiles seem to be born as quadruplets. In the '60s they deployed the SS 7–8–9–11 missiles; the '70s generation was the SS 16–17–18–19 missiles. In the 1980s, they deployed another generation of four missiles. Why always in fours? U.S. experts say that the organization that designs Soviet missiles has four separate design bureaus, and that each is allowed to design a new generation."[56] In 1990, defense secretary Dick Cheney said that "the United States believed that the Soviet Union was developing four new long-range nuclear missiles," and he "expressed concern about the Soviet missile program" to Soviet leaders. Was he aware that the Soviet program possibly had less to do with deep geopolitical strategic designs against the United States than with the more innocuous internal politics of Soviet national defense?[57] In the post-Soviet era, George W. Bush and Russian president Vladimir Putin were asked if they could "say with certainty that your teams will act in the same spirit" of cooperation that the two men seemed to exude. Bush replied that "sometimes the intended [policy] doesn't necessarily get translated throughout the levels of government [due to] bureaucratic intransigence." Putin echoed his words: "Of course, there is always a bureaucratic threat."[58]

Graham Allison and other scholars have noted the tendency of bureaucrats to promote goals that happen to coincide with the organizational mission of their unit. Government agencies may feel as threatened by their own possible extinction as by the extinction of the nation, notwithstanding the remark by a former U.S. secretary of state that "the nearest thing to immortality on Earth is a government bureau."[59] When President Carter attempted to shrink the Washington bureaucracy, his acting budget director said, "Only two federal programs have ever been flatly abolished—Uncle Sam no longer makes rum in the Virgin Islands and no longer breeds horses for the U.S. cavalry."[60] Curiously, the U.S. horse cavalry managed to justify its existence well into the atomic era, with the DOD unit staving off elimination until 1951, and the last army mule retired in 1956. The cavalry units of European defense establishments displayed similar survival instincts, rationalizing the need for horse power alongside more modern modes of firepower.[61]

In democracies especially, not only Executive Branch bureaucracies but also Legislative Branch *committees* and *interest groups* can become heavily involved in foreign policy concerns. American political scientists have studied **iron triangles** (also called subgovernments or policy networks) that are found in several issue-areas (agriculture policy, energy policy, etc.), consisting of mutually supportive back-scratching relationships between the key administrative agencies, key legislative committees, and key interest groups having the greatest stake in a given policy domain. In the case of U.S. defense policy, for example, incestuous relations have been found between the Department of Defense (wanting a bigger budget), the chairs of the House and Senate Armed Services committees (wanting increased dollars spent in their home states and congressional districts), and the major arms manufacturers such as Lockheed Martin and Boeing (wanting larger military weapons contracts). A classic illustration of how such relationships shape foreign policy behavior as important as weapons procurement decisions is the following: When early in the twentieth century the chairman of the House Naval Affairs Committee was asked whether it was a fact that "the navy yard in his district was too small to accommodate the latest battleships," he replied, "That is true, and that is the reason I have always been in favor of small ships."[62]

Irrational as it may seem, such calculations by powerful committee chairpersons, in concert with powerful bureaucratic and interest group actors, can drive national security decisions. Given the growth of intermestic issues, an increasing number of domestic players are becoming involved in the foreign policy process in the United States and elsewhere. Note, for example, the large number of actors involved during the 1980s in the formulation of U.S. policy with regard to the ozone layer, which was deteriorating and threatening to expose Americans and other human beings to ultraviolet radiation. Ambassador Richard Benedick orchestrated an "interagency minuet" in preparation for the Vienna Convention for the Protection of the Ozone Layer, in which "the final U.S. position was drafted by the State Department" but had to be "cleared" by numerous agencies, including the departments of Commerce and Energy, the Environmental Protection Agency, the National Aeronautics and Space Agency, the National Oceanographic and Atmospheric Administration, the Office of Management and Budget, the U.S. Trade Representative, and the Domestic Policy Council. Benedick had to deal with other domestic elements as well.

In the United States in recent years [in the ozone case and other cases], increasing involvement of Congress—and with it nongovernmental organizations and the broader public—has introduced a new range of interests that must ultimately be reflected in the national position. Similar developments seem to be occurring in other democratic countries.[63]

There are growing "domestic-international entanglements" and domestic conflicts over "what the 'national interest' requires."[64] In our examination of diplomacy in the next chapter, we will see more of how chief negotiators must play to both a domestic and an external audience when carrying out negotiations.

Among the *societal interest groups* that had to be accommodated in the ozone layer case were the U.S. chemical industry (manufacturers of chlorofluorocarbons thought to harm the ozone layer) as well as environmental groups. On U.S. Middle East policy, there has been a debate over whether the "Jewish lobby" or "the oil lobby" has been more powerful in influencing American policy in that region.[65] Labor unions and big business groups obviously impact foreign economic policymaking regarding the imposition of tariffs and other decisions. Business groups are more powerful than labor groups and have "a strong, consistent, and, at times, lopsided influence upon U.S. foreign policy" generally.[66] "Epistemic communities" of experts—elites with highly technical knowledge—also influence policymaking, especially on "low politics" issues. Elites are more likely than the general public to influence foreign policy, although the latter is not without influence.[67]

Many scholars have studied the role of *public opinion* as a determinant of foreign policy and have concluded that public opinion acts as "a set of constraints, like dams and dikes, rather than a direct determinant of foreign policy."[68] Leaders in democracies are sensitive to how the public may react to a particular decision. Recall the concern expressed by President Kennedy's advisers during the Cuban missile crisis that inaction by the administration might help the Republicans gain control of Congress in the upcoming elections. However, given the public's general lack of information and short attention span when it comes to foreign policy, leaders often are able to "wave the flag" and, within limits, manipulate the public to accept their decisions or at least accord them wide decision latitude. It is estimated that no more than 25 percent of the American public constitutes the "attentive public," those who regularly pay attention to and become informed about world events. Not surprisingly, the more educated and wealthier one is, the more worldly one is likely to be, although elite views about foreign policy can fluctuate as much as mass attitudes. In most U.S. presidential elections, the mass public normally focuses on domestic concerns and rarely bases electoral choices on the candidates' foreign policy positions, although foreign policy issues become more visible during times of crises, as after the 9/11 attack. To the extent leaders' decisions are affected by public opinion polls, they are apt to be more attuned to mass preferences the louder and more crystallized the expression of majoritarian sentiment is; and they are more likely to heed such sentiment on the eve of an election than the day after.[69]

The Vietnam War provides a good case study in the dynamics of public opinion and how it impacts foreign policy. Initially there was little public opposition to the war, given President Kennedy's explanation to the American people that the "domino theory" and "containment" required the United States to try to stop communist expansion in Southeast Asia. However, as American troop casualties mounted and the public saw televised images of dead soldiers being returned home in body bags, public support for the war gradually waned. With polls sending unmistakable signals to politicians in the 1968 presidential election that an overwhelming majority of Americans wanted peace, it was ultimately public opinion that pressured leaders to end the war a few years later.

The Vietnam War also illustrates the **rally-round-the-flag effect**. President Kennedy's popularity shot up at the start of the Vietnam War, as tends to happen whenever leaders first take their country into war. It is estimated that appearing tough on an adversary produces an upward "bounce" of 4 or 5 percentage points in a president's popularity, although public approval ratings can be sustained only if the policy proves successful.[70] Even if a president does little or nothing in the face of a national crisis, he may still benefit at least momentarily from the country's felt need to come together. One study notes how George W. Bush's approval ratings catapulted immediately following the attacks of September 11, 2001: "Within two weeks of the attacks, Bush's job approval rating was 90 percent—39 percentage points higher than on September 10 (the highest gain . . . in the history of the Gallup poll). . . . There was nothing the Bush administration was actually *doing* in the days following 9/11 . . . that could fully account for the near-universal approval of his job performance. . . . The country simply felt victimized, and it reacted by rallying around its leader."[71] Not only Bush but Congress benefited, as the percentage of Americans indicating "trust" in their government as a whole increased in the aftermath of 9/11 to a level (50 percent) not seen since the pre-Watergate days of the 1960s.[72]

There can be a fine line between a leader, on the one hand, waving the flag for purposes of mobilizing the nation to follow a policy thought necessary in the national interest and, on the other hand, waving the flag for crasser purposes, to pump up precarious domestic support. Patriotism has been called the last refuge of a scoundrel, but it may be the first recourse of a leader in a democracy or a dictatorship wanting to increase personal popularity at home by exploiting the nationalistic impulses present in almost every nation-state. In Chapter 2, in discussing late nineteenth-century international relations, I referred to the ruling coalition of Rye and Iron in Germany offering "foreign adventures instead of domestic reform, circuses in place of bread" in order to prop up the regime. More recently, some observers attributed the 1998 U.S. bombing of Afghanistan and Sudan, seemingly aimed at destroying al Qaeda terrorist training camps, to President Bill Clinton's desire to improve falling poll numbers in the wake of his scandalous affair with a White House intern. The foreign policy of many countries has been linked to internal pressures of the sort depicted in the 1997 movie *Wag the Dog*, where a leadership's sagging popularity at home—whether due to scandal or economic downturn or other negative developments—can lead it to manufacture a conflict against external scapegoats in the hope of producing a rally-round-the-flag effect. The animosity many Middle East governments harbor toward Israel often is explained as a calculated attempt by shaky regimes to divert attention from their own failure to satisfy the political and economic longings of their populations.

Although, based on intuition and anecdotal examples, one would expect to find empirical support for the **scapegoat or diversionary hypothesis**—that internal problems beget external hostility—no clear correlation has been found between these variables.[73] The evidence suggests that governments may be reluctant to risk foreign confrontations when their population is not unified behind them. Indeed, war involvement has often produced the opposite effect that leaders following the logic of the scapegoat hypothesis envision: wars that are relatively long and costly tend to produce electoral defeat for the party in office in a democracy and overthrow for the regime in power in a dictatorship. This is especially true if the leadership loses the war, but it often is true even if the leadership wins the war, as Winston Churchill discovered when he lost the 1945 election to Labor Party leader Clement Attlee by a landslide despite being credited with saving Britain from Nazi conquest during World War II.[74]

Although Alexis de Tocqueville and others have suggested that democracies are disadvantaged in the conduct of foreign policy relative to dictatorships, due to the constraints posed by public opinion in open political systems, one study finds that democracies won over 80 percent of all the wars fought between democracies and autocracies between 1816 and 1990.[75] Some argue that democracies have a special problem successfully fighting "limited wars" of the sort that are most common today, such as the Vietnam or Iraq quagmires, that is, asymmetrical conflicts where one does not use one's entire military arsenal, where the conflict drags on as a war of attrition, and where a restless public opinion eventually demands victory or stoppage of the war. One of the reasons the United States ended the draft after the Vietnam War and instituted an all-volunteer army was the hope that it would help insulate leaders from the vagaries of public opinion and make it easier to fight such protracted conflicts. Nonetheless, mass media coverage of American casualties and other developments still has the potential to influence foreign policy decisions. For example, the so-called **CNN effect** was credited with both getting the United States into the Somalian civil war in 1992 and getting it out; pictures of starving Somalians pressured the Clinton administration to send troops to deliver food aid, while pictures of a murdered GI's body being dragged in the sand of Mogadishu, recounted in the film *Black Hawk Down*, pressured the administration to quit the operation.[76]

Economic and Societal Characteristics

There is a long theoretical tradition, anchored in Marxist analysis, that posits a relationship between type of economic system and foreign policy behavior, with capitalist economic systems, such as the United States and those in Western Europe, thought to generate foreign policies rooted in support of corporate and financial elites.[77] This tradition goes at least as far back as Vladimir Lenin, the father of the Bolshevik Revolution, whose 1916 book *Imperialism* explained World War I as the inevitable product of rivalries between capitalist states competing for overseas raw materials, markets, and cheap labor. Lenin himself drew on the work of the British economist John Hobson, whose 1902 book by the same title argued that capitalist states were inherently expansionist because, given the unequal distribution of wealth that capitalism spawned and the resultant limited purchasing power of the lower classes, such states were constantly faced with economic recession unless they found customers abroad. Colonialism, imperialism, and war all were traced to capitalism. Although Marxists assert that capitalist countries tend to be war-prone, there is little empirical evidence to indicate that communist countries are less so. Indeed, Adam Smith and other liberal thinkers have suggested that wars are often bad for business and that, to the extent capitalism helps to promote a web of economic interdependence worldwide, such economic activity may provide a disincentive and antidote to war.

Radical thinkers point to the presence of economic elites at the center of the **military-industrial complex,** which was President Eisenhower's term for the arms industry and affiliated interests that he feared were gaining "unwarranted influence" over American foreign policy and were creating a permanent war economy. Although many observers have echoed Eisenhower's concerns since he first warned about the complex in 1961, the evidence is mixed as to the extent of its influence on U.S. foreign policy.[78] Moreover, such complexes can be found in noncapitalist states, such as existed in the Soviet Union.

The size of a country's economy, usually measured by GNP (gross national product) or GDP (gross domestic product), is a national-level attribute that clearly affects foreign policy, a large economy tending to increase a nation's interests in and means of influencing events abroad. The smaller economies listed in Table 3.1 generally lack the resources to be global actors. Most states in the international system are regional actors. A country like Chad in Africa is likely to have far more economic, diplomatic, and other contacts with neighboring African states than with, say, Bolivia or other Latin American states or Thailand and other Asian states. Level of economic development, or wealth (usually measured by per capita GNP or per capita GDP), also impacts foreign policy *scope* and other behaviors. Rich countries can better afford the expense of participating in international organizations and maintaining embassies overseas than poor countries. One study of intergovernmental organization membership found that among the twenty-five states having the most IGO memberships, eighteen were wealthy countries of various sizes, with fourteen, including all of those in the top ten, being from West-ern Europe.[79] The wealth of a country obviously is also the main determinant of whether it is a donor or a recipient of foreign aid.

Among the societal attributes that can affect foreign policy are dominant ide-ological or cultural traits. For example, we have noted that historically there has been a moralistic streak running through American foreign policy, grounded in what is sometimes called "American exceptionalism," described as follows by Robert Kagan: "In addition to the common human tendency to seek greater power and influence over one's surroundings, Americans have been driven outward into the world by something else: the potent, revolutionary ideology of liberalism (de-mocracy) that they adopted at the nation's birth. . . . [This] inevitably produced a new kind of foreign policy."[80]

Kagan says that the impulse to intervene in the affairs of others "is embedded in the American DNA." There may be something to such notions as "national character," although we should be cautious about stereotyping entire people, es-pecially when so many nation-states are multiethnic. Only about 10 percent of all countries are ethnically homogeneous, having at least 90 percent of their popu-lation of the same ethnicity. In about a third of all states, no one nationality group constitutes a majority (e.g., in Kazakhstan, Kazakhs constitute only 42 percent of the population). The Minorities at Risk Project has reported that two-thirds of the countries of the world contain sizable ethnic groups that are politically active, counting 284 such groups. Disaffected minorities and separatist movements can be found in less developed countries (the Kurds in Iraq) and developed countries (the Basques in Spain) alike, and can affect foreign policy in important ways.[81] We will examine the growth of ethno-political conflict in Chapter 5.

Just as one must be careful not to exaggerate the importance of international system-level factors as determinants of foreign policy, nation-state level factors—domestic political variables, economic structures, societal values and culture, and the like—also should not be exaggerated. Whether responding to external or in-ternal stimuli in their environment, there is nothing "inevitable" about the deci-sions that foreign policy makers produce. The environment may structure and constrain one's choices, but individual human beings in national capitals must still struggle with reaching judgments about what to do in the world. We now turn to the third level of analysis and the role of *individual* factors.

THE INDIVIDUAL LEVEL

A 1993 newspaper headline read: "Human Factor, Good Wine Played Key Roles in Middle East Accord." Describing what became known as the Oslo peace pro-cess, in which Norwegian diplomats helped to broker a tentative peace agreement between Israelis and Palestinians, the article noted that "good personal chemistry, a disregard for history, and an ample supply of wine and whiskey were key fac-tors" in the success. One Norwegian said, "It shows that individuals can play a key role in history."[82] The peace accord was short-lived as the Israeli-Palestinian conflict resumed within a decade, suggesting that history posed more obstacles than thought at the time. We are not interested here in the role of liquor in influencing international relations. But what about "the human factor"?

Two extreme, opposite views of the role of individual actors in international relations are represented in the **environmental determinism school** and the **great man (or woman) theory**. The former argues that most of the decisions taken by national governments and the fallout from those decisions would have occurred regardless of the identity of the specific individuals empowered to make those decisions. It is argued that the material, objective conditions and historical forces that constrain action are larger than any single individual. For example, environmental determinists would contend that the harsh Versailles peace treaty after World War I, accompanied by a worldwide depression, would have produced a German desire for revenge no matter what leader had come to power in Berlin; in other words, Hitler did not "cause" World War II. One well-known representative of this school of thought was Karl Marx, who said that "men make history, but they do not make it under circumstances chosen by themselves, but under circumstances directly encountered, given, and transmitted from the past."[83] Another member of this school was the great Russian novelist Leo Tolstoy, who, writing about the Napoleonic Wars in *War and Peace*, insisted that even as great a historical figure as Napoleon Bonaparte was merely swept along by the tides of history. According to this view, Winston Churchill, Franklin Roosevelt, Mikhail Gorbachev, and other major leaders of the past were not changers of history but mere caretakers who were creatures of their times.

In contrast, proponents of the great man (or woman) school stress the overriding importance of single individuals in moving history and changing the course of events. Nineteenth-century British commentator Thomas Carlyle is most closely associated with this school of thought, having asserted that "the history of the world is but the biography of great men."[84] Examples of this viewpoint range from Pascal's musings that if Cleopatra's nose had been slightly shorter, the face of the world would have been changed, to Robert Kennedy's aforementioned observation that if six of the fourteen men in the ExCom decision group during the Cuban missile crisis had been president, "the world might have blown up." The great man theory view of Hitler differs from the environmental determinist perspective, reflected in Niall Ferguson's comments about Ian Kershaw's 2000 biography of Hitler: "I recall being struck [in reading the biography] by how often these two words appeared: 'Hitler decided.' . . . Here was a powerful affirmation that, whatever the importance of 'structural factors' in Hitler's rise, these became mere background music after he was in power, and especially after he was at war. The critical decisions that condemned Europe to conflagration, the Jews to annihilation, and Germany to devastation emanated from *one man* [italics mine]."[85]

The truth would seem to lie somewhere between the two schools. On the one hand, the environment often limits what any individual can do. Afghanistan, for

President John F. Kennedy in the Oval Office during the Cuban Missile Crisis, 1962.

George Tames//New York Times/Redux

German Chancellor Adolf Hitler leads Nazi Party officials in Nuremberg in 1935.

United States Holocaust Memorial Museum, courtesy of Richard Freimark

example, is hardly likely to be a great naval power anytime soon regardless of who leads the country, since it is completely landlocked. On the other hand, a vast literature has developed in the international relations field that has focused attention on the individual level of analysis, on such variables as personality traits, cognition, group dynamics, and a host of other psychological phenomena, and forces us to look more deeply inside the foreign policy decision-making process itself—at the decision makers, with all their fortes and foibles.[86] One would expect **idiosyncratic** factors to be particularly important in dictatorships, where there is "one-man rule" or policymaking is dominated by a few people, although such factors can be significant in democracies as well, given the fact that leaders tend to be given greater leeway to make decisions about foreign policy than domestic policy, especially in crisis situations.

In this section, we explore how individual-level determinants of foreign policy operate. We examine (1) images and perceptions, (2) group dynamics, and (3) personality and physiology.

Images and Perceptions

One reason individuals "matter" is that they do not all see their environment in the same way. Harold and Margaret Sprout were among the first to call attention to the distinction between the decision maker's "objective" and "psychological" environments—the difference between reality and one's **image** of reality.[87] Kenneth Boulding also has noted that "we must recognize that the people whose decisions determine the policies and actions of nations do not respond to the 'objective' facts of the situation, whatever that may mean, but to their 'image' of the situation. It is what we think the world is like, not what it is really like, that determines our behavior."[88]

All of us have images—"operational codes," "cognitive maps," belief systems," or whatever you want to call them—that shape our **perceptions** of the world around us. Images help us construct reality, but they also can blind us to reality and bias our assessment of a situation. There is a common tendency to filter out any stimuli—incoming bits of information—that do not square with our image of the world and hence threaten our established mind-set. We tend to see what we want to see, or are predisposed to see. Believing is seeing.

Foreign policy makers are as susceptible to distorting reality as any other decision makers. Robert Jervis has noted in them a tendency to misperceive their environment, particularly to view adversaries as more threatening and better coordinated than may actually be the case, and to assume that not only is the *other* side the more aggressive and devious but also that it is cognizant of this.[89] Boulding notes a tendency to stereotype nations as "good" or "bad"—the enemy is all bad, "one's own nation is of spotless virtue."[90] Mention was made earlier of the conflict spiral that the United States and the Soviet Union found themselves in during the Cold War, created in large measure by the mirror images each side had of the other. Whatever aggressive intentions Moscow might have had, it is highly unlikely that Kremlin leaders saw themselves in that light; indeed, evidence suggests that they saw Washington as the source of the frictions between the two states.[91] The two superpowers "stumbled into a nuclear crisis" in October 1962 because policymakers in both countries "acted on the basis of perceptions deeply informed by their own historical perspectives and experiences, largely oblivious to the fact that their counterparts' perspectives and experiences were radically different. . . . By assuming that others saw the world the same way they did," they came close to a colossal miscalculation.[92] This same mirror imagery may help account for recent tensions in U.S. relations with Muslim countries surrounding 9/11, with much of the Muslim world suspicious of American motives in the Middle East and Americans wondering "why do they hate us?"

Because images color reality for foreign policy makers, it is important to understand how images themselves are formed. There are two main sources of images: *past experiences* and *present circumstances*. As suggested above, some images are based on "historical perspectives and experiences," and as such may be widely shared among the members of a country's foreign policy establishment and even by its populace as a whole. For example, I noted previously the national self-image of "American exceptionalism" that has animated an often messianic American foreign policy. Another example is the memory of the "lessons of Munich" that had a profound impact on an entire generation of Americans after World War II, leading them to equate Korea, Vietnam, and other challenges during the Cold War with Hitler's seizure of the Sudetenland in Czechoslovakia in 1938, resulting in their felt need to resist communist aggression rather than engage in appeasement. Many scholars have argued that a historically based image, wrongly applied, caused a fundamental misreading of the environment and contributed to imprudent U.S. foreign policy decisions.[93]

Some images may be held less widely or less intensely, and may be peculiar to only a few individuals based on their particular past experiences, either their childhood upbringing or some other formative influences. For example, World War II held stronger memories for President George H.W. Bush than for many of his contemporaries, since "as a 19-year-old Navy lieutenant pilot, Bush saw a fellow pilot ripped in two when his plane missed its landing on an aircraft carrier" and "he himself would be shot down after flying fifty-eight missions as the youngest pilot in the Navy." Explaining why Bush was determined to stop Iraq's aggression against Kuwait in 1990, leading him to mobilize a broad military coalition (Desert Storm) that proved victorious in the first Persian Gulf War, Bush's press secretary said that his "war experience was alive in him and was a major factor in his mind which he talked about a lot. It made the question of appeasement and evil dictators vivid, thus altering how he saw the crisis and his approach."[94] It has been said that one reason John Foster Dulles, secretary of state in the Eisenhower administration, was an especially vigorous Cold Warrior was his family background, being a product of a strict Presbyterian upbringing that led him always to see Stalin and the Soviet Union in the worst possible light, as a godless communist regime intent on evil. Even if at times Moscow might attempt to behave cooperatively by offering arms control proposals, Dulles's negative image of the USSR led him to either selectively ignore that information or attribute the behavior to Soviet weakness rather than a possible dovish shift in Soviet policy.[95] Many other examples can be cited of early experiences shaping a decision maker's perception, and often misperception, of his or her environment.

Present circumstances may be an even more fertile source of images than past experiences. I've already noted Graham Allison's observation that where one "stands" on foreign policy issues may well depend on where one "sits" in the bureaucracy, and that bureaucrats tend to develop images of their environment that coincide with the organizational mission and interests of the agency they represent. During the Cold War, it was said that within the U.S. Defense Department "every rival group—the bomber pilots, fighter jockeys, missilemen, carrier admirals— all produced their own interpretation of Soviet behavior to justify their claim for more money."[96] During the Vietnam War, "the organizational interests of the Air Force and the personal interests of career officers tended to generate intelligence reports which exaggerated the effects of the bombing" in terms of how successfully air strikes hit enemy targets. It was not so much a case of a "conscious conspiracy" or "systematically lying" but rather subtle self-delusion in synch with personal and organizational goals.[97]

Although all decision makers approach situations with certain built-in predispositions grounded in their image of reality, some individuals have images that are more *open* images than others, that is, they are more receptive to new information that contradicts their image and are more amenable to revising their image. One way to encourage more open images on the part of decision makers, so that they can more accurately interpret their environment, is to make sure that the decision-making process allows for "multiple advocacy," including a devil's advocate who ensures that all sides of an issue are being adequately explored and analyzed. This is one reason why the U.S. government relies on multiple intelligence agencies, not just the Central Intelligence Agency but also the National Security Agency and several others. However, trying to make foreign policymaking more rational by adding more participants does not always work, given the nature of group and organizational decision making, discussed next.

Group Dynamics

Although groups might be expected to make better decisions than individuals acting alone, two (or more) heads are not necessarily better than one. Irving Janis has pointed out that under certain conditions groups can breed their own brand of irrationality and cause individuals to lose their critical thinking ability and act less rationally than otherwise. He has described a phenomenon called **groupthink**, whereby individuals, feeling group conformity pressures, suppress personal doubts they may have about the emerging group consensus regarding the definition or handling of a situation.[98] For example, in the case of the surprise attack on Pearl Harbor in December 1941, Janis argues that the failure to anticipate the Japanese raid despite numerous prior intelligence clues—including American radar detecting squadrons of planes approaching several miles away—was at least partially due to the clubby atmosphere that prevailed among the American admirals in Hawaii, causing any surfacing of individual reservations about the vulnerability of the naval base to be drowned out by a sense of collective invincibility. In addition to peer pressure, another feature of groupthink is a tendency for members to defer to the group leader and go along with what they assume are the latter's preferences, even if there are serious private doubts about the wisdom of the leader's policy. This helped produce the disastrous Bay of Pigs decision in 1961, when the Kennedy administration's effort to train anti-Castro Cuban exiles for an invasion of the island ended in failure and humiliation.[99] Crisis situations frequently invite groupthink, given the small-group character of decision making, the stressful circumstances, and the need to act quickly, all of which can result in faulty processing of information and a less than exhaustive consideration of all options.

There is some evidence that groupthink was operating in the lead-up to the second Persian Gulf War in 2003, when the administration of George W. Bush claimed that the existence of WMDs in Iraq posed a threat that required the United States to invade Iraq and overthrow Saddam Hussein. National security adviser Condoleezza Rice, a member of Bush's small "war council," declared in 2002: "The problem here is that there will always be some uncertainty about how quickly he can acquire nuclear weapons. But we don't want the smoking gun to be a mushroom cloud."[100] After further deliberations over several months, including CIA director George Tenet telling the president it was "a slam-dunk case" that Iraq had WMD, the United States invaded.[101] No WMDs were subsequently found. As Senator Pat Roberts, a member of the U.S. Senate Intelligence Committee responsible for investigating the handling of WMD intelligence, commented: "Groupthink caused the [intelligence] community to interpret ambiguous evidence as . . . conclusive."[102] Senate committee members agreed that "groupthink led to incorrect intelligence about Iraq's supposed chemical, biological, and nuclear weapons and pushed aside the doubts of dissenting analysts, an attitude that also permeated several big foreign intelligence services."[103] There is debate over how much pressure the CIA felt to skew the intelligence in the direction President Bush was assumed to want. Although the Bush administration was accused of fabricating intelligence data and lying to the American people, it seemed more a case of the administration being victimized by its own self-deception. It was predisposed toward assuming Saddam was hiding WMDs, not only because it wanted to use the WMD claim as an excuse for an invasion but also because Saddam fed such assumptions by giving the impression he had such arsenals; why else, the Bush administration asked, would he deny UN inspectors full access to suspected WMD facilities and fail to file a credible full disclosure report, as had been required by UN Security Council resolutions? Indeed, most observers on the eve of war, including much of the U.S. Congress as well as King Abdullah of Jordan and other foreign leaders, along with the UN inspectors, shared a similar image of Saddam as a leader bent on possessing WMDs and refusing to come clean about having them. Only later, when no WMDs were found, did it occur to observers that Saddam had been bluffing, probably in an effort to maintain Iraq's reputation as a regional power. Had the Bush administration and others not reinforced each other's predispositions and been more open to competing explanations for Saddam's behavior, the rush to war perhaps could have been avoided.

Personality and Physiology: Gender and Other Variables

The philosopher Friedrich Nietzsche once said, "Madness is the exception in individuals; it is the rule in groups." But we cannot forget that irrational behavior from individuals, especially certain personality types, can certainly match, if not surpass, that of groups. About Stalin, his successor, Nikita Khrushchev, remarked: "You see to what Stalin's mania for greatness led. He had completely lost a sense of reality; he demonstrated his suspicion and haughtiness not only in relation to individuals but to whole nations."[104] Some leaders have a milder temperament and are more tolerant of opposing views than others, which can have important implications for the conduct of foreign policy. For example, it has been argued that Woodrow Wilson's authoritarian personality—his unwillingness to compromise, traced to a strict childhood upbringing—affected his relationships with other world leaders and members of the U.S. Senate, and was somewhat responsible for the failure of the Senate to approve U.S. membership in the League of Nations after World War I.[105] American presidents have been classified as "active/passive" and "positive/negative," with active/negative personalities, such as Lyndon Johnson and Richard Nixon, given to paranoia and distrusting not only foreign leaders but even some of their own advisers.[106]

There are many other examples of the role personality plays as a foreign policy determinant. One scholar states that "the British choice in Iraq [in joining the U.S. invasion] has been characterized as 'Tony Blair's War,' with many believing that the personality and leadership style of the prime minister played a crucial part in determining British participation."[107] Given the unpopularity of the war in Britain, a cabinet minister went so far as to say that "had anyone else been leader, we would not have fought alongside Bush."[108] Bush himself has been accused of going to war out of revenge against Saddam for plotting the assassination of his father. Although it is almost impossible to establish any definitive cause-effect relationship here, one would not be surprised to learn that the son had a visceral hatred for his father's nemesis, which might have contributed to his anxiousness to bringing Saddam down. Deeper personal traits might have added to the equation, as one commentator noted that "Bush is more than a little devious and vindictive. . . . I would say that deep down he was determined to overthrow Saddam."[109] Much has been made of how Bush's insular background and deep-seated religiosity may have contributed to his unwavering stance, along with unwarranted optimism, toward the Iraq War. One observer, comparing the president to Vice President Dick Cheney and the senior Bush, remarked: "With his strong religious faith, President Bush has a more upbeat, soul-saving Christian take on life than his somewhat Hobbesian vice-president. Bush [after 9/11] . . . had a providential sense of duty and destiny. . . . Bush Junior, far less worldly [than Senior], is more a creature of Midland [Texas]."[110]

Clearly, one must be circumspect in applying amateur psychology to the study of foreign policy, although such idiosyncratic variables as personality quirks can have impacts no less than balance of power machinations. So, too, can physiological characteristics of leaders, even if, similarly, we must be careful not to indulge too much in amateur medicine. An entire subfield of international relations—**biopolitics**—examines the role played by physical ailments, mental health, and other such characteristics in affecting foreign policy decision making.[111] Woodrow Wilson suffered a stroke that left him incapacitated and unable to function toward the end of his presidency; likewise, Franklin Roosevelt was so sick at the time he was meeting Churchill and Stalin in Yalta in 1945 (shortly before his fatal stroke) that, according to one historian, he was "in no condition to govern the republic" much less make important foreign policy decisions.[112] Boris Yeltsin, who succeeded Gorbachev as Russian president, reputedly suffered from chronic alcoholism. One example of physical factors commonly cited is President Kennedy's constant "crippling back pain." Kennedy injected himself with steroids "twice every day to replace the adrenaline his glands no longer produced because he had Addison's disease."[113] Robert Dallek describes the medical ordeals Kennedy endured in the first six months of his term: "Kennedy suffered stomach, colon, and prostate problems, high fevers, abscesses, and sleeplessness, in addition to his ongoing back and adrenal ailments. His physician administered large doses of . . . Lomotil, Metamucil, Phenobarbital, testosterone [and other drugs] to control his diarrhea and abdominal discomfort; penicillin and other antibiotics for his urinary-tract infections; and Tuinal to help him sleep."[114] It is hard to imagine how Kennedy's mental faculties could possibly be 100 percent under this sort of stress, yet that is what he was coping with at the time of the Cuban missile crisis.

One physiological factor that has attracted increased attention by researchers in recent years, especially those working out of a feminist paradigm, is **gender**.[115] Public opinion polls and other data suggest that women tend to be somewhat more "pacific" than men in terms of being less supportive of not only the death penalty but also the use of armed force. Whether this is due to biological factors (sex) or socialization and the learning of roles (more properly called *gender*), males seem more aggressive in their attitudes and behavior. Francis Fukuyama has argued that the more aggressive tendencies of men cannot be accounted for merely by cultural norms that socialize girls to become "child-bearing and child-caring nurturers" while boys grow up playing with toy guns and become "breadwinners," but rather are mainly the result of genetic predispositions toward violence traced to male testosterone levels and other physical characteristics. He concludes that "a world run by women would follow different rules," and "as women gain power" in societies around the world, the countries "should become less aggressive, adventurous, competitive, and violent."[116]

Although there is some anecdotal evidence supporting such a conclusion—for example, Jeannette Rankin, the first woman elected to the U.S. Congress, was the only congressperson to vote against both declarations of war that brought the United States into World War I and II—we should be wary of stereotyping either women or men. When Mary Caprioli compared the record of male and female heads of state, she found that "female leaders are no more peaceful than their male counterparts." Caprioli pointed to several strong female leaders who took their countries into war, such as Margaret Thatcher of Great Britain, Indira Gandhi of India, and Golda Meir of Israel.[117] Feminist scholars might counter that there have been too few women in positions of power to make true comparisons possible. In the twentieth century, there were no more than a dozen female presidents and twenty prime ministers among heads of state.[118] Feminists could also argue that Thatcher and other women who rose to power in male-dominated, patriarchal societies were forced to "act like men" in order to succeed. However, even feminists disagree among themselves as to whether sex or gender is destiny.[119]

Are men more brash, impulsive, and war-prone? There is evidence that propensity to take high-risk decisions may have less to do with one's anatomical makeup than with the characteristics of the foreign policy problem a leader faces, no matter whether it is a man or a woman. The rational actor model assumes that any decision maker, before acting, will ordinarily do a thorough cost-benefit analysis involving the probable gains relative to possible costs associated with a complete range of options one might choose from as the response to some situation. Although one presumably seeks to *maximize* gains, the tendency is to engage in *satisficing* rather than maximizing behavior, that is, not to do an extensive search to find the best alternative but to settle on the first satisfactory, minimally acceptable solution that appears. Such behavior is not so much "irrational" as amounting to "bounded rationality," since time constraints often preclude the kind of exhaustive search and deliberation necessary to produce an optimal result.[120] **Prospect theory** has provided added insights into how decision makers typically weigh "risks." Supported by considerable empirical evidence, the theory posits that leaders tend to be status-quo oriented. Their fear of losing something they already possess outweighs their longing for what they do not yet have, so that, for example, they are likely to be more willing to take risks to defend against loss of territory than to use force to annex territory.[121]

It should be obvious that anyone attempting to explain foreign policy behavior needs to avoid simplistic analysis that reduces decisions to the work of a single person, whether a man or a woman. Groups, organizations, states, and the globe are all part of the explanatory apparatus. The individual level of analysis, together with the nation-state level and the international system level, can enrich our understanding of why states act as they do, if we are willing to appreciate the complexity of the task and, as Allison said, "think hard" about such matters.

CONCLUSION

Although we have focused in this chapter on *explaining* foreign policy behavior, entailing an examination of the various sources of action, recall that foreign policy analysis also includes *evaluating* the consequences of one's actions and whether they have been positive or negative. It is one thing to ask, for example, why the United States acted as it did in invading Iraq in 2003. It is something else to ask if it was a good decision. (See the *IR* Critical Thinking Box "Doing Empirical and Evaluative Analysis of Foreign Policy: The Case of the 2003 U.S. Decision to Invade Iraq.")

IR Critical Thinking:
Doing Empirical and Evaluative Analysis of Foreign Policy:
The Case of the 2003 U.S. Decision to Invade Iraq

There are several possible modes of foreign policy analysis. Empirical analysis consists of either descriptive or explanatory analysis, whereas evaluative analysis consists of either normative or prescriptive analysis.

Descriptive analysis simply seeks to describe some behavior or occurrence and to give an accurate characterization of what happened. *Explanatory* analysis seeks to go beyond mere description—beyond merely reporting a fact—and tries to account for its existence. It is here where the levels of analysis framework is useful, because it helps steer us toward several possible explanations. For example, the official explanation the Bush administration offered for invading Iraq in 2003 was that Iraq had WMDs that in a post-9/11 world threatened the American homeland, especially given Saddam Hussein's past history of recklessness and alleged ties to terrorist groups. Such anxieties were fed by the immediate aftermath of 9/11, when a month after the attack the president was warned by the CIA that al Qaeda terrorists had smuggled a 10 kiloton nuclear bomb into New York City. Shortly after that an anthrax scare paralyzed Washington, even though both scares proved to be false alarms. From a *rational actor* perspective, one can perhaps understand the U.S. invasion decision as a response to these sorts of security concerns found in the *international environment*. However, many observers traced the decision to other factors, including domestic forces (such as the influence of the Israeli lobby that saw Saddam as a threat to Israel, the influence of oil interests seeking to gain control over Iraq's substantial oil reserves, and the gains in public popularity that the president figured to get in tying the invasion to 9/11) as well as individual-level factors (such as Bush's desire for personal revenge against Saddam's attempt to assassinate his father, Bush's peculiar personality traits, and a groupthink syndrome that prevented members of the president's inner circle from questioning the WMD assumptions).

In contrast to empirical analysis, evaluative analysis engages the student of foreign policy in making *normative* and *prescriptive* judgments—examining whether some decision *ought* to have been made and whether some other foreign policy option(s) *ought* to have been pursued in its place or should be pursued in the future. There are a number of criteria that can aid normative analysis and, in the process, help identify alternative courses of action. First, was the decision or action *legal*—compatible with international law? Second, was it *moral*—consistent with basic canons of ethics relating to fairness, justice, and humanitarianism? Third, was it *smart*—wise in terms of making practical sense in advancing U.S. national security and other national interests?

(continues)

(continued)

Most international lawyers found the U.S. invasion illegal since it seemed to violate the UN Charter, which allows the use of force only in self-defense or if authorized by the UN Security Council, neither of which applied. While some considered the decision moral, equating Saddam with Hitler as among the worst tyrants of the twentieth century and therefore worthy of regime change, others condemned the tragic loss of life and loss of American honor connected with the bombing of Iraqi cities along with human rights and POW violations committed by the U.S. military. As for the wisdom of the war decision, it seemed potentially disastrous, given the loss of over 4,000 American soldiers, the expenditure of hundreds of billions of dollars, and the growing instability of the Middle East.

Just as empirical analysis is complex and must be done carefully, the same is true for evaluative analysis. Different schools of analysis tend to apply different perspectives in both cases. In doing evaluative analysis, realists tend to ask: Was the decision smart? In contrast, liberals tend to be concerned with not only inquiring about the wisdom of a decision but also asking: Was it moral and legal? They would probably agree with Robert Osgood's notion (in *Ideals and Self-Interest in America's Foreign Policy*, 449) of "the expediency of idealism"—that the United States should try to act morally not just because it is the right thing to do but because it is likely to enhance the legitimacy of American power in the eyes of others.

Ask yourself the following:

1. Which level of analysis do you think provides the most potent explanation for the foreign policy behavior of the United States and other countries?

2. If you had to rank-order the three criteria for evaluating foreign policy decisions—legality, morality, and practical wisdom—what would be your ranking? What do you value the most?

3. What is your own take on why the United States invaded Iraq? Which variables do you think played the most important role in shaping the decision?

4. What is your take on the legality, morality, and wisdom of the U.S. decision to invade Iraq?

It is safe to say that one would generally prefer rational to irrational behavior on the part of foreign policymakers. However, one cannot assume that a decision rationally made will necessarily be a "good" one even if a leadership comes close to the ideal type of rational decision making—objectively defining one's situation, carefully articulating goals and objectives, considering a complete menu of possible responses, weighing all potential benefits and costs of each course of action, and choosing a final alternative calculated to produce the greatest utility. Passing judgment on the soundness of some foreign policy decision must ultimately await the response of *other* states. Although the ExCom decision-making process during the Cuban missile crisis was in many ways the model of rationality (Janis observes that "the policy-making group included most of the same key men who participated in the Bay of Pigs decision, but this time they functioned in a much more effective way"), the decision to blockade Cuba could have produced a nuclear catastrophe *if the Soviets had decided to react differently than they did*, if they had not "blinked" first.[122]

I, along with others, have suggested that international relations resembles a game. As in any game, the outcome depends on the moves made by at least two sides. It depends on *your* decision as well as *their* decision and the connection between the two. In the next chapter we will examine "game theory" and the dynamics of *international interactions*, looking at how diplomacy works to keep the game of international politics going short of resorting to violence.

QUESTIONS FOR STUDY AND DISCUSSION

1. How would you define "foreign policy"?
2. In a nutshell, how would you describe U.S. foreign policy today?
3. Which level of analysis do you think is most useful in explaining the foreign policy behavior of countries—the international system level, the nation-state level, or the individual level?
4. At the system level, how often do states behave as unitary, "rational actors," as "billiard balls" interacting with each other?
5. At the nation-state level, in the United States and elsewhere, *does* public opinion affect foreign policy decisions? *Should* it, that is, should leaders take into account public opinion polls when making foreign policy decisions or should they act mainly on the basis of what they deem to be in the national interest, regardless of public sentiment?
6. At the individual level, how important are single individuals, such as an Adolf Hitler or a George W. Bush or a Barack Obama, in determining foreign policy and shaping major international events? Does the great man or woman theory of history risk exaggerating the importance of individual leaders?

SUGGESTIONS FOR FURTHER READING

Graham Allison and Philip Zelikow, *Essence of Decision: Explaining the Cuban Missile Crisis*, 2nd ed. (New York: Longman, 1999).

Walter Carlsnaes, "Foreign Policy," in *Handbook of International Relations* (London: Sage, 2002).

Stephen Dyson, "Personality and Foreign Policy: "Tony Blair's Iraq Decisions," *Foreign Policy Analysis* 2 (July 2006): 289–306.

Morton H. Halperin and Arnold Kanter, eds., *Readings in American Foreign Policy: A Bureaucratic Perspective* (Boston: Little, Brown, 1973).

Valerie Hudson, "Foreign Policy Analysis Yesterday, Today, and Tomorrow," *Mershon International Studies Review* 39 (October 1995): 209–238.

G. John Ikenberry, *American Foreign Policy: Theoretical Essays*, 5th ed. (Pearson, 2005).

Robert Jackson and Alan James, eds., *States in a Changing World* (Oxford: Oxford University Press, 1993).

Irving L. Janis, *Groupthink*, 2nd ed. (Boston: Houghton Mifflin, 1982).

Robert Jervis, *Perception and Misperception in International Politics* (Princeton, NJ: Princeton University Press, 1976).

Charles W. Kegley et al., *American Foreign Policy*, 7th ed. (Belmont, CA: Wadsworth, 2007).

Henry A. Kissinger, "Domestic Structure and Foreign Policy," *Daedalus* 95 (1966): 503–529.

James N. Rosenau, "Pre-Theories and Theories of Foreign Policy," in R. Barry Farrell, ed., *Approaches to Comparative and International Politics* (Evanston, IL: Northwestern University Press, 1966).

Kenneth N. Waltz, *Man, the State, and War* (New York: Columbia University Press, 1959), esp. pp. 1–15.

Arnold Wolfers, *Discord and Collaboration* (Baltimore: Johns Hopkins University Press, 1962).

Steve Yetiv, *Explaining Foreign Policy: U.S. Decision-Making and the Persian Gulf War* (Baltimore: Johns Hopkins University Press, 2004).

4

Diplomacy, Bargaining, and Statecraft

History has shown us all too well that weakness promotes aggression and war, whereas strength preserves the peace.
— Ronald Reagan, 1980 presidential election campaign ad

Diplomacy without force is like music without instruments. It is only as good as the number of guns backing it up.
— Frederick the Great of Prussia, 1712–1786

Speak softly and carry a big stick; you will go far.
— Theodore Roosevelt, Minnesota State Fair, September 2, 1901

A diplomat once said, "Foreign policy is what you do; diplomacy is how you do it."[1] The problem with this distinction is that diplomacy is not the only means whereby foreign policy is carried out and the game of international relations is contested. The use of armed force, for one, is another. Unlike many games, the game of international relations does not come with a set of instructions or a rulebook that prescribes certain ways to comport yourself. Nonetheless, the players tend to follow certain behaviors in conducting their competition and seeking a winning outcome. This chapter examines the way actors *normally* play the game. The basic rule of thumb is "diplomacy before force." In other words, shooting your opponent as a stratagem for achieving victory is usually not the first resort but among the last resorts contemplated in the game of nations.

To many spectators, the game of international relations involves considerable violence. At the very least, countries seem to anticipate the need to use firepower, given the fact that total world military spending exceeds $1 trillion annually, amounting to $190,000 each minute for war *preparation*.[2] However, although there usually is a war going on somewhere in the world at any given moment, interstate violence is not as commonplace as it might appear if one considers the hundreds of interstate transactions that occur daily that are free of hostilities. One study, for example, looked at more than 16,000 recorded observations of interactions among pairs of states (dyads) between 1950 and 1986, and classified 97 percent as peaceful. Another study found that out of 250 serious confrontations involving major powers between 1815 and the mid-twentieth century, fewer than 30 (12 percent) resulted in war. A study surveying conflict involvement between 1816 and 1992 concluded that a majority of all dyads "never have exercised threats, displays, or uses of force," while 87 percent "never fought a war."[3] Much of international relations may be conflictual, but most conflict is *nonviolent* in form. Just as resorting to brawling or gunplay is not the norm in poker or chess or mahjong, resorting to armed force in determining the outcome of the game is not the norm in international relations.

It is especially the case today, in an age of ever more frightening weapons of mass destruction, that national governments, rather than relying on the use of armed force, generally attempt to exercise influence and to achieve desired outcomes through **diplomacy**. To talk of "diplomacy before force" is to raise the question of what exactly is meant by that phrase, what does diplomacy consist of, and what does it take to succeed at it? To address these concerns is to grapple with the essence of statecraft.

WHAT IS DIPLOMACY?

In his classic work *Diplomacy*, British diplomat Sir Harold Nicolson cites a standard dictionary definition of diplomacy: "Diplomacy is the management of international relations by negotiation, the method by which these relations are adjusted and managed by ambassadors and envoys."[4] In this conventional sense, diplomacy refers to the formal practices whereby states conduct their foreign relations, including the creation of embassies and exchange of ambassadors, the transmission of communiqués among official representatives, and the involvement of the latter in negotiations. In recent years, scholars have broadened the concept of diplomacy to mean the general process whereby states seek to communicate, to influence each other, and to resolve conflicts through *bargaining*—either formal or informal—short of the use of armed force. Such a definition can include the *threatened*, as opposed to the *actual*, use of armed force. (The logic of spending so much on armaments may have more to do with the expected utility of weapons stockpiles in bullying rivals into concessions or deterring attacks rather than initiating attacks; their mere possession, rather than delivery, may be the main purpose served by vast arsenals.) Some scholars have stretched the concept of diplomacy even further, suggesting that force itself, when applied in a very limited, discrete, selective way to "send a message," can represent a kind of diplomacy—a "diplomacy of violence."[5]

Karl von Clausewitz, the famous nineteenth-century Prussian military strategist, once defined war as "the continuation of policy by other means," meaning that the use of armed force was merely another instrument, along with diplomacy, that statesmen had available in their toolbox to use in their rivalry with leaders of other states. We will discuss war separately in the next chapter. Although admittedly there can be a fine line between the use of diplomacy and the use of force as bargaining vehicles, that line constitutes one of the most critical distinctions in all of international relations, because crossing it raises the stakes in the game substantially. Force may have been a readily available option for implementing foreign policy in von Clausewitz's day, but it was never as routinely utilized as he suggested, and is arguably even less so in the contemporary nuclear age. Then, as now, leaders generally turned to armed force only when diplomacy failed or appeared likely to fail, although on occasion force has been used before diplomacy has been entirely exhausted.

Again, to equate war with conflict and diplomacy with cooperation is a mistake. Diplomacy is triggered only when there is something in dispute, a disagreement (a conflict) of some sort. After all, if two parties are in total agreement, there is little need for diplomacy. Also, there is a somewhat devious, Machiavellian quality inherent in diplomacy. Much like poker players, diplomats tend to play their cards close to the vest, at times sending confusing signals in an effort to play out their hand as best they can. It has been said that "if a diplomat says yes, he means maybe; if he says maybe, he means no; and if he says no, he is not a good diplomat." In a more positive vein, diplomacy is ultimately the art of compromise, even if one party may win more than another. One way to conceptualize the relationship of diplomacy to force is to imagine a spectrum of interstate relations ranging from total harmony to total disharmony. The absence of conflict would fall at one end of the continuum; diplomacy would generally fall midway on the line, with elements of conflict as well as cooperation; and war and the use of armed force to bludgeon your opponent into accepting your terms of conflict resolution—to take what you want rather than bargain for it—would fall at the opposite end.

Within the category of diplomacy, one can envision another spectrum ranging from relatively dovish to relatively hawkish tactics. One of the most important, interesting puzzles in the field of international relations is: What works best in "winning" at bargaining—a "nice guy" approach (i.e., using *carrots*, such as offers of financial rewards, as positive inducements to shape an adversary's behavior in the desired direction) or a "tough guy" approach (i.e., using *sticks*, such as the threatened use of force or other punishments, to coerce the desired behavior)? The epigraphs at the beginning of this chapter (quoting Ronald Reagan, Frederick the Great, and Teddy Roosevelt) beg the question of, even if we accept the maxim "diplomacy before force," what is the proper mix of dovish (accommodationist) and hawkish (hard-line) diplomatic tactics calculated to achieve a successful outcome? One of the things that separates realists from idealists is that the former tend to be more inclined to utilize sticks. Although the leaders quoted above appear to emphasize sticks over carrots, they can provoke your opponent to engage in the very behavior you are seeking to prevent. At the same time, lacking the ability or will to use certain levers of power and influence can also weaken your bargaining position.

Again, such questions are not merely academic but have real-world relevance. For example, the Bush administration found itself throughout the 2000s struggling with the problem of whether to "talk" at all to North Korea and Iran or instead use armed force in an effort to get those countries to honor their obligation under the Nuclear Nonproliferation Treaty (NPT) to refrain from developing nuclear weapons, and whether, should diplomacy be tried, to apply economic and other sanctions as punishment or offer financial assistance and other rewards in the hope of cooperation. These same issues arose during the 2008 U.S. presidential campaign, when presidential candidates John McCain and Barack Obama debated the merits of talking to Iran and other states that sponsor terrorism and what, if any, preconditions should be attached to opening up a dialogue.

Suffice it to say, diplomacy is a feature of international relations that has a great variety of dimensions, more than the casual student of the subject may realize. Diplomacy can be secretive or public, bilateral or multilateral, formally or informally conducted. It can take place around fancy tables in imposing foreign ministry buildings or mirrored palaces, with pinstriped three-piece suits seated behind bottles of mineral water and notepads (as happened at the Versailles peace conference after World War I), or using ping-pong tables (the aforementioned exchange of table tennis teams between the United States and China in 1971, conceived as a way to break the ice during the Cold War on the eve of Richard Nixon's historic meeting with Mao Zedong in Shanghai). It can occur across great distances using hotline, telephone, or other technologies (as in the case of a ninety-minute phone call between President George H.W. Bush and Soviet premier Mikhail Gorbachev at the height of the 1990–1991 Iraq-Kuwait crisis, placed to obtain Soviet support for Bush's Desert Storm operation), or in intimate, secluded retreats (such as Bill Clinton's "walk in the woods" meetings with Israeli leader Ehud Barak and Palestinian leader Yasser Arafat at Camp David in 2000). It can occur at the highest official level ("summitry") or among junior officials or special envoys, and can even involve private emissaries such as scholars, journalists, or celebrities (what is sometimes called "Track-II diplomacy," as when Jimmy Carter sent heavyweight boxing champion Muhammad Ali on a five-nation tour of Africa to persuade countries to boycott the 1980 Moscow Olympics in retaliation for the Soviet invasion of Afghanistan).[6] Diplomacy can include making promises (the carrot approach) as well as threats (the stick approach), designed either to encourage or extort concessions from the other side, making opponents an offer they won't, or can't, refuse. It can go on between friends over issues on which they are not far apart, or between enemies whose positions seem intractable. And it can be supported by economic, military, or other resources employed to influence states through means other than raw, brute physical compulsion. All of these various aspects of diplomacy will be discussed in this chapter, including their relative effectiveness in enabling one to be a good game-player in international relations. (See the *IR* Critical Thinking Box "Playing the Game of International Relations: What Are the Most Effective Approaches to Diplomacy?")

IR Critical Thinking:
Playing the Game of International Relations:
What Are the Most Effective Approaches to Diplomacy?

A major puzzle in the international relations field revolves around the question of what is likely to produce better results in diplomatic bargaining between states—a soft-line, warm and friendly, flexible, "carrot" approach toward one's adversary, or a hard-line, direct, firm, "stick" approach? This question is perhaps what most separates liberals from conservatives, doves from hawks, and optimists from pessimists. Christopher Wren describes below how the former—especially a casual, informal "walk in the woods" approach—can overcome barriers, such as long-standing hatreds or stuffy protocols, and produce better outcomes for all parties than a more direct, formalized approach. In discussing the 1995 talks that the Clinton administration mediated between Israel and Syria in Wye, Maryland, Wren refers to the "hearty home-cooked meals" served by the Norwegian foreign minister that helped grease the Oslo Accords between Israelis and Palestinians a couple of years earlier, in 1993. (I referred earlier to how "good wine" helped, also.)

> When Syrians and Israelis sat down last week to try to make peace, they did without the traditional trappings of a diplomatic discourse—a formidable table separating the sides, name plates, microphones, and an opening photo-op.
>
> Instead, their American hosts seated them cheek-by-jowl in a cozy room around a circular mahogany table, with only a centerpiece of white tulips dividing them, while a wood fire glowed in the hearth. Outside, cows grazed . . . in the frosty Maryland countryside. Versailles, this was not. Purposely so. . . .
>
> The bucolic ambiance, like the deliberate informality, was intended to break down the kind of barriers of mistrust and distance between negotiators that can wreck deal-making. . . . Such studied mood-making . . . includes encouraging first-name informality, walks in the woods, and bans on both neckties and reporters. . . . It's hard to dislike your adversary when he asks you to pass the butter.
>
> The Norwegian Foreign Minister . . . proved the value of this approach in 1993, throwing in hearty home-cooked meals when he invited Israelis and the Palestinian Liberation Organization for talks at farmhouses, hotels, and his own home. (Christopher Wren, "How to Set a Peace Table," *New York Times*, December 31, 1995.)

Of course, the Oslo Accords ultimately failed to produce a lasting Middle East peace, just as the Wye talks and Bill Clinton's subsequent "walk in the woods" effort to get Israeli and Palestinian leaders to bury the hatchet at Camp David in 2000 proved fruitless as well. Perhaps it is better at times to adopt a tougher, no-nonsense stance, taking the other side out "to the woodshed," so to speak. What do *you* think? Consider the following questions:

(continues)

(continued)

1. What is likely to produce better results in diplomatic bargaining—formality or informality? Can altering the ambiance in a negotiating forum make a difference, or does it simply invite atmospherics?

2. What is more likely to produce a successful diplomatic effort—demonstrations of toughness, including threats if the other side does not cooperate, or gestures of conciliation, including promises and rewards in return for cooperation? Some combination of both?

3. What should the mediator's role be? Is mediation likely to produce better results than direct bilateral talks between the disputants themselves without third-party involvement?

THE CHANGING NATURE OF DIPLOMACY

Our historical overview of the international system traced how technology and other variables have changed the nature of war. The nature of diplomacy has also changed, although, as with war, there are some enduring features as well. Here we examine several ways in which diplomacy today differs from that of previous eras, including (1) the role of ambassadors, (2) the role of public (as opposed to secret) diplomacy, (3) the role of multilateral (as opposed to bilateral) diplomacy, (4) the role of formal (as opposed to informal) diplomacy, and (5) the domestication of diplomacy.

The Role of Ambassadors

Distinguishing diplomacy from force, Nicolson notes that "diplomacy, in the sense of the ordered conduct of relations between one group of human beings and another group alien to themselves, is far older than history. . . . Even in pre-history there must have come moments when one group of savages wished to negotiate with another group of savages, if only for the purpose of indicating that they had had enough of the day's battle and would like a pause in which to collect their wounded and to bury their dead. From the very first, even to our Cromagnon or Neanderthal ancestors, it must have become apparent that such negotiations would be severely hampered if the emissary from one side were killed and eaten by the other side."[7] Such are the roots of the now universally accepted nation-state practice of exchanging **ambassadors** and granting them **diplomatic immunity**— freedom from harm, arrest, and prosecution by the receiving state. (The reader can decide for himself or herself whether we are more civilized than our ancestors.)

The earliest ambassadors had no specialized training. Prior to the Peace of Westphalia and the creation of the modern nation-state system, diplomats were often relatives of the ruling family or high-ranking members of the royal court, although some came from lower stations. Nicolson describes diplomacy in the Middle Ages: "Louis XI sent his barber on a mission to Maria of Burgundy. Florence sent a chemist . . . to Naples, and Dr. de Puebla, who for twenty years represented Spain in London, was so filthy and unkempt that Henry VII expressed the hope that his successor might be a man more fitted for human society."[8] As the nation-state system developed, states gradually established professional, career foreign services from whose ranks ambassadors and lower-level envoys were recruited. However, even today, in the United States and elsewhere, nonprofessionals can be found in ambassadorial positions—for example, John Gavin, a movie star of Hispanic heritage (who performed in the *Tammy* movies of the 1960s), was appointed as U.S. ambassador to Mexico by President Reagan, while Shirley Temple, the famous child actress of the 1930s, was appointed ambassador to Ghana by President Ford. Although most states maintain a professional diplomatic corps, ambassadorial assignments frequently are offered as rewards to major political donors, partly because, as seen below, the job of the ambassador has become increasingly ceremonial.

Although the practice of dispatching emissaries to negotiate with foreign leaders is an ancient one, the **embassy** as an institution—that is, the establishment of *permanent* missions on foreign soil—is a more recent innovation. The concept of a permanent mission to represent a country's interests abroad originated in the Italian city-states during the fifteenth century and was later adopted by France and other nation-states that recognized the growing importance of institutionalized diplomacy in managing relations between states. The Congress of Vienna in 1815, following the Napoleonic Wars, marked the first attempt to develop a standard set of protocols regarding the appointment of ambassadors and the functioning of embassies.

From the start, national governments found embassies to be useful institutions for performing a variety of functions, which included collecting and transmitting information back to the home country concerning conditions in the host country, maintaining a regular line of communication between the home government and the host government, cultivating friendly relations with the host government through ongoing social contacts at embassy balls and other gatherings, providing home government protection to citizens traveling through host countries, expanding commercial interests, and facilitating expeditious, on-the-scene negotiation of mutual concerns shared by the home and host governments. In time, many routine functions were added, such as processing international travel requests (visas) and recording births and deaths of citizens living in the host state.[9]

The twentieth century saw growth in the number and size of embassies. The modern embassy includes specialized staff drawn from many different government agencies, such as information officers (responsible for handling public relations), consular officials (responsible for providing legal assistance and monitoring travel documentation to and from the host country), commercial attachés (responsible for promoting economic relations with the host country), aid and agricultural officers (responsible for economic development assistance), and intelligence personnel (sometimes posing as one of the above officials, responsible for reporting on local political developments). The increased bureaucratization of embassies has reflected the growing volume and complexity of international transactions. It bears repeating, however, that many poorer countries lack the "capacity" to invest the considerable financial resources it takes to maintain embassies around the world. (Recall the example of Tajikistan, which, upon gaining independence in 1991, could only afford a one-man diplomatic corps, consisting of its UN ambassador who had to cook his own state dinners. Another example is Guinea-Bissau, a poor African country whose UN ambassador in 1999 was reduced to "working in darkness" in his New York apartment "because the landlord cut off the electricity" since the government had "not paid the rent in 15 months.")[10] Even rich countries such as the United States cannot afford to have an embassy in every country; the United States maintains embassies in only 142 countries, servicing Vanuatu and several dozen other lesser states through its diplomatic missions in neighboring states.[11]

One key change is that, even as diplomacy has become institutionalized, the diplomatic service in some respects has come to play a reduced role in negotiation, its main historic function. The advanced communications and travel technology of the modern age have made leaders less dependent on their ambassador or envoy on the scene as their chief representative in dealing with a foreign government. As one scholar comments, "In the nineteenth century," if you were an American diplomat abroad, "several thousand miles from Washington, and your instructions arrived in a diplomatic pouch carried by boat across the oceans and then by carriage across land, you had lots of latitude. . . . Today the leash is short and the diplomat's independence of action is drastically reduced."[12] Consider the role played by James Monroe, President Jefferson's special envoy to France in 1803, at a time when a ship could take a month or two to cross the Atlantic. Monroe had been instructed by the president to offer Napoleon $10 million for the port of New Orleans and the immediate surrounding area; when Napoleon offered the entire Louisiana Territory for another $5 million, Monroe had to decide whether to accept such a tantalizing deal even if it meant exceeding his instructions, since he had no way of quickly getting Jefferson's approval and felt, if he was to double the size of the young nation, he had to act without delay. Today telephones, fax machines, and satellite hookups between home office and embassy have reduced the discretion with which ambassadors abroad can make decisions and the need for them to do so.

Ambassadors still perform important functions. However, in an era of supersonic jets and hotlines, many leaders bypass embassy personnel altogether, preferring either to send high-level government ministers on closely monitored "shuttle diplomacy" expeditions (such as Condoleezza Rice's numerous flights between Middle East capitals in 2007 and 2008 as part of the Bush administration's efforts to broker an Israeli-Palestinian peace) or to play the role of diplomat themselves by directly engaging in communications and negotiations with their counterparts in other countries (as in the case of Bill Clinton's "walk in the woods" at Camp David with Israel's Ehud Barak and Palestinian leader Yasser Arafat). When George H.W. Bush was president, in his first year alone (1989), he had 135 face-to-face meetings with world leaders as well as 190 phone calls, including only the third on record between an American president and the head of the Soviet Union (a warm-up to the 90-minute call to Mikhail Gorbachev made during the first Gulf War a couple of years later).[13] The senior Bush suffered a major embarrassment at a state dinner in Tokyo in 1992, when he became ill and vomited on the lap of the Japanese prime minister, suggesting the downside of such diplomacy. Bush's son, upon assuming the presidency in 2001, "departed on his first foreign visit only 27 days after his inauguration," and "during his first six years made 36 trips and visited 58 countries. Additionally, he received visits from 2,190 heads of government or foreign ministers representing 80 countries,"[14] hosting Russian leader Vladimir Putin, Crown Prince Abdullah of Saudi Arabia, and other leaders at the White House or his Texas ranch.

Meetings between heads of state have been called **summitry**. Summit diplomacy is not completely new. European monarchs, for example, would meet on occasion in the pre-Westphalian era and in the early life of the Westphalian system. However, summitry has become much more common in modern times, gaining special attention during the Cold War, epitomized by Richard Nixon's meetings with Chinese leaders Mao Zedong and Chou En-Lai in 1972, Nikita Khrushchev's trip to the United States in 1959 (when President Eisenhower turned down the Soviet leader's request to visit Disneyland in California due to inadequate security), John Kennedy's meeting with Khrushchev in Vienna in 1961 (which by all accounts left Kennedy feeling he had come across as weak and inexperienced in the eyes of his adversary and may have contributed to precipitating the Cuban missile crisis), and Ronald Reagan's four summit meetings with Gorbachev (which produced important nuclear arms control agreements and are generally credited with helping to end the Cold War). As a form of diplomacy, summitry has been both praised and criticized. Summit meetings can amount to little more than media events and photo-ops, but they can also produce some major breakthroughs and, for better or worse, have important effects on interstate relations.

Public Versus Secret Diplomacy

The increase in summitry, with its attendant media fanfare, reflects another trend in diplomacy—the increased role of *public* as opposed to *secret* negotiations. (I am referring here to the diplomatic process, not the public relations governments engage in to burnish their image abroad.) King Louis XIV of France did not hold press conferences; he was more likely to rely on boudoir, behind-the-curtains diplomacy, whose meetings and settlements were not announced to the citizenry. With the rise of mass democracy in the nineteenth century and the mass media (especially cable TV and the twenty-four-hour news cycle) in the twentieth century, states (at least societies possessing a free press) have been under increasing pressure to open up the diplomatic process and publicize the resulting outcomes. Although much diplomacy is still conducted secretly, leaders find it increasingly difficult to do so. The Earth Summit, the global environmental conference held in Rio Janeiro in 1992, attracted not only over 150 heads of state but also 9,000 journalists.

Woodrow Wilson, evidencing his idealist side, hoped to reduce the suspicion, distrust, and insecurity that pervaded international relations by urging states to avoid secret pacts and follow the prescription of "open covenants openly arrived at." Never mind that, in the words of one commentator, Wilson "went on to organize the most closed and conspiratorial peace conference in history," referring to the meeting that produced the Treaty of Versailles after World War I.[15] Whether the conference would have yielded a better outcome had it been more transparent is doubtful. Indeed, it is not clear that open diplomatic practices necessarily produce better international agreements. It could be argued that conducting diplomacy in a fishbowl under the glare of television cameras tends to promote atmospherics—either empty gestures of friendship or outbursts of rhetoric and the adoption of rigid positions for political gain either at home or abroad—rather than the kind of serious discussion and pragmatic give-and-take so essential to effective negotiations. Particularly in the case of highly sensitive, delicate negotiations, even if the final outcome ought to be publicized as a bow to the public's right to know, there may be legitimate reasons for keeping the diplomatic process itself insulated from public scrutiny during the course of the transactions.

As an experienced diplomat states, "Without phases of secrecy and avoidance of publicity, agreements are virtually impossible. The role of secrecy in negotiations is not a mere relic of tradition. It is crucial. If a nation hears of a concession its representatives have offered without hearing of a corresponding concession from the other party, indignation will erupt at the wrong time, with explosive results." The same diplomat concludes that "a wiser," and presumably more realist-minded, "Woodrow Wilson would have opted for 'open covenants secretly arrived at.'"[16]

Multilateral Versus Bilateral Diplomacy

The time-honored practice of pairs of countries exchanging ambassadors and establishing permanent diplomatic missions on each other's soil reflects the traditional emphasis that states have placed on **bilateral** (two-country) diplomacy. It was not until the early twentieth century that **multilateral** diplomacy (the assemblage of several countries) became a common mode of diplomacy. Before that time, multilateral diplomacy was limited mostly to special meetings called at moments of crisis when war threatened (as with the Concert of Europe) or peace conferences after major wars as winners and losers gathered to divide the spoils (as at the Congress of Vienna and Versailles).

However, multilateral diplomacy has become increasingly prevalent, owing to a number of factors: (1) the existence of many problems (not only arms control but economic and environmental concerns and other matters related to the growth of interdependence) that spill over several national boundaries and do not lend themselves to purely bilateral solutions; (2) the proliferation of intergovernmental organizations at the global and regional levels, such as the United Nations and the European Union, that provide ongoing catalysts and institutional forums for the conduct of multilateral diplomacy; and (3) as noted above, the existence of many poor countries that have come to rely on the UN and other multilateral bodies for the bulk of their official diplomatic contacts. Although traditional bilateral relations continue to play a prominent role in modern diplomacy (as exemplified by the many American-Soviet summit meetings during the Cold War), several studies have found that "international organizations are by far the most common method of diplomatic contact for most nations."[17]

Multilateral diplomacy occurs not only through institutions such as the UN but also through ad hoc conferences, such as the wave of global conferences held during the 1970s, 1980s, 1990s, and since on WMD proliferation, population, food, ecology, economic development, and human rights. These conferences have addressed everything from the prevention of nuclear weapons proliferation (discussed at the 1995 NPT Conference) to prevention of graffiti in urban areas (discussed at the 1996 City Summit). What transpires at these conferences has been called "parliamentary diplomacy," since what usually emerges are international agreements that are approved by majority vote among the official state delegates but are not legally binding except on those states that in their sovereign capacity choose to sign and ratify the agreements. We will discuss many of these conferences and the international regimes produced by them when we focus on IGOs and global problem-solving in subsequent chapters. Increasingly, representatives of nongovernmental organizations (NGOs) actively participate in these gatherings as accredited (although nonvoting) delegates. I noted in Chapter 2 that, in addition to the 150 heads of state at the UN-sponsored Millennium Summit in 2000, there were representatives from over 1,300 NGOs. Likewise, the UN-sponsored environmental conferences in recent decades have seen participating NGOs proliferate from some 200 in 1972 (at the first such conference in Stockholm) to 1,400 in 1992 (at the Earth Summit in Rio) to nearly 3,000 in 2002 (at the Johannesburg Summit on Sustainable Development).[18]

Realists tend to be skeptical of the virtues of such large global forums and the inclusion of so many state and nonstate actors in the diplomatic process. Although his father was once the U.S. ambassador to the United Nations, George W. Bush and his "neocon" advisers were also lukewarm toward using global bodies as venues for diplomacy. Some observers believe "minilateral" diplomatic settings, where a few like-minded states interact, such as in the annual economic summits of the Group of Seven major industrialized democracies, are likely to prove more effective vehicles for diplomacy. The number of negotiating parties became an important issue during the Bush administration's efforts to stop North Korea's nuclear weapons program, as Bush argued in favor of "six-party talks" (that included the United States, North Korea, South Korea, China, Russia, and Japan) while the North Koreans preferred direct one-on-one bilateral talks with Washington;

eventually, the inclusion of China and other actors in the diplomatic effort seemed to offer more promise, as China especially was able to exert some leverage on Pyongyang due to North Korea's dependence on China for energy and food supplies. Changing the shape and size of the table can have significant implications for reaching agreements, although it is not always clear what will produce the optimum results. It would seem easier to forge agreement between two parties than six or a couple hundred, but sometimes the inclusion of more states can help grease the wheels of the process.

One other form of multilateral diplomacy is the use of "third parties" as *neutral* participants in the conflict resolution process. In particular, **mediation** is a process whereby a neutral third party (either another state or an IGO or some other actor) undertakes to facilitate discussions between disputants, not only bringing them together but also crystallizing the points of disagreement and offering recommendations for a settlement. Neutrality does not mean the third party has no stake in the outcome, only that the latter is perceived by the disputants as playing the role of honest broker. A classic example of mediation was President Theodore Roosevelt's Nobel Prize–winning treaty ending the Russo-Japanese War in 1905. Another was Jimmy Carter's Camp David accords that produced a peace agreement between Anwar Sadat of Egypt and Menachem Begin of Israel in 1979. Two less successful examples were Bill Clinton's failed effort to broker a peace between the Israeli and Palestinian leaders in 2000, as well as his earlier abortive effort to seal a deal between Arafat and Barak's predecessor, Yitzhak Rabin, in the White House Rose Garden in 1993 following the Oslo Accord. Although mediation efforts do not always succeed, the empirical evidence suggests that they have a good track record in managing and terminating international crises.[19]

Informal Versus Formal Diplomacy

Although in everyday parlance "diplomacy" and "negotiation" are considered synonyms, one should keep in mind that **negotiation**—*formal, direct, verbal* communication through face-to-face meetings, cables and communiqués, or third-party intermediaries—is only one mode of diplomacy. In addition, governments often engage in **tacit bargaining**—*informal, indirect, nonverbal* communication through actions taken outside normal diplomatic channels (e.g., holding press conferences or placing troops on alert) designed to signal intentions or positions, such as the importance attached to some situation.[20]

In practice, states tend to combine the two forms, using tacit bargaining for "posturing" purposes before or during a formal negotiating session to reinforce the messages they wish to convey. For example, during the 1973 Arab-Israeli war, when the Nixon administration sought to persuade Moscow not to enter the conflict on the side of Egypt against Israel, Washington mailed formal diplomatic dispatches warning against Soviet involvement, but also took actions to demonstrate the seriousness of American concern. After Egypt requested Soviet assistance, the Soviet leader Leonid Brezhnev sent a letter to President Nixon in the middle of the

Jimmy Carter's successful Middle East mediation between Anwar Sadat of Egypt and Menachem Begin of Israel at Camp David in 1978.

Bill Clinton's unsuccessful mediation between Yitzhak Rabin of Israel and Yasser Arafat of the Palestinian Liberation Organization on the White House lawn in 1993.

night of October 23, proposing that both American and Soviet troops be inserted in the region to enforce a cease-fire; Brezhnev indicated in the letter that, if Washington did not agree, then Moscow would consider acting unilaterally. The Soviets themselves engaged in posturing, placing several airborne divisions on alert and deploying several naval vessels in the Mediterranean. The United States responded with, on the one hand, a conciliatory formal reply urging mutual restraint and, on the other hand, communicating the depth of American preparedness to use force if necessary by raising the state of defense alert to "DEFCON II—cocked pistol" (not seen since the Cuban missile crisis) and sending American ships to the Mediterranean as a show of force to dissuade Soviet vessels from entering the Bosporous Strait. Moscow ultimately caved into the American request that it stay out of the Arab-Israeli conflict, with the head of the KGB agreeing that "we shall not unleash the Third World War."[21] Hence, in one of the more harrowing moments of the Cold War, a nuclear showdown was avoided through a deft mixture of formal and informal diplomacy.

Tacit diplomacy is not a modern invention. It has always been a part of statecraft along with formal diplomacy. However, it has become a more visible feature of the bargaining process, as the speed of modern communications technology has enabled leaders to exploit the signaling potential of tacit bargaining much more effectively than in the past. Tacit diplomacy allows communication between governments that for ideological or other reasons may not have official diplomatic contacts or whose relations are so strained that they do not wish to be seen formally talking to each other. Such diplomacy, then, can be a useful surrogate for formal diplomacy in managing conflicts. One drawback of tacit bargaining is that although actions such as troop mobilizations may speak louder than words in a formal letter or at a negotiating table, they can also be more easily misinterpreted. We look back on U.S. diplomacy during the 1973 Arab-Israeli war as highly effective and successful; but, again, it takes two to tango in the dance of international relations. Moscow might well have refused to follow the U.S. lead, as U.S. threats to counter Soviet intervention could have hardened Soviet resolve and precipitated an exchange of hostilities neither side wanted.

The Domestication of Diplomacy

Another trend is the growing importance of domestic politics in affecting diplomacy. Whether engaging in formal or informal diplomacy, states can misinterpret each other's cues since officials often are playing to *multiple audiences*, not only an international audience that includes one's bargaining opponents but also a domestic audience back home. Sometimes one talks tough mostly for domestic political consumption, to impress one's own citizens that their leadership is showing backbone, just as one may do the opposite, agreeing to talks and offering conciliatory gestures to convince one's public that their leaders are not warmongers. Moreover, as the game of international relations increasingly has involved multiple "chessboards"—an ever growing agenda of issues, including many "intermestic" concerns that blend foreign and domestic policy matters—domestic political forces tend to play a greater role in foreign policy decision-making processes, making it harder to view states as unitary actors. "Complex interdependence" is also complicating the process of diplomacy as well.

We have already noted the large number of Executive Branch agencies, along with congressional and interest group representatives, involved in preparing for American participation in the 1986 Vienna Conference on the Ozone Layer. These different constituencies were involved in not only the formulation of policy but also the conduct of policy, as they were present on the American delegation that participated in the diplomatic proceedings. Other states had their own internal politics to work out. Internal politics pitted groups concerned primarily with the environmental costs of continuing to produce ozone layer–depleting chemicals (chlorofluorocarbons) against those concerned mainly with the economic costs of discontinuing those chemicals. The external politics pitted those countries most potentially threatened by the harm to the ozone layer against those least threatened, as well as those countries most economically advantaged by a shift to CFC substitutes against those most disadvantaged.

The ozone layer case exemplifies what Robert Putnam has labeled **two-level games**. Putnam argues that when the chief negotiators of countries meet, "the politics of many international negotiations can usefully be conceived as a two-level game," one directed at the international level and the other at the domestic level. He states that "each national political leader appears at both game boards. Across the international table sits his foreign counterparts, and at his elbows sit diplomats and other international advisors. Around the domestic table behind him sit party and parliamentary figures, spokespersons for domestic agencies, representatives of key interest groups, and the leader's own political advisors."[22] Robert Strauss, the chief U.S. official at the Tokyo Round trade talks in the 1970s, is quoted as saying that "during my tenure as Special Trade Representative, I spent as much time negotiating with domestic constituents [both industry and labor groups] and members of the U.S. Congress as I did negotiating with our foreign trading partners."[23] Similarly, former U.S. labor secretary John Dunlop once commented that "bilateral negotiations usually require three agreements—one across the table and one on each side of the table."[24] Realists tend to focus on the international game played between nation-states, while liberal theorists see domestic-level pressures as at least as important. Scholars have shown how in some instances (e.g., negotiations that occur within the European Union, where multinational corporations and NGOs lobby EU officials directly and compete with national governments in determining what decisions are reached in EU institutions on trade policy and other matters), it may be necessary to treat the diplomatic process as a "**three-level game**," in which not only subnational and national actors are involved but also transnational actors.[25] In the case of the United States, one author has called attention to the emergence of "paradiplomacy," the increased involvement of noncentral governmental actors (state governors and city mayors) in meeting and negotiating with foreign officials over trade, investment, and other issues.[26]

THE GOOD DIPLOMAT AND GOOD DIPLOMACY: RULES TO FOLLOW IN NEGOTIATIONS

One can see that diplomacy is all about several "c's"—conflict, communication, and cajoling, if not coercing. The question remains: What makes for a good diplomat and good diplomacy? We are mainly interested here in examining diplomacy in the context of formal negotiations. We will consider the dynamics of bargaining in a more general sense later in the chapter. (See, also, the *IR* Critical Thinking Box "Playing the Game of International Relations.")

Whether it involves tacit bargaining or formal bargaining, diplomacy is "the search for common ground," where each side seeks to achieve key goals short of the use of armed force if possible.[27] A number of writers have prescribed various rules that statesmen can follow to be good diplomats and to conduct successful diplomacy. The sixteenth-century Dutch writer Erasmus, advising envoys on proper etiquette, commented that "vomiting is no disgrace provided one does not dirty others" (a dictum violated by President George H.W. Bush when he threw up on the Japanese prime minister at a state dinner in 1992). Some rules are more important than others. We will first examine the personal qualities thought to be essential to serving as a model diplomat, and then what is essential for model diplomacy.

The Good Diplomat

I stated earlier that diplomacy almost by definition is associated with Machiavellian-like deviousness. Indeed, a diplomat has been described as "an honest man sent abroad to lie for his country."[28] This pejorative view of diplomats is captured in a statement by a Polish official assigned to Moscow during the 1940s, referring to Soviet diplomat Andre Vyshinsky: "In a way, Vyshinsky was the perfect diplomat. He was capable of telling an obvious untruth to your face; you knew it was a lie and he knew that you knew it was a lie, but he stubbornly adhered to it. No other diplomat was able to do this with such nonchalance."[29]

Although a certain amount of guile and deception may be a necessary part of diplomacy, a reputation for honesty, on balance, would seem to benefit a diplomat more than a reputation for dishonesty, if only to retain enough credibility to deliver on whatever proposals are being offered. As Nicolson states, "first among the virtues" a diplomat must demonstrate is truthfulness.[30] The four other virtues Nicolson stresses are precision (clarity of expression), modesty (to avoid the appearance of arrogance), calmness (maintaining one's composure in endeavoring to compose differences even when the other side resorts to threats and refuses to compromise), and loyalty to one's own government (as opposed to "going native" and developing an affinity for the other side, especially if one has spent a long time stationed abroad and developed strong ties to the local culture). At the same time, it is helpful for a diplomat to have deep knowledge of foreign cultures, values, and styles of communication and also to have some capacity for empathy—to be able to walk in the other side's shoes—if one is to understand how to interpret and deal with the bargaining positions of opposing players.

A reputation for honesty is part of a larger moral reputation that a good diplomat cultivates. It was noted in Chapter 2 that the moral reputation of the United States—what Joseph Nye has called its **soft power**—has suffered in recent years. America often has been perceived as arrogant, bullying, intractable in its bargaining positions, and inclined to act unilaterally, instead of being sensitive to the requirements of bilateral and multilateral diplomacy.[31] Whether this is a fair description of U.S. behavior is beside the point; in diplomacy, perception is often reality. There is a limit to which diplomats can overcome the perceived moral failings of their government, but they can, through their body language and communication style, either aggravate such problems or alleviate them.

Good Diplomacy

A good diplomat must also be persistent and patient, although this describes the diplomatic process as much as the person conducting it. First, one must understand that diplomacy can serve several functions, only one of which may be conflict resolution. That is, when diplomats gather around a table, they are not always there for the sole purpose of reaching an agreement; in addition to possible domestic pressures to demonstrate one's readiness to talk, they may be there to feel out other countries' positions and collect information for future bargaining down the road, to communicate to other states not even seated at the table, to spread propaganda, or to pursue some other agenda. Once it has been determined that a serious negotiation is under way, one must be prepared for what can be lengthy, tortuous negotiations. As one example, the UN Law of the Sea Conference, which engaged 149 states in negotiating a single treaty covering 70 percent of the earth's surface, took a decade to conclude, starting in 1973 and ending with the Montego Bay Convention in 1982.

Assuming that a settlement of contested issues is the goal, there are many different tactics that can help grease the diplomatic process. De Callieres, an eighteenth-century student of diplomacy, recommended that envoys "exploit the flush of wine." We have seen how this advice was applied in contemporary times, when "good wine" was credited with helping to produce the 1993 Oslo Accords between Israelis and Palestinians.[32] We have also seen how creating an air of informality, through "walk-in-the-woods diplomacy," can help as well. Beyond setting the proper mood, there are more serious pointers that have been offered by various scholars who have written on the rules of good diplomacy.

Roger Fisher has authored such works as *International Conflict for Beginners*, *Getting to Yes*, and *Beyond Machiavelli*. Among the prescriptions Fisher offers practitioners are the following.

- First, understand exactly what your *own* priorities are—what exactly are you hoping to achieve through negotiation, what outcomes are optimal, and what may not be optimal but may nonetheless be acceptable?
- Second, related to empathy, understand the *other* side's priorities and maximum and minimum positions. "How they feel about the choice we will be asking them to make is just as important to us as how we feel about it. . . . What kind of a decision can we formulate which will be practical for them in their terms,"[33] in satisfying both the international and domestic concerns they may have?
- Third, make it easier for the other side to respond positively by offering not vague proposals but giving them a concrete, "yesable proposition." Not only is there the problem that "the more ambiguous the message the greater the chance for distortion and misunderstanding," but also vague messages can unduly complicate the choices one's negotiating partner is confronted with. Admittedly, there are costs and risks associated with stating terms too plainly, in that you may "sound as if you are delivering an ultimatum" or you "may forfeit the opportunity to ask for more favorable terms," but specificity of proposals helps to expedite the diplomatic process.[34]
- Fourth, "in international conflict as elsewhere our first reaction to somebody's doing something we don't like is to think of doing something unpleasant to them." There is a natural impulse to respond to the other side's negative reply by issuing threats or becoming confrontational. However, "inflicting pain on an adversary government" is "likely to be a poor way of getting them to change their mind." Instead, "mak[e] their choice more palatable" by throwing some sweeteners into the deal.[35]
- Fifth, it follows that humiliating the other side serves no purpose. Again, you want to make it as easy as possible for the other side to accept your terms. Keep your eye on the goal you are striving to achieve. As long as you get what you want, let the other side look good by providing a face-saving way out of a box in which your opponent may find himself. It has been suggested that, during the missile crisis of October 1962, President Kennedy facilitated Nikita Khrushchev's acceptance of the American demand that the Soviets dismantle their nuclear facilities by providing Russia a graceful exit in the form of allowing the Russian leader to claim publicly he had extracted a pledge from the United States never to invade Cuba, even though Kennedy had made no such commitment. Giving the appearance of dictating terms or gloating over diplomatic triumphs can frustrate the diplomatic process and create lingering feelings of bitterness that may occasion another conflict and the need for another round of diplomacy in the future.
- Sixth, if a comprehensive settlement of all the issues in dispute is not possible, then consider "fractionating the problem"—"dividing up a problem

makes it possible for countries to agree on issues on which they have common interests, limiting disagreement to those issues on which they truly disagree."[36] This often makes sense, as in the case of the Camp David Accords that Jimmy Carter mediated between Israel and Egypt, when the diplomacy focused on such matters as Israeli withdrawal from occupied Egyptian territory and normalization of relations between the two states, leaving to another time the tougher issues relating to the future of the Palestinians and Jerusalem. The disadvantage of such an approach can be seen in the fact that the latter issues remain huge sticking points that have festered and prevented an overall Middle East peace. Also, by including more issues together in diplomatic discussions, it may be possible to arrive at a package of proposals that offer various side-deals and quid-pro-quos, which may ultimately facilitate progress toward an agreement, as happened with the 1982 Montego Bay Convention that emerged from the Law of the Sea Conference.

GAME THEORY

The above principles are relevant not just to the game of international relations but to many other, less weighty games all of us play. Few of us are likely to become U.S. secretary of state or find ourselves seated at a diplomatic table, but all of us at one time or another will be in a "bargaining" situation—with a friend, a spouse or lover, our children, or some other persons whose behavior we are trying to influence in a contest of wills around some disagreement. It could be over anything from a divorce settlement to a parent-child squabble over doing school homework. As suggested in the discussion of good diplomacy, the contestants presumably have some idea as to what their maximum and minimum limits are regarding what constitutes an acceptable outcome and how far they are willing to go to reach agreement, although some may have given this more careful thought than others. The bargaining game consists of each side trying to strike a final agreement as far from its own minimum and as close to its maximum demands as possible, although, as indicated at the end of the previous chapter, players—at least nation-states—often engage in "satisficing" behavior more than maximizing behavior.

One way to conceptualize the bargaining process is to picture a "bargaining curve," where along one end of the curve the outcomes represent improvement over the status quo for Player A (with the endpoint on that side of the curve representing the maximum payoff for A), while along the opposite end of the curve the outcomes represent improvement for Player B (with the endpoint there representing the maximum payoff for B). Inside the curve is a zone of potential agreement where both sides stand to gain something, but also another area where neither party gains or where the gains for one party are so superior to those derived by the other that it is difficult to forge agreement. Of course, one player's power may be so much greater than the other's that it may be able to coerce rather than negotiate an agreement.[37]

Let's say a parent is distressed at her son's failing math grades in high school and sits down with the child to discuss how the grades can be improved. Although the parent may hypothetically be in a position of power to dominate the child, simply ordering the child to do more studying is not likely to work. Bargaining, then, may consist of the parent offering several proposals aimed at producing better math grades, backed by some combination of promises or threats, with the child offering some counterproposals. The parent's maximum position would be for the child to attain an A grade, with the parent having to invest as few resources as possible (say, the enticement of a new pair of sneakers rather than a new car), while the kid's maximum position would be to get by with the least amount of extra work and least grade improvement (a C or D) while reaping some reward from the parent. How this bargaining exercise plays out will depend on how effective each side plays the game, although there would seem the potential for a win-win outcome.

A large body of **game theory** exists that provides useful insights into the choices that actors face when bargaining with each other. Grounded in mathematics, game theory offers an analysis of the nature of international bargaining, not only a way to portray strategic interactions between two or more states but also a way of analyzing their interactions in order to predict an outcome and whether cooperation can occur amid conflict.[38] Game theory assumes each state is a unitary actor concerned about promoting its national interests, and rationally calculates the payoffs associated with various options (moves); the payoff from a given move will depend on the move taken by the other player(s). Although these assumptions may oversimplify real-world international relations, they provide a handy tool for thinking about state interaction.

Two types of games are often discussed in regard to international bargaining, one leaning toward confrontation and the other toward cooperation. In a **zero-sum game** what one party wins the other loses, so that there is no hope for a mutually agreeable outcome. An example would be a territorial dispute in which two states claim the same piece of land but it is impossible for both to exercise sovereignty over it. The Palestinian Authority (PA) is not yet a state but seeks to become one, with East Jerusalem as its capital. Israel has insisted that Jerusalem remain undivided and under Israeli rule. Creative diplomacy may turn a zero-sum game into a **positive-sum game** in which both sides can win something, even if one benefits more than the other, if the two sides can coordinate their moves. Various proposals have been floated giving Palestinians at least a sliver of Jerusalem to serve as the capital of a new Palestinian state and awarding them compensation from Israel in the form of both "land for peace" (removal of Israeli settlements in the West Bank or other areas) and money (for resettlement of Palestinians on Arab lands and for economic development). The fact that no such win-win outcome has yet been finalized illustrates the great challenges in attempts to use

FIGURE 4.1 The Prisoner's Dilemma Game

PRISONER B

	No confession (cooperate)	Confession (defect)
No confession (cooperate)	-1, -1	-10, 0
Confession (defect)	0, -10	-6, -6

PRISONER A

*The first number in each cell is the payoff for Prisoner A.
The second number is the payoff for Prisoner B.

diplomacy to resolve conflicts between enemies hardened by decades of mutual hostilities.

Game analysis involves searching for a solution that represents the outcome at which rational players will supposedly arrive. Two classic games often discussed in the study of international relations are the Prisoner's Dilemma and Chicken.

The **Prisoner's Dilemma** is the story of two suspects who have been arrested for armed robbery and are being interrogated separately by the police, who have reason to believe both committed the crime in question but cannot convict them without a confession. Each prisoner is told that if one of them confesses (implicating his partner in crime) and the other does not, the former will be released from jail and go free while the latter will receive a maximum prison sentence (ten years). If both confess, both will get moderately reduced prison terms (six years). If neither confesses, both will serve a short jail sentence due to the lack of evidence and the inability to hold them for anything more than carrying concealed weapons (one year). The choices and outcomes in this game are depicted in the two-by-two matrix in Figure 4.1. The game has the following "solution"—both end up confessing. The reason is that the structure of the payoffs is such that each player understands that the cost of not confessing if the other confesses is incredibly high. From Player A's perspective, the worst possible outcome would be to remain silent while his partner confesses, while the worst possible outcome from Player B's perspective is a similar calculation. Hence, both players, acting rationally, end up producing a less than optimal outcome. Each could have gotten off with a very light sentence had they been able to trust each other not to squeal. However, without being able to talk to each other and not knowing for sure which option the other would choose, the safest choice was to defect rather than cooperate, even if

FIGURE 4.2 The Chicken Game

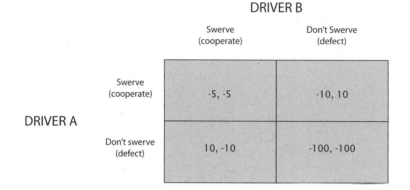

*The first number in each cell is the payoff for Driver A.
 The second number is the payoff for Driver B.

it ultimately left each with a substantially longer prison term. This situation has been compared to international arms races, where both sides would be better off with reduced arms expenditures that could follow from an arms control agreement but neither trusts that the other will fully honor the pact as opposed to seeking an advantage through evading compliance.

The Prisoner's Dilemma seems to contain built-in disincentives to cooperate, given the one-shot nature of the game and the players' concern about the immediate outcome should one make the wrong decision. However, many games played between states, including arms control negotiations, are not one-shot affairs but rather "multiple iterations" in which "the shadow of the future" hovers over the players; these games involve repeated, extended bargaining in which states come to "learn" over time the potential costs of defecting and the potential benefits of cooperating. Members of the liberal school, especially liberal institutionalists, argue that if states communicate their intention to reward cooperative play (say, by following successful arms reductions with further arms reductions) and to penalize noncooperation (by reciprocating noncompliance with rearmament), then such tit-for-tat behavior can produce long-term cooperation.[39] Liberals believe that international organizations can provide ongoing opportunities for states to exchange information, develop trust, and cultivate habits of cooperation.

In the **Chicken** game two teenage boys are trying to impress their girlfriends by daredevil hot-rodding on a country road. With the girls watching, they speed toward each other at 100 miles per hour, as their cars seem destined for a head-on collision. The possible choices and outcomes are depicted in Figure 4.2. Each player is faced with essentially two options—swerve or don't swerve—with neither player knowing which option the other will select and neither one alone able to control the outcome of the game. If one boy swerves and the other does not, then whoever swerves will suffer highly negative payoffs through major humiliation, while the one who continues going straight will score highly positive payoffs by appearing braver. If both swerve, both will suffer minor embarrassment. If neither swerves, then the worst possible outcome of mutual suicide will occur. Given the structure of the payoff matrix, the solution here will be for both to cooperate—swerve. Unlike the Prisoner's Dilemma, rationality here dictates mutual cooperation rather than mutual defection, so as to avoid the worst possible outcome of mutual annihilation. In international relations, the Cuban missile crisis between the United States and the Soviet Union has been compared to a game of chicken—the Soviet ships were coming full-speed toward the American ships maintaining a blockade around Cuba. Even though the Soviets "blinked first," as Kennedy arguably won by seeming willing to risk nuclear war, both sides arguably chose to exercise caution in that the blockade option was far less risky than stronger military responses that were contemplated.

As the Cuban missile crisis episode symbolizes, the games played by nation-states are not abstract exercises or parlor games but have huge implications not only for the direct participants but for humanity as a whole. In the next section, we examine further the dynamics of "strategic bargaining," especially the manipulation of carrots and sticks and the relative utility of economic and military instruments of influence.

THE DYNAMICS OF STRATEGIC BARGAINING

The Manipulation of Carrots and Sticks

Earlier in this chapter I mentioned that a central puzzle in the field of international relations is the question of what works better in winning at bargaining—a nice guy approach (using carrots) or a tough guy approach (using sticks). This question and related questions have been studied extensively by Thomas Schelling, a Nobel Prize–winning economist who, like Roger Fisher, has tried to translate theory into practical advice for statesmen. Schelling's focus has been on the "strategy of conflict" and what could be called **strategic bargaining**—the manipulation of carrots and sticks in pursuit of one's goals vis-à-vis other states.[40] He discusses both formal and tacit bargaining but is especially interested in the latter. While interested in both carrots and sticks, he is more interested in sticks, particularly the *threat* to use force ("coercive diplomacy") and, if necessary, the *actual* use of force in a limited manner for some sort of demonstration purposes (the aforementioned "diplomacy of violence"). Other writers have focused more on the manipulation of carrots.

In practice, states use both carrots and sticks, relying on four types of bargaining tools: threats, punishments, promises, and rewards. Two of these tactics (**threats** and **punishments**) represent the *stick* approach, the former involving a hypothetical action and the latter a real action. The other two tactics (**promises** and **rewards**), which exemplify the *carrot* approach, also involve hypothetical and real actions. Realists tend to place greater faith in the stick, liberals in the carrot. For example, Roger Fisher, an exemplar of the idealist school, has argued against inflicting pain as a strategy of conflict. Liberals point to the lessons of World War I, when, in their judgment, excessive saber rattling on the eve of war—threatening rhetoric and actions on the part of the European powers—created an atmosphere of paranoia and led to a conflagration nobody wanted. In contrast, realists point to the lessons of Munich and how the lack of saber rattling—Britain's reluctance to threaten military action should Germany continue its expansionist policies and its willingness to concede Hitler's annexation of Czechoslovakia—resulted in Hitler's perception of Prime Minister Chamberlain as weak and emboldened Germany to invade Poland, thereby triggering World War II. Realists seem to adopt Al Capone's view that you are likely to get farther with a kind word and a gun than just a kind word. Sometimes, however, as in the case of the run-up to the 2003 Iraq War, the roles are reversed, with realists being the ones calling for restraint in using force. The Bush administration accused war critics of failing to learn the lessons of Munich and supporting appeasement of Saddam Hussein, while the critics argued that the lessons of Munich had been misapplied and that Bush had not given peace a chance in allowing the diplomatic process to play out. Similar debates followed over whether a soft-line or hard-line approach would work better to get North Korea and Iran to renounce nuclear weapons development, a "game" I will discuss below.

There is no clear empirical evidence that one approach is superior to the other. It depends on the situation, the identity and relative power of the bargainers, and other variables. Going back to the example of the parent-child conflict over math grades, if you were the parent, what do you think would work best to achieve your goal of getting your son to improve his math performance—the carrot approach (for example, "Johnny, if you get an A, I will give you a new Mustang car") or the stick approach ("Johnny, if you get an F, I will beat the living daylights out of you")? Chances are that some *mix* of these two strategies—a kind of tough love approach—might work best. That may be true in international relations no less than in parenting. As former UN secretary-general Kofi Annan has said, "You can do a lot with diplomacy, but of course you can do a lot more with diplomacy backed up by firmness and force."[41] Talking or acting tough may convince the other side you mean business and consequently command respect. But if taken too far, it can also get your foe's back up, stiffening his position and making him more hostile, and perhaps even provoking the very behavior you are seeking to deter. Behaving in a more conciliatory way may achieve the desired goal by convincing the other side you are a friendly sort whose accommodating manner should be reciprocated. But if taken too far, it can also make you appear weak, a paper tiger not to be taken seriously, whose demands can be ignored.

If "almost any conflict can be seen as an attempt by one government to influence another government to do something . . . or not to do something," it is often the case that it is harder to *compel* than to *deter*.[42] In the case of **compellence**, one side seeks to persuade the other side to do something it does not wish to do (e.g., the United States persuading Iran to end its nuclear weapons aspirations); in the case of **deterrence**, one side seeks to dissuade the other side from doing something it might wish to do (e.g., Israel discouraging Iran from "wiping Israel off the map," as Iranian leader Mahmoud Ahmadinejad vowed to do in 2005). Compellence and deterrence are most often discussed in terms of military strategy (e.g., painstaking efforts by both the United States and the Soviet Union to deter a first nuclear strike by one against the other during the Cold War), but the terms apply to nonmilitary efforts at influence as well.

In using carrots and sticks, timing is critical. For example, if you have promised to reward an adversary with economic aid for doing what you want, you must not bestow the reward prematurely, or you risk being suckered. Likewise, if you have threatened to punish an adversary with economic or military sanctions if the latter fails to act as you have asked, you need to be certain that the punishment is not meted out prematurely lest you remove any remaining incentive for your foe to cooperate. For promises and threats to work, they must be sufficiently *credible*, as perceived by the *other* side. Regarding **credibility**, State A can intend fully to honor a promise or to carry out a threat; however, both are unlikely to influence State B's behavior unless B believes that A has the capability and willingness to follow through with the promised reward or the threatened punishment. At the same time, promises and threats that are bluffs may well prove effective, since all that counts is that the target state is convinced; as Henry Kissinger once observed, "A bluff taken seriously is more useful than a serious threat [or promise] interpreted as a bluff."[43] Of course, a state may ultimately be called on to make good on a threat or promise, and it must be prepared to do so if it values its future credibility. Recall the importance of a reputation for truthfulness as an element of good diplomacy.

But credibility is not enough. Promises and threats must also be sufficiently *weighty*, again in the eyes of the *other* side. Regarding the element of **potency**, they must be either too attractive to pass up (in the case of a promise) or too potentially injurious to endure (in the case of a threat). In other words, the carrot must be juicy enough for the target state to want to bite, and the stick must be menacing enough for the target state not to want to test it.

The relevance, and also the complexities, of strategic bargaining can be seen in the efforts of the United States to thwart nuclear weapons development by North Korea, which was a party to the 1970 Nuclear Non-Proliferation Treaty obligating nuclear have-nots to refrain from such development. In 1993 North Korea was found to be in breach of its obligations, due to its secret plutonium reprocessing program (a precursor to the manufacture of a nuclear bomb). The Clinton administration thought it had reached an agreement with North Korea to terminate its program, but North Korean leader Kim Jung Il appeared to renege on the agreement, leaving the Bush administration to deal with the problem. A

2006 *Wall Street Journal* article entitled "Weighing Carrots or Sticks for North Korea" quoted Bush officials as criticizing the Clinton administration for not being tough enough on Pyongyang, while former Clinton officials countered that "you need a carrot-and-stick approach—you can't just use the stick."[44] One commentator observed that the Bush administration had "used neither the carrot nor the stick very well."[45] By the end of the Bush presidency, the administration had persuaded China and other concerned states to join Washington in imposing economic sanctions on North Korea, including restrictions on export of military technology, freezing financial assets of businesses associated with the nuclear program, a travel ban on persons working on the program, and an embargo on luxury goods (such as cognac, caviar, and other items known to be favored by Kim and the North Korean leadership), in addition to offering conciliatory gestures that included the promise of fuel aid and economic assistance as well as a nonaggression pact. Although negotiations were progressing, it remained unclear whether such a mix of economic carrots and sticks would be sufficiently weighty to persuade North Korea to change its behavior, and whether the threat of military action as an ultimate tactic would be credible, given North Korea's sizable million-man army and the likelihood of major casualties to American troops and Korean soldiers and civilians in neighboring South Korea should hostilities erupt.

A replay of the North Korean standoff occurred with Iran, which was also a party to the NPT treaty and which by 2002 was also found to be in violation of the treaty because of its uranium enrichment program. Similar news headlines raised the problems that the Bush administration was having in "waving a stick as well as a carrot."[46] Along with Israel, the United States made a veiled threat to attack the Iranian nuclear facilities if Iran did not cease its nuclear program. The threat lacked credibility, however, in that the Iranian nuclear facilities were greatly dispersed and would be difficult to eliminate. In addition, any such attack would enrage Muslims throughout the Middle East and add to American troubles in the region. Bush was eventually able to get the UN Security Council to impose trade and travel sanctions resembling those applied to North Korea, but these did not seem potent enough to alter Iranian behavior. A 2008 newspaper article reported: "Opening a farewell tour of Europe, President Bush won European support" to consider "additional punitive sanctions against Iran, including restrictions on its banks, if Iran rejects a package of incentives to suspend its uranium enrichment program." A joint statement "reaffirmed Western commitments to a 'dual-track strategy,' employing the threat of punitive sanctions along with incentives to Iran. . . . The focus was on the carrot of incentives and the stick of more sanctions."[47] Although another news article opined that "saber-rattling is not a strategy," Bush continued to keep the military option open while exploring peaceful ways to pressure Iran, such as limiting gasoline exports to Iran, trying to exploit the fact that Iran relied on "a half-dozen companies for 40 percent of its gasoline imports."[48] President Obama subsequently faced similar choices.

As the cases of North Korea and Iran suggest, promises and threats that are credible but lack potency are likely to fail, just like promises and threats that may be potent but lack credibility. It is easy for newspaper editorialists to call for "tougher" but "not too tough" sanctions to produce the desired behavior, yet calibrating the proper blend of carrots and sticks can be exceedingly difficult. Success is the mark of exemplary statecraft.

Schelling has suggested a number of ways in which states can increase the credibility of their threats and promises, especially their threats, which he refers to as "the art of commitment."[49] He stresses the importance of reinforcing formal verbal declarations of intent with the kinds of tacit bargaining actions alluded to earlier, such as backing such threats up with troop mobilizations and demonstrations of airlift and sealift capabilities. One strategy that he thinks is especially effective in making threats believable is the "burn all your bridges behind you approach," that is, creating a situation in which you convince the other side that if it takes an action that you wish to deter, you will have no choice but to carry out the threat you have made. An example often cited is that the main reason for stationing 300,000 American troops in Western Europe during the Cold War was to act as a "tripwire," to convince the Soviet Union that any military aggression against America's NATO allies would automatically trigger U.S. involvement, since some American soldiers would surely be killed by enemy troops. Consequently Washington would find it impossible to renege on its commitment to defend Western Europe even if the American homeland was not attacked. Schelling reminds us that the key is to create the element of credibility in the eyes of the other side, while always keeping some options open. As applied to the game of Chicken, a wise bargainer would only pretend to have burned all his bridges—by, say, letting his fellow driver see him throw a steering wheel (a spare) out the window of his car, when in fact the real steering wheel remains fully operable in the vehicle. Throwing beer cans out the window might be another bargaining maneuver worth trying, giving the *appearance* of drunkenness and an inability to swerve even if one wanted to. In the game of international relations, the appearance of recklessness can sometimes work, although a pattern of reckless behavior hardly enhances one's reputation as a reliable partner in diplomacy.

The Utility of Military Versus Economic Instruments in Bargaining

In 1973 President Nixon sent a flotilla of U.S. ships into the Mediterranean as a show of force to dissuade Soviet vessels from entering the Bosporous Strait and to cause Moscow to rethink its threat to intervene in the Arab-Israeli conflict. Nixon was following the time-honored tradition of **gunboat diplomacy** made famous by Teddy Roosevelt and others: the use of military power as a bargaining tool to try to intimidate an adversary into conforming to one's wishes. A more recent example of modern gunboat diplomacy occurred in the 1990s, when China launched a series of naval training exercises in the Taiwan Strait and fired several nuclear warhead-capable missiles off the coast of Taiwan, all aimed at putting Taiwan on notice not to press its campaign for recognition as a sovereign state and UN membership as long as Beijing considered Taiwan to be part of China. Since the United States long had pledged to protect Taiwan from Chinese aggression,

Washington then dispatched two aircraft carrier battle groups into the area. The incident ended without any further confrontation, China satisfied it had made its point to Taiwan, and the United States satisfied it had made its point to China.

Such tactics, where force is not so much "used" as it is "displayed" or "demonstrated," with an implicit *threat* to engage in the actual lethal use of armed force should a future situation require it, have been called **coercive diplomacy**. Alexander George has defined coercive diplomacy as "forceful persuasion," as offering "an opportunity to achieve objectives in a crisis without bloodshed, avoiding the costs of war." It is limited to "those cases in which the use of military force is threatened to persuade an opponent to desist from some unacceptable behavior."[50]

Coercive diplomacy is barely one step removed from **diplomacy of violence**, where deadly force *is* actually employed—guns are fired—albeit in a limited fashion with a tiny loss of life. Some might say that these two terms amount to a distinction without a difference. President Reagan used diplomacy of violence when he dispatched several jet fighters to bomb five targets in Libya in 1986 to "send a message" to Libyan leader Muammar Gaddafi that he should end his support for terrorism; several civilians were killed, including Gaddafi's adopted daughter. Although global terrorism declined over the next decade, it is not clear that "Rambo" Reagan's hard-line "diplomacy" aimed at discouraging state sponsorship of terrorism was the reason.[51] Indeed, the terrorist bombing of New York–bound Pan Am Flight 103 over Lockerbie, Scotland, in 1988, which killed 259 passengers and crew (including 35 Syracuse University students returning from London), was traced to Gaddafi and was assumed to be payback for the 1986 bombing of Libya.

How valid today is Frederick the Great's axiom that diplomacy is likely to be only as effective as the number of guns backing it up? Although the projection of military power can support diplomacy in many instances, the axiom would not seem to be relevant to many diplomatic bargaining situations. First, the threat to use armed force is not a serious option when negotiating with one's allies over various disagreements; the United States is hardly likely to threaten Canada with military reprisals if, say, Canada does not close off its border to terrorists or does not honor trade agreements. Even in the case of nonallies, the growing agenda of economic, environmental, and other nonsecurity issues that states increasingly bargain over do not lend themselves to military saber rattling; it is not plausible that the United States would threaten to nuke OPEC states if they refuse to increase petroleum production and lower the price of a barrel of oil, any more than Washington would threaten military action against states that ban U.S. beef imports or genetically modified corn.

The threat to use military force remains an important element in bargaining situations involving military *deterrence*, preventing military attack by making the potential costs of such action exceed the potential benefits in the eyes of the would-be aggressor. It is generally easier to deter an adversary from attacking one's own homeland than to deter it from attacking another state one has pledged to protect, if only because the commitment to retaliate in the first case (direct deterrence) is inevitably stronger and more credible than in the second case (extended deterrence). However, as seen in the tripwire example of the American defense of Western Europe during the Cold War, extended deterrence can work if the right strategies are put in place. A study of seventeen cases of extended deterrence revealed that the attacker was most likely to refrain from committing aggression when there was both economic interdependence and military cooperation between the threatened state and its patron protector.[52]

A special deterrence problem that preoccupied the United States and the Soviet Union throughout the Cold War is **nuclear deterrence**. Each superpower was horrified at the prospect of the other possibly launching a first nuclear strike at its homeland. Preventing such a catastrophe became the number-one deterrence challenge for both sides. The main strategic doctrine on which Washington and Moscow came to rely during much of the Cold War was **MAD (Mutual Assured Destruction)**. Under MAD, each side communicated to the other that, should one launch a first nuclear strike at the adversary's homeland, however "limited" (e.g., a *counterforce* strike that targeted only intercontinental ballistic missiles in Missouri or Siberia, sparing major cities), the attacked state would then unleash whatever second-strike nuclear weapons it had left in a *countervalue* strike aimed at destroying the aggressor's population and industrial centers. Like two scorpions in a bottle, one could instantly annihilate the other, but it would be mutual suicide. It was hoped that the balance of terror—mutual threats of retaliation—would deter a nuclear exchange.

In the 1980s, MAD evolved into a new doctrine during the Reagan administration, what was called **NUTs (Nuclear Utilization Theory)**. It was a response to American concerns that the MAD deterrent requirements had broken down. Washington thought the Soviets were no longer convinced that, were the United States to be hit with nuclear weapons, (1) it would have a sufficient second-strike retaliatory force left to fire at Russia (since the ICBMs in Missouri and the Dakotas seemed to be sitting ducks in their missile silos); and (2) even if the United States had something left to retaliate with, it could inflict "unacceptable damage" on Soviet cities (since intelligence suggested Moscow had invested heavily in civil defense shelters that could reduce the number of Soviet casualties). In other words, the Reagan administration was worried that deterrence might fail, so it argued that the United States had to be prepared to fight and win a nuclear war by developing counterforce weapons systems as well as civil defense systems.[53] The notion of engaging in a "limited" nuclear war and emerging victorious struck many as odd. Fortunately the Cold War ended, and with it both the MAD and NUTs doctrines.

In the post–Cold War era, nuclear deterrence has remained a major concern of the United States and other countries, although supplemented by other WMD threats (chemical and biological weapons), and has shifted to the threat posed by nonstate actors. There is concern that normal deterrence strategies will not work against an enemy such as al Qaeda that has no specific territorial address to target in retaliation and that may welcome suicide and martyrdom (in order to ascend to heaven and receive seventy-two virgins, which some of bin Laden's followers claimed was the reward that awaited the 9/11 terrorists).

What about the effectiveness of economic tools of influence in international bargaining? As military bargaining has become more problematic and dangerous in the nuclear age, increased attention has been paid to economic levers of influence.[54] As already noted, the Bush administration felt pressure to forgo military measures and instead apply economic sanctions in dealing with North Korea and Iran. The use of such sticks as trade boycotts and embargos, freezing bank assets, and withholding foreign aid can frequently work, just as converting these sticks into carrots (offering most favored nation preferential trade status, additional foreign investment, and additional foreign assistance monies) can also prove effective at times. However, the effectiveness of economic threats depends on whether the country threatened has a sufficient degree of vulnerability to economic pressure. Klaus Knorr asserts that for State A to have coercive economic power over State B, the following conditions must exist: "(1) A must have a high degree of control over the supply of something B values. . . . (2) B's need for this supply must be intensive, and (3) . . . B's cost of compliance must be less than the costs of doing without the supply."[55] The effectiveness of economic promises entails a similar sort of calculus. Neither North Korea nor Iran seemed responsive to either economic threats or promises, even though the Bush administration, recognizing that economic levers would work best if applied not merely by the United States but by the global community, attempted to work through the United Nations. The Obama administration worked even harder to use the United Nations, also with questionable results.

Charles Kindleberger has concluded that "most sanctions are not effective."[56] Several empirical studies have examined the utility of economic sanctions. One study of 103 cases of economic sanctions since 1914 finds only "limited circumstances" in which they work.[57] The same authors, in a study of sanctions from 1846 to 1989, found that sanctions achieved success in only 34 percent of the cases.[58] In a study of eighteen attempts at economic sanctions between 1933 and 1967, the author found that only three could be considered even partial successes.[59] Another study found that, of twenty-two cases of trade sanctions, trade restrictions appeared to work no more than a third of the time.[60] Yet another study also found that success rates did not exceed 33 percent.[61] Margaret Doxy concluded in her extensive study that "in none of the cases analyzed . . . have economic sanctions succeeded in producing the desired result."[62] Not only do economic sanctions usually fail to change behavior, but the state or states imposing sanctions may experience international condemnation for creating economic hardship in the target state, as happened when the United States and others attempted to restrict Iraqi oil exports in the 1990s in order to force Saddam Hussein to relinquish his weapons of mass destruction, something that devastated Iraq's economy and raised a public outcry over the shortage of medical and food supplies for children and other civilians.

However, in a few cases economic sanctions have proved highly successful. Although it took well over a decade, economic pressure applied through the United Nations eventually forced the white minority apartheid government of South Africa to turn over power to the black majority in the 1990s. More recently, the application of creative sanctions that included aviation travel bans against government officials helped pressure the Gaddafi regime to alter Libyan policy and stop its WMD development programs and explore peaceful overtures toward the United States and the West.[63]

CONCLUSION

A U.S. assistant secretary of defense recently explained that a new program that integrates diplomatic personnel into military commands "seeks to integrate our 'soft power' and 'hard power'" by "synching our nation's diplomatic and military instruments."[64] Although frequently there is a fine line between diplomacy and force, they remain important distinctions in international relations. In the words of an Egyptian statesman, "The common objective of players in the Game of Nations is merely to keep the Game going. The alternative to the Game is war."[65] War is rarely the first or even second option states pursue in their disputes. Fundamentally, it represents a breakdown in the game of international relations, in the way it is normally played. However, sometimes the disagreements between states are over such core national values, and are so intractable, that they cannot be resolved through diplomacy. Historically, when such situations have arisen, all-out war has often been the ultimate mode of conflict resolution.

In the next chapter, we will examine trends in war and whether the world has become a more peaceful or more violent place. War has remained an enduring feature of world politics; yet we will also see the changing face of war, including the various forms it now takes and the range of actors—state and nonstate participants—that now dominate this phenomenon. We will also explore the long-standing scholarly debate over the causes of war, as well as the causes of peace.

QUESTIONS FOR STUDY AND DISCUSSION

1. In what ways has diplomacy changed over the years?
2. What is meant by "coercive diplomacy" and "diplomacy of violence"?
3. Based on scholarly evidence, what works better in diplomatic bargaining—sticks or carrots?
4. What insight do the Chicken and Prisoner's Dilemma games provide into the dynamics of international bargaining?
5. Frederick the Great once said that "diplomacy is only as good as the number of guns backing it up." Discuss. What does the scholarly literature tell us about the utility of economic instruments of bargaining as opposed to military instruments?

SUGGESTIONS FOR FURTHER READING

Robert Axelrod, *The Evolution of Cooperation* (New York: Basic, 1984).

Jacob Bercovitch, *Resolving International Conflict: The Theory and Practice of Mediation* (Boulder, CO: Lynne Rienner, 1995).

David Cortright and George A. Lopez, *Sanctions and the Search for Security* (Boulder, CO: Lynne Rienner, 2002).

Gordon A. Craig and Alexander L. George, *Force and Statecraft*, 3rd ed. (New York: Oxford University Press, 1995), pt. 2.

Roger Fisher, *International Conflict for Beginners* (New York: Harper & Row, 1969).

——, *Dear Israelis, Dear Arabs* (New York: Harper & Row, 1972).

Alexander George and Richard Smoke, *Deterrence in American Foreign Policy: Theory and Practice* (New York: Columbia University Press, 1974).

Gary C. Hufbauer et al., *Economic Sanctions Reconsidered*, 2nd ed. (Washington, D.C.: Institute for International Economics, 1990).

Paul Huth and Bruce M. Russett, "What Makes Deterrence Work?" *World Politics* 36 (July 1984): 496–526.

Harold Nicolson, *Diplomacy* (New York: Oxford University Press, 1964).

Robert D. Putnam, "Diplomacy and Domestic Politics: The Logic of Two-Level Games," *International Organization* 42 (Summer 1988): 427–460.

Dennis Ross, *Statecraft* (New York: Farrar, Straus & Giroux, 2007).

Thomas C. Schelling, *Arms and Influence*, rev. ed. (New Haven, CT: Yale University Press, 2008).

——, *The Strategy of Conflict* (Cambridge, MA: Harvard University Press, 1980).

Glenn H. Snyder and Paul Diesing, *Conflict Among Nations* (Princeton, NJ: Princeton University Press, 1977).

Arthur A. Stein, *Why Nations Cooperate* (Ithaca, NY: Cornell University Press, 1990).

I. William Zartman, ed., *Peacemaking in International Conflict*, rev. ed. (Washington, D.C.: U.S. Institute of Peace, 2007).

5

War and
the Use of
Armed Force

Nothing like D-Day [during World War II] will happen again, not because human nature has improved but because weaponry has. Making war on that grand scale is obsolete.
　　　　—Hermann Wouk, "Never Again," *Washington Post,* 1999

In the event of a major war in the nuclear age, you will no longer be dying for your country but with your country.
　　　　—Richard Lamm, Governor of Colorado, 1985

War is on its last legs; and a universal peace is as sure as is the prevalence of civilization over barbarism. . . . The question for us is only how soon?
　　　　—Ralph Waldo Emerson, 1849

I have cited statistics indicating that most conflict in international relations is nonviolent. Still, there is a reason why war has been the single most studied topic in the field of international relations, with more books and articles devoted to it on library shelves than any other subject. First, when war does occur, it produces horrendous human tragedy. Second, while war may constitute only a small fraction of the totality of international interactions, it has been a constant throughout history and still occurs more frequently than we would like to see.

War's origins, as well as its persistent character, go back several millennia. According to one estimate, in the past 3,400 years "humans have been entirely at peace for 268 of them, or just 8 percent of recorded history."[1] Another study calculates that between 3600 B.C. and A.D. 1980, there were "only 292 years of peace."[2] In the past millennium alone, there have been almost 1,000 wars.[3] Although war as a human institution predates the Westphalian state system, Westphalian politics became closely associated with the phenomenon. As noted in Chapter 2, the history of war and the history of the nation-state have been intertwined: "War made the state, and the state made war."[4] Some have suggested that this historic link has been severed, that due to technological and other changes, war as we have known it may have become obsolete. There is a considerable "end of war" literature that has burgeoned in recent years, buoyed especially by the fact that, when the Cold War system gave way to a new international system in 1989, it marked the first time in the annals of Westphalian politics that system transformation had occurred without war being the engine of change.[5] Others are not so sanguine about the future of war, acknowledging some major changes that have occurred but not necessarily for the better:

> We are at a moment in world affairs when the essential ideas that govern statecraft must change. For five centuries it has taken the resources of a state to destroy another state: only states could muster the huge revenues, conscript the vast armies, and equip the divisions required to threaten the survival of other states. Indeed, posing such threats, and meeting them, created the modern state. In such a world, every state knew that its enemy would be drawn from a small class of potential adversaries. This is no longer true, owing to advances in international telecommunications, rapid computation, and weapons of mass destruction. The change in statecraft that will accompany these developments will be as profound as any that the State has thus far undergone.[6]

The above quote relates to our observation that nation-states increasingly are having to compete with nonstate actors on the world stage. It remains to be seen, however, how this competition will play out and how it will affect the phenomenon of war. In this chapter we will look at trends in the use of armed force. We will also discuss what might be done to reduce the incidence of violence, based on a large body of theory on the causes of war.

TRENDS IN THE USE OF ARMED FORCE

Traditionally, those who have studied the use of armed force in world politics have been interested primarily in *interstate war*, most notably war between *great powers*, especially fought over *real estate* (with territorial disputes involved in over half of all wars fought since 1648).[7] Much of the history of international relations has seemed to revolve around these sorts of events. Some of these conflicts have been systemic, involving a wide number of states in the international system (such as the Napoleonic Wars, World War I, and World War II), and some have been more confined (such as the Austro-Prussian War of 1866 and the Russo-Japanese War of 1905). I have noted that throughout the centuries war was considered a legitimate vehicle for expanding national power, which tended to be equated with territorial expansion, and that one of the most profound changes in world politics has been the recent movement away from this historical pattern.

This antiwar thinking began to grow after World War I, but it took World War II for it to deepen. State behavior changed after 1945 due to a variety of factors, including, first, the development of weapons of mass destruction that made great powers gun-shy in using armed force against each other, and, second, the development of democratic, anticolonial norms that made the imposition of foreign rule less acceptable and hence constrained great-power use of armed force against weaker states. During the Cold War the superpowers refrained from open hostilities against each other and territorial annexation objectives against lesser states. The point is that the central problem that preoccupied students and practitioners of international relations over the ages—interstate war, particularly great-power war fought over territory—has become a relatively peripheral concern. As seen below, interstate wars in general have become remarkably infrequent of late, while great-power war has become nonexistent altogether (the so-called long peace). However, I cannot emphasize enough that, as hopeful as these developments are, violence is still prevalent on the planet, and it tends to take a more complex, "messier" form now, which in some respects can be harder to get a handle on conceptually, legally, and otherwise than in the past. How so?

First, to the extent that violence occurs *between* states, it tends to be not so much in the form of what we commonly think of as "war" (large-scale, all-out, sustained armed combat between organized national armies), but rather "force without war" (that is, sporadic, limited hostilities, including border skirmishes and raids, with ill-defined beginnings and endings). Second, the main mode of violence today is not interstate but rather "intrastate," that is, civil wars *within* states, which can become internationalized as external actors are drawn into the fray, making such conflicts hybrid mixes of internal and cross-border conflagrations. Third, there is growing concern over "extrastate" violence, that is, unconventional security threats posed by nonstate actors, including transnational terrorist and criminal organizations, which can potentially disrupt national order and world order through kidnappings, skyjackings, drug trafficking, cyberspace interference, and other means. Sometimes all of these elements can blend together in a volatile stew, as in the case of the Iraq War. Force without war, civil war (purely internal or internationalized), and terrorism are hardly novel features of world politics. What *is* novel is that they seemingly have displaced interstate war as the primary focus of security concerns in the Westphalian state system. As one commentator notes, "U.S. military leaders . . . now recognize that the nature of warfare itself is changing, from conventional conflicts between nations to 'small wars'—counterinsurgency, counterterrorism, religious and ethnic strife."[8]

Although traditional interstate war is being overshadowed today by other forms of violence, we cannot dismiss its continuing existence. The Iraq War started in 2003 as an interstate war between the United States and Iraq, even if it later morphed into a conflict involving intrastate and extrastate elements. In the following section we will examine trends in interstate war, as well as other dimensions of global violence.

Interstate War

When Ralph Waldo Emerson predicted in 1849 that "war is on its last legs," he undoubtedly had **interstate war** in mind. Yale historian Donald Kagan offers a cautionary warning against such optimistic prognoses: "Over the past two centuries the only thing more common than predictions about the end of war has been war itself; . . . statistically, war has been more common than peace, and extended periods of peace have been rare in a world divided into multiple states."[9] Using a standard operational definition of war that has been employed in the Correlates of War Project at the University of Michigan (where war is defined as the onset of sustained military hostilities between at least one recognized state and another state or foreign armed force culminating in at least 1,000 battle deaths), one finds that there were 118 international wars between 1816 and 1980. Some of these were wars between recognized states, and some were colonial wars fought between a state and a foreign army in pursuit of independent statehood. War incidence during this time frame generally declined, although the trend was a modest one.[10] Another study counts 177 interstate armed conflicts between 1648 and 1989, also detecting an overall long-term decline in the incidence of such wars over time.[11] Wars also seem to be getting shorter rather than longer; according to one account, out of nine global (systemic) wars since 1648, the Thirty Years War in the seventeenth century was the longest, and the two world wars in the twentieth century the shortest.[12]

Despite a modest decline in the *occurrence* of interstate war, the *severity* of wars, as measured by casualties, mounted with the invention of new weapons throughout the twentieth century. Although some wars in prior centuries killed large numbers of people (for example, there were 2 million battle deaths caused by the Thirty Years War), at least twice as many soldiers died in twentieth century wars as in all the wars from 1500 to 1899 combined.[13] These totals do not count those wounded on the battlefield, or the millions of civilian casualties. (World War I was the last major war in which there were more military personnel killed than civilians, as the roughly 10 million combat deaths slightly exceeded the number of civilians killed. World War II saw some 15 million soldiers killed, compared to over 40 million civilians.)

If we take into account the proliferation of nation-states since the end of World War II, which has more than tripled the number of potential candidates for interstate war involvement, then a more impressive case can be made that the post–World War II period up to the present has been relatively free of international wars compared with previous eras of world politics. Although "the number of people killed by armed conflicts since World War II is probably twice that of the entire 1900s and perhaps seven times that of the 1800s," fewer and fewer of these conflicts have been waged between states (as opposed to within states).[14]

The decline of interstate war is especially marked since the end of the Cold War. The Uppsala Conflict Data Project reports that between 1989 and 2008, only 6 percent of all armed conflicts worldwide (7 out of a total of 122 wars) were interstate.[15]

One distinct trend is the long-term historical decline in the incidence of *great-power* war. Jack Levy found that wars among great powers in the nineteenth and twentieth centuries were under way only one-sixth of the time, compared with an estimated 80 percent of the time in the sixteenth to eighteenth centuries, reflecting both the diminishing frequency and duration of such wars. Indeed, perhaps the most striking feature of the Cold War era was the paucity of war involvement by major powers, in particular the absence of war *between major powers themselves* (unless one counts the Korean conflict, in which the United States and China fought against each other). Levy has summarized this "long peace" as follows:

> The past five centuries of the modern system have witnessed an average of one great power war per decade, but the frequency of great power wars has declined significantly over time. We have experienced only three such wars in the twentieth century and arguably none in the period since the Second World War, and this constitutes the longest period of great power peace in 500 years. For many centuries war was disproportionately concentrated in the hands of the great powers in Europe, but the twentieth century, and the second half-century in particular, marked a significant shift in warfare from the major powers to minor powers, from Europe to other regions, and from inter-state warfare to intra-state wars.[16]

Again, optimism about the end of great-power war must be tempered. After all, as realists would remind, the other long peace of the recent past—the forty-four year peace after the Franco-Prussian War of 1870—was followed by one of history's most destructive wars in 1914. Still, the probability of great-power war does seem considerably lower today than in earlier times. The explanation for the decline and disappearance of great-power war is at least threefold. First and most importantly, the increasing severity of war over time has made great powers—states having the most to lose in material well-being—less willing to engage each other in hostilities, especially in an age of WMDs. Whether due to the mere existence of WMDs (as liberals would contend) or to a newly internalized norm that major war has become irrational (as constructivists would contend), there is empirical evidence that the increased cost of war has been accompanied by increased inhibitions against great-power war.[17] Second, growing economic interdependence, not only in trade but also capital and investment, has created further inhibitions on the part of national governments about incurring the costs of the disruptive effects of war. Third, related to the "democratic peace" phenomenon, growing democratization has lessened the propensity for great powers to fight each other.

These factors may be contributing to a decline in interstate war generally, not just great-power war. One study found that between 1945 and 1989 highly developed states (both nuclear and nonnuclear) had stopped fighting each other; the author observed that the forty-eight richest industrial states had had no wars against each other except for the British-Argentine Falklands war in 1982 and the Soviet invasion of Hungary in 1956, leading to hope that, as states in the south become wealthier, wars would be averted.[18] Thomas Friedman's "golden arches theory of conflict prevention" posits that "when a country reaches the level of economic development where it has a middle class big enough to support a McDonald's network," it loses its stomach for war. Friedman has found virtually no instance where two countries that have a McDonald's restaurant have gone to war against each other.[19] (The attack by the United States and NATO forces on Serbia in 1999, initiated in order to stop a genocide by the Serb government against ethnic Albanians in Kosovo, was, according to Friedman, an exception that proved the rule, since the United States and its NATO allies were unwilling to shed blood. The United States relied almost entirely on air power, which resulted in no American combat fatalities, while after seventy-eight days the Serbs "wanted McDonalds re-opened much more than they wanted Kosovo re-occupied.")[20] Friedman recently has updated his golden arches theory with his "Dell supply chain theory of conflict prevention," which stipulates that no two countries that are part of the Dell computer global supply chain will go to war against each other, Dell being a metaphor for the ties that bind in an age of globalization.[21] If Friedman is right, then we need not worry about China and the United States facing off in World War III. However, it is sobering to recall similar thoughts uttered by Norman Angell and others on the eve of World War I. Friedman has acknowledged that his theories do not apply to civil wars, where neither Big Macs nor Dell computers have prevented the outbreak of violence. Naive and amusing as Friedman's theories may sound, they help call attention to the causes of war and the causes of peace.

Force Without War

Reports that war is on the decline must be read with care, since counting the number of wars occurring at any given moment is a trickier proposition than it used to be. Distinctions between war and other forms of global violence used to be clearer, because wars in the past were definable in legal terms and had identifiable initiation and termination dates. A war was usually said to start when one state issued a formal declaration of war against another state, as in World War II (when the United States declared war on Japan minutes after Franklin Roosevelt's famous "a date that will live in infamy" speech on December 8, 1941, following the Japanese attack on Pearl Harbor, which in turn was followed by Germany declaring war on the United States). A war normally ended with a formal treaty of peace between the warring parties, as when the Japanese surrendered on board the USS *Missouri* in 1945, bringing a close to World War II. Since World War II, however, states have not issued declarations of war prior to initiating hostilities, perhaps because armed aggression is illegal under the UN Charter. The hostilities that do occur between two or more states can be isolated one-shot affairs or can go on for days, months, and in some cases years, often interrupted by periods of peace, only rarely concluding with a formal peace treaty. The Middle East is emblematic of such hostility patterns, in that the several wars fought between Israel and neighbors such as Syria and Lebanon have never fully ended, with intervals of relative quiet alternating with episodic violence.

To be sure, hostilities occurred in previous eras that were not necessarily preceded by formal declarations. For example, there have been more than 230 instances since 1789 in which an American president has sent U.S. troops into harm's way, only 5 of which were preceded by a formal declaration of war by Congress.[22] Some of these undeclared actions were forays against marauders threatening American shipping (as in the case of Thomas Jefferson's use of the U.S. Navy against the Barbary Coast pirates and their state sponsors) or armed interventions to overthrow foreign governments (as in the case of Woodrow Wilson's interventions in Mexico, Haiti, and Russia). Although the latter uses of armed force were not unlike actions taken in contemporary times in the name of the war on terror or humanitarian intervention, it was assumed in earlier times that any large-scale military action against a foreign power required formal authorization. Since World War II, the intermittent, limited uses of military power (recall the increased use of coercive diplomacy and diplomacy of violence discussed in the previous chapter) have blurred the distinction between war and peace, leading to references in the scholarly literature to **militarized international disputes** and **force without war**.[23]

According to one account, there were more than 200 different incidents during the Cold War in which the United States used armed force in some fashion short of war, and 190 such incidents in the case of the Soviet Union.[24] Not only did the two superpowers refrain from exchanging fire with each other, but even when they resorted to armed force against others, it tended to be in a somewhat restrained, controlled fashion. For example, U.S. jets strafed Muammar Gaddafi's tent headquarters for an hour in 1986 to warn the Libyan leader to cease sponsoring terrorism against American targets. Even when hostilities occurred that were more extensive and had all the earmarks of war, such as the Korean War during the 1950s and the Vietnam War during the 1960s, each of which cost roughly 50,000 American lives and thousands of Asian casualties, or the Afghan War at the end of the 1970s, which likewise resulted in enormous casualties for the Soviet Red Army and its adversaries, only a small fraction of the available arsenal was utilized by the losing side in these undeclared actions.

Many cases of force without war can be found in the post–Cold War era. Note, for example, the border clashes between Peru and Ecuador in 1995 (over a boundary dispute dating back more than fifty years), the periodic skirmishes between India and Pakistan along the Kashmir cease-fire lines (dating back to the partition of the Indian subcontinent in 1947), and the occasional bombing runs by U.S. and British planes over Iraq in the 1990s, following the first Gulf War and the creation of a no-fly zone over northern Iraq aimed at protecting the Kurdish population from Saddam Hussein's military (known as the "whack a mole" policy executed by the Clinton administration, named after an arcade game). Clinton's limited use of force against Iraq included a cruise missile attack against the headquarters of Saddam's intelligence service in Baghdad after the Iraqi leader was discovered plotting to assassinate former president Bush in 1993 during his visit to Kuwait.[25]

Hence, in contrast to the total wars of the past, such as World War I and II, we see references today to "limited wars," "low-intensity conflicts," "police actions," and even such euphemisms as "peaceful engagement." (The latter was the name the Pentagon gave to the American military intervention in Panama in 1989, aimed at removing Manuel Noriega from power after the dictator was linked to drug trafficking in the United States and after economic and other pressures had failed to dislodge him.)

Civil War

Civil wars (internal wars) clearly are not a new phenomenon. As long as there have been nation-states, there have been conflicts within states that have led to internecine fighting between rival groups. For example, the T'ai P'ing rebellion in China in the mid-nineteenth century resulted in an estimated 30 million deaths. Although civil strife is not new, it has been an especially visible feature of world politics since 1945, and has come increasingly to preoccupy the international community in the post–Cold War period. One work notes that "approximately 80 percent of the wars between 1900 and 1941 were of the traditional sort waged by the armed forces of two or more states," whereas "since 1945, about 80 percent of violent conflict has occurred on the territory of only one state and has been internally oriented."[26] K. J. Holsti estimates that "more than two-thirds of all armed conflict in the world since 1945 has taken the form of civil wars."[27] Charles Tilly comments that "since World War II, civil war has displaced interstate war as the dominant setting for large-scale violent death. . . . During the [twentieth] century's second half, civil war, guerrilla and separatist struggles, and conflicts between ethnically or religiously divided populations increasingly dominated the landscape of collective violence. Between 1950 and 2000, civil wars killing half a million people or more occurred in Nigeria, Afghanistan, Sudan, Mozambique, Cambodia, Angola, Indonesia, and Rwanda."[28] The International Commission on Intervention and State Sovereignty notes: "The most marked security phenomenon since the end of the Cold War has been the proliferation of armed conflicts within states."[29] Holsti says that "the assumption that the problem of war is primarily a problem of relations *between* states has to be seriously questioned. . . . Security *between* states . . . has become increasingly dependent upon security *within* those states. . . . The problem of contemporary and future politics, it turns out, is essentially a problem of domestic politics."[30]

Although many civil wars are stoked by outside actors or draw in outside actors once they are under way, as happened with the American-Soviet rivalry dur-

The Rwandan civil war, 1994: Hutu refugees walk past thousands of abandoned machetes used in genocidal and other acts.

ing the Cold War, when the two superpowers used intervention in the internal affairs of Third World states as a surrogate for great-power war, it is the domestic unrest within Third World states that often makes them inviting targets of intervention. It is not surprising that most civil wars have occurred in the south, particularly in Africa and Asia. The decolonialization process after World War II produced new states in those regions that were impoverished and unstable, and many of these states remain underdeveloped both economically and politically. The lack of economic development and democratic institutions, along with the fact that many of these states have arbitrary boundaries that correspond to the lines drawn by colonial mapmakers rather than being based on any historical nationality (ethnic or tribal) groupings, has contributed to powder keg situations.

As of 2008, the Uppsala Conflict Data Project counted twenty-seven ongoing civil wars.[31] Some involve rebels seeking to change the regime, others involve rebels seeking greater autonomy or complete separation from the state, while still others—in failed states where governmental institutions have completely collapsed—involve competing warlords representing rival clans or other groups engaged in what resembles gang warfare. As one writer comments, "Today's typical war is civil, started by rebels who want to change their country's constitution, alter the balance of power between races, or secede."[32] These conflicts usually do "not result from a state's ambitions for regional or global dominance, but from a failure to foster or maintain a society that can provide adequately for its own citizens, either for their political and social rights or for their basic physical needs."[33]

A good example of how such fragile states can attract outside intervention is the Kampuchea (Cambodia) civil war. The war involved state-building more than nation-building issues, insofar as the various parties all thought of themselves as Cambodians. Nobody threatened secession based on national identity claims. But the parties could not agree on the nature of the governing institutions, with communist and noncommunist elements forming rival alliances. The conflict started in the late 1970s with horrendous oppression and violence perpetrated by the ruling Khmer Rouge regime against peasants and professional classes (publicized in the movie *The Killing Fields*), leading to civil warfare between competing factions assisted by external powers (the government in Phnom Penh backed by Vietnam and the rebels backed by China and to an extent the United States), eventually ending in the 1990s when a United Nations–sponsored truce restored a degree of order, although the situation still remains unsettled.

During the Cold War, much of the internationalization of civil wars was driven by the East-West geopolitical competition. The Soviet Union and proxy states often assisted in "wars of national liberation," in which revolutionary groups trying to overthrow colonial rule (for example, against Portuguese domination in Angola and Mozambique) resorted to **guerrilla warfare**. The guerrilla paramilitary, irregular forces used *insurgency* tactics to overcome the stronger conventional military forces of the established authorities, which in turn were trained by the United States or its regional allies in *counterinsurgency* tactics to resist the guerrillas.[34] As Kosovo and other recent cases show, internationalization of civil wars has continued into the post–Cold War era.

However, there are important differences between the pattern seen during the Cold War and the pattern evidenced since. First, civil wars in the post–Cold War era tend to be rooted far more in ethnic differences than ideological differences, represented by recent ethnopolitical conflicts in Rwanda (between Hutus and Tutsis), Sudan (between blacks and Arabs), and the former Yugoslavia (between Bosnians and Kosovars and their Serb rulers). I noted earlier that the problem of "state versus nation" has become accentuated of late, as the Minorities At Risk Project has identified almost 300 substantial ethnic groups found in two-thirds of the countries of the world that are politically active and potential candidates for rebel or separatist movements.[35] Second, interventionism in the post–Cold War era has tended to be multilateral in character, frequently sponsored by regional or global organizations claiming a right of "humanitarian intervention" in chaotic, failed states to relieve mass starvation, stop atrocities, or otherwise provide humanitarian help, as in Somalia, Haiti, Sierra Leone, and Liberia.[36] Intrastate conflict has the potential to become internationalized as refugees flee to neighboring countries to seek sanctuary, as foreign states send arms or supplies to favored factions, and as multilateral efforts are mounted to bring an end to the fighting. A recent example of how civil war can spill over into neighboring states is the Rwandan civil war in the mid-1990s. Hutu extremists committed genocide against hundreds of thousands of Tutsis, leaving one-quarter of Rwanda's population dead or fleeing into the Congo and surrounding areas. It contributed to the onset of the Congo war in 1998, which has become known as "Africa's world war," involving eight African states and resulting in the deaths of some 5 million people.

The "messiness" of conflicts today, especially the concatenation of intranational and international war, can be vividly seen in the Iraq War (the second Gulf War). (For background on the war, particularly competing explanations on why the United States invaded Iraq in 2003, see the *IR* Critical Thinking Box in Chapter 3.) The war started as an interstate war. The United States had attempted to obtain United Nations Security Council approval to use military sanctions to dislodge Saddam Hussein from power as punishment for his violation of UN resolutions following the first Gulf War in the 1990s, particularly for his refusal to grant UN inspectors full access to facilities thought to house WMD arsenals. Having failed to get UN approval, Washington then initiated a "shock and awe" aerial bombing campaign over Baghdad on March, 20, 2003, and dispatched more than 100,000 ground troops (assisted by troops supplied by Britain and a few other countries that comprised "the coalition of the willing"). By May 1, President Bush declared victory on board the USS *Abraham Lincoln*, as Saddam had been ousted from power and America and its allies had seemingly achieved their goals with fewer than 200 combat fatalities.

However, Bush's proclamation proved premature. As one commentator wrote, "The capital descended into a state of chaos, quickly wearing out the welcome that had greeted Baghdad's liberators. . . . By mid-summer, occupation forces were coming under attack by guerrilla bands of Ba'ath loyalists [members of Saddam's party], foreign jihadists," and other resistance forces.[37] Over the next several years, the situation was to deteriorate further as the United States sought to extricate itself from the conflict. Iraq experienced civil war, bitterly divided along ethnic and sectarian lines between its Shiite Muslim population predominantly in the southern part of the country, the Kurds in the north, and the Sunni Muslims in the "Sunni triangle" around Baghdad and the midsection of the country (Saddam's stronghold and the source of his power). These groups disagreed over the distribution of power in the newly constituted Iraqi government, the distribution of oil revenues, and numerous other matters. The conflict was fueled further by Islamic fundamentalists thought to be supported by external actors such as Iran and Syria. By 2009, thousands of Iraqi civilians had died in the fighting along with more than 4,000 American soldiers, with no end in sight.

In many respects, the Iraq War is the prototypical war in the post–Cold War era, other than the fact that it started as an interstate war:

1. The Iraq War was never formally declared, and its end remains elusive.
2. Despite the substantial, tragic loss of life, it is a "limited" war insofar as the United States has used only a very small fraction of its military arsenal, finding much of that arsenal unusable in a war in which the enemy has employed asymmetrical warfare tactics to engage U.S. troops in urban

guerrilla street battles that alter the conventional rules of engagement. For example, militant extremists often embed themselves in heavily populated areas, blending in with civilians and not only targeting noncombatants (at times with suicide bombings) but practically daring their adversary to strike at them in the hope that the latter will suffer devastating public relations fallout from the resulting collateral damage and the appearance of violating international humanitarian law that prohibits indiscriminate attacks on civilians. In 2008, U.S. defense secretary Robert Gates said that "asymmetrical conflict will be the dominant battlefield for decades to come."[38]

3. The U.S. military has found itself in need of greater irregular warfare capabilities, in terms of special forces, intelligence gathering, and "mootwa" (military operations other than war), including training in civil administration, policing, infrastructure repair, and other elements of state building and nation building. American forces have experienced similar challenges in Kosovo, Afghanistan, and elsewhere. Gates was quoted recently as saying that "any soldiers can expect to be tasked with reviving public services, rebuilding infrastructure and promoting good governance. All these so-called nontraditional capabilities have moved into the mainstream of military thinking, planning and strategy, where they must stay."[39] Such statements reflect the new realities of war and are consistent with new norms of "post-conflict peacebuilding" that have been articulated within the United Nations.

4. The civil war has been characterized by a complex, diverse mix of ethnic and religious divisions that seem to defy efforts at reconciliation. Iraq is predominantly an Arab country that includes rival clans as well as many non-Arabs, including the Kurds, who have long sought their own homeland. Iraq also is a Muslim country torn by intra-Muslim disputes between Shiites and Sunnis, as well as fissures within the Shiite community and Sunni community between fundamentalist and more secularized camps. Power-sharing outcomes in such situations are difficult to achieve.[40] Similar tribal, racial, and sectarian differences have complicated efforts by the international community to understand and deal with other conflicts as well, such as in Somalia and Sudan. (Many human rights groups have called for the United States and other countries to engage in humanitarian intervention in the Sudan, where the Arab-controlled government has been accused of committing genocide against black Muslims living in the western region of Darfur and black Christians and animists in the south, but the political complexity there is as great as in Iraq.)

5. Separating the internal dimensions of the conflict from the external dimensions is difficult. It is unclear how much of the resistance to American occupation in Iraq has been indigenous or has been provided from

the outside by Iran and other foreign actors. The foreign actors have included transnational terrorist groups such as al Qaeda, as there have been elements of "extrastate" violence blending with interstate and intrastate violence.

IR Critical Thinking:
Has the Nature of War Changed? Asymmetrical Warfare, Mootwa, and the Blurring of Inter/Intra/Extrastate Violence

John Donnelly describes how, in the wake of recent conflicts in Kosovo, Afghanistan, Iraq, and elsewhere, the U.S. government has been attempting to cope with the changing face of war:

> When Donald H. Rumsfeld became Defense secretary at the start of the Bush administration . . . what he did not foresee was a guerrilla war in the ancient streets of Baghdad that would tie down his Army for years and cost him his job. Iraq required more foot soldiers than the Pentagon had thought, and to be successful, those soldiers had to do jobs for which they were ill-prepared: negotiating with local sheiks, managing municipal governments, fixing sewers, defusing mobs, keeping the lights on and understanding tribal and religious quarrels.
>
> The new doctrine, spelled out in the newest Army and Marine Corps Counterinsurgency Field Manual, is that the Army must be prepared to wage all types of warfare but focus much more on . . . irregular, guerrilla conflicts like that in Iraq. . . . For the Army, the new doctrine means a seismic culture shift. It will still have guns and tanks, but it will also need more people skilled in languages, public affairs, economic development, even anthropology. Instead of grudgingly accepting the task of nation building, as it did in the Balkans and in Iraq at first, the new Army will have to embrace the role. . . .
>
> The "asymmetric" strategy used by today's insurgents is as old as warfare itself, allowing a relatively weak force to tie down a stronger one by exploiting its vulnerabilities rather than meeting it head-on in conventional combat. In Iraq, insurgents do not engage in pitched battles against American armor or aircraft. Instead, they detonate makeshift but powerful roadside bombs when U.S. vehicles happen past, blow up cars near checkpoints and crowds, or hide snipers in Baghdad's alleys. Afterward, they spread their version of events on the Internet before U.S. government spokesmen can get to the microphones.
>
> "These conflicts," according to [Secretary of Defense Robert Gates, Rumsfeld's successor], "will be fundamentally political in nature. Success will be less a matter of imposing one's will and more a function of shaping behavior—of friends, adversaries, and most importantly, the people in between." . . . [According to the Army and Marine Corps field manual] the "center of gravity" in counterinsurgency is the mass of civilians that are not rigidly committed to either the insurgency or the state. Winning them over—rather than just killing insurgents—is the key to success.
>
> At the Command and General Staff College at Fort Leavenworth, where Army majors spend 10 months doing post-graduate work, the curriculum is also changing. Before the Iraq war, less than 20 percent of the course work was geared toward counterinsurgency; now roughly 60 percent is on that subject. . . . The focus of much of the training is on the humanities—history,

(continues)

(continued)

languages, and the like—which teachers and students at the school say are as important to soldiering as military sciences are. . . . An Army War College task force [recently reported] that "future wars will be won by leaders who can succeed at both lethal and non-lethal operations," with the latter skills including "statesmanship, governance, enterprise management, cultural awareness, [and] mental agility." (John M. Donnelly, "Small Wars, Big Changes," *CQ Weekly*, January 28, 2008.)

Donnelly's comments raise the following questions:

1. How "new" is the new face of war? Are we simply seeing a replay of what the United States experienced in the 1960s in Vietnam, when Washington tried unsuccessfully to engage in nation building and win the "hearts and minds" of the people? Or are recent conflicts qualitatively different? Do you think the above commentary underestimates the importance of traditional interstate wars and the continued need for the military to meet those potential challenges?

2. How easy or hard is nation building—promoting economic development, rebuilding highways, electrical grids, and other infrastructure, as well as building democratic institutions and strengthening courts and civil administration in developing countries? To the extent that an outside actor such as the United States engages in such activities, does it risk being accused of "occupation" and meddling in the internal affairs of another country?

3. An army general interviewed by Donnelly said that some officers are "very very uncomfortable" with the new directions called for in the field manual, since "they joined the Army to fight, to break things, to kill things." How compatible is the latter mission with the new mission?

4. Imagine yourself in the shoes of an American GI in Iraq who is part of an armored unit looking for someone identified as a terrorist leader suspected of murdering hundreds of men, women, and children. You receive information that the terrorist is hiding in a crowded apartment building within range of your artillery. You believe that you can eliminate the terrorist with one barrage, but you will also likely be killing dozens of innocent civilians in the process. What do you do? Killing civilians, aside from raising difficult moral and legal issues, is hardly likely to win hearts and minds; yet refraining from shooting will allow the terrorist to continue to terrorize the population.

5. On August 9, 2008, a newspaper headline screamed "Russia Invades Georgia." Three days later, another read: "As the Attacks on Georgia Continue, American and European Officials Wonder What Moscow's Actions Mean for World Politics." What do *you* think it meant? Although this had the appearance of a traditional interstate war, it was triggered by an internal conflict within Georgia, as Russia claimed it was coming to the aid of pro-Russian ethnic groups living in the Georgian regions of South Ossetia and Abkhazia, which had been seeking independence from the former Soviet republic. The subsequent hostilities resulted in hundreds of casualties before the conflict concluded with a cease-fire. Georgia had a McDonald's restaurant in its capital city of Tbilisi, and Russia had several McDonald's franchises in Moscow and throughout the country. How did this episode square with Thomas Friedman's "golden arches theory of war prevention" and with the general view in the IR literature that interstate war is becoming relatively rare?

Terrorism, which occupies a central place in the public consciousness today, deserves special treatment as a category of global violence.

Terrorism and Extrastate Violence

I have noted how "the long peace" exists alongside "the long war" (the U.S. Defense Department's name for the war on terrorism that was undertaken after 9/11). Although **terrorism** attracted special attention in the United States in the wake of the 9/11 attack on the World Trade Center, the phenomenon has a long history. The phenomenon can be traced at least as far back as the first century B.C., when Jews resisting Roman occupation of what is now Israel were called "zealots" to denote the ferocity of their random violence against Roman targets. The term "terrorism" itself owes to the "Reign of Terror" that followed the French Revolution in 1789. Walter Laqueur has noted that by 1900, with the rise of anarchist violence in Russia and other unconventional violence commonplace in other parts of the globe, terrorism had become "the leading preoccupation" of national leaders.[41]

However, he acknowledges that by 9/11, the nature and magnitude of the terrorism phenomenon had changed somewhat, as there seemed to be "new rules for an old game."[42] Although terrorism has been defined as "the substate application of violence or threatened violence intended to sow panic in a society, to weaken or even overthrow the incumbents, and to bring about political change," it is perhaps best thought of as "extrastate," given the fact that such violence increasingly has a transnational dimension, committed by actors organized across state boundaries.[43]

Scholars and policymakers do not agree on a clear definition of terrorism. One study notes that the term had at least 109 different definitions between 1936 and 1981, and many others have appeared since. The search for an authoritative definition has been likened to "the Quest for the Holy Grail."[44] In 1985, the UN General Assembly adopted a resolution that vaguely defined terrorism as any acts that "endanger or take innocent human lives, jeopardize fundamental freedoms, and seriously impair the dignity of human beings." The 2004 *Report of the Secretary-General's High-Level Panel on Threats, Challenges, and Change* defined terrorism as "any action . . . that is intended to cause death or serious bodily harm to civilians or non-combatants, when the purpose of such an act . . . is to intimidate." It is often said that one person's terrorist is another's freedom fighter. Although the United States has been quick to label groups such as Hamas and Hezbollah "terrorists," their supporters have used the term to characterize the American shock and awe aerial bombing over Baghdad in 2003, as well as Israeli attacks against Palestinians in the West Bank and Gaza. Even U.S. strategic bombing over Tokyo during World War II and the dropping of the A-bomb over Hiroshima and Nagasaki in 1945 have been called terrorism by some analysts. If terrorism exists in the eyes of the beholder, however, then any act of violence, however barbarous, can be excused and legitimized as long as someone invents a justification.

One simple, helpful definition considers terrorism "premeditated, politically motivated violence perpetrated against noncombatant targets by subnational groups
or clandestine agents, usually intended to influence an audience."[45] This definition suggests that terrorism entails a combination of at least three elements. First,
terrorism ordinarily involves the threat or use of *unconventional violence*—
violence that is spectacular, violates accepted social mores, and is designed to
shock so as to gain publicity and instill fear in the hope of extorting concessions.
Terrorists generally observe no rules of combat whatsoever. Their tactics can include bombings, hijackings, kidnappings, assassinations, and other acts. Flying
airplanes into office buildings (as in the case of 9/11), committing acts of piracy
at sea (as in the case of the 1985 hijacking of the *Achille Lauro* cruise ship in the
Mediterranean by four Palestinians seeking to gain the release of comrades held
in Israeli jails by holding 400 passengers hostage), and similar acts of savagery are
all part of the terrorist playbook.

Second, terrorism is characterized by violence that is *politically* motivated. The
political context of terrorism distinguishes it from mere criminal behavior such
as armed robbery or gangland slayings, which may be every bit as spectacular
but are driven primarily by nonpolitical motives. The Mafia, for example, is not
known as a terrorist organization, even though it is heavily involved in international drug trafficking and other criminal activities, at times in league with terrorist groups, prompting references to *narcoterrorism.* Most terrorist groups are
clearly motivated by political goals, ranging from the creation of a national homeland to the elimination of foreign cultural influence in a region to the total political and economic transformation of society.

A third key distinguishing characteristic of terrorism, following from the first
two, is the almost incidental nature of the *targets* against which violence is committed. The immediate targets of terrorism—whether persons or property, civilian or military—usually bear only an indirect relation to the larger aims impelling
the terrorist but are exploited for their shock potential. Sometimes the targets are
carefully chosen individuals (prominent business leaders or government officials), while on other occasions the targets are faceless, nondescript masses ran-
domly slaughtered in airports, department stores, and other public places. In
recent times, terrorism has been marked less by the political assassination of national leaders and more by the murder of ordinary men, women, and children.
There are gray areas. When suicide bombers damaged the USS *Cole* in a port in
Yemen in 2000, killing seventeen sailors, Washington deplored the attack as an act
of terrorism, as it did the many roadside bombings of American servicemen in
humvees during the Iraq War, even though the military nature of the targets arguably made them fair game as part of classic guerrilla warfare. When the explicit targets are civilians, or dozens of civilians are consciously and wantonly
sacrificed just to kill one soldier—in violation of the traditional laws of war
limiting civilian attacks to "military necessity"—there is far less question in calling this terrorism.

Osama bin Laden in Afghanistan in 1989: Is one man's terrorist another's national liberation hero?

AP Photo

A fourth component of terrorism has to do with the nature of the *perpetrators* of such violence. It can be argued, with some qualifications, that organized terrorism tends to be the work of nonstate actors: It is mainly the tactic of outgroups—the politically weak and frustrated (e.g., al Qaeda and other Islamic fundamentalists throughout the Middle East and South Asia, the Irish Republican Army (IRA) in Northern Ireland, Shining Path in Peru, or Basque separatists in Spain)—who see terror as the best tool for contesting the sizable armies and police forces of the governments of nation-states. Although certain excessive forms of violence used by government authorities themselves are sometimes referred to as "state terrorism"— in particular the systematic torture and repression a government inflicts on dissidents within its own society, or assassinations and "dirty tricks" committed by secret state agencies abroad—the terrorism label normally does not apply to actions taken by official government bodies. Terrorists generally do not wear uniforms, although many in the past have been indirectly supported and sponsored by governments.[46]

Among the most high-profile terrorist incidents recently, in addition to the 9/11 attack in New York City, were the nerve gas attack in a crowded Tokyo subway in 1995 (when the Japanese Aum Shinrikyo cult succeeded in killing 12 persons and injuring 5,500 others); the bombing of 4 trains in Madrid, Spain, in 2004 that took the lives of some 200 commuters and wounded 1,400 others (thought to be the work of either Basque separatists or al Qaeda); the 2004 killing of 331 people, including 150 children, in a schoolhouse in Beslan, Russia (by militants supporting Chechen independence); and the simultaneous attacks on several luxury hotels in Mumbai, India, in 2008, killing over 150 people and wounding hundreds more (traced to a Pakistani group).

In Chapter 3, we considered rational actor models of state behavior. Do terrorists act rationally? It is hard to understand what motivates people to commit the above acts or to strap hundreds of pounds of explosives to their bodies and then detonate themselves in a crowded marketplace, as has happened frequently in Israeli cities. While such behavior usually entails an element of planning and calculation tied to specific goals that terrorists seek to achieve—"most terrorism is neither crazed nor capricious"[47]—it also usually reflects extreme frustrations and hatreds, at times linked to indoctrination programs conducted by terrorist networks.

Anecdotal accounts of terrorism can distort the magnitude of the terrorism problem. So too can data-based analysis, since the definitional and counting procedures used by researchers can skew the statistical findings considerably. Between 1980 and 2002, based on the procedures used by the U.S. Department of State in its annual *Patterns of Global Terrorism* publication, the world averaged approximately 500 acts of international terrorism a year, peaking at 666 incidents in 1987, and then generally declining to 205 in 2002.[48] Overall, of the roughly 5,000 international terrorist attacks between 1989 and 2003, the regions with the largest number of incidents were Europe (26 percent) and Latin America (34 percent), while the regions with the fewest were Africa (5 percent), Asia (15 percent), and North America (which, aside from 9/11, saw virtually no cases). However, U.S. government findings changed dramatically after 9/11, when a broadened definition was used by a new tracking agency, the National Counterterrorism Center (NCTC), which reported more than a 40 percent increase in the incidence of terrorism from 2005 to 2007, including thousands of incidents in Iraq. Moreover, another government-funded data collection center, the Memorial Institute for the Prevention of Terror (MIPT), noted the growing lethality of terrorism, reporting the annual death toll rising 450 percent between 1998 and 2006, again including Iraq figures. One commentator has said, "Including Iraq massively skews the analysis. In the NCTC and MIPT data, Iraq accounts for 80 percent of all deaths counted. But if you set aside the war there, terrorism has in fact gone way down over the past five years."[49] Indeed, several analysts have argued that the al Qaeda threat and associated terrorist threats have been exaggerated and have largely subsided, although many others question such rosy conclusions.[50]

It is encouraging that some terrorist groups have been eliminated (e.g., the jailing of the Red Brigades, who terrorized Italy in the 1970s, including the kidnapping and murder of former Italian prime minister Aldo Moro) or have agreed to cease their mayhem (e.g., the IRA, whose members had committed numerous acts of violence in Northern Ireland over several decades before recently consenting to join a peace process). The "war on terror" may well wind down, but it is unlikely it will ever end in terms of humanity catching "the last terrorist." The threat can never be completely terminated, only managed. The reality is that modern industrial society remains especially susceptible to nightmarish scenarios, given such inviting targets as jumbo jets, giant skyscrapers, nuclear power stations, electronic grids, and computer networks. Modern communications technology gives terrorists instant publicity through the world's mass media and can contribute to an epidemic effect worldwide, in addition to enabling terrorists to coordinate their efforts across regions. In the past it was assumed that "terrorists want a lot of people watching and a lot of people listening and not a lot of people dead," although that assumption may be open to question given the growing lethality of terrorist attacks.[51] Most worrisome is the rising number of religious-based terrorist groups, who, contrary to the above assumption, appear to prefer a lot of people "dead" to a lot "watching." They could possibly acquire access to weapons of mass destruction through "loose nukes" smuggled from the former Soviet Union, where many nuclear facilities lack adequate security, or through other avenues.[52]

Of course, "the best way to keep weapons and weapons-material out of the hands of nongovernmental entities is to keep them out of the hands of national governments."[53] In 1998, U.S. secretary of state Madeleine Albright, "citing the increasing threat to civil aviation posed by shoulder-fired surface-to-air missiles," issued a call for "an international agreement to place tighter controls on the export of such portable, easily concealed weapons."[54] Of even greater concern are concealed weapons in the form of bags of plutonium, vials of anthrax and Ebola virus, canisters of nerve gas, and the like. In engaging in arms control efforts covering everything from small arms and shoulder-fired surface-to-air missiles to nuclear-tipped ICBMs, the international community today is continuing a long tradition in the Westphalian state system, that is, pursuing humanity's quest to fulfill the biblical prophecy that nations "shall beat their swords into plowshares, and their spears into pruninghooks . . . neither shall they learn war any more" (Isaiah 2:4). We will examine such efforts, as well as other roads to a safer, more peaceful world, later in this book. Meanwhile, what can we conclude about whether the world has become more peaceful or more warlike?

Has the World Become More Peaceful or More Warlike?

What should the reader take away from the above discussion of trends in the use of armed force? Based on the statistical record, there is reason to be both hopeful and concerned about the future level of violence on the planet. On the one hand, there has been no war on a global scale for well over a generation, and the frequency of interstate war in general has greatly diminished. Even taking into account intrastate war, Gregg Easterbrook, citing the research of several scholars associated with the end of war literature, sees significant progress:

> War has entered a cycle of decline. Combat in Iraq and in a few other places is an exception to a significant global trend that has gone nearly unnoticed—namely that, for about 15 years, there have been steadily fewer armed conflicts worldwide. In fact, it is possible that a person's chance of dying because of war has, in the last decade or more, become the lowest in human history.[55]

Likewise, Fareed Zakaria asserts: "Their data show that wars of all kinds have been declining since the mid-1980s and that we are now at the lowest levels of global violence since the 1950s. . . . Harvard's polymath professor Steven Pinker has ventured to speculate that we are probably living 'in the most peaceful time of our species' existence.'"[56] Yet another writer, Nils Gleditsch, concludes: "Overall, there is a clear decline of war" as the world has been "climbing down from a peak of armed violence in the middle of the twentieth century."[57]

On the other hand, the authors of another empirical study that examines all modes of warfare find that their data reveal "a disquieting constancy in warfare and hint at patterns of interchangeability or substitutability among the types of war."[58] Similarly, Worldwatch's *Vital Signs 2007–2008*, relying on a different study, reports "Number of Violent Conflicts Steady."[59] Even *The Human Security Report* adds that "the post-Cold War years have been marked by major humanitarian emergencies, gross abuses of human rights, war crimes, and ever deadlier acts of terrorism. The risk of new wars breaking out . . . or old ones resuming . . . is very real in the absence of a sustained and strengthened commitment to conflict prevention."[60] The contrasting findings of scholars reflect different analytical and coding procedures used by different researchers but also testify to the complexity of the war phenomenon today. In any event, future efforts to reduce the violence worldwide will require "a sustained and strengthened commitment to conflict prevention." Such efforts in turn require a better understanding of the causes of war.

THE CAUSES OF WAR

In investigating the causes of war, it is not so much the immediate triggers we are interested in as the larger conditions that underlie the resort to arms; in other words, we are interested more in the kindling wood than the actual spark that ignites a conflict. For example, it is well known that World War I was precipitated by the assassination of Archduke Franz Ferdinand, the heir to the Austro-Hungarian throne, in June 1914, in Sarajevo by a Bosnian Serb nationalist seeking to strike a blow against the Austrian empire. Austria issued an ultimatum to Serbia and then made a declaration of war, which activated a set of alliances and led to a chain reaction of war declarations by other European countries (Germany supporting Austria, and Russia, Britain, and France supporting Serbia). This all occurred against the backdrop of not only rival alliance systems but also rising nationalism in European societies, growing colonial competition between them, arms races, and internal political unrest, all of which fueled feelings of insecurity and tension. It is these broad, contextual variables, more so than the direct, proximate cause of World War I—the archduke's assassination—that concern us here. I want to focus less on *how* any one specific war started and more on *why* it and other such conflicts arose, that is, with uncovering patterns of causation across several cases that might allow us to develop understandings about war in general.

In Chapter 1, I noted that scholars of international relations attempt to develop theories that can explain the dynamics of world politics and then test these theories against hard evidence. No subject has undergone more theorizing and testing than war. Much of the IR literature is concerned with interstate war, but the theories relate to other dimensions of global violence as well. Despite volumes written on this subject, scholars still do not know for sure exactly which factors, individually or in combination with each other, are the main reasons war occurs and how they can be brought under control, although we can at least contemplate a range of causal factors that appear to be relevant to why people fight.

As with the determinants of foreign policy behavior in general (Chapter 3), it is useful to focus on *individual, nation-state,* and *international system* levels of analysis in considering theories about the causes of war. These levels correspond to the three "images" found in Waltz's *Man, the State, and War.*[61]

Complex linkages across all three levels often account for the occurrence of a given war. For example, as suggested above, World War I has been attributed to a variety of factors operating at the individual, national, and international levels. At the individual level, it has been called the "war nobody wanted," as it seemed to result from spiraling misperceptions of aggressive intentions held by European leaders on the eve of war.[62] Historians have especially found fault with Kaiser Wilhelm II of Germany, who had fired the statesmanlike chancellor Otto von Bismarck in 1890 and clumsily pursued a militaristic policy, antagonizing the British in particular. Wilhelm has been described as "a blusterer, a weak man who was extremely emotional." As for other leaders at the time, Franz Josef of Austria was "a tired old man who was putty in the hands of . . . Count Berchtold, the duplicitous foreign minister. . . . In Russia, Czar Nicholas II was an isolated autocrat . . . served by incompetent foreign and defense ministers and was strongly influenced by his sickly and neurotic wife." Joseph Nye concludes that "personality did make a difference. There was something about the leaders . . . that made them significant contributory causes of the war."[63] However, Nye is quick to cite other factors as well. At the state level, one can point to ethnopolitical tensions in Austria and the Balkan countries, along with the domestic political challenges to the Coalition of Rye and Iron that had ruled Germany for decades and was attempting to fan the flames of nationalism as an alternative to democratic reform. International system-level factors were perhaps the most important, namely the rise of German power, the naval arms race between Germany and Britain, and the increased polarization and rigidity of the alliance systems that rendered balance of power politics less feasible.[64] Of course, we have the benefit of hindsight in understanding the sources of World War I. When German chancellor Bethmann Hollweg was asked shortly after the outbreak of the war "how it all happened," he could only reply, "Oh, if I only knew!"[65]

Our knowledge about war has improved considerably since the Great War, as many studies have been done that enable us to compare World War I with other wars and discern similarities and differences. Let us survey some of the leading causal explanations of war that have been examined at each of the three levels of analysis, starting with the individual level.[66]

Individual-Level Explanations

Some scholars argue that war simply is grounded in *human nature*. Some students of animal behavior (ethologists) see aggression as an innate, instinctual trait of the species, while others (sociobiologists) see it as deriving from evolutionary, Darwinian natural selection processes. It has been said that *Homo sapiens* is one of the rare species whose members kill one another. The psychiatrist Sigmund Freud also viewed war as the inevitable product of humans' psychological makeup. Even some versions of realist theory (particularly classical realism) assume a universal drive for power that translates automatically into competition and war.[67] If such theories are correct and violence is ingrained in the human psyche, there is not much that can be done to reduce man's proclivity toward war. Fortunately the bulk of the evidence runs counter to these views. At the very least, we can say that not all individuals and not all societies are equally violent, as relatively few people commit murder or assault their neighbors, and there are some states that have not engaged in hostilities within memory. Indeed, cooperation is far more common than deadly conflict. Moreover, there is evidence that, just as such long-standing human institutions as slavery and dueling have been "unlearned," so too new norms may develop that make warfare less acceptable. In 1986 several major professional associations representing natural and social scientists on five continents issued the Seville Statement denying the validity of claims that "we have inherited a tendency to make war from our animal ancestors" and that war "is genetically programmed into our human nature."

Even if the human race as a whole is not predisposed toward war, some members may be more inclined toward belligerence than others, based on personality type, gender, or other variables of the sort mentioned in Chapter 3. When these individuals are found in leadership positions in nation-states, the possibilities of their states becoming involved in war increase. I noted earlier that scholars working mainly (although not exclusively) out of the feminist paradigm have hypothesized that *gender* is a key variable—women are more pacifist than men, owing to both physiological factors (the lesser amounts of aggression-inducing testosterone and other related hormones in females) and social-cultural factors (childhood socialization processes and maternal role assignments that promote more nurturing attitudes than those exhibited by males, whose upbringing traditionally has cultivated a "breadwinner" and "warrior as hero" mentality along with more competitive impulses).[68] However, as I also noted earlier, there is little empirical evidence to support the proposition that women are more peaceful than men and that hence female leaders are less prone to war. We have been reminded of this as women increasingly have joined the ranks of suicide bombers, something once thought highly unlikely. As one scholar states, "Both biologically and anthropologically, there is no firm evidence connecting women's caregiving functions (pregnancy and nursing) with any particular kind of behavior such as reconciliation or nonviolence."[69]

What about the importance of *personality* type in the war equation? I made reference to Woodrow Wilson's "authoritarian personality" and the personal characteristics of Josef Stalin and other prominent figures in Chapter 3, and noted above Joseph Nye's characterization of several World War I leaders. Although leadership personality can certainly have a bearing on war decisions, there is no clear empirical evidence that has established such a linkage (aside from anecdotal examples).[70] Many scholars contend that personality traits of individual leaders are less important than the situations leaders find themselves in and the nature of the decision-making processes—groupthink, the misapplication of lessons of history, and the like—that often result in widespread *misperceptions* leading to war. Especially when leaders are under stress, as in crisis situations, there is a tendency to stereotype the enemy and engage in either worst-case thinking (exaggerating the threat) or best-case thinking (being overly optimistic of victory should war break out). Prospect theory suggests that a willingness to take risks has less to do with idiosyncratic risk-taking propensities of individual leaders than with whether what is at stake is the gain or loss of something valued, the assumption being that greater risks are entertained in the latter instance, when defending against loss rather than adding to existing assets.[71]

Still others argue that war, and violence in general, is often the product of anger, frustration, and raw emotions having to do with feelings of deprivation, especially relative to what others have or what one has come to expect.[72] Whole nations can experience anger or resentment contributing to interstate war, as with pre–World War I Germany feeling slighted as an aspiring great power seeking respect from Britain and pre–World War II Germany feeling embittered over the humiliating Treaty of Versailles that followed World War I. Ted Gurr has applied the theory of "revolutions of rising expectations" to the outbreak of rebellion and civil war, finding that the most likely candidates for internal strife are not necessarily the worst-off societies but those with a degree of political or economic progress that has stalled or been dashed by a subsequent setback.[73] Today, many people in the Third World are arguably better off than decades ago, yet their own recent improvement understandably makes them restless for greater well-being, while their exposure to television and the Internet makes them all the more sensitive to how much better others are doing around the globe. This does not mean that a wave of global violence is on the horizon—not all people and societies with grievances, real or perceived, resort to violence—but it does legitimize the concerns of those seeking to reduce oppression and poverty.

The political and economic characteristics of a country are state-level variables discussed in greater detail below. Contrary to those who see war, particularly interstate war, as a kind of spasmodic, emotional response flowing from anger or frustration, others view it as based on rational calculation, as leaders attempt to calculate the expected utility of going to war versus not going to war. Bruce

Bueno de Mesquita has pointed out that, out of fifty-eight interstate wars identified between 1815 and 1974, the attacking nation won forty-two.[74] It would appear that states do not go into war out of a blind rage, but compute the odds of success. However, an important qualifier must be added here. Although the data from the Correlates of War project show that roughly 80 percent of all the wars occurring between 1815 and 1910 were *won* by the initiators, three-fifths of the wars fought between 1910 and 1965 were *lost* by the initiators.[75] Ruth Sivard has observed that "the chances of the starter being victorious are shrinking. In the 1980s only 18 percent of the starters were winners."[76] The two Persian Gulf wars and other conflicts since 1990 have shown war initiation often to be a dubious enterprise. Whether due to miscalculation or other factors, aggression has paid less and less over time.

Indeed, given the increased severity of wars in the twentieth century, the costs of war have been outweighing the benefits lately, even to the "winners." A nation has been called the largest unit that one is willing to die for, but this may be changing. Many liberals and constructivists would argue that war is no longer a rational way of pursuing goals, if it ever was.

State-Level Explanations

To the extent government leaders base war decisions on rational calculations, they calculate not only the costs and benefits for their country but also for themselves.[77] In some *types of political systems*—namely, democracies—they need to factor in electoral consequences. As Winston Churchill discovered after World War II and George H.W. Bush after the First Gulf War, even if you win a war, you can lose power at home. Liberal thinkers from Kant to the present have assumed democracies are more peaceful than dictatorships, precisely because leaders in democratic systems are held more accountable for their decisions, and wars are thought to be generally unpopular with mass publics. It has been suggested that demographic changes in the form of smaller family sizes (families in industrialized countries now average two children compared with five or more in the past) have made publics even less willing than previously to endure the pain of losing sons and daughters to battle.[78] Still, replacing the military draft with all-volunteer armies in most democracies has somewhat cushioned that effect.

I noted in Chapter 3 that no strong correlation has been found between type of government and war participation; democracies have not proven to be decidedly more peaceful than dictatorships.[79] What liberals can point to, however, is the validity of the democratic peace hypothesis, that democracies do not fight other democracies. They virtually never go to war with each other and rarely engage in militarized disputes in which they allow disagreements to escalate to the threatened use of force against one another. At most, one or two exceptions can be found, such as democratic Finland fighting alongside Nazi Germany against the Allies during the early stages of World War II (although this owed to the fact that Finland feared Russia more than Germany) and democratic Britain and Iceland engaging in a "cod war" during the 1970s (when Britain protested Iceland's extension of its exclusive fishing zone out to 200 miles and imposition of limits on the British cod catch in the North Atlantic, resulting in the two countries' naval vessels exchanging a few shots and rammings). Whether due to the special unpopularity of fighting a sister democracy or other factors, the democratic peace proposition is as well proven as any generalization in the IR field.[80] Does this mean that there would be no more war if the entire world were democratic? We can only speculate about such a development; liberals would see hopeful possibilities, whereas realists would remain skeptical.

A state-level variable that has attracted much attention in the war literature over the years is the *degree of internal political instability*, as measured by unpopularity of a country's leadership, rioting, protests, economic unemployment, or other such indicators. Based on the assumption that "nothing ties together the in-group bonds [like] an out-group threat,"[81] the scapegoat (diversionary war) hypothesis posits that the greater the instability in a country, the more prone to war the leadership is likely to be, in terms of pursuing a hostile foreign policy aimed at diverting citizen attention from domestic problems and regime criticism by producing a rally-round-the-flag effect.[82] As suggested in the *Wag the Dog* movie, such pressures can operate in democracies no less than nondemocracies.[83] Rudolph Rummel tested the hypothesis against historical data and found "foreign conflict behavior is generally and completely unrelated to domestic conflict behavior."[84] Subsequent studies have reached similar conclusions, finding little empirical support for the relationship, even if some anecdotal examples can be cited. As one author says, "Seldom has so much common sense in theory found so little support in practice."[85] The logic here may be that there are just as many reasons for a precarious leadership to avoid war as to provoke one, given that it may not be an optimal time to take a country into war when it is experiencing disunity or economic problems.

Almost as much studied as type of political system as a war determinant is *type of economic system*. Marxists are more interested in the economic organization of the state than the political organization, believing that the political structures of a society simply reflect the dominant economic interests. Marxists have long held that capitalist states are prone to war, since their exploitation of the working class leads to underconsumption at home. Workers are not paid enough to purchase the goods produced by their country's factories, which explains the felt need to find overseas markets. To the extent that a capitalist economy can sustain prosperity at home, it supposedly requires large standing armies and arms industries (military-industrial complexes) that tend to put societies on a war footing. In addition, capitalist states seek even cheaper labor abroad as well as access to raw materials to fuel industrialization. These expansionist impulses, Marxists contend, inevitably bring capitalist states into competition with each other, as happened with the scramble for foreign colonies, which in turn leads to war, as with World War I (which Lenin, the father of the communist revolution in Russia, attributed to British, French, and German capitalism).[86] World War I could conceivably be interpreted in this light but hardly World War II, which found the Soviet Union and the capitalists on the same side. Since World War II, capitalist states have mostly cooperated with one another.

Although radical theories help explain colonialism and imperialism, they are less convincing in explaining warfare. The relevance of type of economic system to war making is questionable. War preceded both capitalism and communism in history. More to the point, there is no evidence that communist or socialist states have been less war prone than capitalist states. Marxist theory has simplistically assumed that all capitalist elites benefit from and therefore support war decisions by their governments, whereas in fact some capitalist elements of a society may benefit from war while others suffer along with workers. Indeed, liberals, relying on the market-oriented free trade theories of Adam Smith, argue that capitalist states are likely to be *less* war prone than socialist states, given the growing commercial interdependence among states and the potentially adverse, disruptive effects of war on business, which can include declining exports, unreliable supply chains, increased inflation, and other disadvantages. One study concludes, "Social science research largely supports the link between trade and peace. The more any two states trade with each other, the less likely they are to experience wars or militarized disputes."[87] Although economic interdependence is a system-level variable, economic openness is a nation-state-level variable. While the empirical data must be interpreted with care, there is considerable evidence that open economies, which by definition expand trade and investment, do contribute to reducing interstate conflict.[88]

Realists, in contrast to both Marxist and liberal thinkers, would add their usual caution against exaggerating the importance of state-level factors. They tend to dismiss differences between capitalist and socialist states, since they mainly see war making in all states as a function of strategic national interest calculations. Internal developments may impact foreign policy, but the state's political and economic organization is not seen as a major determinant; due to a growing population and economy requiring increased raw materials and other resources, capitalist and noncapitalist states alike may experience "lateral pressures" resulting in aggressive foreign policies.[89]

International System-Level Explanations

To realists, the inherently anarchic character of the international system invites conflict, including war. However, realists acknowledge that some types of international systems may be more war prone than others, although there is disagreement as to which ones are the most unstable. Earlier I noted the distinction between balance of power realists and hegemonic realists, both of whom focus on the importance of system-level variables such as *polarity* and *polarization* but reach different conclusions about how the *distribution of power* impacts war.[90]

There is a perennial debate in the IR field over whether a concentration of power in the international system is conducive to war or peace. Hegemonic theorists such as Robert Gilpin posit that *unipolar* systems are the most stable and peaceful, since the dominant state is able to deter the expansionist ambitions of others and helps to maintain order and manage the global system through getting others to accept rules and norms governing the world economy, arms control, and other matters, as some argue the Pax Americana did after World War II when the United States enjoyed economic primacy. Others, such as Kenneth Waltz and John Mearsheimer, contend that it was a *bipolar* system after World War II—dominated by the two superpower Cold War rivals—that helped avert systemwide war, since the division of the world into two roughly equal armed blocs riveted the attention of states, especially the bloc leaders, on avoiding what could have been a catastrophic global war; the concentration of power in the hands of only two actors made it relatively simple to balance power and coordinate mutual deterrence, compared to the greater complexity and potential for accidental war if the system would have had multiple poles (as on the eve of World War I). Critics of this view make the point that it was probably nuclear weapons more than the bipolar structure of the system that accounted for the absence of superpower hostilities. Such critics worry about the heightened antagonisms and rigidities of bipolarity and argue that a *multipolar* system of several powers is more stable, since it provides more options for flexible balancing through alliance shifting.[91]

What may matter more than the distribution of power in the international system is the dynamics of great-power rivalries. **Power transition theory**, an offshoot of hegemonic realism, warns that great-power transitions pose the greatest danger, since the probability of a major war is greatest at the moment when a stagnant or declining lead state is being overtaken by an ascendant challenger, as either the challenger will be tempted to start a war in order to achieve an enhanced status commensurate with its increased military power or the fading lead state will start a war as a last-gasp effort to retain its own status and block the challenger.[92] Such a theory assumes that the chances of war occurring increase as the gap in power, especially military capability, narrows.

Recall the puzzle posed by John Ikenberry—whether China's rise as a great power in the twenty-first century will put it on a collision course with the United States in a bid for global leadership, or whether such a power transition can be managed peaceably. Although it is true that "rapid shifts in the global distribution of military power *have* often preceded outbursts of aggression," there is nothing inevitable about this pattern.[93] While Germany's challenge to Britain in the early twentieth century did coincide with the onset of World War I, the American challenge to the declining British Empire after World War II did not result in war. Moreover, it is uncertain how the power transition theory relates to the U.S.-Chinese competition, not only because China lags behind the United States militarily but also because the inhibitions against great-power war are much greater today than in the past. Economic growth in China, as well as Russia, may well facilitate increased arms spending by those countries and increased aspirations of global dominance, as has happened with other newly prosperous states in the past. But it could also lead to a dampening appetite for war, as Thomas Friedman has suggested with his golden arches theory of conflict prevention. (Two of the largest McDonald's restaurants in the world are in Moscow, near Lenin's tomb, and in Beijing, near Mao's portrait on Tiananmen Square.)

Closely related to power transition theory is **long-cycle theory**, which attributes the recurrence of global wars over the past five centuries to uneven rates of economic development and the rise and fall of great powers. The theory holds that major wars result in the appearance of a single hegemon that presides over the international system until economic or other weaknesses (partly tied to the burdens of hegemony and "imperial overstretch") begin to erode its power, making it vulnerable to a new challenger, with global war then producing a new leadership structure that dominates world politics until the next round of power decay and warfare. Among the hegemons (or near hegemons, at least in terms of disproportionate sea power) cited by long-cycle theorists have been Portugal and the Netherlands (at the beginning of the state system in the sixteenth and seventeenth centuries), Great Britain (in the eighteenth and nineteenth centuries), and the United States (after World War II). George Modelski and others find war cycles following a rhythm of roughly 100 years or so, with a "general war" breaking out approximately once every century.[94] According to long-cycle theory, the long peace since World War II may merely be a temporary lull in fighting. Again, though, it remains unclear whether American power is in decline and, if so, whether the current long peace will be shattered by another major war that serves as the engine for system change and the establishment of a new hegemonic order. Also in question is whether hegemony is even a meaningful term today, given the growing ambiguity of power (Chapter 2).

Power relationships can be examined not only at the systemwide level but also in terms of *dyads*. Put simply, are wars more likely to occur between unequals, as balance of power theorists contend, or between equals, as hegemonic theorists suggest? The logic of the former is that, if two sides are equal, neither will feel confident in starting a war, since they cannot be assured of victory; the logic of the latter is that, if one side has a preponderance of power, war will not occur, since "the weaker *dare* not fight and the stronger *need* not" use force to get its way as threats alone should suffice.[95] Which is it that silences war drums—a balance of power or a preponderance of power? Most recent research supports the preponderance hypothesis,[96] although the findings are somewhat mixed. As a general rule, states that have the greatest disparity in power are the least likely to fight each other. Still, history is replete with examples of power imbalances accompanying warfare—either the stronger state issuing demands too excessive for the weaker party to meet and thereby forcing a fight or, at times, the weaker state committing an act of aggression, due to misperception or domestic political pressures or other factors.

Even if superior power does not necessarily prevent war, does it at least translate into victory should war occur? As the question is sometimes framed, is God on the side of the biggest battalions? Bruce Bueno de Mesquita found that the side with the greatest power on paper (as measured by total military and economic resources) did prevail in 75 percent of all the interstate wars between 1815 and 1974.[97] However, it bears emphasizing that the side with the largest army and arsenal does not inevitably win all wars, especially in more recent times, as the American and Soviet experiences in Vietnam and Afghanistan and other cases demonstrate. As seen in the 2003 Iraq War, what might appear to be a quick, easy victory can prove elusive due to the enemy resorting to asymmetrical warfare that neutralizes superior conventional firepower.

One other system-level variable is worth mentioning as a cause of war—**arms races**. Arms races can lead to war, with adversaries driven to match or exceed each other in armaments to protect their respective national security or enhance their position in the world, thereby escalating tension and insecurity (the aforementioned "security dilemma"). Rather than deterring an attack, as the "peace through strength" slogan suggests, an arms buildup can create such paranoia as to provoke a preemptive strike or larger war, as happened in the case of the German-British naval arms race preceding World War I. The link between arms races and war is a complicated one, partly because arms races may be more a symptom than a cause of tension between two or more countries.[98] "Men do not fight because they have arms. They have arms because they deem it necessary to fight."[99]

We saw in the previous chapter on diplomacy that, if one is trying to avoid war, there is a delicate balance one must strike between too much saber rattling and not enough. Although British prime minister Neville Chamberlain will forever be remembered for the latter—for appeasing Hitler at Munich in 1938, emboldening the German leader to make the fateful decision to invade Poland that triggered World War II in 1939—one can sympathize with the quandary Chamberlain was experiencing, as poignantly expressed in his own recollections of the interwar period:

> When I think of four terrible years [1914–1918] and I think of the 7,000,000 young men who were cut off in their prime, the 13,000,000 who were maimed and mutilated, the misery and the suffering of the mothers and fathers, the sons and daughters, and the relatives and friends of those who were killed and wounded, then I am bound to say again what I have said before . . . in war, whichever side may call itself victor, there are no winners, but all are losers. It is these thoughts which have made me feel that it was my prime duty to strain every nerve to avoid repetition of the Great War in Europe.[100]

As costly as war was in Chamberlain's day, it is even more so today. As has been commonly pointed out, in the event of a major war today "the survivors might envy the dead." Based on our analysis of the causes of war, what, then, can be done to address these causes and to increase the prospects of avoiding war?

National Archives Photo No. 111-SC-212342

Survivors of the atomic bomb at Hiroshima, 1945

THE CAUSES OF PEACE:
APPROACHES TO WORLD ORDER

To the extent that arms races are a harbinger of war, then **arms control** may provide a solution to that problem. Arms control is an effort to limit in some fashion the testing, production, possession, deployment, and use of weapons. It can include *cuts* in arsenals (e.g., the START agreement on nuclear weapons negotiated by the United States and the Soviet Union during the Reagan era), *freezes* in existing stockpiles (e.g., the nuclear freeze movement promoted by peace activists in the United States and elsewhere in the 1970s and 1980s), or the establishment of *ceilings* that allow increases in certain kinds of armaments up to a point (e.g., the SALT talks on nuclear weapons held between the United States and the Soviet Union during the Nixon era). **Disarmament**—the total elimination of weapons—is far more ambitious and far less achievable.

The logic of arms control is that it can reduce the danger of war not only by removing some of the instruments of war, but, more importantly, by opening up channels of communication, developing confidence-building attitudes, and reducing mutual insecurity through the very process of forging and verifying arms agreements. The example often cited is the Rush-Bagot Agreement of 1817, one of the oldest and most successful arms control pacts in history, by which the United States and Great Britain agreed to demilitarize the American-Canadian border and the Great Lakes, paving the way for long-term peaceful relations between those countries.

Arms control is one approach to world order. Many others flow from the analysis in the previous section. As we have seen, different paradigms highlight different causal factors related to war, implying different solutions to the problem. Realists, with their theories about the balance and preponderance of power, focus on the wise management of power; but critics note that the balance of power has proven an unreliable antidote to war, and few states are happy with the alternative idea of elevating one state to hegemon over the entire international system. Marxists seek a radical change in global economic relations that dismantles capitalist systems and redistributes wealth from rich to poor states and people; but aside from the unreality of such a scenario, there is no evidence that socialism is any better than capitalism as a cure for war. Feminists want to see more women in positions of leadership; while this is a noble goal, there is little empirical evidence to indicate that states led by women will necessarily be more pacific than those run by men. Constructivists hope humanity has reached the stage where new antiwar norms have been internalized along the lines that have made slavery and colonialism unacceptable; although it is encouraging that in most countries what used to be called "war departments" are now called "defense departments," thinkers from Ralph Waldo Emerson to Alfred Nobel have been predicting for centuries that war was on its "last legs," only to be disappointed.

What is somewhat promising, and worth dwelling on here, is the *liberal* theory of peace, which consists of three legs: (1) the widening of the democratic peace, (2) the growth of free trade and economic interdependence, and (3) the development of international institutions in the form of international organizations and law.[101] Liberals have taken Immanuel Kant's idealist vision articulated in his 1795 book, *Perpetual Peace*, and have tried to provide empirical grounding for the theory. I have already noted the considerable empirical evidence supporting the first two legs. Even if they are not panaceas, the expansion of democracy and economic prosperity tied to trade do offer hopeful possibilities, not only in reducing interstate war but also the other dimensions of global violence, including civil war and terrorism. They are worthwhile goals in their own right, in addition to promoting peace. In the next chapter, I will examine the third leg, the development of international institutions through international organization and law. Where realists seize on the anarchic nature of the international system and the absence of any central authority that can regulate the use of armed force as the core cause of so much violence throughout the history of international relations, and see only limited prospects for ameliorating this problem, liberals envision a way out of the resultant security dilemma through international institution-building.

Karl Deutsch many years ago introduced the concept of a **security community**—the existence of a group of states among which the resort to violence is no longer a serious option for pursuing goals or resolving disputes.[102] The United States and Canada, along with (amazingly, given their record of recurrent warfare during the course of the nineteenth and twentieth centuries) France and Germany, are considered security communities today. They have disagreements on a variety of issues, but it is virtually unthinkable that these conflicts could eventuate in war between them. If states can learn habits of cooperation in solving economic and other problems, it is conceivable that a much wider, perhaps even global, security community could develop in the future. The search for community evidenced by the creation of the United Nations and other international organizations would seem to offer at least a ray of hope as an approach to world order, a subject to which we now turn.

QUESTIONS FOR STUDY AND DISCUSSION

1. Is the world becoming more prone to war, or less? Discuss trends in planetary violence, including "the long peace" and "the long war."
2. Could a military operation like D-Day happen again?
3. It is said that "one person's terrorist is another's national liberation hero." Discuss.
4. Which level of analysis—the individual level, nation-state level, or international system level—seems to offer the best explanations of why wars occur?
5. Based on the "democratic peace" hypothesis, if every country in the world were democratic, we might well witness the total elimination of war. What do you think?
6. Thomas Friedman's "golden arches theory of war prevention" assumes no two countries with a McDonald's restaurant will fight one another, suggesting that humanity will lose its stomach for war once Big Macs are available in every country. Is there anything to this theory?
7. What is more likely to prevent war, a balance of power between disputants or a preponderance of power by one side?

SUGGESTIONS FOR FURTHER READING

Robert J. Art and Kenneth N. Waltz, eds., *The Use of Force: Military Power and International Relations*, 7th ed. (Boulder, CO: Rowman & Littlefield, 2009).
Geoffrey Blainey, *The Causes of War*, 3rd ed. (New York: Free Press, 1988).
Joshua Goldstein, *War and Gender* (Cambridge: Cambridge University Press, 2001).
Ted Gurr and Barbara Harff, *Ethnic Conflict in World Politics*, 2nd ed. (Boulder, CO: Westview, 2004).
Bruce Hoffman, *Inside Terrorism* (New York: Columbia University Press, 1998).
K. J. Holsti, *Peace and War: Armed Conflicts and International Order, 1648–1989* (Cambridge: Cambridge University Press, 1989).
Walter Laqueur, "Postmodern Terrorism," *Foreign Affairs*, September 1996, 24–36.
Jack S. Levy, "War and Peace," in Walter Carlsnaes et al., eds., *Handbook of International Relations* (Thousand Oaks, CA: Sage, 2002).
Marie Lounsbery and Frederic Pearson, *Civil Wars* (Toronto: University of Toronto Press, 2009).

Edward Luttwak, "Toward Post-Heroic Warfare," *Foreign Affairs*, May 1995, 109–122.

John Mueller, *Retreat from Doomsday: The Obsolescence of Major War* (New York: Basic, 1989).

Joseph S. Nye, *Understanding International Conflicts*, 7th ed. (New York: Pearson, 2009), chaps. 2–5.

James Lee Ray, "The Abolition of Slavery and the End of International War," *International Organization* 43 (Summer 1989): 405–440.

Bruce M. Russett and John Oneal, *Triangulating Peace* (New York: Norton, 2001).

Melvin Small and J. David Singer, "Patterns in International Warfare, 1816–1980," in *International War: An Anthology* (Homewood, IL: Dorsey, 1985).

John G. Stoessinger, *Why Nations Go to War*, 10th ed. (Belmont, CA: Wadsworth, 2008).

John A. Vasquez, *The War Puzzle* (Cambridge: Cambridge University Press, 1993).

Kenneth N. Waltz, *Man, the State, and War* (New York: Columbia University Press, 1959).

Ralph K. White, *Nobody Wanted War* (New York: Doubleday, 1970).

6

International
Organization and Law

*No one can observe the international political system without being aware
of the fact that order does exist and that this order is related in important
ways to . . . a body of law and to a process of law-government.*
—Morton A. Kaplan and Nicholas DeB. Katzenbach, *The Strategy of
World Order: International Law,* 1966

*Law is to be found within nations rather than above them. There is no world
state and therefore no world law.*
—David Fromkin, *The Independence of Nations,* 1981

*We should recognize the United Nations for what it is—an admittedly im-
perfect but indispensable instrument of nations in working for a peaceful
evolution towards a more just and secure world order. The dynamic forces
at work in this stage of human history have made world organization
necessary.*
—Dag Hammarskjöld, UN secretary-general, 1957

*There is no such thing as the UN. If the UN Secretariat building in New
York lost 10 stories, it wouldn't make a bit of difference.*
—John Bolton, former U.S. ambassador to the UN (2005–2006),
remarks uttered in a 1994 interview

Opinions about the effectiveness of international law and organization in a decentralized political system have traditionally ranged from extremely harsh cynicism to extremely naive romanticism. Many observers today still view international

UN/DPI Photo

This is a photo of the United Nations Secretariat Building at night, around the time of the UN Millennium Summit in New York City in 2000. As world leaders gathered, there was both hope and skepticism over whether the twenty-first century would mark a new age in global institution-building.

institutions in these terms. Where cynics see international law and organizations as peripheral to the major struggles of world politics or simply as tools of the great powers, used by them to try to perpetuate their dominance, more forward-thinking types see these as noble experiments in world order possibly leading eventually to world government.

The four epigraphs above reflect these divergent views. The first two quotations deal with international *law*, with Kaplan and Katzenbach representing the idealist tradition that stresses the potential for constructing a more peaceful world order built upon the rule of law and Professor Fromkin representing the realist tradition that emphasizes anarchy and lawlessness in world politics. The next two quotations deal with international *organization*, with Secretary-General Hammarskjöld voicing the idealist belief in the United Nations and Ambassador Bolton voicing realist skepticism toward international organizations generally and global ones particularly. Where Hammarskjöld and others have seen the soaring thirty-nine-story

United Nations Secretariat building in New York City as a beacon of hope for humanity, Bolton and his ilk have been less inspired. By the time the new millennium arrived in 2000, the towering Secretariat structure had fallen into disrepair, the neglect of its physical plant reflecting the neglect of the organization on the world stage. According to one news report, with few repairs done over its half-century life, its roof leaking and "a marble wall in the Dag Hammarskjöld Library threatened with collapse," the sad fact was "if the United Nations had to abide by city building regulations, it might well be shuttered."[1] Although the UN complex has undergone renovations over the past decade, many critics of the "architecture" of global organization continue to question the very premise and relevance of the UN.

In this chapter we will examine international institution-building in the form of both international law and international organization. Excessive pessimism or optimism has colored most discussion of this subject over the years, but this chapter aims to avoid both. As I noted in Chapter 1, IR can be pictured as a two-sided coin, displaying both conflict *and* cooperation. The study of international law and organization tends to focus our attention more on the cooperative side, though we should view such phenomena with eyes wide open, not in wonderment but in sober analysis. There is no world government, but opinions differ as to how much "governance without government"[2] is possible and how, at the very least—to use Barry Buzan's phrase—a "more mature anarchy"[3] might be realized.

Where realists talk about "shooting pool" (using the billiard ball metaphor), liberal scholars speak of "pooling" sovereignty. The latter refers to efforts at global governance, as states collaborate in creating international **regimes** aimed at regulating everything from the spread of WMD weaponry to the spread of disease. A "regime" has been defined as a set of "principles, norms, rules, and decision-making procedures around which actors' expectations converge in a given area of international relations,"[4] or, in other words, "governing arrangements,"[5] which allow the international community to function and cope with some set of concerns in the absence of a world government. Drafting treaties, cultivating shared norms, and creating international organizational machinery are all part of regime building. International law and international organization are interrelated in that treaties help found new intergovernmental organizations, while intergovernmental organizations in turn often serve as a catalyst for the development of new treaties. Also serving as a catalyst for the creation of international regimes is the growth of nongovernmental organizations and transnational relations. As more and more people travel, transact business, and interact across national boundaries, states look for ways to coordinate efforts to regulate and routinize these interactions, if only to avoid chaos.

This chapter, then, looks at the problems as well as the possibilities and prospects surrounding international institution-building as an approach to world order. We will start with international organization and then examine international law.

INTERNATIONAL ORGANIZATION

In *Part One* and elsewhere in the text, I have referred to the growing visibility of *nonstate* actors. As one writer notes, "The state-centered view of world affairs, the interstate model which still enjoys so much popularity in the study of international relations, has now become too simplistic," mainly because "nation-states are not the only actors on the world scene. Some NGOs probably have more power and influence in their respective fields than some of the smaller nation-states. The same applies to several IGOs and undoubtedly to many multinational business enterprises which have more employees and a larger production output than most countries."[6] As another writer puts it, "We are not simply confronted with a debate about hypothetical possibilities for the future. The growing complexity of international relations has already produced international organizations; the world *is* engaged in the process of organizing [italics mine]."[7]

Still, what do we make of IGOs and NGOs—in common parlance, **international organizations**? So what if there are now more than 300 IGOs and 20,000 NGOs in the world, compared with less than 200 nation-states? How exactly do they fit into the overall equation of world politics? Even if the proliferation of international organizations is a plain fact that is beyond debate, their significance as actors on the world stage remains open to question, particularly whether they should be considered merely collections of nation-state delegations with no life of their own or, instead, autonomous agents representing supranationalism on the march in a world without borders. Although their growth may be seen as an integrative impulse in human affairs, pulling against the nationalism and subnationalism of the centuries-old Westphalian state system, how likely is it that they will displace national sovereignty and national loyalties?

In Chapter 2, I referred to the tapestries hung in the Palais de Nations in Geneva, Switzerland (League of Nations headquarters between the two world wars), as depicting "the process of humanity combining into ever larger and more stable units for the purpose of governance—first the family, then the tribe, then the city-state, and then the nation—a process which presumably would eventually culminate in the entire world being combined in one political unit."[8] Is this a correct reading of history, and are international organizations the last stage in this process? Harold Jacobson, alluding to the human story depicted in the tapestries, has framed the question as follows: "Few if any serious observers would be willing to accept this view as baldly stated as a comprehensive explanation and forecast except in the broadest historical sense and for the most remote future. . . . [However, if] international organizations are not way stations on the route toward the creation of ever larger territorial sovereignties, what then are they?"[9]

To understand the role of international organizations in the twenty-first century and to evaluate the competing claims, we first need to identify the many different types of international organizations that exist today and to denote their distinguishing characteristics. Not all international organizations look alike, and not all have equal impacts on world politics.

An IO Typology: IGOs and NGOs

The average person equates international organizations with intergovernmental organizations (IGOs) in general and the United Nations in particular. Although the term "international organization" is often synonymous with the United Nations (I may have contributed to that impression with my focus on the UN at the beginning of the chapter), it refers to a much larger phenomenon. The United Nations is only one among thousands of international organizations that come in many different shapes and sizes. If international organization is defined in the broadest possible sense as "any group of individuals from at least two different countries that has a formal institutional apparatus that facilitates regular interactions between members across national boundaries," there is a seemingly endless number of such entities in the world.[10] International organizations can be classified according to at least three criteria: (1) membership type, (2) membership scope, and (3) functional scope.

MEMBERSHIP TYPE (IGOs VERSUS NGOs)

The most fundamental basis for categorizing international organizations is their *membership* characteristics. Some international organizations, **intergovernmental organizations (IGOs)**, have *national governments* as members and are created through treaties between states. Included in the IGO category are such well-known bodies as the United Nations, the World Trade Organization (WTO), the European Union (EU), the Organization of Petroleum Exporting Countries (OPEC), and the North Atlantic Treaty Organization (NATO), along with lesser known entities such as the International Olive Oil Council, the Arab Postal Union, the European Space Agency, and the African Groundnut Council. Other international organizations, labeled **nongovernmental organizations (NGOs)**, are generally composed of *private* individuals or groups. Included in the NGO category are such high-profile organizations as the International Committee of the Red Cross, Amnesty International, and the International Olympic Committee, as well as lower-profile entities such as the International Confederation of Midwives, the Society for the Preservation of and Advancement of the Harmonica, and the International Political Science Association. Few knew or cared about the Harmonica Society holding its forty-fifth annual convention in St. Louis on August 13–15, 2008, whereas the 2008 Summer Games organized by the International Olympic Committee in Beijing that same week captured the world's attention. Visible or not, both are part of the NGO phenomenon.

The *Yearbook of International Organizations*, the most authoritative and comprehensive source of information on international organizations, counts 246 "conventional" IGOs in the world today, although the total exceeds 1,000 if the definition is broadened to include "subsidiary bodies" and other types.[11] The *Yearbook* counts close to 28,000 NGOs, far more than the number of IGOs.[12] Not included are multinational corporations and transnational revolutionary groups, which are special variants of nongovernmental organizations. Although several organizations do not fall neatly into the intergovernmental or nongovernmental categories— for example, the International Telecommunications Satellite Organization (INTELSAT), through which over half of the world's transoceanic telecommunications services are furnished, includes business enterprises as members alongside governments—the rule of thumb is that if it was created by a treaty or an intergovernmental agreement of some sort, as was INTELSAT, it is an IGO.

MEMBERSHIP SCOPE (UNIVERSAL VERSUS LIMITED MEMBERSHIP)

Another important dimension on which international organizations differ is *membership scope*—the extent to which all states are hypothetically eligible to join or access is restricted in some way. Some international organizations are *universal* in terms of being potentially open to representatives from all states; the most notable example is the United Nations and its affiliated agencies such as the Universal Postal Union and the World Health Organization. Others have *limited* membership, restricting members based on geographical or other criteria.

Consider for a moment the geographical scope of international organizations. Although it is common to think of IGOs in global terms, along the lines of the United Nations, only a quarter of all IGOs are *global*, drawing their members from every region of the world. (Furthermore, most global IGOs are not fully universal in the sense of having every country in the world on their membership roster. Even the UN, although open to all recognized states, has been missing a few states, such as Switzerland, which did not choose to join until 2002, and Vatican City, which has yet to apply for membership.) The vast majority of IGOs, roughly 75 percent of the total, are *regional* in scope (e.g., the European Union), and in some cases subregional (e.g., the Nordic Council).

Indeed, **regionalism** has been a more powerful force than globalism in the development of intergovernmental organizations, perhaps not surprising given the tendency for states to have more intense ties at the regional level than the global level as well as the generally greater ease and lower expense of regional organizational participation.[13] Such IGOs as military alliances and customs unions typically are found at the regional level rather than the global level. According to one observer, "the interwar period [between WWI and WWII] was clearly the high tide of universalism,"[14] in that global IGOs as a percentage of all IGOs peaked at that time, as distinct regional subsystems in Asia, Africa, and other parts of the globe did not become fully developed and did not create their own regional institutions until the decolonialization period after World War II. It remains to be seen whether globalization today will revive the growth of global IGOs relative to regional IGOs.

Not all regions are equally represented in the IGO network. Africa, Asia, and Latin America tend to be underrepresented. A 1986 study found that sixteen of the twenty states that belonged to the greatest number of IGOs were in either Western Europe or North America (along with Australia and Japan).[15] A study a decade later found a similar pattern, with the IGO network "dominated by literate, wealthy, and democratic states," as these states had become "more enmeshed in the IGO network" while the poorest and least democratic states had "drifted toward the network's periphery."[16] In recent years Western Europeans have occupied the top ten spots, led by France and Denmark, owing not only to their heavy participation in global IGOs but, more importantly, to the proliferation of regional IGOs associated with the growth of the European Union. Although less developed countries belong to many IGOs and rely on them for diplomatic contacts—both global organizations such as the UN and regional organizations such as the African Union, the Arab League, the Organization of American States (OAS), and the Association of Southeast Asian Nations (ASEAN)—the countries with the smallest number of IGO memberships overall tend to be found in the developing world, owing to limited state capacity (scarce financial resources and other factors).[17]

A similar pattern can be seen in the NGO network. Although NGOs "vary in size from a few dozen members from only three countries to millions of members from close to 200 countries," only about one-fourth of all NGOs are global.[18] Even more so than the network of IGOs, the NGO network draws its members overwhelmingly from Western, industrialized countries. In the past, citizens from Eastern bloc and Third World countries were inhibited from fuller participation in the NGO world. One reason was the lack of democracy in these states, since authoritarian governments have been reluctant to permit their citizens active involvement in private, voluntary associations with the citizens of more open societies. A second reason was the lack of economic resources, since NGO participation can entail considerable travel and other expenses that poor people can ill afford. However, as democratization and economic growth has expanded in the post–Cold War era, Africa and Asia are being brought increasingly into the NGO system.[19]

The European Union and the African Union are examples of international organizations that are "limited-membership" organizations based on geography. Many others limit membership based on very different criteria. For example, OPEC includes a dozen member states from virtually every region of the world, not only the Middle East but also Africa, Asia, and Latin America, but invites only major oil-exporting countries to join. The Commonwealth of Nations spans the globe but is restricted to countries with former colonial ties to the British Empire. The Group of Eight (G8) is an elite club composed of the leading industrialized countries from North America, Europe, and Asia.

FUNCTIONAL SCOPE (MULTIPURPOSE VERSUS SINGLE PURPOSE)

International organizations are established to serve a great variety of purposes. In terms of *functional scope*, some international organizations are general, *multipurpose* organizations, and others have more specific, *single-purpose* missions. In the case of both IGOs and NGOs, single-purpose organizations far outnumber multipurpose ones. Among IGOs, a few institutions such as the United Nations, the Organization of American States (OAS), the African Union, the Arab League, and the Association of Southeast Asian Nations (ASEAN) have mandates to address a wide range of political, economical, and social concerns of members. The OAS, African Union, Arab League, and ASEAN are sometimes referred to as regional security organizations insofar as they are designed to facilitate general cooperation and peaceful settlement of disputes among their members. General-purpose IGOs are only about 2 percent of all IGOs. Most IGOs have more narrow, specialized functions, either military (e.g., NATO), economic (e.g., the World Bank), social and cultural (e.g., the UN Educational, Scientific, and Cultural Organization), or technical (the World Meteorological Organization). Among single-purpose IGOs, two-thirds focus on economic tasks, 25 percent on social welfare tasks, and less than 10 percent on military matters.[20]

NGOs tend by nature to be single-purpose organizations even more than IGOs, given the fact that they ordinarily serve a clientele that shares specialized interests, drawn from a particular occupation, profession, industry, technical field, religious or social group, or sport or hobby. The largest numbers of NGOs (not counting multinational corporations) are found in the areas of commerce and industry (one-fourth of all NGOs) and science and medicine (over a third of the total).[21]

Trying to classify international organizations according to function can be difficult. For example, the European Union started as an economic IGO called the European Economic Community but has evolved into a general governance arrangement among European countries dealing with everything from border and immigration control to transportation, labor, and social welfare policy. The World Bank has become involved increasingly in environmental concerns through its funding of development projects in Latin America and elsewhere, so that calling it a single-purpose economic organization hardly does it justice. As with the other key dimensions of international organizations, fitting particular institutions into particular pigeonholes on the functional dimension is less important than knowing what the various pigeonholes look like. Table 6.1 summarizes the classification scheme presented here and includes examples in each category.

The Causes and Effects of International Organizations

What lies behind the assorted names and statistics found in the universe of "IO"? When all is said and done, *do international organizations matter?*

Some have referred to the study of IO as similar to the "Mt. Everest syndrome," that is, we study international organizations because "they are there." However, international organizations require expenditures of money and effort to create and maintain. They exist not for their own sake but to serve certain purposes, as noted in the discussion of functional scope. Although IGOs and NGOs each have a distinct logic, the common thread running through both types of organizations is a

TABLE 6.1 A Typology of International Organizations

FUNCTIONAL SCOPE

	Multi-Purpose	Single-Purpose
Universal	United Nations	World Health Organization Universal Postal Union
	World Federation of United Nations Associations	International Olympic Committee International Council of Scientific Unions
Limited	European Union Organization of American States African Union	Central American Common Market North American Free Trade Agreement (NAFTA) North Atlantic Treaty Organization (NATO)
	Afro-Asian Peoples Solidarity Organization	Pan American Association of Ophthalmology Arab Lawyers Union

MEMBERSHIP SCOPE

☐ IGOs   ▨ NGOs

set of concerns that transcend national frontiers. If IGOs are a bridge between governments, NGOs are a bridge between peoples. IGOs are generally considered more important actors on the world stage than NGOs, since IGOs tend to be of more immediate interest to national governments and tend to be more directly associated with the development of international regimes. Admittedly, neither the Society for the Preservation and Advancement of the Harmonica nor the International Confederation of Accordionists is likely to produce greater world harmony, any more than the World Federation of Master Tailors is likely to alter the course of world affairs. However, certain nongovernmental organizations such as the Roman Catholic Church, multinational corporations such as Shell Oil or General Motors, and revolutionary groups such as al Qaeda can have a significant impact insofar as they are often in a position to act independently of national governments in shaping major events in the international arena.

THE LOGIC OF NGOS

Transnational relations—interactions between private individuals and groups across national boundaries—have existed for centuries, represented by the early travels of European explorers, missionaries, and traders to the far corners of the earth. Long before Westphalia, intercontinental trade was occurring along sea routes and such land corridors as the Silk Road, which ancient Rome used to pursue commerce with China. Marco Polo journeyed from Venice to Mongolia in the thirteenth century, and the bubonic plague traveled from Central Asia to Europe in the fourteenth century. Nevertheless, it was not until the improved communications and transportation technology that accompanied industrialization in the nineteenth century (during "the first era of globalization" discussed in Chapter 2) that large numbers of people were able to interact more readily across borders. Industrialization also created specialized economic groups for which national boundaries posed artificial barriers. Not only business executives but also labor union activists, artists, and others were added to the ranks of what James Field describes below as the "new tribe":

> Among the humanitarians there developed an international peace movement and international campaigns for the abolition of . . . slavery, for women's rights, and for temperance. Working class groups supported the international labor movement. . . . From the managers there came a network of . . . trusts, cartels, and the like. . . . Among the actors, governments were the most visible. But while the apparatus of the state continued to grow throughout the period, and particularly from the latter part of the nineteenth century, its role . . . was less one of initiating policy than of responding to conditions produced by nongovernmental actors whose influence transcended national boundaries.[22]

As "global civil society" expanded, these ties increasingly became *institutionalized* in the form of nongovernmental organizations designed to provide more durable bonds and more regularized contact between transnational actors. There were only 5 NGOs in 1850.[23] The number grew to 200 by 1900, 800 by 1930, 2,000 by 1960, and 4,000 by 1980.[24] According to some accounts, there are now almost 30,000 NGOs (not-for-profit organizations, as opposed to for-profit multinational firms) in the world.

Curiously, when the United Nations Charter was drafted in 1945, nongovernmental organizations were mentioned only once in the entire document. It was only around the 1970s that the acronym NGO entered the IR lexicon and became the subject of extensive scholarship. Today, it is a commonplace term now found in mass media worldwide from the *China Daily* to the *New York Times*. The following scene, a description of an NGO gathering at the 1995 UN World Summit for Social Development held in Copenhagen, Denmark, is being played out regularly across the globe at numerous international conferences every year:

> It started in Rio de Janeiro, with the 1992 Earth Summit. Now no big United Nations conference takes place without it. It is called the NGO Forum, a gathering of private organizations on the edges of the main event. . . . This week, as [government] delegates to the World Summit were bickering over phrases on touchy issues like debt cancellation . . . the NGO Forum was . . . itself lobbying and sometimes attacking the establishment.
>
>   Along Main Street of the Global Village . . . women's organizations from Africa set up shop selling handicrafts near European advocates for greater AIDS awareness. A Danish neocommunist distributed leaflets in front of a Pakistani self-help project's stall. Two rows of little blond children from a local school dressed in exotic foreign costumes tried gamely to sing about humankind above the din of a thousand voices. Strollers could buy a tiny symbolic plant to help raise money for refugees, hear from Zapatista rebels about their plight in southern Mexico, and listen to Swami Agnivesh talking about slave labor in India.[25]

The same forces that spurred NGO growth in the past—technological developments, industrialization, and urbanization—are likely to continue in the future. If it is simple to understand why nongovernmental organizations exist, assessing the effects of such institutions is more difficult. NGOs are thought to have a number of impacts on world politics.

In an empirical study that examined hundreds of examples of "transnational participation," Robert Angell concluded that sustained exposure to other cultures through NGO membership tends to produce a more cosmopolitan, less nationalistic outlook in participants. Business executives or other elites with access to the corridors of power can promote greater understanding among governments. However, many scholars question the impact of such socialization experiences, particularly the extent to which business executives and other types of transnational actors are truly capable of shedding their national identity and thinking in broader terms. The fact is that several NGOs are dominated by the citizens of one country, if not the government. Even Angell acknowledges that certain kinds of transnational organizations (e.g., multinational corporations or religious movements) can foster resentment and tension rather than empathy and brotherhood among peoples. In other words, as the saying goes, familiarity can breed contempt, although on balance Angell finds that transnational relations represent "peace on the march."[26]

A second NGO impact is based on the special consultative status that many NGOs have been accorded in IGOs, enabling them to have input into the latter's decision making. Whereas in 1948, only forty-one nongovernmental organizations were listed with the UN Economic and Social Council (ECOSOC), today over 2,000 NGOs have been formally accredited to participate in UN diplomatic proceedings—sharing information, advancing proposals, and helping implement agreements as part of a web of governmental, intergovernmental, and nongovernmental efforts aimed at global problem-solving. For example, many transnational scientific bodies have played an important role in getting environmental issues on the global agenda and providing technical expertise at such conferences as the 1987 Montreal Conference on the Ozone Layer and the 1997 Kyoto Conference on Climate Change. One such NGO is the International Council of Scientific Unions, whose members include the main national academies in the physical sciences in more than seventy countries and whose committees on ocean research, Antarctic research, and space research have dealt with politically sensitive concerns. Amnesty International, which is credited with conducting accurate, impartial monitoring of human rights violations, is viewed by some as "almost an arm of the UN."[27] Likewise, CARE and other NGOs have become major vehicles for delivering economic assistance to poor countries, as donor governments and UN agencies often prefer channeling aid through these bodies rather than through the host governments, which are thought to be corrupt and less likely to transfer the funds to those in need at the grassroots level. It should be added that many NGOs do not enjoy a privileged consultative status in IGOs (witness most of the groups that comprised the NGO Forum in Copenhagen in 1995 and participated only informally in the World Summit there) but nonetheless are active in trying to shape outcomes in the international arena.

As with IGOs, NGOs are likely to have greater influence and be accorded greater autonomy of action by states the more an issue is "low politics" in nature. However, some argue that NGOs "are muscling their way [even] into areas of high politics . . . that were once dominated by the state."[28] Referring to the key role played by the International Campaign to Ban Land Mines in lobbying for the 1997 Ottawa Treaty that outlawed such devices, the Canadian foreign minister commented: "Clearly, one can no longer relegate NGOs to simple advisory or advocacy roles. . . . They are now part of the way decisions have to be made."[29]

Indeed, a third impact that NGOs have on world politics is more sizable and has nothing to do with socialization or consultative processes. This impact, alluded to earlier, is the role of some NGOs as distinct, independent actors that compete directly with national governments, at times contributing to world order and at times playing havoc with it. In some instances, the part played by NGOs in the international political system can be quite visible—perhaps the most obvious recent example is al Qaeda. In other instances, NGOs might have a lower profile but nonetheless significant implications—for example, the role of the International Federation of Airline Pilots Associations, a transnational labor union, in pressing governments to adopt stronger air safety and anti-skyjacking measures. Then, too, there is the multinational corporation (MNC), seen by some observers as an alternative form of human organization to the nation-state, pursuing its own objectives apart from those of any national government and undermining (or at least complicating) traditional notions of sovereignty, citizenship, and patriotism. At the very least, one cannot ignore the role played by a handful of multinational agribusiness corporations and oil companies in determining the world distribution of grain and energy supplies and possibly the success or failure of government-imposed grain or oil embargoes. I will look more closely at the MNC phenomenon when we focus on the international economy in Chapter 9.

THE LOGIC OF IGOs

I noted in Chapter 2 that the first IGO was the Central Commission for the Navigation of the Rhine River, created in 1815, and that a few other IGOs appeared during the nineteenth century, such as the International Telegraphic Union (ITU) in 1865 and the Universal Postal Union (UPU) in 1874. One scholar, counting off-shoots of existing IGOs, notes that the number of IGOs grew 5,000 percent in the twentieth century, from only 37 in 1909 to 1,850 by 1997.[30] Counting only "conventional" IGOs, there is some evidence that the raw number of them may have peaked during the 1980s, but in any case it is safe to say that the long-term trend has been a proliferation of IGOs and that there are hundreds of IGOs in existence today. IGOs deserve attention, however, not because they are readily counted but because they appear to be part of an evolutionary process at work in world politics. Rather than being viewed as experimental, failed, or at best marginal responses to human problems, intergovernmental organizations may more cogently be seen as structures that are deeply imbedded in historical forces. Inis Claude, a leading student of international organization, has said:

> The expectation of international organization, the habit of organizing, the taking for granted of international bodies . . . are permanent results of the movement [that began almost from scratch a century or so ago]. . . . We cannot ignore the successful implantation of the idea of international organization. International organization may not have taken over the system, but it has certainly taken hold in the system. The twentieth century [saw] the establishment of the prescription that multilateral agencies are essential to the conduct of international affairs.[31]

Claude primarily attributes the growth of intergovernmental organizations in the twentieth century, particularly the creation of broad multipurpose organizations such as the League of Nations and the United Nations, to the scourge of war: "The organizing movement of the twentieth century can be interpreted as a reaction to the increasingly terrible consequences of armed conflict."[32] While the League and UN can be considered a direct reaction to World War I and World War II, single-purpose IGOs can be traced to other roots. Recalling the origins of the ITU and the UPU, these and other UN "Specialized Agencies" owe their existence to the expansion of interstate commerce and the need for new structures to assist national governments in promoting orderly economic relations in an emergent world capitalist economy. Regarding the latter IGOs (sometimes called "international public unions"), their arrival on the scene in the late nineteenth century coincided not only with the growth of an internationalist-oriented capitalist class and the "new tribe" of transnational actors but also the growth of the welfare state and modern industrial society, with national governments experiencing mounting pressures to produce a better standard of living for their citizenry and recognizing that material well-being could only be maximized through enhanced international cooperation. Other forces also contributed to IGO growth, notably scientific and intellectual elites ("epistemic communities") seeking to improve the human condition through social engineering that took advantage of new technologies spanning national boundaries.[33]

States today form intergovernmental organizations for the same practical reasons that have always provided the rationale behind IGOs: Problems exist that either cannot be handled unilaterally by one state or can be dealt with more efficiently through collaboration with others. The bottom line is that states turn to IGOs so that they "are able to achieve goals that they cannot accomplish [alone]."[34] Neoliberals stress the utilitarian character of international institutions and how mutual interests drive states to create IGOs. For example, even the leader of a "rogue state" wants to send and receive overseas mail and be able to fly abroad without accident, simple but essential routines made possible only through international regimes developed by the Universal Postal Union and International Civil Aviation Organization.[35]

When a problem arises, the first inclination of governments ordinarily is not to create an organization but to try to address the concern simply through a treaty or informal ad hoc arrangement, which is less costly; however, if the problem is viewed as an ongoing one, more elaborate machinery may be felt necessary, and an IGO is born. Some problems may involve only two states and hence a two-member IGO (e.g., the Great Lakes Fishery Commission established by the United States and Canada), whereas other problems may be defined as regional in scope (e.g., the North-West Atlantic Fisheries Organization) or requiring global approaches (e.g., the International Maritime Organization).

Although IGOs are generally conceived to be instruments of cooperation, it is important to keep in mind the realist caveat that they also inevitably involve conflict, that they can be thought of as forums for managing interstate disagreements as well as mutual problem-solving, and that member states vie for control of IGOs as they attempt to use international organizations as tools for legitimizing various national policies. It is also important to keep in mind the high politics–low politics distinction, with multipurpose IGOs generally dealing with the former and functionally specific IGOs dealing with the latter, which by definition tend to involve relatively narrow, technical, noncontroversial matters (although even setting international mail rates or sharing AIDS research data or managing fisheries can become quite politicized).

The typical IGO has a plenary assembly or conference in which all member governments discuss and vote on policies, along with a secretariat or bureau that is responsible for implementing decisions and running the organization's administrative apparatus. However, IGOs differ considerably in the amount of decision-making power that states vest in them. A few IGOs approach a **supranational** model: The organization is empowered to make decisions that are binding on the entire membership. All member states are required to abide by the collective will, even if they were on the losing side of a roll-call vote. In such cases, sovereignty is not merely "pooled" but to some extent is surrendered. Far more IGOs are at the opposite extreme, empowered by member states merely to offer recommendations or resolutions of an advisory nature that each government is free to accept or reject. States are more willing to cooperate robustly and entrust decision-making competence in organizations having narrow, well-defined goals (functionally specific IGOs) than in organizations having broader, more open-ended missions (multipurpose IGOs). In the case of the Universal Postal Union, for example, governments even have allowed secretariat officials ("technocrats") to exercise considerable discretion in making and implementing decisions on behalf of the entire membership. The "higher" the politics, the more likely states will insist on retaining full sovereignty. Indeed, the most powerful states will often seek to impose their own agenda on the organization, although IGO secretariats have at times played an important, independent role, even in situations involving war and peace or other volatile concerns.

Liberals associated with the **functionalist school** hypothesize that as states collaborate and surrender some measure of sovereignty to IGOs in low-politics issue-areas, their governments will learn habits of cooperation that will gradually induce further collaboration in high-politics areas, leading ultimately to a possible supranational community (i.e., a regional or world government).[36] In other words, willingness to cooperate robustly in, say, locust control (through the International Red Locust Control Organization for Central and Southern Africa) may be the beginning of a process that could eventually "spill over" into the realm of arms control. Spillover is especially likely where beneficial cooperation in one sector (e.g., managing fisheries) cannot be sustained without more ambitious cooperation across other sectors (e.g., managing water pollution). Although the available evidence indicates that the spillover process does not lead inexorably to supranationalism, the European Union (to be discussed below) does provide at least partial support for the functionalist logic.[37]

Even if functionalist theory is wrong about supranationalism, there is evidence that "entanglement in a web of IGOs" tends to "make states less bellicose."[38] The latter proposition is the "third leg" of liberal peace theory (along with the democratic peace and economic interdependence)—the notion that shared IGO memberships are associated with a reduction in interstate war.

Thus IGOs play a role both as *arenas* for interstate conflict and cooperation and as *actors* that affect state behavior and outcomes in world politics. In the next section of this chapter, I focus on two specific IGOs that are among the most important in world affairs, the United Nations at the global level and the European Union at the regional level.

THE UNITED NATIONS AND THE UN SYSTEM

Historian John Keegan has written, "Four times in the modern age men have sat down to reorder the world—at the Peace of Westphalia in 1648 after the Thirty Years War, at the Congress of Vienna in 1815 after the Napoleonic Wars, in Paris in 1919 after World War I, and in San Francisco in 1945 after World War II."[39] Created out of the ashes of World War II, the **United Nations** represented the most ambitious attempt yet at global institution-building. Led by the United States, the World War II Allies called themselves "the United Nations" and as early as 1943 had already drafted a charter envisioning what the postwar world might look like. When President Franklin Roosevelt died just two weeks before the San Francisco conference convened to finalize the UN Charter in April 1945, it was left to his vice president and successor, Harry Truman, to represent the United States and guide the negotiations. Ever since he was a small boy growing up in Independence, Missouri, Truman had carried in his wallet a copy of the famous 1837 poem by Alfred, Lord Tennyson, "Locksley Hall," which dreamed of "the Parliament of Man, the Federation of the World."[40] Shortly before the San Francisco conference, Truman had addressed a gathering in Jefferson City, Missouri, to build support for a global organization; he offered what he thought was the central rationale for the UN, warning that "the only rational alternative to existing international anarchy lies in some reasonable form of international organization among so-called sovereign states."[41]

The League of Nations, founded at the 1919 Paris Peace Conference after World War I, set the precedent of a large assembly of nations meeting in regular annual session. Like the League, the United Nations was created to great fanfare and euphoria. President Truman opened the San Francisco conference with the bold prediction that the delegates were about to construct "machinery which will make future peace not only possible, but certain."[42] Former U.S. secretary of state Cordell Hull proclaimed, "There will no longer be need for spheres of influence, for alliances, balances of power, or any other of the special arrangements through which, in the unhappy past, the nations strove to safeguard their security or to promote their interests."[43]

However, idealism mixed with realism in shaping the UN, no less than the League. As realists would predict, the war winners, not losers, were the main architects of the organizations. Truman and the other Allied leaders were sincere in wanting to end war, but they designed an organization that would also promote their own interests in maintaining the postwar status quo. The UN, like the League, was founded on the principle of **collective security**, which meant that, should any state commit aggression and threaten the existing order, the entire international community—the entire membership of the organization—was obligated to come together in a grand coalition and punish that state through the application of military or economic sanctions. Like the founders of the League, the UN founders assumed that collective security would be implemented primarily through the leadership of a handful of major powers. Thus the concept was modeled after the concert of great powers approach to world order inspired by the Concert of Europe created at the Congress of Vienna in 1815.

Where the Concert of Europe and League of Nations failed, the UN hoped to succeed. The "Big Five"—the United States, the Soviet Union, the United Kingdom, France, and China—assumed the role of the "world police" under the new UN Charter. The initial hope was that great-power unity would enable the UN to function better than its predecessor, which had been hampered by the absence of several important countries, including the United States, from its membership. Although most of the major powers in 1945 were represented in the UN, expectations about great-power cooperation quickly dissolved as the Cold War between the American-led Western bloc and Soviet-led Eastern bloc began no sooner than the Charter was signed and took effect. Even with the end of the Cold War a half century later, the UN has struggled to achieve its original aims and aspirations.

Structure and Operations

Figure 6.1 is an organization chart of the United Nations and its affiliated agencies that together make up "the UN system." As one can see, there is a complex array of councils, commissions, committees, programs, and other bodies. As the chart shows, also, the UN is involved in a host of issues in addition to war and peace. I will try to reduce the UN to its essentials here, focusing on the half dozen "principal organs" and the dozen or so "specialized agencies."[44]

Under the UN Charter, the **Security Council** was assigned the main responsibility for peace and security matters. Chapter VII of the Charter stipulated that, if **peaceful settlement** procedures (such as mediation, arbitration, and adjudication) under Chapter VI fail to resolve a dispute, the Council could, in the name of collective security, authorize military and economic sanctions against any states engaging in actions that were "a threat to the peace." The powers granted the Security Council in this area exceeded the powers given any other UN organ, since the Council was empowered to take decisions under Chapter VII that were *binding* on all UN members. However, the collective security provisions of Chapter VII have rarely been implemented to mete out economic sanctions, much less organize a UN military force, against an aggressor.

The Security Council has fifteen member states. This includes the Big Five (sometimes called the "Perm Five"), who were given permanent seats under the Charter, along with ten other states serving two-year terms on a rotating basis. (The Chinese seat originally held by Taiwan has been occupied by the People's Republic of China since 1971.) Although many have questioned the composition of

FIGURE 6.1 The United Nations System

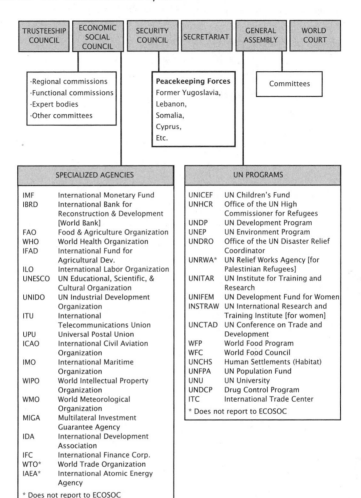

the Security Council—for example, whether countries such as Germany and Japan are not at least as deserving of permanent seats as Britain and France, or why emerging economic powerhouses such as India and Brazil do not merit consideration, or whether any states should be accorded special status as permanent members—the present arrangement is difficult to change not only because recent efforts at UN reform have been unable to reach consensus on this issue but, additionally, the Charter gives each of the Perm Five the power to *veto* any decision regarding collective security measures, Charter amendments, or other substantive matters requiring Security Council approval.

In other words, the Security Council cannot take decisions of any importance unless the permanent members are in unanimous agreement (along with at least four other votes needed for passage of a Council resolution). Therefore the veto power gives each permanent member the ability to block a move to terminate its Security Council seat. Likewise, the veto enables any one member of the Perm Five to frustrate Council attempts to enforce the collective security provisions of Chapter VII or to take any other actions it finds objectionable. Both the Soviet Union and the United States used the veto numerous times during the Cold War. Although the veto often had the effect of paralyzing the UN's ability to act, it arguably helped to preserve the organization, ensuring that neither superpower felt threatened by the organization and impelled to walk out.

Use of the veto has declined since the end of the Cold War. Between 1946 and 1989, some 270 vetoes were cast, whereas between 1990 and 2003, only 14 were cast.[45] It is still true that paralysis occurs at times, and the mere threat of a veto often has sufficed to block submission of a resolution (e.g., the threat by Russia, China, and France to veto a 2003 resolution contemplated by the United States that would have sought authorization to use armed force against Iraq; the threat by China to block any resolution in 2007 condemning genocide by the Sudanese government in Darfur; or a similar threat by Russia in 1998 to frustrate Council efforts to end ethnic cleansing by the Serb government in Kosovo). As a result, watered-down resolutions rather than resolutions with teeth have been passed. Moreover, as happened in Kosovo and Iraq, Council members at times have acted without Security Council approval, in violation of the Charter. Nonetheless, scholars generally agree that the Council in the post–Cold War era has begun to approach the role the founders envisioned. "In recent years the workload of the Security Council has increased dramatically; taking into account both its daily formal sessions and the literally continuous informal interactions among delegations, the Security Council today is never out of session. So, too, has the agenda . . . broadened to regularly include questions of human rights, human security, and humanitarian intervention that would not have been taken up even ten years ago."[46]

In the words of another observer:

With the end of the Cold War, there has been greater cooperation within the Council. . . . The Council's activity and output have both expanded enormously since the end of the Cold War. In 2002 there were 238 formal meetings of the Council, and sixty-eight resolutions were adopted. The corresponding figures for 1989 were sixty-five meetings and twenty resolutions. In the decade between January 1990 and December 1999, the Council adopted 638 resolutions, an average of sixty-four a year, compared with an average of fourteen a year over the preceding forty-four years.[47]

The clubby nature of the Perm Five has led other members to call for greater transparency of Council proceedings, along with enlarging the Council and broadening its composition. However, Perm Five unanimity and consensus building may be difficult to sustain in the future, given growing frictions between the United States, Russia, and China; adding new members would only complicate consensus building. Also, as discussed below, recent UN efforts in the peace and security field have included a number of failures, leading some critics to continue to question UN effectiveness in conflict management and resolution. Meanwhile, the Security Council remains shrouded in mystery to much of the public, with only 16 percent of the American public able to name the five members with veto power, and mass publics in other countries not faring much better.[48]

The public knows even less about the other principal organs of the UN. The **General Assembly** is the UN's plenary body in which each member country has a seat. The Assembly conducts its work mainly through several committees, including Disarmament and Security, Economic and Financial, Political and Decolonialization, and three others. Although the Charter calls for the Assembly to deal with a broad range of issues, its power is limited because virtually all resolutions passed by the body are *nonbinding*; they are merely recommendations, carrying no legal obligations. For example, in 2007, the General Assembly debated and passed a resolution calling for a moratorium on the use of the death penalty worldwide. The vote was 104 countries in support of the resolution, 54 against (including the 6 countries in which 90 percent of all executions occur annually—China, Iran, Iraq, Pakistan, Sudan, and the United States), and 29 abstaining. Since the resolution was nonbinding, countries were free to ignore the Assembly's decision and did so. Although it is easy to dismiss the work of the Assembly, its resolutions at the very least often have symbolic significance and moral weight and therefore can create pressure for change in the international system.

The General Assembly is the primary forum used by smaller, poorer states to articulate their positions on a wide number of concerns. In 1945 the Assembly had only fifty-one members, with a clear majority being pro-Western. Western influence declined in the General Assembly during the Cold War as the decolonialization process brought dozens of newly independent states from Africa and Asia into the world body. By 1980, there were more than 150 members of the General Assembly, with more than 100 of these being less developed countries, most of which were far more interested in north-south issues than east-west issues. Third World states formed a coalition, the **Group of 77**, to push their agenda. In the 1970s, the Third World tried, with little success, to use its majority in the General Assembly to demand a **New International Economic Order** (NIEO) that would give poor countries greater power and wealth through a change in the rules governing international trade, investment, and foreign aid. (The NIEO will be discussed in Chapter 8 in connection with economic development issues.)

The ranks of the Third World in the United Nations have been swelled in recent years by the addition of such ministates as Palau (having a population of less than 25,000 when it was admitted in 1994). In the past two decades many other states have entered the UN, including some tiny Western European countries (e.g., the aforementioned Monaco, Liechtenstein, and Andorra, each smaller than Little Rock, Arkansas) as well as almost twenty states created out of the breakup of the Soviet Union and Yugoslavia. As of 2009, the total UN membership was 192. The admission of so many new members, especially ministates, has occasioned renewed controversy about General Assembly voting procedures. Voting in the General Assembly is based on majority rule (a two-thirds majority required for "important" questions), with each state having one vote. Thus a country such as Palau with fewer than 25,000 people has the same voting power as China with over 1 billion inhabitants, representing roughly one-fifth of humanity. The one state, one vote principle is based on the traditional norm of sovereign equality among nations. The problem is that the voting formula reflects neither power realities nor democratic principles of representation nor fairness in terms of who pays the organization's bills. The absurdity lies in the fact that a two-thirds majority can be formed in the General Assembly by a coalition of states representing less than 10 percent of the world's population and an even smaller percentage of UN budget contributions. (The United States' annual dues assessment is 22 percent of the entire UN operating budget, compared to only .001 percent for Palau.) Various weighted voting schemes based on population and other criteria have been proposed, but the problem remains intractable.

Over 70 percent of the UN budget is spent on economic and social concerns. The Charter established the **Economic and Social Council (ECOSOC)** as the principal organ charged with providing leadership in the economic and social field. The fifty-four-member body offers recommendations, issues reports, organizes conferences, and attempts to coordinate the activities of various UN agencies addressing economic development, population, environmental concerns, disaster relief, and other problems. Much of its work is carried out through five regional economic commissions (for Europe, Latin America, the Pacific, Africa, and western Asia) and several functional commissions (including, for example, commissions on the status of women and narcotic drugs). There is a general view that ECOSOC has been one of the least powerful and least effective bodies in the UN system, a victim of structural flaws and the unwillingness of the rich countries to provide sufficient resources to meet the many challenges in the economic and social area. The **Trusteeship Council**, on the other hand, has been a victim of its own success, having completely fulfilled the Charter's mandate that it supervise the dismantling of colonial empires and bring trust territories to independence. With Palau, the last trust territory, achieving independence and joining the UN in 1994, the Trusteeship Council suspended operations after that year.

The **Secretariat** is the administrative hub of the UN. It is headed by the secretary-general, who is selected through nomination by the Security Council, and then election by a majority of the General Assembly for a five-year term that can be renewed. The United Nations has had eight secretaries-general: Trygve Lie of Norway (1946–1952), Dag Hammarskjöld of Sweden (1953–1961), U Thant of Burma (1961–1971), Kurt Waldheim of Austria (1972–1982), Javier Perez de Cuellar of Peru (1982–1992), Boutros Boutros-Ghali of Egypt (1992–1997), Kofi Annan of Ghana (1997–2007), and Ban Ki-moon of South Korea (2007–). Hammarskjöld (who died in a plane crash while on a UN mission to Congo) elevated the secretary-general post to one that went well beyond chief administrator, bringing conflicts to the attention of the Security Council and engaging in "good offices" (bringing disputants together for talks) and more active mediation efforts. His successors have struggled with defining their role either as organizational manager or global diplomat or both. The secretary-general must walk a fine line between not alienating the Perm Five and not alienating the bulk of the UN membership, and also not alienating his own bureaucracy.

The international civil service that the secretary-general heads consists of some 30,000 employees (9,000 core staff of economists, planners, researchers, and managers, plus support personnel), half of whom work at UN headquarters in New York City, with the remainder scattered among UN offices in Geneva, Vienna, and elsewhere. Although the UN bureaucracy often is criticized for being bloated, the fact is that, even if one adds the thousands of staff who work for the specialized agencies that are separate from the UN proper, it is smaller than the civil service of Stockholm, Sweden, or the state of Wyoming or, for that matter, the workforce of Disney World.[49] The problem is not so much the size of the administrative apparatus as the lack of efficiency, which owes both to the heavily politicized appointment process as well as the sprawling, unwieldy nature of the UN system. The Charter calls for appointments to be based on "efficiency, competence, and integrity," but it also stipulates that "due regard shall be paid to the importance of recruiting the staff on as wide a geographical basis as possible." While a global organization understandably would want its civil service to be broadly representative of the peoples of the world, the Charter language tends to undermine the merit principle, invites cronyism as the delegates of member countries lobby the secretary-general to hire fellow countrymen and at times close associates and relatives, and points up a contradiction that has plagued the Secretariat: It is expected to be an independent body of technocrats responsible for serving impartially the interests and needs of the UN organization as a whole, even as they remain citizens of particular countries subject to potential pressures from their national governments.

It is impossible to discuss the UN, especially its technical activities, without mentioning the **specialized agencies** that are affiliated with it. As shown in Figure 6.1, there are more than a dozen of these, each a separate IGO having its own charter, membership, secretariat, headquarters location, budget, and decision-making machinery apart from the United Nations but closely linked to ECOSOC and other UN organs. For example, the Universal Postal Union is headquartered in Berne, Switzerland, and includes states that are not necessarily members of the United Nations, such as the Vatican. Despite efforts to coordinate the work of the specialized agencies with that of the UN itself, through a chief executives board headed by the UN secretary-general, the UN system continues to be characterized by overlap, duplication, and general inefficiency. Some parts of the system work better than others, notably a number of the highly technical, low-politics IGOs.

Among the most important of the specialized agencies are several economic IGOs (to be discussed at greater length in Chapters 8 and 9). The **International Monetary Fund (IMF)**, headquartered in Washington, D.C., is a 185-member organization created to promote international monetary cooperation, including stabilizing exchange rates of national currencies and providing temporary financial assistance to countries in order to help them address economic problems and facilitate world trade. The **World Bank**, also headquartered in Washington with 185 member states, provides low-interest loans and other multilateral foreign aid to developing countries for education, health care, and other needs. Although the IMF and the Bank have contributed billions of dollars for economic development, developing countries long have complained that decision making in both the IMF and the Bank is dominated by major donors led by the United States, and has not been entirely sensitive to their concerns. The IMF and the World Bank were created after World War II as key pieces in the postwar international economic order (often called "the Bretton Woods system," named after the site of the 1944 conference at which UN economic institutions were first planned). The third leg of the Bretton Woods system established in the immediate postwar period was the **General Agreement on Tariffs and Trade (GATT)**, designed to lower tariff and other barriers to international trade in manufactured and agricultural goods. In 1995, GATT was replaced by the **World Trade Organization (WTO)**, which aimed to expand trade further by eliminating remaining barriers, including in the service sector (banking, insurance, and the like). Headquartered in Geneva, Switzerland, and consisting of over 150 members, the WTO has become a center of controversy in the politics of globalization, with have and have-not groups and countries squaring off against each other in attempts to shape trade regimes.

Most of the other specialized agencies have near-universal membership. The **International Labor Organization (ILO)**, originally a part of the League of Nations, was established to monitor and improve working conditions and the standard of living of workers worldwide through the drafting of an international labor code and other activities. The **Universal Postal Union (UPU)** and the **International Telecommunications Union (ITU)**, as noted earlier, predated even the League. The UPU, in accordance with its mandate to treat the world as "a single postal territory," facilitates the flow of mail across national boundaries through setting the rules for international mail exchanges, developing procedures to expedite mail delivery, and providing technical assistance in postal service. The ITU similarly helps to manage the flow of telegraph, telephone, radio, and television communications across the globe and above the globe, including regulating space satellite broadcasting and the assignment of radio frequencies for use by commercial radio stations and other users. The ITU's World Summit on the Information Society has been the chief forum in which Internet governance has been debated and global norms developed. The **United Nations Educational, Scientific, and Cul-**

tural Organization (UNESCO) engages in a variety of activities, including im-proving literacy rates in poor countries, promoting scientific and cultural ex-changes, and developing standards of press freedom. UNESCO attempted in the 1980s to promote a "new world information order," drafting a set of controver-sial guidelines governing regulation of the mass media, at least partly in response to Third World complaints that Western news agencies dominated the dissemi-nation of news even in Third World countries. The effort was abandoned when countries could not agree on the degree of government control over freedom of the press and the international flow of news.

The **Food and Agriculture Organization (FAO)** has engaged in research and technical assistance aimed at improving agricultural productivity and addressing the needs of food deficit countries. FAO has sponsored global conferences that have attempted to address the problem of global hunger and malnutrition. Although FAO helped foster the Green Revolution that yielded miracle strains of rice and wheat in the Third World and has partnered with the World Food Program to al-leviate starvation, famine can still be found in some countries despite the prediction by U.S. secretary of state Henry Kissinger at the 1974 World Food Conference that by the end of the decade "no child will go to bed hungry." The **World Health Organization (WHO)** has made substantial progress in controlling communicable diseases, including the virtual elimination of smallpox and a dramatic reduction in malaria, in addition to promoting public health services in developing countries. Through its international health regulations, it has helped to control the spread of cholera and yellow fever and pandemics such as the SARS virus, avian flu, and swine flu. WHO also has played the lead role in the global fight against AIDS.

The **International Civil Aviation Organization (ICAO)** has been responsi-ble for drafting a series of conventions establishing uniform practices and stan-dards regarding aircraft specifications, air traffic control, airport safety, and anti-skyjacking measures, all of which have contributed to making the skies friend-lier to air travelers around the globe. The **International Maritime Organization (IMO)** has performed a similar function in regard to the oceans, helping to man-age traffic on the two-thirds of the earth's surface that is covered with water. The **World Meteorological Organization (WMO)** engages in the collection and ex-change of global weather forecasting data and monitors conditions relating to the global environment and climate change.

There are many other parts of the UN system, too numerous to detail here. The system is a labyrinthine network of organizations with complex linkages. In the case of both the United Nations and its specialized agencies, the organizations ultimately work only as well as the member governments will permit, recalling the remark of Lord Caradon, the former British UN ambassador, that "there is noth-ing fundamentally wrong with the United Nations—except its members."[50] Some-times the level of effectiveness can be quite high, as with those specialized agencies whose officials are given considerable discretion to act within their circumscribed sphere of responsibility. Other times, talking far exceeds action, although to quote another British statesman, Winston Churchill, "jaw-jaw is better than war-war."[51] To gain proper perspective on the UN, let us do a quick cost-benefit analysis.

An Assessment of the UN: Benefits and Costs

The United Nations is commonly evaluated based on its record in the area of war and peace. That record has been at best mixed, with failures outnumbering successes. Despite the UN Charter's proscription against armed aggression, according to one estimate, between 1945 and 1999, two-thirds of the members of the United Nations were involved in interstate "militarized disputes" of some sort.[52] However, some scholars have offered empirical evidence indicating that the UN's performance may be better than generally thought, especially in the recent past. A Rand Corporation study of "major UN-led nation-building operations from 1945 to the present" concludes that the UN was successful in two-thirds of the cases studied; successes included Namibia (1989–1990), El Salvador (1991–1996), Cambodia (1991–1993), Mozambique (1992–1994), Eastern Slavonia (1996–1998), Sierra Leone (1999), and East Timor (1999); failures included, most notably, the Congo (1960–1964).[53] In another study, Ernst Haas examined 123 disputes submitted to the UN for settlement during the Cold War period between 1945 and 1981 and concluded that the organization helped to resolve or at least manage (ameliorate) conflict, through reducing hostilities, in 51 percent of the cases.[54] In a subsequent study, Haas found that the early 1980s marked a low point in the life of the UN, with the "lowest share" of "all disputes involving military operations and fighting" being referred to that body "in the history of the organization."[55] With the end of the Cold War, though, the UN became increasingly active in hot spots all over the globe, scoring a number of successes. As one study, *Human Security Report*, noted (consistent with the Rand report), "the number of armed conflicts around the world declined by more than 40 percent" after 1990, at least partly because "with the Security Council no longer paralyzed by Cold War politics, the UN spearheaded a veritable explosion of conflict prevention, peacemaking, [peacekeeping], and post-conflict peace-building activities."[56]

In order to provide an overall assessment of the degree of success (or lack thereof) the UN has experienced in peace and security matters, it is helpful to utilize as a conceptual framework the spectrum of conflict management roles identified by former UN secretary-general Boutros Boutros-Ghali, in his 1992 *Agenda for Peace* report to the Security Council.[57] See Figure 6.2 for an overview.

Ghali pointed out that the UN often is able to play a constructive role in **peace maintenance**, defusing a crisis *before* it has escalated and deteriorated into hostilities. The UN in fact has engaged at times in "preventive diplomacy" by dispatching fact-finding teams to relieve tensions and encouraging disputants to make use of Chapter VI peaceful settlement procedures ranging from mediation and good offices on the part of the secretary-general or another third party (e.g., U Thant's assistance during the Cuban missile crisis and his intervention in the 1962 West Irian conflict between the Netherlands and Indonesia) to adjudication

FIGURE 6.2 Spectrum of UN Conflict Management Roles

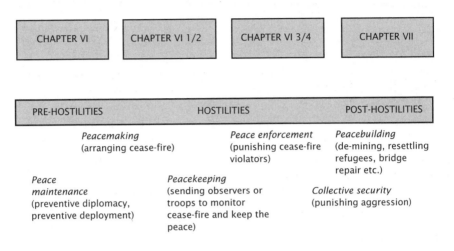

through the World Court (e.g., Libya and Chad submitting a border dispute to the Court in 1990). There was a sixfold increase in the number of preventive diplomacy missions mounted by the UN between 1990 and 2002, and there have been several others since, along with a growing number of disputes submitted to the World Court.[58] Even so, conflicts at times are not ripe for settlement until each side has tested each other's resolve through the use of armed force and has incurred fatalities. As will be seen in the discussion of international law, the World Court especially has been grossly underutilized as a peaceful settlement device.

Boutros-Ghali calls attention to two UN roles that may come into play once a dispute has erupted into violence, referring to **peacemaking** and **peacekeeping**— sending diplomats to help broker a cessation of hostilities and then dispatching blue-helmeted peacekeeping troops to monitor and support the cease-fire. Peace-keeping missions have ranged in size from the 224 observers sent to the Sinai to supervise the uneasy truce following the first Middle East war in 1948 (UNTSO) and the 40 observers placed on the India-Pakistan border during the conflict over Kashmir in 1949 (UNMOGIP), to the 6,000 soldiers sent to the Middle East during the Suez crisis of 1956 (UNEF, which was the first major deployment of UN peacekeeping troops) and the 2,000 soldiers sent to maintain the cease-fire in the Cyprus civil war in 1964 (UNFYCIP), to the 22,000 troops sent to the former Yugoslavia during the Bosnian conflict in 1992 (UNPROFOR) and the 26,000 authorized to go to Sudan in 2008 to deter further bloodshed in Darfur (UNAMID, jointly mounted with the African Union and constituting the largest peacekeeping operation in UN history). As noted above, the end of the Cold War saw a huge expansion of UN peacekeeping activities, with more peacekeeping missions authorized between 1988 and 1992 than in the entire previous history of the organization; included here was a UN role in facilitating the withdrawal of Soviet troops from Afghanistan (UNGOMAP) and the removal of Cuban and South African forces from Angola and Namibia (UNAVEM and UNTAG), the restoration of peace between Nicaragua and its neighbors (ONUCA) and the monitoring of elections in El Salvador (ONUSAL), and the end of the Cambodian civil war (UNTAC). All told, there has been more than a fourfold increase in peacekeeping since 1990.[59] As of 2009, the UN had 19 different peacekeeping operations around the world, totaling over 100,000 troops, police, and civilian personnel drawn from 119 countries.[60]

"Peacekeeping" is an innovation that was never mentioned in the UN Charter, falling somewhere between the peaceful settlement procedures provided for in Chapter VI and the collective security role envisioned in Chapter VII. Often labeled "Chapter VI ½" action, peacekeeping goes far beyond a mediating role yet falls short of collective security. Peacekeepers are sent to provide a neutral military presence and buffer between belligerents rather than punish an aggressor. They cannot be dispatched to the soil of the conflicting parties without their consent and can be ordered out at any time the host countries desire (as happened when Egypt ordered UNEF to withdraw in 1967). In line with their aura of neutrality, peacekeepers traditionally have been unarmed except in a few instances (e.g., the UNTAG troops dispatched to Namibia in 1989 were permitted to carry weapons so as to protect themselves from wild animals). Often placed in harm's way, 2,500 UN peacekeepers have been killed since 1948.

Peacekeeper deaths are a reminder of the dangerous work they do and the lack of cooperation the UN frequently faces. Notwithstanding many successful peacekeeping efforts of late, such as in Nambia in 1990 (which allowed for that country's independence from South Africa) and East Timor in 1999 (which allowed the latter's independence from Indonesia), there also have been conspicuous failures. During the 1990s, the world witnessed UN futility in Bosnia (where NATO forces had to step in and compensate for the inability of UN troops to prevent ethnic cleansing by Serbs of Muslims), Somalia (where UN troops could not stop a brutal civil war between rival clans), and Rwanda (where a small, belated peacekeeping effort could not stem a genocide by Hutus against Tutsis).

The UN's problems in these and other cases can be attributed to a variety of factors. First, sometimes the peacekeepers have been sent in before the peacemakers have done their job, so that there has been no peace to keep. Second, the Charter envisioned that the UN would deal mainly with traditional interstate wars, but most conflicts the UN has been asked to manage in the post–Cold War era have been of the intrastate variety. Third, in many of these conflicts, the UN has been put in the challenging position of having to do postconflict **peace building**. As defined by Ghali and others, this entails creating the conditions necessary for a long-term, durable peace, such as rebuilding destroyed bridges and infrastructure and removing land mines as well as conducting democratic elections in societies that have never experienced democracy and that in some instances are failed states teetering on anarchy. Fourth, at times, peacekeeping has morphed into **peace enforcement,** as UN neutrality is called into question when peace-keepers become embroiled in a messy civil war in which they have to take actions against one faction that gets branded as an aggressor for its interference with de-livery of humanitarian aid and other mission objectives; some have suggested such actions fall under "Chapter VI ¾" insofar as they come close to amounting to a Chapter VII collective security response. Fifth, UN peacekeeping frequently has suffered from a poor organizational structure tying the military chain of com-mand in the field with the political leadership of the Security Council and Sec-retariat, as well as inadequate funding and resolve on the part of the UN membership. (A small standing UN rapid deployment force of 60,000 soldiers has been proposed, but it has not yet materialized.)

In regard to **collective security**, only once during the Cold War did the Secu-rity Council take military action under Chapter VII to punish an aggressor. That was during the Korean War in 1950, when a UN expedition under the command of General Douglas MacArthur, launched against North Korea for its invasion of South Korea, was possible only because the Soviet Union happened to be boy-cotting Council meetings (to protest Taiwan's occupying the Chinese seat rather than the People's Republic of China). The other times Chapter VII was invoked during the Cold War involved economic sanctions (an arms embargo and trade sanctions against the apartheid government in South Africa in the 1960s, 1970s, and 1980s, and similar sanctions against the white minority regime in Rhodesia in the 1960s). However, in response to the first post–Cold War crisis, when Iraq invaded and attempted to annex Kuwait in 1990, the Security Council passed res-olutions under Chapter VII obligating the entire UN membership to participate in economic sanctions against Iraq and authorizing the use of armed force by any individual states coming to the defense of Kuwait, thereby legitimizing the mo-bilization of a multinational force (Desert Storm) led by the United States.

Desert Storm in many respects was a model of collective security in the way the UN's founders had envisioned, as the Iraqi invasion was repelled and Kuwait's sovereignty restored. The post–Cold War period has seen a greater willingness on the part of the Security Council to consider collective security measures. Ninety percent of all Chapter VII resolutions passed since 1945 have been since 1990; in over two dozen instances a variety of military and economic sanctions (includ-ing trade and travel bans) have been authorized against states such as Libya, Haiti, Iraq, the former Yugoslavia, North Korea, and Iran, and even nonstate actors such as rebel groups in Sierra Leone and other African countries. Although, as one au-thor remarks, "UN sanctions now form a prominent feature of the international relations landscape,"[61] the success of the UN role must not be exaggerated, given both the questionable effectiveness of the sanctions in some cases (e.g., as pun-ishment for North Korea's and Iran's suspected development of nuclear weapons in violation of the Nuclear Nonproliferation Treaty) and their total absence in other cases (e.g., UN inability to punish U.S. aggression against Iraq in 2003 or Russian aggression against Georgia in 2008).

The United Nations has played a more subtle conflict management role as a forum in which countries can vent hostilities verbally rather than physically. There is no way of knowing how many outbreaks of violence the United Nations has averted in this fashion. It is difficult to assess, also, how much the UN has contributed to war prevention through its work in addressing various economic and social ills that often underlie the resort to violence. As noted above, the UN devotes over 70 percent of its total budget to economic and social problem-solving. In conjunction with the specialized agencies, the United Nations has sponsored global conferences to address a litany of concerns, including, to name a few, the environment (1972, 1992, and 2002), population (1974, 1984, 1994), food (1974 and 1996), women's and human rights (1975, 1980, 1985, 1993, 1995, and 2005), trafficking of children for prostitution and slavery (2000 and 2004), and economic development issues generally (2000 and 2005).

If the *benefits* produced by the United Nations are modest, the *costs* associated with it are even more modest. Its regular annual operating budget is approximately $2 billion, which is smaller than the annual budget of the Tokyo Fire Department. If the $7 billion currently being spent annually on peacekeeping (which is a special budget) is added, UN expenses still barely exceed the cost of running the New York City police and fire departments, and are less than the money spent by the New York City Board of Education. Considering the fact that the world's governments today spend over $1 trillion a year on weapons of war, with the Pentagon alone spending $2 billion every thirty hours, the amount spent on the UN would seem a bargain. Even if the money spent in the entire UN system is added— the voluntary contributions to organizations such as the UN International Children's Emergency Fund (UNICEF) and the assessments paid to the specialized agencies, a total of some $20 billion annually—the UN would seem to earn its keep. The latter translates into costing each of the world's inhabitants about $3.00, less than the price of renting a home video.

The future of the United Nations remains uncertain. Notwithstanding the flurry of UN activity in peacekeeping and collective security in the post–Cold War era and pockets of success in the economic and social field, one observer, based on extensive interviews with UN diplomats and officials, questions whether "multilateral responses to global problems" can be "cobbled from the combative factions and less than compatible interests of a politically fragmented world. Although the UN has seemingly always been in crisis, even the UN's most ardent supporters insist that the 'crisis of multilateralism' in the early twenty-first century 'is different' and that today the continuing relevance of the entire institution is at stake."[62] Declaring in 2003 that the world body was at a "fork in the road," former secretary-general Kofi Annan issued a report two years later, *In Larger Freedom*, which called for major institutional reform in order to achieve the interrelated goals of collective security, economic development, and human rights.[63] The report remains to be implemented. Lest one leave this discussion of the UN hopelessly skeptical, it is worth quoting a former Israeli ambassador to the UN, who, after expressing his own skepticism, concludes as follows: "With all its imperfections, the United Nations is still the main incarnation of the global spirit. . . . At no other time have so many people crossed frontiers and come into contact with people of other faiths and nationalities. . . . In light of these slow but deep currents of human evolution, the idea of an international organization playing an assertive role in the pacification of this turbulent world may have to bide its time, but it will never disappear from view. History and the future are on its side."[64]

THE EUROPEAN UNION

Regionalism remains a more powerful force than globalism. The most ambitious regional institution-building project in the world is in Europe, where a regional organization has been established complete with its own flag and anthem (although the anthem—the "Ode to Joy" theme from Beethoven's Ninth Symphony—has no words, reflecting the twenty-three official languages that are spoken in the member countries). The **European Union** (EU) is an IGO consisting of twenty-seven member states—France, Germany, the United Kingdom, Italy, Belgium, the Netherlands, Luxembourg, Ireland, Denmark, Greece, Spain, Portugal, Austria, Sweden, Finland, Poland, the Czech Republic, Hungary, Slovakia, Lithuania, Latvia, Estonia, Slovenia, Cyprus, Malta, Romania, and Bulgaria—that together constitute the third-largest demographic unit in the world (its population of almost 500 million exceeded only by China and India) and account for 30 percent of the world's gross domestic product ($15 trillion) and nearly half of global trade.[65] The key question surrounding the European Union is the extent to which it can be considered a *single* unit or actor. In some respects it comes close to being a unified, supranational entity, whereas in other respects it seems little more than a fragile collection of sovereign states.

The Formation of the Union

The dream of a United States of Europe can be traced as far back as Dante in the fourteenth century. However, it was not until after World War II that the idea of a "European Community" was seriously pursued. At first, only six states on the Continent (the "inner six," which included France, West Germany, Italy, and the Benelux countries) joined together to form the **European Coal and Steel Community** in 1951. The same six countries expanded their cooperation by signing the **Treaty of Rome** in 1957, creating the **European Economic Community** (EEC or Common Market). The Community expanded to nine in 1973, with the addition of the United Kingdom, Ireland, and Denmark, then to ten with the admission of Greece in 1981, and to twelve with the entrance of Spain and Portugal in 1986 (with Spanish television marking the event with the words, "Good evening, citizens of Europe"). German unification brought the former East Germany into the Community in 1990, and Austria, Sweden, and Finland were added in 1995. The next large expansion came in 2004, when ten new members were welcomed, mostly former Soviet bloc Eastern European states that were judged to have made sufficient progress in adopting Western political and economic reforms to merit membership. The last expansion was in 2007, when Romania and Bulgaria were added. A number of other states have applied for membership and remain on a waiting list, most notably Turkey.

Although some of the founders of the European Community envisioned eventual *political* unification among the members, most of the national leaders have viewed the undertaking in more narrow terms as a vehicle for *economic* integration. A main rationale behind the project from the start was the desire to emulate the economic model of the United States, where the absence of trade and other barriers to interstate commerce (between, say, Illinois and Missouri) made for a single large market that permitted economies of scale and resulted in greater efficiency and prosperity for Americans as a whole. Although economic integration was not as ambitious a goal as political unification, it nonetheless represented an unprecedented attempt at cooperation on a continent whose members had fought two major wars in the twentieth century.

The plan was to proceed in several stages: (1) a free trade area, in which all tariff barriers would be eliminated between the member states; (2) a customs union, whereby all member states would impose a common external tariff on all goods exported to the Community from nonmember states; (3) a common market, in which not only goods and services but also workers and capital would be able to move freely across national boundaries (so that, for example, Belgian beer could be sold in the German market even if it did not meet "beer purity" standards specified by the German government, and a Dutch physician could practice medicine in Italy without worrying about work permit, licensing, or other obstacles); and (4) an economic and monetary union in which all member states would harmonize their economic policies and accept a single European currency in place of their individual national currencies.

The last two stages, in particular, posed daunting challenges. The European experiment seemed to stall during the 1970s, leading "Euroskeptics" to ask whether European integration could be described as "forward march, parade rest, or dismissed?"[66] However, by 1993, with the signing of the **Treaty of Maastricht** (the Treaty of European Union), all four stages were moving toward completion, and what had been called the European Community changed its name to the European Union. Still, the EU has not fully achieved the goal of total economic integration and is a long way from realizing the larger aspiration of political unification harbored by some founders. Despite substantial progress, a number of problems have persisted, especially given the uneven levels of economic development between the original members of the Community and the latest entrants (e.g., the UK has a per capita income of $38,000, compared to Bulgaria's $3,450).

Continued Challenges

One problem involves the dismantling of travel restrictions across national boundaries. Under the Maastricht Treaty, all nationals of the twenty-seven member states are "EU citizens" while retaining their individual national citizenship. The treaty gives all EU citizens the right of free movement and residence throughout the Union and the right to apply for work subject to certain restrictions. When traveling abroad, all EU citizens carry a similar burgundy-colored passport that has the words "European Union" on it along with the name of their country. Within the EU, under the Schengen Agreement, virtually all internal border controls have been eliminated (so that cars and trucks can cross expeditiously between, say, France and Germany without border checks) and a common set of controls of external borders have been established (so that the EU member states have a common visa policy). However, to date, the United Kingdom and Ireland are still not part of the Schengen Agreement, while Cyprus, Romania, and Bulgaria do not yet fully participate. This has been an extremely difficult issue, given the sensitivity national governments have toward ensuring secure borders and regulating the movement of would-be terrorists, drug traffickers, and illegal aliens and refugees. Even among the Schengen members, there have been some snags in implementation because of concern about liberal drug policies in the Netherlands and lax enforcement of immigration restrictions on the part of some members; the fear is that the end of border controls could mean that drug traffickers and terrorists might be free to roam around the Continent.

A second problem involves the common currency. A common EU currency, the euro, was introduced in 1999, with the aim of replacing French francs, German deutschmarks, and other national currencies of EU members. Currently, only fifteen states are part of "Euroland," the United Kingdom, Denmark, and Sweden having opted out and the remainder of the EU membership having not yet met the conditions for adopting the single currency (e.g., reducing their governmental budget deficits). While the euro has enjoyed considerable success, it has complicated economic policymaking at the national level and reduced national autonomy, since the existence of a common currency means that individual governments are less able to use the traditional levers of monetary policy to help fine-tune their national economy (such as lowering interest rates to stimulate a recovery during a recession or devaluing currency to stimulate exports). According to one expert, "economic policy in Europe is no longer made in national capitals" but through EU institutions based in Brussels.[67] Others worry that the lead economy in the EU, Germany, will dictate policy as states lose their "independence to a new central bank dominated by the Germans."[68]

A third problem has been the harmonization of product standards as well as social standards among the twenty-seven member states. Although Belgian beer no longer has to meet German beer purity standards to be sold in Germany, there have been ongoing controversies over myriad issues, for example, whether there should be a uniform EU-wide standard for pasta (the Italian government having insisted at one time that all pasta sold in Italy had to be made from hard wheat of the sort Italians used) and a standard EU-wide condom (the British insisting that the recommended specifications would not fit most British men).[69] In addition to its absence from the Schengen Agreement and Euroland, Britain has also been one of the major holdouts against the imposition of a EU-wide Social Charter that would guarantee all workers throughout the Union the same minimal set of welfare, unemployment, work safety, and other benefits. The British have viewed these regulations as representing excessive interference in national affairs and as antithetical to the concept of a continental free market on which the EU was founded. Among the more difficult problems the EU continues to face is the need to reconcile the demands of member governments that tend ideologically to favor a large welfare state and those that favor a more laissez-faire, deregulated state.

A fourth problem has been the formation of a common foreign policy. Under the Treaty of Rome that created the European Community, the decision-making competence of EU institutions generally extended only to economic matters, with the Community having no authority to deal with defense issues. Attempts to coordinate foreign policy through a process called "European political cooperation" have at times produced some degree of unity, but more often have resulted in disarray, as in the case of disagreements between so-called Old Europe and New Europe over whether to support the U.S. invasion of Iraq in 2003. The Treaty of Maastricht called for "a common foreign and security policy including the eventual framing of a common defense policy which might in time lead to a common defense [a single European army]." Even though in 2000 the EU announced that "a single foreign and security policy czar would speak for Europe," none has yet been appointed other than a powerless high representative for foreign policy.[70] Even so, there is growing evidence that the member countries "are acting as a unit" in the United Nations and that "the European Union is being viewed increasingly as a distinct actor to be negotiated with not only over economic issues but also over international environmental, narcotics, and other issues."[71] Moreover, EU contingents of soldiers have been sent as peacekeepers to various fronts in recent years, including to Bosnia in 2004 and to Georgia in 2008. Questions have been raised about the future of NATO should an EU army be created, although that remains an unlikely development anytime soon.

A fifth, and core, problem has to do with the decision-making machinery of the European Union, headquartered in Brussels. The Treaty of Maastricht and subsequent treaties (the Treaty of Nice and Treaty of Lisbon) have attempted to promote, first, greater transparency and accountability (as the EU has suffered from a "democratic deficit" in that European publics feel far removed from the EU institutions, and power seems to be exercised as much by EU bureaucrats as by elected officials) and, second, greater efficiency (as EU decision-making procedures have been extremely cumbersome and prone to "Eurosclerosis," a condition exacerbated by the addition of so many new members).

The European Council, comprising the heads of state of the twenty-seven member countries, conducts summit meetings a few times each year to set broad policy. Brussels, the "capital" of the EU, is where the Council of Ministers meets. The Council of Ministers, composed of members of the national cabinets from each state (usually the foreign ministers but sometimes agriculture or environmental ministers or other cabinet officials, depending on the issues to be discussed at monthly meetings), is the most powerful decision-making body in the EU other than the European Council. On paper, the Council of Ministers seems to operate in an almost supranational fashion, with each state allocated weighted votes based on population (e.g., Germany, France, Italy, and the United Kingdom each have 29 votes, while Poland and Spain have 27, Romania 14, Malta 3, and so forth) and decisions on most issues based on a qualified majority rule formula requiring a triple majority. A proposal passes only if a majority of the 27 member states approve, plus it receives at least 73 percent of the total weighted votes (255 out of 345), and the majority coalition must represent at least 62 percent of the EU population. The voting formula is expected to be simplified in the future. In actual practice, most decisions are taken by consensus. Moreover, on a few high-politics issues, such as foreign and security policy, taxation, and immigration, decisions still require unanimous approval. While consensus and unanimity procedures are designed to safeguard sovereignty, such procedures become a potential recipe for paralysis as more member states are added to the Union.

The Council of Ministers increasingly is having to share power with the European Parliament, the legislative arm of the EU. The Parliament used to be merely a watchdog institution with little legislative power. However, recent EU reforms have made it practically coequal with the Council of Ministers insofar as its consultation and concurrence with Council decisions is needed on many issues before the decisions can become EU "law." The members of the Parliament were appointed from the individual legislatures of each country until 1979, when citizens were allowed to vote directly for their representatives in the European Parliament (with seats allocated to countries based on population). There are now 785 members serving 5-year terms, although voting turnout in most countries is considerably lower than for national elections, given continued public uncertainty over the Parliament's role. An interesting feature of the European Parliament is that the political parties are organized across national lines, with Socialists from Italy sitting with Socialists from France and other states, with Christian Democrats sitting together, and so forth. The Parliament has been criticized for its "traveling circus" dysfunctionality, since its committee meetings are held in Brussels, its plenary sessions in Strasbourg, France, and its administrative secretariat situated in Luxembourg, requiring "$200 million (more than 10 percent of the EU budget)" to move "MEPs, staff, and files back and forth."[72]

The European Commission, the executive arm of the EU in Brussels, plays an important role in the EU political process, both at the front end (where it helps set the agenda of issues to be discussed by the Council of Ministers) and the rear end (where it is charged with implementing Council decisions). Each of the twenty-seven member states is entitled to nominate a commissioner. (If the EU expands beyond twenty-seven members, this is expected to change, due to concerns about the unwieldy nature of such a large body.) Although nominated by their governments for renewable 5-year terms, these "Eurocrats," along with the 25,000 EU employees under them, are expected to represent the interests of the EU as a whole and, indeed, tend to exercise considerable independence. Each commissioner is assigned a portfolio for which he or she is responsible (e.g., fisheries, transport, health).

Important decisions are increasingly being taken in Brussels across a wide range of issue-areas that affect people throughout the Union. Consequently business, labor, and other interest groups have been organizing transnationally and establishing offices in Brussels to lobby at the EU level. The EU political process, then, is a complicated one that involves governmental, intergovernmental, and nongovernmental actors. In addition to the political institutions just described, there is also a European Court of Justice that sits in Luxembourg and adjudicates disputes related to the Treaty of Rome and other EU treaties. The Court has handled hundreds of cases ranging from hiring and firing grievances filed by EU civil servants to equal pay suits filed by airline stewardesses and other female employees against their own governments.

The Future of the EU

The question remains whether the substantial progress made thus far toward *economic* integration will lead to *political* integration and whether that progress is sustainable without further development of the Union's political institutions. The tensions surrounding this issue were evident in the disagreements over the wording of the 1993 Maastricht Treaty, particularly the use of the "F word." While most states agreed to an early draft containing the word "federal" as an eventual goal of the treaty, the United Kingdom rejected any mention of the term, thus resulting in the following substitute language: "This treaty marks a new stage in the process of creating an ever closer union among the peoples of Europe."[73] Federalism reentered the discussion in 2002, when Germany urged the creation of a "European Federation"[74] and a draft European Constitution was submitted to the member states for ratification in 2004.[74] However, the Constitution, which required unanimous approval by the entire EU membership, proved to be too supranational even for such a staunch EU advocate as France and never took effect. In its place, in 2007 the Lisbon Treaty was approved, which attempted to salvage some of the key elements of the Constitution (e.g., the creation of a new post of EU president) but without posing as direct a threat to sovereignty.

As one observer writes, "The work of the EU is compromised by the competing sense of affiliation that Europeans have toward their home states and toward the EU; most Europeans still feel closer to their home states, owe them their primary allegiance, and often think of the members states as competing with one another rather than being involved in a joint endeavor. About two in every three EU residents feels an identity with the European Union, with rates ranging from a high of 60–64 percent in Italy, Luxembourg, Hungary, Poland, and Belgium, to a low of 27–34 percent in Lithuania, the Netherlands, Finland, Estonia, and Cyprus."[75] The blurred, competing identities were evident in the recent complaints of fans of the Barcelona soccer team, which has often led the "Spanish first-division," over the fact that there have been more Dutch players than Spanish players on the team since a 1995 EU ruling that, even though teams are limited in the number of foreigners they can field, players from other EU countries are not counted as foreigners.[76]

For the foreseeable future, it is likely that the EU will continue muddling along in what has become a halfway house between a collection of sovereign states and a supranational actor. New challenges may complicate the community-building process. For example, Turkey's application for membership has raised alarm bells. Not only is Turkey a predominantly Islamic country different in culture from much of Europe, but it would be the second-largest state in population after Germany and would have heavy influence in weighted voting in the Council of Ministers. There is the more basic question about the optimal size of the Union: How large and diverse can it become and still remain viable in terms of the ability to reach mutually agreeable decisions? This has become known as the "widening vs. deepening" dilemma—the more states that are added, the harder it will be to develop a closer sense of community and build fully supranational institutions. Further complicating the picture are subnational ethnic tensions and pressures for greater regional autonomy *within* some EU states (e.g., Scotland and Wales seeking greater home rule from the British Parliament in London and, in the heart of the EU, French-speaking Belgians in Wallonia and Dutch-speaking Belgians in Flanders threatening to split Belgium in half).[77] As the European Union endeavors to advance its experiment in regional integration and governance, other regions of the world are conducting their own, more modest experiments with much to learn from European successes and disappointments.

INTERNATIONAL LAW

Treaties such as the UN Charter and the Treaty of Rome, international regimes such as the postal regime and nuclear nonproliferation regime, and institutions such as the World Court (officially known as the International Court of Justice, listed in Figure 6.1) are all part of **international law**. During the Cold War, international relations textbooks typically distinguished between Western, Marxist, and Third World views of international law. After the Cold War, many hoped that there would be more consensus surrounding human rights and other aspects of international law. On November 17, 1989, immediately following the fall of the Berlin Wall, the UN General Assembly declared the 1990s the "UN Decade of International Law," urging that the post–Cold War era should promote the further

IR Critical Thinking
How Much Progress in International Law Is Possible?

Louis Henkin has said that "in relations between nations, the progress of civilization may be seen as movement from force to diplomacy, from diplomacy to law." Henkin was essentially referring to the development of international "regimes"—norms, rules, and institutions that govern various areas of human activity across national boundaries. An example of how regimes develop, and the challenges and opportunities they present for the creation of "new rules of the game," is provided by Daniel Yergin and Joseph Stanislaw, *The Commanding Heights* (Simon & Schuster, 2002, 399–401):

> Late one afternoon in July 1876, along one of Ireland's main railways, a Scottish-born engineer missed his train. As a result, Sir Sandford Fleming spent the night in the station, thus failing to make the ferry connection that was supposed to carry him to England. It was not his fault. The problem was with the times on the railway schedule. . . .
>
> Railways in the United States, for instance, operated according to the time in their headquarters city. Twelve noon on the schedule of the New York Central took place a little earlier than noon on the one of the Philadelphia Railroad. . . . High noon in Boston was twelve minutes earlier than high noon in New York City. These differences put enormous pressure on travelers—and created great distress. . . . Europe suffered from the same indignities. As commerce became regional, national, and international, the differences created great turmoil—and worse. Railroad accidents were frequent because trains operating on different times shared the same tracks. And ships at sea could not communicate their position to each other because they were working on different times. . . . The need for something new was critical. . . .
>
> Chief engineer of the two biggest railway projects in Canada, [Fleming] set out to create "standard time"—a global system for time. . . . His labors paid off eight years later when an international conference, with representatives from twenty-six independent nations, gathered in Washington, D.C. It created what is still the world's time system—twenty-four time zones defined by longitude lines, with the prime meridian passing through Greenwich, England. Agreement was not easily achieved. The French vigorously objected to the meridian's line being through Greenwich, rather than Paris. . . . But all obstacles were overcome, and the Prime Meridian Conference of 1884 provided new rules for time that a much more connected world required.
>
> There is a lesson here from this development of global rule-making. . . . New circumstances . . . create the need for new rules of the game. . . . Today, in sector after sector, the revision of existing regimes and the creation of new ones are at the top of the international agenda. They typically involve complex negotiations among governments, private companies, international organizations, and nongovernmental organizations. The rapid pace of globalization . . . requires new rules of the game—to harmonize existing systems, to ensure efficient functioning of the marketplace, and to provide legitimacy and guidance.

What is described above is more what legal analysts call "soft law" than "hard law." The 1884 conference did not produce a treaty containing binding obligations but rather a set of new understandings and norms that had the same effect insofar as the world came to accept a common set of rules governing time. Greenwich was selected as the basis for the global system not only because Britain was a leading power that also enjoyed the support of the United States on this issue, but also because two-thirds of global commerce already depended on maps and charts that used Greenwich as the prime meridian.

Consider the following questions and try to answer them:

1. Recalling Henkin's remarks, how much progress do you think humanity has made thus far toward the rule of law in international relations, and how much do you think is possible in the future?

2. Just because there is a need for rules in some area, does that mean an international regime will develop? What factors are likely to affect successful development of international law in a given area? What is the role of individual leaders, power politics, epistemic communities of expert problem solvers, commercial elites, and the practical needs of everyday people?

3. The 1884 conference did not create a new IGO to handle the problem of standardizing time. When there is a problem that seems to cry out for a new international regime, what determines whether new international organizations will be created, in addition to new rules? Do you think it is easier or harder to develop global regimes today compared with the past?

4. The Yergin and Stanislaw case study is an example of regime-making in a relatively technical, "low politics" issue-area. What are some examples today of issue-areas where similar rule making may be possible due to technological and other pressures that are creating a mutually felt need around the world for some sort of global regulation and governance? What about, for example, the Internet? How easy or hard do you think it is to develop a new international regime in this area? What about in "high politics" areas?

5. Do you subscribe to the functionalist theory that if countries cooperate in technical sectors, such as setting standard time zones, they will develop habits of cooperation that will eventually spill over into cooperation in high politics fields, ultimately producing greater peace and perhaps even a supranational community?

6. What explains the willingness of countries to enter into agreements and abide by them, when there is no central police body in the world to enforce agreements and punish violators, and no world court with compulsory jurisdiction? Why do *you* obey rules?

---

development of the international legal system. This challenge was in keeping with Louis Henkin's observation quoted earlier that "in relations between nations, the progress of civilization may be seen as movement from force to diplomacy, from diplomacy to law."[78]

As we assess the magnitude of this challenge and how much progress has been made, it is worth going back in time to a moment just ten years prior to the 1989 UN declaration. On November 4, 1979, sixty-six Americans in the U.S. embassy in Tehran were seized by an angry mob of Iranian militants protesting Washington's grant of asylum to the recently deposed Shah. After a few escaped or were released, fifty-two remained imprisoned. Their captors intended to use the hostages to force the extradition of the Shah back to Iran to stand trial, an endeavor that had the blessing of the new regime in Iran headed by Ayatollah Khomeini. It was not until January 20, 1981, after 444 days in captivity, that the American diplomatic personnel were finally released by the Iranian government, coinciding with the inauguration of President Ronald Reagan, who had warned of possible military action by his administration. This event preoccupied the nation for over a year and raised interesting questions about the role of international law in international affairs.

To many, the Iranian hostage crisis seemed a vivid illustration of the lawless character of international relations. However, rather than reflecting the nonexistence or impotence of international law, the episode in some respects illustrated its general reliability. In particular, what made the incident so noteworthy was precisely the fact that it involved a virtually unprecedented violation of one of the most sacred rules of international conduct, namely, the immunity of diplomats from host government seizure. The actions of the Iranian government represented such a departure from the routinely honored canons of state practice that observers at the time feverishly searched through history books to determine the last time such a violation had occurred. Although the timing of the release of the hostages perhaps reflected Iran's fear of U.S. military action, it may also have reflected Iran's concern about its growing isolation as a pariah nation. When the United States brought suit against Iran before the World Court in 1979, Iran's blatantly illegal behavior prompted the Court to issue a rare unanimous judgment (15 to 0) in favor of the United States that included support even from the Soviet judge. Iran ignored the Court's verdict but faced mounting international pressure to end the standoff, so that it might well have eventually relented even if "Rambo" Reagan had not won election.

Still, long after the hostages were returned, questions remained as to what kind of legal system depends for its success on the threat of retaliation by one party to a dispute, or would allow a court order to be ignored and a major violation of law to go unpunished. Those who believe in international law may ask a number of questions: Why, if international law were a farce, would the U.S. State Department's Office of the Legal Adviser maintain a staff of 130 international lawyers, and why would multinational corporations employ hundreds more?[79] Why would a Canadian secretary of state remark that "in my office and in my department, we are, first of all, students of international law"?[80] The skeptic might respond that much of international law is a charade in which states pick and choose to obey those rules that happen to coincide with their interests at a given moment:

> The first time that states break a rule of international law, they apologize and claim that they were unaware the rule existed. The second time, they claim that the rule is ambiguous. The third time, they claim that the rule has changed.[81]

Even if international law is grudgingly acknowledged to exist, it is said to work effectively only in areas of low politics that "do not strike at the core security concerns of states."[82] Where core interests are at stake, the golden rule is that those who have the gold—power—rule, as in the case of Perm Five politics on the UN Security Council. Cynics could note, for example, that the United States, which was so quick to invoke international law in the Iranian hostage case, chose to flout it in 1986, when the Reagan administration refused to acknowledge that its mining of Nicaraguan harbors violated the rule against aggression despite widespread condemnation by international legal experts and a World Court ruling against the United States.

Hence, we are still left with the nagging question as to whether international law is *really* law. The discussion below examines the case for and against international law, elucidating the manner in which it operates and the degree to which it impacts international affairs.[83]

Is International Law Really Law?

To answer this question, we need first to define what law is. "Law" can be defined as a set of rules or expectations that govern the relations between the members of a society, that have an obligational basis, and whose violation is punishable through the application of sanctions by society.[84] The definition implies at least three fundamental conditions that must be present if law can be said to exist in a society: (1) a process for developing an identifiable, legally binding set of rules that prescribe certain patterns of behavior among societal members (a lawmaking process); (2) a process for punishing illegal behavior when it occurs (a law enforcement process); and (3) a process for determining whether a particular rule has been violated in a particular instance (a law adjudication process).

These are the three conditions normally associated with domestic law in national societies. Certainly, such conditions exist in the United States or any other nation-state. Although some national legal systems might be much more effective than others—for example, in achieving compliance with the law—all have the basic elements noted above, as manifested by legislatures, law enforcement agencies, and courts; even so-called failed states have these basic structures in place, at least on paper.

What about *international* law, traditionally defined as the body of rules that are binding on states in their relations with one another? How does it compare with law in *national* political systems (commonly called *municipal* law)? The most obvious difference is that the central governmental institutions that are associated with law within nation-states do not exist in relations between nation-states. There is no world government, no supreme lawgiver, no police squads patrolling international affairs and directing traffic, and no court (at least not one that has all of the normal attributes of a court). International law does not meet what some consider the "Five C's" test of law: congress, code, court, cop, and clink:

First, the rule must be produced by a centralized legislative body—a "Congress," or parliament, or whatever. Second, this legislative body must produce a written "Code." Anyone should be able to pull out a statute book and read precisely what the rule says. Third, there must be a "Court"—a judicial body with complete compulsory jurisdiction to resolve disputes about the rules or to determine culpability for violation of the rules. Fourth, there must be a "Cop," some centralized means of enforcing violations of the rule. Finally, there has to be a "Clink." There must be some kind of sanctions that will be imposed on those who choose to violate the rule.[85]

However, a willingness to overlook the lack of strong central authoritative institutions in the international system—to abandon the stereotype of law as "a centralized constraint system backed by threat of coercive sanctions" and adopt instead the more relaxed definition of law I offered at the outset—would leave open the possibility of accepting international law as law.[86] One must still be prepared to demonstrate how law can operate in a decentralized political system such as the international system. One can rightly ask, "If international law is really law, who enacts, construes, and enforces it?"[87]

The Making of International Law: Where Does the Law Come From?

Clearly, the lawmaking process in the international political system is far more complicated and disjointed than that which is found typically in national political systems. If one were the legal adviser in the foreign ministry of a country involved in an international dispute over maritime boundaries or illegal trade practices or some other such matter, there is no single body of world statutes that can be consulted to discover what the relevant law is. However, there is an identifiable set of rules accepted by states as legally binding, derived from *sources* of international law specified in Article 38 of the International Court of Justice (ICJ) Statute that is attached to the United Nations Charter. The two most important, widely recognized sources are *custom* and *treaties*.

Customary rules of international law are those practices that have been widely accepted as binding by states over time as evidenced by repeated usage. In the early life of the international system, custom was an especially important source of international law. Hugo Grotius, the seventeenth-century Dutch scholar, noted even in his day the development of certain common practices whose routine observance by governments led to their acceptance as required behavior in relations between states. One such custom, already referred to, was the practice of diplomatic immunity granted by a host government to a foreign government's ambassadors. Another was the designation of a three-mile limit within which coastal states were assumed to exercise sovereignty over "territorial waters" adjacent to their land, beyond which there was to be "freedom of the sea"; the three-mile limit was based on the effective range of cannon fired from shoreline fortifications. Numerous other rules developed.

Rarely were any of these rules written down, but they were nonetheless understood to constitute rules of prescribed conduct. Given the decentralized nature of the international system, a customary rule technically became binding only on those states that, through their compliance over time, indicated their willingness to be bound by the rule in question, so that a "persistent objector" generally was exempted from any such legal obligation. For example, Sweden long insisted on maintaining a four-mile territorial sea, whereas practically all other states observed the three-mile limit. That did not mean a state could make any legal claim to ocean space it wanted—early claims by Spain to the Pacific Ocean and Portugal to the Atlantic Ocean were not recognized by other states—only that it was not automatically bound by the behavior of a majority of states.

Today many customary rules continue to form part of the body of international law. An example commonly cited to illustrate the workings of customary law is the state practice that developed in immediate response to the first artificial satellite that was put into orbit around the earth on October 4, 1957—the Sputnik spacecraft launched by the Soviet Union—and the subsequent satellites launched shortly thereafter by the United States. Since no state protested this as a violation of its air space, there was general acquiescence to claims by the United States and the Soviet Union that they had the right to place satellites over the territory of other states, effectively creating customary law on this subject: The circling of objects overhead, as long as they were in outer space and not flying through national air space, was permitted.

Customary rules of law are to be distinguished from rules of etiquette, known as *comity*. In the case of customary law, an established pattern of conduct (e.g., diplomatic immunity) is based on a sense of legal obligation (*opinio iuris*) and invites legal penalties if breached, whereas in the case of comity, it is merely a matter of courtesy (e.g., two ships saluting each other's flag while passing at sea). Admittedly, when states engage in certain standard practices toward each other, it is not always clear whether they do so out of a sense of legal obligation or simply out of politeness. Moreover, given the unwritten nature of customary law, there is great potential for ambiguity and misinterpretation of the rules. For these reasons, there has been a distinct trend in recent years to *codify* customary law—to embody customary rules in precise, written documents to which states can explicitly give or withhold consent.

Treaties are formal written agreements between states that create legal obligations for the governments that are parties to them. Written agreements between societies can be found from the beginnings of human history ("archeologists have discovered a treaty between the city-states of Umma and Lagosh written in the Sumerian language on a stone monument and concluded about 3100 B.C.").[88] Their importance has grown as the modern nation-state system has evolved. As with customary law, treaties are binding only on those states that consent to be bound by them. A state normally indicates its consent by a two-step process in which its authorized representative *signs* the treaty and its legislature or other constitutionally empowered body *ratifies* the agreement. For example, President Carter in 1977 signed a landmark human rights treaty, the International Covenant on Civil and Political Rights, but failed to win approval of the U.S. Senate; the treaty was not ratified by the Senate until 1992, when it finally became binding on the United States. The Convention on Biological Diversity was signed by President Clinton in 1993 but has yet to be ratified by the U.S. Senate; hence it is not yet technically binding on the United States.

Those international instruments known as "conventions," "protocols," or "covenants" are essentially the same as treaties, at least in their binding quality. (Many students find it surprisingly difficult to understand that a "convention" here refers not to a conference but to a paper document.) Once a state becomes a party to such an agreement, it is expected to honor the fundamental principle associated with treaties—*pacta sunt servanda*, which means that treaties are to be obeyed. Many treaties are simply bilateral agreements between two states seeking, for example, to establish trade relations or an alliance, or regarding the use of each other's air space or the extradition of criminals from each other's territory. Other treaties are multilateral—between three or more states—and can involve such subjects as international commerce, patent and copyright regulations, regulation of mail and other communications, use of the oceans for fishing and exploration, treatment of prisoners of war, and development or deployment of various kinds of weapons. The past century has witnessed much more multilateralism than previous eras. Over 4,000 new multilateral treaties were concluded between 1945 and 1995, an average of almost 90 per year.[89] Nonetheless an overwhelming majority of treaties are bilateral. It is estimated that multilateral treaties are "only 10% of all treaty activity in the world."[90] Multilateral agreements, though, are the ones of greatest relevance to international law, especially multilateral treaties that deal with issues of broad importance and seek to involve as many members of the international community as possible, such as the UN Charter.

As already noted, there have been increased efforts to use treaties to codify traditional, customary rules of international law. For example, the Vienna Convention on Diplomatic Relations of 1961, ratified by almost every country, reiterated the long-standing rule of international law requiring that the immunity and inviolability of embassies and diplomats be respected. Iran, a party to the treaty, was in violation, then, of both customary law and treaty law when it seized the fifty-two Americans in the U.S. embassy in 1979. Among the provisions of the treaty are the following: Diplomatic agents and members of their families cannot be arrested and prosecuted by the host government for any crimes committed, even a blatant act of murder or a hit-and-run accident; diplomatic agents are immune not only from host state criminal jurisdiction but also from civil claims, which means that they cannot be punished for damaging personal property or passing bad checks and cannot be evicted by landlords for failure to pay the rent. In New York City alone, where diplomats abound at UN headquarters, in some years an estimated 140,000 parking tickets worth $15 million have gone unpaid as diplomats continue to triple park, block major thoroughfares, and generally go about their business blissfully free from the restrictions that apply to most motorists.[91]

However, what might seem to be a grossly unfair system of rules to the New York City cab driver or the person on the street is necessitated by the desire of national governments to ensure that their diplomats are not harassed in any fashion by the host country to which they are assigned. If a diplomat were to abuse such diplomatic immunity, by becoming a mass murderer or a notorious check bouncer, the remedy would be for the host state to request a waiver of immunity from the diplomat's government or to declare the diplomat persona non grata and expel that individual from the country.

Although some treaties simply transcribe customary law into written form, keeping the traditional rules intact, other treaties are designed to revise the customary law. For example, the 1982 UN Convention on the Law of the Sea, a 200-page document negotiated by 150 countries, incorporated some elements of the traditional law of the sea—such as the right of "innocent passage" enjoyed by all ships in the territorial waters of coastal states, the right of "hot pursuit" by coastal state vessels against foreign ships violating the laws of the coastal state, and absolute freedom of navigation for all ships on the "high seas" outside any state's boundaries—but also modified some existing rules, such as extending the width of the territorial seas from 3 to 12 miles.

In some instances, treaties have been used to develop rules in new areas of concern for which no law has existed or been necessary before. For example, the Outer Space Treaty of 1967, now ratified by some 100 states, requires the signatories to refrain from deploying weapons of mass destruction in outer space and to recognize the moon and other celestial bodies as beyond any state's sovereign control. Had the United States, as a party to the treaty, attempted to declare the moon its sovereign territory when it was the first to land there in 1969, the government would have been acting in violation of the 1967 agreement.

It is evident that even in the absence of a world legislature, machinery exists to create written rules that are considered legally binding, with bilateral treaties drafted by the foreign ministries of individual countries and multilateral treaties drafted by the UN International Law Commission or bodies such as the Law of the Sea Conference, the UN specialized agencies, or other entities. There are literally thousands of treaties in effect around the world, and the number is growing not only as a function of the proliferation of states but, more importantly, as the increased volume and complexity of international interactions lead governments to seek more formalized arrangements in regulating intercourse between states. An estimated 40,000 international agreements have been concluded since 1900, most of them since 1945.[92] The growth of treaties in modern times is reflected in the fact that "treaties concluded between 1648 and 1919 fill 226 thick books, between 1920 and 1946 some 205 more volumes, and between 1946 and 1978, 1,115 more tomes."[93]

Still, because state sovereignty means that no state can be forced to endorse any treaty, a common indictment of international law is its essentially voluntary nature.[94] Individuals in the United States and other municipal legal systems do not have the prerogative of deciding whether to agree to be bound by the law. The consent basis of law is generally unheard of in such systems; once a legal rule is promulgated, everyone in the society is expected to abide by it regardless of whether everyone agrees with it. As Michael Glennon says, "One can hardly decide that one will no longer be bound by the rule prohibiting bank robbery."[95] However, the effectiveness of a legal system may consist not so much in how many members of the society have an obligation to obey the law as how many actually *do* obey the law. We will next examine the extent to which international law is obeyed and enforced.

The Breaking of International Law: How Is the Law Enforced?

Another common indictment of international law is the lack of enforcement—the complaint that international law is broken regularly with impunity because of the lack of a central policing agent. True, there are frequent violations of international law, most notably those serious breaches that are reported on the front pages of newspapers, such as the seizure of the U.S. embassy in Iran, the genocidal acts committed in Rwanda and elsewhere in recent years, and various acts of violent aggression at odds with the UN Charter. Critics often point to the cavalier comment by Germany's chancellor, Theobald von Bethmann-Hollweg, on the eve of World War I, that the treaty guaranteeing Belgium's neutrality and safety from invasion was merely a "scrap of paper." The tendency to notice the conspicuous failures of international law, though, obscures the ordinary workings of international law in the everyday life of the international system. What is most striking is not how often international law is broken but how often it is *obeyed*, despite the lack of "traffic cops" to provide a central coercive threat of punishment against would-be offenders. The fact is, if one takes into account the plethora of treaties and customary rules of international law that exist today, it can be said that "almost all nations observe almost all principles of international law and almost all of their obligations almost all of the time."[96] In other words, international law gets "enforced" in its own way.

To understand why this is so, we need to consider the basic reasons why people obey laws in any society. The first is the threat of punishment for illegal behavior, something that realists tend to dwell on. A second is the mutual interests that individuals have in seeing that laws are obeyed, something that idealists or liberals tend to stress. A third is the internalization of the rules by the members of the society—habits of compliance; people obey the law because that is what they have come to accept as the legitimate, right thing to do, something that constructivist thinkers highlight. All of these elements can operate to produce obedience to the law. Consider for a moment why most people bother to obey a stop sign at a busy intersection. One reason is the coercive element—the possibility that a police officer may be lurking around the corner and may stop you if you do not stop yourself. Another is the utilitarian motive—the possibility that another car may accidentally collide with your vehicle if you pass through the intersection without stopping. As powerful as these two motives are, the main driving force behind the inclination to stop at a stop sign is probably the simple habitual nature of the act, which has been inculcated as part of the "code of the road." (Even if someone were driving through the middle of Death Valley in California, where no police cars or other vehicles were visible for several miles, there would be a tendency to stop if a red stop sign were somehow sticking out of the desert sand!)

The point is that law and order can function to some extent even in the absence of police; indeed, any society that relies primarily on coercive threats as the basis for order is terribly fragile. Although habits of compliance—the most solid basis for law—are not well developed in the international system, the mutual interests of states in having a set of rules that prescribe as well as proscribe patterns of behavior provide a foundation for the international legal order. States are willing to tolerate certain constraints on their own behavior because it is widely recognized that international commerce, travel, and other forms of international activity would be exceedingly difficult otherwise. A state will be reluctant to violate a particular rule in a particular instance in order to achieve an expedient, short-term gain if the effect is to weaken an area of law that it wishes to preserve in the long term.

But there are more weighty reasons why all states experience pressure to obey rules. Some might ask, If treaties are merely pieces of paper, to be discarded at the whim of the signatories when it no longer suits their needs, then why do so many diplomats haggle over the fine print during the drafting stage, and why do so many states frequently resist intense lobbying from the international community to commit to an agreement? The answer is that states understand quite well the concept of *pacta sunt servanda*, that, with ratification, they incur legal obligations that can be ignored only at the risk of developing a reputation as a "cheater" and suffering the penalty of finding few takers willing to enter into agreements with such an unreliable partner the next time (what liberals call "the shadow of the future"). This logic of reciprocity is at odds with the cynical view that "peace is a period of cheating between two periods of fighting."[97] Some scholars argue that, to the extent countries violate treaties, it is often due more to a lack of adequate technical, financial, and other resources to carry out their obligations than to willful disobedience.[98] Poor countries face many strains in trying to comply with their international obligations, whether it is filing annual reports with the UN on efforts to combat terrorism or submitting records to the International Maritime Organization regarding the volume of pollutants dumped overboard by ships that sail under their flag.

Curiously, critics argue that international law is virtually nonexistent because it is frequently broken. Anyone who applied the same test of effectiveness to municipal law that is generally demanded of international law—100 percent conformity to and enforcement of the law, or close to it—would have to conclude that there is no law anywhere in the world, not only between nation-states but also within them. Even in as highly developed a legal system as the United States, "the fact is that only about a third of all serious crimes [ranging from murder to auto theft] . . . are ever even reported to the police by the victims. Of all serious crimes reported, in only 19 percent of cases is a suspect ever arrested, although the figure can go as high as 78 percent for murder. Only about half of all suspects arrested are ever convicted. And only a quarter of those convicted actually ever 'do time' for their crime."[99] A murder is committed in the United States every thirty-one minutes, a forcible rape every five minutes, and a burglary every fourteen seconds.[100]

If the number of people who exceed the speed limit on America's highways is added, then the effectiveness of law enforcement in the United States becomes that much more dubious. It is worth noting, however, that law can have an impact in constraining behavior even when it is broken. Before the U.S. Congress (in response to the energy crisis) lowered the speed limit on most U.S. interstates in 1974 from 70 to 55 miles per hour, motorists often went 75 or 80, compared with a typical speed of 65 or 60 after the reduction. Some observers have argued that in the international system as well, international law can have a braking effect that curbs excessive behavior: Many states will try to bend the law without breaking it or will try to limit the extent of their departure from the law so as to be able to claim they were acting at least within the spirit of the law. Abram Chayes has shown, for example, that even in as "high-politics" a situation as the Cuban missile crisis in 1962, American decision-makers were sensitive to the requirements of international law and took it into account in mounting a naval blockade against Russian ships steaming toward Cuba. Although the blockade was technically a violation of international law, it was not as blatant a violation or as provocative an act as other options would have been.[101]

One is hard pressed to find many examples where a state admitted that any of its actions were illegal, precisely because states recognize the value of being perceived as a law-abider. When was the last time you heard a head of state saying, "Yes, we acted illegally, and we are proud of it"? In order to be positioned even to remotely make the claim of legality for their actions, national leaders have a felt need to try to operate within the rough parameters of the law as much as possible, stretching it more often than brazenly, openly showing contempt for the law. In this way, through at least token bows to the rules more than through slavish devotion to them, states enable international law to subtly impact international politics.

While the problem of law enforcement in international law should not be overlooked, we should be aware that unfair and unrealistic standards are sometimes applied in evaluating the effectiveness of international law relative to national law.

The Adjudicating of International Law: Who Are the Judges?

In municipal legal systems, courts are used to determine whether a particular law has been violated in a particular instance when one party accuses another party of an infraction. In the international system, judicial institutions also exist, such as the International Court of Justice (the ICJ, or World Court), which can be used when one state accuses another of violating the law. However, such international institutions are extremely weak insofar as the disputants tend to judge for themselves whether an offense has occurred, or at least tend to reserve for themselves the decision whether to go to court. Whereas in municipal systems one disputant can normally compel the other party to appear in court, international tribunals such as the World Court generally lack compulsory jurisdiction. As in the *United States Diplomatic and Consular Staff in Tehran* case, which the United States brought before the World Court in 1979, one party—in this instance, Iran—can simply refuse to acknowledge the jurisdiction of the Court and to participate in the judicial proceedings. The United States itself refused to accept the jurisdiction of the Court in the 1986 case in which Nicaragua filed suit criticizing the United States for mining Nicaraguan harbors and intervening illegally.

The World Court consists of fifteen judges whose term of office is nine years. Elected by the UN membership, requiring the approval of both the UN Security Council and General Assembly, the judges are generally drawn from every major legal system in the world, with certain countries, such as the United States, each assured of one seat at all times. Only states are eligible to appear as litigants before the Court in its normal proceedings, based on the traditional view that only states have rights and obligations under international law. However, the Court has shown a growing willingness to accord some nonstate actors limited standing before the Court and to issue "advisory opinions" in their favor, such as the 2004 *Legal Consequences of the Construction of a Wall in the Occupied Palestinian Territory* case, which the UN General Assembly brought against Israel.

The World Court sits in The Hague, Netherlands. Some wags say that all the Court seems to do is sit. Despite the fact that 192 states are parties to the ICJ Statute that established the Court (all signatories to the UN Charter automatically accept the statute), the Court has not had a busy docket. The ICJ received a total of only 138 "contentious" cases (nonadvisory in nature) between 1946 and 2008; in roughly one-third of them, it did not render a judgment.[102] There has been an increase in the Court's caseload in recent years, thanks to the innovative use of a "chambers" procedure that permits cases to be heard more efficiently and cheaply by a subset of five or fewer judges. As of 2009, there were twelve cases pending, including boundary disputes such as the altercation between Nicaragua and Colombia over ownership of several Caribbean islands and the disagreement between Romania and Ukraine over division of the Black Sea.[103] However, many observers question whether the Court's docket will be crowded anytime soon.[104]

The lack of business, again, has been largely a function of the lack of compulsory jurisdiction. As of 2009, only sixty-seven countries—about one-third of the international system—had signed the Optional Clause of the ICJ Statute, agreeing to give the Court compulsory jurisdiction in certain kinds of disputes. Moreover, even states that have signed have attached so many reservations to their acceptance of the Court's jurisdiction as to render the clause feeble. The United States, for example, before it formally withdrew its declaration of acceptance in

1986 over the Nicaraguan incident, had agreed to give the Court compulsory jurisdiction except for those "disputes . . . which are essentially within the domestic jurisdiction of the United States *as determined by the United States of America*" (the so-called Connally Amendment).

Where the Court has reached a judgment in a case, its decision has usually been obeyed, even though the ICJ "has no bailiffs . . . to ensure compliance."[105] Some exceptions have already been noted. A few other acts of defiance by states can be cited as well, such as Albania refusing to pay the damages awarded by the Court to the United Kingdom for destruction of British ships in the Corfu channel in 1946, but the bulk of Court rulings have been honored.[106] The ICJ's overall favorable compliance record should not be surprising, since "states do not, as a general rule, refer their more sensitive legal disputes to the ICJ."[107] The fundamental problem remains that, in disputes involving vital interests, states have generally been unwilling to entrust a third party with binding decision-making competence; and in disputes over more trivial matters, states have not felt the need to use the Court because it is far simpler and more economical to settle out of court.

In fairness to the Court, it might be said that most disputes that arise in domestic law are also settled out of court through a process of bargaining not unlike that found in the international system. At times, the very act of one state bringing suit against another state before the Court has put pressure on the parties to reach a settlement on their own, such as Nauru's 1989 ICJ filing against Australia asking it to pay for the rehabilitation of one-third of the island damaged by phosphate mining during the colonial era, which resulted in Australia paying $75 million in restitution in 1993 to avoid further litigation. Still, even the most charitable apologist for the Court would have to admit that it has been an extremely ineffective, largely ignored international institution despite its representing the "highest legal aspiration of civilized man."[108]

Fortunately for the international legal system, the World Court is not the only adjudication vehicle. A variety of other courts exist, including several at the regional level, such as the European Court of Justice. More importantly, *national* courts play a key role in the application of international law in those instances in which international issues arise in domestic suits. The constitutions of most countries stipulate that treaties and other elements of international law are considered to be the supreme law of the land, at least coequal with the highest national statutes. An unusually strong statement of the priority that might be given in the future to international law over national law recently came from U.S. Supreme Court Justice Sandra Day O'Connor: "I suspect that over time we will rely increasingly—or take notice, at least—on international and foreign courts in examining domestic issues [such as capital punishment]."[109] Not all observers shared Justice O'Connor's enthusiasm for international law trumping national law, and the jury is still out on how the relationship between international courts and national courts will evolve.

Adjudication, then, like lawmaking and law enforcement, tends to occur in a more convoluted fashion in the international system than in national systems. In the end, the reader will have to reach his or her own verdict on whether international law, imperfect as it is, qualifies as "law."

The Future of International Law

In the international system, as in national societies, law is essentially based on politics.[110] That is, the legal rules developed by a society tend to reflect the interests of those members of society who have the most resources with which to influence the rule-making process. Although the law in some societies may be based on a wider, more just set of values and interests than in other societies, underlying political realities invariably shape the law. Much of the current body of international law, for example, evolved from the international politics of the nineteenth and early twentieth centuries, when Western states dominated the international system. The traditional rules that were created to promote freedom of the sea, protection of foreign investment, and many other international activities tended to reflect the needs and interests of these powers.

However, when political realities change along with technological conditions and other factors, pressures mount to *alter* the law so that it better reflects the new environment. The contemporary international system can be thought of as a society in ferment, with weapons of mass destruction, globalization and the growth of multinational corporations, and revolutionary advances in travel and communications threatening to make many of the existing rules obsolete. An equally important impetus for change in the legal order is provided by the shifting power equation in world politics, as traditional powers find it difficult to impose their will on former colonies clamoring for a rewriting of the rules more compatible with their interests, and all states are facing challenges posed by nonstate actors. Then, too, as constructivists argue, sometimes the law changes in response not to material conditions but to ideational factors—normative progress.

CONCLUSION

We have seen that international law, along with international organization, have developed not merely as handmaidens of the great powers but as responses to the felt need by all states to "pool" sovereignty and collaborate in addressing various problems. *Part Three* will examine the politics of global problem-solving and efforts to produce international regimes in three issue-areas: (1) *improving international security* (with a focus especially on controlling the proliferation of weapons of mass destruction), (2) *enhancing human rights and human development* (including not only expanding democracy but closing the rich-poor gap and improving "human security"), and (3) *managing the world economy and promoting prosperity* (with a focus on globalization and the international politics of trade and investment). We will see how some 200 nation-states, thousands of international

organizations, and over 6 billion people are engaging in both conflict and cooperation in an ever more complex world system.

QUESTIONS FOR STUDY AND DISCUSSION

1. What is meant by "global governance" and the "pooling" of sovereignty?
   What role do "international regimes" play in such processes?
2. Give examples of IGOs and NGOs, global and regional international organizations, and multipurpose and unipurpose international organizations.
3. What explains the growth of IGOs? NGOs? Which are more important
   actors in IR?
4. What is meant by "functionalism"? Do you agree with functional theorists about the dynamics of international cooperation and international
   institution-building?
5. What is meant by "collective security"? What is the record of the United
   Nations in this area? What about "peacekeeping"?
6. How do you see the "widening versus deepening" debate in the European
   Union and the future of the EU? Can the EU regional integration experiment be duplicated elsewhere? What variables seem critical to successful regional integration?
7. How do lawmaking, law enforcement, and law adjudication occur in the
   international system? How effective is international law? Is international
   law really "law"?

SUGGESTIONS FOR FURTHER READING

Abram Chayes, *The Cuban Missile Crisis and the Role of Law* (Oxford University Press, 1974).
Inis Claude, *Swords into Plowshares*, 4th ed. (New York: Random House, 1984).
Paul F. Diehl, ed., *The Politics of Global Governance*, 3rd ed. (Boulder, CO: Lynne Rienner,
   2005).
Linda Fasulo, *An Insider's Guide to the UN* (New Haven, CT: Yale University Press, 2004).
Louis Henkin, *How Nations Behave: Law and Foreign Policy* (New York: Columbia Univer-
   sity Press, 1979).
Harold K. Jacobson, *Networks of Interdependence*, 2nd ed. (New York: Knopf, 1984).
Margaret Karns and Karen Mingst, *International Organizations* (Boulder, CO: Lynne Rien-
   ner, 2010).
Margaret E. Keck and Kathryn Sikkink, *Activists Beyond Borders* (Ithaca, NY: Cornell Uni-
   versity Press, 1998).
Paul Kennedy, *The Parliament of Man* (New York: Random House, 2006).
Robert O. Keohane and Joseph S. Nye, eds., *Transnational Relations and World Politics*
   (Cambridge, MA: Harvard University Press, 1971).
Stephen D. Krasner, ed., *International Regimes* (Ithaca, NY: Cornell University Press, 1983).
John McCormick, *Understanding The European Union*, 3rd ed. (New York: Palgrave, 2005).
John Mearsheimer, "The False Promise of International Institutions," *International Security*
   19 (Winter 1994/1995): 5–49.

J. Martin Rochester, *Between Peril and Promise* (Washington, D.C.: CQ Press, 2006).

Thomas Weiss et al., *The United Nations and Changing World Politics*, 5th ed. (Boulder, CO: Westview, 2007).

Thomas Weiss and Leon Gordenker, eds., *NGOs, the UN, and Global Governance* (Boulder, CO: Lynne Rienner, 1996).

"What Good Is International Law?" special issue of *Wilson Quarterly,* Autumn 2003.

Mark W. Zacher and Brent A. Sutton, *Governing Global Networks: International Regimes for Transportation and Communication* (Cambridge: Cambridge University Press, 1996).

PART THREE

GLOBAL PROBLEM-SOLVING:

Issue-Areas

Only six or seven thousand years ago civilization emerged, enabling us to build a human world and to add to the marvels of art, of science, of social organization, or spiritual attainment. But, as we built higher and higher, the evolutionary foundation beneath our feet became more and more shaky, and now in spite of all we have learned and achieved—or, rather, because of it—we hold this entire terrestrial creation hostage to nuclear destruction, threatening to hurl it back into the inanimate darkness from which it came.

—Jonathan Schell, *The Fate of the Earth*, 1982

In the Cold War, the most frequently asked question was: "How big is your missile?" In globalization, the most frequently asked question is: "How fast is your modem?"

—Thomas Friedman, *The Lexus and the Olive Tree*, 1999

Welfare, not warfare, will shape the rules [and] dictate the agenda.

—Josef Joffe, 1993

We are fast approaching many of the earth's limits.

—World scientists' Warning to Humanity signed by over 1,600 scientists, including a majority of Nobel Prize laureates, 1992

7

Improving
International
Security

*An essential part of the consensus we seek must be agreement on when
and how force can be used to defend international peace and security. . . .
[States] have disagreed about whether States have the right to use military
force pre-emptively, to defend themselves against imminent threats; whether
they have the right to use it preventively to defend themselves against la-
tent or non-imminent threats, and whether they have the right—or perhaps the obligation—to use it protectively to rescue citizens of other States
from genocide or comparable crimes.*

—Kofi Annan, *In Larger Freedom* (Report of the Secretary-General
on UN Reform), 2005

*Nations . . . shall beat their swords into plowshares, and their spears into
pruninghooks . . . neither shall they learn war any more.*

—Isaiah 2:4

A former Speaker of the U.S. House of Representatives, Thomas "Tip" O'Neill, once
observed that "all politics is local." Although many problems, along with the politics of problem-solving, continue to be local, increasingly they are national, regional, and global in scope. *Part Three* engages in a discussion of problem-solving
on a global scale. There is some disagreement as to which global problems are most
challenging and serious. Is it managing the proliferation of weapons of mass destruction (WMDs)? Closing the gap between rich and poor and lifting millions
of human beings out of dire poverty? Reducing global warming and other environmental threats? Not everyone sees these issues as problems, at least not equally
so. Yet they have attracted sufficient attention as planetary concerns to merit a place
on the global agenda and to stimulate efforts at multilateral institution-building
and regime-making. Many other concerns, of course, can be identified as well. We

will examine several of these problems in a survey of various issue-areas in this part of the book. We begin in Chapter 7 with a discussion of efforts to improve international security, including the rules governing the possession of armaments and their use.

THE PROBLEM

Chapter 5 reported trend data on whether the world has become more warlike or less so, with the record being a mixed bag. What remains highly problematical is the continued existence of lots of lethal firepower scattered about the planet, both small arms and big arms. Although the post–Cold War era at first saw a "peace dividend" as total global military spending declined somewhat in the 1990s, world military expenditures since have risen roughly to the level that existed at the end of the Cold War, currently hovering over $1 trillion.[1] Even if such arsenals are never used, they represent enormous opportunity costs in terms of health care and other societal benefits forgone due to resources spent elsewhere. (See the *IR* Critical Thinking Box "The Guns Versus Butter Debate.") Worse, if they were to be used, there is the potential for unprecedented destruction in the nuclear age.

IR Critical Thinking:
The Guns Versus Butter Debate

A lively, long-standing debate in the international relations discipline, as well as in public discourse, has revolved around the costs of defense spending—the impact of defense spending on the overall health of the national economy, including the diversion of vital resources that could be used for other societal needs. This is known as the "guns versus butter" debate. President Dwight Eisenhower, who was among the first to raise concerns about a growing "military-industrial complex" in the United States, framed this problem in a speech to the American Society of Newspaper Editors in 1953:

> Every gun that is made, every warship launched, every rocket fired signifies in the final sense a theft from those who hunger and are not fed, those who are cold and are not clothed. This world in arms is not spending money alone. It is spending the sweat of laborers, the genius of its scientists and the hopes of its children.

Eisenhower was referring to the opportunity costs of arms spending for not only Americans but others. The 1980 Brandt report, *North-South* (p. 14), stated:

> The military expenditure of only half a day would suffice to finance the whole malaria eradication programme of the World Health Organization. . . . A modern tank costs about one million dollars; that amount could improve storage facilities for 100,000 tons of rice [and thus reduce spoilage by 4,000 tons annually]. The same sum of money could provide 1,000 classrooms for 30,000 children.

One can add numerous other statistics during the Cold War and since that suggest the folly of arms spending. However, such statistics beg the twofold question of (1) whether arms spending necessarily is bad for an economy and (2) whether arms spending necessarily diverts resources that would otherwise be definitely used for more productive societal purposes.

Regarding the first question, Marxist scholars long have argued that peacetime military spending is often used by governments to stimulate capitalist economies with high unemployment. Indeed, many Marxists and non-Marxists alike have argued that heavy military spending during World War II helped get the United States out of the Great Depression. However, many liberals argue that defense spending is not only unnecessary for a healthy economy (witness the impressive growth of Germany and Japan after World War II, achieved with relatively little defense spending) but can weaken an economy in terms of increasing inflationary pressures, making localities overly dependent on the vagaries of defense industry jobs, and encouraging waste through costly overruns for weapons systems. Based on the evidence in the scholarly literature, there is no clear impact, positive or negative, that defense spending has on a national economy. (See Steve Chan, "Grasping the Peace Dividend: Some Propositions on the Conversion of Swords Into Plowshares," *Mershon International Studies Review*, August 1995.)

But what about the second question, regarding the trade-offs between defense spending and welfare spending? Here, too, there is no clear finding in the literature that a reduction in defense spending translates into more spending on health, education, and social welfare concerns. U.S. defense spending has fluctuated substantially over time, mainly as a function of wars and foreign policy crises, whereas social spending has remained fairly level, suggesting that one is independent of the other and that the military slice of the pie does not necessarily come at the expense of the welfare slice, although social spending did rise somewhat during the 1990s era of the post–Cold War "peace dividend" as military bases were closed and other downsizing occurred. The trade-offs would seem more a matter of political choices than economic imperatives.

Think about the following questions:

1. If you were a congressman or senator and you had to vote on a bill that would close a major military installation or cut appropriations for a weapons system manufactured in your home district or state, how would you vote? Would you look at the big picture in terms of how such spending cuts might free up money for other national needs (either more important national security needs or domestic needs), or would you be guided mainly by parochial interests in maintaining local jobs? How do you think elected representatives normally act when making such decisions? How, as a constituent, would you want your elected representative to act?

2. How do you weigh the relative importance of national defense and security spending versus domestic welfare spending? How does this relate to your general philosophy about the proper role of government?

3. The United States now spends roughly $500 billion a year on the military. How much is enough in terms of defense spending? Would you be willing to spend less on national defense so that more could be spent on the poor at home and abroad?

4. Does it matter that the United States is now the leading arms merchant in the world? If the U.S. refrained from selling arms to other countries, including poor

(continues)

(continued)

countries that can ill afford to use scarce resources for weaponry, would it make a difference? Or would other countries simply benefit by filling the weapons orders instead of the United States?

5. Almost every country has become a party to the Nuclear Nonproliferation Treaty, which, if you do not have nuclear weapons, obligates you not to acquire them. Given the fact that the vast majority of countries are nuclear have-nots, what explains their willingness to deny themselves arguably the ultimate badge of national power and prestige? Discuss realist, liberal, and constructivist explanations of such behavior.

In 1989, as the Cold War was ending, world military expenditures totaled $1.3 trillion.[2] Commenting on wasteful military spending at the time, one analyst noted that the outlay for just a single U.S. Trident submarine could fund a five-year program for universal child immunization against the six deadliest diseases, thereby preventing 1 million deaths annually. Even more wasteful, in terms of "overkill" capacity, was the existing stockpile of nuclear weapons, whose mega-tonnage (95 percent of which was possessed by the United States and the Soviet Union) equaled "1 million Hiroshima-size bombs and 3.2 tons of TNT for everyone on earth."[3] Over the next ten years, between 1989 and 1999, world military expenditures decreased by 35 percent, highlighted by a dramatic drop in nuclear arsenals resulting from bilateral agreements between Washington and Moscow.[4]

However, the period from 1999 to 2009 saw a reversal of these trends. The Stockholm International Peace Research Institute's (SIPRI) annual yearbook on world armaments reported in 2008 that "military spending, arms production and international arms transfers are all on the rise," with world military spending totaling $1.3 trillion, corresponding to 2.5 percent of world GDP and $202 for each person in the world. "This is a real-terms increase of 45 percent since 1998. The factors driving increases . . . include aspiration to global or regional power status, actual or potential conflicts, and the availability of economic resources."[5]

The United States now accounts for almost half of all world military spending, followed far behind by the United Kingdom, China, France, and Japan (with 4–5 percent each). High-income countries account for 75 percent of the total, although their share of world spending has been shrinking over time as many lower-income countries, led by China, have enlarged their military establishments. Developing countries that are among the top fifteen spenders in the world are China, Saudi Arabia, India, South Korea, and Brazil. Aside from North America, Europe is the biggest-spending region (28 percent of the total), followed by Asia (16 percent) and the Middle East (7 percent). The subregions outside North America that have experienced the greatest increases over the past ten years are Eastern Europe (including Russia), the Middle East (fueled by ongoing Israeli-Arab/Muslim tensions), South Asia (fueled by the India-Pakistan conflict), and East Asia (fueled by problems on the Korean peninsula along with rapid Chinese economic growth permitting expansion of its military forces).[6]

The largest arms-producing companies in the world have tended to be private firms, especially in the United States, where Boeing, Lockheed, and a handful of other corporations dominate. Whether private or state-owned (as in Russia and in some Western European countries), defense industries have close ties to their home governments. Arms are produced not only for the home country but also for sale abroad. International **arms transfers** are actively promoted by firms when domestic sales are inadequate to keep production lines going, as well as by their home governments, which see such transfers as a way to sustain a national arms industry and help the defense of allies and gain influence over other states.[7] Some believe that the military-industrial complex in the United States—incestuous relations between large munitions makers and the U.S. Department of Defense— has created a larger than necessary U.S. arms budget and positioned the United States as the world's largest arms merchant.

During the Cold War, the two superpowers competed for the latter title, with two-thirds of all arms exports worldwide provided by the United States and the Soviet Union, going mostly to less developed countries. Although the United States surged ahead of Russia in the 1990s, Russia has recently begun to compete again. The U.S. share of major conventional weapons exports is now approximately 30 percent, while Russia's is 25 percent, followed by Germany (10 percent), France (9 percent), and the United Kingdom (4 percent). Two-thirds of all arms still flow to the developing world, in some cases to countries saddled with extreme poverty. The leading arms-importing countries have been China (12 percent of the total), India (8 percent), United Arab Emirates (7 percent), Greece (6 percent), and South Korea (5 percent). Asia, Europe, and the Middle East have been the largest recipient regions. Although the current annual $50 billion value of the global arms trade is well below the peak of $87 billion reached toward the end of the Cold War (1987), the trend over the past decade has been in the direction of increasing arms transfers.[8]

For those concerned about gun control on a global level, the challenge of limiting weapons proliferation ranges from the ubiquity of small arms, particularly assault rifles that flow freely into the hands of irregular armies fighting in civil conflicts, to the slow spread of nuclear weapons possibly to not only "rogue" states but also "rogue" nonstate actors. Regarding the former, it is estimated that there are 500 million small arms in circulation worldwide—one for every twelve people; these arms are thought to be responsible for over half a million deaths annually.[9] A former Canadian foreign minister has called these "small arms of mass destruction."[10] (The weapon of choice is the AK-47 automatic rifle, which can fire thirty rounds in three seconds.) The problem is described as follows: "Small arms and light weapons have been the primary instruments of the many intrastate conflicts that have plagued the globe since the end of the Cold War. They are inexpensive and widely available, which makes it easy for aggrieved groups to take up arms against governments or other nonstate actors. . . . Their ease of use and small size make small arms ideal for untrained combatants and even child soldiers. . . . Furthermore, the existence of transnational criminal organizations trafficking in drugs and persons [has] provided a ready-made network of dealers for the illicit weapons trade."[11]

Regarding larger weapons of mass destruction—commonly called WMDs or ABC weapons (atomic [nuclear], biological, and chemical weapons)—there is concern about their growing availability as well, along with their ending up in the hands of criminal or terrorist groups. The United States and Russia possess 98 percent of the world's stockpile of chemical weapons (nerve gas, mustard gas, and other deadly munitions). Although the Chemical Weapons Convention (CWC) bans such weapons and the United States and Russia along with other signatories are in the process of disposing of them, only 25 percent of the world's declared stockpile of 70,000 metric tons of chemical agents had been verifiably destroyed as of 2009, while several states in the Middle East and elsewhere remain nonsignatories and are thought to have undeclared chemical arsenals.[12] The Biological Weapons Convention (BWC) bans the possession of bacteriological weapons (smallpox, anthrax, and the like) but contains even weaker verification and enforcement machinery than the CWC. At least thirteen countries are thought to have active biological weapons programs.[13] Concerns have been raised in recent years about "an international black market in 'hot strains'—deadly organisms—such as anti-biotic resistant strains of anthrax and Black Death [bubonic plague] as well as botulinum toxin and possibly the Ebola virus."[14] (The CWC, BWC, and other arms control treaties are discussed in detail later in the chapter.)

Concerns also have been raised about "loose nukes" that might be acquired by terrorists in countries such as Russia and Pakistan, whose security systems are considered relatively lax.[15] The progress made during the 1990s in scaling down the superpower nuclear arsenals—the United States and Russia each lowered its stockpile of **strategic** nuclear weapons (warheads deliverable by long-range bombers, intercontinental ballistic missiles, or submarine-launched missiles) from approximately 9,000 to 3,000, with pledges to reduce further down to 2,000—was offset by three developments. First, arms control talks between the United States and Russia have remained stalled, with further cuts in question and the two countries still possessing huge strategic nuclear arsenals along with many other **tactical** nuclear weapons (shorter-range weapons). Second, despite the Nuclear Nonproliferation Treaty (NPT), nuclear weapons have spread to other states. Where the "**nuclear club**" for many years had consisted of the United States, Russia, China, Britain, and France, the 1990s saw India and Pakistan join the club (each with some 60 warheads), while North Korea (through plutonium reprocessing) and Iran (through uranium enrichment) were on the brink of joining the club and may be close to possessing nuclear weapons capability. North Korea is thought to have exploded a number of nuclear devices since 2006, and Iran is suspected of planning to do the same by the end of the decade.[16] (Israel long has been considered a de facto member of the club, since it is assumed to have a nuclear capability even though it never has acknowledged such.) Third, the loose nuke problem has become even more alarming, given the unstable regimes in Pyongyang and Islamabad. The former chief scientist of the Pakistani nuclear program was so cavalier in shopping nuclear secrets to various state and nonstate actors, as if he were selling toys, that critics called his operation "Nukes R Us."

In total, the eight current nuclear weapons states possess over 10,000 operational nuclear weapons; if all nuclear warheads are counted, the number is over 25,000, a significant decrease from the 60,000 that existed during the Cold War but still equivalent to the explosive power of 200,000 Hiroshima bombs.[17] As noted earlier, deterrence may work to prevent a nuclear attack by one state against another, but it is less feasible against nonstate actors, which often do not have clear addresses to retaliate against and which in the case of religious groups may even welcome death as martyrdom. Given such a threat, several former high-level American policymakers have urged movement "toward a nuclear-free world," issuing the following warning: "The accelerating spread of nuclear weapons, nuclear know-how and nuclear material has brought us to a nuclear tipping point. We face a very real possibility that the deadliest weapons ever invented could fall into dangerous hands."[18] Although the Stockholm Peace Research Institute notes that "efforts to prevent the proliferation of weapons of mass destruction—nuclear, biological or chemical—are increasingly focused on individuals and nonstate groups rather than states," governments remain the main custodians of WMDs. The more states that have WMDs, the greater the possibility of a catastrophic incident.[19] For example, the authors of the article "Toward a Nuclear Free World" write, "Mistakes are made in every other human endeavor. Why should nuclear weapons be exempt? . . . [In August 2007] six cruise missiles armed with nuclear warheads were loaded on a U.S. Air Force plane, flown across the country and unloaded. For 36 hours, no one knew where the warheads were, or even that they were missing."[20] If the United States, with its supposed secure, fail-safe systems, is prone to nuclear negligence, what does this say about other countries with fewer safeguards?

Are the two staples of Cold War management of aggression and WMD threats still relevant in the post–Cold War era, or, as one observer suggests, are "deterrence and arms control in decline"?[21] To answer this question, we need to examine the status of international regimes governing the use of armed force and arms control, as well as how the changing face of global violence has created special problems, and opportunities, for global governance in the security issue-area.

USE OF FORCE REGIMES

Although the great body of international law consists of rules governing intercourse among nations during peacetime, there is also a corpus of law having to do with war. As noted in the previous chapter, these rules have been unevenly observed. Some of these rules pertain to the *start* of war—the circumstances under which

National Archives Photo no. 111-SC-259370

The second atomic bomb test at Bikini Atoll in the Pacific, July 24, 1946. Is a nuclear-free world possible?

it is legal for a state to resort to the use of armed force against another state (what is called *jus ad bellum*). Other rules pertain to the *conduct* of war—the kinds of behavior that are permissible by governments once a war is under way, regardless of how it began (what is called *jus in bello*).

Efforts to Regulate the Outbreak of War

Throughout history there have been attempts to regulate the outbreak of war, going back to the **just war** doctrine advanced by St. Augustine in the fourth century A.D. and later Grotius in the seventeenth century; this position held that the use of violence was legitimate as long as the purpose was not self-aggrandizement or petty revenge but rather correction of some major wrong (and as long as the means used were proportionate to the provocation). In the eighteenth and nineteenth centuries, legal efforts were devoted more to making war a more civilized affair than actually banishing or restricting its occurrence. Not until the twentieth century, with the **League of Nations Covenant** and the **Kellogg-Briand Pact** (the Pact of Paris) following the horrors of World War I, were efforts made to explicitly *outlaw* war.[22] The 1919 Covenant contained a modest prohibition on war, stating that the only obligation of states to refrain from the use of armed force was that they at least first exhaust all peaceful settlement procedures and "in no case resort to war until three months after the award by the arbitrators or the judicial decision or the report of the Council." Member states that violated this rule were to be subject to collective security sanctions by the League, a threat that failed to deter or punish acts of aggression in the interwar period, such as Italy's attack on Ethiopia in 1935, which was met with only "a brief boycott of Italian-made shoes."[23] The 1928 Kellogg-Briand treaty, ratified by most nations, was a more ambitious denunciation of war but one with even less teeth; it declared that "the settlement of all disputes . . . shall never be sought except by pacific means." World War II showed the ineffectiveness of such pious denunciations of violence.

The **United Nations Charter** in 1945 sought to specify more clearly the proscription against the use of armed force in international relations, and to provide stronger enforcement machinery should the norm be violated. Article 2(4) states that all members are obligated to "refrain . . . from the threat or use of force against the territorial integrity or political independence of any state." In other words, *any first use of armed force by one state against another state*—no matter how limited—constitutes aggression and is *illegal*. Force may be used legally only under the following two conditions: (1) if a state is attacked, it is entitled to use force in *self-defense*, either individually or as part of an alliance; and (2) even if a state is not attacked, it is entitled, indeed obligated, to use armed force in the service of the UN or a regional security organization, as long as it is authorized by the UN Security Council under the "threat to the peace" collective security provisions of Chapter VII.

We saw in the previous chapter that compliance with UN rules governing the use of armed force has been erratic. Michael Glennon, expressing the realist view, has argued that state practice (in effect, customary law) has superseded the UN Charter; the ban on the first use of armed force has "collapsed" as "the rules of the Charter do not today constitute binding restraints on intervention by states."[24] Glennon was referring to the many military interventions by the United States and the Soviet Union during the Cold War as well as the numerous interventions in the post–Cold War era. A contrary, liberal view has been voiced by Louis Henkin. Echoing Mark Zacher's views about the "territorial integrity" norm, Henkin contends that, even though the use of armed force continues to be a feature of contemporary world politics, "the norm against the unilateral national use of force has survived. Indeed . . . the norm has been largely observed . . . and the kinds of international wars which it sought to prevent and deter [wars between states] have been infrequent."[25]

However—and this is the rub—the norm against unilateral force has been less effective in the gray areas discussed earlier, such as "force without war," and is especially problematic in dealing with the most common forms of global violence today—intrastate and extrastate hostilities. As Joseph Nye comments, "The doctrine of collective security enshrined in the UN Charter is state-centric, applicable when borders are crossed but not when force is used against peoples within a state."[26] Similarly, another writer remarks that the institutions we have to combat security problems are "still wired for the sovereign, often state-to-state military confrontations of a bygone era."[27] Some authors have examined "the challenges to the Charter paradigm" and called for a "post-Charter paradigm" to rectify the inadequacy of the current regime governing the use of armed force.[28]

WHAT RULES APPLY TO CIVIL WARS?

The rules governing the outbreak of hostilities have been inadequate to cope with internal wars and mixed internal/external conflicts (internal wars involving outside intervention). The obligations that outside actors have in situations of civil strife are hard to sort out because of the inherent complexities of these situations. In these conflicts, it is often the case that, rather than one state engaging in an armed attack on another state, there is a government seeking foreign support to suppress a rebellion or a rebel group seeking foreign support to overthrow a government or to secede. The rules governing the right of a state to intervene militarily in an internal conflict in another state are fairly straightforward, based on customary law: The former can intervene only if it has the permission of the latter's government. The intrusion of foreign troops or clandestine agents into a domestic conflict on the side of the rebels to subvert an established government constitutes aggression and is a violation of the UN Charter. However, neither can foreign military assistance be provided to a government on the brink of collapse, since a government has a legal right to invite such assistance only if it can claim to exercise effective control and authority over its own population. The problem is this is the very condition that is often in dispute during a civil war.

The rules failed to regulate the insurgency/counterinsurgency dance played by the United States and the Soviet Union during the Cold War. They continue to be plagued by difficulties in the post–Cold War era, as seen, for example, in the case of Russia's 2008 intervention in Georgia. Rebel groups in South Ossetia and Abhazia had been resisting Georgian rule and seeking self-determination. When Georgian troops escalated the use of force in an effort to restore order in the two breakaway provinces, Russia intervened militarily, claiming it had a right to protect ethnic Russians and others from the violence being inflicted on them. Russian tanks advanced all the way to the Georgian capital of Tbilisi, reinforcing suspicions in the European Union and the United States that Moscow was attempting to undermine an emergent democratic regime that was friendly to the West and to gain control over the oil pipeline in the region rather than rescue civilians in harm's way and stabilize Russia's border as a defensive measure. From Russia's perspective, its intervention seemed little different from NATO's military intervention in Kosovo in 1999, which had the effect of stopping ethnic cleansing of an Albanian minority by the Serb government and facilitating Kosovar independence from Serbia.

WHAT RULES APPLY TO HUMANITARIAN INTERVENTION?

As noted earlier, foreign involvement in civil wars in the post–Cold War era, not only in Kosovo but also in Somalia, Haiti, Sierra Leone, and other places, frequently has been justified as **humanitarian intervention**.[29] The so-called Clinton Doctrine stated that "if somebody comes after innocent civilians and tries to kill them *en masse* because of their race, ethnic background, or religion, and it's within our power to stop it, we will stop it."[30] Similarly, UN secretary-general Kofi Annan became closely associated with humanitarian intervention, when he said that the protection of human rights must "take precedence over concerns of state sovereignty," that sovereignty cannot provide "excuses for the inexcusable," and that the UN Charter "was issued in the name of 'the peoples,' not the governments, of the United Nations."[31] In his report *In Larger Freedom* (2005), Annan noted that the International Commission on Intervention and State Sovereignty described "an emerging norm that there is a collective responsibility to protect" against genocide, ethnic cleansing, and crimes against humanity.[32]

Annan sparked much debate over this "emerging norm." The traditionalist view is that international law grants "no general right unilaterally to charge into another country to save its people from their own leaders."[33] But what about multilateral intervention—an action taken by the international community at large, triggered by ethnic cleansing or other atrocities committed by a dictatorial regime (as in the case of the 1992 UN-authorized intervention to protect Bosnians in the former Yugoslavia) or the collapse of civil order and the spread of starvation in failed states (as in the case of the UN-authorized intervention in Somalia that same year)? If the international community waits for an invitation before acting in these situations, a humanitarian response may be impossible. No repressive regime would welcome external oversight in the first case, and there would be no functioning regime to extend the invitation in the second case. There is a widely held view that "humanitarian intervention now must be multilateral to be legitimate," yet international law is not entirely clear on this point.[34] As one international lawyer has observed, "The permissible contours of humanitarian intervention have not been defined in a way that represents a meaningful State consensus. An essential reason is that . . . neither word has been precisely defined."[35] The failure of the UN to respond effectively to genocide in Rwanda in the 1990s (by Hutus against Tutsis) and Sudan in the 2000s (by the Khartoum government against non-Arabs in Darfur) reflected the uncertainty surrounding the principle of humanitarian intervention.

Realists and other critics have noted that humanitarian intervention threatens Westphalian ordering arrangements and is at odds with the UN Charter, insofar as it contradicts Article 2(7), which stipulates that "nothing contained in the Charter shall authorize the UN to intervene in matters which are essentially within the domestic jurisdiction of any state." Although Article 2(7) adds that "this principle shall not prejudice the application of enforcement measures under Chapter VII," many UN members fear that such language is an invitation for Security Council members to interfere in the domestic affairs of smaller, weaker states. Of greatest concern is a state or group of states using the humanitarian intervention norm as a pretext to bring about regime change without UN approval, as happened with NATO bombing of Kosovo in 1999 that ended the reign of Slobodan Milosevic and led to the separation of Kosovo from Serbia. The 114 members of the nonaligned movement, representing the developing countries, have condemned such intervention, declaring it has "no legal basis under the Charter."[36] The theory and practice of humanitarian intervention remain mired in controversy.

WHAT RULES APPLY TO "SELF-DEFENSE" AGAINST STATES AND NONSTATE ACTORS?

Also controversial recently has been the definition of "self-defense." When the United States attacked Afghanistan in 2001 and Iraq in 2003, Washington invoked a right of self-defense among its main legal arguments to support the invasions. The Bush administration found it easier to claim international law was on its side in the Afghanistan War than the Iraq War, although both raised thorny legal questions.

Regarding Afghanistan, the United States clearly was attacked on September 11, 2001, when airplanes struck the World Trade Center and the Pentagon. However, the attack was perpetrated not by another state but by al Qaeda, a nonstate actor hiding in Afghanistan. This raised the following question: To what extent can State A (e.g., the United States) enter the territory of State B (e.g., Afghanistan) to capture or kill actors (such as Osama bin Laden and his followers) thought to have been responsible for a terrorist attack on State A? International law ordinarily does not condone a state trespassing into another state to abduct alleged criminals, assassinate individuals, or pursue terrorists. Although state practice has been inconsistent, the general rule is that, if State B is not clearly sponsoring or harboring the terrorists but merely finds itself used as a refuge, State A cannot intrude upon its sovereignty by engaging in military activity on its soil without its permission. On the other hand, if State B can be shown to be a close collaborator giving succor to the terrorists and not taking adequate steps to prevent terrorism, then State A is on stronger legal footing in taking military action. Given the Taliban government's close ties to al Qaeda and its refusal to surrender bin Laden to the United States after 9/11, the American bombing of al Qaeda bases was widely accepted as justifiable self-defense, although some critics complained that it amounted to retaliation rather than defense and that the regime change that forced the removal of the Taliban from power violated Afghan sovereignty. (It helped Washington that the UN Security Council passed resolutions after 9/11 affirming the U.S. right of self-defense.) These same issues arose later in the decade, as al Qaeda reconstituted itself in Pakistan along the Afghan border and Washington claimed the right to send Special Operations forces into Pakistan to kill terrorists there even if the Pakistani government denied permission.[37]

In the case of the American invasion of Iraq in 2003, Secretary-General Annan said it was "illegal" since the United States could not invoke the right of self-defense (the U.S. had not been attacked by Iraq or any groups within Iraq) and could not invoke the collective security provisions of the Charter (the Security Council had not authorized the use of armed force).[38] The most intriguing legal argument advanced by Washington was the right of anticipatory or *preemptive* self-defense, which seemed to be at odds with the UN Charter's ban on the first use of armed force. To the extent any such right exists, the onus is on the attacker to justify the resort to force, with the so-called *Caroline* standard (based on an 1837 case involving customary law) being the generally accepted requirement that must be met: The preemptive use of armed force is legal only if "the necessity of that self-defense is instant, overwhelming, and leaving no choice of means, and no moment of deliberation."[39]

The Bush administration claimed in 2003 that there was reason to believe that Iraq had weapons of mass destruction, that Saddam Hussein was a serial aggressor as well as state sponsor of terror, and that he posed a threat to U.S. security that could not be ignored in the post-9/11 era. Bush went so far as to enunciate what came to be known as the **Bush Doctrine**, which asserted the right of the United States to engage in the preemptive use of military force against any country thought to *possibly* pose a threat to U.S. security.[40] However, critics of the Iraq invasion argued that it did not meet the *Caroline* test, since it was a *preventive* war rather than a *preemptive* war—a war Washington wanted to fight rather than one it needed to fight. They pointed out that no attack by Iraq was imminent, there was no unequivocal evidence it still possessed WMDs, and there was no clear connection between Iraq and the 9/11 terrorists. Moreover, critics worried that the Bush Doctrine, if embraced by other states, could invite and legitimize all kinds of first strikes, including an attack by Pakistan against nuclear-armed India, or India against nuclear-armed Pakistan.

On the one hand, it perhaps was reasonable for the Bush administration to take the position that, after 9/11, the United States could not afford to be a sitting duck waiting for a state or nonstate actor to initiate a WMD attack on New York City or another American target before retaliating. On the other hand, the loose definition of self-defense implied in the Bush Doctrine threatened to unravel the entire Charter regime that had been developed to control the outbreak of war. In 2004, the UN Secretary-General's High-Level Panel on Threats, Challenges, and Change attempted to address the problem by calling for legalizing the use of military force in a "preventive" manner to eliminate the potential for horrific terrorist attacks as long as such use of force against terrorist sanctuaries is authorized by the Security Council. The proposal failed to gain acceptance by the United States and others who were wary of entrusting their fate to the Security Council. The international community may yet seize the opportunity to expand global governance in this area of mutual threat posed by nonstate actors by revising the existing regime on the use of armed force, but consensus is hard to achieve when the "highest" politics issues are at stake.

The war on terror has no ending in sight. Also uncertain is the question of which laws of war should apply in conducting the war, in terms of the scope of the battlefield, the treatment of captured prisoners, and other issues. The *Caroline* case had suggested standards governing not only the *resort* to force but also the *proportionality* of force, recognizing the long-standing just-war prescription that, no matter how a war commences, there is an obligation to refrain from using force in a manner that is excessive or inhumane. Earlier we noted how asymmetrical warfare today poses challenges for the operation of what is called *international humanitarian law*. The changing nature of global violence is making the rules governing the *conduct* of war no less of a legal minefield than those governing the onset of war.

Efforts to Regulate the Conduct of War

Over the centuries, humanity, having failed to ban war altogether, has attempted to make it at least more humane by regulating its conduct through agreed-upon rules of engagement. Some of the efforts to inject a dose of civility into warfare have seemed paradoxical and slightly comical, such as the prohibition (embodied in the Hague Convention of 1907) against the use of "dum-dum" expanding bullets and the use of "deceit" in the form of misrepresenting a flag of truce or wearing Red Cross uniforms as a disguise—especially at a time when using poisonous gas and other horrendous weapons were legally permissible. However, absurd as they might appear and as erratic as their observance has been, the laws governing the conduct of war (*jus in bello*) have often succeeded in limiting the brutal nature of war to some extent.[41] The International Committee of the Red Cross describes the essence of *jus in bello*, or **international humanitarian law**, as follows:

> International humanitarian law is a set of rules which seek . . . to limit the effects of armed conflict. It protects persons who are not or are no longer participating in the hostilities and restricts the means and methods of warfare. International humanitarian law is also known as the law of war or the law of armed conflict.[42]

One of the main things that distinguishes nation-state armies from terrorist cells is that the former are held to a higher standard of conduct based on customary and treaty law, dating back at least to the mid-nineteenth century. The first major multilateral instrument that tried to regulate modern warfare was the Declaration of Paris in 1856, which placed restrictions on naval warfare, prohibiting privateering, circumscribing contraband goods subject to seizure, and delimiting the conditions for implementing naval blockades against enemy coastlines. Other treaties followed that resulted from several factors, including the mutual interests states shared in managing hostilities (the liberal explanation), the agendas of great-power states concerned about other states gaining military advantage through newly emerging weapons technology (the realist explanation), and new norms and sensibilities (the constructivist explanation).

Important milestones included the Geneva Convention of 1864 that codified rules for treatment of battlefield wounded, the Hague Conventions of 1899 and 1907 that specified the parameters of land warfare and delineated the rights and duties of belligerents and neutrals, and the Geneva Conventions of 1929 and

1949 that developed guidelines for humane treatment of prisoners of war (POWs). Normative progress can be seen in the fact that, whereas POWs in ancient and medieval times were either killed or enslaved, important safeguards had been instituted by the twentieth century. The four 1949 **Geneva Conventions**, which have been universally accepted, further elaborated the POW protections (e.g., limiting the amount of information that prisoners were obligated to give to name, rank, date of birth, and serial number) and added new rules for protecting civilians from indiscriminate violence, after World War II saw widespread abuse of captured soldiers as well as widespread killing of innocent civilians through strategic bombing of population centers.

As military technology and strategy have evolved with ever more lethal weaponry and with whole societies and economies involved in war efforts and considered legitimate targets, it has become harder to maintain the distinction between combatants and noncombatants. In World War I, which witnessed indiscriminate sinking of ships by submarines, almost as many civilians as soldiers were killed. In World War II, which witnessed aerial bombardment of British cities by the German Luftwaffe and aerial attacks on German and Japanese cities by the U.S. Air Force, more civilians died than soldiers. The United States was criticized for its "shock and awe" bombing campaign over Baghdad at the outset of the 2003 Iraq War. However much American pilots attempted surgical strikes aimed only at targets of "military necessity," as international humanitarian law requires, the air attack inevitably resulted in substantial collateral damage of civilian areas with heavy loss of innocent lives. Intrastate and extrastate conflicts exacerbate these problems, since rival factions in civil wars often sack towns and villages, brutalizing the sympathizers of each side, and terrorists tend to select noncombatants as their primary targets.

WHAT RULES APPLY TO THE PROTECTION OF CIVILIANS AND POWS IN WARFARE?

Intrastate and extrastate conflicts pose special problems today for implementation of POW conventions and other rules governing treatment of combatants. In guerrilla warfare, armies do not ordinarily confront each other across well-defined fronts, and soldiers do not always wear uniforms. Not only are customary distinctions between civilians and combatants blurred, but so too are distinctions between soldiers and common criminals. A national government experiencing rebellion is understandably reluctant to extend to rebels the same status normally accorded enemy soldiers, preferring to dismiss them as "thugs" rather than legitimizing them as "freedom fighters." There is even greater reluctance to accord POW status to terrorists, who observe no Geneva Convention rules regarding the wearing of proper insignia, functioning through a regular chain of command, or honoring humanitarian law in their use of force. Common Article 3 of the four 1949 Geneva Conventions requires all captured soldiers to be treated humanely, even if not formally granted POW status. The United States, upon capturing al Qaeda fighters in Afghanistan after 9/11, branded most of the prisoners as "enemy combatants" (also termed "unlawful combatants") not entitled to POW protection, jailed them at the U.S. naval base at Guantanamo Bay, Cuba, and in some cases subjected them to interrogation methods that included torture. Human rights watchers were critical of American behavior, not only at Guantanamo but also at Abu Ghraib prison in Iraq, where American military personnel abused and humiliated Iraqi prisoners captured in the 2003 Iraq War.[43] (On the dilemmas experienced by U.S. policymakers and soldiers in meeting the requirements of international humanitarian law after 9/11, see the problems raised in the *IR* Critical Thinking Boxes in Chapters 1 and 5 of this book.)

As with other areas of international law, the laws of war suffer at times from major violations. However, the Geneva Conventions and other rules at least provide a baseline of expectations against which state behavior can be measured. Moreover, it is probably true that most states observe most rules during warfare and, at the very least, are sensitive to being accused of committing "war crimes." For example, even in the case of the American shock and awe air campaign over Iraq in 2003, the *New York Times* reported that the American commanders took "extraordinary steps to limit collateral damage. The Army's Third Infantry Division [had] a team of lawyers to advise on whether targets are legitimate under international conventions—and a vast database of some 10,000 targets to be avoided, such as hospitals, mosques, and cultural or archaeological treasures. . . . The allies deserve credit for conducting the most surgically precise bombing effort in the history of warfare."[44] A more salient example of the impact of the laws of war is the fact that chemical weapons (mustard gas and other agents) were used extensively during World War I, causing horrible effects, but—after the signing of the 1925 **Geneva Gas Protocol** that banned the first use of lethal chemical weapons—were not employed at all during World War II. Whether due to new norms or the mutual fears associated with unpredictable chemical arsenals, or both, the ban has held (other than Saddam Hussein's usage in the 1980s).[45]

ARMS CONTROL REGIMES

The 1925 Geneva Gas Protocol is just one of many international regimes that impose restrictions on the use of various kinds of weapons, including both conventional weapons and weapons of mass destruction. Other regimes are more comprehensive, restricting not only the use but also the testing, production, stockpiling, and transfer of weaponry. Whether serving as a mechanism to humanize war, curb arms races and promote confidence building, or conserve scarce resources for more positive, productive purposes, **arms control** can entail reduction or elimination of certain classes of weapons (sometimes called **disarmament**), freezes in existing arsenals, or ceilings that place upper limits on stockpiles (see Chapter 5). Arms control negotiations and agreements can be either *bilateral* (e.g., the SALT and START strategic nuclear weapons talks between the United States and Russia during and after the Cold War) or *multilateral* (e.g., the BWC, CWC, and NPT treaties). This discussion will focus on the latter—broad global pacts.

Arms control has a long history. In 600 B.C. "the Chinese states formed a disarmament league that produced a peaceful century for the league's members,"[46] while in 431 B.C. "Sparta and Athens negotiated over the length of the latter's defensive walls."[47] In 1139 the Second Lateran Council attempted to outlaw the use of crossbows between Christian armies. The first known international agreement to limit chemical weapons dates back to 1675, shortly after the Peace of Westphalia, when the French and Germans signed a pact in Strasbourg not to use poison bullets in warfare. Many other examples of "beating swords into plowshares," or at least making them less plentiful and deadly, can be cited. Arms control regimes have proliferated since World War II, with negotiations occurring through the Geneva-based Conference on Disarmament, at the United Nations, and in other settings. These regimes represent considerable progress but, as suggested in the statement of the problem at the outset of this chapter, are imperfect, with several states refusing to ratify treaties, compliance spotty even among the legally bound parties, and many issues not as yet covered by any agreements. Let us first examine conventional weapons regimes, and then regimes relating to weapons of mass destruction.

Controlling Conventional Weapons

An example of conventional weapons arms control is the 1980 Convention on Prohibitions or Restrictions on the Use of Certain Conventional Weapons Which May Be Deemed to Be Excessively Injurious and to Have Indiscriminate Effects, which placed limits on the use of napalm, booby traps, and other devices. Only 106 countries had ratified the treaty as of 2009. A more prominent treaty has been the 1997 **Anti-Personnel Land Mine Treaty (Ottawa Treaty)**, which sought to outlaw the use of land mines in warfare. The Campaign to Ban Land Mines, a network of 1,400 NGOs in 90 countries, in combination with Canada and a few other states, led the way in calling attention to the problem and mobilizing support for the treaty. In the 1990s, it was estimated that in over 60 countries there were some 100 million land mines buried in the ground, left over from various conflicts. Land mines tend to claim innocent civilians, often children, as their main victims as the latter accidentally trigger the devices. They have been called the "Saturday night special of civil wars," and Cambodia—one of the most land mine–littered landscapes in the world—has been called a "nation of amputees" as a result of its internal conflict during the 1970s and 1980s (depicted in the movie *The Killing Fields*).[48] In Angola, another victimized country, "roughly 40 percent of the population has experienced amputations due to land-mine accidents."[49] As of 2009, 156 states had ratified the Ottawa Treaty, with the United States, Russia, and China among the most conspicuous absentees (Washington claiming it needed to continue to rely on land mines to deter a potential attack by waves of North Korean soldiers against South Korea).

A land mine victim in the
Nicaraguan Civil War during the
1980s.

AP Photo/Eugene Hoshiko

At the UN Conference on the Illicit Trade in Small Arms in 2001, over 100 countries agreed to a program of action aimed at limiting small-arms sales to rebel groups and civilians in conflict zones, although the United States (a chief exporter of light weapons that was also concerned about infringement of the right to bear arms protected in the U.S. Constitution) insisted that only military weapons be covered rather than the firearms that typically are the main source of the problem. Subsequent conferences have failed to achieve stronger measures beyond vague commitments to eradicate the illicit arms trade.

Toward the end of the Cold War, NATO and Warsaw Pact countries engaged in arms control talks that resulted in the 1990 **Treaty on Conventional Armed Forces in Europe** (CFE), aimed at reducing the number of tanks, artillery, aircraft, and other forms of conventional weaponry in the Atlantic to Urals region. Although substantial cuts have been made, the treaty has been threatened recently by Russia's resurgent militarism in Georgia and elsewhere. A wider regime is the 1996 **Wassenaar Arrangement**, consisting of forty countries across several regions (including all the Perm Five members except China), which attempts to promote transparency in monitoring and restricting the export of conventional weapons and advanced weapons technology, particularly missile technology that could deliver weapons of mass destruction. In 2008 a **Convention on Cluster Munitions** was adopted at a conference attended by over one-hundred states, which sought to ban the use as well as production and stockpiling of cluster munitions, defined as "a conventional munition that is designed to disperse or release explosive submunitions each weighing less than 20 kilograms." The concern with cluster bombs, which Israel used in its war with Hezbollah in Lebanon in 2006, is that they "cannot discriminate between a military and civilian target," inviting a violation of the "proportionality test in international humanitarian law," and that "many unexploded cluster munitions cause death and disabilities among civilians."[50] It remains to be seen whether leading cluster bomb manufacturers and users, such as the United States, Israel, India, and China, will join the treaty.

Controlling Weapons of Mass Destruction

The Geneva Gas Protocol of 1925 banned the first use of chemical weapons by any state, but was interpreted to permit the use of chemical weapons in retaliation for another state's prior use. In an effort to outlaw chemical weapons altogether, the 1993 **Chemical Weapons Convention (CWC)** obligated states party to the treaty "never under any circumstances to develop, produce, otherwise acquire, stockpile or retain chemical weapons, or transfer, directly or indirectly, chemical weapons to anyone" or "to use chemical weapons." Any parties that already had chemical weapons were obligated to destroy them within ten years following the treaty entering into force (after the necessary number of ratifications had been obtained). A verification system was established in the form of a new IGO headquartered in The Hague, the Organization for the Prohibition of Chemical Weapons (OPCW). In response to a challenge from a member state, the OPCW was allowed to do on-site inspections in any state suspected of violating the treaty. The treaty took effect in April 1997, six months after the sixty-fifth ratification (by Hungary), and by 2009 it had over 180 parties. The CWC is considered a landmark agreement since it is "the first comprehensively verifiable multilateral treaty that completely bans an entire class of weapons, and firmly limits activities that may contribute to the production of those weapons."[51]

A look at the politics that went into the CWC treaty offers a window into the politics of regime-making generally.[52] The combination of concern about Iraqi use of chemical weapons in the 1980s opening up a Pandora's box of chemical warfare, along with improved American-Russian relations following the end of the Cold War, helped put a new chemical weapons pact on the global agenda in the early 1990s. It was in the interest of both Moscow and Washington to take the lead in calling for the elimination of chemical weapons, since "the poor person's nuclear bomb" was superfluous to the nuclear-armed states yet potentially menacing in the hands of others. Other states played an important role as well in formulating proposals during the negotiations that followed in the Conference on Disarmament, including Australia and Germany stressing both security and humanitarian imperatives, along with India and Iran representing the views of developing countries concerned about retaining access to civilian chemical technology. Hence from a "billiard ball politics" perspective, there were a variety of national interests in play. The story would be incomplete without mentioning domestic factors, nonstate actors, and the kind of "two-level diplomacy games" discussed in Chapters 3–4.[53] For example, the Chemical Manufacturers Association (CMA), the trade association that represents Dow, DuPont, and other major American chemical companies, was invited by the U.S. delegation to participate in the internal U.S. policy deliberations during the CWC talks. Chemical plants manufacture insecticides, dyes, and other products containing agents that can readily be precursors to weapons, and Washington wanted to be careful not to take decisions on restricting the production and export of chemicals that could adversely affect the U.S. chemical industry (the largest in the world, employing almost a million people). Initially the chemical industry was lukewarm to the treaty, wary of costly governmental regulations and intrusive on-site inspections that might encourage industrial espionage. However, once it became resigned to a treaty, it worked to protect its interests as best it could and ultimately supported an agreement, urging a uniform industry-wide set of rules in conjunction with trade associations in other countries and the EU. (CMA feared that if the United States failed to become a party, American chemical companies could stand to lose $600 million in annual export sales under the proposed sanctions for noncompliance.) Similar dynamics were at work on other national delegations at the series of meetings that culminated in the signing of the 1993 Chemical Weapons Convention. Added to the mix of actors were environmental NGOs that articulated concerns about incineration procedures for destroying chemical munitions. One such group, the Chemical Weapons Working Group, contended, "Our position is not NIMBY— 'not in my backyard.' . . . It is NOPE—'not on Planet Earth.'"[54]

The CWC also offers a window into the various stages of regime-making, what could be called "the global public policy process."[55] Even if some issue (e.g., chemical weapons proliferation) manages to make it through the *agenda-setting* stage and not only makes it onto the global agenda but also past the *policy formulation* and *policy adoption* stages resulting in the formation of a regime, there is still the matter of *policy implementation*. Put simply, how effective is a regime, in this case the chemical weapons regime? Disposal and other problems continue to hamper implementation of the chemical weapons treaty. Although almost all countries are parties to the CWC, including the two with by far the largest chemical arsenals (the United States and Russia), several states thought to have such weapons remain nonparties, including Israel, Egypt, Lebanon, Syria, and North Korea. Furthermore, as noted earlier, only a quarter of the world's declared chemical weapons stockpile had been destroyed as of 2009, as the United States and Russia, along with some other parties, requested an extension beyond the 2007 deadline (until 2012) so as to meet financial and environmental obstacles. In addition, given the ease of concealing chemical weapons (it is easy to make and store them in a basement or garage, or to hide them in dual-use facilities such as paint factories), concerns have been raised about the "transparency" of the verification regime and whether cheating can be detected by the OPCW. The United States has accused

China, Iran, Russia, and Sudan of violating the treaty. Finally, there are gaps in the regime, as riot control agents and other nonlethal but incapacitating chemical agents are not covered by the treaty.

Similar problems have plagued the 1972 **Biological Weapons Convention (BWC)**. Now ratified by over 160 countries, including the United States and Russia, the treaty prohibits developing, producing, and stockpiling toxins and other bacteriological weapons for use in germ warfare. The United States and Russia claim to have terminated their biological weapons programs in the 1970s, although there is still some question whether they and a few other states (the same parties and nonparties suspected of developing chemical weapons) continue to possess some stockpiles and whether biodefense programs (e.g., the Pentagon's storage of anthrax strains used to test the effectiveness of vaccines) are permitted by the treaty.[56] A major weakness of the treaty is the absence of verification procedures, so that determining how much compliance has occurred is difficult.[57] An attempt in 2001 to produce a biological weapons protocol that would have created a counterpart to the OPCW failed, mainly due to lack of U.S. trust in the detection apparatus and concern about inspection possibly damaging the American biotech industry. BWC parties periodically hold review conferences to examine the functioning of the regime, such as one in 2008 that included presentations on "biosecurity" by representatives from both IGOs (e.g., WHO and UNEP) and NGOs (e.g., the International Biosafety Working Group and the Inter-Academy Panel of experts from over 70 national scientific academies).[58] Despite many problems, the regime can be considered a success in that states generally have refrained from using biological weapons against other states.[59]

At the center of efforts to control WMDs is the nuclear nonproliferation regime, the centerpiece of which is the 1970 **Nuclear Nonproliferation Treaty (NPT)**. The treaty has been endorsed by the entire UN membership, with the exception of India, Pakistan, and Israel. The NPT has been one of the most successful arms control treaties in history, insofar as much of the international system has defied realist expectations in denying themselves the ultimate badge of national power and prestige. The NPT obligates states that do not have nuclear weapons to refrain from developing them, and obligates existing nuclear weapons states to refrain from transferring such weaponry to the nuclear have-nots. A tremendous achievement was the 1995 agreement (as the NPT was about to expire) to renew the NPT in perpetuity. The nuclear powers had to overcome objections from many states, which contended that the United States and other members of the nuclear club had not done enough to reduce their own nuclear arsenals and to adopt a comprehensive ban on any future nuclear testing.

The **Partial Test Ban Treaty** of 1963 prohibited atmospheric testing of nuclear weapons but permitted underground testing. It was followed up in 1996 with a **Comprehensive Nuclear Test Ban Treaty** that was scheduled to take effect upon ratification by not only the members of the nuclear club but all forty-four countries possessing nuclear energy reactors. This treaty has been called "the longest-sought, hardest-fought prize in the history of arms control," since an elimination of all nuclear testing might effectively put the nuclear genie back in the bottle.[60] However, the United States and some other states have yet to sign on. The United States, in particular, has expressed concerns about adequate verification mechanisms as well as adequate alternative technologies for determining whether existing arsenals are in working order should they be needed for credible deterrence or actual use in self-defense or collective security. (The NPT is silent on the *use* of nuclear weapons—the treaty contains no explicit ban on use—although many commentators maintain that nuclear weapons are covered under the body of customary and treaty law prohibiting indiscriminate attacks on civilians.)

As indicated above, the nuclear club currently consists of eight states—the United States, Russia, China, Britain, France, India, Pakistan, and (de facto) Israel, with North Korea and Iran possibly knocking on the door. Brazil, Argentina, and South Africa had active programs in the 1980s, but have renounced any intention to build nuclear weapons, as have states such as Japan and Germany that clearly have the technological ability to go nuclear if they chose to but have thus far "abstained." The so-called **Nuclear Suppliers Group** is a set of forty-five countries, including the Perm Five, which have attempted to regulate the export of nuclear technology and materials, notably "dual use" equipment that could be converted to weapons development. Whether the current global stockpile of 25,000 nuclear weapons can be reduced will depend on the willingness of the United States and Russia to decrease their warheads below the 2,200 level promised in the 2002 U.S.-Russian Nuclear Arms Treaty (due to expire in 2012) and on the decisions taken in other national capitals. At issue is whether the existing nuclear nonproliferation regime is still effective in limiting the spread of nuclear weapons or whether the entire edifice is on the brink of collapse.

As already noted, two parties to the NPT—North Korea and Iran—have attempted over the past decade to establish active nuclear weapons programs in violation of their treaty commitments. Under the NPT, states are allowed to pursue peaceful nuclear energy programs, including either uranium enrichment or plutonium production from reprocessing spent fuel (both potential bomb-making materials), as long as they report their activities and submit to inspections by the **International Atomic Energy Agency (IAEA)**, the UN agency charged with monitoring NPT compliance. The IAEA, along with the UN Security Council, has continued to apply pressure on both North Korea and Iran to honor their NPT obligations, with the outcome of negotiations and sanctions as yet uncertain. Past North Korean sponsorship of terrorism and Iranian ties to Islamic fundamentalists considered terrorist groups are of special concern, as well as the potential for nuclear arms races to follow in East Asia and the Middle East. Graham Allison has proposed a "three no's" policy, urging "no loose nukes" (securing the nuclear weapons facilities in the former Soviet Union and Pakistan that are now vulnerable to theft and sabotage due to poor surveillance), "no new nascent nukes" (closing the loophole in the NPT treaty that allows member states to start up the nuclear fuel cycle), and "no new nuclear weapons states" (preventing the admission of new members into the nuclear club).[61] As one analyst says, "Either the international community will succeed in stopping the spread of nuclear weapons, or we could soon find ourselves in a world of twelve or fifteen or even more nuclear weapons states."[62]

Arms control will continue to pose enormous challenges for international security as well as opportunities for confidence-building and institution-building in international affairs. Clearly there is the need to manage weapons proliferation. Yet there are many other "needs," too—problems that cry out for solutions in world politics. The question here and in other issue-areas is, as Stanley Hoffmann has phrased it, "Will the need forge a way?"[63]

CONCLUSION

Peace researchers distinguish between negative peace (the reduction and elimination of armaments and war) and positive peace (the creation of improved living standards for growing numbers of people, thereby helping to alleviate conditions that are often the underlying sources of violence). In this same vein, commentators speak of addressing not only physical violence (bombings and other forms of hostilities) but also **structural violence** (starvation, poor health care, and other forms of economic deprivation that can maim and kill no less than war, along with institutionalized racism, sexism, and other systemic barriers that breed resentment and prevent individuals from realizing their full potential).[64] Another formulation of the problem is the distinction between *order* (peace) and *justice* (peaceful change). The haves tend to dwell on the former, the have-nots on the latter. Both are important values; it is hard to maintain order without justice, and it is hard to promote justice in the absence of order. Hoffmann, a realist, has said that, as a general rule, "in world affairs, order has to be achieved first" even if "it is established at the cost of justice."[65] However, recognizing that it may not be possible to separate these concerns, he adds that "it is difficult to conceive of a future international system remaining moderate if the inequality among its members incites recurrent violence." He acknowledges that "there shall be no world order unless some progress is made toward worldwide equity."[66] By that is meant equity both among nations and within nations.

In Chapter 2, I noted that the term "national security" has been broadened in recent years beyond its traditional military connotation to include economic well-being, protection from environmental threats and disease, energy security, and other issues. Josef Joffe may have been exaggerating the growing importance of such welfare issues in the post–Cold War era when he said, in 1992, that "welfare, not warfare, will shape the rules [and] dictate the agenda" of nations. However, at the very least, such issues are increasingly competing for attention with traditional peace and security matters. In the next two chapters we will focus on "welfare" concerns. Chapter 8 will examine the politics of enhancing human security, both human rights and human development, especially as it relates to the most impoverished nations and people on the planet. Chapter 9 will examine global governance of the world economy in general, including the politics of trade, investment, and other aspects of international political economy that are part of globalization.

QUESTIONS FOR STUDY AND DISCUSSION

1. What rules today govern the *start* of war (*jus ad bellum*) and the *conduct* of war (*jus in bello*)? In other words, under what circumstances today can states resort to the use of armed force, and, once war is under way, what use of force is permissible?
2. Describe trends in military spending and arms transfers in the post–Cold War era.
3. How many countries currently are members of "the nuclear club"? What international regimes exist to regulate the proliferation and use of nuclear weapons, and what are their main provisions? What about biological and chemical weapons?
4. Do you think a "nuclear-free world" is possible, as several former high-ranking American officials and Barack Obama have urged?
5. Discuss "structural violence" and the relationship between order (peace) and justice (peaceful change).

SUGGESTIONS FOR FURTHER READING

Graham Allison, *Nuclear Terrorism* (New York: Times Books, 2004).
Anthony Clark Arend and Robert J. Beck, *International Law and the Use of Force* (New York: Routledge, 1993).
Richard Betts, "The New Threat of Mass Destruction," *Foreign Affairs,* January 1998, 26–41.
Barry Buzan and Eric Herring, *The Arms Dynamic in World Politics* (London: Lynne Rienner, 1998).
Kurt Campbell et al., *The Nuclear Tipping Point* (Washington, D.C.: Brookings Institution, 2004).
Lori Damrosch and David Scheffer, eds., *Law and Force in the New International Order* (Boulder, CO: Westview, 1991).
Jayantha Dhanapala, *Multilateral Diplomacy and the NPT: An Insider's Account* (Geneva: UN Institute for Disarmament Research, 2005).
Michael J. Glennon, *Limits of Law, Prerogatives of Power: Intervention After Kosovo* (New York: Palgrave, 2001).
Scott Kagan and Kenneth N. Waltz, *The Spread of Nuclear Weapons: A Debate,* 2nd ed. (New York: Norton, 2003).
Keith Krause, *Arms and the State: Patterns of Military Production and Trade* (Cambridge: Cambridge University Press, 1992).
John F. Murphy, "Force and Arms," in Christopher Joyner, ed., *The United Nations and International Law* (Cambridge: Cambridge University Press, 1997).

Frederic Pearson, *The Global Spread of Arms: The Political Economy of International Security* (Boulder, CO: Westview, 1994).

J. Martin Rochester, *Between Two Epochs* (Upper Saddle River, NJ: Prentice-Hall, 2002), 138–145.

Jonathan Schell, *The Fate of the Earth* (New York: Knopf, 1982).

George P. Schultz et al., "Toward a Nuclear-Free World," *Wall Street Journal,* January 15, 2008.

Thomas Weiss and Cindy Collins, *Humanitarian Challenges and Intervention,* 2nd ed. (Boulder, CO: Westview, 2000).

8

Enhancing
Human Rights and
Human Development

Usually we speak of violence only when it has reached an extreme. But it is also violence when children are dying of malnutrition, when there is no freedom of unions, where there is not enough housing, and enough health care.

—Adolfo Perez Esquivel, Argentine human rights activist and recipient of the 1980 Nobel Peace Prize

Growing inequality is divisive. It polarizes societies, it divides regions within countries, and it carves up the world between rich and poor. . . . Ignoring increasing inequality is not an option.

—Angel Gurria, General Secretary of the Organization for Economic Cooperation and Development (OECD), 2008

We have been more or less brought up to believe that the bonds of community, responsibility, and obligation run only to the [national] frontiers. Should we extend our vision to include all of the people of our planet?

—Barbara Ward Jackson, *The Lopsided World*, 1968

This chapter is concerned with "positive peace"—improving human dignity and satisfying basic economic needs. The chapter focuses, first, on *human rights* (promoting the rights of women, children, and others) and, second, on *human development* (addressing issues of poverty and rich-poor gaps between and within countries). As in the previous chapter, the discussion starts with a definition of the problem, followed by an examination of the politics of problem-solving and efforts by the international community to respond to the problem in the form of international regimes and other remedies. In pondering these matters, the reader should consider how far individuals and nation-states should go in accepting the challenge posed by Barbara Ward Jackson above, calling on leaders and publics to take responsibility for the well-being of not only their fellow citizens but also foreigners.

THE PROBLEM

Human Rights

Consider the following news headline from 2008: "Switzerland's Green Power Revolution: Ethicists Ponder Plants' Rights." It refers to a plant scientist's need to obtain government approval for experimentation with genetically modified wheat, based on a Swiss constitutional amendment safeguarding "flora's dignity" and "lifestyle."[1] That same year, another newspaper article reported the passage of a bill in a committee of the Spanish parliament "to grant rights to our closest biological relatives—the great apes" that would forbid "torture and arbitrary imprisonment, including for circuses or films."[2] Many years earlier, in 1978, an article entitled "UN Espouses Animal's Lib" reported the adoption at a UNESCO conference of an "animal charter" that proclaimed "all animals are born with an equal claim on life and the same rights to existence" and, among other provisions, stated it "was wrong to abandon one's dog in the street when one goes on vacation" and it "is unfeeling to gas stray cats" and "hideous to keep pigs or cattle locked inside container trucks, sweating or freezing." The article noted that "signing of the charter by the 142 member states of UNESCO does not mean that blue-capped UN troops will now be rushed to the defense of persecuted pooches," only that it "will help animal lovers pressing for animal rights legislation."[3] In 1990 the Animal Liberation Front claimed responsibility for the bombings of several British department stores in protest against the fur trade. It seems that sometimes plant and animal rights get more serious attention than *human* rights.

Human rights is a branch of international law that seeks to extend fundamental political, social, and economic rights to all individual human beings in the world regardless of where they live. Anne-Marie Slaughter maintains that "international law is undergoing profound changes that will make it far more effective than it has been in the past. By definition, international law is a body of rules that regulates relations among states, not individuals. Yet over the course of the 21st century, it will increasingly confer rights and responsibilities directly on individuals."[4] Realists might question whether this is an empirical statement of what is likely to happen, or a normative statement of what a desirable future might look like. Still, idealists can point to some progress that supports Slaughter's prediction.

Human rights advocates face daunting challenges. In Chapter 7 I noted great resistance to the emerging norm of humanitarian intervention and Kofi Annan's claim that UN members have a "responsibility to protect" individuals who are threatened by their own government with genocide, ethnic cleansing, and gross human rights atrocities, as has occurred recently in Kosovo, Rwanda, and Darfur.[5] There is disagreement, also, over whether individuals have a right to elemental freedoms, such as freedom of speech and assembly, and elemental material goods, such as the right to shelter. Human rights remains a weak area of international law. Tension exists between the concept of sovereignty and the concept of human rights. On the one hand, sovereignty implies the existence of a government that claims complete authority to regulate all persons within its borders, while, on the other hand, human rights implies certain "rights one has simply because one is a human being"—rights which even one's own government cannot deny and which can be protected by the international community.[6] Sovereignty remains a core legal precept in international relations, despite pressures to pool sovereignty. The international legal system has attempted to resolve this tension by creating numerous human rights treaties that countries in their sovereign capacity can sign and ratify, although problems persist in that many states refuse to join such treaties while some that are parties do not fully comply with their treaty commitments.

At the outset of this book, there are statistics on the progress that has occurred over the past thirty years in the growth of democracy, as documented by Freedom House.[7] However, Freedom House has raised concerns of late that the march of freedom and democracy may be stalling. Although almost half of the world's population, living in ninety countries, is "free," that leaves the other half only "partly free" (in sixty countries) or "not free" (in forty-three countries). Moreover, "the year 2007 was marked by a notable setback for global freedom. The decline . . . was most pronounced in South Asia, but also reached significant levels in the former Soviet Union, the Middle East and North Africa, and sub-Saharan Africa. It affected a substantial number of large and politically important countries—including Russia, Pakistan, Kenya, Egypt, Nigeria, and Venezuela."[8] Problems continue in these and other countries, and even in democracies, "human rights abuses occur every day."[9]

Some groups are especially vulnerable to human rights violations. **Women's rights** have been an area of growing concern. Most cultures around the world have been traditionally patriarchal, male-dominated societies in which women have routinely experienced political and economic discrimination. Even a progressive Western democracy such as France did not extend the right to vote to women until 1944. The United Nations has developed a measure of gender inequality called the gender empowerment measure, which monitors female office holding in government (both legislative and executive branches) and female representation in the managerial, professional, and technical economic sectors. A recent UN report notes that, despite considerable progress of late, women occupy less than 17 percent of parliamentary seats worldwide (with ten countries having no females in their national legislatures), 14 percent of government cabinet posts (with only Chile, Spain, and Sweden exhibiting gender parity in ministerial portfolios), and less than one in ten mayoral positions in the world's city halls.[10]

The photo shows Burqa-clad women in Afghanistan in 2001, when the Taliban government that was then in power forced women to cover themselves from head to toe. Strict dress codes are still enforced for women in many Islamic countries.

Regarding economic inequality, it has been said that "women do two-thirds of the world's work, receive 10 percent of the world's income and own 1 percent of the means of production."[11] In industrialized nations, women's earnings are only 57 percent of men's earnings; the figures for the developing world are even lower, such as 40 percent in Latin America and 28 percent in the Middle East.[12] This does not, of course, fully take into account women's unpaid work performing household duties. (Norway, where women earn 75 percent of what men earn, has the best record on equal pay.) Globally, 70 percent of those living in extreme poverty are women, at least partly related to the fact that two-thirds of all adult illiterates are women, given their inferior access to primary and secondary education. Hence women continue to experience roadblocks to political participation, educational opportunity, occupational advancement, and access to health care and basic needs.

Gender discrimination and mistreatment of women are more egregious in some regions than others, notably the Middle East, sub-Saharan Africa, and South Asia. Note such practices as the "giraffe women" in Myanmar (where six-year-old girls are made to wear five-pound coils of brass rings around their necks), female genital mutilation in Kenya, Sierra Leone, and other African societies (where circumcision of adolescents and pre-adolescents is considered a coming-of-age ritual), gang rapes or honor killings of women in Pakistan and other Islamic fundamentalist societies in order to avenge adultery by them or their relatives, the prohibition against women not only voting but even driving a car in Saudi Arabia, and the selective abortion of female fetuses and murder of female infants in cultures where girls are viewed as a burden and boys are valued more highly (e.g., as happens at times in India, where scalding hot soup is poured down the throats of baby girls).[13] In Swaziland, according to one recent report, as punishment for playing loud music the king's daughter and beauty queen Miss Swaziland were "whipped by a palace official at a party of teenage virgins ahead of a festival where more than 50,000 maidens [were made] available to become her father's 13th wife."[14] Women are frequently the victims of rape and violence not only in terms of domestic spousal abuse but also in armed conflicts, reflected in a UN report's firsthand observations noting, "Wombs punctured with guns. Women raped and tortured in front of their husbands and children. Rifles forced into vaginas. Pregnant women beaten to induce miscarriages."[15] In addition, as many as 2 million women, many of them young girls, are subjected annually to "sex trafficking" and what amounts to slavery as they are coerced into becoming prostitutes to service the international sex tourism industry. (The International Labor Organization has estimated that as much as 14 percent of the GNP of Indonesia, Malaysia, the Philippines, and Thailand may be derived from sex tourism.)[16]

Boys are also victimized by human trafficking and what has been called "the new global slave trade," as "it is likely that more people are being trafficked across borders against their will now than at any point in the past."[17] As several of the above examples of human rights abuses indicate, **children's rights** in general have been a growing problem attracting increased attention. Ethan Kapstein notes that half of all the "slaves on the global market" who do forced labor of some sort, usually the result of incurring debts brought on by shady job recruiters, are under eighteen years of age. He cites a UN report stating that the victims span the globe, being trafficked "from 127 countries to be exploited in 137 countries." He adds: "Most of the slaves come from countries such as Albania, Belarus, China, Romania, Russia, and Thailand, while the most frequent destinations . . . are in Asia, followed by the advanced industrial states of western Europe and North America."[18] Whether coerced or not, the International Labor Organization counts approximately 218 million child laborers between the ages of five and seventeen in poor countries. Seventy percent of them toil in agriculture but some in industrial sweatshops, half of whom are engaged in hazardous work, often working "long hours, in dangerous and unhealthy conditions, exposed to lasting physical and psychological harm." Working at rug looms "has left children disabled with eye damage, lung disease, stunted growth, and a susceptibility to arthritis," while "children harvesting sugar cane in El Salvador use machetes to cut cane for up to nine hours a day in the hot sun, injuries to their hands and legs are common, and medical care is often not available."[19] Especially worrisome has been the estimated 300,000 child soldiers (as young as eight years of age) who have been forcibly recruited, abducted, or economically pressured to fight in various armed conflicts in Africa and elsewhere.[20]

Another human rights category that has aroused concern is **minority rights**. Based on race, ethnicity, or religion, certain groups have experienced oppression and discrimination by their governments. Perhaps no case has attracted more attention recently than the Sudan, where, since 2003, an Arab government has committed atrocities against non-Arab, black Muslims seeking greater autonomy in the western region of Darfur, with Arab militia killing not only rebel soldiers but civilians numbering in the hundreds of thousands. This followed an earlier Sudanese civil war during the 1980s and 1990s that was fought over religion more than ethnic or tribal differences and that left 2 million civilians (mostly black Christians and animists in the south of the country) dead. The worst genocide since World War II occurred in Rwanda during the 1990s, when almost a million Tutsis were murdered at the hands of Hutu militias, recounted in movies like *Hotel Rwanda* and books like *We Wish to Inform You That Tomorrow We Will Be Killed with Our Families*. Racism and religious discrimination are not limited to Africa and the developing world, as evidenced by the recent problems between Catholics and Protestants in Northern Ireland, growing anti-Semitism in parts of Europe, the persecution of Gypsies in Romania, and the ethnic cleansing of Albanian Kosovars and Bosnian Muslims in the former Yugoslavia in the 1990s. On the subject of respecting cultural diversity, a particular problem has been the **rights of indigenous peoples**—native, often primitive, cultures, such as the Yanomami tribes found in the Amazon jungles of South America or the Aborigines of Australia—who seek to maintain their traditional ways against encroachment by government agencies enforcing national regulations and developers coveting their lands.

There is a long-standing debate over whether human rights refer primarily to political rights—civil liberties and civil rights—or also include economic rights. The United States, more than most democracies, has been particularly resistant to the idea that human beings have a right to, say, a job or shelter. In the American political culture and jurisprudence, there is no constitutional, much less universal, right to housing or to other socioeconomic benefits such as health care or education (although some U.S. states may include such rights in their state constitutions). Many countries, including some authoritarian regimes, claim that they consider certain economic rights as fundamental human rights but do not actually enforce such rights. Before examining the effectiveness of global responses to human rights problems in both the political and economic spheres, let us first look at the problem of "human development" and the degree of rich-poor gaps between and within nation-states.

Human Development: Rich-Poor Gaps

During the summer of 1985, capacity crowds filled London's Wembley Stadium and Philadelphia's John F. Kennedy Stadium to hear the simulcast "Live Aid" concert, while another 400 million people in sixty countries watched the live broadcast via satellite. The concert, organized by musicians Bob Geldof and Midge Ure, featured some of the world's best-known bands, who played to benefit Ethiopian famine relief. At the time over 30,000 children a day were dying of hunger and disease in Africa and the world. Despite the charitable contributions from the concerts and the *We Are the World* album produced by Bruce Springsteen and over thirty other recording artists, it was unclear whether the issues of global poverty and starvation had struck a chord among the more prosperous citizens of the planet.

Twenty years later, with thousands of children still dying daily for lack of food and basic necessities, Geldof and Ure organized another set of concerts for July 2, 2005, called "Live 8." It was timed to coincide with the annual economic summit of the **G8** countries—the world's leading industrialized states (the United States, Britain, France, Germany, Italy, Canada, Japan, plus Russia)—scheduled to convene in Gleneagles, Scotland, on July 6. Led by Bono, Paul McCartney, Elton John, and over 1,000 musicians, the concerts were held in each of the G8 countries and were viewed by 3 billion people worldwide over 182 television networks and 2,000 radio networks. Thirty million people sent text messages in support of the "make poverty history" theme, and hundreds of thousands of protestors and NGO members gathered at Gleneagles to demand debt relief and development assistance for the poor in Africa and elsewhere.[21]

THE RICH-POOR GAP BETWEEN COUNTRIES

Statistics on poverty, as well as efforts to combat poverty, can sometimes be numbing. It is important to put these numbers in perspective, particularly to assess whether poverty is getting better or worse over time. As noted in the historical overview in Chapter 2, there have always been gaps between rich and poor *within* societies, but starting in the nineteenth century the Industrial Revolution created an unprecedented rich-poor gap *between* societies. The Northern Hemisphere rapidly developed and accumulated large amounts of wealth, while the Southern Hemisphere remained almost untouched by these developments. (Although there is some controversy today in using the term "less developed countries," the phrase refers to the gap in industrialization and the attendant well-being commonly associated with industrialization.) By the 1970s, the "North-South" gap had widened to the point where the United Nations created the Brandt Commission to study the problem. The Brandt Commission's 1980 report *North-South* described the gap as follows:

> The North including Eastern Europe has a quarter of the world's population and four-fifths of its income; the South including China has three billion people—three-quarters of the world's population but living on one-fifth of the world's income. In the North the average person can expect to live for more than seventy years; he or she will rarely be hungry, and will be educated at least up to secondary level. In the countries of the South the great major-

ity of people have a life expectancy of closer to fifty years; in the poorest countries one out of every four children dies before the age of five; one-fifth or more of all the people in the South suffer from hunger and malnutrition; fifty percent have no chance to become literate.[22]

What has happened since 1980? Has the gap widened or closed? The picture is complicated.[23] Different analysts cite different statistics to demonstrate that the problem is worsening or improving. For example, Joseph Stiglitz has commented that "a growing divide between the haves and the have-nots has left increasing numbers in the Third World in dire poverty, living on less than a dollar a day."[24] In contrast, Fareed Zakaria notes that the percentage of people living on $1 a day "plummeted from 40 percent in 1981 to 18 percent in 2004."[25] Part of the problem is that a continuing population explosion in parts of the Third World (in some countries the fertility rate, or average number of children per family, can be as high as seven) means that the absolute numbers of people living in poverty may be going up even as economic progress makes a dent in the overall percentage experiencing such conditions. Competing assessments can be found, depending upon which dimensions of poverty and which regions of the world one examines.

On the one hand, the World Bank reported in 2003 that the past thirty years had seen "considerable progress in improving human well-being. . . . Average income per capita . . . in developing countries grew from $989 in 1980 to $1,354 in 2000. Infant mortality was cut in half, from 107 per 1,000 live births to 58, as was adult illiteracy, from 47 to 25 percent."[26] The World Bank's *World Development Indicators 2008* noted that "average growth of low-income economies [defined as those countries with per capita income of $905 or less] and lower middle-income economies [per capita income of under $3,596] has been rising, surpassing that of upper middle-income [per capita income under $11,116] and high-income [per capita income of $11,116 and above] economies in the last three decades. Since 2000 annual GDP [gross domestic product] growth in low-income economies has averaged 6.5 percent, compared with 5.6 percent in middle-income economies and 2.3 percent in high-income economies."[27]

However, the 2008 report was careful to point out that the remarkable growth of just a few less developed countries (LDCs), particularly huge countries like China and India (expanding at almost double-digit rates), accounted for a disproportionate share of the growth in the developing world and that "growth remains uneven across regions," with some regions (e.g., Latin America) generally stagnant and others (e.g., much of Africa) retrogressing since globalization took off in 1990.[28] Per capita income in high-income economies is more than five times higher than that in middle-income economies and more than nineteen times higher than that in low-income economies.[29] There are still almost 3 billion people, roughly half of humanity, living on less than $2 a day. Of special concern are "the bottom billion" living on less than $1 a day.[30] The absolute number of people living in extreme poverty has increased since 1990 in sub-Saharan Africa and South

Asia due to population growth despite a slight decline in the overall poverty rate.[31] All told, "828 million go to bed hungry, 114 million children of primary school age are not in school, [and] 11 million children die each year of preventable causes."[32] Life expectancy at birth ranges on average from 77 in North America and Europe to 50 in sub-Saharan Africa (where AIDS has taken an enormous toll in such countries as Botswana, with almost 40 percent of its adult population infected with HIV in recent years); AIDS aside, much of the developing world has seen a significant increase in life expectancy, which now averages 73 in Latin America, 71 in East Asia, 70 in the Middle East, and 64 in South Asia.[33] Youth literacy rates range from 99 percent in North America and Europe (for males and females) to 76 percent (for males) and 64 percent (for females) in sub-Saharan Africa.[34]

As mentioned in Chapter 2, the "South" is no longer a singular entity whose members share a high degree of poverty and solidarity. What is today called "the two-thirds world" or "global South"—the collection of states aspiring to join the ranks of the "first world" (in wealth, if not westernization)—consists of several different groups of countries in various stages of economic development. These include: (1) **NICs** (newly industrializing countries, such as Singapore and South Korea, whose per capita income now equals or exceeds that of some highly developed countries); (2) **next NICs** (next-tier LDCs, such as Malaysia and Thailand, which are approaching NIC status); (3) **BRICs** (the big emerging markets of Brazil, Russia, India, and China); (4) former Soviet bloc countries, such as Romania and Bulgaria, transitioning from communism to capitalism; (5) **OPEC** members (countries such as Saudi Arabia, Kuwait, and United Arab Emirates, whose oil-fueled economies have created tremendous wealth even if their societies do not yet have all the trappings of development in terms of high-quality mass education and health care); (6) middle-income LDCs (countries such as Egypt and Paraguay, which continue to suffer from extensive poverty but not as great as some other LDCs); and (7) the fifty **Fourth World** countries—the poorest of the poor—designated by the United Nations as "least developed countries," found mostly in sub-Saharan Africa (e.g., Angola, Burundi, and Niger) and South Asia (e.g., Afghanistan, Bangladesh, and Nepal).

The United Nations Development Program (UNDP) annually publishes a ranking of states according to a **Human Development Index (HDI)**, a measure that assesses a country's overall quality of life based on its per capita income, average life expectancy, and adult literacy rate. Table 8.1 shows the extremes of wealth and poverty found in the North and South, with the twenty "most livable" countries found exclusively in North America and Europe (along with Japan, Australia, and New Zealand) and all of the twenty "least livable" ones found in sub-Saharan Africa. (A few countries, such as Afghanistan in South Asia, were not listed due to lack of data.) *The 2007/2008 Human Development Report* showed Iceland (with the world's longest life expectancy, men reaching 79 and women 83) and Norway (with the largest per capita income, $66,000) leading the pack, while at the other

TABLE 8.1. Human Development Index Rankings: The Twenty Most and Least Livable Countries

Most Livable Countries	Least Livable Countries
1. Iceland	1. Sierra Leone
2. Norway	2. Burkina Faso
3. Australia	3. Guinea-Bissau
4. Canada	4. Niger
5. Ireland	5. Mali
6. Sweden	6. Mozambique
7. Switzerland	7. Central African Republic
8. Japan	8. Chad
9. Netherlands	9. Ethiopia
10. France	10. Congo, Dem. Rep.
11. Finland	11. Burundi
12. United States	12. Côte d'Ivoire
13. Spain	13. Zambia
14. Denmark	14. Malawi
15. Austria	15. Benin
16. United Kingdom	16. Angola
17. Belgium	17. Rwanda
18. Luxembourg	18. Guinea
19. New Zealand	19. Tanzania, U. Rep. of
20. Italy	20. Nigeria

SOURCE: UN Development Program, *Human Development Report 2007/2008*. The rankings are based on per capita income, life expectancy, and adult literacy rate data for each country.

end were the likes of the Central African Republic (with life expectancy of 39 and 40 for men and women), Sierra Leone (with per capita income of $240), and Burkina Faso (with a literacy rate of 24 percent).[35]

Rich and poor states alike were shaken by the global financial panic that began in October 2008, with the prospects for the world economy over the next decade and beyond remaining uncertain. Although globalization in the early post–Cold War era created winners and losers, with some states regressing rather than advancing, on balance most saw economic improvements. These included not only such behemoths as China and India (fueled by exports and outsourcing of services to the North) and Russia and OPEC countries (fueled by a growing world economy and high oil prices) but even Third World states bordering on the Fourth World, such as Ghana, which, immediately prior to the world financial crisis, was reported to have "joined a long list of developing countries in Africa and beyond enjoying record periods of economic growth, with the robust economy leaving it no longer in need of more IMF [International Monetary Fund] cash."[36] However, in the wake of the 2008 global financial crisis, all bets were off for both poor states like Ghana and rich states at the very top of the HDI rankings, including two that had hitched their sails to globalization with great success (Iceland, which experienced a "meltdown" due to bank collapses, and Ireland, which went "bust" for similar reasons).[37] As of 2010, it was too soon to tell how quickly the world economy would rebound, and which countries would rebound the quickest.

THE RICH-POOR GAP WITHIN COUNTRIES

In world politics, we still tend to see the world in Westphalian, state-centric terms, so that when we think of economics, we generally think in terms of the economic well-being of countries. However, as Robert McNamara noted when he was president of the World Bank in the 1970s, "Development is about people. The only criterion for measuring its ultimate success or failure is what it does to enhance the lives of individual human beings."[38] McNamara was calling attention to the need not only to target assistance to the poorest countries but to ensure that aid gets to the poorest people within those countries.

Rich-poor gaps exist not only between countries but also *within* countries. In addition to publishing HDI rankings of states, UNDP has collected data on per capita income, life expectancy, and literacy rates for different geographical regions, ethnic groups, or other categorical subgroups within a given state. For example, a recent Human Development Report asked, "Why in Nepal do Muslims have less than half the level of human development of Newars? Why in China is the HDI in the province of Qinghai barely half that of Shanghai?"[39] Commenting on another Human Development Report, the *New York Times* pointed out that even in postapartheid South Africa, "the white and black sections of the population are not just two different peoples but 'almost two different worlds.' If white South Africa were a separate country it would rank 24th in the world in terms of human development, while black South Africa would be in 123rd place, just above Congo. . . . In Brazil, the report highlights the discrepancy in living standards between the more prosperous south and the impoverished northeast, where life expectancy is 17 years shorter, adult literacy 33 percent lower, and average incomes 40 percent lower."[40]

In both developed and less developed countries, one finds rich as well as poor people. For decades, Latin America has been the region with the greatest disparity in wealth within societies. Brazil is the clearest example, where the richest 20 percent of the population accounts for roughly 65 percent of the national income—in the United States, the comparable figure is 45 percent, which is actually less egalitarian than many developed states. Globalization has brought uneven benefits to not only countries but various groups within countries. Even within the United States and some other industrialized states the rich-poor gap lately has been widening considerably. The **Organization for Economic Cooperation and Development (OECD)**, an umbrella IGO that facilitates data collection and monitoring of economic conditions in the developed world, reported in 2008 that "the gap between rich and poor has widened in most developed countries over the past two decades as economic growth has benefited the wealthy more than the poor. . . . A few countries bucked the trend, with France, Greece, and Spain all enjoying a narrowing of the gap between rich and poor over the past 20 years." The report added that although rich households were "leaving both middle and poorer income groups behind" in most developed economies, "nowhere has this trend been so stark as in the United States."[41] Globalization has had the effect of further widening gaps in much of the developing world as well. The World Bank reported in 2008 that societal inequalities were highest in Latin America and sub-Saharan Africa (where the income share of the richest 20 percent of the population was 18 times that of the poorest 20 percent) and lowest in South and Central Asia (where the ratio was less than 7). [42]

Just as one can examine the extremes of wealth and poverty between countries, one can look at such extremes between individuals. In 1989, as the Cold War ended and the age of globalization began, there were an estimated 187 billionaires and 2 million millionaires, along with 100 million homeless, in the world.[43] By 2008, there were over 1,000 billionaires and 10 million millionaires in the world; there were still 100 million homeless, excluding the roughly 600 million with inadequate shelter, as well as the 30 million refugees and "people of concern" identified by the Office of the UN High Commissioner for Refugees.[44] Globalization coincided with what Kofi Annan called the "ultra rich" (the three richest people in the world) owning "assets that exceed the combined gross domestic product of the 48 least developed countries," and the "super rich" (the world's 225 richest individuals) having "a combined wealth of over $1 trillion—equal to the annual income of the poorest 47 percent of the entire world's population."[45]

In 2008, according to *Forbes*, the three richest persons were Warren Buffett, Carlos Slim Helu, and Bill Gates. Buffett and Gates were Americans, Helu a Mexican. Helu, worth $60 billion, was a telecom tycoon and was one of two dozen billionaires in Mexico (up from only one in 1989) who together represented more wealth than the 50 million Mexicans at the bottom of that country's economic ladder. The developing world was well represented among the "filthy rich," as *Forbes* noted that India, home to millions of "untouchables" and others lacking basic sanitation facilities, had four of the top ten billionaires, more than any other country (although Americans were 42 percent of the total number of 1,125 billionaires).[46] Again, even billionaires suffered huge losses after the 2008 global financial crisis, given the fact they had the most to lose. Like nation-states, they waited to see if those losses would be recouped in the future as the world's financial house attempted to put itself back in order.

HUMAN RIGHTS REGIMES

Before examining the politics of economic problem-solving and efforts by the international community to address issues of poverty, we will focus on the politics of human rights and efforts to develop human rights regimes relating to women, children, and humanity generally.

Human Rights Conventions

World War II marked a watershed moment in the history of human rights. As one writer puts it, "The Second World War marked the ultimate transition of international law from a system dedicated to State sovereignty to one also devoted to the protection of human dignity."[47] At the **Nuremberg Trials** immediately following World War II, leaders of Nazi Germany were charged with having committed, along with other crimes, "crimes against humanity." German officials were convicted of having violated the rights of the indigenous Jewish population in Germany and neighboring states by engaging in genocide, killing an estimated 6 million Jews; as a result, several German leaders were sentenced to life imprisonment or execution. Nuremberg was a landmark event in setting an important precedent supporting the proposition that individuals have rights (as well as obligations) under international law.

Critics of the Nuremberg Trials have argued that they did not reflect the evolution of international law but simply amounted to "victors' justice," the winners of a war arbitrarily asserting the existence of certain rules that were used as a pretext to punish the leaders of a vanquished state. These critics point out that the United States, which supported such strong penalties against German leaders at Nuremberg, resisted any calls for international tribunals to hold American officials accountable for atrocities allegedly committed by American forces during World War II (and later in Vietnam) in the form of strategic bombing of population centers. Although the United States was not guilty of atrocities on the scale of the Germans, certainly not toward its own people (notwithstanding the internment of Japanese Americans on the West Coast after Pearl Harbor), Washington invited charges of hypocrisy in refusing to permit any scrutiny of its own behavior by an international body. These issues surfaced again in the 1990s, when the United States joined other countries under the auspices of the United Nations to organize special tribunals (the first since Nuremberg) to consider alleged acts of genocide and war crimes committed by the leadership in the former Yugoslavia and Rwanda. Yet Washington refused to endorse the establishment of the new **International Criminal Court**, designed as a permanent Nuremberg-type institution, fearing that its sovereignty might be compromised.

Despite the uneven application of the Nuremberg principles, the significance of Nuremberg is that it clearly challenged the traditional notion that only states are subjects of international law. Nuremberg was followed by the **Universal Declaration of Human Rights**, a resolution passed by the UN General Assembly in

1948 by a vote of 48 to 0, with eight abstentions that included the Soviet Union, Saudi Arabia, and South Africa. The declaration, which was a moral pronouncement ("soft law") rather than a legally binding decree, called on governments to promote a variety of rights, both civil and political (e.g., the right to a fair trial, protection from cruel and inhumane punishment, freedom of expression and religion) as well as economic and social (e.g., the right to an adequate standard of living, the right to work, the right to an education). The declaration subsequently triggered efforts to create legally binding treaties that would obligate states to honor such rights.

Over the next several decades, more than a dozen multilateral treaties were produced, including separate conventions dealing with genocide, racial discrimination, discrimination against women, children's rights, human trafficking, political and civil rights, and economic and social rights.[48] The latter two conventions, along with the Universal Declaration, are often referred to as the **International Bill of Human Rights**. The following list summarizes the key provisions and current status of major human rights treaties (with the number of state parties, as of 2009, indicated in parentheses).

- The first important human rights treaty after World War II was the 1948 **Genocide Convention** (ratified by 140 parties); approved the day before the Universal Declaration, the treaty bans killing and other acts that intend to "destroy a national, ethnic, racial or religious group."
- The 1965 **International Convention on the Elimination of All Forms of Racial Discrimination** (173 states) requires each member country to "review governmental, national, and local policies, and to . . . nullify any laws and regulations which have the effect of creating or perpetuating racial discrimination" and to "prohibit . . . racial discrimination by any persons, group or organization."
- The 1966 **Covenant on Civil and Political Rights** (161 states) and the 1966 **Covenant on Economic, Social, and Cultural Rights** (157 states) reiterate many of the rights enunciated in the Universal Declaration.
- The 1979 **Convention on Elimination of All Forms of Discrimination Against Women** (185 states) followed earlier women's rights treaties that had dealt with political participation, marriage, and other issues.
- The 1984 **Convention Against Torture** (145 states) attempts to define torture, bans torture under any circumstances, and requires states to ensure that "the victim of an act of torture obtains redress."
- The 1989 **Convention on the Rights of the Child** (193 states) stipulates inalienable rights enjoyed by children, including the establishment of a minimum age (18) under which minors cannot be recruited for military service and sent into combat.
- The 2000 UN **Convention Against Transnational Organized Crime** and the **Protocol to Prevent, Suppress, and Punish Trafficking in Persons,**

Especially Women and Children (110 parties) obligate states to pass national legislation to address the human trafficking problem and to enforce criminal penalties against traffickers.

Many states have not yet ratified several of these conventions, and many that are parties have interpreted the requirements loosely or failed altogether to observe the rules. Even the United States, an early catalyst behind the Universal Declaration (led by Eleanor Roosevelt), did not ratify the Covenant on Civil and Political Rights until 1992. President Carter had signed it in 1977, but fifteen years elapsed before it was finally ratified, after the U.S. Senate was satisfied with various "reservations" that the United States attached, which addressed Washington's concerns about provisions of the treaty limiting capital punishment, infringing on First Amendment rights through imposition of speech codes, and otherwise conflicting with U.S. law. The United States has never ratified the Covenant on Economic, Social, and Cultural Rights, also signed by Carter in 1977, because it is viewed by conservative members of the U.S. Senate as promoting an expanded welfare state and excessive governmental regulation, for example by guaranteeing paid leave for women before and after childbirth. Similarly, the United States has not yet ratified the Convention on Discrimination Against Women, since it contains language considered stronger than that contained in the Equal Rights Amendment, which failed to gain the necessary support to be added to the U.S. Constitution in the 1980s. Indeed, the United States did not become a party to the Genocide Convention until 1988, forty years after its inception, when it decided that the anti–capital punishment provisions did not violate states' rights under U.S. domestic law. The United States remains, with Somalia, the only nonparty to the Convention on the Rights of the Child, a main sticking point being the treaty language thought to interfere with the rights of parents to discipline their kids and the rights of states to execute juvenile offenders. (Once it was assured that it could meet its volunteer army's numerical recruitment goals, the United States belatedly agreed to raise its military combat age requirement from 17 to 18 by ratifying a 2002 protocol on child soldiers, but still remains outside the parent treaty.) Commenting on the spotty American participation in human rights treaties, Michael Ignatieff has characterized the United States as "a nation with a great rights tradition that leads the world in denouncing human rights violations but which behaves like a rogue state in relation to international legal conventions."[49]

Arguably far worse behavior is displayed by those countries that *are* parties to human rights treaties but flout their obligations. In 2002, UN secretary-general Kofi Annan reported that twenty-three parties to the Convention on the Rights of the Child, including Liberia, Burundi, and the Congo, were guilty of treaty violations in recruiting child soldiers.[50] Although there is still considerable sexism in American society, the U.S. record of gender equality is superior to that of countries such as Chad, Ghana, Kenya, Nigeria, China, Japan, Myanmar, and Saudi Arabia, all of which, unlike the United States, are parties to the Convention on Discrimination Against Women. Saudi Arabia is one of the 145 states that have acceded to the 1984 Convention Against Torture, yet this has not ended the weekly floggings, stonings, and beheadings in Riyadh's "Chop-Chop Square."[51] Of course, the United States was itself criticized for violating the Convention Against Torture (in addition to the Geneva Convention POW rules) in its treatment of prisoners at the Guantanamo Bay detention center after 9/11. Then, too, there is the example of Russia and Iraq as original members of the Covenant on Civil and Political Rights, having joined in 1976 (long before American ratification), and Cuba having joined in 2008, despite never permitting even the semblance of a free press.

Obviously there are grounds for much cynicism toward human rights law. Oona Hathaway has researched the question, "Do human rights treaties make a difference?" Hathaway examined a database of 166 countries over a nearly forty-year period to determine whether ratification of such treaties improves a state's human rights record. She found that ratifiers do not differ significantly in their behavior from nonratifiers, and some countries that have joined human rights treaties have worse records than those that have not joined.[52] Data on human rights abuses are difficult to obtain from highly repressive societies because of government secrecy and distortion. However, various NGOs have managed to improve the monitoring of governments' human rights records worldwide; these include Amnesty International, Freedom House, and Human Rights Watch. IGO involvement through the UN Human Rights Commission and the Office of the UN High Commissioner for Human Rights has also been a core element of human rights regime enforcement. Although each convention has its own rapporteur and monitoring apparatus to receive and investigate complaints about noncompliance, the Human Rights Commission was established as the main UN watchdog body. An especially sad commentary on respect for human rights occurred when Libya, long under the dictatorial yoke of Muammar Gaddafi, was elected to chair the Human Rights Commission in 2003, thanks to support from commission members like Saudi Arabia, Sudan, Cuba, and Zimbabwe. The latter debacle resulted in the creation of a new **UN Human Rights Council** in 2006, which replaced the commission and adopted reforms aimed at improving membership qualifications.

Even though enforcement machinery remains weak, increased attention from NGOs and other watchdog groups has given human rights issues more importance on the global agenda than many realists might have predicted. The growing role of NGOs in agenda setting as well as regime formation in the human rights field is described by Margaret Karns and Karen Mingst in their discussion of global efforts to curb violence against women:

> The 1993 World Conference on Human Rights [organized by the UN] . . . put the issue of violence against women on the agenda. The success of the Vienna conference in marrying human rights and women's rights can be attributed to the ninety or so human rights and women's NGOs that organized the Global Campaign for Women's Human Rights. A key element in that

campaign was the focus on gender-based violence. At the NGO forum, the Global Campaign organized [a tribunal that] . . . heard testimony of women from twenty-five countries. . . . [Their efforts helped] produce Article 18 of the Vienna Declaration and Programme of Action that declared: "The human rights of women and of the girl-child are an alienable . . . part of universal human rights."[53]

The same themes were reiterated at the 1995 UN World Conference on Women, held in Beijing as a follow-up to the first three UN women's conferences held in 1975 in Mexico City, 1980 in Copenhagen, and 1985 in Nairobi. Since Mexico City, "the number of NGOs [had] increased exponentially and shifted percepti-bly from women in the North to women in the South," with the number of women NGO Forum participants jumping from over 6,000 in 1975 to an estimated 25,000 in 1995.[54]

Similar efforts to advance human rights have occurred in regard to indigenous peoples (through the work of the World Council on Indigenous Peoples and its links to the UN Permanent Forum on Indigenous Peoples, which led to the Gen-eral Assembly declaring 2005–2014 the International Decade of the Indigenous Peoples), human trafficking, and other human rights fields. It would be a mistake to exaggerate either the power of NGOS or the significance of the platitudinous wording of the assorted declarations, action plans, and other outputs that emanate from UN conferences. Nor, however, should they be dismissed as irrelevant.

Human Rights Challenges in the Twenty-first Century

The post–Cold War era presents numerous obstacles to the future development of human rights, but also new opportunities. As noted in Chapter 6, after 1989 there was some hope of forging a global consensus on human rights built around Western, liberal-democratic principles, in place of the Western, Marxist, and Third World divisions that had existed during the Cold War. However, such optimism did not adequately take into account the "clash of civilizations" that Samuel Hunt-ington called attention to in his 1993 article.[55] As one observer noted at the time, referring to Francis Fukuyama's "end of history" thesis, "the self-congratulatory, simplistic, and sanctimonious tone of much Western commentary at the end of the Cold War and the current triumphalism of Western values grate on East and Southeast Asians," whose model of "Asian democracy" did not fully square with the Western version.[56] It also grated on adherents of Islam in the Middle East and elsewhere, whose political systems had a strong theocratic bent that prevented the elevation of secular legal precepts above religious law, especially over matters such as the status of women and privacy rights. In addition, disagreement remained surrounding the concept of economic and social rights ("second-generation" human rights), with even West-West conflict increasingly apparent between the United States and many Western European countries over the relative importance of civil liberties, property rights, and free markets versus welfare state entitlements.

All of these divergent viewpoints were expressed at the aforementioned 1993 UN World Conference on Human Rights in Vienna, where national delegations debated everything from "the rights of the disabled" and "the rights of gays and lesbians" to "the right to development" and "the right to a clean environment" ("third generation" human rights). According to one commentator, the conference "appeared to take a step backward in terms of *globally* defining human rights. China and Indonesia were the front-runners in the final conference statement. It [contended] that Western-derived human rights standards should now be tempered by 'regional peculiarities and various historical, cultural and religious backgrounds.'"[57] The meeting ultimately produced a declaration embodying a fragile, uneasy consensus. The Vienna Declaration's affirmation of human rights as "universal, indivisible, and interdependent" papered over, on the one hand, the charges of cultural imperialism leveled against the West by "the rest" and, on the other hand, the criticisms leveled against the developing world for spinning off yet another generation of new rights before earlier ones had been consolidated.

By January 2001, Thomas Franck and other veteran human rights watchers were asking, "Are human rights universal?"[58] By September of that year, following the attack on the World Trade Center in New York City, larger questions loomed. Michael Ignatieff went so far as to suggest that "the question after Sept. 11 is whether the era of human rights has come and gone,"[59] referring to the fact that the need for the United States and other countries to fight the war on terrorism gave China, Russia, and other authoritarian regimes excuses to crack down on political dissidents and separatist movements, made it less likely that Washington would pressure these governments to liberalize their political systems, and raised concerns about undermining of civil liberties even in Western democracies (e.g., the Patriot Act's possible threat to privacy and due process in the United States).

Where, then, does this leave human rights in the twenty-first century? Despite Ignatieff's lament, there are some hopeful signs. First, certain human rights gains seem irreversible, as divine right of kings hardly figures to make a comeback as a basis for exercising authority. Even in Saudi Arabia, there is growing pressure for the royal family to begin to open up the political system to electoral politics. Second, even if human rights globally have been lagging, there are regional human rights regimes worth noting, particularly in Europe. For example, the European Court of Human Rights allows individual citizens to sue their own government for violating the European Convention on Human Rights. Among the recent rulings have been decisions ordering Britain to rescind its ban on homosexuals serving in the military and admonishing Britain for failing to protect a nine-year-old boy from severe corporal punishment by his parents.[60] "Remarkably, sovereign states have respected the adverse judgments of the Court . . . [and] have reformed or abandoned police procedures, penal institutions, child welfare practices, . . . and many other important public matters."[61] In addition, Turkey and other would-be entrants to the European Union are feeling pressure to improve their human rights records if they wish to be considered for EU admission.

Third, despite the resistance of the United States and some other countries, there is a growing movement worldwide to institutionalize punishment for the worst atrocities through the establishment of the aforementioned International Criminal Court that was created in 2002 as a permanent "Nuremberg trial" judiciary. (See the *IR* Critical Thinking Box "The International Criminal Court and the Future of Human Rights.") Fourth, through the articulation and pursuit of the Millennium Development Goals that emerged from the 2000 UN Millennium Summit, there has been a strengthened commitment to the proposition that basic economic rights are part of the human rights project.

IR Critical Thinking:
The International Criminal Court and the Future of Human Rights

There is some question whether there is a definition and suite of human rights that is universally accepted. For example, are there minimal standards governing treatment of women that all states should observe, including Pakistan, with its allowance of honor killings for adultery, Saudi Arabia, with its no-driving laws and segregated shopping malls for women, and Swaziland, with its custom of parading 50,000 virgins at a national festival as a mating ritual whereby the king selects his wives? What about children's rights? Although almost every country on earth has ratified the Convention on the Rights of the Child, which bans corporal punishment and affords children other protections, many African countries still practice female genital mutilation. Clearly there is disagreement regarding the exact content of human rights when it comes to women, children, and other persons. Even the subject of genocide and "crimes against humanity" remains a contested area, as seen in the politics of the International Criminal Court.

In the 1990s the United Nations charged former Serb president Slobodan Milosevic with ethnic cleansing of Bosnian civilians in Bosnia-Herzegovina and Albanian civilians in Kosovo, while Rwandan prime minister Jean Kambanda was charged with genocide against ethnic Tutsis. They were tried by ad hoc tribunals established solely to hear those two cases. Kambanda was found guilty and Milosevic died in his cell before a guilty verdict could be rendered in what were the first international trials of heads of state and high-level government officials since Nuremberg. Recognizing that a permanent, sitting, Nuremberg-style court might deter future atrocities and, if deterrence failed, punish those individuals responsible, many states and NGOs worked to create an International Criminal Court (ICC). These efforts culminated in a gathering of almost 150 states in 1998 to finalize the drafting of the Rome Statute establishing the Court in The Hague, Netherlands. A total of 120 countries voted in favor, 20 abstained, and 7 opposed, including the United States, Israel, China, Iraq, and Libya. The ICC officially came into existence in 2002; as of 2009, over 100 countries were parties.

The Rome Statute authorizes prosecution of individuals (private citizens, military personnel, and former or current public officials from member or nonmember states) who are accused of war crimes, genocide, or crimes against humanity. In addition to cases that may be referred by the U.N. Security Council, proceedings may be initiated by any ICC member state on whose territory the alleged crime occurred or by the state of the nationality of the accused. The state whose national has been charged with a crime is given the first opportunity to try that individual, but must defer to the ICC if it is unwilling or unable to take action.

The United States has not yet ratified the treaty, despite the fact that most European nations and U.S. allies have. The main American objections are: (1) the Statute undermines the primacy of the UN Security Council, and hence the American veto power, by permitting cases to be initiated by any member state or by the ICC prosecutor; (2) American leaders or American soldiers might well be prime targets of an ICC investigation, given the relatively heavy involvement of U.S. armed forces in peacekeeping, humanitarian intervention or other overseas military operations (so that, say, George Bush might conceivably be apprehended while traveling abroad and indicted over alleged Iraq War transgressions); and (3) ICC procedures under the Rome Statute are to be determined by a majority of states party to the treaty, so that, assuming the ultimate goal is to make the treaty universal, the majority of the world's countries that are "not free" or "partly free" might be positioned to dominate the court over the will of its democratic members.

Consider the following questions:

1. Two dozen African and Latin American states with questionable human rights records are ICC parties. How would they likely view accusations of genocide against the current Sudan leadership, compared with, say, complaints against the United States (for possible war crimes in Iraq) and Israel (for its treatment of Palestinians)? How realistic is it for politics to be kept out of ICC deliberations? Also, how can the ICC function while a major actor such as the United States remains outside its purview?

2. Should the United States join the International Criminal Court? What are the pros and cons?

3. When Western human rights groups criticize such customs as women wearing head-to-toe burqas in Islamic fundamentalist societies or female genital mutilation in some African societies, are they guilty of "cultural imperialism" in imposing their values on other peoples, or are they rightly calling attention to universal rights that all states should observe? Also, what happened to sovereignty?

4. Are you optimistic or pessimistic about the future of human rights? Do you agree with constructivist theorists that we have already seen considerable global progress in the internalization of new norms against not only colonialism but also racism and sexism and other forms of discrimination, and that more progress will occur in the twenty-first century, or is that an unrealistic assessment?

HUMAN DEVELOPMENT REGIMES

The World Bank's homepage trumpets, "Our dream is a world free of poverty." Not surprisingly, poverty-related issues have not made their way to the top of the global agenda and resulted in major "global policy" adoption any more than they have been given the highest priority on national domestic agendas. However, they are at least on the radar screen, as evidenced by the creation of the **Millennium Development Goals** (**MDGs**) adopted at the 2000 Millennium Summit, the largest gathering of heads of state in history, accompanied by officials of the UN and several specialized agencies, along with representatives from over 1,000

NGOs. The chief output of the conference was the Millennium Declaration, which set 2015 as the target date for reaching most of the MDGs, including halving the number of people living on one dollar a day, the number suffering from hunger, and the number lacking access to safe drinking water; ensuring universal primary education and elimination of gender inequality in all schooling; and halting the spread of HIV/AIDS, malaria, and other major diseases. Additional goals aimed at addressing debt relief and other "special needs of the least developed countries."[62] Such aspirations were reaffirmed in a 2005 report issued by the UN Millennium Project, which laid out a vision that some considered "utterly affordable" and others considered "utopian."[63] A midpoint assessment by the World Bank in 2008 claimed "a mixed picture of significant progress and formidable challenges," with the goal of halving dollar-a-day extreme poverty within reach but others less so.[64]

Whether current international economic regimes will be able to deliver on this promise remains open to question. On the one hand, there is considerable global governance in the economic field. Comparing regime-building in the economic sphere with that in the peace and security field, Charles Lipson notes: "Conflict and cooperation are, of course, commingled in both [sets of] issues, but . . . economic issues are characterized far more by elaborate networks of rules, norms, and institutions."[65] Lipson is referring primarily to the "Bretton Woods system" institutions created after World War II—the **World Bank**, the **International Monetary Fund (IMF)**, and the **General Agreement on Tariffs and Trade (GATT)**— that are mentioned in the Chapter 6 discussion of the United Nations. However, these institutions were designed more to promote international economic *order* than *justice*. This chapter will focus mainly on the World Bank and IMF, leaving GATT (and its successor IGO, the World Trade Organization) for further discussion in the next chapter.

The World Bank, IMF, and GATT

A variety of paradigms can be used to understand the politics of global governance in the economic arena. For example, Marxists see the North-South conflict in class struggle terms, as revolving around the exploitation of the working class by national and transnational elites, while feminist theorists are inclined to focus on the exploitation of women especially. A lot of the politics, though, can be conceptualized simply in classic realist, billiard ball terms—as a game played between nation-states that involves power and national interests.[66] Southern countries have long complained that the Bretton Woods institutions have been dominated by Northern states, especially the G7 (now the G8, with Russia added). For example, the World Bank and the IMF are both headquartered in Washington, D.C., four blocks from the White House; an American has always headed the Bank, and a European the IMF.

Although all of the World Bank's 185 member governments are represented on its board of governors, decision making is based on weighted voting, with voting power assigned according to the size of a state's capital contribution to the Bank. G8 states account for almost half of the total shares in the Bank, the United States being the largest contributor. The Bank was conceived as a key multilateral aid institution to supplement the foreign aid that states gave bilaterally; funds were to be loaned to needy governments on generous terms, particularly by the International Development Association, the "soft loan window" of the Bank, which was authorized to offer fifty-year repayment periods at low interest rates. Although the Bank over the years has played an important role in providing capital to poor countries, many problems have arisen, not the least of which has been the servicing of the more than $1 trillion debt that borrowing countries have accumulated, leading to periodic calls for debt cancellation. The IMF also consists of 185 member states and operates based on a weighted voting system tied to financial clout, with the United States, Germany, and Japan accounting for approximately one-third of the total votes. The IMF was created to promote global monetary cooperation and financial stability by, first, furnishing temporary assistance to countries to ease balance of payments problems (where lack of hard currency might inhibit trade) and, second, providing a central forum for negotiating adjustments in currency values (where fluctuations in exchange rates might disrupt international economic activity). The World Bank and IMF increasingly have found themselves with overlapping missions, competing to serve as the major global IGO in the economic development field, supported by the UN Development Program (UNDP) and other multilateral agencies.

Initial efforts to create an International Trade Organization (ITO) alongside the World Bank and IMF foundered when the 1947 Havana Conference could not agree on how much power to permit the trade body to have in regulating commerce. Under traditional international law, based on sovereignty, states were "free to discriminate in their economic dealings," deciding which states received favored treatment.[67] The ITO aimed to create a single multilateral nondiscriminatory trade regime, but the United States and other states raised concerns about possible infringements on sovereignty. In lieu of the ITO, GATT was created in 1948 as an interim institution that could provide a global forum for multilateral negotiations aimed at reducing tariffs and nontariff barriers. For nearly 50 years, GATT, headquartered in Geneva, Switzerland, and consisting of over 100 member states, remained the major international trade forum, with decision making—agenda setting as well as policy formulation and adoption—dominated by the United States and developed countries. It was replaced in 1995 by the World Trade Organization (WTO), a body that has sparked renewed debate over international economic governance arrangements and relations between North and South.

For historical perspective on this debate, it is helpful to revisit the failed effort of the Third World to transform the Bretton Woods economic order into a **New International Economic Order** (NIEO) during the 1970s, when the less developed countries (LDCs) attempted to use their newfound majority control of the UN General Assembly to redistribute wealth from the North (headed by the G7) to the South (represented by the so-called **Group of 77**).[68] Many of the NIEO demands made by the South are still on the table today, even though the stridency of the rhetoric has subsided and even though the Group of 77 (now more than 100 states) has found it harder to sustain itself as a cohesive bargaining group given the diversity that now separates, for example, NICs and Fourth World countries.

In the *trade* sector, the South attempted to establish the **UN Conference on Trade and Development (UNCTAD)** as their preferred forum for global trade negotiations, since LDCs enjoyed greater power there than in GATT. They sought better terms of exchange for their raw material and primary commodity exports that were hurt by depressed prices, along with greater market access for their manufactured, cheap-labor exports that were hampered by "voluntary export restrictions" (quotas). In the *capital* sector, specifically in regard to *foreign aid*, the South urged greater efforts by the North to meet the aid target established during the first UN development decade of the 1960s (i.e., at least 0.7 percent of the North's combined GNPs allocated for official development assistance), greater Northern willingness to cancel debts of Southern countries in serious balance of payments difficulties or to negotiate longer repayment schedules, and more loans at cheaper interest rates with fewer strings attached. As for *foreign private investment*, the South pushed for a code of conduct for multinational corporations (MNCs) that would limit the profits companies could repatriate to their home country and would strengthen host country ability to retain control over its natural resources and to regulate foreign subsidiaries. Led by communist states such as Cuba, the Third World attempted to rewrite the rules governing seizure of foreign holdings through passage of a General Assembly resolution (the 1974 Charter of Economic Rights and Duties of States) that stated, "Every state has . . . full permanent sovereignty . . . over its wealth, natural resources, and economic activities," including the right "to nationalize, expropriate, or transfer ownership of foreign property." In the *currency* sector, the South objected to the IMF's tendency to withhold benefits from developing countries unless their governments agreed to adopt often painful "structural adjustment" policies calling for draconian cuts in their public expenditures and services aimed at enforcing sounder fiscal management. The South, above all, urged a greater LDC role in the governance of the IMF and other economic IGOs. They went so far as to propose a world development authority and other new bodies in which voting would be less tied to financial contributions and economic power.

The South's NIEO demands largely went unmet as the United States and other G7 members during the 1980s resisted calls for what they saw as a global welfare state being pushed by a would-be global parliament. The 1990s saw some rapprochement, with, for example, LDCS recognizing the need to tone down their militancy toward MNCs in order to attract foreign capital, and the MNCs recognizing the need to reach some accommodation with Third World governments in order to do business in secure environments free of the threat of expropriation of MNC assets.[69] Meanwhile, the **Washington Consensus** became the accepted development model, requiring LDCs to promote free markets internally and externally, reducing bloated government budgets and regulations as well as opening up their economies to foreign trade and investment.

The 1995 UN World Summit for Social Development in Copenhagen (see Chapter 6) drew government officials from 180 countries, as well as over 2,500 NGO representatives, dozens of MNC executives, and hundreds of IGO secretariat staff (from not only the World Bank and IMF but also other UN specialized agencies having a stake in economic development issues). Over the objection of many LDCs, the summit encouraged the practice of the World Bank and other aid donors at times bypassing LDC governments, instead channeling aid to poor countries through NGOs (feminist groups, village cooperatives, or other nongovernmental entities such as CARE), on the assumption that NGOs "can better reach the grassroots level" and "involve less bureaucratic red tape" and are less prone to corruption.[70]

The summit issued a nonbinding declaration reiterating the plea for rich nations to spend 0.7 percent of their GNP on foreign aid and provide debt relief for poor countries. Such entreaties have been repeated almost annually, including in the Millennium Project reports since 2000. Scaling down expectations, the director of the Millennium Project recently urged at the very least a doubling of aid from the current 0.25 percent of rich country GNPs to 0.50 percent, arguing that "we're talking about rich countries committing 50 cents out of every $100 of income to help the poorest people in the world get a foothold on the ladder of development."[71] As of 2008, however, only Sweden, Norway, the Netherlands, Luxembourg, and Denmark among the twenty richest states had met the target; the United States, the biggest aid donor in absolute terms (giving roughly $20 billion annually in official assistance), ranked at the bottom among the leading industrial nations in terms of aid as a percentage of GNP, donating only 0.16 percent.[72] In the wake of the 2008–2009 global financial crisis, the foreign assistance challenge became more daunting, as IMF was being asked to provide emergency loans and extended credit lines even to "such emerging-market stalwarts as Brazil, South Africa, and Turkey."[73]

FAO and WHO

It should be evident from the previous discussion that, even if much of the history of the North-South confrontation can be understood in simple state-centric terms as a contest between rich and poor states, *nonstate* actors also have played an important role. In addition to the World Bank and IMF, other IGOs have had substantial involvement in combating poverty, both as arenas of conflict and as agents of problem-solving. Let us look briefly at FAO and WHO, two functionally specific IGOs with heavy technical missions. Although decision making is less clearly dominated by the wealthiest, most powerful states, these IGOs nonetheless depend on them for the bulk of their funding.

The **Food and Agriculture Organization (FAO)**, with 191 member states, is the UN specialized agency that has primary responsibility for addressing both systemic food problems (the estimated 800 million people worldwide who are chronically hungry and undernourished) and food emergencies (the roughly 80 million people a year facing starvation due to natural disasters, refugee dislocations, armed conflict, or other humanitarian crises). Ever since Thomas Malthus predicted worldwide famine due to world population outstripping food production in *Essay on the Principle of Population* (1798), the specter of famine has haunted humanity. However, Malthusian predictions have proven erroneous, thanks largely to improvements in agricultural technology. Although world population has exploded since Malthus's time, so has food output, due to advances in wheat and rice seed (the Green Revolution), genetic engineering, increased use of pesticides and chemical fertilizers, and other innovations. While local pockets of famine have occurred periodically, they have resulted from maldistribution of food supplies rather than from global food shortages. Lately, though, Malthusian fears have recurred over the fact that production of the three major grain crops that humans depend on for almost half their calories—wheat, corn, and rice—has declined in recent years, with some observers worrying that the planet has reached its agricultural carrying capacity.[74]

FAO's World Food Program, in partnership with CARE, Save the Children, and other NGOs, has been responding to an average of thirty emergencies annually in recent years. Regarding systemic problems, FAO's Committee on Food Security tracks food security in the eighty-eight states, mostly in Africa and Asia, which have been identified as low-income food-deficit countries.[75] The deficits are caused by a variety of factors, including LDC government policies, such as price controls and inadequate investment in rural communities, that discourage local farmers from growing more food; unfair competition from farmers in developed countries, including the large agribusiness grain dealers (e.g., Cargill, Continental, Louis Dreyfus)[76] and producers of genetically modified foods (e.g., Monsanto) that benefit from home government subsidies and whose cheaper exports then undermine food self-sufficiency in importing countries; population pressures combining with water shortages, soil erosion, climate change, and other environmental constraints to produce food scarcity; further strain on world food supplies due to conversion of cropland to biofuel production and the growing appetite for grain-fed beef in China and elsewhere; and lack of purchasing power by the poor to buy the food that is available on the world market.[77]

One might hope that politics stops at the edge of starvation, but there is a politics of food, even if it is relatively low-politics compared to, say, conflicts over missile silos and WMD proliferation. Indeed, food fights can be quite politicized. Politics has been at work at FAO-sponsored conferences, such as the 1974 World Food Conference in Rome, which saw "two and three level games" pitting not only nations against nations but also various domestic constituencies, UN secretariats, and NGOs against each other in turf wars over who would bear the burdens and reap the benefits of new food regimes. FAO's 1996 World Food Summit, which attracted 185 states, two dozen UN agencies, and 500 NGOs to Rome, issued a declaration on food security that affirmed "the fundamental right of everyone to be free from hunger" and a plan of action that stressed national-level responses. On the eve of the World Food Summit: Five Years Later Conference in 2002, the FAO director-general could only lament the stale nature of such calls to action, noting that there was little evidence of "the large-scale purposive action needed to get to grips with the underlying causes of hunger."[78]

In some respects, the world has addressed health care issues more effectively than hunger issues, although many problems persist in the health issue-area too. The **World Health Organization (WHO)** is the 193-member UN specialized agency that has played a major role in promoting public health worldwide. Infectious diseases long have posed a global threat, exemplified by the bubonic plague (Black Death) that started in Asia and ultimately decimated a third of Europe's population in the fourteenth century, as well as the Spanish flu that killed 600,000 Americans and 20 million to 40 million people worldwide in 1918–1919. Diseases can now travel more quickly across national boundaries, given the speed of airliners, but there are also quicker global response mechanisms. As one writer notes, WHO, "acting through its Health Assembly, has express authority—acting by simple majority—to adopt regulations binding on all members except those that notify the director-general of rejections or reservations within a designated time. . . . [The International Health Regulations] are of major importance. The Health Regulations try to preclude the international spread of such diseases as cholera, the plague, and yellow fever."[79] WHO recently was given authority to issue global alerts against health threats and to send inspection teams to countries of origin so as to prevent outbreaks from becoming planetary pandemics, as happened in 2003–2005, when WHO successfully managed the containment of the SARS (severe acute respiratory syndrome) and avian flu epidemics. The year 2009 saw efforts by WHO to contain the swine flu epidemic.

Although WHO serves both rich and poor countries, it has focused on improving health in LDCs, where government expenditures on medical care can be as low as $20 a person, compared to $6,000 in many developed countries. Perhaps WHO's greatest success story has been the eradication of smallpox, which once afflicted 50 million people a year, mostly in the Third World, but by 1979 had been totally eliminated through the organization's immunization efforts. In 1973, WHO started an expanded program on immunization to immunize children against six leading causes of child deaths in the Third World—tuberculosis (TB), measles, diphtheria, whooping cough, tetanus, and polio; whereas only 20 percent of children had been immunized in 1981, the rate had improved to 80 percent by 1995. WHO's global polio eradication initiative, launched in 1988, has achieved a 99 percent reduction in infections, with the disease practically conquered. Unfortunately TB and malaria have resisted prevention and cure, each claiming over 1 million lives annually. There is hope that the former (newly resurgent due to the rise in

HIV infections and drug-resistant strains) can be reduced through development of new vaccines, and the latter through widespread use of insecticides (particularly DDT, which has made a comeback after earlier environmental bans) and inexpensive mosquito-repelling bed nets. WHO has had greater success in disseminating oral rehydration therapy to control diarrhea, a leading childhood killer in poor countries.

As in the food issue-area, there is a politics of health. It can be clearly observed in WHO's global campaign to curb the spread of AIDS and improve treatment along with prevention of the disease, an effort coordinated with another UN body, UNAIDS, supported by such NGOs as the International AIDS Society and the Bill and Melinda Gates Foundation. An estimated 33 million people worldwide are living with HIV/AIDS, nearly two-thirds of them in sub-Saharan Africa. Although progress has been made in some countries, each year 2 million new infections occur (largely transmitted through unprotected sex or illicit drug use) and 2 million deaths are attributed to the disease. Many governments are still reluctant to acknowledge the extent of the AIDS epidemic within their borders, for fear of discouraging foreign tourist traffic and foreign investment. In many of these same countries, condom use remains a cultural taboo, as does homosexuality—stigmas that increase the incidence of the disease and decrease the reporting of it. Until recently, WTO intellectual property rules limited the sale of cheap generic antiretroviral drugs for AIDS treatment that violated the patents of global pharmaceutical companies. Merck, Eli Lilly, and other firms claimed they needed patent protection to preserve incentives for them to invest in medical research and development that might provide cures, even though the effect was to deny treatment to desperately sick people. However, more generic drugs are beginning to make their way onto the market, providing better access to treatment and offering hope that the AIDS scourge can be substantially reduced.[80] These and other issues were aired at the seventeenth annual International AIDS Conference in Mexico City in 2008, which attracted 22,000 scientists, policymakers, and activists. Along with panels organized by epistemic communities of medical experts on such subjects as HIV transmission and pathogenesis, there were numerous other panels dealing with women's rights (including the rights of sex workers), gay rights, reproductive rights, and other matters more political than medical in nature.[81]

Politics has also been at work in the WHO campaign against cigarette smoking. There are some 1 billion smokers in the world (80 percent of whom are in LDCs), with 5 million tobacco-related deaths a year. Supported by the World Medical Association, an NGO comprising 10 million doctors from 117 countries, WHO in 2003 produced the Framework Convention on Tobacco Control, its first treaty. The treaty obligated all parties (now over 160 states) to take steps to ban cigarette advertising, impose higher taxes on cigarettes, and restrict smoking in public places. WHO found an ally in the World Bank, which was concerned about the economic costs of smoking, since each pack of cigarettes contributes to skyrocketing health care expenses borne by society. Not surprisingly, the treaty was opposed by Phillip Morris and other MNCs representing tobacco interests. The United States, where 20 percent of adults smoke, has signed but not yet ratified the treaty, due to concerns about overregulation infringing on free speech and trademark laws (e.g., the convention's ban on use of package wording such as "light" or "low tar"). In the American federal system, individual states, such as California and New York, have taken the lead in outlawing cigarettes in the workplace. In 2003 Norway became the first country to approve a national ban on smoking in restaurants and bars, with several other states following suit since. In South Asia, Bhutan has banned cigarettes altogether. As one observer has commented, "Only a few years ago the idea that citizen groups, national governments, medical associations, WHO, and the World Bank would be working together to create a tobacco-free world would have seemed far-fetched. Today, it is becoming a reality."[82]

CONCLUSION

The crusade to promote both human dignity and human development is embodied in the **Global Compact**, a partnership between the United Nations and the global business community that was started by Secretary-General Kofi Annan in 2000 and counted over 1,000 corporate members in 2009. What is most intriguing about the Global Compact is that it appears to be an end run around the state system. Frustrated with the slow pace of government commitments to end human rights abuses and poverty, Annan sought to enlist the direct participation and resources of the private sector. As reported by the *New York Times*, large companies like Cisco Systems and Microsoft have become "unlikely allies with the United Nations," as they fund community development projects in poor countries in the name of good global corporate citizenship. They rely on the UN Development Program and other IGOs to help administer these projects.[83] The Business Council for the UN is "engaging technology companies to help bridge the digital divide" and is "working with policy experts to deal with debt and financial crises in the developing world."[84] At a recent meeting of the World Congress of the International Chamber of Congress (ICC), Kofi Annan's call for the United Nations as "the global institution" and the ICC as "the global business association" to join together to give globalization "more of a human face" met with a warm response from ICC members who supported the concept even if they were lukewarm to any new regulations.[85]

Such IGO-NGO-MNC links may seem incongruous with the organizational logic of the Westphalian state system, but they are increasingly common. It remains to be seen if corporations will prove any more selfless than nations. The world is nowhere near to accepting some of the more idealistic, utopian proposals that have been floated at recent UN conferences, such as a world income tax or a global tax on currency exchanges that would be used to support a UN development fund. But the architecture of global economic governance is already evolving beyond what many realist, state-centric theorists could have predicted.[86]

In the next chapter we will examine the functioning and management of the world economy as a whole. With the advent of globalization, we are witnessing a great drama unfolding in the twenty-first century between two powerful forces that are in tension with each other—a persistent welfare state nationalism versus an emergent world-without-borders capitalism. This is commonly referred to as the contest of "states vs. markets." [87] We will see how states and markets are interacting in the international economy (more precisely, the international *political* economy) as we explore the politics of trade and investment. We will also explore the role played by international institutions and regimes in resolving these tensions and keeping the world economy running.

QUESTIONS FOR STUDY AND DISCUSSION

1. How does the concept of human rights square with the concept of sovereignty?
2. What international regimes have been developed to promote women's rights, minority rights, and children's rights? What about political, economic, and social rights? How effective have these been? What roles have nonstate actors played in the development of these regimes?
3. Is the rich-poor gap between countries widening or narrowing? What about the rich-poor gap within countries? What obligations do you think national governments have to narrow these gaps?
4. What international institutions and regimes exist to promote economic development and improvement in the lives of the world's poor? How effective are these? Discuss the politics of global governance and problem-solving in this field, including the role of nonstate actors?

SUGGESTIONS FOR FURTHER READING

Lloyd Axworthy, "Human Security and Global Governance: Putting People First," *Global Governance* 7 (2001): 19–23.

Brandt Commission, *North-South* (Cambridge: MIT Press, 1980).

J. Peter Burgess et al., "What Is Human Security?" *Security Dialogue* 35 (September 2004): 345–385.

Paul Collier, *The Bottom Billion* (Oxford: Oxford University Press, 2007).

Jack Donnelly, *International Human Rights*, 3rd ed. (Boulder, CO: Westview, 2007).

Jean Dreze et al., eds., *The Political Economy of Hunger* (Oxford: Oxford University Press, 1995).

David P. Forsythe, *Human Rights and World Politics*, 2nd ed. (Lincoln: University of Nebraska Press, 1989).

Thomas M. Franck, "Are Human Rights Universal?" *Foreign Affairs* 80 (January–February 2001): 191–204.

Fen Osler Hampson et al., *Madness in the Multitude: Human Security and World Disorder* (Oxford: Oxford University Press, 2002).

Arie M. Kacowicz, "Globalization, Poverty, and the North-South Divide," *International Studies Review* 9 (Winter 2007): 565–580.

Ethan Kapstein, "The New Global Slave Trade," *Foreign Affairs* 85 (November–December 2006): 103–115.

Stephen D. Krasner, *Structural Conflict: The Third World Against Global Liberalism* (Berkeley: University of California Press, 1985).

Robin Meredith, *The Elephant and the Dragon: The Rise of India and China* (New York: Norton, 2007).

John Rapley, *Understanding Development* (Boulder, CO: Lynne Rienner, 1996).

Robert Rothstein, *Global Bargaining: UNCTAD and the Quest for a New International Economic Order* (Princeton, NJ: Princeton University Press, 1979).

Amartya Sen, *Development as Freedom* (Oxford: Oxford University Press, 2001).

Caroline Thomas, *Global Governance, Development, and Human Security* (London: Pluto, 2000).

UNDP, *Human Development Report*, published annually.

9

Managing the
World Economy
and Promoting Prosperity

You can't go home again.
    —Thomas Wolfe, *You Can't Go Home Again*, 1940

In the world of globalization, you won't be able to leave home again.
    —Thomas Friedman, *The Lexus and the Olive Tree*, 1999

The word **globalization** was first used in a Western dictionary in 1961.[1] It has a much longer lineage. If the term simply refers to the cultural diffusion of ideas and customs (e.g., washing with soap and shaving, invented by the ancient Gauls and Egyptians), then it goes back to antiquity.[2] More recently, the late nineteenth century has been called the first era of globalization, since it was marked by expanded transnational flows of people, goods, and services fueled by innovations in communications and transportation (see Chapter 2). By the 1970s, respected observers such as Charles Kindleberger, George Ball, and Raymond Vernon were saying that "the state is about through as an economic unit," that "the nation-state is a very old-fashioned idea and badly adapted to serve the needs of our complex modern world," and that **multinational corporations (MNCs)** posed a threat to state independence and were putting "sovereignty at bay."[3] These commentators were calling attention to the growing penetration of national economies by external forces that were making the national identity of products and producers less and less clear. However, globalization as a phenomenon did not fully take off until the 1990s, following the end of the Cold War. As one author remarks, globalization

has become one of the catchwords of the new millennium. In fact, globalization is shorthand for a cluster of interrelated changes: economic, ideological, technological, political, and cultural. [Most importantly,] economic

288

changes include the increasing integration of economies around the world, particularly through trade and financial flows. This integration takes place through the internationalization and de-territorialization of production [and] the greatly increased mobility of capital and of transnational (multinational) corporations. . . . Ideological changes involve investment and trade liberalization, de-regulation, privatization, and the adoption of political democracy. . . . Technological changes refer to information and communication technologies that have shrunk the globe. Finally, cultural changes involve trends toward a harmonization of tastes and standards, epitomized by a world culture that transcends the nation-state.[4]

Today, we can speak of a world economy even if there is no world government. True, national boundaries still matter (e.g., the volume of trade between Toronto and Vancouver, two Canadian cities, is far greater than that between Toronto and Seattle, just across the border from Vancouver), but they seem to be receding in importance. The author Thomas Wolfe said, "You can't go home again." But Thomas Friedman has countered that "in the world of globalization, you won't be able to leave home again."[5] A single, homogeneous marketplace has emerged and is increasingly encountered wherever one roams in the world, whether it is in former communist states once insulated behind the Iron Curtain or in Middle East states still governing behind the veil of Islam. This global marketplace is sustained not only by transnational *trade* flows but also transnational *capital* flows, as firms in one country increasingly operate subsidiaries in other countries. McDonald's does business in 119 countries, serving 50 million customers daily in its 30,000 restaurants, earning two-thirds of its revenue outside the United States; the largest McDonald's on the planet is now found in Beijing, China (one of 80 in the city). Starbucks now operates 4,500 coffeehouses in 47 countries; in China alone, there are more than 250 Starbucks coffee shops, including one at the Great Wall and another in the Forbidden City. Coca-Cola is served 600 million times a day in virtually every country on earth (including North Korea); 70 percent of its income is derived from overseas bottlers. MTV spans 5 continents, is beamed into over 100 countries, and attracts 80 percent of its viewership from abroad.[6]

Globalization is not to be equated with Americanization. Dr. Pepper, 7-Up, Ben and Jerry's ice cream, and countless other American brand names are owned by companies that have their headquarters abroad. Although the United States is still the base of operations for the largest number of MNCs in the world, with Microsoft and other U.S. firms continuing to expand their reach into overseas markets, its lead as a headquarters country is shrinking as American businesses increasingly fall prey to corporate buyouts by foreign interests, for example, Amoco being taken over by British Petroleum (the headquarters shifting from Chicago to London), Ralston-Purina being purchased by Nestlé (Checkerboard Square relocating from St. Louis to Lake Geneva, Switzerland), and Anheuser-Busch being sold to Inbev (the headquarters of Budweiser, long billed as "the Great American Lager," moving to Leuven, Belgium, under the management of a Brazilian CEO).

"Hostile takeover" has a different meaning today in international relations than it once had in an earlier era. It is somewhat ironic that, at a time when the territorial integrity norm[7] (against the forcible annexation of territory) has become sacrosanct in regard to international security, borders in the international economy are becoming so porous and blurred that some observers go so far as to talk about "the end of geography."[8] The implications of globalization for the nation-state (whether "there appears to be a diminution of state autonomy, and a disjuncture between the notion of a sovereign state directing its own future and the dynamics of the contemporary world economy")[9] can be debated, but what is nondebatable is the heightened interest among international relations scholars and practitioners in the subject of **international political economy (IPE)**. If you were to look at the best-selling IR textbooks in the decades following World War II, for example Hans Morgenthau's *Politics Among Nations*, you would find scant attention to international economics other than its importance to the exercise of power. In contrast, no contemporary textbook would fail to include extensive treatment of trade, foreign investment, and other such topics as deserving their own issue-area coverage.

This chapter examines the problems associated with the coordination of an increasingly interdependent international economy, the politics of economic problem-solving, and the various regime-building efforts that have been undertaken. There is disagreement not only over how much coordination of the international economy is possible or desirable, but also what purposes coordination should serve—greater overall economic growth and efficiency, or also greater economic justice. There is disagreement as well over what role international institutions should play in this process. In conducting this examination, it is helpful to conceptualize the international economy as consisting of two distinct but interrelated components: the *trade* sector (exports and imports of goods and services) and the *capital* sector (foreign private investment). It is also helpful, indeed necessary, to review a number of widely different, conflicting perspectives on the nature of international economic relations.

THE PROBLEM

Three Schools of International Political Economy: Mercantilism, Liberalism, and Marxism

There are two basic ways to organize an economy—around the *state* (government) or the free *market* (the private sector). There has been an ongoing historical drama pitting these two organizing principles against each other, with much economic thought over the years revolving around the search for the proper balance. Virtually all states today adopt a mixed form in practice, although some

© James Andanson/Sygma/Corbis

A Chinese boy at the Great Wall of China: The Coca-Colonization of the world.

lean more heavily toward the statist end of the spectrum (notably communist states such as Cuba and China) while others tilt more heavily toward markets (notably states with a strong capitalist tradition such as the United States). This drama has played out not only within states but on the international stage as well, where it has shaped the evolution of international economic regimes. There are three main schools of thought about the role of states and markets in the international economy: mercantilism, liberal internationalism, and Marxism. Each of these intellectual traditions offers its own set of explanations of the workings of the international economy and its own prescriptions for improving it.

MERCANTILISM

The first nation-states in the early life of the Westphalian system during the seventeenth and eighteenth centuries were mercantilist in character. As Robert Gilpin has written, **mercantilism** meant economic nationalism. "Its central idea [was] that economic activities are and should be subordinate to the goal of state building and the interests of the state."[10] The mercantilist state was interested in economic matters mainly as they related to using government levers, particularly tariffs and other trade policies, in support of military power and conquest. Exports were to be promoted as a way to generate gold bullion and other currency to pay for an army, while imports were to be discouraged in order to deny potential adversaries such financial resources. Epitomized by France, the mercantilist state was far less concerned about the general welfare of the nation and citizenry at large.

The welfare state had not yet been born, as only the privileged few were thought to be entitled to enjoy the fruits of the nation's economic growth. Louis XIV and other rulers could hardly conceive of such notions as a "human development index" for their own people, much less for people living abroad. As the welfare state developed in the twentieth century, protectionist government economic policies were aimed at maximizing not only national security but also national employment and well-being.

Mercantilism is consistent with realist thinking. Mercantilist theory sees international economics as a zero-sum game, as inherently conflictual and not very conducive to interstate cooperation. To the extent that institution-building occurs, "nations continually try to change the rules or regimes governing international economic relations to benefit themselves disproportionately. . . . [Therefore, an open international economy] cannot develop unless it is supported by the dominant states."[11] Many observers today see the international economy still being driven primarily by national interests and power, as reflected in the dominance of the United States and the richest states in the governance of global economic institutions such as the WTO, World Bank, and IMF.

Liberal Internationalism

The mercantilist model, which stressed the role of the state as a mode of organizing economic activity, was challenged by a competing model in 1776, when Adam Smith wrote *The Wealth of Nations*, which stressed free market, laissez-faire principles as an alternative basis for economic relations. Smith became known as the father of "free trade," and his model became known as **liberal internationalism**. The liberal internationalist school of thought holds that there are benefits to be derived from cooperation between national governments. States share certain mutual interests in collaborating to open up trade and investment opportunities for each other in order to maximize the special economic advantages of each country. Some countries might have particularly low labor costs, others abundant raw materials, and so forth. Ultimately, producers as well as consumers in all nations can expect to benefit from an international economy based on the most efficient use of resources. To this end, Smith called on governments to reduce tariffs and other artificial barriers to international economic activity and to allow goods and services to flow as freely as possible based on supply and demand market factors, so that the boundary between, say, England and France would be no more an impediment to commerce than the boundary separating Paris and Marseilles.

Although Smith's views initially met with resistance, the idea of **free trade** proved to be very powerful. With the repeal of its protectionist Corn Laws in 1846, Great Britain became the champion of free trade in the nineteenth century, helping to stimulate a tremendous expansion of worldwide commercial activity. The first transatlantic telegraph cable, completed in 1866, allowed money to be moved from London to New York and back in a matter of minutes, and presaged the $1 trillion a day computerized transactions that were to fuel global financial markets much later. Between 1870 and 1910, the British invested roughly a quarter of their savings overseas in railroads, mines, and other enterprises in the colonies and in the United States. Economic ties between the major powers of Europe had become so expansive by the early 1900s that these states recorded unprecedented levels of exports and imports as a percentage of gross national product.

However, between 1914 and 1945, three major events produced a revival of economic nationalism (neomercantilism) and interrupted the nascent globalization trends that had been building previously. Erstwhile trading partners were trading bullets in World War I and World War II, and were trading little of anything during the Great Depression in the interwar period. Domestically, the Great Depression led to the growth of the welfare state, associated foremost with another Englishman, John Maynard Keynes. He argued that governments everywhere should actively intervene in their national economy, using monetary and fiscal policy (manipulation of interest rate, tax, and spending measures) to stimulate the economy (during recession) or cool it off (at a time of inflation), as well as developing "national industrial policy" around collaborative links between management, labor, and government to promote homegrown industry. Aside from promoting jobs, the welfare state also had an obligation to protect public health, protect consumers from shoddy products, and protect citizens generally from the vagaries of life (including social security). The mixed economy became the main model for industrial democracies, which remained committed to market-oriented capitalism but permitted a growing role for the state in socioeconomic planning and problem-solving. Internationally, there remained the question of how compatible the welfare state was with free trade and Adam Smith's vision of a liberal international economic order. It seemed incompatible, judging from the Smoot-Hawley tariff and other highly protectionist measures taken by the United States and other governments in the interwar period to shield domestic industries from foreign competition, policies that led to a general contraction of world trade and a deepening of global recession, contributing in turn to the outbreak of World War II.

The second half of the twentieth century proved more conducive to Adam Smith's ideas than the first half. After World War II, there was a new determination to lower trade and other economic barriers so that the "beggar thy neighbor" mistakes of the interwar period would not be repeated. Given the "acute collective consciousness of the economic disaster of the Great Depression," free trade became internalized as a core norm in international economics.[12] The United States, as the lead economy, became the chief supporter of open borders in the postwar period. Whether due to U.S. hegemony or, at least as importantly, the power of the idea of free trade and the calculus of mutual interests, world trade increased more than twentyfold between 1945 and 1990.

In pushing for an open world economy, the United States along with other capitalist countries had to confront the legacy of the Keynesian welfare state and the right of national governments to adopt policies that in some instances might restrict trade and foreign investment in the name of protecting jobs, the environment, or other values demanded by their citizenry. In an effort to reconcile the seemingly contradictory requirements of a liberal international economic order on the one hand and what amounted to welfare state nationalism on the other hand, states entered into what John Ruggie has called the "compromise of embedded liberalism."[13] States agreed that they would work together to maximize free trade and open borders, recognizing, however, that each state retained the right to pursue protectionist policies whenever conditions warranted. As much as possible, when open borders threatened job loss at home, the government would respond not with trade protectionism but with unemployment insurance and other safety net programs to help those adversely affected. The idea of free trade was refined to accommodate the idea of the welfare state, which might even expand under a free trade regime. Driving much of this bargain was the attempt by countries such as the United States to satisfy two competing sets of domestic interests: export-oriented industries and efficient agricultural producers that had a stake in opening up foreign markets, juxtaposed against steel, textiles, and other older industries and farm lobbies seeking to protect their predominately domestic markets from foreign competition. The hope was that using the Bretton Woods international institutions—the General Agreement on Tariffs and Trade (GATT), the World Bank, and the International Monetary Fund (IMF)—states could collaborate and peaceably adjust their differences so as to avoid the mercantilist tensions of earlier eras.

As described below, globalization has played havoc with the compromise of embedded liberalism. Over the past thirty years, the ideological debate over states versus markets has swung between an extreme faith in markets during the 1980s (the privatization, deregulation, and "market fundamentalism" views exemplified by Ronald Reagan and Margaret Thatcher), the more centrist "Third Way" views of Bill Clinton and Tony Blair in the 1990s (with Clinton proclaiming that "the era of big government is over," while still promoting a nationalized health care program), and the more recent backlash against markets and a return to massive government intervention in the economy worldwide (including bailouts of banks) in the wake of the 2008 global financial crisis. Liberal internationalists continue to view the role of international institutions as maintaining as much stability as possible in the international economy, helping to facilitate transnational economic activity and expand the planetary product, a role that is likely to be increasingly tested in the future.

MARXISM

The recent ideological ferment, especially the rethinking of the excesses of free market capitalism, has sparked a renewed interest in a third school of IPE: **Marxism**. Marxism has always represented an alternative to the realist and liberal paradigms as an approach to understanding world politics. After being largely discarded following the defeat of the communist bloc in the Cold War, Marxism has experienced a bit of a revival through the rise of Hugo Chavez and some other radical-left leaders in Latin America who have used mass resentment against rich-poor gaps to inveigh against global capitalism.

As an IPE school, Marxism has several variants, including dependency theory and world systems theory. What unites all versions of Marxist thought are at least two central tenets. One is that economic structures determine politics within and between states. A second, which follows from the first, is that the global economy revolves not so much around states and their concerns about national security and national interests or around the invisible, neutral hand of the market but around an inherently exploitive set of relationships between capitalist classes and working classes worldwide. **Dependency theory** traces poverty in less developed countries to colonialism, as a colony's economic activities were geared toward serving the needs of the mother country, and later to neocolonialism. After World War II the newly independent countries of the South saw their economies controlled by Northern-based MNCs seeking their raw materials, cheap labor, and other factors of production that contributed to MNC profits more than LDC prosperity. Dependency is perpetuated through Northern political and economic elites co-opting local officials to accept foreign domination of their economies as well as unequal terms of trade and investment: High-value activities are kept in the North and less valuable activities relegated to the South. **World system theory** takes a longer historical perspective, tracing global inequalities to the Industrial Revolution that created a Western-dominated "core" exploiting the "periphery," with MNCs and IGOs being simply the latest institutional responses of modern capitalist elites to a changing world, just as economic elites in an earlier age developed the nation-state as the chief mode of human organization. Marxists contend that the role of international institutions should not be to help order and manage international economic relations but rather to change those relations in pursuit of greater economic justice.

Trends in International Trade and Foreign Investment

Although the second half of the twentieth century saw a growing web of economic interdependence, it was unevenly concentrated among the industrialized democracies, which accounted for the bulk of world trade and investment. Through much of the post–World War II period, the world economy reflected First, Second, and Third World divisions associated with the Cold War, as barriers persisted between Western bloc and Eastern bloc and developing countries. Trade and investment flows predominantly followed a West-West pattern. As one writer described it, "North America, Japan, and Europe [dominated] as originators and destinations of most international [trade] and investment."[14] However, since 1990, according to an IMF study that reinforces points made in Chapter 8:

> Profound changes have been taking place in the global economy. . . . First, trade and financial linkages between developed countries [DCs], the North, and developing countries [LDCs], the South, have become much stronger.

Second, a number of developing countries have differentiated themselves from the others in the South by growing at an extraordinary pace while rapidly integrating themselves into the global economy. Moreover, some of these developing economies have become increasingly important players in the global economy as they have begun to account for a substantial share of the world output.[15]

Looking at the direction of *trade*, by 1990, the Western industrialized democracies accounted for roughly 70 percent of all exports worldwide, selling mostly to each other. In terms of North-South trade, approximately one-third of DC exports went to LDCs, while 70 percent of the exports of the latter went to the former, with relatively little South-South trade occurring, due mainly to lack of purchasing power.[16] However, in the post–Cold War era, LDCs have been gradually brought into the global trading system, if unevenly. The World Bank has reported that between 1990 and 2006 the LDC share in world trade rose from 16 percent to 30 percent, led by China, India, and Brazil. "Developing country trade integration, measured by the share of imports and exports in GDP [gross domestic product], has been rising rapidly, increasing from 40 percent of GDP in 1990 to almost 67 percent in 2006, surpassing the share in high-income economies."[17]

Trends in *private foreign investment* flows have followed the pattern of trade flows. There is a need here to distinguish between **portfolio investment** (simply putting money in a foreign bank and foreign bonds, or an investor acquiring an ownership interest in a foreign firm through buying stocks but not a stake large enough to exercise control over the firm's operations) and **foreign direct investment** (acquiring at least 10 percent of the voting stock in the enterprise so as to permit a degree of controlling interest). It is the latter—FDI, where a firm headquartered in one country establishes and manages subsidiaries (production plants or other facilities) in another country—that has attracted the most interest among IPE scholars and that has been most associated with the globalization phenomenon described at the outset of this chapter. Thomas Friedman has referred to the ease with which capital now moves across borders as "the electronic herd," with portfolio investors called "short-horn cattle" and direct investors "long-horn cattle" with deeper involvement in foreign enterprises. [18] Although multinational corporations (MNCs) have a long history—for example, Singer Sewing Machines already had an overseas factory in Scotland in 1878, while Ford Motors had an assembly plant in Europe in 1911—the MNC phenomenon did not become highly visible until after World War II, when the United States spread the gospel of an open world economy, large profits were to be made through a rationalization of production and sales across many markets, and speedier communications and travel technology as well as containerization of cargo and computerized storage of data greatly facilitated the expansion of MNC operations. By the 1980s, nearly half of the Fortune 500 list of the largest corporations depended on international operations for over 40 percent of their profits.[19] Globalization since 1990 has only accelerated the "Coca-Colonization" of the world.

There are now roughly 50,000 multinational corporations in the world. MNCs account for half of the 100 largest economic units in the world. As Table 9.1 indicates, Walmart is "bigger" than Denmark and Norway. Not surprisingly, over 400 of the Fortune 500 companies are headquartered in G7 states. In recent years, 90 percent of all FDI has *originated* in DCs. Perhaps more surprisingly, DCs also have overwhelmingly been the *targets* of FDI, receiving over 75 percent of the total. As one writer notes, "The Triad of the United States, the European Union, and Japan has been the main source and recipient of the world's FDI for more than half a century. . . . The most consistent theme in the where-FDI-is-going and where-it-is-coming-from statistics is that in both directions it is concentrated in a relatively few countries."[20] However, as with trade, LDCs are gradually being integrated into the world finance sector. Still, to the extent FDI has gone to LDCs, only about a dozen have benefited significantly. China alone has been getting one-third of the annual total of all LDC inflows lately; China and just the next 4 largest recipients (Hong Kong, Singapore, Mexico, and Brazil) attract over half of all FDI destined for the developing world. The poorest countries get little FDI, as the 50 "least developed countries" account for only a tiny 1 percent of the world total.[21] As another writer characterized FDI flows, in recent years "about 70 percent went from one rich country to another, 8 developing countries received about 20 percent, and the remainder was divided among more than 100 poor nations."[22]

These data are somewhat at odds with Marxist theories, which assume that LDCs will be the main targets of MNC investment, as firms supposedly prey on the weak and relocate manufacturing facilities overseas in search of the cheapest labor available in order to reap the highest profits. If that were the case, countries like Haiti and Somalia would be swimming in FDI. To the contrary, "those Triad countries with the world's best-paid workers"—the United States, Canada, Germany, France, the United Kingdom, and the like—"dominate the list of largest recipients of FDI,"[23] mainly because MNCs are attracted to economies that have buying power and to polities that are stable. Although past foreign direct investment in LDCs in the Middle East, Latin America, and elsewhere was mostly limited to their extractive sectors (oil, mining, and agriculture, as with the holdings of Standard Oil, Alcoa Aluminum, and United Fruit), current investments in places like China are focused in manufacturing. MNCs are increasingly building plants to take advantage of inexpensive labor in producing labor-intensive goods (shoes, clothing, etc.) for both export and local markets. Known as export platform FDI, this investment has helped countries such as China, Singapore, and South Korea attain higher levels of growth than most LDCs. Again, however, the countries receiving this investment are not the poorest, most vulnerable LDCs.[24] Despite frequent criticisms of MNCs for promoting sweatshops and other questionable practices, most LDCs seek more, not less, FDI. Over the past decade or so, LDCs have relied on foreign private investment, rather than foreign aid, for four-fifths of their capital inflows.[25]

There remains some ambivalence about inviting foreign-based MNCs into one's borders and allowing them to take over large sectors of one's economy.

298

TABLE 9.1 Ranking of Countries and Corporations According to Size of Annual Product

Countries are ranked according to gross national income. Corporations (headquarters in parentheses) are ranked according to gross revenues. Although not exactly comparable, they are sufficiently close to illustrate size relationships.

Rank	Economic Entity	$ Millions
1.	United States	13, 886,472
2.	Japan	4,813,341
3.	Germany	3,197,029
4.	China	3,120,891
5.	United Kingdom	2,608,513
6.	France	2,447,090
7.	Italy	1,991,284
8.	Spain	1,321,756
9.	Canada	1,300,025
10.	Brazil	1,133,030
11.	Russia	1,070,999
12.	India	1,069,427
13.	S. Korea	955,802
14.	Mexico	878,020
15.	Australia	755,795
16.	Netherlands	750,526
17.	Turkey	592,850
18.	Switzerland	452,121
19.	Belgium	432,540
20.	Sweden	421,342
21.	**Wal-Mart** (US)	378,799
22.	Poland	374,633
23.	Saudi Arabia	373,490
24.	Indonesia	373,125
25.	**Exxon Mobil** (US)	372,824
26.	Norway	360,038
27.	**Shell Oil** (Neth.)	355,782
28.	Austria	355,088
29.	Greece	331,658
30.	Denmark	299,804
31.	**British Petroleum** (UK)	291,438
32.	South Africa	274,009
33.	Iran	246,544
34.	Argentina	238,853
35.	Finland	234,833
36.	**Toyota** (Japan)	230,201
37.	Thailand	217,348
38.	**Chevron** (US)	210,783
39.	Ireland	210,168
40.	**ING Group** (Neth.)	201,516
41.	Venezuela	201,146
42.	Portugal	201,079

(continues)

TABLE 9.1 *(continued)*

Rank	Economic Entity	$ Millions
43.	**Total** (France)	187,280
44.	**General Motors** (US)	182,347
45.	**Conoco Phillips** (US)	178,558
46.	**Daimler** (Germany)	177,167
47.	**General Electric** (US)	176,656
48.	Malaysia	173,705
49.	**Ford Motor** (US)	172,468
50.	**Fortis** (Belgium)	164,877
51.	**AXA** (France)	162,762
52.	**Sinopec** (China)	159,250
53.	**Citigroup** (US)	159,229
54.	Israel	157,065
55.	Colombia	149,934
56.	Czech Republic	149,378
57.	**Volkswagen** (Germany)	149,054
58.	Singapore	148,992
59.	**Dexia Group** (Belgium)	147,648
60.	**HSBC** (UK)	146,500
61.	Philippines	142,623
62.	Pakistan	141,009
63.	**BNP Paribas** (France)	140,728
64.	**Allianz** (Germany)	140,618
65.	Chile	138,630
66.	**Credit Agricole** (France)	138,155
67.	Nigeria	137,091
68.	**State Grid** (China)	132,885
69.	Romania	132,502
70.	**China National Petroleum** (China)	129,798
71.	**Deutsche Bank** (Germany)	122,644
72.	Algeria	122,465
73.	New Zealand	121,708
74.	**ENI** (Italy)	120,565
75.	Egypt	119,405
76.	**Bank of America** (US)	119,130
77.	**AT&T** (US)	118,928
78.	Ukraine	118,445
79.	**Berkshire Hathaway** (US)	118,245
80.	**UBS** (Switzerland)	117,206
81.	**J.P. Morgan** (US)	116,353
82.	Hungary	116,303
83.	**Carrefour** (France)	115,565
84.	**Ass. General** (Italy)	113,813
85.	**American International** (US)	110,064
86.	**Bank of Scotland** (UK)	108,392
87.	**Siemens** (Germany)	106,444
88.	**Samsung** (S. Korea)	106,008
89.	**Arcelor** (Luxembourg)	105,216

(continues)

TABLE 9.1 *(continued)*

Rank	Economic Entity	$ Millions
90.	**Honda** (Japan)	105,102
91.	**Hewlett-Packard** (US)	104,286
92.	**Pemex** (Mexico)	103,960
93.	**Societe Generale** (France)	103,443
94.	**McKesson** (US)	101,703
95.	**HBOS** (UK)	100,267
96.	**IBM** (US)	98,786
97.	**Gazprom** (Russia)	98,642
98.	**Hitachi** (Japan)	98,306
99.	**Valero** (US)	96,758
100.	Peru	96,241

SOURCE: Gross national income data are from World Bank, *World Development Indicators 2008*; gross revenues data are from *Fortune*, July 21, 2008.

However, such apprehensions are not limited to LDCs. Perhaps nowhere is there a better example of foreign penetration of a developed country economy and the resentment it can engender than in Canada, where U.S. companies alone in recent years have produced over 90 percent of the films shown in Canada, supplied 75 percent of the magazines read, and controlled 55 percent of its manufacturing sector.[26] Even the United States has felt such concerns. The United States long had been the #1 *home* country of MNCs, with more world headquarters than any other nation-state; by 1980, it had also become the #1 *host* country, attracting more FDI than anyone else. A 1978 issue of *Newsweek* had a cover story on "The Buying of America," showing the Statue of Liberty with a "For Sale" sign, raising fears of a foreign takeover of the American economy, both its farmland and its industrial base.[27] The 1980s saw Japanese, European, and Arab interests buying up iconic American properties and assets such as Rockefeller Center in New York, Columbia Pictures, Capitol and RCA Records, Roy Rogers Restaurants, and other slices of Americana. The next two decades saw foreigners purchasing a controlling interest in Amoco, Ralston-Purina, Anheuser-Busch, and other brand names. By 2008, as a weak dollar was encouraging still greater FDI in the United States, worries were expressed about "foreigners buying stakes in the U.S. at a record pace, reigniting debate on America's place in the global economy."[28] Although foreign interests owned a relatively small fraction of the huge American economy, and majority foreign ownership was banned altogether in certain strategically important sectors (e.g., defense, airlines, media communications), there was nonetheless a concern that U.S. sovereignty was potentially threatened.

FDI is a double-edged sword. On the one hand, foreign capital can pump fresh money into a nation's economy and help save jobs in failing industries or create new jobs. On the other hand, the more a host state depends on foreign capital, the more sensitive and vulnerable it can be to decisions taken externally, leaving it with less autonomy and less of a sense of its own identity. For example, in recent decades, Japanese car companies have built plants ("transplants") throughout the United States (Honda in Ohio, Toyota in Kentucky, Nissan in Tennessee) that employ thousands of American workers and have allowed the United States to regain its position as the lead automaking country in the world. In 2008 Asian autos outsold Detroit's in the U.S. market for the first time ever. This begs the following question: If your boss tells you to "buy American" when shopping for a car, does that mean purchasing a Honda made in Maryville, Ohio, or a Ford made in Ontario, Canada (where Ford has a major production plant)? Since Hondas are made with American labor, they are arguably American cars, even though the profits ultimately are repatriated back to Japan and their capture of the American market may well undermine the Big Three indigenous producers and American household names. These issues took on special significance in 2009, as the U.S. government spent billions of dollars to save Ford, General Motors, and Chrysler from bankruptcy amid a growing recession.

Just as a *host* government may suspect foreign enterprises of being Trojan horses potentially harmful to its national interests, so too the *home* government cannot be sure whether its own firms are primarily loyal to country or company. Although MNCs are commonly portrayed by Marxists and other critics as agents of home government imperialism, the evidence is mixed as to whether MNCs fully act in the interest of and under the direction of the home state. As they do with host governments, MNCs tend to have a love-hate relationship with home governments. For example, while Washington sees itself as having some responsibility to promote American business abroad, it has criticized U.S.-based MNCs for "runaway shops" that abandon American workers for cheaper overseas labor (e.g., Rawlings's decision to supply Major League Baseball with baseballs from its assembly plant in Costa Rica), outsourcing services to India, and setting up tax havens in the Bahamas. Whereas traditionally the boards of directors and top management of MNCs have been dominated by nationals of the headquarters country, they are becoming more internationalized. For example, in 2008 Unilever, the giant English-Dutch conglomerate (which owns Ben and Jerry's, Good Humor, Popsicles, Breyers, and Slim-Fast Foods, among others) had a French CEO and a six-member executive board that included two Indians, a South African, and two Americans. In 2005 Howard Stringer, an American citizen of Welsh extraction who had run the CBS television network, was named the new CEO of Sony Corp., the Japanese electronics company, even though he could not speak Japanese.[29] In 2006 the head of IBM said that "state borders define less and less the boundaries of corporate thinking or practice."[30] Although the "stateless corporation" is not yet a reality, such is the growing complexity that globalization introduces into national and international life.[31]

Globalization further complicates the functioning of the Keynesian welfare state. As noted above, free trade exposes workers to greater risk of job loss and hence

Is globalization the new patriotism?

can place more demands on government to help globalization's losers with un-employment insurance, retraining, and other programs. Yet at the same time, globalization increases pressures on national governments to downsize their welfare states—reducing taxes and regulations—in order to attract FDI (jobs) to their shores and keep their own footloose firms from relocating overseas. It also makes it harder for governments to unilaterally manipulate Keynesian monetary and fiscal policy levers.[32] Many commentators speak of growing "loss of control" on the part of national governments.[33] Granted there has never been any "golden age of state control"[34]; nonetheless the multinational corporation and unprecedented capital mobility pose extraordinary contemporary challenges to the viability of nation-states, even the most powerful ones, which are increasingly held hostage to external economic forces. This was evident in the crash of world financial markets in 2008, which, precipitated by the collapse of housing prices and risky lending policies in the United States, snowballed from one state to another and sparked headlines such as "Nations Weighing Global Approach as Chaos Spreads."[35]

Friedman has written that "the defining document of the Cold War system was 'The Treaty'" whereas "the defining document of the globalization system is 'The Deal.'"[36] However, deals cannot be made without treaties—without a larger set of rules governing international economic transactions, that is, international regimes. International regimes are looked to by states more than ever as a vehicle for coping with loss of control and managing the relationship between states and markets: "As the global system becomes more integrated, there is a demand for international public goods that neither markets nor nation-states will provide. . . . These are roughly as follows: systematic financial stability; the rule of law and dispute settlement needed for an open system of trade and investment; common standards of weights and measures; management of global communications networks like aviation, telecommunications, and sea-lanes to prevent congestion and disasters. . . . All these require some sort of institutional development beyond the nation-state."[37] Although "there is a complex but rich system of governance growing up to manage globalization," is it enough?

INTERNATIONAL ECONOMIC REGIMES

As liberals would predict, states have developed international regimes in order to facilitate international commerce. They have pooled sovereignty in a number of areas—postal service, air transport, shipping, and the like—in support of furthering mutual economic interests and other goals.[38] Space does not permit us to consider the entirety of global economic governance, and in this section we will focus on regimes regulating the flow of capital and trade, especially trade.

As world leaders met at an economic summit in Washington in November 2008, as "a first step to new rules to prevent financial meltdown and market mayhem," there was a general sense that the Bretton Woods system needed a major overhaul, what some called "Bretton Woods II."[39] The Washington gathering brought together the presidents and prime ministers of the **Group of 20 (G20)**, a recently formed consultative group composed of the G7 states plus the BRICs, Saudi Arabia, and several other important actors. The G20 reflected the growing stature of China, India, and some other developing countries in the world economy. Just days before the Washington conference, G20 finance ministers and central bankers had convened in São Paulo, Brazil, to set the agenda for the Washington conference, with the LDCs blaming the DCs for the crisis and insisting that developing countries should be given a bigger role in shaping "a new global financial architecture." The G20 São Paulo communiqué called for "increased regulation, common accounting standards, and the need to explore ways to restore access to credit," along with urging "the IMF to enhance its early warning capabilities, surveillance, and policy advice."[40] Of special concern to the G20 officials was the historic memory of the Great Depression and the tendency for states to revert to mercantilist, protectionist policies in the face of hard economic times. The head of the World Bank worried about a possible "stunning drop" in world trade if states resorted to economic nationalism, as had happened during the interwar period.[41]

From GATT to the WTO

The **General Agreement on Tariffs and Trade (GATT)** was created after World War II as the key trade component of the Bretton Woods system, designed to provide the forum for bargaining over and expanding free trade. In the words of one official, GATT's creation in 1948 "provided a rule of law for world trade" and represented "an attempt to banish into history the jungle of restrictions and bilateral dealings that strangled world trade in the 1930s like jungle weed."[42] Although GATT membership barely exceeded 100 states, they represented over 80 percent of total world trade. The flowering of postwar trade occurred through a series of seven GATT negotiations, including the Kennedy Round (1963–1967) and Tokyo Round (1973–1979), which succeeded in substantial tariff reductions, particularly on industrial goods. However, by the 1980s, it was clear that if the liberal trade regime was to be strengthened further, there was a need not only to involve more states but also to address protectionist practices in areas where GATT rules were weak or nonexistent, such as agriculture and services (insurance, information technology, etc.), and to improve dispute settlement procedures. The **Uruguay Round** was initiated in September 1986 in Punta del Este, Uruguay, where "chilling winds greeted the two thousand delegates from seventy-two countries."[43] It culminated almost a decade later in the 22,000-page Marrakesh Agreement establishing the **World Trade Organization (WTO)** as GATT's successor, after "without question the most complex and protracted multilateral trade negotiation in history."[44]

Ernest Preeg describes the critical bargaining that went on even before the formal opening of Uruguay Round talks:

> An informal group of industrialized countries, the "Dirty Dozen," held a series of private meetings and produced the first comprehensive ministerial declaration. For tactical reasons, the three large members—the United States, the EC [the European Community], and Japan—temporarily withdrew from the group while the smaller industrialized countries joined with about twenty moderate developing countries to further develop and circulate the draft. Other developing countries joined, the big three rejoined, and the now forty-eight participants formally constituted themselves as the G-48 [cochaired by a Swiss and a Colombian]. . . . The cohesion of the G-48 [which included the likes of Singapore, Malaysia, South Korea, Chile, and Mexico], cutting across North/South lines, put the hardliners [a group of ten developing countries, led by Brazil and India] on the defensive and forced them to produce their own G-10 draft. . . . A separate yet overlapping country realignment that took place during the summer of 1986 related to the agricultural sector. . . . [Six] agricultural exporters—Australia, Chile, Colombia, Thailand, New Zealand, and Uruguay—submitted a joint paper calling for substantial trade liberalization in this sector. The group expanded to fourteen, adding Argentina, Brazil, Canada, Fiji, Hungary, Malaysia, and the Philippines [the so-called Cairns Group].[45]

Over the next eight years, "economic dichotomy between North and South would fade, between East and West disintegrate," as globalization would become the motto "for a brave new world of traders and diplomats."[46] Before that outcome, however, much bargaining remained to be done, and not just between nation-states but among a host of actors engaged in two-level and three-level games.

For example, the U.S. delegation at Punta Del Este consisted of members drawn from various Executive Branch agencies and congressional committees, as well as

corporate, labor, and farm interest groups. U.S. negotiators had to consider foreign interests articulated by their diplomatic counterparts across the table from
them while representing American national interests, at the same time looking
over their shoulder trying to reconcile the diverse interests of various domestic pressure groups and bureaucracies (e.g., U.S. rice, soybean, and other growers seeking
to open up Japanese and European markets, contrasted with U.S. cotton growers
and the textile lobby seeking to keep the American market closed to foreign competition). Similar internal conflicts were played out within other delegations.

Coalitions of strange bedfellows formed to support and oppose the treaty. On
one side, opposing the agreement, were conservatives such as Pat Buchanan and
Ross Perot joined by liberals such as Ralph Nader and various environmental
and labor union groups. The conservatives were mainly concerned about the
threat to U.S. sovereignty posed by the proposed majority-rule voting procedures
in the WTO and the binding nature of the dispute settlement procedures that, in
the words of Buchanan, empowered "foreign bureaucrats [three-judge panels
in Geneva] who will meet in secret to demand changes in U.S. laws" when such
laws violated WTO rules.[47] The liberals were not concerned about a nascent world
government so much as the failure of the Marrakesh Agreement to include adequate international labor and environmental standards that would protect American workers from a flood of cheap imports made in some cases by children or
prisoners and would protect American consumers from tainted fruits and vegetables
and other products that possibly threatened environmental harm. They predicted
a "race to the bottom" if, in order to remain competitive in an open world economy, businesses and governments had to lower wages or safety and environmental regulations. For example, Teamsters president James Hoffa asked how American
truckers could be expected to compete when "a fifteen-year-old sitting on an or-
ange crate may be driving an eighteen-wheeler truck from Mexico into the U.S.
now that trucking safety rules at the border were being relaxed." He was referring
to the parallel negotiations occurring over the creation of the **North American
Free Trade Agreement** (**NAFTA**), a regional free trade pact between the United
States, Canada, and Mexico that aspired to regional economic integration along
the lines of the EU.[48]

On the other side, endorsing the WTO agreement, were conservatives such as
Ronald Reagan and George H.W. Bush (who had initiated the Uruguay Round
talks) siding with the Wall Street corporate community, along with liberals, such
as Jimmy Carter and Bill Clinton (who had concluded the talks). The conservatives were driven mainly by their belief in the private sector and the promise of
expanded investment opportunities, while the liberals were driven by a commitment to internationalism and a determination to promote multilateral cooperation that could avert future trade wars. This coalition argued that allowing China
and other protectionist states into the WTO could provide a wedge to force their
closed economies to become more market driven and their closed political systems to become more democratic.

Jeff Danziger. Reproduced with permission from the July 31, 1992, issue of The Christian Science Monitor (www.CSMonitor.com) © 1992 The Christian Science Monitor.

NAFTA, globalization, and runaway shops: The Smith-Corona Typewriter Company moves its North American operations to Mexico.

Trade politics included not only subnational actors but transnational actors. Although NGOs were not permitted nearly the direct access to participation in the trade talks as they were in other UN forums, they nonetheless were heard. Earlier, in 1990, 30,000 European farmers had marched in protest against trade liberalization discussions in Brussels, which at the time was playing host to GATT meetings and where the European Union's Commission was engaged in trying to work out a common EU trade policy. Greenpeace and environmental NGOs attempted to soften WTO proposals allowing free trade imperatives to override environmental protection. Many MNCs, supported by the World Intellectual Property Organization, a UN specialized agency, worked to strengthen intellectual property rights so as to combat piracy of copyrighted films, music, books, and other materials in China and other countries. The GATT secretariat chaired the various working groups during the Uruguay Round. According to one account, the executive head of GATT, Director-General Peter Sutherland, played an indispensable role in moving the proceedings along, developing "a detailed negotiating strategy for the complex diplomatic endgame ahead."[49]

The pro-globalization, pro-WTO forces ultimately prevailed. Among the provisions contained in the WTO treaty that finally was approved in 1995 were the following: (1) tariffs would be reduced on over 80 percent of world trade; (2) dumping goods on another country's market at below-cost prices in order to eliminate that country's domestic producers would be banned; and (3) farm subsidies that artificially make one's domestic producers more competitive would be reduced, and quotas on imported textiles would be phased out.

A key innovation was the establishment of a compulsory dispute-resolution process. Under the WTO regime, any state accusing another state of being in violation of WTO rules can take the latter before an independent panel of trade experts, which is entrusted with investigating the complaint and rendering a judgment that may be subject to further review by a three-member appellate panel. If the defendant state is found guilty of violating free trade obligations and refuses to comply with the panel's judgment, member states can then legally impose trade sanctions against the state in question.

The WTO in Action

Based in Geneva, Switzerland, the WTO had 152 member states as of 2009, with many other countries seeking to join but whose economies have not been sufficiently liberalized to meet the membership criteria. Policy decisions in the WTO are made through majority rule but by consensus as much as possible, with each state having one vote, unlike the weighted voting procedures of the World Bank and IMF. However, rich countries such as the United States are advantaged insofar as most developing countries lack the financial resources, first, to "afford an embassy in Geneva" (to participate fully in the agenda-setting and policy formulation stages that precede formal voting on trade reforms) and, second, to afford the substantial expense of bringing disputes before trade tribunals.[50] Still, as seen below, LDC voices are being increasingly heard in WTO trade discussions, and LDCs at times do bring successful cases before WTO judges.

Over 350 cases have been brought before trade tribunals in Geneva, with the plaintiff states winning 85 percent of the time. Interestingly, the U.S. has brought more challenges than any other country (bringing suit in over one-quarter of all the cases in recent years) and, given the pro-plaintiff bias of the system, has won 78 percent of the time; however, the U.S. also has been a frequent defendant, losing in 83 percent of the cases filed against it. For example, while the U.S. won in its suit challenging the European ban on U.S. hormone-treated beef imports, it was found to be in violation of WTO rules when Brazil complained about the U.S. government subsidizing its cotton farmers and when the small island state of Antigua and Barbuda challenged a U.S. federal law banning Internet gambling. The United States has seen several other congressional statutes ruled illegal by WTO trade experts, such as laws banning the import of tuna caught with driftnets that kill dolphins and banning petroleum products containing high-level pollutants. In these cases, the practices authorized by Congress have been "ordered" ended, with failure to comply inviting economic sanctions by WTO members. As some observers have noted, the WTO is "potentially [very] intrusive on national policies because it is now making rules . . . that override the preexisting national laws of members."[51] Despite concerns about the threat to national sovereignty, compliance with Geneva decisions "has been close to 100 percent."[52]

Many state and nonstate actors have expressed dissatisfaction with current global economic governance. Annual WTO gatherings have been disrupted by antiglobalization rallies organized by protest groups, such as "the battle of Seattle" in 1999. That year, the summit meeting of WTO, World Bank, and IMF officials and government representatives was marked by angry street demonstrations on the part of thousands of "environmentalists, human rights activists, the anti-sweatshop movement, and a whole grab bag of groups concerned about everything from saving the sea-turtles to saving teamster jobs."[53] The protestors were attacking what they saw as an elite alliance between "GATTzilla" (their name for the WTO) and the multinational corporations, arguing that the meetings had been largely closed to NGOs and grassroots movements and were obsessed with free trade to the exclusion of other issues.[54] Even though the protestors claimed to be speaking for the world's poor, the developing countries represented in Seattle did not see it that way. LDC governments resisted any attempt to put global minimum wage or environmental standards on the agenda lest they be used to ban imports from developing countries. President Zedillo of Mexico spoke for many LDCs in his statement that "self-appointed representatives of civil society" were "determined to save developing countries from development."[55]

While the WTO has claimed to promote a level playing field between the North and South, some in the South, echoing the NIEO debate of the 1970s, still see it as "not the GATT of the whole world but that of the rich and powerful."[56] A revival of North-South trade tensions occurred during the **Doha Development Round** talks that began in 2001. The talks were supposed to take Adam Smith's free trade vision to the next level, further reducing tariff and other trade barriers, especially in the area of agriculture. However, in 2008, the talks collapsed over the refusal of developed countries, particularly the United States and EU states, to eliminate trade-distorting farm subsidies that advantaged their growers, and the refusal of less developed countries, led by China, India, and Brazil, to eliminate tariff protection for their own farmers threatened by a surge of food imports. Commentators referred to "a rich-poor deadlock" in "the latest sign of India's and China's growing might on the world stage and the decreasing ability of the United States to impose its will globally."[57] Protectionist sentiment had been mounting in the United States due to concern about record annual trade deficits and the failure of China and other countries to open up their economies fully to American exports, at the same time that those same countries were demanding greater trading privileges themselves. All countries were talking out of both sides of their mouths, professing to support free trade principles while practicing selective protectionism, leading to a fear that the global commitment to free trade was weakening.[58] There was hope that the talks could be put back on track, although it was not clear if the postwar free trade momentum could be sustained, especially if the worldwide recession of 2008–2009 deepened. Policymakers and publics throughout the world were debating the pros and cons of not only free trade but globalization generally. (See the *IR* Critical Thinking Box "The Pros and Cons of Globalization.")

IR Critical Thinking:
The Pros and Cons of Globalization

Globalization poses many interesting dilemmas. At the core of the debate there is tension between an expansive "world without borders" free market capitalism versus welfare state nationalism. As one example of this, note the following case:

Although the United States remains the premier agricultural exporter in the world, whose farmers have an important stake in an open world economy, increasingly Americans are eating foods imported from abroad. It is estimated that, given the growing appetite for fresh produce year-round, some 40 percent of the fruit consumed by Americans is now imported, along with 15 percent of the vegetables. In 1997, because of concerns about food safety in the wake of recent outbreaks of diseases tied to Guatemalan raspberries, Mexican cantaloupes, and Thai coconut milk, President Clinton announced that he would ask Congress to require the U.S. Food and Drug Administration (FDA) "to ban imports of fruit and vegetables from countries that did not meet American food safety standards." The president's announcement seemed a reasonable assertion of a national government's right to protect the public health of its citizenry. However, there was a slight problem—it was questionable whether requiring foreign agricultural producers to meet U.S. standards was compatible with the free trade rules embodied in the Marrakesh Agreement that created the WTO, and it was likely that any such policy would be challenged in a WTO trade tribunal in Geneva. The United States itself, in 1997, had used the new WTO rules to force European countries to lift their ban on beef from cattle treated with growth hormones, arguing that the ban was aimed at protecting European farmers by keeping out American meat products rather than preventing mad cow disease or other ailments; the United States used a similar argument to force its beef exports into South Korea in 2008, sparking a massive demonstration by 80,000 Koreans in the streets of Seoul in protest over their government's relaxation of trade restrictions. Washington also has been demanding that Europeans and others lift their ban on the import of genetically modified crops that American agribusinesses are anxious to sell abroad, despite foreign objections to possible health risks associated with GMOs.

Globalization has been blamed for lax government regulations that have allowed Chinese-made toys with lead-based paint and poisonous dog food and tainted milk to enter the United States and other countries, for trade rules that elevate free trade over the lives of dolphins and sea-turtles and the environmental well-being of the planet, for sweatshops and the widening of rich-poor gaps, and for cultural imperialism that has undermined non-Western cultures and produced a monotonous uniformity of consumer tastes and lifestyles worldwide. At the same time, even as some people and societies have been retrogressing economically ("the bottom billion"), globalization has been credited elsewhere with lifting millions of people out of abject poverty and making several developing countries major players in the world economy. As Nils Gleditsch of the International Peace Research Institute in Oslo, Norway, has stated: "In fact, on a global basis, individual economic inequality has undergone a massive decrease, thanks to the phenomenal economic growth of poor countries like China, India, Vietnam and many others." ("The Liberal Moment Fifteen Years On," *International Studies Quarterly*, December 2008, 704.)

Where do you stand in this debate? Consider the following:

1. Do you approve of President Clinton's proposal to require U.S. food imports to meet FDA standards? Would you approve of other governments imposing similar standards on U.S. exports entering their countries? To what extent are governments motivated by genuine public health concerns as opposed to protectionist impulses?

(continues)

(continued)

Are both equally legitimate? How does the United States avoid accusations of a double standard when it imposes tight regulations on American imports but demands reduction of barriers to American exports? What constitutes fair trade?

2. William Greider and other globalization critics have condemned Third World sweatshops as "dark satanic mills" because of often horrendous work conditions and low wages. (Greider, *One World, Ready or Not*, 337.) Yet Nobel Prize–winner Paul Krugman has written: "Could anything be worse than having children work in sweatshops? Alas, yes. In 1993, child workers in Bangladesh were found to be producing clothing for Wal-Mart, and Senator Tom Harkin proposed legislation banning [such] imports. The direct result was that Bangladeshi textile factories stopped employing children. But did the children go back to school? [No, they] ended up in even worse jobs, or on the streets, or forced into prostitution." ("Heads and Hearts," *New York Times*, April 22, 2001.) Where do you stand on the sweatshop issue? If it were possible to pass a global minimum wage and set of work safety standards, would Third World jobs dry up? Do MNC sweatshops in Africa, Asia, and the Caribbean offer a win-win situation by providing jobs that would not otherwise exist for poor people in poor countries while enabling modest wage earners and others in the United States and DCs to purchase inexpensive goods at places like Walmart? Or are they an affront to civilization, especially given the huge profits Nike and other companies make from such enterprises?

3. Virtually every U.S. president in the past several decades, both liberal and conservative as well as Democrat and Republican, has supported free trade. Why? Which arguments do you believe are the strongest in support of the WTO and free trade? Which against?

CONCLUSION

A theme repeated throughout this book is that a hallmark of the contemporary international system is growing complexity that includes not only a diffusion of power and fluidity of alignments but also a proliferation of new actors as well as new issues beyond the traditional elements of the Westphalian state system.

Among the actors seeking to play a role in global trade politics are subnational government entities, such as state-level governments in the case of the United States federal system. Although the U.S. Constitution forbids states from entering into treaties with foreign countries, this has not stopped state governors and legislatures from becoming involved in international political economy. Ever since New York State opened an international trade office in 1954 to represent its interests abroad, virtually every other state in the union has followed suit, with states now having over 200 such offices overseas. Twenty-eight states authorized sanctions against U.S. and foreign businesses operating in South Africa during the apartheid era before Congress passed sanctions legislation. In 2003 30 state attorneys general signed a letter "calling for greater protections of state interests in trade agreements" negotiated by the U.S. Trade Representative.[59] Following the "first business delegation to western Europe in search of direct investment," led by Governor

Luther H. Hodges of North Carolina in 1959, many other state missions followed. By 1979 thirty-three governors had led eighty-four missions, a phenomenon that has now become commonplace.[60] In 2006 Governor Arnold Schwarzenegger of California entered into an "agreement" with Prime Minister Tony Blair of the United Kingdom to "share ideas and information" on clean-energy technologies to combat climate change. Although he was careful to say "it is not a treaty," he added that "California will not wait for our federal government to take strong action on global warming."[61]

As suggested by Arnold Schwarzenegger, among the many increasingly important issue-areas in play in the game of international politics is the environment. The preamble of the Marrakesh Agreement establishing the WTO states that trade relations are aimed at "raising standards of living . . . and expanding the production of and trade in goods and services, while allowing for the optimal use of the world's resources in accordance with the objective of sustainable development." The phrase "sustainable development" was an artful compromise reached at the 1992 Earth Summit in Rio de Janeiro, Brazil, which brought together over a hundred heads of state along with thousands of IGO and NGO representatives. The phrase called for balancing environmental and economic interests, at a time when 1,600 of the world's leading scientists had just issued a "warning to humanity" that "we are fast approaching many of the earth's limits."

In *Part Four*, a concluding chapter offers some final thoughts on environmental and other concerns that are likely to dominate world politics for the foreseeable future.

QUESTIONS FOR STUDY AND DISCUSSION

1. What are the major schools of thought in the study of "international political economy"? Which do you find most useful in understanding the workings of the world economy?

2. Define "globalization." Give pros and cons. If we wanted to stop globalization, could we?

3. Whom do you see winning the contest between "states vs. markets"? How do multinational corporations (MNCs) complicate state sovereignty and the capacity of national governments (both home and host governments) to make economic policy and operate welfare states? How powerful are MNCs in world politics?

4. Discuss the World Trade Organization (WTO) and the politics of "free trade." Where do you stand in the free trade debate?

5. Discuss trends in international trade and foreign investment, including patterns in the direction of trade and capital flows between developed and developing countries.

6. The global financial crisis in 2008–2009 raised questions about whether the architecture of global governance of the world economy—built around

the Bretton Woods institutions—needed a major overhaul, what some called "Bretton Woods II." Discuss.

SUGGESTIONS FOR FURTHER READING

Jagdish Bhagwati, *In Defense of Globalization* (New York: Oxford University Press, 2004).

Vincent Cable, "The Diminished Nation-State," *Daedalus,* Spring 1995. Special issue: "What Future for the State?"

Paul Doremus et al., *The Myth of the Global Corporation* (Princeton, NJ: Princeton University Press, 1998).

Jeffry A. Frieden and David A. Lake, eds., *International Political Economy: Perspectives on Global Power and Wealth*, 4th ed. (New York: St. Martin's, 2000).

Thomas L. Friedman, *The Lexus and the Olive Tree* (New York: Farrar, Straus, Giroux, 1999).

————, *The World Is Flat* (New York: Farrar, Straus, Giroux, 2006).

Geoffrey Garrett, "Global Markets National Politics: Collision Course or Virtuous Circle?" *International Organization* 52 (Autumn 1998): 787–824.

Robert Gilpin, *The Political Economy of International Relations* (Princeton, NJ: Princeton University Press, 1987).

William Greider, *One World, Ready or Not* (New York: Simon & Schuster, 1997).

Joseph Grieco and G. John Ikenberry, *State Power and World Markets* (New York: Norton, 2003).

David Held et al., *Global Transformations* (Stanford, CA: Stanford University Press, 1999).

Bruce E. Moon, *Dilemmas of International Trade*, 2nd ed. (Boulder, CO: Westview, 2000).

Dani Rodrik, "Sense and Nonsense in the Globalization Debate," *Foreign Policy,* Summer 1997.

Joan E. Spero and Jeffrey A. Hart, *The Politics of International Economic Relations*, 5th ed. (New York: St. Martin's, 1997).

Joseph E. Stiglitz, *Globalization and Its Discontents* (New York: Norton, 2002).

Susan Strange, "The Defective State," *Daedalus,* Spring 1995. Special issue: "What Future for the State?"

Lori Wallach and Patrick Woodall, *Whose Trade Organization?* (New York: New Press, 2004).

Daniel Yergin and Joseph Stanislaw, *The Commanding Heights: The Battle for the World Economy* (New York: Simon & Schuster, 2002).

PART FOUR

CONCLUSION

Thinking About

the New Millennium

We live in a world of transformations, affecting almost every aspect of what we do. For better or worse, we are being propelled into a global order that no one fully understands, but which is making its effects felt upon all of us.

—Anthony Giddens, *Runaway World*, 2003

Good planets are hard to find.

—Graffito scribbled on a bridge in Rock Creek Park in Washington, D.C. (cited by Lester Brown in *State of the World 1989*)

On the eve of most revolutions, they are thought to have been impossible, whereas the morning after they are thought to have been inevitable.

—Remarks by Richard Benedick, the chief U.S. negotiator at the 1987 Montreal Protocol ozone layer talks, at a meeting of the International Studies Association

Go forth to meet the shadowy future.

—Henry Wadsworth Longfellow, *Hyperion*, 1852

10

The Future of
International Relations

SOVEREIGNTY,
GLOBAL GOVERNANCE,
AND THE
HUMAN PROSPECT
IN THE TWENTY-FIRST CENTURY

Look, I have nothing against globalization, just as long as it's not in my backyard.

—Robert Mankoff, *New Yorker* cartoonist

The age of nations is past; the task before us, if we would survive, is to build the earth.

—Pierre Teilhard de Chardin

The study of international relations ultimately is about how human beings organize and conduct their political affairs. The two epigraphs above embody two competing worldviews. The NIMBY quip reflects parochialism, while the musing of a Jesuit philosopher reflects cosmopolitanism. We have seen that the history of the world can be likened to a giant pendulum swinging back and forth between these two impulses, moving in a localistic direction one moment and a universalistic direction the next. What is perhaps most striking, and perplexing, about our current time is that these opposite tendencies seem to be occurring all at once. As Benjamin Barber observes in *Jihad vs. McWorld* (see the *IR* Critical Thinking Box in Chapter 2), "The planet is both falling apart and coming together." Returning to this puzzle and similar questions raised in *Part One* of this book, what is the dominant world order trend today, integration or disintegration? What should be our dominant mood today, optimism or pessimism? What is the future of the nation-state and the state system? This last chapter is an opportunity to tie up loose ends and encourage critical thinking about the future and where humanity might be headed.

WHITHER THE NATION-STATE SYSTEM?
ALTERNATIVE WORLD ORDER MODELS

Earlier I suggested that the central question of our time is whether we are witnessing merely a shift from bipolarity of the Cold War to multipolarity, the more usual form the international system took prior to 1945, *or* a more fundamental shift of the Westphalian system itself into something completely different. In other words, is the early twenty-first century a "Westphalian moment" similar to 1648?

Some observers see the combination of centrifugal and centripetal forces today as marking possibly the beginning of the end of the nation-state system. Barber, for example, believes that "the national state based on territory and political sovereignty looks to be a mere transitional development" between "the two axial principles of our age—tribalism and globalism."[1] Others argue otherwise, that the nation-state is not a passing fad but is deeply ingrained in the human DNA, and that the more things change the more they stay the same. According to realist Kenneth Waltz, "Challenges at home and abroad test the mettle of states. Some states fail, and other states pass the tests nicely. In modern times, enough states always make it to keep the international system going as a system of states. The challenges vary; states endure. They have proved to be hardy survivors."[2] Ditto Robert Jackson and Alan James: "Nowadays no less than previously the population of the world is divided into separate, independent States each with their own identities, territories, and symbols which mark them off from one another. The vast majority of people still owe their allegiance to [these entities]. . . . There is nothing to indicate that in the foreseeable future such entities will not continue to be the preferred and predominant form of political organization. . . . The fundamental characteristics of the international society formed by such . . . entities therefore give no indication of soon changing into something different."[3]

It is possible that *both* sides are right, that we are truly straddling two epochs, a Westphalian one struggling to survive and a post-Westphalian one struggling to be born.[4] Obviously we still live in a state system, but it is being challenged daily. We can only guess how this will ultimately play out, how long we will be in limbo between two epochs, or even if these tensions will ever be resolved and a post-Westphalian system will ever fully materialize. We also cannot be certain that a successor to a nation-state system would be superior in terms of meeting human needs for security, economic well-being, environmental quality of life, and other aspirations.

Let us speculate about the future for a moment: If not the nation-state, then *what*? How else might, or should, human affairs be organized? In other words, what **alternative world order models** are possible (empirically) and desirable (normatively)?[5] Regarding the empirical question, it is almost as difficult today for the average person to envision a world without nation-states as it was for people in an earlier time to envision a world that was round rather than flat. Yet the historical record shows that the nation-state and state system have not always existed, and logic dictates that they will not necessarily be with us for all time. Regarding the normative question, many arguments can ensue over the criteria to be applied in evaluating the merits of alternative world order models. Most people would want world order to promote such values as peace, individual freedom, economic prosperity, and ecological balance. Still, an order that is conducive to one goal might be detrimental to another, or at least might maximize certain values more than others.

Regionalism

Should the integrative, centralizing forces currently at work prove dominant, then one possible world order model that could materialize in the twenty-first century is *regionalism*. Instead of some 200 nation-states, the world's people might be organized in 5 or 6 region-states. The most obvious candidate to lead the way is Europe, where the European Union has taken on many attributes of a supranational entity, including not only a common currency but a common decision-making apparatus whereby economic and other important decisions increasingly are made by EU-wide institutions. However, the EU has failed to take the next step toward a federation based on a new European constitution, and other regionalism candidates are much farther behind in their integration experiment, including NAFTA, the African Union, and counterpart efforts in Asia and Latin America.

As a world order model, would regionalism be an improvement on the current nation-state system? Because it would be a somewhat more centralized political system in which agreement would have to be reached among fewer actors, it would probably be a more manageable world in many respects. Such a system would be particularly effective in dealing with problems that are primarily regional rather than global in scope. However, one can argue that regional entities would simply be nation-states writ large, with the same propensity for conflict, so that conflicts that today might be confined to a localized area would in a future regionalized system pit very large areas of the globe against each other. Hence peace might not necessarily be maximized; the same can be said for individual freedom and democracy, given the "democratic deficit" criticism leveled at EU institutions.[6]

World Government

If "McWorld" trends were to be carried to their ultimate endpoint, we could see *world government*—a political system in which one set of institutions would preside over the entire earth. Several variants of this model have been proposed. The most ambitious proposal calls for nation-states surrendering total sovereignty to a supreme global authority that would rule directly over all citizens of the world. Almost equally ambitious would be a federation in which nation-states would share power and authority with a central world government; somewhat along the lines of the U.S. Constitution, the world government would be delegated specific powers in certain areas (e.g., maintaining an army, regulating interstate commerce) and the nation-states allowed to exercise power in other areas (e.g., education or health care). Yet another possibility would be a confederation in which a world government would enjoy a limited degree of power and authority, but the bulk would be exercised by the constituent nation-state units.

Various model constitutions have been drafted over the years to flesh out what the elements of a world government might look like. For example, Grenville Clark and Louis Sohn of the Harvard Law School, in *World Peace Through World Law*, envisioned a permanent world police force with a monopoly on the legitimate use of force. Richard Hudson of the Center for War/Peace Studies has proposed a "binding triad" arrangement that would empower the UN General Assembly to make binding decisions upon approval of three concurrent majorities, one based on the current one state, one vote formula, another based on a formula weighted by a state's contribution to the regular UN budget, and a third proportioned by national population. Marc Nerfin, a former staff member of the UN Secretariat, has proposed a tripartite assembly consisting of a princes chamber, in which national governments would be represented and security issues would predominate; a merchants chamber, in which major economic actors would be represented, including multinational corporations; and a citizens chamber, representing grassroots associations.[7] Jan Tinbergen, a Nobel Prize–winning economist, has called for a world treasury, a world central bank, a world ministry of agriculture, and other global executive agencies,[8] while another Nobel laureate economist, James Tobin, has suggested a global tax on all foreign exchange transactions, to be utilized by the UN to combat global poverty. Other suggested global taxes have been a world income tax (for general revenue purposes), a global carbon tax (to fund environmental programs), a global tax on arms sales (to fund peacekeeping), a global tax on international air or sea travel (to fund air and ocean safety programs), and a global tax on distant e-mails (to fund the Internet wiring of developing countries).[9]

Fanciful as all this sounds, it is not just ivory tower academics who are sounding like world federalists. Bottom-line-oriented multinational corporation executives have written about "the twilight of sovereignty."[10] One writer notes "the new generation of planetary visionaries, unlike globalists of earlier days, come to their prophetic calling not by way of poetic imagination, transcendental philosophy, or Oriental mysticism but by solid careers in electrical circuitry, soap, mayonnaise, and aspirin."[11] Even those with the most vested interests in sovereignty-based institutions sometimes seem prepared to write off the nation-state. A U.S. deputy secretary of state for global affairs in the 1990s was quoted as saying that "I'll bet that within the next hundred years . . . nationhood as we know it will be obsolete; all states will recognize a single, global authority. [The phrase] 'citizen of the world' will have assumed real meaning. . . . It has taken the events in our own wondrous and terrible century to clinch the case for world government."[12]

Still, notwithstanding the growing globalization of the international economy, the spread of the World Wide Web, and other globalizing trends, speculating about the prospects for world government at this moment admittedly borders on science fiction and betting on it seems foolhardy. By the year 2500—the setting for *Star Trek*—humankind's sense of the universe may have expanded to the point where earthlings will view each other as one people with a common destiny. However, short of a Martian invasion, the vision of a single supranational community under one roof is not likely to materialize anytime soon.

Even if a world government were possible, though, would it necessarily be a panacea for all our problems? A centralized system would facilitate a more concerted global effort to deal with environmental and other problems. Such a system also might allow for a more equitable distribution of wealth, although probably at the expense of some individuals and states that are now in a privileged position. There is a serious concern whether such a system would promote freedom and democracy. Where would the capital be located, and how far away from the grassroots, from where you live? A world government would be in a better position to enforce the Universal Declaration of Human Rights and other human rights regimes than the UN is today, yet nondemocratic elements might be the ones controlling the world government and defining the nature of those rights. The one value that a world government would most likely maximize, according to conventional wisdom, is peace. However, just as central governments of nation-states today are often incapable of preventing the outbreak of civil war (and sometimes find themselves presiding over failed states), there is no assurance that a world government could necessarily avoid a global "internal war."

City-States

Should the "jihad," disintegrative trends become more pronounced, another possibility is increased decentralization, with political life revolving around even smaller and more fragmented units than the current nation-states. Each of the roughly 1,500 distinct nationality or ethnic groups in the world might seek to form its own state.[13] This scenario, unlikely as it is, has gained a measure of credibility in the post–Cold War era with the growing ethnic unrest from Rwanda to Georgia, calls for greater home rule in Scotland (UK), Catalonia (Spain), and other subnational entities in Europe, and the breakup of such countries as Yugoslavia, Czechoslovakia, and the Soviet Union. Ethnic-based secessionist movements could add substantially to the proliferation of ministates that already exist. Two-thirds of the nation-states of the world are smaller in population than Ohio, with many (like Monaco and Micronesia) smaller than several Ohio cities.

On the "rebirth" of *city-states*, Robert Kaplan comments: "Nations as we know them have existed for only a few hundred years. But cities have been with us since the dawn of civilization. And while the future of the city is not in doubt, modern nations will probably continue to weaken in the 21st century. By 2100, the organizing principle of the world will be the city-state. . . . Indeed, loyalty toward the polis will gradually overwhelm the traditional state patriotism of the 20th century."[14] Some observers have noticed a trend toward the evolution of "microregions" emerging not only within national boundaries but in some cases across national boundaries, based on intense economic and other ties (e.g., the San Diego-Tijuana corridor across the U.S.-Mexican border). James Rosenau points to a cooperation pact signed in 1988 by Lyon (France), Milan (Italy), Stuttgart (Germany), and Barcelona (Spain) that, in combination with the "Alpine Diamond" (Lyon plus Geneva, Switzerland, and Turin, Italy) and other such developments, has led one analyst to observe that "a resurrection of 'city-states' and regions is quietly transforming Europe's political and economic landscape, diminishing the influence of national governments and redrawing the continental map of power for the twenty-first century" and another to forecast that "cities, not nations, will become the principal identity for most people in the world."[15]

Still, a world order system composed of subnational local entities or transnational microregions as the dominant political units seems at least as unlikely as world government. Although some utopian thinkers long for smaller, human-scale communities, such a model could prove dystopian. While decentralization might well maximize individual freedom, democracy, and economic justice, some central guidance mechanism would still be needed to address global issues such as greenhouse warming and other ecological problems. Traditional security concerns would also have to be addressed somehow. The specter of Peoria or Poughkeepsie or the San Diego-Tijuana corridor saber rattling with nuclear weapons is hardly any more reassuring than the likes of the United States and Russia doing it. As hard as it is to forge agreement on nuclear arms control among 200 sovereign actors, it would be all the more cumbersome and daunting a task if several hundred or thousand actors had to be consulted.

Other World Order Models: An MNC-Centric World or a New Feudalism?

All of the models discussed so far tend to assume a territorial basis for human organization. Even world government models generally assume that, in addition to a global orientation, people will retain some degree of identity with smaller territorial units, be they regional, national, or subnational. However, other futures are conceivable. Many globalization thinkers already see the world organized around nonterritorial principles, with transnational economic elites and the pursuit of corporate interests overshadowing national governments and the pursuit of national interests. If the multinational corporation phenomenon continues to grow, the world political map might consist of units defined more by company logos than geographical boundaries. As Stephen Kobrin and others have suggested, the "strategic alliances" between MNCs across nations and regions (e.g., the partnership formed between Delta, Singapore, and Swissair airlines) may render mute the concept of home country.[16] So too the growth of global civil society—the NGO network of not-for-profit voluntary associations occupying the space between the governmental and the corporate sectors—may mean "the end of geography."[17]

As noted in the *IR* Critical Thinking Box in Chapter 2, the mix of jihad and McWorld tendencies today may be taking humanity back to a pre-Westphalian, medieval-type system of overlapping hierarchies of authority and multiple loyalties and identities.[18] Although the European Union is commonly seen as a manifestation of a new regionalism, it could just as easily be viewed as the leading edge of a "new feudalism." Brussels is a symbol of this complexity, at one level the headquarters of the major EU-wide supranational institutions, at another level the capital of the nation-state of Belgium, and at yet another level the site of subnational ethnic tensions between Walloons and Flemish. While it may be true that "one may entertain serious doubts about whether the competitive, often violent nation-state system" is "any longer safe for the human race," would an MNC-centered or feudalistic world order be any safer or more hospitable to other values?[19] It would surely be more muddled in terms of lines of accountability.

The Continuation of the Nation-State System

One distinct possibility—indeed probability—is that the nation-state system will persevere well into the twenty-first century and beyond. Paul Kennedy echoes the view of Kenneth Waltz, Robert Jackson, and Alan James when he writes that despite "pressures for a relocation of authority both upward and downward," the nation-state "is still at the center of things, engaging in a ceaseless jostling for advantage against other nation-states," that "the nation-state remains the primary locus of identity of most people," and that "as new challenges emerge" "no adequate substitute has emerged to replace it as the key unit in responding to global change."[20] Still, this begs the question raised by John Ikenberry and others mentioned at the outset of this book: What kind of nation-state system will it be? Will it be a unipolar system dominated by a single hegemon? And, if so, will it be the United States? China? Or some other state? Might we possibly return to the bipolar system of two superpowers that characterized the Cold War era? More likely, as a recent U.S. intelligence forecast predicted, "We're projecting [by 2025] a multipolar world."[21]

Whether the state system survives will depend on whether it can create "a more mature anarchy" that will enable it to respond to global changes.[22] Will it be able to continue "the long peace" and extend it beyond developed states to less developed ones, address rich-poor gaps between and within countries, avert environmental disaster, and solve other problems? In short, will it be up to the challenge of global governance?

LIVING WITH PARADOXES:
TOWARD A MORE MATURE ANARCHY

As the World Commission on Environment and Development stated in *Our Common Future* (which provided the basis for the 1992 Rio Summit), "The Earth is one but the world is not."[23] Meanwhile, we have to live and cope with the paradoxes that define the contemporary international system. It is possible that IGOs will be the key that allows nation-states to retain their sovereignty as they function in a global political space in which human transactions and concerns increasingly transcend national borders. As Inis Claude said about the historic role of IGOs such as the UN, it is best to think of them not as precursors to world government but rather as an adaptation of the state system that could make world government unnecessary, if such arrangements among sovereign states could be made to work in a way that responds to human needs.[24] Although some problems can be handled unilaterally by a national government, many cannot be. Whether through IGOs or some other mechanism, states will be pressured to develop international regimes to deal with a new agenda of issues that require multilateral approaches. For an example, let us look at two sets of issues that have been the focus of regime-building efforts recently and see how the state system has responded: (1) combating global warming and ozone layer deterioration and (2) regulating Internet usage.

Environmental Concerns: Global Warming and the Ozone Layer

The environment has been called "the national security issue of the early twenty-first century. The political and strategic impact of surging populations, spreading disease, deforestation and soil erosion, water depletion, and, possibly, rising sea levels . . . —developments that will prompt mass migrations and, in turn, incite group conflicts—will be the core foreign policy challenges from which most others will emanate."[25] While the latter statement, along with the Warning to Humanity issued by over 1,500 scientists worldwide, may overstate the importance of environmental issues, it seems safe to predict that global ecology is likely to gain greater visibility as a global governance concern.

Although environmental concerns and consciousness are not new—for example, one can read accounts of air pollution as far back as ancient times, in Seneca's references to "the heavy air of Rome"—the modern era of environmental policy firmly positioned on national and international agendas did not really begin until the 1970s. The United Nations Charter in 1945 did not contain a single reference to the environment. The United States did not establish its national environmental protection agency until 1970, the same year as the first Earth Day celebration. The first global conference on the environment was not until 1972, when the UN sponsored the **Conference on the Human Environment** in Stockholm, which created the **UN Environmental Program** (**UNEP**). The Stockholm Conference coincided with the publication of the Club of Rome's landmark book *The Limits to Growth*, which warned that unless population and economic growth rates were reduced to near zero, the world would witness in the coming century a catastrophic exhaustion of petroleum and other finite, nonrenewable resources, resulting in the end of civilization.[26] The Stockholm Conference and UNEP were catalysts for the development of many international environmental regimes that attempted to address problems that were global in scope. Of the hundreds of international environmental agreements that currently exist, the vast majority were initiated after 1972. The 1992 **Earth Summit (UN Conference on Environment and Development)** in Rio de Janeiro added further impetus to the growth of environmental regimes. Since neither rich nor poor countries had enthusiastically embraced the limits to growth message, the Earth Summit sought a middle ground that championed economic growth sensitive to environmental concerns. The result was the concept of **sustainable development**, now a central theme of environmental problem-solving.

One outcome of Rio was the **Framework Convention on Climate Change**. Prior to the summit, there were growing concerns that burning fossil fuels and other human activities were creating a buildup of carbon dioxide and other gases in the earth's atmosphere, a process thought to cause a "greenhouse effect" leading to global warming. The Intergovernmental Panel on Climate Change (IPCC), a UN body created in 1988 to assess data on climate change, had issued warnings that inaction might result in the polar ice caps melting, which in turn would flood dozens of coastal cities such as Miami and New York and decimate entire low-lying nations like Bangladesh and the Maldives. Other fears included severe drought adding to food supply concerns, along with an increase in hurricanes and wildly erratic weather patterns. As evidence of the earth's temperature rising, almost each year in the 1980s and 1990s seemed to bring the news headline "hottest year ever," accompanied by hard data supporting the headline. In response, the Framework Convention on Climate Change contained a nonbinding set of principles acknowledging that global warming was a serious concern deserving continued monitoring. It called upon countries to try to reduce their greenhouse gas emissions to 1990 levels by 2000 and urged industrialized countries in particular to take immediate steps to curb their emissions and to help developing countries do likewise. The convention was signed and quickly ratified by almost the entire UN membership present at the conference, including the three biggest CO_2 emitters in the industrialized world—the United States (responsible for almost 25 percent of the worldwide total), Russia (7 percent), and Japan (5 percent). The framework convention represented "soft law." It was essentially hortatory in nature, merely urging rather than requiring action, although the hope was it would grease the way for "hard law" to follow.

At the follow-up Kyoto Conference in 1997, the United States joined with Saudi Arabia and other OPEC countries to try to block any treaty provisions that would adversely affect major oil-producing or oil-consuming economies, while Japan and most EU states joined with the thirty-two nation Alliance of Small Island States (the Maldives and others especially vulnerable to the rise of sea levels) to press for tougher measures. The foot-dragging states were backed by the oil industry and other groups worried about reductions in fossil fuel use, while most scientific and environmental NGOs lobbied for the other side. The resulting **Kyoto Protocol** obligated industrialized countries to meet specific targets (averaging approximately 5 percent below their 1990 levels) by 2010, while less developed countries for the most part were exempted from any obligations. The protocol, which required the ratification of at least 55 states accounting for at least 55 percent of developed-country CO_2 emissions before it could take effect, finally came into force when Russia ratified the agreement in 2005. Although over 180 states had become parties by 2009, the United States has refused to join, mostly due to concerns about economic costs and the free ride given to China and India, which are now among the world's top 5 CO_2 emitters. (By 2008, China had become number 1.) With the protocol due to expire in 2012, there is general agreement that the treaty is too weak to remedy global warming, given not only the absence of the United States and several other major contributors of carbon emissions but also the fact that many parties themselves are not on track to meet their commitments. Meanwhile, each year sees record carbon emissions and more ominous warnings. IPCC has estimated that without vigorous action, global average temperatures could rise as much as 11 degrees Fahrenheit by the end of the century.[27]

One of the greenhouse gases, chlorofluorocarbons (CFCs), has also been blamed for contributing to the depletion of the ozone layer, which shields us from the sun's ultraviolet rays and helps prevent skin cancer. However, where regime-making in the area of global warming has been largely unsuccessful, "ozone diplomacy" is credited with producing a landmark environmental treaty.[28] The story begins in the 1950s, as CFCs were being produced in large quantities by chemical companies as coolants in refrigeration systems, propellants in aerosol spray cans, Styrofoam packaging in fast food restaurants, and for other purposes. When scientists established the link between CFCs and ozone depletion in the 1970s, the international community responded with a meeting in 1985 in Vienna that produced the **Framework Convention for the Protection of the Ozone Layer**. Ratified by virtually all the major CFC-producing industrialized states, the treaty was a modest instrument that merely obligated the parties to take "appropriate measures" to protect the ozone layer and to monitor the problem and exchange data. However, it paved the way for the subsequent protocol produced in Montreal two years later that would set explicit, mandatory CFC phase-out targets and timetables.

As described by Richard Benedick, the chief U.S. negotiator in Montreal, "On September 16, 1987, representatives of countries from every region of the world reached an agreement unique in the annals of international diplomacy."[29] The **Montreal Protocol on Substances that Deplete the Ozone Layer** has been hailed as "the most significant international agreement in history" and "unparalleled as a global effort."[30] The protocol called for CFCs to be cut by 50 percent from 1986 levels by 1998, with developing countries given a grace period of an additional ten years to phase out their CFCs, along with financial aid in weaning themselves off of CFCs. In addition, the agreement contained an unusual provision for periodic review whereby fast-track revisions of the protocol could occur without lengthy negotiations if the scientific evidence revealed the necessity for amendments. Along with key states such as Norway and Sweden, nonstate actors played an important role in development of the regime. It was scientific NGOs, along with the UNEP's executive director, Mostafa Tolba, who helped put the issue on the agenda; it was an American MNC, DuPont, that discovered the key substitute for CFCs (HCFCs), facilitating the switch in technology and also encouraging the United States to become a strong supporter of the protocol; and it was Greenpeace, Friends of the Earth, and other NGOs that provided pressure group support in mobilizing publics.[31]

By the late 1990s, the Montreal Protocol had attained nearly universal adherence, including acceptance by the United States, the EU membership, India, and China. Ultimately, in the face of alarming scientific data about the widening of the ozone "hole," the parties agreed to a total ban on CFC production by 1996, with LDCs given until 2010 to phase out the chemicals. The goals of the protocol have been largely accomplished. However, despite the success of the ozone regime, concerns remain about its effectiveness, given gaps in the regime (i.e., the harm caused by methyl bromide as well as the HCFC chemicals substituted for CFCs) and the fact that CFCs already deposited in the upper atmosphere may not become inert for another fifty years.

Governance of the Internet

A major challenge today is the governance of cyberspace, a space that knows no borders and "wherein the continued tension between globalist flows and statist claims to territorial sovereignty are being renegotiated."[32] The nascent global governance of electronic information flows thus far has included ICANN (the Internet Corporation for Assigned Names and Numbers), a U.S.-based private body that manages the Internet domain system; a network of NGOs and epistemic communities seeking to shape norms in the digital world; the International Telecommunications Union (ITU), the UN specialized agency with 191 members that regulates satellite uses of outer space and promotes uniform standards in the operation of transborder communications systems; and the UN World Summit on the Information Society (WSIS) conferences organized by the ITU in an effort to develop uniform rules and standards for using the Internet and World Wide Web.

The WSIS conference held in Geneva in 2003, attended by government officials and civil society representatives from 175 countries, produced a declaration of principles promoting the "idea of universal, accessible, equitable, and affordable ICT [Information and Communications Technology] infrastructure" and "an enabling environment at the national and international level based on the rule of law with a transparent, predictable policy and regulatory framework." A plan of action called for bringing at least half of the world's people online by 2015. A follow-up WSIS meeting was held in Tunis in 2005, although little progress was made in regard to Internet governance and funding. Much work remains to be done not only in addressing the many complex technical challenges associated with coordinating Internet usage across boundaries but also in dealing with issues relating to closing the digital divide, promoting freedom of speech and artistic expression, regulating e-commerce, and improving cyber security. Developing countries have complained about information hegemony—domination of Internet routines by the English-speaking world in general and the United States in particular.[33] Regarding cyber security, there are millions of "cyber attacks" (viruses, worms, and other cyber incidents) committed annually, with increasing potential for cyber criminals and cyber terrorists to create havoc by disrupting governmental and financial systems worldwide.[34] Hence global governance of the infosphere remains a work in progress, which will require not only multilateral cooperation between governments but also public-private partnerships between states, corporations, and civil society, all of which are stakeholders in this enterprise.

Global Governance and the Global Commons

Cyberspace can be thought of as part of the **global commons**—that area of the globe that is under the sovereignty of no one state. Other parts of the global commons include the *high seas* (outside the territorial waters of any state), *air space* (above the high seas and beyond the national air space over the territory of any state), *outer space*, and *Antarctica*. The 1982 UN Law of the Sea Treaty governs the high seas and establishes rules regulating fishing and other activities in the world's oceans. The Tokyo Convention and other treaties drafted by the International Civil Aviation Organization govern the use of air space. The 1967 Outer Space Treaty and related treaties govern the use of outer space, including the moon. The 1959 Antarctic Treaty created a regime whereby a dozen states agreed to repudiate or suspend claims of sovereignty and to provide joint stewardship over the South Pole. These regimes have been generally successful in muting conflict and permitting states to function in "the commons." Interestingly, there is no regime as yet governing the Arctic at the North Pole, and growing friction over ownership of Arctic resources (e.g., an estimated 90 billion barrels of oil), claimed by the United States, Russia, Canada, Denmark, and several other states, has been called potentially "the most important territorial dispute of the century."[35] In the latter area and other areas, the capacity of the state system to promote global governance will be increasingly tested in the future.

As realists would predict, developed, powerful countries have had more impact on the politics of governance of the global commons than less developed, less powerful countries. However, many of the commons regimes reflect more than raw power at work. Idealists, or liberals, would note that the most powerful states, such as the United States, did not get everything they wanted out of the negotiations leading to, say, the Tokyo Convention or Antarctic Treaty, but settled for compromises based on mutual interests. Constructivists could argue that the Outer Space Treaty, in repudiating any claims to sovereignty over the moon or celestial bodies, was a visionary document representing considerable normative progress compared to the discovery-based titles to ownership staked out by explorers sent to distant reaches of the earth by great-power states in earlier ages.

THINKING ABOUT THE FUTURE

In 1948 it was thought that "once a photograph of the Earth, taken from the outside is available . . . a new idea as powerful as any other in history will be let loose,"[36] namely, that humanity shares a common destiny. Yet neither Sputnik's orbiting of the planet in 1957, nor the Apollo moon landing in 1969, nor thousands of satellite photos taken since have fundamentally altered our image of the human species as organized around a competitive state system, exhortations about Spaceship Earth to the contrary. In an amusing twist of events, Brazil recently marketed its nascent space program as an ideal one for other countries or organizations to use for payload delivery because of its unique equatorial location, which gives it a competitive edge over "temperate zone competitors." It is actually emphasizing the benefits found within its specific nation-state to further use of a global common. Furthermore, it is building its own version of Cape Canaveral at Alcantara on the edge of the tropical rainforest, often asserted to be the common heritage of mankind due to the vast biodiversity contained within it, again using a global common for national gain.[37]

In contemplating what is possible, there is a tendency to become either overly cynical and resigned to the current reality or overly optimistic and given to wishful thinking in presuming what ought to be, could be. The field of international relations has had its share of both "bad realists" and "bad idealists."[38] Observers of late have seemed to err more on the side of the former than the latter. In 1945, at the end of World War II, who foresaw that France and Germany, centuries-old rivals, would within a dozen years be engaged in a regional integration project that would reduce the probability of war between them to almost zero, and would by the end of the century share a common currency and an open border? And in 1981, when a Cold Warrior entered the White House decrying the "evil empire," who foresaw that both the Cold War and the Soviet Union would be gone within a decade and that this transformation of the bipolar international system would occur so quietly, without a shot being fired?

Indeed, as Thomas Schelling has said, perhaps "the most astonishing development" in international relations—"a development that no one I have known could have imagined—is that during the rest of the twentieth century, or fifty-five years after Hiroshima and Nagasaki suffered the world's first nuclear bombs, not a single nuclear weapon was exploded in warfare." Schelling calls it "a stunning achievement" that we have now "enjoyed [over] sixty years without nuclear weapons exploded in anger." He notes that "in 1960 the British novelist C.P. Snow said on the front page of the *New York Times* that unless the nuclear powers drastically reduced their nuclear armaments, thermonuclear war within the decade was a 'mathematical certainty.' . . . We now have mathematical certainty compounded more than four times, and no nuclear war. Can we make it through another half dozen decades?"[39]

As I have suggested throughout this book, there are grounds for both pessimism and optimism, as we live today in arguably the worst and best of times.

It is easy enough to adopt a gloom-and-doom mentality, given the possibility of growing numbers of rogue states and nonstate actors acquiring weapons of mass destruction. Then, too, the current global economic crisis elicits memories of the Great Depression; as of this writing, it is too soon to know how it will end. Thus the future may well be bleak. At the same time, however, there are many positive trends, not only the long peace and growing democratization but some we take for granted, for example, the increase in the world average for life expectancy from twenty-six years in the early nineteenth century to over sixty-five today.[40] Whose prediction will prove valid: Alan Goodman's proclamation that the twenty-first century "will encompass the longest period of peace, democracy, and economic development in history" or Robert Heilbroner's dismissing "the human prospect" with the baleful lament, "Is there hope for man?"[41]

Among the guarded optimists, Fareed Zakaria envisions a "post-American world" in which the United States, China, and other states engage in a healthy competition that mutually benefits them and much of humanity.[42] With the 2008 election of the first African American president in U.S. history, Barack Obama, many people around the globe hoped for a new era in U.S. foreign policy, one associated with a growth in American soft power and willingness to lead or share in the burdens of multilateralism. We could be on the brink of a new era in international politics, although—mindful of the great complexity of IR that this textbook has attempted to communicate to the reader—such thinking may exaggerate the importance of single actors, whether states or individuals. Because of this complexity, it is impossible to foretell with any certainty what the future holds. The most any of us can do—professors, policymakers, publics, and students—is to try as best we can to understand how the world works and to build our hopes and expectations on those assumptions and analyses. That is the challenge of our time.

Malcolm Hancock

QUESTIONS FOR STUDY AND DISCUSSION

1. Discuss the politics of global governance in the environmental issue-area, particularly the development of regimes dealing with the ozone layer and global warming. Are there any lessons to be learned from successes or failures in global environmental problem-solving that might help humanity progress toward a "more mature anarchy"?

2. Some observers see globalization and other trends possibly leading to the end of the nation-state as the basis for human political organization. If not the nation-state, then how else might people be organized? Discuss "alternative world order models" (regionalism, world government, etc.) in terms of both their likelihood and desirability.

3. Assuming the nation-state remains the primary mode of human political organization, what will the nation-state system look like in the future in terms of the power distribution and other key features?

4. In *A Brief History of the Future*, Allan Goodman predicts that "the twenty-first century will encompass the longest period of peace, democracy, and economic development in history." What basis can you think of for such a rosy forecast? Are you optimistic or pessimistic about the future of the world? *Your* future? Do you think the world will be a better place, say, in the year 2050, than it is today?

SUGGESTIONS FOR FURTHER READING

Benjamin Barber, "Jihad vs. McWorld," *Atlantic,* March 1992.

Richard E. Benedick, *Ozone Diplomacy* (Cambridge, MA: Harvard University Press, 1998).

"Fighting Climate Change." Special issue of *Human Development Report 2007/2008.*

Robert Kaplan, "The Coming Anarchy," *Atlantic,* February 1994.

Paul Kennedy, "The Future of the Nation-State," in *Preparing for the 21st Century* (New York: Random House, 1993).

Stephen D. Krasner, "Sovereignty," *Foreign Policy,* January–February 2001, 20–29.

Maryann Cusimano Love, *Beyond Sovereignty: Issues for a Global Agenda*, 3rd ed. (Belmont, CA: Wadsworth, 2007).

Jessica T. Matthews, "Power Shift," *Foreign Affairs,* January–February 1997, 50–66.

Stephen D. McDowell et al., *Managing the Infosphere* (Philadelphia: Temple University Press, 2008).

Joseph S. Nye and John D. Donahue, eds., *Governance in a Globalizing World* (Washington, D.C.: Brookings, 2000).

Roland Paris, "The Globalization of Taxation? Electronic Commerce and the Transformation of the State," *International Studies Quarterly* 47 (June 2003): 153–182.

John Rapley, "The New Middle Ages," *Foreign Affairs,* May–June 2006, 95–103.

James N. Rosenau, *Turbulence in World Politics* (Princeton, NJ: Princeton University Press, 1990).

Paul Starobin, "Beyond Hegemony," *National Journal,* December 1, 2006, 18–25.

Strobe Talbott, *The Great Experiment: The Story of Ancient Empires, Modern States, and the Quest for a Global Nation* (New York: Simon & Schuster, 2008).

Mary Ann Tetreault and Ronnie D. Lipschutz, *Global Politics As If People Mattered* (Lanham, MD: Rowman & Littlefield, 2005).

Fareed Zakaria, *The Post-American World* (New York: Norton, 2008).

NOTES

CHAPTER 1: UNDERSTANDING INTERNATIONAL RELATIONS, OR GETTING A HANDLE ON THE WORLD

1. George Santayana, *Life of Reason* (New York: Scribner's, 1954), 1:12.

2. Karl W. Deutsch, *The Analysis of International Relations*, 3rd ed. (Englewood Cliffs, NJ: Prentice-Hall, 1988), ix.

3. G. John Ikenberry, "The Rise of China and the Future of the West," *Foreign Affairs,* January–February 2008, 23.

4. Parag Khanna, "Waving Goodbye to Hegemony," *New York Times Magazine,* January 27, 2008, 36.

5. The term "postinternational politics," referring to the transformation of the state system into a completely new set of relationships not predicated on the nation-state as the preeminent actor and instead involving multinational corporations and other nonstate actors, was coined by James Rosenau in *Turbulence in World Politics* (Princeton, NJ: Princeton University Press, 1990), 6.

6. Zbigniew Brzezinski, *Game Plan: A Geostrategic Framework for the Conduct of the US-Soviet Contest* (Boston: Atlantic Monthly Press, 1986), xiii. On the failure of international relations theory to anticipate and account for the end of the Cold War, see John Lewis Gaddis, "International Relations Theory and the End of the Cold War," *International Security* 17 (Winter 1992–1993): 5–58.

7. Gorbachev's statement was published in *Pravda* on December 5, 1989. Bush's statement appeared in his State of the Union address, January 29, 1991.

8. Francis Fukuyama, "The End of History?" *National Interest* 16 (Summer 1989): 3–16.

9. Notable dissenters were Samuel P. Huntington and John J. Mearsheimer. See note 12 below.

10. The "holiday from history" line is attributed to Charles Krauthammer, "The *Real* New World Order," *Jewish World Review*, November 7, 2001.

11. Allan E. Goodman, *A Brief History of the Future* (Boulder, CO: Westview, 1993); Fareed Zakaria, *The Post-American World* (New York: Norton, 2008); John Mueller, *Retreat from Doomsday: The Obsolescence of Major War* (New York: Basic

Books, 1989); Mueller, *Overblown* (New York: Free Press, 2006). Also see Max Singer and Aaron Wildavsky, *The Real World Order*, rev. ed. (Chatham, NJ: Chatham House, 1996).

12. John J. Mearsheimer, "Why We Will Soon Miss the Cold War," *Atlantic Monthly*, August 1990, 35–50; Mearsheimer, *The Tragedy of Great Power Politics* (New York: Norton, 2001); Samuel P. Huntington, "The Clash of Civilizations," *Foreign Affairs*, Summer 1993, 22–49; Robert D. Kaplan, *The Coming Anarchy: Shattering the Dreams of the Post–Cold War Era* (New York: Random House, 2000).

13. The quote is attributed to Richard Lamm, former governor of Colorado, cited in the *Christian Science Monitor*, April 24, 1985, 5.

14. Negative economic, environmental, and other trends are tracked in *Vital Signs*, published annually by the Worldwatch Institute.

15. According to the World Bank, "the past 30 years . . . [has seen] considerable progress in improving human well-being. Average income per capita . . . in developing countries grew from $989 in 1980 to $1,354 in 2000. Infant mortality was cut in half, from 107 per 1,000 live births to 58, as was adult illiteracy, from 47 to 25 percent." World Bank, *World Development Report 2003* (New York: Oxford University Press, 2003), 1.

16. Freedom House, *Freedom in the World 2008* (Washington, D.C.: Freedom House, 2008). The report did express some concerns that thirty years of dramatic progress might be slowing down and becoming flat, if not stagnating, in the past year or two.

17. Lawrence Summers, commencement address, Harvard University, June 9, 2005.

18. John Lewis Gaddis, "The Long Peace: Elements of Stability in the Postwar International System," *International Security* 10 (1986): 99–142.

19. CNN.com report on May 4, 2006. Half of the eighteen- to twenty-four-year-olds also could not find New York State on a map.

20. See www.nationalgeographic.com/roper2006/.

21. National Geographic–Roper 2002 Global Geographic Literacy Survey, November 2002.

22. See the 1981 Washington Post–ABC News poll, reported in *Interdependent* 7 (November 1981): 1; the 1983 CBS–New York Times poll cited in *National Journal*, August 8, 1983, 1658; the 1987 Overseas Development Council poll reported in *Interdependent* 13 (April-May 1987): 1.

23. Thomas Friedman, *The Lexus and the Olive Tree*, rev. ed. (New York: Anchor, 2000), xviii. Global Internet use can be monitored by accessing the Internet world stats website.

24. Thomas Friedman, *The World Is Flat*, exp. ed. (New York: Picador/Farrar, Straus & Giroux, 2007), 13, 24–25.

25. Joel Krieger, *Globalization and State Power* (New York: Pearson, 2005), 1.

26. "Foreigners Buy Stakes in the U.S. At Record Pace," *New York Times*, January 20, 2008, 1.

27. "Belgians, Adrift and Split, Sense a Nation Fading," *New York Times*, September 21, 2007.

28. On ethno-political conflict in world politics, see Ted Robert Gurr and Barbara Huff, *Ethnic Conflict in World Politics*, 2nd ed. (Boulder, CO: Westview, 2003).

29. Harold D. Lasswell, *Politics: Who Gets What, When, and How?* (Cleveland: World, 1958).

30. For example, see John Spanier, *Games Nations Play*, 4th ed. (New York: Holt, Rinehart & Winston, 1978); Mark Amstutz, *The Rules of the Game* (Boulder, CO: Paradigm, 2008).

31. Kenneth Oye, ed., *Cooperation Under Anarchy* (Princeton, NJ: Princeton University Press, 1986).

32. John G. Stoessinger, *The Might of Nations*, 10th ed. (New York: McGraw Hill, 1993), 4.

33. See Thomas S. Kuhn, *The Structure of Scientific Revolutions*, 2nd ed. (Chicago: University of Chicago Press, 1970). Also see the work of Imre Lakatos.

34. James N. Rosenau and Mary Durfee, *Thinking Theory Thoroughly* (Boulder, CO: Westview, 1995), 2, 7.

35. The idealist tradition is discussed in Louis Rene Beres and Harry Targ, *Reordering the Planet: Constructing Alternative World Futures* (Boston: Allyn & Bacon, 1974).

36. Robert O. Keohane and Joseph S. Nye, *Power and Interdependence*, 3rd ed. (New York: Longman, 2001).

37. Robert O. Keohane, *After Hegemony: Cooperation and Discord in the World Political Economy* (Princeton, NJ: Princeton University Press, 1984); Robert Axelrod, *The Evolution of Cooperation* (New York: Basic Books, 1985).

38. E. H. Carr, *The Twenty Years' Crisis, 1919–1939* (London: Macmillan, 1939).

39. Hans J. Morgenthau, *Politics Among Nations* (New York: Knopf, 1948). Morgenthau's influence is discussed in William D. Coplin et al., "Color It Morgenthau: A Data-Based Assessment of Quantitative International Relations Research" (paper presented at the annual meeting of the International Studies Association, New York City, March 14–17, 1973).

40. Kenneth N. Waltz, *Theory of International Politics* (Reading, MA: Addison-Wesley, 1979).

41. Joseph Grieco, "Anarchy and the Limits of Cooperation: A Realist Critique of the Newest Liberal Institutionalism," *International Organization* 42 (Summer 1988): 486–507.

42. John J. Mearsheimer, "The False Promise of International Institutions," *International Security* 19 (1994–95): 5–49.

43. Randall L. Schweller, "Unanswered Threats: A Neoclassical Realist Theory of Underbalancing," *International Security* 29 (Fall 1999): 159–201. Also see Bruce Bueno de Mesquita, *Principles of International Politics: People's Power, Preferences, and Perceptions*, 2nd ed. (Washington, D.C.: CQ Press, 2003).

44. Immanuel Wallerstein, *The Capitalist World-Economy* (Cambridge: Cambridge University Press, 1979).

45. Alexander Wendt, "Constructing International Politics," *International Security* 20 (Summer 1995): 71–81.

46. John Ruggie, ed., *Constructing the World Polity* (London: Routledge, 1998), 11.

47. Martha Finnemore, "Constructing Norms of Humanitarian Intervention," in Peter J. Katzenstein, ed., *The Culture of National Security: Norms and Identity in World Politics* (New York: Columbia University Press, 1996), 153.

48. This view was expressed by Hurst Hannum of Tufts University in a talk at the University of Missouri–St. Louis on February 6, 2003.

49. On the end of slavery and colonialism, see James Lee Ray, "The Abolition of Slavery and the End of International War," *International Organization* 43 (Summer 1989): 405–439; on free trade as an idea, see Judith Goldstein and Robert O. Keohane, eds., *Ideas and Foreign Policy: Beliefs, Institutions, and Political Change* (Ithaca, NY: Cornell University Press, 1993).

50. Inis L. Claude, "The Record of International Organizations in the Twentieth Century," Tamkang Lecture Series 64 (1986), 25; Martha Finnemore, *National Interests in International Society* (Ithaca, NY: Cornell University Press, 1996), 5.

51. These and other such hypotheses are discussed in V. Spike Peterson and Anne Sisson Runyan, *Global Gender Politics*, 2nd ed. (Boulder, CO: Westview, 1999); Cynthia Enloe, *Bananas, Beaches, and Bases: Making Feminist Sense of International Politics* (Berkeley: University of California Press, 1990).

52. See note 5.

53. Charles A. McClelland, "International Relations: Wisdom or Science?" in James N. Rosenau, ed., *International Politics and Foreign Policy*, rev. ed. (New York: Free Press, 1969), 4.

54. For realist and liberal takes on the Iraq War, see J. Martin Rochester, *U.S. Foreign Policy in the Twenty-First Century: Gulliver's Travails* (Boulder, CO: Westview, 2008); Tony Smith, *A Pact with the Devil* (New York: Routledge, 2007). Also see "Intellectual Left's Doves Take on Role of Hawks," *New York Times*, March 14, 2003.

55. See Jeffrey Pickering and Mark Peceny, "Forging Democracy at Gunpoint," *International Studies Quarterly* 50 (September 2006): 539–559.

56. For a realist view of the Middle East and what policy prescriptions flow from a realist analysis, see Stephen M. Walt, *Taming American Power* (New York: Norton, 2005).

CHAPTER 2: THE HISTORICAL DEVELOPMENT OF THE INTERNATIONAL SYSTEM: FROM THE BIRTH OF THE NATION-STATE TO GLOBALIZATION

1. Alexander Wendt, "Why a World State Is Inevitable" (paper presented at the annual meeting of the International Studies Association, New Orleans, March 24,

2002), 1. Also see Claudio Cioffi-Revilla, "Ancient Warfare: Origins and Systems," in Manus I. Midlarsky, ed., *Handbook of War Studies*, vol. 2 (Ann Arbor: University of Michigan Press, 2000).

2. For a discussion of the early Greek and Chinese state systems, see K. J. Holsti, *International Politics: A Framework for Analysis*, 3rd ed. (Englewood Cliffs, NJ: Prentice-Hall, 1977), 31–45.

3. Harold K. Jacobson, *Networks of Interdependence*, 2nd ed. (New York: Knopf, 1984), 14.

4. Lynn Miller, *Global Order*, 3rd ed. (Boulder, CO: Westview, 1994), 21–23.

5. Holsti, *International Politics*, 54.

6. See Charles Tilly, *Coercion, Capital, and European States: A.D. 900–1990* (Cambridge: Basil Blackwell, 1990); Bruce Bueno de Mesquita, "The Concordat of Worms and Westphalia" (paper presented at the annual meeting of the International Studies Association, Washington, D.C., February 18, 1999).

7. Stephen D. Krasner, "Westphalia and All That," in Judith Goldstein and Robert O. Keohane, eds., *Ideas and Foreign Policy* (Ithaca, NY: Cornell University Press, 1993), 240–246. Also see John H. Herz, *International Politics in the Atomic Age* (New York: Columbia University Press, 1959).

8. Henrik Spruyt, *The Sovereign State and Its Competitors* (Princeton, NJ: Princeton University Press, 1994).

9. K. J. Holsti, *Peace and War: Armed Conflicts and International Order, 1648–1989* (Cambridge: Cambridge University Press, 1991), 25.

10. Leo Gross, "The Peace of Westphalia, 1648–1948," *American Journal of International Law* 42 (January 1948): 28.

11. The "law of nations" was mentioned in Jeremy Bentham's *An Introduction to the Principles of Morals and Legislation*, published in 1789.

12. Miller, *Global Order*, 203.

13. See Hedley Bull and Adam Watson, eds., *The Expansion of International Society* (Oxford: Oxford University Press, 1985).

14. Stephen D. Krasner, "Economic Interdependence and Independent Statehood," in Robert Jackson and Alan James, eds., *States in a Changing World* (Oxford: Clarendon, 1993), 305.

15. Cited in Vincent Cable, "The Diminished Nation-State: A Study in the Loss of Economic Power," *Daedalus*, Spring 1995, 25.

16. Adam Markham, *A Brief History of Pollution* (New York: St. Martin's, 1994), 10.

17. Charles Tilly, "Reflections on the History of European State-Making," in *The Formation of National States in Western Europe* (Princeton, NJ: Princeton University Press, 1975), 42.

18. The evolution of military technology is discussed in William H. McNeill, *The Pursuit of Power* (Chicago: University of Chicago Press, 1984).

19. Thomas Schelling, *Arms and Influence* (New Haven, CT: Yale University Press, 1966), 27–28.

20. On the history of U.S. foreign policy, including early isolationist tendencies, see J. Martin Rochester, *U.S. Foreign Policy in the 21st Century: Gulliver's Travails* (Boulder, CO: Westview, 2008); David A. Lake, *Entangling Relations* (Princeton, NJ: Princeton University Press, 1999).

21. Joseph S. Nye, *Understanding International Conflicts*, 5th ed. (New York: Pearson, 2005), 72.

22. Thomas L. Friedman, *The Lexus and the Olive Tree* (New York: Farrar, Straus, Giroux, 1999), xiv.

23. Kenneth N. Waltz, *Theory of International Politics* (Reading, MA: Addison-Wesley, 1979), 158–160.

24. The words are those of Asa Briggs, cited in Waltz, *Theory,* 140.

25. The words are those of Erich Marcks in 1911, cited in Geoffrey Barraclough, *An Introduction to Contemporary History* (Baltimore: Penguin, 1967), 53.

26. On the growth of transnational actors, see James A. Field, "Transnationalism and the New Tribe," in Robert O. Keohane and Joseph S. Nye, eds., *Transnational Relations and World Politics* (Cambridge, MA: Harvard University Press, 1971), 3–22.

27. Barraclough, *Introduction,* 110–111.

28. Donald M. Snow, *Cases in International Relations* (New York: Longman, 2003), 181.

29. George Will, "From Bayonets to Tomahawks," *Newsweek,* January 28, 1991, 66.

30. David Fromkin, *The Independence of Nations* (New York: Praeger, 1981), 4.

31. Charles P. Kindleberger, "Hierarchical Versus Inertial Cooperation," *International Organization* 40 (Autumn 1986): 841.

32. See Stanley Hoffmann, *Gulliver's Troubles, Or the Setting of American Foreign Policy* (New York: McGraw-Hill, 1968), 17.

33. The containment doctrine was inspired by George Kennan, the U.S. ambassador to the Soviet Union in the late 1940s, who wrote an article calling for such a policy. George F. Kennan ["X"], "The Sources of Soviet Conduct," *Foreign Affairs,* July 1947, 566–582.

34. Walter Millis, cited in Stephen E. Ambrose, *Rise to Globalism,* 2nd ed. (New York: Penguin, 1980), 180–181.

35. Frederic S. Pearson and J. Martin Rochester, *International Relations: The Global Condition in the Twenty-First Century,* 4th ed. (New York: McGraw-Hill, 1998), 66–75. This discussion of the gradual unraveling of the post–World War II bipolar system draws on the latter work.

36. Mark W. Zacher, "The Territorial Integrity Norm: International Boundaries and the Use of Armed Force," *International Organization* 55 (Spring 2001): 215–250.

37. "I still believe he [President Johnson] found it viscerally inconceivable that what Walt Rostow [a chief national security adviser] kept telling him was 'the greatest power in the world' could not dispose of a collection of night-riders in

black pajamas." Quoted from Arthur Schlesinger Jr., "The Quagmire Papers," *New York Review of Books*, December 16, 1971, 41.

38. Ronald Steel, *The End of Alliance* (New York: Viking, 1964).

39. Richard N. Rosecrance, "Bipolarity, Multipolarity, and the Future," *Journal of Conflict Resolution* 10 (September 1966): 314–327.

40. Cited by Fouad Ajami in the *New York Times*, October 17, 2003, referring to comments in Kissinger's memoirs. It was more the threat to cut off oil than actual cutoffs that caused panic in the United States, since U.S. multinational oil companies were able to route needed oil supplies to the American economy. For this aspect of the crisis as well as other features, see Raymond Vernon, ed., *The Oil Crisis* (New York: Norton, 1976).

41. Stanley Hoffmann, "Choices," *Foreign Policy,* Fall 1973, 5.

42. See notes 8–12, Chapter 1.

43. Charles Krauthammer. "The Unipolar Moment," *Foreign Affairs* 70 (1991): 23–33.

44. Kennedy was quoted in Charles Krauthammer, "An American Foreign Policy for a Unipolar World" (speech given to the American Enterprise Institute, February 10, 2004). The Walt quote is from Stephen M. Walt, "American Primacy: Its Prospects and Pitfalls," *Naval War College Review,* Spring 2002, 1. Also see Stephen G. Brooks and William Wohlforth, "American Primacy in Perspective," *Foreign Affairs*, July–August 2002, 20–25.

45. Stephen M. Walt, *Taming American Power* (New York: Norton, 2005), 31.

46. Statistics on American power can be found in Walt, *Taming*, 31–39; the quotes are from page 38.

47. On soft power and the decline of American power, see Joseph S. Nye, *The Paradox of American Power* (New York: Oxford University Press, 2002); Nye, *Soft Power* (New York: PublicAffairs, 2004).

48. On potential rivals and the emergent international power structure, see Nye, *The Paradox of American Power*, 18–33; Charles A. Kupchan, *The End of the American Era* ((New York: Random House, 2003), 28–29; Niall Ferguson, *Colossus* (New York: Penguin, 2004).

49. Samuel P. Huntington, "The Lonely Superpower," *Foreign Affairs,* March–April 1999, 40–49.

50. Ferguson, *Colossus*, 288.

51. The unit veto system, in which each state has nuclear weapons, is one of the models discussed in Morton A. Kaplan, *System and Process in International Politics* (New York: Wiley, 1957).

52. Friedman, *Lexus*, 13.

53. Ferguson, *Colossus*, 295.

54. Nye, *Paradox*, 40.

55. See Joseph S. Nye, "U.S. Security Policy: Challenges for the 21st Century," *Agenda* 3 (July 1998): 20; Richard N. Haass, *The Reluctant Sheriff* (New York: Council on Foreign Affairs, 1997), 6.

56. Abba Eban, "The UN Idea Revisited," *Foreign Affairs,* September–October 1995, 50.

57. See Nicholas Kristof, "China Sees 'Market-Leninism' As Way to Future," *New York Times,* September 6, 1993.

58. Nye, *Paradox,* 18. On the "tragedy of the great powers," see note 12, Chapter 1.

59. The quotes are from Walt, *Taming American Power,* 111.

60. The poll was reported in Fareed Zakaria, "Why We Don't Get No Respect," *Newsweek,* July 10, 2006, 49. The quote by Mayor Ken Livingston is cited in Walt, *Taming American Power,* 69.

61. Dominique Moisi, cited in Richard N. Haass, *The Opportunity* (New York: PublicAffairs, 2005), 145.

62. www.news.com.au/story, accessed on September 17, 2006.

63. Kupchan, *End,* 51, citing the historian Paul Kennedy.

64. John G. Stoessinger, *The Might of Nations,* 7th ed. (New York: Random House, 1982), 5.

65. Samuel P. Huntingon, "The Clash of Civilizations," *Foreign Affairs,* Summer 1993, 48.

66. On this point, see Michael Mandelbaum, "David's Friend Goliath," *Foreign Policy,* January–February 2006, 33.

67. Haass, *Opportunity,* 6. Michael Mandelbaum, along with others, adds that for all its brusque, arrogant behavior, the United States is not perceived by any other would-be great power as a "predatory" state bent on their destruction. See Michael Mandelbaum, *The Case for Goliath* (New York: PublicAffairs, 2005).

68. The quote is from Daniel Bell in the Fall 1990 issue of *Dissent,* cited in Samuel P. Huntington, "Why International Primacy Matters," *International Security* 17 (Spring 1993): 81. Clausewitz famously defined war as "the continuation of policy by other means."

69. On the growing importance of NGOs in world politics, see Jessica Matthews, "Power Shift," *Foreign Affairs,* January–February 1997, 50–66. On the role of epistemic communities, see Peter Haas, *Saving the Mediterranean: The Politics of International Environmental Cooperation* (New York: Columbia University Press, 1990); Richard E. Benedick, *Ozone Diplomacy* (Cambridge, MA: Harvard University Press, 1998).

70. Gordon Smith and Moises Naim, *Altered States* (Ottawa: International Development Research Centre, 2000), 10; cited in Nye, *Paradox,* 74.

71. Raymond Vernon, *Sovereignty at Bay* (New York: Basic Books, 1971).

72. Charles Kindleberger, *American Business Abroad* (New Haven, CT: Yale University Press, 1969), 207.

73. George W. Ball, "The Promise of the Multinational Corporation," *Fortune,* June 1, 1967, 80.

74. See Joseph A. Camilleri and Jim Falk, *The End of Sovereignty?* (London: Edwin Elgar, 1992); Kenichi Ohmae, *The End of the Nation-State* (New York: Touchstone, 1996); Kimberly Weir, "The Waning State of Sovereignty," in John T.

Rourke, ed., *Taking Sides: Clashing Views in World Politics*, 12th ed. (New York: McGraw-Hill, 2007), 40–48. For a counterpoint, see Stephen D. Krasner, "Sovereignty," *Foreign Policy*, January–February 2001; Paul Kennedy, "The Future of the Nation-State," in *Preparing for the Twenty-First Century* (New York: Vintage, 1993), chap. 7. Also see the symposium on "What Future for the State?" in *Daedalus*, Spring 1995.

75. The first quote is from Nicholas Negroponte, cited in Keith Shimko, *International Relations: Perspectives and Controversies*, 2nd ed. (Boston: Houghton Mifflin, 2007), 215; the second is from Anthony Giddens, cited in Shimko, *International Relations*, 216.

76. Pearson and Rochester, *International Relations*, 114, 116.

CHAPTER 3: STATES AND FOREIGN POLICY

1. Ronald Steele, interview, *New York Review of Books*, March 13, 1963, 22.

2. Graham T. Allison, "Conceptual Models and the Cuban Missile Crisis," *American Political Science Review* 63 (September 1969): 689.

3. Hedley Bull, *The Anarchical Society* (New York: Columbia University Press, 1977), 8.

4. Boutros Boutros-Ghali, *An Agenda for Peace*, UN Doc. A/47/277 and S/24111, June 17, 1992, 5.

5. Geraldine Brooks, "It's UN Protocol: No Chair No Office for Tajikistan's Man," *Wall Street Journal*, September 20, 1993, 1.

6. The Reagan quote is from the *St. Louis Post-Dispatch*, June 14, 1981, 1. The George H. W. Bush quote is from *Time*, January 1, 1990, 20. The article about Clinton was in *Harpers*, January 1994, 57–64. The reference to George W. Bush is from Charles Kupchan, *The End of the American Era* (New York: Random House, 2003), 12. The McCain headline is from *Newsweek*, April 7, 2008, 27–29; the Obama headline, from *Weekly Standard*, March 27, 2008, 15.

7. Thomas A. Bailey, *A Diplomatic History of the American People*, 7th ed. (New York: Appleton-Century-Crofts, 1964), 1.

8. Henry A. Kissinger, "Bureaucracy and Policymaking: The Effects of Insiders and Outsiders on the Policy Process," in Morton H. Halperin and Arnold Kanter, eds., *Readings in American Foreign Policy: A Bureaucratic Perspective* (Boston: Little, Brown, 1973), 85; the essay originally appeared in a 1968 volume shortly before Kissinger entered the Nixon administration.

9. John G. Ruggie, "International Structure and International Transformation: Space, Time, and Method," in Ernst-Otto Czempiel and James N. Rosenau, eds., *Global Changes and Theoretical Challenges* (Lexington, MA: Lexington Books, 1989), 32.

10. Roger Hilsman, *To Move a Nation* (Garden City, NY: Doubleday, 1967), 5.

11. Margaret Hermann and Charles F. Hermann, "Who Makes Foreign Policy Decisions and How? An Empirical Inquiry," *International Studies Quarterly* 33 (December 1989): 361–387.

12. K. J. Holsti, *International Politics: A Framework for Analysis*, 7th ed. (Englewood Cliffs, NJ: Prentice-Hall, 1995), 267, based on testimony from U.S. State Department officials.

13. This definition of crisis decision making draws on the pioneering work of Charles F. Hermann, ed., *International Crises: Insights from Behavioral Research* (New York: Free Press, 1972); Hermann, "International Crisis As A Situational Variable," in James N. Rosenau, ed., *International Politics and Foreign Policy*, rev. ed. (New York: Free Press, 1969), 409–421.

14. See the work of Michael Brecher and Jonathan Wilkenfeld, for example, Brecher, *Crisis in World Politics: Theory and Reality* (New York: Pergamon, 1993).

15. Ian Clark and Christian Reus-Smit, "Preface," *International Politics* 44 (March-May 2007): 153.

16. Reported in Charles W. Kegley Jr., *World Politics: Trend and Transformation*, 12th ed. (Belmont, CA: Wadsworth, 2009), 490, based on the work of Jonathan Wilkenfeld.

17. See the discussion in Frederic S. Pearson and J. Martin Rochester, *International Relations: The Global Condition in the Twenty-First Century*, 4th ed. (New York: McGraw-Hill, 1998), 222–225.

18. The phrase appeared in Jefferson's correspondence with George Rogers Clark, December 25, 1780; cited in Niall Ferguson, *Colossus* (New York: Penguin, 2004), 2.

19. Robert Osgood, *Ideals and Self-Interest in America's Foreign Relations* (Chicago: University of Chicago Press, 1953), 18.

20. Realist criticism of "American exceptionalism" goes back a long time; see George F. Kennan, *American Diplomacy* (Chicago: University of Chicago Press, 1951). On the history of America's missionary tendencies, see Robert Kagan, *Dangerous Nation* (New York: Knopf, 2006).

21. Deborah J. Gerner, "Foreign Policy Analysis: Exhilarating Eclecticism, Intriguing Enigmas," *International Studies Notes*, Winter 1992, 4.

22. Arnold Wolfers, *Discord and Collaboration* (Baltimore: Johns Hopkins University Press, 1962), 37.

23. Democritus of Abder; cited in Bruce Russett, Harvey Starr, and David Kinsella, *World Politics: The Menu for Choice*, 8th ed. (Belmont, CA: Wadsworth, 2006), 1.

24. Graham T. Allison, *Essence of Decision: Explaining the Cuban Missile Crisis* (Boston: Little, Brown, 1971).

25. Wolfers, *Discord*, 19.

26. Allison, *Essence*, 4–5.

27. Morton H. Halperin, *Bureaucratic Politics and Foreign Policy* (Washington, D.C.: Brookings Institution, 1974), ix.

28. Theodore Sorenson, *Kennedy* (New York: Harper & Row, 1965), 675.

29. Kenneth N. Waltz, *Man, the State, and War* (New York: Columbia University Press, 1959). Also see J. David Singer, "The Level-of-Analysis Problem in

International Relations," in Klaus Knorr and Sidney Verba, eds., *The International System: Theoretical Essays* (Princeton, NJ: Princeton University Press, 1961), 77–92.

30. G. John Ikenberry, ed., *American Foreign Policy: Theoretical Essays*, 5th ed. (New York: Longman, 2005), 3.

31. See James N. Rosenau, *The Scientific Study of Foreign Policy,* rev. ed. (London: Pinter, 1980), chap. 6.

32. On the reciprocity of conflictual or cooperative behavior, see, for example, Lewis Richardson, *Arms and Insecurity* (Pittsburgh: Boxwood, 1960); Robert Axelrod, *The Evolution of Cooperation* (New York: Basic Books, 1984); David W. Larson, "The Psychology of Reciprocity in International Relations," *Negotiation Journal* 4 (1988): 281–301.

33. See Will H. Moore and David J. Lanoue, "Domestic Politics and U.S. Foreign Policy: A Study of Cold War Conflict Behavior," *Journal of Politics* 65 (2003): 376–397; Joshua S. Goldstein, "Reciprocity in Superpower Relations: An Empirical Analysis," *International Studies Quarterly* 35 (June 1991): 195–209; Matthew Evangelista, *Innovation and the Arms Race* (Ithaca, NY: Cornell University Press, 1988), which argues that systemic determinants account for some superpower behavior but not all.

34. Douglas M. Gibler, "Bordering on Peace: Democracy, Territorial Issues, and Conflict," *International Studies Quarterly* 51 (September 2007): 509–532.

35. Frank M. Russell, *Theories of International Relations* (New York: Appleton-Century-Crofts, 1936), 45.

36. The Washington quote is from Daniel Smith, ed., *Major Problems in American Diplomatic History: Documents and Readings* (Boston: D.C. Heath, 1964), 1:104. The French ambassador, Jules Jusseraud, is cited in Stephen M. Walt, *Taming American Power* (New York: Norton, 2005), 39. The Hoover quote is from David A. Lake, *Entangling Relations* (Princeton, NJ: Princeton University Press, 1999), 3.

37. See Bruce Russett and John Oneal, *Triangulating Peace* (New York: Norton, 2001), chap. 4; Mark J. Gasiorowski, "Economic Interdependence and International Conflict: Some Cross-National Evidence," *International Studies Quarterly* 30 (March 1986): 23–38.

38. Russett and Oneal, *Triangulating*, 125. On the democratic peace—the general absence of war between democracies—see Michael W. Doyle, *Ways of War and Peace* (New York: Norton, 1997).

39. Russett and Oneal, *Triangulating*, 87.

40. On polarity, see Kenneth N. Waltz, *Theory of International Politics* (Reading, MA: Addison-Wesley, 1979), 97–99.

41. David R. Rapkin and William R. Thompson with Jon A. Christopherson, "Bipolarity and Bipolarization in the Cold War Era: Conceptualization, Measurement, and Validation," *Journal of Conflict Resolution* 23 (June 1979): 263.

42. On the balance of power, see Edward V. Gulick, *Europe's Classical Balance of Power* (Ithaca, NY: Cornell University Press, 1955); John Vasquez and Colin Elman, eds., *Realism and the Balancing of Power: A New Debate* (Englewood Cliffs,

NJ: Prentice-Hall, 2003). On bandwagoning, see Randall L. Schweller, "Bandwagoning for Profit: Bringing the Revisonist State Back In," *International Security* 19 (Summer 1994): 72–107.

43. On the sometimes confused meaning of "balance of power," see Ernst B. Haas, "The Balance of Power: Prescription, Concept, or Propaganda?" *World Politics* 5 (July 1953): 442–477. A. F. Pollard, in "The Balance of Power," *Journal of the British Institute of International Affairs* 2 (1923): 58, said that the term "may mean almost anything; and it is used not only in different senses by different people, or in different senses by the same people at different times, but in different senses by the same person at the same time."

44. Among the leading hegemonic realists are A. F. K. Organski and Jacek Kugler, *The War Ledger* (Chicago: University of Chicago Press, 1980); Robert Gilpin, *War and Change in World Politics* (New York: Cambridge University Press, 1981).

45. See Michael Mandelbaum, *The Case for Goliath* (New York: PublicAffairs, 2005); chap. 2. 66–67

46. Benjamin Miller, *States, Nations, and the Great Powers: The Source of Regional War and Peace* (Cambridge: Cambridge University Press, 2008).

47. Indexes of national power, based on material capabilities, are treated in Richard L. Merritt and Dina A. Zinnes, "Alternative Indices of National Power," in Richard J. Stoll and Michael D. Ward, eds., *Power in World Politics* (Boulder, CO: Lynne Rienner, 1989); also see Ashley J. Tellis et al., *Measuring National Power in the Postindustrial Age* (Santa Monica, CA: RAND, 2000) and measurements of power found in the Correlates of War (COW) Project writings produced by J. David Singer and colleagues at the University of Michigan.

48. Quincy Wright, *A Study of War* (Chicago: University of Chicago Press, 1942); Melvin Small and J. David Singer, "The War-Proneness of Democratic Regimes, 1816–1965," *Jerusalem Journal of International Relations* 1 (1976): 50–69.

49. See Zeev Maoz and Nasrin Abdolali, "Regime Types and International Conflict, 1816–1976," *Journal of Conflict Resolution* 33 (1989): 3–35; also see Joe D. Hagan, "Domestic Political Systems and War Proneness," *Mershon International Studies Review* 38 (October 1994): 183–207.

50. Bruce Bueno de Mesquita states that "statistical patterns have uncovered a law of nature." See de Mesquita, "Domestic Politics and International Relations," *International Studies Quarterly* 46 (March 2002): 5. See the works cited in note 38; Zeev Maoz, "The Controversy Over the Democratic Peace," *International Security* 22 (1997): 162–198.

51. See Bruce Bueno de Mesquita, *Principles of International Politics: People's Power, Preferences, and Perceptions*, 2nd ed. (Washington, D.C.: CQ Press, 2003); Raymond Dacey and Lisa J. Carlson, "Traditional Decision Analysis and the Poliheuristic Theory of Foreign Policy Decision Making," *Journal of Conflict Resolution* 48 (2004): 38–55.

52. On the influence of domestic politics on foreign policy, see Bueno de Mesquita, "Domestic Politics"; Peter Gourevitch, "Domestic Politics and Inter-

national Relations," in Walter Carlsnaes et al., eds., *Handbook of International Politics* (Thousand Oaks, CA: Sage, 2002), 309–328. In the case of the United States, see Charles W. Ostrom and Brian L. Job, "The President and the Political Use of Force," *American Political Science Review* 80 (1986): 541–566; Bruce W. Jentelson, *American Foreign Policy: The Dynamics of Choice in the 21st Century*, 3rd ed. (New York: Norton, 2007), chap. 2.

53. Kiron K. Skinner, Serhiy Kudelia, Bruce Bueno de Mesquita, and Condoleezza Rice, "Politics Starts at the Water's Edge," *New York Times*, September 15, 2007.

54. Henry A. Kissinger, "America at the Apex," *National Interest,* Summer 2001): 15. Also see Kissinger, "Domestic Structure and Foreign Policy," *Daedalus* 95 (1966): 503–529.

55. On bureaucratic politics and the Cuban missile crisis, see Allison, *Essence of Decision*; Timothy J. McKeown, "Plans and Routines: Bureaucratic Bargaining and the Cuban Missile Crisis," *Journal of Politics* 63 (2001): 1163–1191.

56. Deborah Shapley, "Technological Creep and the Arms Race: ICBM Problem a Sleeper," *Science*, September 22, 1978, 105. On the reasons behind U.S. weapons procurement policies during the Cold War, see James Kurth, "Why We Buy the Weapons We Do," *Foreign Policy* 11 (Summer 1973): 33–56; Matthew Evangelista, "Why the Soviets Buy the Weapons They Do," *World Politics* 36 (July 1984): 597–618. On the role of bureaucratic politics generally in American foreign policymaking, including defense budgets, see Halperin and Kanter, *Readings*.

57. "U.S. Accuses Soviets of Developing 4 New Long Range Missiles," *St. Louis Post-Dispatch*, October 18, 1990.

58. Transcript of joint press conference, October 21, 2001, on the White House website at www.whitehouse.gov.

59. The remark has been attributed to James Byrnes, secretary of state under President Truman.

60. Cited in David V. Edwards, *The American Political Experience* (Englewood Cliffs, NJ: Prentice-Hall, 1979), 223.

61. Edward L. Katzenbach, "The Horse Cavalry in the Twentieth Century," *Public Policy* 8 (1958): 120–149.

62. James L. Sundquist, *The Decline and Resurgence of Congress* (Washington, D.C.: Brookings Institution, 1981), 452.

63. Abram Chayes and Antonia Chayes, "On Compliance," *International Organization* 47 (Spring 1993): 180–181.

64. Robert Putnam, "Diplomacy and Domestic Politics: The Logic of Two-Level Games," *International Organization* 42 (Summer 1988): 427–460.

65. On the Jewish lobby, see John Mearsheimer and Stephen Walt, "The Israel Lobby," *London Review of Books,* March 23, 2006.

66. Lawrence R. Jacobs and Benjamin I. Page, "Business Versus Public Influence in U.S. Foreign Policy," in G. John Ikenberry, ed., *American Foreign Policy: Theoretical Essays*, 5th ed. (New York: Pearson, 2005), 376.

67. On the influence of epistemic communities and other elite opinion, compared with public opinion, see Jacobs and Page, "Business," 357–383. On interest groups generally, see David Skidmore and Valerie M. Hudson, eds., *The Limits of State Authority: Societal Groups and Foreign Policy Formation* (Boulder, CO: Westview, 1992).

68. Joseph S. Nye, *The Paradox of American Power* (New York: Oxford University Press, 2002), 136.

69. For the view that public opinion does not have much influence on foreign policy, see Gabriel A. Almond, *The American People and Foreign Policy* (New York: Praeger, 1960). For another view, see Benjamin Page and Robert Y. Shapiro, *The Rational Public: Fifty Years of Trends in American Policy Preferences* (Chicago: University of Chicago Press, 1992); Thomas Knecht and M. Stephen Weatherford, "Public Opinion and Foreign Policy: The Stages of Presidential Decisionmaking," *International Studies Quarterly* 50 (September 2006): 705–727.

70. On the rally-round-the-flag effect, see Russett, Starr, and Kinsella, *World Politics*, 154–160. Also see Philip J. Powlick and Andrew Z. Katz, "Defining the American Public Opinion/Foreign Policy Nexus," *Mershon International Studies Review* 42 (May 1998): 29–61; John E. Mueller, *War, Presidents, and Public Opinion* (New York: Wiley, 1973).

71. Russett, Starr, and Kinsella, *World Politics*, 157.

72. See Thomas Dye, *Politics in America*, 5th ed. (Upper Saddle River, NJ: Prentice-Hall, 2003), 6–7.

73. On the link between domestic political instability and war, see Jack Levy, "The Diversionary Theory of War: A Critique," in Manus L. Midlarsky, ed., *Handbook of War Studies* (Boston: Unwin Hyman, 1989), 259–288; T. Clifton Morgan and Kenneth N. Bickers, "Domestic Discontent and the External Use of Force," *Journal of Conflict Resolution* 36 (1992): 25–52.

74. Bruce Bueno de Mesquita and Randolph M. Siverson, "War and the Survival of Political Leaders: A Comparative Study of Regime Types and Political Accountability," *American Political Science Review* 89 (December 1995): 841.

75. David A. Lake, "Powerful Pacifists: Democratic States and War," *American Political Science Review* 86 (March 1992): 30–31.

76. See Eytan Gilboa, "Global Television News and Foreign Policy: Debating the CNN Effect," *International Studies Perspectives* 6 (August 2005): 325–341.

77. On the role of capitalist elites driving American foreign policy in an expansionist, often war-prone direction, see William Appleman Williams, *The Roots of the Modern American Empire* (New York: Vintage, 1969); Gabriel Kolko, *The Roots of American Foreign Policy* (Boston: Beacon, 1969); Richard J. Barnet, *Roots of War* (Baltimore: Penguin, 1973).

78. On the military-industrial complex, see C. Wright Mills, *The Power Elite* (New York: Oxford University Press, 1956); on mixed evidence regarding its influence, see Skidmore and Hudson, *Limits*, 36–38.

79. Harold K. Jacobson, William M. Reisinger, and Todd Mathers, "National Entanglements in International Governmental Organizations," *American Political Science Review* 80 (March 1986): 148–149.

80. Robert Kagan, "Against the Myth of American Innocence: Cowboy Nation," *New Republic*, October 23, 2006, 20–22.

81. Data on ethnic divisions within each country can be found in the annual editions of the *CIA World Factbook*. Also see Tanja Ellingsen, "Colorful Community or Ethnic Witches' Brew? Multiethnicity and Domestic Conflict During and After the Cold War," *Journal of Conflict Resolution* 44 (2000): 228–249; and the Minorities at Risk website maintained by the University of Maryland.

82. *St. Louis Post-Dispatch*, October 15, 1993.

83. Stated in the beginning of *The Eighteenth Brumaire of Louis Bonaparte*, cited in Robert Tucker, ed., *The Marx-Engels Reader*, 2nd ed. (New York: Norton, 1978), 595.

84. E. D. Hirsch, *The New Dictionary of Cultural Literacy*, 2nd ed. (Boston: Houghton Mifflin, 2002).

85. Niall Ferguson, "Review of Ian Kershaw's *Fateful Choices*," *Times Literary Supplement*, September 19, 2007.

86. A pioneering study that focused on the decision-making process was Richard C. Snyder, H. W. Bruck, and Burton Sapin, *Foreign Policy Decision-Making: An Approach to the Study of International Politics* (New York: Free Press, 1962). Other studies examining psychological variables include Irving Janis, *Groupthink*, 2nd ed. (Boston: Houghton Mifflin, 1982); Robert Jervis, *Perception and Misperception in International Politics* (Princeton, NJ: Princeton University Press, 1976); David G. Winter, "Personality and Political Behavior," in D. O. Sears et al., eds., *Oxford Handbook of Political Psychology* (Oxford: Oxford University Press, 2003); Margaret G. Hermann, "Effects of Personal Characteristics of Political Leaders on Foreign Policy," in Maurice A. East et al., eds., *Why Nations Act* (Beverly Hills: Sage, 1978), 49–68.

87. Harold and Margaret Sprout, *Man-Milieu Relationship Hypotheses in the Context of International Politics*, research monograph, Center for International Studies, Princeton University, 1956.

88. Kenneth Boulding, "National Images and International Systems," *Journal of Conflict Resolution* 3 (June 1959): 120.

89. Robert Jervis, "Hypotheses on Misperception," *World Politics* 20 (April 1968): 475–476; Jervis, *Perception*, pt. 3.

90. Boulding, "National Images," 130.

91. See note 33; William A. Gamson and Andre Modigliani, *Untangling the Cold War* (Boston: Little, Brown, 1971), 108.

92. Don Munton and David Welch, *The Cuban Missile Crisis: A Concise History* (New York: Oxford University Press, 2007), 4.

93. Ernest R. May, *"Lessons" of the Past: The Use and Misuse of History in American Foreign Policy* (New York: Oxford University Press, 1973); Deborah W. Larson,

Origins of Containment: A Psychological Explanation (Princeton, NJ: Princeton University Press, 1985).

94. These quotes are from Steve A. Yetiv, *Explaining Foreign Policy: U.S. Decision-Making and the Persian Gulf War* (Baltimore: Johns Hopkins University Press, 2004), 62–63.

95. Ole Holsti, "The Belief System and National Images," *Journal of Conflict Resolution* 6 (September 1962): 244–252.

96. Les Aspin, "Misreading Intelligence," *Foreign Policy*, Summer 1981, 168.

97. Morris Blachman, "The Stupidity of Intelligence," in Halperin and Kanter, *Readings*, 328–329.

98. Janis, *Groupthink*.

99. On the Pearl Harbor and Bay of Pigs cases, see Janis, *Groupthink*.

100. The reference to the war council is found in the *New York Times*, September 23, 2001. The Rice quote is from an interview with Wolf Blitzer on CNN on September 8, 2002. On the members of the war council, see J. Martin Rochester, *U.S. Foreign Policy in the Twenty-First Century: Gulliver's Travails* (Boulder, CO: Westview, 2008), 46–48.

101. Reported in Bob Woodward, *Plan of Attack* (New York: Simon & Schuster, 2004).

102. Cited in *Newsweek*, July 19, 2004, 38.

103. www.sfgate.com/cgi-bin/article.cgi?file=/c/a/2004.

104. Nikita Khrushchev, special report to the twentieth Congress of the Communist Party of the Soviet Union, February 24, 1956. See Raymond Birt, "Personality and Foreign Policy: The Case of Stalin," *Political Psychology* 14 (December 1993): 607–625.

105. See Alexander L. George and Juliette George, *Woodrow Wilson and Colonel House* (New York: John Day, 1956). For discussion of the role of personality, see Lloyd S. Etheredge, "Personality Effects on American Foreign Policy 1898–1968: A Test of Interpersonal Generalization Theory," *American Political Science Review* 72 (June 1978): 435–436; Etheredge, *A World of Men: The Private Sources of American Foreign Policy* (Cambridge: MIT Press, 1979).

106. James D. Barber, *Presidential Character*, 3rd ed. (Englewood Cliffs, NJ: Prentice-Hall, 1985).

107. Stephen Benedict Dyson, "Personality and Foreign Policy: Tony Blair's Iraq Decisions," *Foreign Policy Analysis* 2 (2006): 289.

108. Phillip Stephens, *Tony Blair: The Making of a World Leader* (New York: Viking, 2004), 234.

109. Stanley Hoffmann, *Gulliver Unbound* (Lanham, MD: Rowman & Littlefield, 2004), 55.

110. Evan Thomas, "The 12-Year Itch," *Newsweek*, March 31, 2003.

111. See Gordon Hilton et al., *Leaders Under Stress: A Psychophysiological Analysis of International Crises* (Durham, NC: Duke University Press, 1985); Thomas Wiegele, *Biopolitics* (Boulder, CO: Westview, 1979).

112. Robert Ferrell, *The Dying President: Franklin D. Roosevelt, 1944–1945* (Columbia: University of Missouri Press, 1998), xi.

113. Richard Reeves, "Kennedy's Private Ills," *New York Times*, December 21, 2002.

114. Robert Dallek, "The Medical Ordeals of JFK," *Atlantic*, December 2002.

115. See the citations in note 51, Chapter 1; Joshua S. Goldstein, *War and Gender* (Cambridge: Cambridge University Press, 2001).

116. Francis Fukuyama, "Women and the Evolution of World Politics," *Foreign Affairs*, September–October 1998, 27; for a counterpoint, see "Fukuyama's Follies: So What If Women Ruled the World," *Foreign Affairs*, January–February 1999, 118–129.

117. Mary Caprioli, "The Myth of Women's Pacifism," in John T. Rourke, ed., *Taking Sides: World Politics*, 11th ed. (New York: McGraw-Hill, 2004), 245.

118. V. Spike Peterson and Anne Sisson Runyan, *Global Gender Issues*, 2nd ed. (Boulder, CO: Westview, 1999), 73.

119. See Peterson and Runyan, *Global*, chap. 5.

120. Herbert A. Simon, *Models of Man* (New York: Wiley, 1957).

121. See Jack S. Levy, "Prospect Theory, Rational Choice, and International Relations," *International Studies Quarterly* 41 (March 1997): 87–112.

122. Janis, *Groupthink*, 132.

CHAPTER 4: DIPLOMACY, BARGAINING, AND STATECRAFT

1. Paul Gore-Booth, *With Great Truth and Respect* (London: Constable, 1974), 15.

2. Charles W. Kegley Jr., *World Politics: Trend and Transformation*, 12th ed. (Belmont, CA: Wadsworth, 2008), 429.

3. The first study is Patrick James, Eric Solberg, and Murray Wolfson, "An Identified Systemic Test of the Democracy-Peace Nexus" (paper presented at the annual meeting of the Peace Science Society [International], Columbus, Ohio, October 1995), 9. The second study is J. David Singer, "Accounting for International War: The State of the Discipline," *Annual Review of Sociology* 6 (1960): 353. The third study is Zeev Maoz, "Pacificsm and Fightaholism in International Politics: A Structural History of National and Dyadic Conflict, 1816–1992," *International Studies Review* 6 (December 2004): 110. Further data on the incidence of war are presented in Chapter 5.

4. Sir Harold Nicolson, *Diplomacy* (New York: Oxford University Press, 1964), 4–5.

5. Thomas C. Schelling, *Arms and Influence* (New Haven, CT: Yale University Press, 1966), chap. 1.

6. See Hussein Agha et al., *Track II Diplomacy: Lessons from the Middle East* (Cambridge, MA: MIT Press, 2003).

7. Nicolson, *Diplomacy*, 5–6.

8. Sir Harold Nicolson, *The Evolution of Diplomacy* (London: Constable, 1956), 50–51.

9. Here and elsewhere in this chapter I draw on Frederic S. Pearson and J. Martin Rochester, *International Relations: The Global Condition in the Twenty-First Century*, 4th ed. (New York: McGraw-Hill, 1998), chap. 7.

10. See note 5 in Chapter 3; "Landlords Around the UN Find Diplomacy Doesn't Pay," *New York Times*, December 25, 1999.

11. For data on embassies, see Joel Krieger, ed., *Globalization and State Power* (New York: Longman, 2005), 36; David Held et al., *Global Transformations* (Stanford, CA: Stanford University Press, 1999), 53.

12. Lincoln P. Bloomfield, *The Foreign Policy Process: A Modern Primer* (Englewood Cliffs, NJ: Prentice-Hall, 1982), 144.

13. *Washington Post*, April 13, 1990, A7.

14. John T. Rourke, *International Politics on the World Stage*, 12th ed. (New York: McGraw-Hill, 2008), 264.

15. Abba Eban, "The UN Idea Revisited," *Foreign Affairs*, September–October 1995, 42.

16. Eban, "UN Idea," 48. The "open covenants secretly arrived at" phrase is attributed to Canadian prime minister Lester Pearson.

17. Patrick J. McGowan and Howard B. Shapiro, *The Comparative Study of Foreign Policy* (Beverly Hills, CA: Sage, 1973), 140.

18. Statistics on NGOs are from Jacqueline V. Switzer, *Environmental Politics: Domestic and Global Dimensions* (New York: St. Martin's, 1994), xv; UNEP, *World Resources 2002–2004* (New York: Oxford University Press, 2004), 166.

19. Derrick V. Frazier and William J. Dixon, "Third-Party Intermediaries and Negotiated Settlements, 1946–2000," *International Interactions* 32 (December 2006): 385–408.

20. On the use of nonverbal "signaling," see Raymond Cohen, *Theatre of Power: The Art of Diplomatic Signalling* (New York: Longman, 1987).

21. The quote is attributed to Yuri Andropov. The source is Abraham Rabinovich, *The Yom Kippur War* (New York: Schocken, 2005), 484.

22. Robert D. Putnam, "Diplomacy and Domestic Politics: The Logic of Two-Level Games," *International Organization* 42 (Summer 1988): 434. Also see Peter B. Evans, Harold K. Jacobson, and Robert D. Putnam, eds., *Double-Edged Diplomacy: International Bargaining and Domestic Politics* (Berkeley: University of California Press, 1993); Robert O. Keohane and Helen V. Milner, eds., *Internationalization and Domestic Politics* (Cambridge: Cambridge University Press, 1996).

23. Cited in ibid., 433.

24. Cited in Putnam, "Diplomacy and Domestic Politics," 433.

25. James Caporaso, Maria Green Cowles, and Thomas Risse, *Europeanization and Domestic Structural Change* (Ithaca, NY: Cornell University Press, 2000).

26. Samuel Lucas McMillan, "Subnational Foreign Policy Actors: How and Why Governors Participate in U.S. Foreign Policy," *Foreign Policy Analysis* 4 (July 2008): 234.

27. See Pearson and Rochester, *International Relations*, 267.

28. The definition is attributed to Sir Henry Wooten, an ambassador of King James I of England in the seventeenth century, cited in Arthur Lall, *Modern International Negotiation* (New York: University Press, 1966), 151.

29. Cited in David J. Dallin, *Soviet Foreign Policy After Stalin* (Philadelphia: Lippincott, 1961), 9.

30. Nicolson, *Diplomacy*, 58.

31. See note 47, in Chapter 2.

32. The quote is from William F.G. Mastenbroek, "Development of Negotiating Skills," in Victor A. Kremenyuk, ed., *International Negotiation* (San Francisco: Jossey-Bass, 1991), 382. For the newspaper headline about the role played by wine in the 1993 Oslo Accords, see note 82 in Chapter 3.

33. Roger Fisher, *International Conflict for Beginners* (New York: Harper & Row, 1969), 11.

34. Fisher, *International Conflict*, 15–19. Also see Roger Fisher et al., *Beyond Machiavelli* (Cambridge, MA: Harvard University Press, 1994), 96–97.

35. Fisher, *International Conflict*, 27–29, 47.

36. Fisher, *International Conflict*, 90, 94–95.

37. Formal models of bargaining are discussed in Howard Raiffa, *The Art and Science of Negotiation* (Cambridge, MA: Harvard University Press, 1982). Also see Glenn H. Snyder and Paul Diesing, *Conflict Among Nations* (Princeton, NJ: Princeton University Press, 1977), 69.

38. See James D. Morrow, *Game Theory for Political Scientists* (Princeton, NJ: Princeton University Press, 1994); Steven Brams, *Superpower Games: Applying Game Theory to Superpower Conflict* (New Haven, CT: Yale University Press, 1985).

39. See Robert Axelrod, *The Evolution of Cooperation* (New York: Basic Books, 1984). Also see Duncan Snidal, "Coordination vs. Prisoner's Dilemma: Implications for International Cooperation and Regimes," *American Political Science Review* 79 (1985): 923–942.

40. See Thomas C. Schelling, *The Strategy of Conflict* (Cambridge, MA: Harvard University Press, 1980); Schelling, *Arms and Influence*.

41. *New York Times*, February 24, 1998.

42. Fisher, *International Conflict*, 9.

43. Henry A. Kissinger, *American Foreign Policy* (New York: Norton, 1974), 61.

44. *Wall Street Journal*, October 13, 2006.

45. Statement from Graham Allison of Harvard University in a public lecture at the University of Missouri–St. Louis on April 7, 2005.

46. See "Iran's Nuclear Threat," editorial, *New York Times*, October 22, 2004.

47. "Europeans Back Bush on Iran Nuclear Curbs," *New York Times*, June 11, 2008.

48. "Threatening Iran," editorial, *New York Times*, June 10, 2008.

49. Schelling, *Arms and Influence*, chap. 2.

50. Alexander George, interview, *U.S. Institute of Peace Journal*, October 1991, 1. Also see George et al., *The Limits of Coercive Diplomacy* (Boston: Little, Brown,

1971); Gordon A. Craig and Alexander George, *Force and Statecraft* (New York: Oxford University Press, 1995), chap. 15.

51. The decline was reported in *Patterns of Global Terrorism, 1998* (Washington, D.C.: U.S. Department of State, 1999), 91.

52. Bruce M. Russett, "The Calculus of Deterrence," *Journal of Conflict Resolution* 7 (June 1963): 97–109; Paul Huth and Bruce M. Russett, "What Makes Deterrence Work?" *World Politics* 36 (July 1984): 496–526.

53. Richard Pipes, "Why the Soviet Union Thinks It Could Fight and Win a Nuclear War," *Commentary* 64 (July 1977).

54. See David A. Baldwin, *Economic Statecraft* (Princeton, NJ: Princeton University Press, 1985); Jean-Marc Blanchard et al., eds., *Power and the Purse: Economic Statecraft, Interdependence, and National Security* (London: Frank Cass, 2000).

55. Klaus N. Knorr, "International Economic Leverage and Its Uses," in Klaus N. Knorr and Frank N. Trager, eds., *Economic Issues and National Security* (Lawrence: Regents Press of Kansas, 1977), 103.

56. Charles Kindleberger, *Power and Money* (New York: Basic Books, 1970), 97.

57. Gary C. Hufbauer and Jeffrey J. Schott, *Economic Sanctions in Support of Foreign Policy Goals* (Washington, D.C.: Institute for International Economics, 1983).

58. Gary C. Hufbauer, Jeffrey J. Schott, and Kimberly Ann Elliott, *Economic Sanctions Reconsidered*, 2nd ed. (Washington, D.C.: Institute for International Economics, 1990), 49–73.

59. Peter Wallensteen, "Characteristics of Economic Sanctions," *Journal of Conflict Resolution* 5 (1968): 248–267.

60. Klaus N. Knorr, *The Power of Nations* (New York: Basic Books, 1975).

61. Kimberly Ann Elliott and Barbara I. Oegg, "Economic Sanctions Reconsidered—Again" (paper presented at the International Studies Association annual meeting, New Orleans, March 23–25, 2002).

62. Margaret P. Doxey, *Economic Sanctions and International Enforcement* (New York: Oxford University Press, 1971), 139.

63. For a more mixed view of sanctions, both military and economic, see David Cortright and George A. Lopez, *Sanctions and the Search for Security* (Boulder, CO: Lynne Rienner, 2002).

64. *Washington Times*, January 18, 2008, 1.

65. The quote belongs to Egyptian vice president Zakaria Mohieddin, speaking to the Egyptian War College in 1962; cited in Miles Copeland, *The Game of Nations* (London: Weidenfeld & Nicolson, 1969), 9. I am indebted to Frederic Pearson for calling my attention to this passage.

CHAPTER 5: WAR AND THE USE OF ARMED FORCE

1. Chris Hedges, "What Every Person Should Know About War," *New York Times*, July 6, 2003.

2. The quote is based on the findings of Norman Cousins and is reported in Francis A. Beer, *Peace Against War* (San Francisco: Freeman, 1981), 20.

3. John T. Rourke, *International Politics on the World Stage*, 12th ed. (New York: McGraw-Hill, 2008), 306.

4. See note 17 in Chapter 2.

5. See, for example, James Lee Ray, "The Abolition of Slavery and the End of International War," *International Organization* 43 (Summer 1989): 405–440; John Mueller, *Retreat from Doomsday: The Obsolescence of Major War* (New York: Basic Books, 1989); Mueller, *The Remnants of War* (Ithaca, NY: Cornell University Press, 2004); Mark W. Zacher, "The Decaying Pillars of the Westphalian Temple: Implications for International Order and Governance," in James N. Rosenau and Ernst-Otto Czempiel, eds., *Governance Without Government* (Cambridge: Cambridge University Press, 1992), 58–100.

6. Philip Bobbitt, *The Shield of Achilles* (New York: Anchor, 2002), xxi.

7. K. J. Holsti, *Peace and War: Armed Conflicts and International Order, 1648–1989* (Cambridge: Cambridge University Press, 1989). Also see Paul D. Senese and John A. Vasquez, "Assessing the Steps to War," *British Journal of Political Science* 35 (October 2005): 607–634.

8. John Donnelly, "Small Wars, Big Changes," *CQ Weekly*, January 28, 2008, 252. U.S. secretary of defense Robert Gates has said, "I have noticed too much of a tendency toward what might be called Next War-itis–the propensity . . . to be in favor of what might be needed in a future conflict [say, a great-power war between the United States and China or a war against states such as North Korea or Iran]. But . . . the Pentagon must concentrate on building a military that can defeat the current enemies: smaller, terrorist groups and militias waging irregular warfare." Quoted in *Philadelphia Inquirer*, May 14, 2008.

9. Cited in George Will, "Defense Cuts Reflect Liberals' Blind Optimism in Lasting Peace," *St. Louis Post-Dispatch*, July 17, 1995.

10. Melvin Small and J. David Singer, "Patterns in International Warfare, 1816–1980," in *International War: An Anthology and Study Guide* (Homewood, IL: Dorsey, 1985). Also see Meredith Reid Sarkees, "The Correlates of War Data: An Update to 1997," *Conflict Management and Peace Science* 18, no. 1 (2000): 123–144.

11. Holsti, *Peace*.

12. Bruce Russett, Harvey Starr, and David Kinsella, *World Politics: The Menu for Choice*, 8th ed. (Belmont, CA: Wadsworth, 2006), 201.

13. Jack S. Levy and T. Clifton Morgan, "The Frequency and Seriousness of International War: An Inverse Relationship," *Journal of Conflict Resolution* 28 (December 1984): 742.

14. Charles W. Kegley Jr., *World Politics: Trend and Transformation*, 12th ed. (Belmont, CA: Wadsworth, 2009), 378.

15. Lotta Harbom and Peter Wallensteen, "Armed Conflict: 1989–2006," *Journal of Peace Research* 44 (2007): 624.

16. Jack S. Levy, "War and Peace," in Walter Carlsnaes et al., eds., *Handbook of International Relations* (Thousand Oaks, CA: Sage, 2002), 351. On the long peace, see John L. Gaddis, *The Long Peace* (New York: Oxford University Press, 1987); Charles Kegley Jr., ed., *The Long Postwar Peace* (New York: HarperCollins, 1991).

17. Ray, "Abolition," argues that the "end of war" has more to do with a new internalization of norms than with the mere existence of destructive weaponry.

18. Mueller, *Retreat from Doomsday*, 78. Also see Max Singer and Aaron Wildavsky, *The Real World Order: Zones of Peace/Zones of Turmoil* (Chatham, NJ: Chatham House, 1993).

19. Thomas L. Friedman, *The Lexus and the Olive Tree* (New York: Farrar, Straus, Giroux, 1999), 196.

20. Thomas L. Friedman, "Was Kosovo World War III?" *New York Times*, July 2, 1999.

21. Thomas L. Friedman, *The World Is Flat* (New York: Farrar, Straus, Giroux, 2005), chap. 14.

22. Richard Holbrooke, interview, C-SPAN, September 28, 2002.

23. See Barry M. Blechman and Stephen S. Kaplan, *Force Without War: U.S. Armed Forces as a Political Instrument* (Washington, D.C.: Brookings Institution, 1979); Kaplan, *Diplomacy of Power: Soviet Armed Forces as a Political Instrument* (Washington, D.C.: Brookings Institution, 1981). Also Faten Ghosn, Glenn Palmer, and Stuart Bremer, "The MID3 Data Set, 1993–2001," *Conflict Management and Peace Science* 21 (2004): 133–154.

24. Blechman and Kaplan, *Force*; Kaplan, *Diplomacy*.

25. "Whack a mole" was the name given to the policy by an adviser in the Clinton White House: "Saddam would stick his head up, and we'd whack him." Reported by Evan Thomas in "The 12-Year Itch," *Newsweek*, March 31, 2003.

26. Russett et al., *World Politics*, 213.

27. K. J. Holsti, "War, Peace, and the State of the State," *International Political Science Review* 16 (October 1995): 320.

28. Charles Tilly, "Violence, Terror, and Politics As Usual," *Boston Review*, Summer 2002, www.bostonreview.net/BR27.3/tilly.html.

29. International Commission on Intervention and State Sovereignty, *The Responsibility to Protect* (Ottawa: International Research Development Research Centre, 2001), 4.

30. K. J. Holsti, *The State, War, and the State of War* (New York: Cambridge University Press, 1996), 21.

31. Harbom and Wallensteen, "Armed Conflict," 623–624.

32. "The World's Wars," *Economist*, March 12, 1988, 19–20.

33. Project Ploughshares, *Armed Conflicts Report 1995* (Waterloo, Canada: Institute of Peace and Conflict Studies, 1995), 3. On the conditions that promote civil war, see James D. Fearon and David Lattin, "Ethnicity, Insurgency, and Civil War," *American Political Science Review* 97 (2003): 75–90.

34. On the record of military intervention during the Cold War, see Herbert K. Tillema, *Overt Military Intervention in the Cold War Era* (Columbia: University of South Carolina Press, 2008).

35. See note 28 in Chapter 1 and note 81 in Chapter 3.

36. On "failed states," see William Zartman, ed., *Collapsed States* (Boulder, CO: Lynne Rienner, 1995); Tonya Langford, "Things Fall Apart: State Failure and the Politics of Intervention," *International Studies Review* 1 (Spring 1999): 59–79.

37. David Kinsella, *Regime Change: Origins, Execution, and Aftermath of the Iraq War*, 2nd ed. (Belmont, CA: Wadsworth, 2007), 1.

38. *New York Times*, April 23, 2008.

39. "Gates Says Military Faces More Unconventional Wars," *New York Times*, October 11, 2007. The term "mootwa" is from James Traub, "Making Sense of the Mission," *New York Times Magazine*, April 11, 2004.

40. See James D. Fearon, "Iraq's Civil War," *Foreign Affairs*, March–April 2007, 2–15.

41. Walter Laqueur, "Postmodern Terrorism," *Foreign Affairs*, September–October 1996, 24.

42. Laqueur, "Postmodern Terrorism," 24–25.

43. Ibid.

44. Anthony Clark Arend and Robert J. Beck, *International Law and the Use of Force* (New York: Routledge, 1993), 140. Arend and Beck cite Alex Schmid as the source of the study counting 109 definitions.

45. *Patterns of Global Terrorism 2001* (Washington, D.C.: U.S. Department of State, 2002), xvi. A similar definition can be found in Arend and Beck, *International Law*, 140.

46. See Claire Sterling, *The Terror Network* (New York: Holt, Rinehart & Winston, 1981).

47. Bruce Hoffman, *Inside Terrorism* (New York: Columbia University Press, 1998), 157; see chap. 6 for "the modern terrorist mindset." Also see Jerrold Post, *The Mind of the Terrorist* (New York: Palgrave, 2007).

48. *Patterns of Global Terrorism 2002* (Washington, D.C.: U.S. Department of State, 2003).

49. Fareed Zakaria, "The Only Thing We Have to Fear . . . ," *Newsweek*, June 2, 2008, 37.

50. See, for example, John Mueller, *Overblown* (New York: Free Press, 2006); Mueller, "A Not Very Private Feud over Terrorism," *New York Times*, June 8, 2008, describing the disagreement between terrorism experts Bruce Hoffman and Marc Sageman, the former believing that al Qaeda is alive and well and the latter arguing otherwise.

51. The "watching and listening" statement is attributed to Brian Jenkins of the Rand Corporation; cited in Hoffman, *Inside Terrorism*, 198. Hoffman questions whether this assumption still holds.

52. See Graham Allison, *Nuclear Terrorism* (New York: Times Books, 2004).

53. Thomas C. Schelling, "Thinking About Nuclear Terrorism," *International Security* 6 (Spring 1982): 76.

54. www.acda.gov/factshee/conwpn/small.htm (accessed on November 24, 1999).

55. Gregg Easterbrook, "The End of War?" *New Republic,* May 30, 2005. Easterbrook cites data from Mueller, *Remnants of War,* and the series of *Peace and Conflict* reports published by Ted Gurr and Monty Marshall and colleagues at the Center for International Development and Conflict Management at the University of Maryland. Also see other authors mentioned in note 5.

56. Fareed Zakaria, *Newsweek,* May 12, 2008, 27; excerpted from Zakaria, *Post-American World.*

57. Nils Petter Gleditsch, "The Liberal Moment Fifteen Years On," *International Studies Quarterly* 52 (December 2008): 691, 696. Also see Edith Lederer, "Global Violence Has Decreased, UN Says," washingtonpost.com, October 18, 2005.

58. Meredith Reid Sarkees, Frank Wayman, and J. David Singer, "Inter-State, Intra-State, and Extra-State Wars: A Comprehensive Look at Their Distribution Over Time, 1816–1997," *International Studies Quarterly* 47 (March 2003): 49. Also see Mikael Eriksson and Peter Wallensteen, "Armed Conflict, 1989–2003," *Journal of Peace Research* 41 (2004): 625–636.

59. Worldwatch Institute, *Vital Signs, 2007–2008* (New York: Norton, 2007), 76. The conclusion is based on research done at the University of Hamburg in Germany.

60. Lederer, "Global Violence."

61. See note 29 in Chapter 3.

62. See Ralph K. White, *Nobody Wanted War* (New York: Doubleday, 1970); Ole R. Holsti, Robert C. North, and Richard A. Brody, "Perception and Action in the 1914 Crisis," in J. David Singer, ed., *Quantitative International Politics* (New York: Free Press, 1968).

63. Joseph S. Nye, *Understanding International Conflicts,* 5th ed. (New York: Pearson, 2005), 74.

64. See Nye, *Understanding,* chap. 3.

65. Bernhard von Bulow, *Memoirs of Prince Von Bulow 1909–1919* (Boston: Little, Brown, 1932), 165–166; cited in Nye, *Understanding,* 68.

66. An overview of the "causes of war" literature can be found in Greg Cashman and Leonard C. Robinson, *An Introduction to the Causes of War* (Lanham, MD: Rowman & Littlefield, 2007); John A. Vasquez, *What Do We Know About War?* (Lanham, MD: Rowman & Littlefield, 2000); Jack S. Levy, "The Causes of War and the Conditions of Peace," *Annual Review of Political Science* 1 (1998): 139–165.

67. Ethologists include Konrad Lorenz, *On Aggression* (New York: Harcourt, Brace, 1966); and Robert Ardrey, *The Territorial Imperative* (New York: Atheneum, 1966), while sociobiologists include Edward O. Wilson, *Sociobiology: The New Synthesis* (Cambridge, MA: Harvard University Press, 2000). Freud's views are ex-

pressed in *Civilization and Its Discontents*, edited and translated by J. Strachey (New York: Norton, 1962). Realist views can be seen in Reinhold Niebuhr, *The Children of Light and Children of Darkness* (New York: Scribner, 1945).

68. See the cited works in note 51 in Chapter 1. Also, see notes 115 and 116 in Chapter 3.

69. Joshua S. Goldstein, *International Relations*, 5th ed. (New York: Longman, 2004), 131; Goldstein, *War and Gender* (Cambridge: Cambridge University Press, 2001). Also see note 117, in Chapter 3.

70. On the role of personality, see notes 86 and 105 in Chapter 3; Scott Bennett and Allan C. Stam, *The Behavioral Origins of War* (Ann Arbor: University of Michigan Press, 2004). One author who argues emphatically that individual personalities have had a major impact on the outbreak of war is John Stoessinger, in *Why Nations Go to War*, 10th ed. (Belmont, CA: Thomson, 2008).

71. On psychological variables, see especially Robert Jervis, *Perception and Misperception in International Politics* (Princeton, NJ: Princeton University Press, 1976); Irving Janis, *Groupthink*, 2nd ed. (Boston: Houghton Mifflin, 1982). For a comparison of "psychological" and "realist" perspectives, see Russell J. Leng, "Escalation: Competing Perspectives and Empirical Evidence," *International Studies Review* 6 (December 2004): 51–64. On how leaders in crisis situations can fall into war, see Ole R. Holsti, *Crisis, Escalation, War* (Toronto: McGill-Queens, 1972). On prospect theory, see note 121, in Chapter 3.

72. For example, see Paul D. Senese, "Territory, Contiguity, and International Conflict: Assessing a New Joint Explanation," *American Journal of Political Science* 49 (2005): 769–791; Ivo K. Feierabend et al., eds., *Anger, Violence, and Politics* (Englewood Cliffs, NJ: Prentice-Hall, 1972).

73. Ted Gurr, *Why Men Rebel* (Princeton, NJ: Princeton University Press, 1970).

74. On war as a calculated decision, see Bruce Bueno de Mesquita, *The War Trap* (New Haven, CT: Yale University Press, 1981); de Mesquita and David Lalman, *Reason and War* (New Haven, CT: Yale University Press, 1992); Michael Howard, *The Causes of War* (London: Ashgate, 1983), 22.

75. Lloyd Jensen, *Explaining Foreign Policy* (Englewood Cliffs, NJ: Prentice-Hall, 1982), 217.

76. Ruth L. Sivard, *World Military and Social Expenditures 1991* (Washington, D.C.: World Priorities, 1991), 20.

77. See note 51 in Chapter 3; de Mesquita and Lalman, *Reason*, 13–19.

78. Edward Luttwak, "Where Are the Great Powers?" *Foreign Affairs*, July–August 1994, 23–29. The "graying" of America and other countries (the growth in the aged population relative to younger age-groups, due to lower birth rates and lower death rates) may also make it more difficult for governments to go to war if they have to divert funds to social security and health care. See Mark Haas, "Pax Americana Geriatrica," *Miller-McCune* (August 2008): 31–39. This argument is also taken up in Niall Ferguson, *Colossus* (New York: Penguin, 2004), chap. 8.

79. See notes 48 and 49 in Chapter 3. However, some authors find support for the notion that democracies tend to be less prone to war than dictatorships. See Dan Reiter and Allan C. Stam, *Democracies at War* (Princeton, NJ: Princeton University Press, 2002).

80. On the "democratic peace," see Michael W. Doyle, *Ways of War and Peace* (New York: Norton, 1997); de Mesquita and Lalman, *Reason*, 156; Steve Chan, "Mirror, Mirror on the Wall . . . Are the Free Countries More Pacific?" *Journal of Conflict Resolution* 28 (December 1984): 617–648; David A. Lake, "Powerful Pacifists: Democratic States and War," *American Political Science Review* 86 (March 1992): 24–37; Bruce Russett, *Grasping the Democratic Peace* (Princeton, NJ: Princeton University Press, 1993); Karen A. Rasler and William R. Thompson, *Puzzles of the Democratic Peace* (London: Palgrave, 2005).

81. Desmond Morris, *The Human Zoo* (New York: Dell, 1969).

82. See note 73 in Chapter 3.

83. See John Oneal and Jaroslav Tir, "Does the Diversionary Use of Force Threaten the Democratic Peace?" *International Studies Quarterly* 50 (December 2006): 755–779. On American presidents and the rally-round-the-flag effect, see Charles W. Ostrom and Brian L. Job, "The President and the Political Use of Force," *American Political Science Review* 80 (June 1986): 541–566; James Meernik, "Domestic Politics and the Political Use of Military Force by the United States," *Political Research Quarterly* 54 (2001): 889–904.

84. Rudolph Rummel, "Dimensions of Conflict Within and Between Nations," *General Systems* 8 (1963): 24.

85. Patrick James, "Conflict and Cohesion: A Review of the Literature and Recommendations for Future Research," *Cooperation and Conflict* 22 (1987): 22.

86. For Marxist explanations of war, see the works cited in notes 77 and 78 in Chapter 3.

87. Russett et al., *World Politics*, 321.

88. On free trade and economic interdependence contributing to the decline of warfare, see Bruce Russett and John Oneal, *Triangulating Peace* (New York: Norton, 2001), chap. 4. The authors cite research (p. 132) indicating that open economies and expanding trade do reduce conflict. Also see John Oneal and Bruce Russett, "Assessing the Liberal Peace with Alternative Specifications: Trade Still Reduces Conflict," *Journal of Peace Research* 36 (July 1999): 423–442; Erik Gartze, "The Capitalist Peace," *American Journal of Political Science* 51 (January 2007): 166–191.

89. On how lateral pressures rooted in the economic need for resources can lead to war, see Nazli Choucri and Robert C. North, *Nations in Conflict: National Growth and International Violence* (San Francisco: Freeman, 1975).

90. See notes 42–44 in Chapter 3.

91. On the stability of hegemonic, unipolar systems, see Robert Gilpin, *War and Change in World Politics* (Cambridge: Cambridge University Press, 1981). On the stability of bipolar systems, see Kenneth N. Waltz, "The Stability of a Bipolar World," *Daedalus*, Summer 1964, 881–909; John Mearsheimer, "Back to the Fu-

ture: Instability in Europe After the Cold War," *International Security* 15 (Summer 1990): 5–56. On the stability of multipolar systems, see Karl W. Deutsch and J. David Singer, "Multipolar Power Systems and International Stability," *World Politics* 16 (April 1964): 390–406.

92. A. F. K. Organski and Jacek Kugler, *The War Ledger* (Chicago: University of Chicago Press, 1980); Jacek Kugler and Douglas Lemke, eds., *Parity and War* (Ann Arbor: University of Michigan Press, 1996).

93. Kegley, *World Politics*, 412.

94. George Modelski, *Long Cycles in World Politics* (Seattle: University of Washington Press, 1987); Modelski and William R. Thompson, *Leading Sectors and World Powers* (Columbia: University of South Carolina Press, 1996); Paul Kennedy, *The Rise and Fall of the Great Powers* (New York: Random House, 1997).

95. J. David Singer, "Accounting for International War: The State of the Discipline," *Journal of Peace Research* 18, no. 1 (1981): 10.

96. Organski and Kugler, *War Ledger*; Kugler and Lemke, *Parity*; R. I. Tammen et al., *Power Transitions: Strategies for the 21st Century* (Chatham, NJ: Seven Bridges, 2000). Also see Bruce Bueno de Mesquita, "Domestic Politics and International Relations," *International Studies Quarterly* 46 (March 2002): 6.

97. See Bueno de Mesquita, *War Trap*, chap. 5.

98. The findings are summarized in Frederic S. Pearson and J. Martin Rochester, *International Relations: The Global Condition in the 21st Century*, 4th ed. (New York: McGraw-Hill, 1998), 314–317.

99. Hans J. Morgenthau, *Politics Among Nations*, 5th ed. (New York: Knopf, 1973), 400.

100. Duncan Keith Shaw, *Prime Minister Neville Chamberlain* (London: Wells Garden, updated), 111–112, as quoted by Randolph M. Siverson, "War and Change in the International System," in Ole R. Holsti et al., eds., *Change in the International System* (Boulder, CO: Westview, 1980), 216.

101. Russett and Oneal, *Triangulating Peace*.

102. Karl W. Deutsch et al., "Political Community and the North Atlantic Area," *International Political Communities: An Anthology* (Garden City, NY: Doubleday, 1966), 1–91.

CHAPTER 6: INTERNATIONAL ORGANIZATION AND LAW

1. Christopher Wren, "An International Symbol of Neglect," *New York Times*, October 24, 1999.

2. James N. Rosenau and Ernst-Otto Czempiel, eds., *Governance Without Government* (Cambridge: Cambridge University Press, 1992).

3. Barry Buzan, *People, States, and Fear* (Chapel Hill: University of North Carolina Press, 1983), 97.

4. Stephen D. Krasner, ed., *International Regimes* (Ithaca, NY: Cornell University Press, 1983), 2.

5. Robert O. Keohane and Joseph S. Nye, *Power and Interdependence* (Boston: Little, Brown, 1977), 19.

6. Kjell Skjelsbaek, "The Growth of International Nongovernmental Organizations in the Twentieth Century," *International Organization* 25 (Summer 1971): 435–436.

7. Inis L. Claude, *Swords into Plowshares*, 4th ed. (New York: Random House, 1984), 3.

8. See note 3 in Chapter 2. Harold K. Jacobson, *Networks of Interdependence*, 2nd ed. (New York: Knopf, 1984), 14.

9. Ibid.

10. Frederic S. Pearson and J. Martin Rochester, *International Relations: The Global Condition in the 21st Century*, 4th ed. (New York: McGraw-Hill, 1998), 367. The author draws on chapter 10 in writing this chapter.

11. *Yearbook of International Organizations*, 42nd ed. (Brussels: Union of International Associations, 2005–2006), 5:33. Reports of IGO totals can vary, depending not only on whether one counts IGOs that are spin-offs of other IGOs but also other criteria as well. For example, some definitions of IGOs require at least three member countries (i.e., multilateral organizations), while others allow for two (i.e., bilateral organizations). Jon Pevehouse et al., "Intergovernmental Organizations," in Paul F. Diehl, ed., *The Politics of Global Governance*, 3rd ed. (Boulder, CO: Lynne Rienner, 2005), define an IGO as a formal entity (created by treaty), with at least three sovereign states as members, and possessing a permanent headquarters structure.

12. *Yearbook of International Organizations*, 42nd ed. (Brussels: UIA, 2005/2006), 5:33. There is considerable variation in NGO totals reported by different sources, due to varying measurement procedures. For example, the report of the Commission on Global Governance, in *Our Global Neighborhood* (New York: Oxford University Press, 1995), 32, lists 28,000 international NGOs, whereas Margaret Karns and Karen Mingst, *International Organizations: The Politics and Processes of Global Governance* (Boulder, CO: Lynne Rienner, 2004), 11, report 6,500.

13. On regionalism in general, see Louise Fawcett and Andrew Hurrell, eds., *Regionalism in World Politics* (New York: Oxford University Press, 2002). On regional organizations, see Karns and Mingst, *International Organizations*, chap. 5. For data comparing global and regional IGO growth, see Jacobson, *Networks*, 47–50; Jacobson et al., "National Entanglements in International Governmental Organizations," *American Political Science Review* 80 (March 1986):145–147; Cheryl Shanks et al., "Inertia and Change in the Constellation of International Governmental Organizations, 1981–1992," *International Organization* 50 (Autumn 1996): 593–627.

14. Jacobson, *Networks*, 49.

15. Jacobson et al., "National Entanglements," 149.

16. Shanks et al., "Inertia and Change," 594, 607.

17. Shanks et al., "Inertia and Change," 611; Jacobson et al., "National Entanglements," 149.

18. John Boli and George M. Thomas, "INGOs and the Organization of World Culture," in Paul F. Diehl, ed., *The Politics of Global Governance*, 2nd ed. (Boulder, CO: Lynne Rienner, 2001), 64.

19. When I visited China in 2007, I came across a newspaper article entitled "NGOs Have More Room to Develop" reporting on efforts by the Beijing government to ease restrictions on NGO operations in the country. *China Daily*, May 25, 2007.

20. Shanks et al., "Inertia and Change," 601.

21. Boli and Thomas, "INGOs," 84–85.

22. James A. Field, "Transnationalism and the New Tribe," *International Organization* 25 (Summer 1971): 355–356.

23. Jacobson, *Networks*, 10.

24. Boli and Thomas, "INGOs," 63.

25. Barbara Crossette, "Once a Sideshow, Private Organizations Star at UN Meetings," *New York Times*, March 12, 1995.

26. Robert C. Angell, *Peace on the March* (New York: Van Nostrand, 1968).

27. UN official, remarks cited in Donald Puchala and Roger Coate, *The Challenge of Relevance: The United Nations in a Changing World Environment* (Hanover, NH: Academic Council on the UN, 1989), 95.

28. P. J. Simmons, "Learning to Live with NGOs," *Foreign Policy,* Fall 1998, 84; Jessica T. Mathews, "Power Shift," *Foreign Affairs,* January–February 1997, 50–66.

29. Simmons, "Learning to Live with NGOs," 91.

30. Maryann K. Cusimano, *Beyond Sovereignty* (New York: St. Martin's, 2000), 21. See note 9. Also see Jacobson et al., "National Entanglements"; Richard Cupitt et al., "The (Im)mortality of International Governmental Organizations," in Paul F. Diehl, ed., *The Politics of Global Governance*, 2nd ed. (Boulder, CO: Lynne Rienner, 2001), 54–58.

31. Inis L. Claude, "The Record of International Organizations in the Twentieth Century," Tamkang Chair Lecture Series 64, Tamkang University, Taiwan, January 1986, 25. Mimeo.

32. Claude, "Record of International Organizations," 2.

33. Craig N. Murphy, *International Organization and Industrial Change: Global Governance Since 1850* (New York: Oxford University Press, 1994).

34. Kenneth W. Abbott and Duncan Snidal, "Why States Act Through Formal International Organizations," *Journal of Conflict Resolution* 42 (February 1998): 29.

35. See Mark W. Zacher and Brent A. Sutton, *Governing Global Networks* (Cambridge: Cambridge University Press, 1996). On the role of international regimes in reducing cheating and lowering transaction costs for states seeking to cooperate under anarchy, see Robert O. Keohane, *After Hegemony: Cooperation and Discord in the World Political Economy* (Princeton, NJ: Princeton University Press,

1984); Andreas Hasenclever et al., *Theories of International Regimes* (Cambridge: Cambridge University Press, 1997), esp. chap. 2.

36. The classic functionalist work is David Mitrany, *A Working Peace System: An Argument for the Functional Development of International Organization* (London: Royal Institute of International Affairs, 1943).

37. James A. Caporaso, *Functionalism and Regional Integration* (Beverly Hills: Sage, 1972).

38. Jacobson et al., "National Entanglements." Also see Jon Pevehouse and Bruce Russett, "Democratic International Governmental Organizations Promote Peace," *International Organization* 60 (October 2006): 969–1000; Steve Chan, "Influence of International Organizations on Great-Power War Involvement: A Preliminary Analysis," *International Politics* 41 (March 2004): 127–143.

39. *Washington Post,* national weekly edition, December 15–21, 2002.

40. See Paul Kennedy, *The Parliament of Man* (New York: Random House, 2006), xi–xii.

41. Cited in Stephen C. Schlesinger, *Act of Creation: The Founding of the United Nations* (Boulder, CO: Westview, 2003), 7.

42. *U.S. Department of State Bulletin,* April 29, 1945, 789.

43. Cited in Abba Eban, "The UN Idea Revisited," *Foreign Affairs,* September–October 1995, 39–40.

44. A good overview of the UN is provided in Lawrence Ziring, Robert Riggs, and Jack Plano, *The United Nations,* 3rd ed. (New York: Harcourt Brace, 2000); see chapter 2 for a summary of the institutional structure. Also see A. Leroy Bennett and James K. Oliver, *International Organizations,* 7th ed. (Upper Saddle River, NJ: Prentice-Hall, 2002), esp. chaps. 3–5.

45. Susan C. Hulton, "Council Working Methods and Procedures," in David M. Malone, ed., *The UN Security Council: From the Cold War to the 21st Century* (Boulder, CO: Lynne Rienner, 2004), 238–239.

46. Donald J. Puchala et al., *United Nations Politics* (Upper Saddle River, NJ: Prentice-Hall, 2007), 56.

47. Hulton, "Council Working Methods," 237–240; Peter Wallensteen and Patrik Johansson, "Security Council Decisions in Perspective," in David M. Malone, ed., *The UN Security Council: From the Cold War to the 21st Century* (Boulder, CO: Lynne Rienner, 2004), 17–33. Also see Linda Fasulo, *An Insider's Guide to the UN* (New Haven, CT: Yale University Press, 2004), 44.

48. Erik Voeten, "The Political Origins of the UN Security Council's Ability to Legitimize the Use of Force," *International Organization* 59 (Summer 2005): 538–539. For example, only 5 percent of the Portuguese public could name the Big Five, and only 24 percent of the German public.

49. Madeleine Albright, "Think Again: The United Nations," *Foreign Policy,* September–October 2003, 24.

50. Cited in Richard Gardner, "To Make the World Safe for Interdependence," *UN* 30 (1975): 16.

51. Cited in *Chronicle* 2 (March 1982): 12. Published by the Dag Hammarskjöld Information Centre on the Study of Violence and Peace.

52. Cited in Steven L. Kenny, "The National Security Strategy Under the United Nations and International Law," in John T. Rourke, ed., *Taking Sides: Clashing Views in World Politics,* 12th ed. (New York: McGraw-Hill, 2007), 224; also see Michael J. Glennon, *Limits of Law, Prerogatives of Power* (New York: Palgrave, 2001), 67–70.

53. James Dobbins et al., *The UN's Role in Nation-Building: From the Congo to Iraq* (Santa Monica, CA: Rand Corporation, 2005).

54. Ernst B. Haas, "Regime Decay, Conflict Management, and International Organizations, 1945–1981," *International Organization* 37 (Spring 1983): 189–256. In many of these cases, though, the UN contribution was judged to be "limited" rather than "great."

55. Ernst B. Haas, *Why We Still Need the UN* (Berkeley: University of California Press, 1986), 20.

56. Human Security Centre, *Human Security Report* (New York: Oxford University Press, 2005), 8.

57. *An Agenda for Peace: Report of the Secretary-General on the Work of the Organization,* UN Doc. S/24111, June 17, 1992.

58. *Human Security Report,* 9.

59. Ibid., 10.

60. www.un.org/Depts/dpko/dpko/bnote.htm. Data provided by the UN Department of Peacekeeping Operations.

61. Jeremy Farrall, *United Nations Sanctions and the Rule of Law* (Cambridge: Cambridge University Press, 2007), 1.

62. Puchala et al., *United Nations Politics,* 182.

63. Kofi Annan, "'In Larger Freedom': Decision Time at the UN," *Foreign Affairs,* May–June 2005, 63–74.

64. Eban, "UN Idea," 55.

65. John McCormick, *The European Union,* 4th ed. (Boulder, CO: Westview, 2008), 8.

66. Roger Hansen, "European Integration: Forward March, Parade Rest, or Dismissed?" *International Organization* 27 (Spring 1973): 225–254.

67. Jeffry Frieden, comment at a seminar at the University of Missouri–St. Louis on March 26, 1998.

68. Nathaniel C. Nash, "What Fits in Europe's Wallet?" *New York Times,* July 11, 1995.

69. Dana Milbank, "Will Unified Europe Put Mules in Diapers and Ban Mini-Pizza?" *Wall Street Journal,* June 22, 1995.

70. "European Union Vows to Become Military Power," *New York Times,* June 4, 1999.

71. Puchala and Coate, *Challenge of Relevance,* 36.

72. McCormick, *European Union,* 161. McCormick offers an overview of the entire EU institutional structure in part 2. Also see George Tsebelis and Geoffrey

Garrett, "The Institutional Foundations of Intergovernmentalism and Supranationalism in the European Union," *International Organization* 55 (Spring 2001):
357–390.

73. Neill Nugent, *The Government and Politics of the European Union*, 3rd ed.
(Durham, NC: Duke University Press, 1994), 65.

74. "Germany's Foreign Minister Urges European Federation," *New York Times*,
May 15, 2000; "Germans Offer Plan to Remake European Union," *New York Times*,
May 1, 2001.

75. McCormick, *European Union*, 223.

76. Thomas Kamm, "You Won't Find Fans of a Borderless Europe in This Soccer Arena," *Wall Street Journal*, February 12, 1999.

77. "A Spat in the Family," *New York Times*, August 31, 2008, noting that "Scottish nationalists are pushing for a divorce from England"; "Belgians Adrift and Split,
Sense a Nation Fading," *New York Times*, September 21, 2007.

78. Louis Henkin, *How Nations Behave*, 2nd ed. (New York: Columbia University Press, 1979), 1.

79. The figure is cited on the website of the U.S. Department of State's Office
of the Legal Advisor at www.state.gov/s/1/3190.htm (accessed August 22, 2004).

80. Paul Martin, Canadian secretary of state for external affairs, cited in *External
Affairs* 16 (1964).

81. Graham Allison, comment made during visit to the University of
Missouri–St. Louis on April 7, 2005. The skeptical view is represented by Jack L.
Goldsmith and Eric A. Posner, *The Limits of International Law* (New York: Oxford
University Press, 2004).

82. Michael J. Glennon, "Sometimes a Great Notion," *Wilson Quarterly*, Autumn 2003, 49.

83. My discussion of international law draws on Pearson and Rochester, *International Relations*, chap. 9.

84. William D. Coplin, *The Functions of International Law* (Chicago: Rand Mc-
Nally, 1966), 1–3.

85. Anthony Clark Arend, *Legal Rules and International Society* (New York:
Oxford University Press, 1999), 29. Arend credits Inis Claude with this phrasing.

86. This is the traditional notion of law attributed to John Austin, a nineteenth-
century British writer.

87. George Will, "The Perils of Legality," *Newsweek*, September 10, 1990, 66.

88. Richard Bilder, *Managing the Risks of International Agreement* (Madison:
University of Wisconsin Press, 1981), 5.

89. On the growth in multilateral treaties, see Shirley Scott, *International Law
in World Politics* (Boulder, CO: Lynne Rienner, 2004), 5; John King Gamble, "Reservations to Multilateral Treaties: A Macroscopic View of State Practice," *American
Journal of International Law* 74 (April 1980): 372–394; James P. Muldoon, *The Architecture of Global Governance* (Boulder, CO: Westvew, 2004), 155–157.

90. Charlotte Ku, *Global Governance and the Changing Face of International Law*, ACUNS Reports and Papers 2 (New Haven, CT: Academic Council on the United Nations System, 2001), 5.

91. See Clyde Haberman, "Diplomatic or Not, Mayor Gets Results with His War on Scofflaws," *New York Times*, March 30, 2000. Although Mayor Rudolph Giuliani managed to reduce traffic violations by the diplomatic community in New York City during the 1990s, diplomats could not be forced to pay fines or towing fees.

92. Based on University of Washington Treaty Research Center Studies, reported in Bilder, *Managing the Risks*, 232.

93. Mark W. Janis, *An Introduction to International Law* (Boston: Little, Brown, 1988), 11.

94. It is sometimes argued that there are a few rules of international law that states cannot ever contract of, that is, cannot choose to circumvent whether a party to a treaty or not. This is the concept of *jus cogens*, or "peremptory norms," such as the norm against aggression embodied in the UN Charter. *Jus cogens* remains controversial due to its seeming incompatibility with sovereignty.

95. Glennon, "Sometimes a Great Notion," 45.

96. Henkin, *How Nations Behave*, 47.

97. Ambrose Bierce, *Devil's Dictionary* (1911).

98. Abram Chayes and Antonio Chayes, "On Compliance," *International Organization* 47 (Spring 1993): 175–206.

99. David V. Edwards, *The American Political Experience*, 4th ed. (Englewood Cliffs, NJ: Prentice-Hall, 1988), 372–373.

100. Reported in *Washington Post*, September 16, 2008, based on the U.S. Federal Bureau of Investigation's Uniform Crime Statistics.

101. Abram Chayes, *The Cuban Missile Crisis: International Crises and the Role of Law* (New York: Oxford University Press, 1974).

102. Data on trends in the Court's caseload can be found in A. Leroy Bennett and James K. Oliver, *International Organization*, 7th ed. (Englewood Cliffs, NJ: Prentice-Hall, 2002), 189–193. Also see the ICJ homepage, www.icj-cij .org/docket/index.

103. On the use of the chambers procedure and the growth in caseload, see J. Alan Beesley, *New Frontiers of Multilateralism* (Hanover, NH: Academic Council on the UN, 1989), 9. For the current Court caseload, see note 102.

104. For example, see Eric Posner, "All Justice, Too, Is Local," *New York Times*, December 30, 2004; Goldsmith and Posner, *Limits*.

105. William R. Slomanson, *Fundamental Perspectives on International Law*, 3rd ed. (Belmont, CA: Wadsworth, 2000), 378.

106. In a study of all ICJ cases involving territorial, river, or maritime boundary disputes, Paul Hensel found virtually total compliance with court decisions on the part of the parties. See Paul Hensel, "International Institutions and Compliance with Agreements," www.paulhensel.org/comply.html.

107. Ibid., 376.

108. These are the words of Benjamin Civiletti, former U.S. attorney general, in his oral argument presented before the World Court on December 10, 1979, during the proceedings of the *US Diplomatic and Consular Staff in Tehran* case.

109. Based on a 2003 article in the *Atlanta Journal Constitution*, www .washtimes.com/national/20031030–120613–3167r.htm.

110. On the relationship between international law and international politics, see J. Martin Rochester, *Between Peril and Promise* (Washington, D.C.: CQ Press, 2006).

CHAPTER 7: IMPROVING INTERNATIONAL SECURITY

1. See note 2 in Chapter 4. For statistics on world military spending, see Stockholm Peace Research Institute, *SIPRI Yearbook 2008: Armaments, Disarmament, and International Security* (Stockholm: SIPRI, 2008).

2. *World Military Expenditures and Arms Transfers, 1999–2000* (Washington, D.C.: U.S. State Department, 2003), 1.

3. Ruth Leger Sivard, *World Military and Social Expenditures, 1987–1988* (Washington, D.C. World Priorities, 1987), 16, 35.

4. *World Military Expenditures and Arms Transfers*, 1.

5. See SIPRI Press Release, June 9, 2008; *SIPRI Yearbook 2008*, 10.

6. See *SIPRI Yearbook 2008*, 10; *World Military Expenditures and Arms Transfers*, 1–2.

7. On the arms industry, including production and trade, see Ethan Kapstein, *The Political Economy of National Security* (New York: McGraw-Hill, 1992); Keith Krause, *Arms and the State: Patterns of Military Production and Trade* (Cambridge: Cambridge University Press, 1992).

8. See *SIPRI Yearbook 2008*, 14–15; *World Military Expenditures and Arms Transfers*, 9–11; Richard Grimmett, *Conventional Arms Transfers to Developing Nations, 1999–2006* (Washington, D.C.: Congressional Research Service, 2007).

9. William Hartung and Rachel Stohl, "Hired Guns," *Foreign Policy* 142 (May–June 2004): 29; Elisabeth Olson, "Globally, Number of Small Arms Has Risen Sharply," *New York Times*, June 30, 2002.

10. Lloyd Axworthy, speech, 1999; cited by Dan Caldwell and Robert E. Williams Jr., *Seeking Security in an Insecure World* (Lanham, MD: Rowman & Littlefield, 2006), 27.

11. Ibid.

12. OPCW, *Report of the Organization for the Prohibition of Chemical Weapons*, June 2008; David Fidler, "The Chemical Weapons Convention After Ten Years: Successes and Future Challenges," *ASIL* [American Society of International Law] *Insight*, April 27, 2007.

13. Arms Control Association, "Chemical and Biological Weapons at a Glance," www.armscontrol.org/factsheets.

14. Richard Peterson, "Biology Gone Bad," *New York Times*, November 7, 1997. On biological terrorism, see Barry Kellman, *Bioviolence* (Cambridge: Cambridge University Press, 2008).

15. On nuclear terrorism, including loose nukes, see Graham Allison, *Nuclear Terrorism* (New York: Times Books, 2004).

16. The International Atomic Energy Agency, an agency affiliated with the United Nations, accused Iran in 2008 of trying to hide its nuclear development program. See "Atomic Monitor Signals Concern over Iran's Work," *New York Times*, May 27, 2008.

17. Data on nuclear arsenals are found in *SIPRI Yearbook 2008*, 16–17; and the Carnegie Endowment for International Peace, "Nuclear Weapons Status 2005," www.carnegieendowment.org/images/npp/nuke.jpg.

18. George P. Schultz et al., "Toward a Nuclear-Free World," *Wall Street Journal*, January 15, 2008.

19. *SIPRI Yearbook 2008*, press release, June 9, 2008.

20. Shultz et al., "Toward a Nuclear-Free World." They were quoting California governor Arnold Schwarzenegger in referring to "mistakes."

21. Richard K. Betts, "The New Threat of Mass Destruction," *Foreign Affairs*, January–February 1998, 26–41.

22. On *jus ad bellum* and attempts to regulate the outbreak of war, see Gerhard von Glahn and James Larry Taulbee, *Law Among Nations*, 8th ed. (New York: Pearson, 2007), chap. 20.

23. William R. Slomanson, *Fundamental Perspectives on International Law*, 3rd ed. (Belmont, CA: Wadsworth, 2000), 119.

24. Michael J. Glennon, *Limits of Law, Prerogatives of Power* (New York: Palgrave, 2001), 84. Glennon cites numerous empirical studies, including a study by Herbert Tillema that counted 690 "overt military interventions" between 1945 and 1996.

25. Louis Henkin, *How Nations Behave*, 2nd ed. (New York: Columbia University Press, 1979), 146. John F. Murphy, "Force and Arms," in Christopher C. Joyner, ed., *The United Nations and International Law* (Cambridge: Cambridge University Press, 1997), 102, supports Henkin. On Zacher's "territorial integrity norm," see the citation in note 36, Chapter 2.

26. Joseph S. Nye, "What New World Order?" *Foreign Affairs*, Spring 1992, 90.

27. Maryann Cusimano Love, ed., *Beyond Sovereignty*, 2nd ed. (Belmont, CA: Wadsworth, 2003), 4.

28. Anthony Clark Arend and Robert Beck, *International Law and the Use of Force* (New York: Routledge, 1993).

29. On humanitarian intervention, see Gary Bass, *The Origins of Humanitarian Intervention* (New York: Knopf, 2008); Morton Abramowitz and Thomas Pickering, "Making Intervention Work," *Foreign Affairs*, September–October 2008, 100–107.

30. Quoted in Walter McDougall, "America and the World at the Dawn of a New Century," *WIRE*, December 1999.

31. Cited in Judith Miller, "Sovereignty Isn't So Sacred Anymore," *New York Times*, April 18, 1999.

32. Kofi Annan, *Report on UN Reform: In Larger Freedom* (A/59/2005), March 21, 2005.

33. David J. Scheffer, "Use of Force After the Cold War," in Louis Henkin et al., eds., *Right vs. Might* (New York: Council on Foreign Relations Press, 1991), 144.

34. Martha Finnemore, "Constructing Norms of Humanitarian Intervention," in Peter J. Katzenstein, ed., *The Culture of National Security: Norms and Identity in World Politics* (New York: Columbia University Press, 1996), 170.

35. Slomanson, *Fundamental Perspectives*, 463.

36. Cited in Glennon, *Limits of Law*, 158.

37. In 2008 President Bush approved orders that "for the first time allowed American Special Operations forces to carry out ground assaults inside Pakistan without the prior approval of the Pakistani government." *New York Times*, September 11, 2008, 1.

38. "UN Chief Ignites Firestorm by Calling Iraq War 'Illegal,'" *New York Times*, September 17, 2004.

39. See von Glahn and Taulbee, *Law Among Nations*, 599–600; Arend and Beck, *International Law*, chap. 5; Arend, "International Law and the Preemptive Use of Military Force," *Washington Quarterly*, Spring 2003, 89–103.

40. George W. Bush, "The National Security Strategy of the United States of America," annual report to the U.S. Congress, September 2002.

41. On *jus in bello* and efforts to regulate the conduct of war, see von Glahn and Taulbee, *Law Among Nations*, chap. 21.

42. Quoted in ibid., 628.

43. Seymour Hersh, "The Gray Zone," *New Yorker*, May 24, 2004.

44. "How Precise Is Our Bombing?" editorial, *New York Times*, March 31, 2003.

45. There have been reports of a few other exceptions where such weapons have been used, such as Japan against China during World War II, but these are not fully documented.

46. Charles W. Kegley Jr., *World Politics: Trend and Transformation*, 12th ed. (Belmont, CA: Wadsworth, 2009), 517.

47. John T. Rourke, *International Politics on the World Stage*, 11th ed. (New York: McGraw-Hill, 2007), 345.

48. Virginia Nesmith, "Landmines Are a Lingering Killer," *St. Louis Post-Dispatch*, December 31, 1995.

49. Dan Caldwell and Robert E. Williams, *Seeking Security in an Insecure World* (Lanham, MD: Rowman & Littlefield, 2006), 28.

50. Priya Pillai, "Adoption of the Convention on Cluster Munitions," *ASIL Insight*, October 1, 2008.

51. Robert J. Mathews and Timothy L.H. McCormack, "Entry into Force of the Chemical Weapons Convention," *Security Dialogue* 26, no. 1 (1995): 93.

52. A short case study is presented in J. Martin Rochester, *Between Two Epochs* (Englewood Cliffs, NJ: Prentice-Hall, 2002), 138–145.

53. See note 64 in Chapter 3 and note 22 in Chapter 4.

54. David Morrison, "Political Chemistry," *National Journal,* May 14, 1994, 1133.

55. Rochester, *Between Two Epochs,* 99–104; J. Martin Rochester, "Global Policy and the Future of the United Nations," *Journal of Peace Research* 27 (May 1990): 141–154.

56. See "Briefing on Biological Weapons," provided by the Arms Control Association, www.armscontrol.org/factsheets/bwissuebrief.asp.

57. See notes 13–14.

58. Information accessed at www.acronym.org.uk/bwc/Mx08-03.htm.

59. As with chemical weapons, there are sketchy reports of biological weapons having been used on rare occasions, such as Soviet germ warfare in Afghanistan in the 1980s, but these, too, are not fully documented. See John Barry, "Planning a Plague?" *Newsweek,* February 1, 1993, 40–41.

60. Remark by President Clinton in his address to the UN General Assembly on September 22, 1997.

61. Allison, *Nuclear Terrorism,* 141.

62. Richard N. Haass, *The Opportunity* (New York: PublicAffairs, 2005), 82.

63. Stanley Hoffmann, *Primacy or World Order* (New York: McGraw-Hill, 1978), 193.

64. Johan Galtung, "Violence, Peace, and Peace Research," *Journal of Peace Research* 6, no. 3 (1969): 167–191.

65. Hoffmann, *Primacy,* 108.

66. Ibid., 184–186.

CHAPTER 8: ENHANCING HUMAN RIGHTS
AND HUMAN DEVELOPMENT

1. *Wall Street Journal,* October 10, 2008.

2. "When Human Rights Extend to Nonhumans," *New York Times,* July 13, 2008.

3. *St. Louis Post-Dispatch,* October 16, 1978.

4. Anne-Marie Slaughter, "Leading Through Law," *Wilson Quarterly,* Autumn 2003, 42–43.

5. On humanitarian intervention, see notes 29–36 in Chapter 7.

6. Rhoda E. Howard and Jack Donnelly, eds., *International Handbook of Human Rights* (New York: Greenwood, 1987), 1.

7. See note 16, in Chapter 1.

8. Arch Puddington, "Findings of *Freedom in the World 2008*–Freedom in Retreat? Is the Tide Turning?" Freedom House, *Freedom in the World 2008* (London: Freedom House, 2008), www.freedomhouse.org/template.cfm?page= 130&year=2008.

9. *Freedom in the World* (London: Freedom House, 1993), 4.

10. *The State of the World's Children 2007* (New York: UNICEF, 2007), www.unicef.org/sowc07/profiles/inequality_politics.php.

11. Richard H. Robbins, *Global Problems and the Culture of Capitalism* (New York: Allyn & Bacon, 1999), 354.

12. *State of the World's Children 2007*, 41.

13. "Female Infanticide: Old Reasons, New Recipes," *Hindu*, June 24, 2001.

14. "Report: Swazi Princess Whipped for Loud Music," August 28, 2005, www.cnn.com/2005/WORLD/africa.

15. UN Development Fund for Women, *War, Women, and Peace* (New York: UN, 2002), 9.

16. International Labor Organization, *World of Work*, September–October 1998.

17. Ethan Kapstein, "The New Global Slave Trade," *Foreign Affairs*, November–December 2006, 103.

18. Ibid., 105–106.

19. Human Rights Watch, October 27, 2008, www.hrw.org/children/labor.htm.

20. Jill M. Gerschutz and Margaret P. Karns, "Transforming Visions into Reality: Actors and Strategies in the Implementation of the Convention on the Rights of the Child," in Mark Ensalaco and Linda Majka, eds., *Children's Human Rights: Progress and Challenges* (Lanham, MD: Rowman & Littlefield, 2005).

21. See the Live-8 website, www.thedatareport.org/pdf/execSumm2007.

22. Brandt Commission, *North-South* (Cambridge, MA: MIT Press, 1980), 32.

23. On the competing interpretations of data, see Arie M. Kacowicz, "Globalization, Poverty, and the North-South Divide," *International Studies Review* 9 (Winter 2007): 565–580.

24. Joseph Stiglitz, *Globalization and Its Discontents* (New York: Norton, 2002), 5.

25. Fareed Zakaria, "The Post-American World," *Newsweek*, May 12, 2008, 30.

26. See note 15, in Chapter 1.

27. World Bank, *World Development Indicators 2008* (Washington, D.C.: World Bank, 2008), 194. On operational definitions of low-, middle-, and high-income economies, see *World Development Report 2008* (Washington, D.C.: World Bank, 2007), 331.

28. On China and India, see Robin Meredith, *The Elephant and the Dragon: The Rise of India and China* (New York: Norton, 2007). For lagging countries and regions, see *World Development Indicators 2008*, 194.

29. *World Development Indicators 2008*, 4.

30. Paul Collier, *The Bottom Billion* (Oxford: Oxford University Press, 2007).

31. See Worldwatch Institute, *Vital Signs 2007–2008* (New York: Norton, 2007), 108; *World Development Report 2008*, 3.

32. UN Development Program, *Human Development Report 2004* (New York: Oxford University Press, 2004), 30.

33. "Facts and Figures from World Development Indicators 2008," http://site resources.worldbank.org/DATASTATISTICS/Resources/reg_wdi.pdf.

34. Ibid.

35. The rankings are listed in UN Development Program, *Human Development Report 2007/2008* (New York: Oxford University Press, 2008). The data on per capita income (based on the GNI World Bank Atlas method), life expectancy, and literacy rates are from *World Development Report 2008*, 334–335.

36. "As Global Wealth Spreads, the IMF Recedes," *Washington Post*, May 24, 2008.

37. See Thomas Friedman, "The Great Iceland Meltdown," *New York Times*, October 19, 2008; Gauti Kristmannsonn, "The Ice Storm," *New York Times*, October 16, 2008; John Banville, "Erin Go Bust," *New York Times*, October 16, 2008.

38. Robert S. McNamara, *One Hundred Countries, Two Billion People* (New York: Praeger, 1973), 8.

39. FAQs on the Human Development Indexes, www.undp.org/hdr2000/english/FAQs.html#15.

40. Paul Lewis, "UN Lists 4 Lands at Risk Over Income Gaps," *New York Times*, June 2, 1994.

41. "Rich-Poor Divide Widens, Says OECD," *Financial Times*, October 21, 2008.

42. *World Development Indicators 2008*, 5.

43. Alan B. Durning, "Ending Poverty," *State of the World 1990* (New York: Norton, 1990), 135.

44. The data on billionaires is from "World's Billionaires," *Forbes*, March 5, 2008; data on millionaires is from *World Wealth Report 2007*, published by Merrill Lynch; data on homeless is from the UN Center for Human Settlements, accessed at www.un.org/Conferences/habitat/unchs/press; data on refugees and "people of concern" is from UNHCR, *Protecting Refugees and the Role of the UNHCR* (2007).

45. "Kofi Annan's Astonishing Facts," *New York Times*, September 27, 1998.

46. "World's Billionaires."

47. David Bederman, *International Law Frameworks*, 2nd ed. (New York: Foundation Press, 2006), 99.

48. See David P. Forsythe, "The United Nations and Human Rights, 1945–1985," *Political Science Quarterly* 100 (Summer 1985): 249–270. Forsythe examines the politics of human rights in *Human Rights and World Politics*, 2nd ed. (Lincoln: University of Nebraska Press, 1989). A comprehensive list of conventions and protocols can be found on the homepage of the UN Office of the High Commissioner for Human rights, www.unhchr.ch/html/intlinst.htm.

49. Michael Ignatieff, "Human Rights: The Midlife Crisis," *New York Review of Books*, May 20, 1999, 61.

50. Cited in "U.S. Bans Child Soldiers," CBS News, www.cbsnews.com/stories/2002/12/24/national.

51. Alan Philips, "Public Beheadings Carried Out Weekly, Rights Group Says," Amnesty Report on Saudi Arabia, www.ukar.org/philips01.html.

52. Oona Hathaway, "Do Human Rights Treaties Make A Difference?" *Yale Law Journal* 111 (June 2002).

53. Margaret P. Karns and Karen A. Mingst, *International Organizations* (Boulder, CO: Lynne Rienner, 2004), 452–453.

54. Martha Alter Chen, "Engendering World Conferences: The International Women's Movement and the UN," in Thomas G. Weiss and Leon Gordenker, eds., *NGOs, the UN and Global Governance* (Boulder, CO: Westview, 1996). On the politics of the global women's movement, see V. Spike Peterson and Anne Sisson Runyan, *Global Gender Issues*, 2nd ed. (Boulder, CO: Westview, 1999).

55. See note 1 in Chapter 1 and note 65 in Chapter 2.

56. Bilahari Kausican, "Asia's Different Standard," *Foreign Policy*, Fall 1993, 34.

57. William R. Slomanson, *Fundamental Perspectives on International Law*, 3rd ed. (Belmont, CA: Wadsworth, 2000), 504.

58. Thomas M. Franck, "Are Human Rights Universal?" *Foreign Affairs*, January–February 2001, 191. Franck answered in the affirmative.

59. Michael Ignatieff, "Is the Human Rights Era Ending?" *New York Times*, February 5, 2002.

60. "European Court Orders Britain to Restrict Beatings by Parents," *New York Times*, September 24, 1998; "European Identity: Nation-State Losing Ground," *New York Times*, January 14, 2000.

61. Mark Janis and Richard Kay, *European Human Rights Law* (Hartford: University of Connecticut Law School Foundation Press, 1990), vii; cited in Slomanson, *Fundamental Perspectives*, 511.

62. "Millennium Development Goals: A Compact Among Nations to End Human Poverty," in UN Development Program, *Human Development Report 2003* (New York: UNDP, 2003), 1–2.

63. Jeffrey Sachs, director of the UN Millennium Project and author of the 2005 report, said that doubling aid to reduce poverty was "utterly affordable." Critics called it "utopian." See "UN Proposes Doubling of Aid to Cut Poverty," *New York Times*, January 18, 2005.

64. "Progress on the MDGs: September 2008 Update," *Global Monitoring Report 2008*, web.worldbank.org/WBSITE/EXTERNAL/EXTDEC/EXTGLOBAL/MONITOR. Also see "Progress Toward the MDGs Is Mixed," in *Vital Signs 2007–2008*, 108.

65. Charles Lipson, "International Cooperation in Economic and Security Affairs," *World Politics* 37 (October 1984): 12. A similar observation is made by Robert Jervis in "Security Regimes," *International Organization* 36 (Spring 1982): 357–378.

66. As an example of realist analysis of these issues, see Stephen D. Krasner, *Structural Conflict: The Third World Against Global Liberalism* (Berkeley: University of California Press, 1985).

67. Slomanson, *Fundamental Perspectives*, 585.

68. In addition to Krasner, *Structural Conflict*, see Roger D. Hansen, *Beyond the North-South Stalemate* (New York: McGraw Hill, 1979); John Toye and Richard Toye, *The UN and Global Political Economy* (Bloomington: Indiana University Press, 2004). Krasner takes a realist approach to analyzing the North-South conflict, Hansen a liberal approach, and the Toyes a constructivist approach.

69. See Charles Lipson, *Standing Guard: Protecting Foreign Capital in the Nineteenth and Twentieth Centuries* (Berkeley: University of California Press, 1985).

70. Maryann Cusimano, *Beyond Sovereignty* (New York: St. Martin's, 2000), 262.

71. Jeffrey Sachs is quoted in "UN Proposes Doubling of Aid to Cut Poverty," *New York Times*, January 18, 2005.

72. "Failing the World's Poor," editorial, *New York Times*, September 24, 2008.

73. "West Is in Talks on Credit to Aid Poorer Nations," *New York Times*, October 23, 2008.

74. *Vital Signs, 2007–2008*, 20–21.

75. See www.fao.org/wfs/index.

76. See Dan Morgan, *Merchants of Grain* (New York: Penguin, 1980).

77. An overview of world food trends can be found in L. T. Evans, *Feeding the Ten Billion* (Cambridge: Cambridge University Press, 1998).

78. The quote is from the *United Nations Chronicle* 3 (2001).

79. Frederic Kirgis, "Specialized Law-Making Processes," in Christopher C. Joyner, ed., *The United Nations and International Law* (Cambridge: Cambridge University Press, 1997), 74.

80. On trends in AIDS, as well as the politics of AIDS, see the annual *AIDS Epidemic Updates* published by WHO; also see *Vital Signs 2007–2008*, 120–121.

81. See Katherine Bliss, "XVII International AIDS Conference in Mexico City: Implications for Latin America and the Caribbean," *Hemisphere Focus,* September 15, 2008.

82. Lester Brown, "U.S. Leading World Away from Cigarettes," www.earth/policy.org/Updates/Update34.htm (accessed February 18, 2004).

83. "Unlikely Allies with the United Nations," *New York Times*, December 10, 1999.

84. "In Shadow of Iraq, UN's Development Agenda Evolves, Expands," *Interdependent,* Spring 2003, 25.

85. The meeting occurred on May 4, 2000. "Business Supports Kofi Annan Global Compact but Rejects Prescriptive Rules," www.iccwbo.org/home/news_archives/2000/buda_global.asp.

86. On Nobel laureate economist James Tobin's proposed tax on currency transactions, first mentioned in 1978, see Hilary French, "Reshaping Global Governance," in Christopher Flavin et al., eds., *State of the World 2002* (New York: Norton, 2002), 188–189. On the world income tax, proposed by Nobel laureate Jan Tinbergen in the *Human Development Report 1994* (p. 88), see "World Income Tax: Report Floats Idea," *New York Times*, June 12, 1994.

87. For example, see Herman M. Schwartz, *States Versus Markets* (New York: St. Martin's, 1994).

CHAPTER 9: MANAGING THE WORLD ECONOMY
AND PROMOTING PROSPERITY

1. For a history of globalization, see Nayan Chanda, *Bound Together: How Traders, Preachers, Adventurers, and Warriors Shaped Globalization* (New Haven, CT: Yale University Press, 2007).

2. See Ralph Linton, *The Study of Man* (Englewood Cliffs, NJ: Prentice-Hall, 1936), esp. 326–327.

3. See notes 71–73 in Chapter 2.

4. Arie Kacowicz, "Globalization, Poverty, and the North-South Divide," *International Studies Review* 9 (Winter 2007): 567. For a good overview of the contemporary globalization phenomenon, see David Held et al., *Global Transformations* (Stanford, CA: Stanford University Press, 1999).

5. Thomas Friedman, *The Lexus and the Olive Tree* (New York: Farrar, Straus, Giroux, 1999), 221.

6. These statistics can be found on the homepages of these companies on the World Wide Web, which now reaches over 200 million people in over 100 countries.

7. See note 36 in Chapter 2.

8. For example, see Richard O'Brien, *Global Financial Integration: The End of Geography* (London: Pinter, 1992); John Agnew, "The Territorial Trap: The Geographical Assumptions of International Relations Theory," *Review of International Political Economy* 1 (Spring 1994): 60–65.

9. David Held and Anthony McGrew, "Globalization and the Liberal Democratic State," in Y. Sakamoto, ed., *Global Transformation* (New York: United Nations Press, 1994), 66.

10. Robert Gilpin, *The Political Economy of International Relations* (Princeton, NJ: Princeton University Press, 1987), 31. Chapter 2 of the Gilpin book offers an excellent summary of the three IPE schools, or "ideologies."

11. Ibid., 33–34.

12. John Toye and Richard Toye, *The UN and Global Political Economy* (Bloomington: Indiana University Press, 2004).

13. John G. Ruggie, "International Regimes, Transactions, and Change: Embedded Liberalism in the Postwar Economic Order," in Stephen D. Krasner, ed., *International Regimes* (Ithaca, NY: Cornell University Press, 1983), 195–231. Also see Dani Rodrik, *Why Do More Open Economies Have Bigger Governments?* Working Paper 5537 (Cambridge, Mass: National Bureau of Labor Research, 1996).

14. Norman Lewis, "Globalization and the End of the Nation-State" (paper presented at the annual meeting of the International Studies Association, San Diego, April 16, 1996).

15. Cigdem Akin and M. Ayhan Rose, *Changing Nature of North-South Linkages: Stylized Facts and Explanations*, IMF Working Paper WP/07/280 (2007), 4.

16. See Joan E. Spero, *The Politics of International Economic Relations*, 4th ed. (New York: St. Martins, 1990), chaps. 3, 7.

17. World Bank, *World Development Indicators 2008* (Washington, D.C.: World Bank, 2008), 318. Also see IMF, *Direction of Trade Statistics Yearbook 2007* (Washington, D.C.: IMF, 2007).

18. Friedman, *Lexus*, chap. 6.

19. Duane Kujawa, "International Business Education and International Studies" (paper presented at annual meeting of the International Studies Association, Cincinnati, March 25, 1982).

20. Stephen D. Cohen, *Multinational Corporations and Foreign Direct Investment* (New York: Oxford University Press, 2007), 150–151.

21. Ibid. Although Hong Kong, after long British rule, has been reincorporated into China and is now under the sovereignty of the People's Republic, it is often listed by the World Bank as a separate entity.

22. Bruce R. Scott, "The Great Divide in the Global Village," *Foreign Affairs*, January–February 2001, 164.

23. Cohen, *Multinational Corporations*, 150.

24. Some critics of MNCs question whether the success of Singapore and other LDCs as export platforms can be duplicated. They attribute the success of such countries more to their impressive domestic savings rate than their link to MNCs. See, for example, Scott, "Great Divide."

25. Joseph M. Grieco and G. John Ikenberry, *State Power and World Markets* (New York: Norton, 2003), 259.

26. Peter Kresl, "Canada-United States Investment Linkages" (paper presented at annual meeting of the International Studies Association, Cincinnati, March 26, 1982), 6; Cohen, *Multinational Corporations*, 346–348; Grieco and Ikenberry, *State Power*, 231–235.

27. *Newsweek*, November 27, 1978.

28. *New York Times*, January 20, 2008.

29. "In Hiring, Europeans Go Global," *New York Times*, June 4, 2008; *St. Louis Post-Dispatch*, March 7, 2005; "Seeking Leaders, U.S. Companies Think Globally," *New York Times*, December 12, 2007.

30. Samuel Palmisano, "The Globally Integrated Enterprise," *Foreign Affairs*, May–June 2006, 129.

31. Robert Reich raises the question "Who are us?" in *The Work of Nations* (New York: Knopf, 1991). For a counterpoint that challenges the idea of the "stateless corporation," see Paul Doremus et al., *The Myth of the Global Corporation* (Princeton, NJ: Princeton University Press, 1998). Also see Paul Hirst and Grahame Thompson, *Globalization in Question*, 2nd ed. (New York: Wiley, 2001).

32. Thomas Friedman calls this "the golden straitjacket." See Friedman, *Lexus*, chap. 5. On how the bargain contained in "the compromise of embedded liberalism" has been breaking down due to globalization, posing dilemmas for governments, see Dani Rodrik, "Sense and Nonsense in the Globalization Debate," *Foreign Policy*, Summer 1997, 19–37.

33. For example, see Vincent Cable, "The Diminished Nation-State: A Study in the Loss of Economic Power," *Daedalus,* Spring 1995, 23–53.

34. Janice E. Thomson and Stephen D. Krasner, "Global Transactions and the Consolidation of Sovereignty," in Ernst-Otto Czempiel and James N. Rosenau, eds., *Global Changes and Theoretical Challenges* (Lexington, MA: Lexington Books, 1989), 198.

35. *New York Times,* October 10, 2008.

36. Friedman, *Lexus,* 8.

37. Cable, "Diminished Nation-State," 37.

38. See Mark W. Zacher and Brent A. Sutton, *Governing Global Networks* (Cambridge: Cambridge University Press, 1996).

39. "World Leaders Confront Global Crisis," CNNMoney.com, November 15, 2008.

40. "Demand for a Say on a Way Out of Crisis," *New York Times,* November 10, 2008.

41. Ibid. The quote is from Robert Zoellick.

42. Sir Roy Denman, head of the European Community mission to the United States, cited in *Washington Post* national weekly edition, September 22, 1986, upon the opening of the Uruguay Round talks leading to the creation of the World Trade Organization.

43. Ernest H. Preeg, *Traders in a Brave New World* (Chicago: University of Chicago Press, 1995), 2.

44. Ibid., 185.

45. Ibid., 58.

46. Ibid., 10.

47. Quoted in Robert Dodge, "Grappling with GATT," *Dallas Morning News,* August 8, 1994; cited in Bruce Moon, *Dilemmas of International Trade* (Boulder, CO: Westview, 1996), 91.

48. The remark was made on *Both Sides,* a television show hosted by Jesse Jackson, on April 4, 1999.

49. Preeg, *Traders,* 161.

50. See Toye and Toye, *UN,* 288–293; Richard H. Steinberg, "In the Shadow of Law or Power?" *International Organization* 56 (Spring 2002): 339–374.

51. Toye and Toye, *UN,* 287–288.

52. On compliance statistics as well as statistics on the overall caseload, see *International Judicial Monitor,* April 2008; Lori Wallach and Patrick Woodall, *Whose Trade Organization?* (New York: New Press, 2004).

53. Molly Ivins, "Time to Begin Building Labor, Human, and Environmental Rights on a Global Scale," *St. Louis Post-Dispatch,* November 30, 1999.

54. On "GATTzilla," see Wallach and Woodall, *Whose Trade,* 242.

55. Quoted in "Clinton Gives a Pass to Globaphobia," *Wall Street Journal,* January 31, 2000.

56. See comments in Preeg, *Traders,* 176.

57. *New York Times*, July 30, 2008.

58. Lawrence Summers, "The Global Consensus on Trade Is Unraveling," *Financial Times*, August 25, 2008.

59. The examples cited here are from Samuel Lucas McMillan, "Subnational Foreign Policy Actors: How and Why Governors Participate," *Foreign Policy Analysis* 4 (July 2008): 230–231.

60. Ibid., 231–232.

61. "Calif., Britain to Address Global Warming," *New York Sun*, August 1, 2006. On the limits of state legal capacity to make foreign policy in the U.S. federal system, see "Justices Weigh Issue of States' Making Foreign Policy," *New York Times*, March 23, 2000. On the role of U.S. states, and also cities, in foreign affairs, see Earl Fry, *The Expanding Role of State and Local Governments in U.S. Foreign Affairs* (New York: Council on Foreign Relations, 1998).

CHAPTER 10: THE FUTURE OF INTERNATIONAL RELATIONS: SOVEREIGNTY, GLOBAL GOVERNANCE, AND THE HUMAN PROSPECT IN THE TWENTY-FIRST CENTURY

1. Benjamin Barber, "Jihad Vs. McWorld," *Atlantic Monthly*, March 1992, 53.

2. Kenneth N. Waltz, "Globalization and Governance," *PS*, December 1999, 697.

3. Robert H. Jackson and Alan James, "The Character of Independent Statehood," in Jackson and James, eds., *States In A Changing World* (Oxford: Clarendon Press, 1993), 6–7. Also see Stephen Krasner, *Sovereignty: Organized Hypocrisy* (Princeton, NJ: Princeton University Press, 1999).

4. See J. Martin Rochester, *Between Two Epochs* (Englewood Cliffs, NJ: Prentice-Hall, 2002).

5. Alternative world order models were first discussed by scholars in the World Order Models Project (WOMP) in the 1970s. For example, see Saul H. Mendlovitz, *On the Creation of a Just World Order* (New York: Free Press, 1975).

6. On the implications of regionalism for peace and other values, see Joseph S. Nye, *Peace in Parts* (Boston: Little, Brown, 1971).

7. See Grenville Clark and Louis Sohn, *World Peace Through World Law*, 3rd ed. (Cambridge, MA: Harvard University Press, 1966); Richard Hudson, "Give the UN The Power to Make Peace," *St. Louis Post-Dispatch*, July 20, 1990; Marc Nerfin, "The Future of the UN System," *Development Dialogue* 1 (1985): 21.

8. See UN Development Program, *Human Development Report 1994* (New York: Oxford University Press, 1994), 88.

9. Various tax proposals are discussed in Christopher Stone, *The Gnat Is Older Than Man* (Princeton, NJ: Princeton University Press, 1993), 206–211.

10. Walter Wriston, *The Twilight of Sovereignty* (New York: Scribner's, 1992). Wriston is the former head of Citicorp.

11. Richard J. Barnet and Ronald E. Muller, *Global Reach* (New York: Simon & Schuster, 1974), 19–20.

12. Comments made by Strobe Talbott in "The Birth of the Global Nation," *Time,* July 20, 1992, 70. Also see Talbott, *The Great Experiment: The Story of Ancient Empires, Modern States, and the Quest for a Global Nation* (New York: Simon & Schuster, 2008).

13. James N. Rosenau, *Turbulence in World Politics* (Princeton, NJ: Princeton University Press, 1990), 406.

14. Robert D. Kaplan, "Could This Be the New World?" *New York Times,* December 27, 1999.

15. James N. Rosenau, "Governance in the Twenty-First Century," *Global Governance* 1 (Winter 1995): 25–26; John Newhouse, "Europe's Rising Regionalism," *Foreign Affairs,* January–February 1997, 67–84.

16. On "strategic alliances," see Stephen J. Kobrin, "Strategic Alliances and State Control of Economic Actors" (paper given at annual meeting of the International Studies Association, Chicago, February 21, 1996).

17. On global civil society, see Ronnie D. Lipschutz, "Power, Politics, and Global Civil Society," *Millennium* 33, no. 3 (2005): 747–769; Mary Ann Tetreault and Lipschutz, *Global Politics As If People Mattered* (Lanham, MD: Rowman & Littlefield, 2005). On "the end of geography," see note 8 in Chapter 9.

18. On "the new feudalism" and "new medievalism," see Susan Strange, "The Defective State," *Daedalus,* Spring 1995, 55–74; John Rapley, "The New Middle Ages," *Foreign Affairs,* May–June 2006, 95–103.

19. Robert C. North, *The World That Could Be* (New York: Norton, 1976), 136.

20. Paul Kennedy, *Preparing for the Twenty-First Century* (New York: Vintage, 1993), 127, 131, 134. On the continuing need for national governments, including welfare states, in an age of globalization, see Geoffrey Garrett, "Global Markets and National Politics: Collision Course or Virtuous Circle?" *International Organization* 52 (Autumn 1998): 787–824.

21. "Global Forecast by American Intelligence," *New York Times,* November 21, 2008. The study stated that "the unipolar moment is over, or certainly will be over by 2025."

22. The phrase is Barry Buzan's. See note 3 in Chapter 6.

23. World Commission on Environment and Development (Brundtland Commission), *Our Common Future* (Oxford: Oxford University Press, 1987), 27.

24. Inis Claude, "The Record of International Organizations in the Twentieth Century," Tamkang Chair Lecture Series no. 64, Tamkang University, Taiwan, 4–5; mimeo.

25. Robert Kaplan, "The Coming Anarchy," *Atlantic Monthly,* February 1994, 58. For an overview of global environmental politics and regimes, see Pamela Chasek et al., *Global Environmental Politics,* 4th ed. (Boulder, CO: Westview, 2006); Peter M. Haas et al., eds., *Institutions for the Earth* (Cambridge, MA: MIT Press, 1993).

26. Club of Rome, *The Limits to Growth* (New York: Universe Books, 1972).

27. Based on the assessments of the Intergovernmental Panel on Climate Change, the UN *Human Development Report 2007/2008* devoted the entire issue

to "fighting climate change," which it called "the greatest challenge facing humanity." On climate change, see David G. Victor, *Climate Change* (New York: Council on Foreign Relations, 2004); and John Browne, "Beyond Kyoto," *Foreign Affairs*, July–August 2004, 20–32.

28. Richard E. Benedick, *Ozone Diplomacy* (Cambridge, MA: Harvard University Press, 1998).

29. Richard E. Benedick, "Ozone Diplomacy," *Issues in Science and Technology*, Fall 1989, 43.

30. Comments made by Lee Thomas in testimony before the U.S. Senate, Committee on Foreign Relations hearings, February 19, 1988, and George Mitchell, statement in U.S. Senate, 1988; cited in Benedick, *Ozone Diplomacy*, 1.

31. The key factors behind the success of the Montreal Protocol are summarized by Benedick in *Ozone Diplomacy*, 5–7. Also see Edward A. Parson, "Protecting the Ozone layer," in Haas et al., *Institutions*, chap. 2. On the role played by domestic politics and the need to reconcile the positions of competing interest groups and bureaucracies in the United States and elsewhere, see notes 63 and 64 in Chapter 3.

32. Stephen D. McDowell et al., *Managing the Infosphere* (Philadelphia: Temple University Press, 2008), 118. One example of the complex challenges posed by Internet governance is in the area of taxation; see Roland Paris, "The Globalization of Taxation? Electronic Commerce and the Transformation of the State," *International Studies Quarterly* 47 (June 2003): 153–182.

33. On the politics of regime-making in this area, see McDowell et al., *Managing*; Marcus Franda, *Launching Into Cyberspace* (Boulder, CO: Lynne Rienner, 2002); Derrick Cogburn, "Partners or Pawns? The Impact of Elite Decision-Making and Epistemic Communities in Global Information Policy on Developing Countries and Transnational Civil Society" (paper presented at annual meeting of the International Studies Association, Montreal, March 17, 2004).

34. For statistics on cyber attacks and an overview of the problem, see Maryann Cusimano Love, *Beyond Sovereignty*, 3rd ed. (Belmont, CA: Thomson Wadsworth, 2007), chap. 9.

35. "Countries in Tug-of-War over Arctic Resources," cnn.com, accessed on January 2, 2009. On governance of the global commons, see J. Martin Rochester, *Between Peril and Promise: The Politics of International Law* (Washington, D.C.: Congressional Quarterly Press, 2006), chap. 7.

36. The quote is attributed to Frank Hoyle.

37. *New York Times*, May 23, 2000.

38. These terms were coined by Giovanni Sartori in *Democratic Theory* (New York: Praeger, 1965).

39. Thomas Schelling, *Arms and Influence*, rev. ed. (New Haven, CT: Yale University Press, 2008), vii, 287.

40. Nils Gleditsch, "The Liberal Moment Fifteen Years On," *International Studies Quarterly* 52 (December 2008): 697. Gleditsch's survey of recent trends reports several positive developments.

41. Alan E. Goodman, *A Brief History of the Future* (Boulder, CO: Westview, 1993); Robert L. Heilbroner, *An Inquiry Into the Human Prospect: Looked At Again for the 1990s* (New York: Norton, 1991), 11.

42. Fareed Zakaria, *The Post-American World* (New York: Norton, 2008).

GLOSSARY

Administrative decision. A type of foreign policy decision involving concerns that are relatively narrow in scope, low threat in nature, and tend to be handled by lower level officials in the bureaucracy (e.g., processing a visa request).

Alternative world order models. Alternative ways in which humanity might be organized politically (e.g., a world government vs. regionalism vs. a city-state system).

Ambassador. A high-level diplomatic official appointed as a representative by one government to another.

Anarchy. In international relations, the absence of any overarching, hierarchical authority, a lack of a central government that can enforce rules.

Apolarity. A type of international system where there is a power vacuum, i.e., there are virtually no actors or centers of power that dominate world politics.

Arms control. Agreements to limit the production, testing, stockpiling, or use of certain types of weapons or their deployment in certain areas. Can include reductions, freezes, or ceilings on the size and/or makeup of arsenals.

Arms race. An arms competition between two or more countries in which each builds up military arsenals in response to the other.

Arms transfers. The movement of armaments between countries through sales or foreign aid.

Asymmetrical warfare. A form of warfare usually pitting opponents that are grossly uneven in military power. To counter the gap in military power, the ostensibly weaker side often changes the rules of engagement through the use of unconventional tactics (insurgency, guerrilla warfare, suicide bombings, etc.) to negate the military capabilities of the more powerful foe (e.g., the 2003 Iraq War).

Balance of power. A theory that assumes that in a system where capabilities are fairly evenly distributed among the major actors, states will be deterred from committing aggression by the prospect of having to fight a coalition of states at least as powerful as they are.

Bandwagoning. A strategy of joining the stronger alliance of states in order to share the spoils of victory (as opposed to balancing, which refers to joining the weaker coalition in order to counter the power of the stronger state or alliance of states and forestall aggression by the latter).

Behavioralists. In international relations, theorists who employ rigorous social science methods, including the collection and analysis of quantitative data, to formulate and test hypotheses explaining the behavior of international actors.

Bilateral diplomacy. Negotiations between two countries.

Bi-multipolar system. An international system in which two major powers predominate but other actors have significant freedom of maneuver (sometimes called a loose bipolar system).

Biological Weapons Convention of 1972. A treaty banning not only the use of bacteriological agents in warfare but also their production and stockpiling, outlawing their very existence.

Biopolitics. A theory that examines the role of physiological factors, particularly physical and mental health, in shaping human behavior in foreign policy and other fields.

Bipolar system. An international system in which there are two power centers, or poles, with countries tending to align themselves into two blocs around those poles.

BRICs. Brazil, Russia, India, and China—considered big emerging markets and rising powers in the global economy.

Bush Doctrine. A policy enunciated by President George W. Bush in 2002 after the 9/11 attacks on the United States. The United States claimed the right to engage in the preemptive use of armed force in "self-defense" against any enemy that was thought to possibly pose a threat to American national security in the future, even if the latter had not yet committed aggression and an attack was not imminent.

Chemical Weapons Convention of 1993. A treaty banning not only the use of chemical agents in warfare but also their production and stockpiling, outlawing their very existence.

Chicken. A game in which each of two opponents threatens the other with serious harm in an attempt to extract concessions and thereby achieve certain gains. The payoff structure of the game tends to promote mutual cooperation more than defection (a conflictual outcome).

Civil war. Sustained violent conflict between organized political factions within a state.

CNN effect. The role played by major news media in shaping events in world politics through agenda setting and other impacts. For example, CNN's pictures of starving Somali babies increased pressure on the first Bush administration to engage in humanitarian intervention in 1992; in turn, pictures of dead American GIs dragged through the streets of Mogadishu raised a public outcry, forcing the Clinton administration eventually to retreat from Somalia.

Coercive diplomacy. "Forceful persuasion": the threatened use of armed force in an effort to persuade an adversary to refrain from engaging in undesirable behavior.

Cold War. The global geopolitical competition between the two superpowers, the United States (leading the Western bloc of mostly industrialized democracies) and the Soviet Union (leading the Eastern bloc communist countries), between 1945 and 1990. Characterized by great tension, it never resulted in actual direct military engagement.

Collective security. A system of world order in which the power of the entire international community is turned against any state committing aggression, as provided for in Chapter VII of the UN Charter. An attack against one is considered an attack against all and must be countered as such.

Communism. A political ideology originating with Karl Marx, it calls for the oppressed class of workers (the proletariat) to rise up against the owners of the means of the production (the bourgeoisie). As envisioned, the initial state ownership of property and centralized planning would lead eventually to a stateless and classless society; this stage has never been achieved.

Compellence. The attempt by one state to persuade another state to do something it might otherwise not wish to do. The opposite of deterrence.

Comprehensive Nuclear Test Ban Treaty. A treaty that bans all testing of nuclear weapons. Signed by many states in 1996, it has not yet been ratified by the United States and other major nuclear powers and thus is not yet in effect.

Concert of Europe. A system of great-power consultations created by Britain, Prussia, Russia, and other European powers at the Congress of Vienna in 1815, following the end of the Napoleonic Wars. Designed to defuse and resolve disputes that threatened to erupt into war, it was somewhat successful until the late nineteenth century. It subsequently became a model for the council of great powers in the League of Nations and UN.

Congress of Vienna. The 1815 peace conference after the Napoleonic Wars that created the Concert of Europe and produced important rules governing the exchange of ambassadors and diplomatic relations among states.

Constructivist paradigm (Constructivism). A body of IR theory, which posits that changing ideas and norms held by "agents" (individuals, epistemic communities, and the like) shape the content of state interests and "structures" (international law, international organizations, and other features of international relations).

Containment. The U.S. foreign policy designed to prevent the expansion of communism and Soviet influence during the Cold War, relying on military alliances, economic aid, and other instruments.

Convention. See treaty.

Credibility. The extent to which threats or promises made by one state are believed by another state.

Crisis decision. A type of foreign policy decision made in situations normally characterized by a sense of high threat, an element of surprise, a short time frame (urgency), and involvement of the highest levels of the foreign policy establishment.

Customary rules. Practices that have been widely accepted as legally binding by states over a period of time as evidenced by repeated usage (e.g., the three-mile territorial sea in the eighteenth through twentieth centuries); along with treaties, customary rules are considered the main source of international law.

Democratic peace. The theory, generally confirmed by empirical evidence, that democracies are highly unlikely to go to war against other democracies.

Dependency theory. A theory that traces poverty and the lack of economic progress in the South to unequal economic relationships through which the industrialized countries of the North exploit nonindustrialized countries.

Deterrence. An attempt by one state to dissuade another state from doing something it might otherwise wish to do. The opposite of compellence.

Diplomacy. The general process states use to communicate through government officials, to influence each other, and to resolve conflicts through bargaining.

Diplomacy of violence. The use of armed force in a limited fashion to demonstrate resolve and "send a message," that is, to persuade an adversary that more force might be forthcoming should the latter not behave properly.

Diplomatic immunity. The freedom from arrest or prosecution enjoyed by foreign diplomats in a host country, based on the Vienna Convention on Diplomatic Relations.

Disarmament. Agreement by states to reduce or eliminate an entire class of weapons.

Domino theory. The rationale used by the Kennedy administration as the basis for American intervention in Vietnam in the 1960s: the idea that failing to stop communist aggression in Vietnam would lead to the toppling of other "dominoes" in Cambodia, Laos, and elsewhere. The theory recalled the lessons of Munich, when the decision to meet Hitler's aggression with appeasement rather than military resistance on the eve of World War II seemingly invited further aggression by Germany.

East-West conflict. The main axis of conflict of the Cold War between 1945 and 1990, which pitted the Western industrialized, capitalist democracies (the United States, Western European countries, Japan, Canada, Australia, and others) against the Eastern bloc communist states (consisting of the Soviet Union and its allies in Eastern Europe and elsewhere).

Economic and Social Council (ECOSOC). The UN organ charged with offering recommendations, organizing conferences, and coordinating the activities of various UN agencies in the economic and social field.

Embassy. A permanent outpost of diplomats established in a foreign country to represent the interests of the home (sending) government in that country.

Ethnopolitical conflict. Conflict between ethnically distinct groups over issues of self-determination or other such goals.

European Union (EU). The intergovernmental organization (IGO) of over two dozen countries in Western Europe engaged in a regional integration effort that began with the creation of the Common Market and European Economic Community under the Treaty of Rome in 1957. It became the EU under the Maastricht Treaty in 1993, and has a number of supranational institutions, including the European Commission, European Parliament, and European Court of Justice.

Failed state. A state whose governmental institutions have virtually collapsed and ceased to function, leaving the country in a state of near anarchy. In most cases, a failed state is unable to provide even minimal levels of security and well-being to its citizens.

Fascism. An ideology or type of political system built around a totalitarian dictatorship that stresses nationalism, often tied to ethnic identity. Nazi Germany under Hitler and Italy under Mussolini represent the clearest examples of this political system.

Feminism. A body of thought, which holds that the discrimination against women in political and economic life is reflected in IR theory, which is based on male-oriented and gendered views of the world, and in the IR scholarly literature, which ignores the contributions of women as well as women's issues while privileging male actors and concerns.

Feudal system. A complex mode of political organization featuring overlapping hierarchies of authority and multiple loyalties (e.g., between the pope and the Holy Roman Emperor) that existed in Western Europe and other parts of the world in the Middle Ages, prior to the creation of the modern nation-state system in the seventeenth century.

Food and Agriculture Organization (FAO). The specialized agency of the UN charged with addressing food security needs, agricultural development, and other food-related issues, especially as they relate to developing countries.

Force without war. The use of armed force short of all-out war, for example, intermittent border raids or air strikes in limited or low-intensity conflict situations.

Foreign direct investment. The acquisition by investors in one country of a controlling interest in a foreign economic enterprise in another country.

Foreign policy. A guide to action that drives a country's behavior toward other states and includes both the basic goals a national government seeks to pursue in the world as well as the instruments used to achieve those goals.

Fourth World. The poorest, least developed countries in the world—approximately fifty countries found mostly in sub-Saharan Africa and South Asia.

Framework Convention on Climate Change. A treaty produced at the Earth Summit in Rio de Janeiro in 1992, which committed states to modest obligations aimed at attempting to curb greenhouse gas emissions and monitoring global warming.

Free trade. The theory and practice, traced to Adam Smith's *Wealth of Nations* in 1776, of encouraging international flow of imports and exports by removing government-imposed tariffs and nontariff barriers (quotas, state subsidies, etc.) between states.

Functionalism. The idea that as states collaborate in trying to solve specific, relatively technical problems (e.g., facilitating more efficient transnational mail delivery), their governments will learn habits of cooperation, leading to collaboration on broader, more politically sensitive issues (e.g., arms control) and, possibly, eventual surrender of sovereignty to supranational institutions.

Game theory. A mathematical way of analyzing strategic interactions between two or more players, used in IR to predict outcomes in various situations where one country's success in making a choice depends on the choices made by the other country, or countries, involved.

Gender. A set of male-female differences—grounded not only in biology but also in social role construction—and seen by some IR theorists as important variables that explain certain behaviors of foreign policy decision-makers and other actors in world politics.

General Agreement on Tariffs and Trade (GATT). A global intergovernmental organization established in 1947 to promote free trade, succeeded by the World Trade Organization in 1995.

General Assembly. The main plenary body of the United Nations, in which each member country has one vote and decisions are based on a one state, one vote formula but resolutions are nonbinding. It is authorized by the UN Charter to address a broad range of political, economic, and social issues.

Geneva Conventions of 1949. Four treaties that further developed international humanitarian law, obligating states to refrain from mistreating prisoners of war, from engaging in indiscriminate bombing of civilians in wartime, and from committing other acts during wartime that fell below standards of civilized behavior.

Geneva Gas Protocol of 1925. A treaty that prohibited the first use of lethal chemical weapons in warfare, although it did permit the production and possession of such weapons. Later the 1993 Chemical Weapons Convention banned the very existence of chemical weapons.

Geopolitics. A school of thought in IR, popular in the late nineteenth and early twentieth centuries, that stresses the importance of geographical factors, such as physical locale, terrain, and access to raw materials, in shaping foreign policy and international politics.

Global commons. Those areas of the earth that are not under any country's sovereign control, such as the high seas, the air space above the high seas, outer space, and Antarctica.

Global Compact. A partnership started by former UN secretary-general Kofi Annan. It includes linkages between the UN, multinational corporations, and NGOs cooperating to address issues such as the "digital divide" that especially affect developing countries.

Globalization. The internationalization of production, trade, and finance as well as the integration of the world in terms of communications and culture—a process involving the growth of multinational corporations and other transnational relations that increase interdependence among countries.

Global South. The name given to the NICs, next NICs, OPEC countries, middle-income developing countries, Fourth World countries, and other countries in various stages of development, as distinct from First World (rich, highly industrialized) countries.

Great man (or woman) theory. The belief that a single individual is capable of shaping major events and creating history.

Greenhouse effect. A rise in the earth's temperature caused by the accumulation of carbon dioxide and other gases in the atmosphere due primarily to the burning of coal and other fossil fuels.

Group of Eight (G8). See Group of Seven.

Group of Seven (G7). The leading industrialized democracies (the United States, Britain, France, Germany, Italy, Canada, and Japan), which hold an annual economic summit to discuss trade and other related issues affecting the world economy. After the Cold War ended, Russia was invited to participate in the 1990s, creating what has been called the G8.

Group of 77. A group of more than 100 Third World countries (at its founding in 1964, there were 77 members) that in the UN and in other arenas has sought to promote reform of the international economic order aimed at redistributing wealth from the North to the South.

Group of Twenty (G20). An informal group of finance ministers and central bank governors from the major industrialized states (including the G7) along with big emerging markets and economic powers (such as Brazil, India, China, Mexico, and Saudi Arabia), which meets periodically to discuss global financial regimes and related issues. Its role expanded after 2008.

Groupthink. A phenomenon often found in small-group decision making, first observed by the psychologist Irving Janis, in which group conformity pressures may lead individuals to suppress personal doubts about an emerging group consensus.

Guerrilla warfare. Warfare involving irregular forces that tend to use unconventional tactics, including mixing with civilian populations, against a regular army.

Higher-order decision. A type of foreign policy decision involving relatively broad, general concerns that may be of great importance but usually allow a lengthy time frame for decision making and engage many elements of the political system (e.g., the size of the defense budget or foreign aid budget).

High politics. Issues that involve core national interests, such as arms control and national security.

Human Development Index (HDI). An annual ranking of countries' quality of life, based on their per capita income, life expectancy, and literacy rate, compiled by the UN Development Program.

Humanitarian intervention. The insertion of military force by the international community into a country whose government may be engaging in genocide or failing to provide basic human rights and services, which former UN secretary-general Kofi Annan called "the responsibility to protect."

Human rights. The set of rights possessed by all human beings, regardless of their nationality, based on treaties and customary rules.

Idealist paradigm (Idealism). See liberal paradigm.

Idiosyncratic factors. Variables that operate at the individual level of analysis, such as personality and gender, which can affect foreign policy decisions and behavior.

Image. A view of the world that tends to color, and may distort, an individual's perception of reality.

Imperialism. The acquisition of colonies through conquest, typically aimed at economic exploitation of conquered territories, closely associated with the colonization of the Americas, Africa, Asia, and the Middle East by European and Western powers.

Intercontinental ballistic missiles (ICBMs). Guided land-based rockets able to deliver nuclear payloads at distances of over 3,000 miles.

Interdependence. A relationship of mutual sensitivity and vulnerability in which changes or developments in one part of the system impact other parts of the system. In the international system, some interdependent countries may be unevenly (asymmetrically) impacted.

Intergovernmental organizations (IGOs). International organizations whose members are national governments (states) and that are normally created through a treaty.

Intermestic issues. Issues that combine domestic and international dimensions (e.g., energy or agricultural policy).

International Atomic Energy Agency (IAEA). The UN agency responsible for maintaining safeguards pertaining to nuclear energy and monitoring compliance with the Nuclear Nonproliferation Treaty and other nuclear arms control agreements.

International Bank for Reconstruction and Development. See World Bank.

International Bill of Human Rights. Includes the Universal Declaration of Human Rights, the Covenant on Civil and Political Rights, and the Covenant on Economic, Social, and Cultural Rights.

International Civil Aviation Organization (ICAO). The UN specialized agency responsible for establishing uniform practices and standards governing international air safety.

International Court of Justice. See World Court.

International Criminal Court (ICC). A permanent Nuremberg Trials court in The Hague, Netherlands, established by the Rome Statute in 1998 to prosecute individuals alleged to have committed war crimes, crimes against humanity, and genocide.

International humanitarian law. See *jus in bello*.

International Labor Organization (ILO). The UN specialized agency responsible for monitoring working conditions worldwide and improving labor wages and standards through drafting of an international labor code and other activities.

International law. The body of rules governing relations between states, based mainly on treaties and custom.

International Maritime Organization (IMO). The UN specialized agency responsible for promoting international maritime standards and safety.

International Monetary Fund (IMF). The UN specialized agency responsible for promoting international monetary cooperation, stabilizing exchange rates, and providing foreign exchange funds for needy states to facilitate global commerce.

International organizations. Intergovernmental and nongovernmental organizations (IGOs and NGOs), created on a regional or global basis in response to problems that transcend national boundaries.

International political economy (IPE). An IR subfield that examines the politics of trade, aid, and investment flows across national boundaries.

International regimes. Norms, rules, and institutions that govern various aspects of international relations (e.g., air or maritime safety) and create a degree of world order.

International relations. The study of interactions primarily between nation-states, but also nonstate actors as well—the study of who gets what, when, and how in the international arena.

International system. The political, economic, and social environment in which international politics occur at any point in time, including the distribution of power and other key characteristics that structure world affairs.

International Telecommunications Union (ITU). The UN specialized agency charged with managing the flow of telegraph, radio, and television communications across the globe, including developing rules governing the Internet.

Interstate war. Sustained armed combat between states, to be distinguished from intrastate and extrastate violence.

Iron triangles. Mutually supportive relationships among interest groups, executive branch agencies, and legislative committees in a given policy area (e.g., agriculture or defense spending).

Jus ad bellum. The body of international law containing the rules governing the commencement of war, that is, the circumstances under which it is legal for a state to resort to the use of armed force against another state.

Jus in bello. The body of international law containing the rules governing the conduct of war, that is, the kinds of behavior that are permissible once a war is under way.

Just war doctrine. A set of principles indicating the circumstances under which the use of armed force may be justified (e.g., in self-defense) and, once war has begun, what kinds of armed force are permissible (e.g., the rule of proportionality).

Kellogg-Briand Pact. A 1928 multilateral treaty that attempted to outlaw war as a means of resolving disputes among nations. The treaty was considered highly idealistic and devoid of enforcement mechanisms.

Kyoto Protocol. A 1997 treaty drafted as a follow-up to the 1992 Framework Convention on Climate Change, obligating developed countries that were parties to reduce greenhouse gas emissions by roughly 5–7 percent below their 1990 levels by 2012.

League of Nations Covenant. The treaty that created the League of Nations after World War I, which the United States failed to ratify despite the key role played by U.S. president Woodrow Wilson in founding the organization.

Levels of analysis. A framework for examining explanations of foreign policy and international politics, based on looking at variables that operate at the individual, state, and systemic levels.

Liberal internationalism. See free trade.

Liberal paradigm (liberalism). A major school of international relations that focuses on the role of international law and organization, as well as morality, in shaping world politics, viewing the latter as offering great potential for cooperation based on mutual interests.

Long-cycle theory. An IR theory that views the modern state system as exhibiting the following pattern: a systemwide war gives rise to hegemonic dominance by one state (e.g., Portugal, the Netherlands, Britain, or the United States) lasting approximately one century, followed by the decline of the latter's economic and military power, leading to the rise of new challengers, one of which then becomes the successor hegemon through another systemwide war.

Low politics. Issues that are relatively narrow, technical, and noncontroversial in nature, such as regulating international mail traffic.

Marshall Plan. An American foreign aid program that helped rebuild the war-torn economies of Western Europe after World War II.

Marxist paradigm (Marxism). An IR school that views international relations through the lens of class struggle and the exploitation of workers by those who own the means of production—capital (the bourgeoisie)—within and between countries.

Mediation. A form of peaceful settlement of disputes in which a third party facilitates a resolution to a conflict by listening to both sides and offering recommendations.

Mercantilism. An economic theory that prefers the use of tariffs and other governmental policies that promote national interests over free trade.

Military-industrial complex. The linkages between a country's military establishment and its economic elite, each supporting the other.

Millennium Development Goals. A series of goals established at the UN Millennium Summit in 2000. These include halving, by 2015, the number of people living on less than a dollar a day as well as the number suffering from hunger and malnutrition.

Montreal Protocol on the Ozone Layer of 1987. The landmark environmental treaty, which committed countries that were the major producers of ozone layer–depleting CFC chemicals to eliminate CFC production by the end of the twentieth century.

Multilateral diplomacy. Negotiations among three or more countries.

Multinational corporation (MNC). A firm that is headquartered in one country and has subsidiaries in one or more countries.

Multipolar system. An international system with multiple power centers.

Mutual Assured Destruction (MAD). A nuclear deterrent doctrine used by the two superpowers during the Cold War. Each sought to dissuade the other from launching a first nuclear strike against its homeland by threatening to retaliate with a second-strike nuclear attack against the aggressor's cities, thereby representing mutual suicide.

Nation. A group of people who share a common history and a common sense of future destiny, usually grounded in a common language or ethnicity. It is a social-cultural entity that may or may not coincide with a formal-legal political entity.

National interests. The core set of concerns that dominate a country's foreign policy, including physical security, political independence, and economic well-being.

Nationalism. The set of emotional and cultural beliefs that sustain the attachment and loyalty of members to the nation and to national symbols.

Nation-state. A political unit with a relatively well-defined territory and population over which a central government exercises sovereignty; often used by IR scholars as a synonym for "state."

NATO. See North Atlantic Treaty Organization.

Negotiation. Formal, direct face-to-face or written diplomatic communication and bargaining between parties seeking to pursue goals short of the use of armed force.

New International Economic Order (NIEO). A series of proposals, first presented during the 1970s in the UN General Assembly, aimed at improving the economic well-being of the South, including commodity price stabilization and more favorable terms of trade, more foreign aid and debt relief, a code of conduct for multinational corporations, and a rearrangement of voting power in international economic institutions.

NICs. Newly industrializing countries—less developed countries, such as Singapore and South Korea, that have developed a sizable manufacturing sector and now have per capita incomes approaching those of the First World.

Nongovernmental organizations (NGOs). International organizations whose members are private actors, either individuals or groups.

Nonstate actor. An actor other than a national government that has an impact on international relations (e.g., IGOs, NGOs, MNCs).

North American Free Trade Agreement (NAFTA). An economic agreement between Canada, Mexico, and the United States, established in 1994, aimed at reducing barriers to trade and investment across those countries' borders.

North Atlantic Treaty Organization (NATO). A military alliance established in 1949 by a dozen countries in North America and Western Europe. Members pledged that an attack on one would be considered an attack on all. Initially aimed at deterring a Soviet attack, NATO now has twenty-six member states, including several former Soviet republics.

North-South conflict. The rich-poor axis of conflict that developed alongside the East-West axis of conflict during the Cold War and continued into the post–Cold War era.

Nuclear club. Countries officially known to have detonated a nuclear device and to possess nuclear arsenals of some size; includes the United States, Russia, China, Britain, France, India, and Pakistan, with Israel considered an unofficial member of the club and North Korea and Iran on the brink of joining.

Nuclear deterrence. A form of military dissuasion whereby a nuclear-armed nation threatens to use nuclear weapons if an adversary initiates a nuclear strike or aggressive conventional attack.

Nuclear Nonproliferation Treaty (NPT). Signed in 1968 and put in force in 1970, the NPT obliges parties that do not have nuclear weapons to refrain from developing them, and parties that have nuclear weapons to refrain from transferring them to nuclear have-nots. Renewed in 1995, the NPT has almost 190 member states.

Nuclear Utilization Theory (NUTs). An alternative to MAD, NUTs presumes that a nuclear war is fightable, survivable, and winnable; thus a country such as the United States must be prepared to wage such a war if deterrence fails.

Nuremberg Trials. The venue at which the victorious Allies prosecuted Nazi war criminals after World War II. The Nazis were tried for crimes against the peace, war crimes, and crimes against humanity, including the extermination of millions of Jews in the Holocaust—a landmark moment in the history of human rights.

Organization of Economic Cooperation and Development (OECD). An intergovernmental organization created after World War II that has provided a forum for economic cooperation among the industrialized democracies, including the United States, Canada, Japan, and Western Europe.

Organization of Petroleum Exporting Countries (OPEC). A cartel of less developed countries that together account for roughly half of the world's oil exports.

Ottawa Land Mine Treaty. A 1997 treaty aimed at outlawing the use of antipersonnel land mines in warfare.

Pacta sunt servanda. The international legal principle that treaties, once signed and ratified, are to be obeyed by the parties.

Paradigm. An intellectual framework that structures our thinking about a set of phenomena.

Partial Test Ban Treaty of 1963. A treaty that bans the testing of nuclear weapons in the atmosphere but allows limited testing underground.

Peace building. The role played by the United Nations in creating postconflict conditions conducive to a long-term durable peace following civil war, through facilitating infrastructure repair, removing land mines, restoring police and judicial institutions, disarming the former combatants, holding elections, and other such measures.

Peace enforcement. The use of armed force by UN military personnel who may have begun their mission as neutral peacekeepers but find themselves having to enforce the peace against one or more actors that have violated the UN Charter rules against aggression.

Peaceful settlement procedures. Procedures such as mediation and adjudication that are outlined in Chapter VI of the UN Charter and are designed to forestall the use of armed force in disputes between states.

Peacekeeping. The role played by the United Nations when it sends troops into a conflict—to provide a neutral buffer between warring sides but not to punish or confront an aggressor.

Polarity. The number of major powers or poles in the international system.

Polarization. The degree of rigidity of alignments in the international system.

Portfolio investment. Foreign investment that does not attempt to gain controlling interest in a foreign enterprise but seeks to realize a capital return on foreign transactions (e.g., the purchase of foreign stocks and bonds).

Positive-sum game. In game theory, a type of game in which both players can simultaneously win, although one may reap a bigger payoff than the other.

Potency. The weightiness of a promise or a threat—in terms of potential attraction or harm—as perceived by the other side in a bargaining situation.

Power. The ability to influence the behavior of others, based on various tangible or intangible assets.

Power transition theory. A theory, which posits that eras of great-power transitions pose the greatest likelihood for war, as a declining hegemon is challenged by a rising power.

Prisoner's Dilemma (game). A game in which the optimal, rational strategy for both players is to betray the other, even though engaging in mutual cooperation would leave each player better off.

Promise. In international bargaining, a statement of intent to reward desirable behavior by the other side.

Prospect theory. A theory, which predicts that foreign policy makers will tend to take greater risks in defending against loss than in seeking gains.

Punishment. In international bargaining, a penalty imposed on actors who refuse to engage in desirable behavior.

Rally-round-the-flag effect. The phenomenon in which a leadership gathers public support for foreign policy decisions, particularly involving the use of armed force, by appealing to the public's patriotism or nationalism.

Rational actor model. A model of decision making in which the decision maker follows several successive steps, which include carefully defining the situation, articulating goals, considering a range of options, weighing possible consequences, and choosing an option calculated to maximize a successful outcome.

Realist paradigm (realism). A major school of international relations that focuses on the role of power and competing national interests in shaping state behavior in an anarchic environment; realists see greater potential for conflict than cooperation in world politics.

Regionalism. A model of world order that stresses the growth of international organizations, economic transactions, and other ties among states at the regional level.

Reward. In international bargaining, a benefit afforded to actors who behave in a desirable manner.

Scapegoat (diversionary) hypothesis. A supposition that a government experiencing domestic unpopularity or unrest may engage in externally hostile behavior in order to use a foreign adversary as a scapegoat in order to deflect public criticism away from the government.

Secretariat. The administrative arm of the United Nations; more generally, the administrative organ of IGOs.

Secretary-general. The chief administrative officer of the United Nations.

Security community. A political space (territory), possibly encompassing multiple nation-states, in which institutions and community building have progressed to the point where there is very little probability or expectation that a conflict among its members would be resolved by the resort to armed force.

Security Council. The UN organ with primary responsibility for peace and security, consisting of fifteen members, including five (the United States, Russia, China, the United Kingdom, and France) that have permanent seats and veto power.

Security dilemma. The situation in international relations where, due to the lack of any central authority to enforce agreements—international anarchy— states feel compelled to increase their power, only to find that such competition increases insecurity for all.

Soft power. The ability to exercise influence through the attractiveness of one's political system, culture, values, or accomplishments. Soft power can prompt states to follow one's lead by example rather than due to coercion.

Sovereignty. The existence of a government that claims supreme authority over everyone within its borders and recognizes no higher authority outside its borders.

Specialized agencies. Intergovernmental organizations that are affiliated with the UN but have their own separate memberships, budgets, headquarters, and decision-making machinery in addressing relatively narrow, technical problems (e.g., WHO and IMF).

Strategic bargaining. The manipulation of carrots and sticks in order to shape an opponent's behavior in international relations.

Strategic nuclear weapons. Large-scale, long-range nuclear weapons, such as ICBMs and long-range bombers.

Structural violence. Starvation, poor health care, and other forms of systemic deprivation traced to poverty that kill people no less effectively than bombs and other instruments of physical violence.

Summitry. The practice of heads of state or other high-level officials from different countries meeting and communicating directly in the conduct of foreign policy.

Supranational. A type of organization or community in which nation-states surrender sovereignty to a higher authority.

Tacit diplomacy. Informal, indirect communications through words and deeds designed to signal intentions, engage in posturing, and affect international bargaining outcomes.

Tactical nuclear weapons. Nuclear weapons with a range of less than 3,000 miles, intended for use on the battlefield or in regional theaters at shorter distances than ICBMs and strategic nuclear weapons.

Terrorism. Unconventional violence designed to shock for psychological effect, normally perpetrated by nonstate actors, usually targeted at civilians or noncombatants, for the purpose of achieving some political goal such as self-determination or a remaking of economic and social structures.

Third World. The term that was used during the Cold War to refer to the economically less developed countries of the Southern Hemisphere, many of which were nonaligned in the East-West conflict; considered somewhat passé in the post–Cold War era, although still used by some analysts.

Threat. In international bargaining, a statement of intent to penalize undesirable behavior by the other side.

Three-level games. See two-level games. The difference between two- and three-level games is that the latter includes not only interstate level and domestic level bargaining but also transnational (nonstate) actors, such as IGO, NGO, or multinational corporation representatives, participating in conference diplomacy.

Transnational relations. Interactions that occur across national boundaries, particularly by nongovernmental actors.

Treaty. A formal written agreement between states (sometimes called a convention or protocol) that creates legal obligations for the governments that are parties to it.

Treaty of Rome. The 1957 agreement that created the European Economic Community (Common Market), now called the European Union; the original members were France, West Germany, Italy, Belgium, Netherlands, and Luxembourg.

Treaty on European Union (Treaty of Maastricht). Adopted by members of the European Union in 1993, designed to take Western European integration to the next level in terms of consolidating the common internal market and establishing a single economic and monetary union around the euro.

Trusteeship Council. A UN organ charged with dismantling colonial empires after World War II. It is no longer functioning, as it succeeded in its mission.

Two-level games. The term used to denote two levels of bargaining that often occur at diplomatic conferences, one in which the head of a state's delegation negotiates across the table with official counterparts from other countries (each trying to maximize its own nation's interests) and the other in which the head delegate negotiates behind his or her shoulder with the members of one's own national delegation (trying to reconcile the demands of competing domestic constituencies). Thus negotiations are aimed at both an international audience and a domestic audience.

Unipolar system. An international system with only one dominant, hegemonic power.

United Nations (UN). The global intergovernmental organization formed in 1945 as the successor to the League of Nations after World War II, designed to promote peace and international security as well as cooperation in the economic and social field.

United Nations Charter. The treaty that is the founding document of the UN, enumerating its various organs and specifying the rights and obligations of member states.

United Nations Conference on Environment and Development. The Earth Summit held in Rio de Janeiro in 1992, which sought to address a wide range of global environmental and economic development issues around the theme of sustainable development.

United Nations Conference on the Human Environment. The first global environmental conference, organized by the UN in Stockholm in 1972 and resulting in the creation of the UN Environmental Program.

United Nations Conference on Trade and Development (UNCTAD). A UN General Assembly organization established in 1964 to supplement GATT as a world trade forum, especially to give voice to the concerns of less developed countries.

United Nations Educational, Scientific, and Cultural Organization (UNESCO). The UN specialized agency responsible for improving literacy in developing countries, promoting information and scientific exchanges, and protecting cultural monuments and heritage sites worldwide.

United Nations Environmental Program (UNEP). The major global environmental agency, created after the UN Conference on the Human Environment in 1972.

Universal Postal Union (UPU). The UN specialized agency responsible for drafting and implementing rules governing mail traffic worldwide.

Warsaw Pact. The military alliance comprising the Soviet Union and its Eastern European satellite states during the Cold War as a counterpart to NATO. It was terminated in the 1990s.

Washington Consensus. The term used to describe the neoliberal, market-oriented economic policies that the United States and other Western countries urged upon less developed countries and the world economy as a whole after 1990. These included downsizing national government budgets and welfare states and promoting private sector solutions to economic problems.

Wassenaar Arrangement. A 1996 agreement among forty countries that attempts to promote transparency in monitoring and restricting the export of conventional weapons and advanced missile technology.

World Bank (IBRD). The UN specialized agency responsible for providing loans and other forms of aid to less developed countries to support building of bridges, roads, and other developmental needs.

World Court (ICJ). A global institution for adjudicating international disputes, situated in The Hague, Netherlands. It consists of fifteen judges and bases its procedures on the ICJ Statute attached to the UN Charter.

World Health Organization (WHO). The UN specialized agency responsible for controlling communicable diseases and promoting health standards and public health services in less developed countries and worldwide.

World Meteorological Organization (WMO). The UN specialized agency responsible for collecting and disseminating global weather forecasting data and monitoring conditions related to the global environment and climate change.

World system theory. A theory of the evolution and workings of the world economy that stresses the relationships of dominance and dependence linking the "center" (the North) with the "periphery" (the South).

World Trade Organization (WTO). UN agency that promotes free trade worldwide; replaced GATT in 1995.

Zero-sum game. In game theory, a game in which whatever one player wins the other must automatically lose.

INDEX

War and Peace (Tolstoy), 100
War on terror, 245–246
Warsaw Pact, 52, 58
Washington, George, 41
Washington Consensus, 281
Wassenaar Arrangement, 250
The Wealth of Nations (Smith), 19,
    39, 292
Weapons, 141, 163. *See also*
    Conventional weapons; Nuclear
    weapons; Weapons of mass
    destruction
Weapons of mass destruction
    (WMDs), 7, 8, 9, 61–62,
    105–106
  and arms control, 238, 239,
    251–255
  and bargaining, 141–142
  and interstate war, 149
  See also Weapons
Welfare issues, vs. military issues, 65,
    235, 236
Welfare state, 50, 293–294, 301–302
West vs. the rest axis, 64
Westphalian state system, 36, 38, 59.
    See also Nation-states; Peace of
    Westphalia
WHO. *See* World Health
    Organization
Wilhelm II, 46, 165
Wilson, Woodrow, 19, 28, 50, 107
  and diplomacy, 122
  and force without war, 151
  personality traits of, 167
WMDs. *See* Weapons of mass
    destruction
WMO. *See* World Meteorological
    Organization
Women's rights, 260–262,
    273–274

World Bank, 52, 200
  and human development,
    278–279, 281, 284–285
World Court. *See* International
    Court of Justice
World Economy. *See* Global
    economy
World government, 317–319
World Health Organization (WHO),
    201, 281, 283–285
World Meteorological Organization
    (WMO), 201
World order, 174–176, 189–190
World Summit on the Information
    Society (WSIS), 325
World system theory, 295
World Trade Organization (WTO),
    59, 200, 279, 304–306, 307–308,
    309
World War I, 46–50, 147
  causes of, 164, 165, 167, 169–170
  and economic nationalism, 293
  Europe after, 49 (map)
  Europe before, 48 (map)
  severity of, 148
World War II, 47, 48, 51, 147, 150
  causes of, 170, 173
  and economic nationalism, 293
  and liberal paradigm, 19–20
  and realist paradigm, 21
  severity of, 148
WSIS. *See* World Summit on the
    Information Society
WTO. *See* World Trade Organization

*Yearbook of International
    Organizations,* 182–183
Yeltsin, Boris, 107

Zero-sum game, 132